Criminal Justice

Contemporary Literature in Theory and Practice

Series Editors

Marilyn McShane
Frank P. Williams III
California State University – San Bernardino

GARLAND PUBLISHING, INC.
New York & London
1997

Contents of the Series

Criminological Theory

Edited with introductions by

Marilyn McShane
Frank P. Williams III
California State University – San Bernardino

GARLAND PUBLISHING, INC.
New York & London
1997

Library of Congress Cataloging-in-Publication Data

Criminological theory / edited with introductions by Marilyn McShane
    and Frank P. Williams III.
        p.   cm. — (Criminal justice ; v. 3)
    Includes bibliographical references.
    ISBN 0-8153-2509-6 (alk. paper)
    1. Criminology. 2. Crime. I. McShane, Marilyn D., 1956–   .
II. Williams, Franklin P.   III. Series: Criminal justice (New York,
N.Y.) ; v. 3.
HV6018.C73 1997
364 —dc21   96-39144
                                                CIP

Printed on acid-free, 250-year-life paper
Manufactured in the United States of America

Contents

Series Introduction

At the turn of the century the criminal justice system will be confronting many of the same demons, although the drugs of choice, the technology of crime fighting, and the tools and techniques of management have evolved. Despite the enhancements of twenty-first century technologies, funding, crowding, and public concerns about effectiveness continue to be discussed in "crisis" terminology, and criminal justice scholars remain somewhat cynical about the ability to reform the criminal justice system. This pessimistic attitude may be fueled, at least in part, by the drama of real-life crime that plays itself out in courtrooms, newspapers, and talk shows across America every day. The combination of emotional political maneuvering and campaigning on punitive rhetoric assures us of a steady stream of legislation designed to reflect a zero tolerance for crime.

Testing the constitutional limits of our times, we have devised even more ways of imposing severe punishments, seizing assets, reinstituting corporal punishment, and penalizing the parents of delinquents. We have also created new offenses, such as recruiting someone into a gang, transmitting "indecent" images on the Internet, and knowingly passing along a disease. Despite these politically popular solutions to crime, problems of enforcement, equity, and affordability remain. The public's preoccupation with "what works?" and quick fixes to crime problems have never been reconciled with the more realistic ideas of "what can we live with?" and long-range preventive solutions.

Ironically, despite public perceptions that crime has been getting worse, statistics seem to indicate that the rates for virtually all offenses are either no worse than they were in 1980 or are now lower. Drug-related arrests and the rates for most forms of adult crime (in particular, most violent crimes) have actually decreased. Against this general backdrop, the rate of violent juvenile crime appears to be the sole increasing trend, leading to a situation in which risks of victimization by violent crime have also increased for juveniles. The contrary public perception of a massive and growing crime problem has created a situation in which the number of cases of juveniles transferred to adult court has increased, as has the proportion of inmates facing life sentences, life in prison without parole, and death sentences. On the other hand the risk of incarceration also appears to have increased for minorities, directing attention to questions of racial and economic disparity in the quality of protection and justice available in this country today.

While all this has been happening over the past two decades, academia has rather quietly developed an entire discipline dedicated to the study of crime and the criminal justice system. Though crime policy is still dominated largely by political interests swayed by public opinion, crime scholars have begun to have an impact on how crime is viewed and what can be done about it. While this impact is not yet a major one, it continues to gain weight and shows promise of some day achieving the influence that economists have come to wield in the realm of public policy-making.

Simultaneously with this growing scholarship comes an irony: academic journals, the major repository of scholarly wisdom, are being discontinued by libraries. Access, although ostensibly available in an electronic form, is decreasing. In many academic libraries, only a few select, "major" journals are being retained. Clearly, there is so much being done that the few "top" journals cannot adequately represent current developments (even if these journals were not focused in particular directions). Thus, the knowledge of the field is being centralized and, at the same time, more difficult to obtain. The multitude of criminal justice and criminology degree programs now face an interesting dilemma: how do students and faculty access current information? Or put differently, how does the field distribute its hard-gained knowledge to both assure quality of education and pursue efforts to offset the often ill-informed myths of public opinion?

Electronic access would appear to be one possible answer to the problem, especially with libraries facing yet another squeeze, that of space. On-line and media-based (CD-ROM) services promise quick availability of periodical literature, but remain futuristic. The costs associated with downloading articles can approximate the cost of the journal subscriptions themselves and many libraries cannot afford to participate in on-line periodical services. In addition, there is the inconvenience of translating the electronic images into the user's still-preferred paper-based format. Moreover, the paper-based serendipitous value of "browsing" decreases as only specific articles appear on-line, without surrounding materials.

An alternative solution is to review the range of journals and collect the "best" of their articles for reprinting. This is the approach this criminal justice periodical series has taken. By combining both depth and scope in a series of reprints, the series can offer an attractive, cost-effective answer to the problem of creating access to scholarship. Moreover, such a compact format yields the added advantage that individuals searching for a specific topic are more likely to experience the serendipity of running across related articles. Each of the six volumes presents a comprehensive picture of the state of the art in criminal justice today and each contains articles focused on one of the major areas of criminal justice and criminology: Police, Drugs, Criminological Theory, Corrections, Courts, and Victimology. Each volume contains approximately twenty articles.

The Article Selection Process

The articles appearing in the series represent the choices of the editors and a board of experts in each area. These choices were based on four criteria: (1) that the articles were from the time period of 1991–1995, (2) that they represent excellent scholarship, (3) that collectively they constitute a fair representation of the knowledge of the period, and (4) that where there were multiple choices for representing a knowledge area, the articles appeared in journals that are less likely to be in today's academic library holdings. We believe the selection criteria and the board of experts were successful in compiling truly representative content in each topical area. In addition, the authors of the selected articles constitute a list of recognizable experts whose work is commonly cited.

Finally, there is one other advantage offered by the volumes in this series: the articles are reprinted as they originally appeared. Scholars using anthologized materials are commonly faced with having to cite secondary source pages because they do not have access to the original pagination and format. This is a difficulty because mistakes in reprinting have been known to alter the original context, thus making the use of secondary sources risky (and synonymous with sloppy scholarship). In order to overcome this problem, the series editors and the publisher made the joint decision to photoreproduce each article's original image, complete with pagination and format. Thus, each article retains its own unique typesetting and character. Citations may be made to pages in confidence that the reproduced version is identical in all respects with the original. In short, the journal article is being made available exactly as if the issue had been on a library shelf.

We believe this series will be of great utility to students, scholars, and others with interests in the literature of criminal justice and criminology. Moreover, the series saves the user time that would have otherwise been spent in locating quality articles during a typical literature search. Whether in an academic or personal library, the only alternative to this collection is having the journals themselves.

Volume Introduction

From classical concepts to modern theoretical frameworks, this volume seeks to provide the reader with an overview of some of the major contributions to our understanding of criminality. Indeed, those contributions have been rather abundant over the past eight years after a period of stagnation lasting through the 1970s and most of the 1980s. As a result, several new perspectives have been developed, much commentary has taken place, and there is even a new journal devoted exclusively to criminological theory (*Theoretical Criminology*).

Having noted the reinvigoration, however, we also must comment on the general thrust of contemporary theorizing. Virtually all of the more popular works have been restatements or adaptations of older theories. Newer, alternative perspectives have been, for the most part, not given the consideration they deserve. Indeed, an observer might conclude that the field is more interested in maintaining theoretical traditions than in developing new ideas and concepts. On the alternative front, most radical criminology has become "postmodern" criminology, with a multitude of approaches falling under this rubric. Chaos, peacemaking, symbolic imagery, and left realism are but a few of the individual theoretical threads that are now postmodern perspectives.

The selections in this volume are designed to cover a wide range of theoretical concepts from the normalcy of crime to the cycle of crime. Selected works include reconsideration of strain theory, Gottfredson and Hirschi's general theory of crime, and interactional theory. Also covered are new approaches to female criminality, juvenile delinquency, violent crime, and white collar crime. New techniques for collecting and analyzing data are also explored. The works presented here will no doubt caution and direct empirical testing of criminological theories in the years to come.

Traditional Perspectives

In one sense, most criminological perspectives have been able to withstand the test of time: we have returned to their concepts again and again. The oldest of the modern era perspectives, the Classical School, is reexamined by Piers Beirne through a review of Cesare Beccaria's classic work *Dei delitti e delle pene*. Beirne presents evidence that Beccaria was less influenced by humanist and rational philosophies than by a Scottish "science of man." This would recast Beccaria's work and question the existence of a

Classical School.

Another essay on the most popular Classical School concept, deterrence, is authored by Mark Stafford and Mark Warr. They examine general and specific deterrence, proposing that the former is better viewed as punishment avoidance and the latter as both punishment and punishment avoidance. This allows for a separation of punishment and avoidance behavior, thereby increasing the complexity of deterrence but allowing it to be interpreted by modern learning theory.

Lawrence Cohen and Richard Machalek critique one of the giants of sociology, Emile Durkheim and his concept of the normalcy of crime. They find various logical flaws in his approach and ultimately conclude that Durkheim explained crime through individual characteristics, rather than social facts. Reinterpreting normalcy of crime through evolutionary game theory, Cohen and Machalek believe that they have adequately specified property-oriented crime as a byproduct of normal social structure/organization. Further, they feel that the theory uniquely combines both micro- and macro-level forces.

New Theoretical Perspectives

The combination of adapting old theories and proposing new ones is exemplified by most of the selections here. In perhaps one of the most well-received attempts, Robert Agnew extends Merton's strain theory by adding the avoidance of negative situations to the seeking of positive goals. When both positive blockage and negative avoidance are combined, stress levels suggest we can expect the highest rates of crime or delinquency. Agnew believes that the new theory better accounts for different adaptations to strain.

John Braithwaite makes a contribution to a general understanding of crime. He argues that both street crime and white-collar crime can be understood through differentiating between needs and wants. Powerlessness and poverty affect needs by making it likely that needs are not satisfied. Street crime, then, becomes a way to satisfy these needs and punishment is largely ignored by those who have little to lose. On the other hand, those with power and wealth have satisfied their needs but not their wants. Those wants are conducive to white-collar crime as expressed through greed. Braithwaite believes that greater inequality in society increases the chances of both forms of crime.

Drawing upon a reanalysis of the Glueck's classic delinquency study, Robert Sampson and John Laub have proposed a general theory of informal social control. In their essay in this volume they test the interaction of social structure with processual variables in delinquency. They find that poverty and other structural variables are mediated by family controls, with antisocial tendencies also exerting some effect.

John Hagan combines a "drift" version of social control theory with life-course concepts. He uses a thirteen-year panel study to examine the effects of adolescent drift and subcultural choices on later adult status attainment. Adolescents in drift are more likely to develop deviant subcultural affiliations, which he designates as delinquent subculture and party subculture. Working-class adolescents tend to move toward the delinquent subculture with negative results for adult status attainment. Non-working-class adolescents prefer the party subculture, which ultimately has a net positive result on attainment.

In the only selection in this section that is truly an alternative to traditional approaches, Dragan Milovanovic provides a comparison of modernist (positivist) and postmodernist perspectives. Using eight comparative dimensions, he argues that postmodernism represents a new paradigm of social thought that will propose better practical applications as well as a new understanding of social action.

Intervention in Criminal or Delinquent Behavior

Translating theoretical knowledge into practice and policy is one of the avowed purposes of criminology. Unfortunately, this work has proven rather difficult for two reasons. First, there is a remarkable complexity of situations, environment, and variables that affect behavior. Second, the translating of theoretical components into program elements often suffers from the use of "convenient" and inappropriate versions of the theoretical variables and a program that is not sensitive to theory. Still, there are some interesting programs in operation. In a research report, Joan McCord reviews data from a followup of an old (1939–40) delinquency prevention program that combined both biological and sociological variables. Her analysis suggests that parental competence is sufficient to offset biological propensities toward antisocial behavior. Thus, she proposes programs designed to develop parental warmth and competence during early childhood socialization.

Empirical Testing of Theories

One of the tasks of the research field is to provide evidence in support of theoretical concepts. The first half of the 1990s found researchers taking the task seriously. Indeed, research on theories has been a staple for the past two decades and much of the research has focused on social control theories. Pursuing this avenue, Terence Thornberry, Alan Lizotte, Marvin Krohn, Margaret Farnworth, and Sung Joon Jang use the Rochester Youth Development study to examine three elements of the social control bond. They conclude that, while weakened bonds help predict delinquency, delinquent behavior itself serves to further weaken these bonds. Harold Grasmick, Charles Tittle, and Robert Bursik test a newer version of social control theory: Gottfredson and Hirschi's low self-control theory. They find some support and some inconsistencies, including a large share of unexplained variance. Their conclusions suggest modifying the low self-control theory.

Strain theory is another of the traditional theories that has received renewed attention (as the work of Agnew indicates). Velmer Burton, Francis Cullen, David Evans, and Gregory Dunaway examine the argument that support for strain theory depends on how the variables are measured. Using three measures of strain and controlling for variables from other theories, they report no relationships with self-reported adult criminality for any of the measures.

Social disorganization (social area theory) represents another of the major perspectives of the past. Denise Gottfredson, Richard McNeil, and Gary Gottfredson investigate the effects of social area on self-reported juvenile behavior, thus combining both aggregate and individual-level effects. They find that, overall, the effect of social areas was rather small. However, more disorganized areas were more closely associated with the variables in other theories and seemed to produce more aggressive crime. Juveniles from more organized areas reported more property crime.

Steven Messner and Reid Golden look at the relationship between racial inequality in socioeconomic status and crime. Using Uniform Crime Report data to establish homicide rates, they find a relationship between racial inequality and both total homicide rates and race-specific homicide rates. Theories that predict a more general effect of racial inequality on urban crime should receive the greatest support.

Theory Development

Some criminologists have criticized criminological theories as lacking in specificity and logic. When the criterion of empirical evidence is added to this mix, one might begin to conclude that most of our theories begin to come up short. Don Gibbons has periodically offered comments on theory development and in his essay focuses on the viability of general theories of crime. Examining recent contributions to integrative and general theory, Gibbons remains pessimistic about the value of their contributions. He concludes that time would be better spent on theories of specific lawbreaking.

Gender is now viewed as an important part of theory development, particularly because it was so rarely treated in the past. Sally Simpson discusses gender as a theoretically important variable and cautions theorists that it is a mistake to treat females as if they were all the same. She notes especially the interaction between race and gender, discussing the potential sources of those differences. After evaluating three existing theoretical perspectives, Simpson provides suggestions for adding more complex understandings of gender to their mix.

Daniel Nagin and Raymond Paternoster explore the relationship between theories of individual propensities and theories that require situational choices. Analyzing data from a scenario given to college students, they find evidence that both types of theories are useful in explaining self-reported offenses. They conclude that theories should contain both propensity and choice variables.

* * * * * *

We would like to thank the board members of this volume who assisted us in the selection of articles. Because only a limited number of pieces could be selected for this volume, an expanded bibliography is included to provide additional materials. Articles marked with an asterisk (*) are included in this anthology.

Agnew, Robert (1991). A longitudinal test of social control theory and delinquency. *Journal of Research in Crime and Delinquency* 28: 126–56.

*Agnew, Robert (1992). Foundation for a general strain theory of crime and delinquency. *Criminology* 30: 47–66.

Agnew, Robert (1995). Determinism, indeterminism, and crime: An empirical exploration. *Criminology* 33(1): 83–109.

Akers, Ronald (1991). Self-control as a general theory of crime. *Journal of Quantitative Criminology* 7: 201–11.

*Beirne, Piers (1991). Inventing criminology: The "science of man" in Cesare Beccaria's *Dei Delitti E Delle Pene* (1764). *Criminology* 29: 777–820.

Benda, Brent and Frederick A. DiBlasio (1991). Comparison of four theories of adolescent sexual exploration. *Deviant Behavior* 12: 235–57.

Bennett, Richard and Peter Basiotis (1991). Structural correlates of juvenile property crime: A cross-national, time-series analysis. *Journal of Research in Crime and Delinquency* 28: 262–87.

Benson, Michael and Elizabeth Moore (1992). Are white-collar and common offenders the same? An empirical and theoretical critique of a recently proposed general theory of crime. *Journal of Research in Crime and Delinquency* 29: 251–72.

Booth, Alan and Wayne Osgood (1993). The influence of testosterone on deviance in adulthood: Assessing and explaining the relationship. *Criminology* 31: 93–117.

*Braithwaite, John (1991). Poverty, power, white-collar crime and the paradoxes of criminological theory. *Australian and New Zealand Journal of Criminology* 24: 40–48.

Brown, Sandra and Liqun Cao (1993). The impact of race in criminal justice ideology. *Justice Quarterly* 9(4): 685–701.

Brownfield, David and Kevin Thompson (1991). Attachment to peers and delinquent behaviour. *Canadian Journal of Criminology* 33: 45–60.

Burkett, Steven and David Ward (1993). A note on perceptual deterrence, religiously-based moral condemnation, and social control. *Criminology* 31: 119–34.

*Burton, Velmer, Francis Cullen, David Evans, and Gregory Dunaway (1994). Reconsidering strain theory: Operationalization, rival theories and adult criminality. *Journal of Quantitative Criminology* 10(3): 213–39.

Cappel, Charles and Gresham Sykes (1991). Prison commitments, crime and unemployment: A theoretical and empirical specification for the United States, 1933–1985. *Journal of Quantitative Criminology* 7(2): 155–99.

Carey, Gregory (1992). Twin imitation for antisocial behavior: Implications for genetic and family environment research. *Journal of Abnormal Psychology* 101: 18–25.

Cernkovich, Stephen and Peggy Giordano (1992). School bonding, race, and delinquency. *Criminology* 30: 261–91.

Chilton, Roland (1991). Urban crime trends and criminological theory. *Criminal Justice Research Bulletin* 6(3):1–10.

*Cohen, Lawrence and Richard Machalek (1994). The normalcy of crime: From Durkheim to evolutionary ecology. *Rationality and Society* 6: 286–308.

Dekeseredy, Walter and Martin Schwartz (1991). British and U.S. left realism: A critical comparison. *International Journal of Offender Therapy and Comparative Criminology* 35: 248–62.

Dick, Andrew (1995). When does organized crime pay? A transactional analysis. *International Review of Law and Economics* 15(1): 25–46.

Ferrell, Jeff and Clinton Sanders, eds. (1995). *Cultural criminology.* Boston: Northeastern University Press.

Ferrell, Jeff (1993). *Crimes of style: Urban graffiti and the politics of criminality.* New York: Garland.

*Gibbons, Don (1992). Talking about crime: Observations on the prospects for causal theory in criminology. *Criminal Justice Research Bulletin* 7(6): 1–10.

*Gottfredson, Denise, Richard McNeil III, and Gary Gottfredson (1991). Social area influences on delinquency: A multilevel analysis. *Journal of Research in Crime and Delinquency* 28: 197–226.

Grasmick, Harold, Robert Bursik Jr., and Bruce Arneklev (1993). Reduction in drunk driving as a response to increased threats of shame, embarrassment, and legal sanctions. *Criminology* 31: 41–67.

Grasmick, Harold, Robert Bursik Jr., and Karyl Kinsey (1991). Shame and embarrassment as deterrents to noncompliance with the law: The case of an antilittering campaign. *Environment and Behavior* 23: 233–51.

*Grasmick, Harold, Charles Tittle, Robert Bursik Jr., and Bruce Arneklev (1993). Testing the core empirical implications of Gottfredson and Hirschi's general theory of crime. *Journal of Research in Crime and Delinquency* 30: 5–29.

*Hagan, John (1991). Destiny and drift: Subcultural preferences, status attainments, and the risks and rewards of youth. *American Sociological Review* 56: 567–82.

Henry, Stuart and Dragan Milovanovic (1991). Constitutive criminology: The maturation of critical theory. *Criminology* 29: 293–315.

Henry, Stuart and Dragan Milovanovic (1996). *Constitutive criminology: Beyond postmodernism.* Thousand Oakes, Calif.: Sage.

Horney, Julie and Ineke Haen Marshall (1992). Risk perceptions among serious offenders: The role of crime and punishment. *Criminology* 23: 575–92.

Junger-Tas, Josine (1992). An empirical test of social control theory. *Journal of Quantitative Criminology* 8: 9–28.

Kandel, Denise and Mark Davies (1991). Friendship networks, intimacy, and illicit drug use in young adulthood: A comparison of two competing theories. *Criminology* 29: 441–69.

Kowalski, Gregory and Thomas Petee (1991). Sunbelt effects on homicide rates. *Sociology and Social Research* 75: 73–79.

Krohn, Marvin and William Skinner (1992). Age and gender differences in a social process model of adolescent cigarette use. *Sociological Inquiry* 62: 56–82.

Lester, David (1991). Crime as opportunity: A test of the hypothesis with European homicide rates. *British Journal of Criminology* 31: 186–91.

Liska, Allen and Barbara Warner (1991). Functions of crime: A paradoxical process. *American Journal of Sociology* 96: 1441–63.

Lynch, James and David Cantor (1992). Ecological and behavioral influences on property victimization at home: Implications for opportunity theory. *Journal of Research in Crime and Delinquency* 29: 335–62.

Mak, Anita (1991). Psychosocial control characteristics of delinquents and nondelinquents. *Criminal Justice and Behavior* 18: 287–303.

Makkai, Toni and John Braithwaite (1991). Criminological theories and regulatory compliance. *Criminology* 29: 191–220.

McCarthy, Bill and John Hagan (1992). Mean streets: The theoretical significance of situational delinquency among homeless youths. *American Journal of Sociology* 98(3): 597–627.

*McCord, Joan (1991). The cycle of crime and socialization practices. *Journal of Criminal Law and Criminology* 82: 211–28.

*Messner, Steven and Reid Golden (1992). Racial inequality and racially disaggregated homicide rates: An assessment of alternative theoretical explanations. *Criminology* 30: 421–45.

Miethe, Terance, Michael Hughes, and David McDowall (1991). Social change and crime rates: An evaluation of alternative theoretical approaches. *Social Forces* 70: 165–85.

*Milovanovic, Dragan (1995). Dueling paradigms: Modernist versus postmodernist thought. *Humanity and Society* 19: 19–44.

Morris, Allison and Loraine Gelsthorpe (1991). Feminist perspectives in criminology: Transforming and transgressing. *Women and Criminal Justice* 2: 3–26.

Mugford, Stephen and Pat O'Malley (1991). Heroin policy and deficit models: The limits of Left Realism. *Crime, Law and Social Change* 15: 19–36.

*Nagin, Daniel and Raymond Paternoster (1993). Enduring individual differences and rational choice theories of crime. *Law and Society Review* 27: 201–30.

Nagin, Daniel and Raymond Paternoster (1991). The preventive effects of the perceived risk of arrest: Testing an expanded conception of deterrence. *Criminology* 29: 561–85.

Nagin, Daniel and Raymond Paternoster (1991). On the relationship of past to future participation in delinquency. *Criminology* 29: 163–89.

Newton, Carolyn (1994). Gender theory and prison sociology: Using theories of masculinities to interpret the sociology of prisons for men. *Howard Journal of Criminal Justice* 33(3): 193–202.

O'Brien, Robert (1991). Sex ratios and rape rates: A power control theory. *Criminology* 29: 99–114.

Perkins, Douglas, Abraham Wandersman, Richard Rich, and Ralph Taylor (1993). The physical environment of street crime: Defensible space, territoriality, and incivilities. *Journal of Environmental Psychology* 13: 29–50.

Riedel, Mark (1993). *Stranger violence: A theoretical inquiry.* New York: Garland.

Roncek, Dennis and Pamela Maier (1991). Bars, blocks and crimes revisited: Linking the theory of routine activities to the empiricism of "hot spots." *Criminology* 29: 725–53.

Ross, Lee (1994). Religion and deviance: Exploring the impact of social control elements. *Sociological Spectrum* 14(1): 65–86.

Rowe, David and Chester Britt III (1991). Developmental explanations of delinquent behavior among siblings: Common factor vs. transmission mechanisms. *Journal of Quantitative Criminology* 7: 315–32.

Rowe, David and Daniel Flannery (1994). An examination of environmental and trait influences on adolescent delinquency. *Journal of Research in Crime and Delinquency* 31(4): 374–89.

Sampson, Robert and John Laub (1991). The Sutherland-Glueck debate: On the sociology of criminological knowledge. *American Journal of Sociology* 96: 1402–40.

*Sampson, Robert J. and Robert J. Sampson (1994). Urban poverty and the family context of delinquency: A new look at structure and process in a classic study. *Child Development* 65: 523–40.

Schwartz, Martin and Walter Dekeseredy (1991). Left realist criminology: Strengths, weaknesses and the feminist critique. *Crime, Law and Social Change* 15: 51–72.

Schwartz, Martin and David Friedrichs (1994). Postmodern thought and criminological discontent: New metaphors for understanding violence. *Criminology* 32(2): 221–46.

*Simpson, Sally (1991). Caste, class, and violent crime: Explaining differences in female offending. *Criminology* 29: 115–36.

*Stafford, Mark and Mark Warr (1993). A reconceptualization of general and specific deterrence. *Journal of Research in Crime and Delinquency* 30(2): 123–35.

*Thornberry, Terence, Alan Lizotte, Marvin Krohn, Margaret Farnworth, and Sung Joon Jang (1991). Testing interactional theory: An examination of reciprocal causal relationships among family, school, and delinquency. *Journal of Criminal Law and Criminology* 82: 3–35.

Triplett, Ruth and Roger Jarjoura (1994). Theoretical and empirical specification of a model of informal labeling. *Journal of Quantitative Criminology* 10(3): 241–76.

Tygart, Clarence (1991). Juvenile delinquency and number of children in a family: Some empirical and theoretical updates. *Youth and Society* 22: 525–36.

Tunnell, Kenneth, ed. (1993). Political crime in contemporary America: A critical approach. New York: Garland.

Vila, Bryan (1994). A general paradigm for understanding criminal behavior: Extending evolutionary ecological theory. *Criminology* 32(3): 311–59.

Vila, Bryan and Lawrence Cohen (1993). Crime as strategy: Testing an evolutionary ecological theory of expropriative crime. *American Journal of Sociology,* 98: 873–912.

Warr, Mark (1993). Age, peers and delinquency. *Criminology* 31: 17–40.

Warr, Mark and Mark Stafford (1991). The influence of delinquent peers: What they think or what they do? *Criminology* 29: 851–66.

Wooldredge, John, Francis Cullen, and Edward Latessa (1992). Victimization in the workplace: A test of routine activities theory. *Justice Quarterly,* 9(2): 325–35.

FOUNDATION FOR A GENERAL STRAIN THEORY OF CRIME AND DELINQUENCY*

ROBERT AGNEW
Emory University

This paper presents a general strain theory of crime and delinquency that is capable of overcoming the criticisms of previous strain theories. In the first section, strain theory is distinguished from social control and differential association/social learning theory. In the second section, the three major types of strain are described: (1) strain as the actual or anticipated failure to achieve positively valued goals, (2) strain as the actual or anticipated removal of positively valued stimuli, and (3) strain as the actual or anticipated presentation of negatively valued stimuli. In the third section, guidelines for the measurement of strain are presented. And in the fourth section, the major adaptations to strain are described, and those factors influencing the choice of delinquent versus nondelinquent adaptations are discussed.

After dominating deviance research in the 1960s, strain theory came under heavy attack in the 1970s (Bernard, 1984; Cole, 1975), with several prominent researchers suggesting that the theory be abandoned (Hirschi, 1969; Kornhauser, 1978). Strain theory has survived those attacks, but its influence is much diminished (see Agnew, 1985a; Bernard, 1984; Farnworth and Leiber, 1989). In particular, variables derived from strain theory now play a very limited role in explanations of crime/delinquency. Several recent causal models of delinquency, in fact, either entirely exclude strain variables or assign them a small role (e.g., Elliott et al., 1985; Johnson, 1979; Massey and Krohn, 1986; Thornberry, 1987; Tonry et al., 1991). Causal models of crime/delinquency are dominated, instead, by variables derived from differential association/social learning theory and social control theory.

This paper argues that strain theory has a central role to play in explanations of crime/delinquency, but that the theory has to be substantially revised to play this role. Most empirical studies of strain theory continue to rely on the strain models developed by Merton (1938), A. Cohen (1955), and Cloward and Ohlin (1960). In recent years, however, a wealth of research in several fields has questioned certain of the assumptions underlying those theories and pointed to new directions for the development of strain theory. Most notable in this area is the research on stress in medical sociology and psychology, on equity/justice in social psychology, and on aggression in psychology—particularly recent versions of frustration-aggression and social

---

* I would like to thank Helene Raskin White and Karen Hegtvedt for their comments.

1

learning theory. Also important is recent research in such areas as the legitimation of stratification, the sociology of emotions, and the urban underclass. Certain researchers have drawn on segments of the above research to suggest new directions for strain theory (Agnew, 1985a; Bernard, 1987; Elliott et al., 1979; Greenberg, 1977), but the revisions suggested have not taken full advantage of this research and, at best, provide only incomplete models of strain and delinquency. (Note that most of the theoretical and empirical work on strain theory has focused on delinquency.) This paper draws on the above literatures, as well as the recent revisions in strain theory, to present the outlines of a general strain theory of crime/delinquency.

The theory is written at the social-psychological level: It focuses on the individual and his or her immediate social environment—although the macroimplications of the theory are explored at various points. The theory is also written with the empirical researcher in mind, and guidelines for testing the theory in adolescent populations are provided. The focus is on adolescents because most currently available data sets capable of testing the theory involve surveys of adolescents. This general theory, it will be argued, is capable of overcoming the theoretical and empirical criticisms of previous strain theories and of complementing the crime/delinquency theories that currently dominate the field.

The paper is in four sections. In the first section, there is a brief discussion of the fundamental traits that distinguish strain theory from the other two dominant theories of delinquency: social control and differential association/ social learning theory (in the interest of brevity, the term *delinquency* is used rather than *crime and delinquency*). In the second section, the three major sources of strain are described. In the third section, guidelines for the measurement of strain are provided. And in the final section, the major adaptations to strain are listed and the factors influencing the choice of delinquent versus nondelinquent adaptations are discussed.

STRAIN THEORY AS DISTINGUISHED FROM CONTROL AND DIFFERENTIAL ASSOCIATION/SOCIAL LEARNING THEORY

Strain, social control, and differential association theory are all sociological theories: They explain delinquency in terms of the individual's social relationships. Strain theory is distinguished from social control and social learning theory in its specification of (1) the type of social relationship that leads to delinquency and (2) the motivation for delinquency. First, strain theory focuses explicitly on *negative relationships with others*: relationships in which the individual is not treated as he or she wants to be treated. Strain theory has typically focused on relationships in which others prevent the individual from achieving positively valued goals. Agnew (1985a), however, broadened the focus of strain theory to include relationships in which others present the individual with noxious or negative stimuli. Social control theory, by contrast, focuses on the *absence of significant relationships with conventional others and institutions.* In particular, delinquency is most likely when (1) the adolescent is not attached to parents, school, or other institutions; (2) parents and others fail to monitor and effectively sanction deviance; (3) the adolescent's actual or anticipated investment in conventional society is minimal; and (4) the adolescent has not internalized conventional beliefs. Social learning theory is distinguished from strain and control theory by its focus on *positive relationships with deviant others.* In particular, delinquency results from association with others who (1) differentially reinforce the adolescent's delinquency, (2) model delinquent behavior, and/or (3) transmit delinquent values.

Second, strain theory argues that adolescents are *pressured into delinquency by the negative affective states—most notably anger and related emotions— that often result from negative relationships* (see Kemper, 1978, and Morgan and Heise, 1988, for typologies of negative affective states). This negative affect creates pressure for corrective action and *may* lead adolescents to (1) make use of illegitimate channels of goal achievement, (2) attack or escape from the source of their adversity, and/or (3) manage their negative affect through the use of illicit drugs. Control theory, by contrast, denies that outside forces pressure the adolescent into delinquency. Rather, the absence of significant relationships with other individuals and groups *frees the adolescent to engage in delinquency.* The freed adolescent either drifts into delinquency or, in some versions of control theory, turns to delinquency in response to inner forces or situational inducements (see Hirschi, 1969:31–34). In differential association/social learning theory, the adolescent commits delinquent acts because group forces lead the adolescent to *view delinquency as a desirable or at least justifiable form of behavior* under certain circumstances.

Strain theory, then, is distinguished by its focus on negative relationships with others and its insistence that such relationships lead to delinquency through the negative affect—especially anger—they sometimes engender. Both dimensions are necessary to differentiate strain theory from control and differential association/social learning theory. In particular, social control and social learning theory sometimes examine negative relationships— although such relationships are not an explicit focus of these theories. Control theory, however, would argue that negative relationships lead to delinquency not because they cause negative affect, but because they lead to a reduction in social control. A control theorist, for example, would argue that physical abuse by parents leads to delinquency because it reduces attachment to parents and the effectiveness of parents as socializing agents. Likewise, differential association/social learning theorists sometimes examine negative relationships—even though theorists in this tradition emphasize that imitation, reinforcement, and the internalization of values are less likely in negative relationships. Social learning theorists, however, would argue that negative relationships—such as those involving physically abusive parents—lead to delinquency by providing models for imitation and implicitly teaching the child that violence and other forms of deviance are acceptable behavior.

Phrased in the above manner, it is easy to see that strain theory complements the other major theories of delinquency in a fundamental way. While these other theories focus on the absence of relationships or on positive relationships, strain theory is the only theory to focus explicitly on negative relationships. And while these other theories view delinquency as the result of drift or of desire, strain theory views it as the result of pressure.

THE MAJOR TYPES OF STRAIN

Negative relationships with others are, quite simply, relationships in which others are not treating the individual as he or she would like to be treated. The classic strain theories of Merton (1938), A. Cohen (1955), and Cloward and Ohlin (1960) focus on only one type of negative relationship: relationships in which others prevent the individual from achieving positively valued goals. In particular, they focus on the goal blockage experienced by lower-class individuals trying to achieve monetary success or middle-class status. More recent versions of strain theory have argued that adolescents are not only concerned about the future goals of monetary success/middle-class status, but are also concerned about the achievement of more immediate goals—such as good grades, popularity with the opposite sex, and doing well in athletics (Agnew, 1984; Elliott and Voss, 1974; Elliott et al., 1985; Empey, 1982; Greenberg, 1977; Quicker, 1974). The focus, however, is still on the achievement of positively valued goals. Most recently, Agnew (1985a) has argued that strain may result not only from the failure to achieve positively valued goals, but also from the inability to escape legally from painful situations. If one draws on the above theories—as well as the stress, equity/justice, and aggression literatures—one can begin to develop a more complete classification of the types of strain.

Three major types of strain are described—each referring to a different type of negative relationship with others. Other individuals may (1) prevent one from achieving positively valued goals, (2) remove or threaten to remove positively valued stimuli that one possesses, or (3) present or threaten to present one with noxious or negatively valued stimuli. These categories of strain are presented as ideal types. There is no expectation, for example, that a factor analysis of strainful events will reproduce these categories. These categories, rather, are presented so as to ensure that the full range of strainful events are considered in empirical research.

STRAIN AS THE FAILURE TO ACHIEVE POSITIVELY VALUED GOALS

At least three types of strain fall under this category. The first type encompasses most of the major strain theories in criminology, including the classic strain theories of Merton, A. Cohen, and Cloward and Ohlin, as well as those modern strain theories focusing on the achievement of immediate goals. The other two types of strain in this category are derived from the justice/equity literature and have not been examined in criminology.

STRAIN AS THE DISJUNCTION BETWEEN ASPIRATIONS AND EXPECTATIONS/ACTUAL ACHIEVEMENTS

The classic strain theories of Merton, A. Cohen, and Cloward and Ohlin argue that the cultural system encourages everyone to pursue the ideal goals of monetary success and/or middle-class status. Lower-class individuals, however, are often prevented from achieving such goals through legitimate channels. In line with such theories, adolescent strain is typically measured in terms of the disjunction between *aspirations* (or ideal goals) and *expectations* (or expected levels of goal achievement). These theories, however, have been criticized for several reasons (see Agnew, 1986, 1991b; Clinard, 1964; Hirschi, 1969; Kornhauser, 1978; Liska, 1987; also see Bernard, 1984; Farnworth and Leiber, 1989). Among other things, it has been charged that these theories (1) are unable to explain the extensive nature of middle-class delinquency, (2) neglect goals other than monetary success/middle-class status, (3) neglect barriers to goal achievement other than social class, and (4) do not fully specify why only *some* strained individuals turn to delinquency. The most damaging criticism, however, stems from the limited empirical support provided by studies focusing on the disjunction between aspirations and expectations (see Kornhauser, 1978, as well the arguments of Bernard, 1984; Elliott et al., 1985; and Jensen, 1986).

As a consequence of these criticisms, several researchers have revised the above theories. The most popular revision argues that there is a youth subculture that emphasizes a variety of immediate goals. The achievement of these goals is further said to depend on a variety of factors besides social class: factors such as intelligence, physical attractiveness, personality, and athletic ability. As a result, many middle-class individuals find that they lack the traits or skills necessary to achieve their goals through legitimate channels. This version of strain theory, however, continues to argue that strain stems from the inability to achieve certain ideal goals emphasized by the (sub)cultural system. As a consequence, strain continues to be measured in terms of the disjunction between *aspirations* and *actual achievements* (since we are dealing with immediate rather than future goals, actual achievements rather than expected achievements may be examined).

It should be noted that empirical support for this revised version of strain theory is also weak (see Agnew, 1991b, for a summary). At a later point, several possible reasons for the weak empirical support of strain theories focusing on the disjunction between aspirations and expectations/achievements will be discussed. For now, the focus is on classifying the major types of strain.

STRAIN AS THE DISJUNCTION BETWEEN EXPECTATIONS AND ACTUAL ACHIEVEMENTS

As indicated above, strain theories in criminology focus on the inability to achieve *ideal* goals derived from the cultural system. This approach stands in contrast to certain of the research on justice in social psychology. Here the focus is on the disjunction between *expectations* and *actual achievements* (rewards), and it is commonly argued that such expectations are existentially based. In particular, it has been argued that such expectations derive from the individual's past experience and/or from comparisons with referential (or generalized) others who are similar to the individual (see Berger et al., 1972, 1983; Blau, 1964; Homans, 1961; Jasso and Rossi, 1977; Mickelson, 1990; Ross et al., 1971; Thibaut and Kelley, 1959). Much of the research in this area has focused on income expectations, although the above theories apply to expectations regarding all manner of positive stimuli. The justice literature argues that the failure to achieve such expectations may lead to such emotions as anger, resentment, rage, dissatisfaction, disappointment, and unhappiness—that is, all the emotions customarily associated with strain in criminology. Further, it is argued that individuals will be strongly motivated to reduce the gap between expectations and achievements—with deviance being commonly mentioned as one possible option. This literature has not devoted much empirical research to deviance, although limited data suggest that the expectations-achievement gap is related to anger/hostility (Ross et al, 1971).

This alternative conception of strain has been largely neglected in criminology. This is unfortunate because it has the potential to overcome certain of the problems of current strain theories. First, one would expect the disjunction between expectations and actual achievements to be more emotionally distressing than that between aspirations and achievements. Aspirations, by definition, are *ideal* goals. They have something of the utopian in them, and for that reason, the failure to achieve aspirations may not be taken seriously. The failure to achieve expected goals, however, is likely to be taken seriously since such goals are rooted in reality—the individual has previously experienced such goals or has seen similar others experience such goals. Second, this alternative conception of strain assigns a central role to the social comparison process. As A. Cohen (1965) argued in a follow-up to his strain theory, the neglect of social comparison is a major shortcoming of strain theory. The above theories describe one way in which social comparison is important: Social comparison plays a central role in the formation of individual goals (expectations in this case; also see Suls, 1977). Third, the assumption that goals are culturally based has sometimes proved problematic for strain theory (see Kornhauser, 1978). Among other things, it makes it difficult to integrate strain theory with social control and cultural deviance theory (see Hirschi, 1979). These latter theories assume that the individual is weakly tied to the cultural system or tied to alternative/oppositional subcultures. The argument that goals are existentially based, however, paves the way for integrations involving strain theory.[1]

STRAIN AS THE DISJUNCTION BETWEEN JUST/FAIR OUTCOMES AND ACTUAL OUTCOMES

The above models of strain assume that individual goals focus on the achievement of specific outcomes. Individual goals, for example, focus on the achievement of a certain amount of money or a certain grade-point average. A third conception of strain, also derived from the justice/equity literature, makes a rather different argument. It claims that individuals do not necessarily enter interactions with specific outcomes in mind. Rather, they enter interactions expecting that certain distributive justice rules will be followed, rules specifying how resources should be allocated. The rule that has received the most attention in the literature is that of equity. An equitable relationship is one in which the outcome/input ratios of the actors involved in an exchange/allocation relationship are equivalent (see Adams, 1963, 1965; Cook and Hegtvedt, 1983; Walster et al., 1978). Outcomes encompass a broad range of positive and negative consequences, while inputs encompass the individual's positive and negative contributions to the exchange. Individuals in a relationship will compare the ratio of their outcomes and inputs to the ratio(s) of specific others in the relationship. If the ratios are equal to one another, they feel that the outcomes are fair or just. This is true, according to equity theorists, even if the outcomes are low. If outcome/input ratios are

---

1. One need not assume that expectations are existentially based; they may derive from the cultural system as well. Likewise, one need not assume that aspirations derive from the cultural system. The focus in this paper is on *types* of strain rather than *sources* of strain, although a consideration of sources is crucial when the macroimplications of the theory are developed. Additional information on the sources of positively valued goals—including aspirations and expectations—can be found in Alves and Rossi, 1978; Cook and Messick, 1983; Hochschild, 1981; Jasso and Rossi, 1977; Martin and Murray, 1983; Messick and Sentis, 1983; Mickelson, 1990; and Shepelak and Alwin, 1986.

not equal, actors will feel that the outcomes are unjust and they will experience distress as a result. Such distress is especially likely when individuals feel they have been underrewarded rather than overrewarded (Hegtvedt, 1990).

The equity literature has described the possible reactions to this distress, some of which involve deviance (see Adams, 1963, 1965; Austin, 1977; Walster et al., 1973, 1978; see Stephenson and White, 1968, for an attempt to recast A. Cohen's strain theory in terms of equity theory). In particular, inequity may lead to delinquency for several reasons—all having to do with the restoration of equity. Individuals in inequitable relationships may engage in delinquency in order to (1) increase their outcomes (e.g., by theft); (2) lower their inputs (e.g., truancy from school); (3) lower the outcomes of others (e.g., vandalism, theft, assault); and/or (4) increase the inputs of others (e.g., by being incorrigible or disorderly). In highly inequitable situations, individuals may leave the field (e.g., run away from home) or force others to leave the field.[2] There has not been any empirical research on the relationship between equity and delinquency, although much data suggest that inequity leads to anger and frustration. A few studies also suggest that insulting and vengeful behaviors may result from inequity (see Cook and Hegtvedt, 1991; Donnerstein and Hatfield, 1982; Hegtvedt, 1990; Mikula, 1986; Sprecher, 1986; Walster et al., 1973, 1978).

It is not difficult to measure equity. Walster et al. (1978:234–242) provide the most complete guide to measurement.[3] Sprecher (1986) illustrates how

---

2. Theorists have recently argued that efforts to restore equity need not involve the specific others in the inequitable relationship. If one cannot restore equity with such specific others, there may be an effort to restore "equity with the world" (Austin, 1977; Stephenson and White, 1968; Walster et al., 1978). That is, individuals who feel they have been inequitably treated may try to restore equity in the context of a totally different relationship. The adolescent who is inequitably treated by parents, for example, may respond by inequitably treating peers. The concept of "equity with the world" has not been the subject of much empirical research, but it is intriguing because it provides a novel explanation for displayed aggression. It has also been argued that individuals may be distressed not only by their own inequitable treatment, but also by the inequitable treatment of others (see Crosby and Gonzalez-Intal, 1984; Walster et al., 1978.) We may have, then, a sort of vicarious strain, a type little investigated in the literature.

3. The equity literature has been criticized on a number of points, the most prominent being that there are a variety of distribution rules besides equity—such as equality and need (Deutsch, 1975; Folger, 1984; Mikula, 1980; Schwinger, 1980; Utne and Kidd, 1980). Much recent research has focused on the factors that determine the preference for one rule over another (Alves and Rossi, 1978; Cook and Hegtvedt, 1983; Deutsch, 1975; Hegtvedt, 1987, 1991a; Hochschild, 1981; Lerner, 1977; Leventhal, 1976; Leventhal et al., 1980; Schwinger, 1980; Walster et al., 1978). Also, the equity literature argues that individuals compare themselves with similar others with whom they are involved in exchange/allocation relations. However, it has been argued that individuals sometimes compare themselves with dissimilar others, make referential (generalized) rather than local (specific) comparisons, make internal rather than external comparisons, make group-to-group comparisons,

equity may be measured in social surveys; respondents are asked who contributes more to a particular relationship and/or who "gets the best deal" out of a relationship. A still simpler strategy might be to ask respondents how fair or just their interactions with others, such as parents or teachers, are. One would then predict that those involved in unfair relations will be more likely to engage in current and future delinquency.

The literature on equity builds on the strain theory literature in criminology in several ways. First, all of the strain literature assumes that individuals are pursuing some specific outcome, such as a certain amount of money or prestige. The equity literature points out that individuals do not necessarily enter into interactions with specific outcomes in mind, but rather with the expectation that a particular distributive justice rule will be followed. Their goal is that the interaction conform to the justice principle. This perspective, then, points to a new source of strain not considered in the criminology literature. Second, the strain literature in criminology focuses largely on the individual's outcomes. Individuals are assumed to be pursuing a specific goal, and strain is judged in terms of the disjuntion between the goal and the actual outcome. The equity literature suggests that this may be an oversimplified conception and that the individual's *inputs* may also have to be considered. In particular, an equity theorist would argue that inputs will condition the individual's evaluation of outcomes. That is, individuals who view their inputs as limited will be more likely to accept limited outcomes as fair. Third, the equity literature also highlights the importance of the social comparison process. In particular, the equity literature stresses that one's evaluation of outcomes is at least partly a function of the outcomes (and inputs) of those with whom one is involved in exchange/allocation relations. A given outcome, then, may be evaluated as fair or unfair depending on the outcomes (and inputs) of others in the exchange/allocation relation.

---

or avoid social comparison altogether (see Berger et al., 1972; Hegtvedt, 1991b; Martin and Murray, 1983; see Hegtvedt, 1991b, and Suls and Wills, 1991, for a discussion of the factors affecting the choice of comparison objects). Finally, even if one knows what distribution rule individuals prefer and the types of social comparisons they make, it is still difficult to predict whether they will evaluate their interactions as equitable. Except in unambiguous situations of the type created in experiments, it is hard to predict what inputs and outcomes individuals will define as relevant, how they will weight those inputs and outcomes, and how they will evaluate themselves and others on those inputs and outcomes (Austin, 1977; Hegtvedt, 1991a; Messick and Sentis, 1979, 1983; Walster et al., 1973, 1978). Fortunately, however, the above three problems do not prohibit strain theory from taking advantage of certain of the insights from equity theory. While it is difficult to predict whether individuals will define their relationships as equitable, it is relatively easy to measure equity after the fact.

9

56   AGNEW

SUMMARY: STRAIN AS THE FAILURE TO ACHIEVE POSITIVELY VALUED GOALS

Three types of strain in this category have been listed: strain as the disjunction between (1) aspirations and expectations/actual achievements, (2) expectations and actual achievements, and (3) just/fair outcomes and actual outcomes. Strain theory in criminology has focused on the first type of strain, arguing that it is most responsible for the delinquency in our society. Major research traditions in the justice/equity field, however, argue that anger and frustration derive primarily from the second two types of strain. To complicate matters further, one can list still additional types of strain in this category. Certain of the literature, for example, has talked of the disjunction between "satisfying outcomes" and reality, between "deserved" outcomes and reality, and between "tolerance levels" or minimally acceptable outcomes and reality. No study has examined all of these types of goals, but taken as a whole the data do suggest that there are often differences among aspirations (ideal outcomes), expectations (expected outcomes), "satisfying" outcomes, "deserved" outcomes, fair or just outcomes, and tolerance levels (Della Fave, 1974; Della Fave and Klobus, 1976; Martin, 1986; Martin and Murray, 1983; Messick and Sentis, 1983; Shepelak and Alwin, 1986). This paper has focused on the three types of strain listed above largely because they dominate the current literature.[4]

Given these multiple sources of strain, one might ask which is the most relevant to the explanation of delinquency. This is a difficult question to answer given current research. The most fruitful strategy at the present time may be to assume that all of the above sources are relevant—that there are several sources of frustration. Alwin (1987), Austin (1977), Crosby and Gonzalez-Intal (1984), Hegtvedt (1991b), Messick and Sentis (1983), and Tornblum (1977) all argue or imply that people often employ a variety of standards to evaluate their situation. Strain theorists, then, might be best advised to employ measures that tap all of the above types of strain. One might, for example, focus on a broad range of positively valued goals and, for each goal, ask adolescents whether they are achieving their ideal outcomes (aspirations), expected outcomes, and just/fair outcomes. One would expect strain to be greatest when several standards were not being met, with perhaps greatest weight being given to expectations and just/fair outcomes.[5]

---

4. To add a still further complication, it has been suggested that anger may result from the violation of *procedural* as well as distributive justice rules (Folger, 1984, 1986; Lind and Tyler, 1988). Procedural justice does not focus on the fairness of outcomes, but rather on the fairness of the procedures by which individuals decide how to distribute resources. A central issue in procedural justice is whether all individuals have a "voice" in deciding how resources will be distributed. One might, then, ask adolescents about the fairness of the procedures used by parents, teachers, and others to make rules.

5. This strategy assumes that all standards are relevant in a given situation, which

STRAIN AS THE REMOVAL OF POSITIVELY VALUED STIMULI FROM THE INDIVIDUAL

The psychological literature on aggression and the stress literature suggest that strain may involve more than the pursuit of positively valued goals. Certain of the aggression literature, in fact, has come to de-emphasize the pursuit of positively valued goals, pointing out that the blockage of goal-seeking behavior is a relatively weak predictor of aggression, particularly when the goal has never been experienced before (Bandura, 1973; Zillman, 1979). The stress literature has largely neglected the pursuit of positively valued goals as a source of stress. Rather, if one looks at the stressful life events examined in this literature, one finds a focus on (1) events involving the loss of positively valued stimuli and (2) events involving the presentation of noxious or negative stimuli (see Pearlin, 1983, for other typologies of stressful life events/conditions).[6] So, for example, one recent study of adolescent stress employs a life-events list that focuses on such items as the loss of a boyfriend/girlfriend, the death or serious illness of a friend, moving to a new school district, the divorce/separation of one's parents, suspension from school, and the presence of a variety of adverse conditions at work (see Williams and Uchiyama, 1989, for an overview of life-events scales for adolescents; see Compas, 1987, and Compas and Phares, 1991, for overviews of research on adolescent stress).[7]

Drawing on the stress literature, then, one may state that a second type of strain or negative relationship involves the actual or anticipated removal (loss) of positively valued stimuli from the individual. As indicated above, numerous examples of such loss can be found in the inventories of stressful life events. The actual or anticipated loss of positively valued stimuli may lead to delinquency as the individual tries to prevent the loss of the positive stimuli, retrieve the lost stimuli or obtain substitute stimuli, seek revenge

---

may not always be the case. In certain situations, for example, one may make local comparisons but not referential comparisons (see Brickman and Bulman, 1977; Crosby and Gonzales-Intal, 1984). In other situations, social comparison processes may not come into play at all; outcomes may be evaluated in terms of culturally derived standards (see Folger, 1986).

6. The stress literature has also focused on positive events, based on the assumption that such events might lead to stress by overloading the individual. Accumulating evidence, however, suggests that it is only undesirable events that lead to negative outcomes such as depression (e.g., Gersten et al., 1974; Kaplan et al., 1983; Pearlin et al., 1981; Thoits, 1983).

7. Certain individuals have criticized the stress literature for neglecting the failure of individuals to achieve positively valued goals. In particular, it has been charged that the stress literature has neglected "nonevents," or events that are desired or anticipated but do not occur (Dohrenwend and Dohrenwend, 1974; Thoits, 1983). One major distinction between the strain literature in criminology and the stress literature in medical sociology, in fact, is that the former has focused on "nonevents" while the latter has focused on "events."

against those responsible for the loss, or manage the negative affect caused by the loss by taking illicit drugs. While there are no data bearing directly on this type of strain, experimental data indicate that aggression often occurs when positive reinforcement previously administered to an individual is withheld or reduced (Bandura, 1973; Van Houten, 1983). And as discussed below, inventories of stressful life events, which include the loss of positive stimuli, are related to delinquency.

STRAIN AS THE PRESENTATION OF NEGATIVE STIMULI

The literature on stress and the recent psychological literature on aggression also focus on the actual or anticipated presentation of negative or noxious stimuli.[8] Except for the work of Agnew (1985a), however, this category of strain has been neglected in criminology. And even Agnew does not focus on the presentation of noxious stimuli per se, but on the inability of adolescents to escape legally from noxious stimuli. Much data, however, suggest that the presentation of noxious stimuli may lead to aggression and other negative outcomes in certain conditions, even when legal escape from such stimuli is possible (Bandura, 1973; Zillman, 1979). Noxious stimuli may lead to delinquency as the adolescent tries to (1) escape from or avoid the negative stimuli; (2) terminate or alleviate the negative stimuli; (3) seek revenge against the source of the negative stimuli or related targets, although the evidence on displaced aggression is somewhat mixed (see Berkowitz, 1982; Bernard, 1990; Van Houten, 1983; Zillman, 1979); and/or (4) manage the resultant negative affect by taking illicit drugs.

A wide range of noxious stimuli have been examined in the literature, and experimental, survey, and participant observation studies have linked such stimuli to both general and specific measures of delinquency—with the experimental studies focusing on aggression. Delinquency/aggression, in particular, has been linked to such noxious stimuli as child abuse and neglect (Rivera and Widom, 1990), criminal victimization (Lauritsen et al., 1991), physical punishment (Straus, 1991), negative relations with parents (Healy and Bonner, 1969), negative relations with peers (Short and Strodtbeck, 1965), adverse or negative school experiences (Hawkins and Lishner, 1987), a wide range of stressful life events (Gersten et al., 1974; Kaplan et al., 1983; Linsky

---

8.   Some researchers have argued that it is often difficult to distinguish the presentation of negative stimuli from the removal of positive stimuli (Michael, 1973; Van Houten, 1983; Zillman, 1979). Suppose, for example, that an adolescent argues with parents. Does this represent the presentation of negative stimuli, (the arguing) or the removal of positive stimuli (harmonious relations with one's parents)? The point is a valid one, yet the distinction between the two types of strain still seems useful since it helps ensure that all major types of strain are considered by researchers.

and Straus, 1986; Mawson, 1987; Novy and Donohue, 1985; Vaux and Ruggiero, 1983), verbal threats and insults, physical pain, unpleasant odors, disgusting scenes, noise, heat, air pollution, personal space violations, and high density (see Anderson and Anderson, 1984; Bandura, 1973, 1983; Berkowitz, 1982, 1986; Mueller, 1983). In one of the few studies in criminology to focus specifically on the presentation of negative stimuli, Agnew (1985a) found that delinquency was related to three scales measuring negative relations at home and school. The effect of the scales on delinquency was partially mediated through a measure of anger, and the effect held when measures of social control and deviant beliefs were controlled. And in a recent study employing longitudinal data, Agnew (1989) found evidence suggesting that the relationship between negative stimuli and delinquency was due to the *causal* effect of the negative stimuli on delinquency (rather than the effect of delinquency on the negative stimuli). Much evidence, then, suggests that the presentation of negative or noxious stimuli constitutes a third major source of strain.

Certain of the negative stimuli listed above, such as physical pain, heat, noise, and pollution, may be experienced as noxious largely for biological reasons (i.e., they may be unconditioned negative stimuli). Others may be conditioned negative stimuli, experienced as noxious largely because of their association with unconditioned negative stimuli (see Berkowitz, 1982). Whatever the case, it is assumed that such stimuli are experienced as noxious regardless of the goals that the individual is pursuing.

THE LINKS BETWEEN STRAIN AND DELINQUENCY

Three sources of strain have been presented: strain as the actual or anticipated failure to achieve positively valued goals, strain as the actual or anticipated removal of positively valued stimuli, and strain as the actual or anticipated presentation of negative stimuli. While these types are theoretically distinct from one another, they may sometimes overlap in practice. So, for example, the insults of a teacher may be experienced as adverse because they (1) interfere with the adolescent's aspirations for academic success, (2) result in the violation of a distributive justice rule such as equity, and (3) are conditioned negative stimuli and so are experienced as noxious in and of themselves. Other examples of overlap can be given, and it may sometimes be difficult to disentangle the different types of strain in practice. Once again, however, these categories are ideal types and are presented only to ensure that all events with the potential for creating strain are considered in empirical research.

Each type of strain increases the likelihood that individuals will experience one or more of a range of negative emotions. Those emotions include disappointment, depression, and fear. Anger, however, is the most critical emotional reaction for the purposes of the general strain theory. Anger results when individuals blame their adversity on others, and anger is a key emotion because it increases the individual's level of felt injury, creates a desire for retaliation/revenge, energizes the individual for action, and lowers inhibitions, in part because individuals believe that others will feel their aggression is justified (see Averill, 1982; Berkowitz, 1982; Kemper, 1978; Kluegel and Smith, 1986: Ch. 10; Zillman, 1979). Anger, then, affects the individual in several ways that are conducive to delinquency. Anger is distinct from many of the other types of negative affect in this respect, and this is the reason that anger occupies a special place in the general strain theory.[9] It is important to note, however, that delinquency may still occur in response to other types of negative affect—such as despair, although delinquency is less likely in such cases.[10] The experience of negative affect, especially anger, typically creates a desire to take corrective steps, with delinquency being one possible response. Delinquency may be a method for alleviating strain, that is, for achieving positively valued goals, for protecting or retrieving positive stimuli, or for terminating or escaping from negative stimuli. Delinquency may be used to seek revenge; data suggest that vengeful behavior often occurs even when there is no possibility of eliminating the adversity that stimulated it (Berkowitz, 1982). And delinquency may occur as adolescents try to manage their negative affect through illicit drug use (see Newcomb and Harlow, 1986). The general strain theory, then, has the potential to explain a broad range of delinquency, including theft, aggression, and drug use.

Each type of strain may create a *predisposition* for delinquency or function as a *situational event* that instigates a particular delinquent act. In the words of Hirschi and Gottredson (1986), then, the strain theory presented in this paper is a theory of both "criminality" and "crime" (or to use the words of Clarke and Cornish [1985], it is a theory of both "criminal involvement" and "criminal events"). Strain creates a predisposition for delinquency in those cases in which it is chronic or repetitive. Examples include a continuing gap

---

9. The focus on blame/anger represents a major distinction between the general strain theory and the stress literature. The stress literature simply focuses on adversity, regardless of whether it is blamed on another. This is perhaps appropriate because the major outcome variables of the stress literature are inner-directed states, like depression and poor health. When the focus shifts to outer-directed behavior, like much delinquency, a concern with blame/anger becomes important.

10. Delinquency may still occur in the absence of blame and anger (see Berkowitz, 1986; Zillman, 1979). Individuals who accept responsibility for their adversity are still subject to negative affect, such as depression, despair, and disappointment (see Kemper, 1978; Kluegel and Smith, 1986). As a result, such individuals will still feel pressure to take corrective action, although the absence of anger places them under less pressure and makes vengeful behavior much less likely. Such individuals, however, may engage in inner-directed delinquency, such as drug use, and if suitably disposed, they may turn to other forms of delinquency as well. Since these individuals lack the strong motivation for revenge and the lowered inhibitions that anger provides, it is assumed that they must have some minimal disposition for deviance before they respond to their adversity with outer-directed delinquency (see the discussion of the disposition to delinquency).

between expectations and achievements and a continuing pattern of ridicule and insults from teachers. Adolescents subject to such strain are predisposed to delinquency because (1) nondelinquent strategies for coping with strain are likely to be taxed; (2) the threshold for adversity may be lowered by chronic strains (see Averill, 1982:289); (3) repeated or chronic strain may lead to a hostile attitude—a general dislike and suspicion of others and an associated tendency to respond in an aggressive manner (see Edmunds and Kendrick, 1980:21); and (4) chronic strains increase the likelihood that individuals will be high in negative affect/arousal at any given time (see Bandura, 1983; Bernard, 1990). A particular instance of strain may also function as the situational event that ignites a delinquent act, especially among adolescents predisposed to delinquency. Qualitative and survey data, in particular, suggest that particular instances of delinquency are often instigated by one of the three types of strain listed above (see Agnew, 1990; also see Averill, 1982, for data on the instigations to anger).

MEASURING STRAIN

As indicated above, strain theory in criminology is dominated by a focus on strain as goal blockage. Further, only one type of goal blockage is typically examined in the literature—the failure to achieve *aspirations*, especially aspirations for monetary success or middle-class status. The general strain theory is much broader than current strain theories, and measuring strain under this theory would require at least three sets of measures: those focusing on the failure to achieve positively valued goals, those focusing on the loss of positive stimuli, and those focusing on the presentation of negative stimuli. It is not possible to list the precise measures that should be employed in these areas, although the citations above contain many examples of the types of measures that might be used. Further, certain general guidelines for the measurement of strain can be offered. The guidelines below will also highlight the limitations of current strain measures and shed further light on why those measures are typically unrelated to delinquency.

DEVELOPING A COMPREHENSIVE LIST OF NEGATIVE RELATIONS

Strain refers to negative or adverse relations with others. Such relations are ultimately defined from the perspective of the individual. That is, in the final analysis adverse relations are whatever individuals say they are (see Berkowitz, 1982). This does not mean, however, that one must employ an idiosyncratic definition of adverse relations—defining adverse relations anew for each person one examines. Such a strategy would create serious problems for (1) the empirical study of delinquency, (2) the prediction and control of delinquency, and (3) efforts to develop the macroimplications of the general

15

strain theory. Rather, one can employ a strategy similar to that followed by stress researchers.

First, one can draw on theory and research to specify those objective situations that might reasonably be expected to cause adversity among adolescents. This parallels stress research, which relies on inventories of stressful life events, and several standard inventories are in wide use. The items in such inventories are based, to varying degrees, on the perceptions and judgments of researchers, on previous theory and research, and on reports from samples of respondents (see Dohrenwend, 1974). In developing inventories of strainful events, criminologists must keep in mind the fact that there may be important group differences in the types of strain or negative relations most frequently encountered. A list of negative relations developed for one group, then, may overlook certain negative relations important for another group (see Dohrenwend, 1974). It may eventually be possible, however, to develop a comprehensive list of negative relations applicable to most samples of adolescents.

Second, criminologists must recognize that individuals and groups may experience the strainful events in such inventories differently (see Thoits, 1983). Limited data from the stress literature, for example, suggest that the impact of family stressors is greatest among young adolescents, peer stressors among middle adolescents, and academic stressors among old adolescents (Compas and Phares, 1991). Stress researchers have responded to such findings not by abandoning their inventories, but by investigating those factors that determine why one group or individual will experience a given event as stressful and another will not. And researchers have identified several sets of variables that influence the perception and experience of negative events (e.g., Compas and Phares, 1991; Pearlin, 1982; Pearlin and Schooler, 1978). Many of the variables are discussed in the next section, and they represent a major set of conditioning variables that criminologists should consider when examining the impact of strainful events on delinquency.

EXAMINING THE CUMULATIVE IMPACT OF NEGATIVE RELATIONS

In most previous strain research in criminology, the impact of one type of negative relation on delinquency is examined with other negative relations ignored or held constant. So, for example, researchers will examine the impact of one type of goal blockage on delinquency, ignoring other types of goal blockage and other potential types of strain. This stands in sharp contrast to a central assumption in the stress literature, which is that stressful life events have a cumulative impact on the individual. Linsky and Straus (1986:17), for example, speak of the "accumulation theory," which asserts that "it is not so much the unique quality of any single event but the *cumulation* of several stressful events within a relatively short time span" that is consequential. As a result, it is standard practice in the stressful life-events literature to measure stress with a composite scale: a scale that typically sums the number of stressful life events experienced by the individual.

The precise nature of the cumulative effect, however, is unclear. As Thoits (1983:69) points out, stressful events may have an additive or interactive effect on outcome variables. The additive model assumes that each stressor has a fixed effect on delinquency, an effect independent of the level of the other stressors. Somewhat more plausible, perhaps, is the interactive model, which assumes that "a person who has experienced one event may react with even more distress to a second that follows soon after the first . . . two or more events . . . results in more distress than would be expected from the simple sum of their singular effects."

Whether the effect is additive or interactive, there is limited support for the idea that the level of stress/strain must pass a certain threshold before negative outcomes result (Linsky and Straus, 1986; Thoits, 1983). Below that level, stress/strain is unrelated to negative outcomes. Above that level, stress/strain has a positive effect on negative outcomes, perhaps an additive effect or perhaps an interactive effect.

Given these arguments, one should employ a composite index of strain in all analyses or examine the interactions between strain variables. Examining interactions can become very complex if there are more than a few indicators of strain, although it does allow one to examine the differential importance of various types of strain. If stressors have an interactive effect on delinquency, the interaction terms should be significant or the composite index should have a nonlinear effect on delinquency (see the discussion of interactions and nonlinear effects in Aiken and West, 1991). If the effect is additive, the interaction terms should be insignificant or the composite index should have a linear effect on delinquency (after the threshold level is reached). These issues have received only limited attention in the stress literature (see the review by Thoits, 1983), and they should certainly be explored when constructing measures of strain for the purpose of explaining delinquency. At a minimum, however, as comprehensive a list of negative events/conditions as possible should be examined.

There is also the issue of whether positive events/experiences should be examined. If prior stressors can aggravate the negative effect of subsequent stressors, perhaps positive events can mitigate the impact of stressors. Limited evidence from the stress literature suggests that lists of negative events predict better than lists examining the balance of negative and positive events (usually negative events minus positive events) (see Thoits, 1983:58–59; Williams and Uchiyama, 1989:101; see Gersten et al., 1974, for a possible exception). This topic, however, is certainly in need of more research. In addition to looking at the *difference* between desirable and undesirable events, researchers may also want to look at the *ratio* of undesirable to desirable events.

It should be noted that tests of strain theory in criminology typically examine the disjunction between aspirations and expectations for one or two goals and ignore all of the many other types of strain. The tests also typically assume that strain has a linear effect on delinquency, and they never examine positive as well as negative events. These facts may constitute additional reasons for the weak empirical support given to strain theory in criminology.

EXAMINING THE MAGNITUDE, RECENCY, DURATION, AND CLUSTERING OF ADVERSE EVENTS

Limited research from the stress and equity literatures suggest that adverse events are more influential to the extent that they are (1) greater in magnitude or size, (2) recent, (3) of long duration, and (4) clustered in time.

MAGNITUDE

The magnitude of an event has different meanings depending on the type of strain being examined. With respect to goal blockage, magnitude refers to the size of the gap between one's goals and reality. With respect to the loss of positive stimuli, magnitude refers to the amount that was lost. And with respect to the presentation of noxious stimuli, magnitude refers to the amount of pain or discomfort *inflicted*.[11] In certain cases, magnitude may be measured in terms of a standard metric, such as dollars or volts delivered. In most cases, however, there is no standard metric available for measuring magnitude and one must rely on the perceptions of individuals (see Jasso, 1980, on quality versus quantity goods). To illustrate, researchers in the stress literature have asked judges to rate events according to the amount of readjustment they require or the threat they pose to the individual (see Thoits, 1983, for other weighting schemes). Such judgments are then averaged to form a magnitude score for each event. There is evidence, however, of subgroup differences in weights assigned (Thoits, 1983:53–55).

Magnitude ratings are then sometimes used to weight the events in composite scales. A common finding, however, is that lists of life events weighted by magnitude do *not* predict any better than unweighed lists (e.g., Gersten et al., 1974). This is due to the fact that the correlation between lists of

---

11. As Empey (1956) and others have pointed out, magnitude may also be measured in *relative* terms. For example, suppose an individual earning $10,000 a year and an individual earning $100,000 both lose $100 in a burglary. In absolute terms, the magnitude of their loss is the same. Relative to their current income, however, the magnitude of their loss is quite different. In most cases, it would be difficult to develop precise measures of relative magnitude. Nevertheless, researchers should at the very least be sensitive to this issue when analyzing and interpreting data.

weighted and unweighted events is typically so high (above .90) that the lists can be considered virtually identical (Thoits, 1983). Williams and Uchiyama (1989:99–100) explain this high correlation by arguing that severe life events, which are heavily weighted, have a low base rate in the population and so do not have a significant impact on scale scores. Studies that consider major and minor events separately tend to find that major events are in fact more consequential than minor events (Thoits, 1983:66).

It should be noted that the previous research on strain theory has paid only limited attention to the dimension of magnitude, even in those cases in which standard metrics for measuring magnitude were available. Samples, in fact, are often simply divided into strained and nonstrained groups, with little consideration of variations in the magnitude of strain.

RECENCY

Certain data suggest that recent events are more consequential than older events and that events older than three months have little effect (Avison and Turner, 1988). Those data focus on the impact of stress on depression, and so are not necessarily generalizable to the strain-delinquency relationship. Nevertheless, the data suggest that the recency of strain may be an important dimension to consider, and findings in this area might be of special use in designing longitudinal studies, in which the issue of the appropriate lag between cause and effect is central (although the subject of little research and theory).

DURATION

Much theory and data from the equity and stress literatures suggest that events of long duration (chronic stressors) have a greater impact on a variety of negative psychological outcomes (Folger, 1986; Mark and Folger, 1984; Pearlin, 1982; Pearlin and Lieberman, 1979; Utne and Kidd, 1980). Some evidence, in fact, suggests that discrete events may be unimportant except to the extent that they affect chronic events (Cummings and El-Sheikh, 1991; Gersten et al., 1977; Pearlin, 1983). Certain researchers in the equity/justice literature have suggested that the expected duration of the event into the future should also be considered (Folger, 1986; Mark and Folger, 1984; Utne and Kidd, 1980; see especially the "likelihood of amelioration" concept).

CLUSTERING

Data from the stress literature also suggest that events closely clustered in time have a greater effect on negative outcomes (Thoits, 1983). Such events, according to Thoits (1983), are more likely to overwhelm coping resources than events spread more evenly over time. Certain data, in particular, trace negative outcomes such as suicide and depression to a series of negative events clustered in the previous few weeks (Thoits, 1983).

INVENTING CRIMINOLOGY: THE "SCIENCE OF MAN" IN CESARE BECCARIA'S *DEI DELITTI E DELLE PENE* (1764)*

PIERS BEIRNE
University of Southern Maine

This paper challenges existing images of the context and object of Cesare Beccaria's (1764) Dei delitti e delle pene. It offers textual and other evidence that the chief object of Beccaria's famous treatise was the application to crime and penality not of humanism and legal rationality, as convention holds, but of the Scottish-inspired "science of man." This latter was a deterministic discourse whose key principles—utilitarianism, probabilism, associationism, and sensationalism—implicitly defy conventional assumptions about the volitional basis of classical criminology. The paper thus questions Dei delitti's proper place in the history of criminology and, in so doing, casts doubt on the very existence of a distinctive "classical criminology."

When you have any thing to obtain of present dispatch, you entertain; and amuse the party, with whom you deal, with some other Discourse; that he be not too much awake, to make Objections.

> Francis Bacon in *Sermones Fideles* (1632)

In recent work I have tried to uncover the process of concept formation in the early history of criminology (Beirne, 1987a, 1987b, 1988; Beirne and Hunt, 1990). About the origin and development of positivist criminology, in particular, I have opposed two sets of conventional claims. First, against externalist claims, I have argued that the origins of the conceptual content and explanatory structure of positivist criminology cannot adequately be understood either as mere representations of the power relations peculiar to modernity or as unmediated expressions of the epistemological divisions wrought by state practices in the asylum, the clinic, and the prison. Second, against internalist claims, I have argued that the key concepts and discursive techniques of positivist criminology did not develop as logical or even inevitable products of scientific development. Rather, the key concepts emerged from some of the focal concerns of the domains of penality and the statistical

---

* This paper was presented at the annual meetings of the American Society of Criminology, Baltimore, Maryland, November 1990. Research for it was enabled by the generosity of the National Endowment for the Humanities (Fellowship #FB-26796) and by the provision of a Visiting Scholarship at the Institute of Criminology at Cambridge University. For their cautions, I am most grateful to Susan Corrente, David Garland, Alasdair MacIntyre, Jim Messerschmidt, Ray Michalowski, and Graeme Newman.

movement, which, during the Restoration (1814–1830) in France, coincided in the issue of the regulation of the "dangerous classes." Positivist criminology, I have suggested, was originally a multifaceted, nineteenth-century discourse based on economism, biologism, and mental hereditarianism; its chief objects ("criminal man," "criminality," and "criminal character") were demarcated by epistemological boundaries dividing the "normal" from the "pathological."[1]

In developing this description I have assumed, as have most other scholars (e.g., Vold and Bernard, 1986:10–15), the truth of the hallowed distinction between positivist criminology and the dominant discourse about crime that preceded it, namely, classical criminology. By convention, classical criminology was a mid- to late-eighteenth-century discourse couched in the rhetoric of classical jurisprudence; its chief object, as found in the works of Beccaria, Bentham, Romilly, and others, is held to have been the construction of a rational and efficient penal calculus directed to the actions of the volitional legal subject.[2]

In this paper, I reconsider the merits of the key text in the development of classical criminology, namely, Beccaria's *Dei delitti e delle pene* (*Of Crimes and Punishments*—henceforth, *Dei delitti*) of 1764. I do so not only because descriptions of classical criminology invariably focus on the life and labors of its anonymous author, the shy and enigmatic member of the Milanese patriciate Cesare Bonesana, Marchese di Beccaria (1738–1794), but also because, as I argue here, the discursive objects of Beccaria's famous treatise have been persistently misrepresented by friend and foe alike.

My thesis about *Dei delitti* unfolds in four stages. First, I claim that in the past 200 years the predominant images of *Dei delitti* have been constructed more in terms of its practico-juridical effects in Europe and colonial America

---

1. By the term "positivist" criminology, I refer loosely to a discourse about crime and criminality that is predicated on the belief that there is a fundamental harmony between the methods of the natural and the social sciences. This discourse views its observational categories as theory independent, and it can assume several forms, each of which, according to its context and object, can be more or less appropriate as a method of inquiry (Beirne, 1987a:1141, n. 3).

2. Some scholars nowadays suggest that because concepts such as "crime," "criminal," and "criminality" were absent from their epistemological universe, classical criminologists such as Beccaria and his followers were not representative of a criminology of *homo criminalis* as such. Rather, the suggestion is that because their concepts were directed to *homo penalis* their labors should be categorized as either "classical penology" or "administrative penology" or even "a theory of social control." For example, Garland argues that it is altogether misleading to designate the work of writers such as Beccaria, Voltaire, Bentham, and Blackstone as "criminology": "their work is essentially the application of legal jurisprudence to the realm of crime and punishment, and it bears no relation to the "human sciences" of the nineteenth century that were to form the basis of the criminological enterprise", (1985:14–15; similarly, see Foucault, 1979:102, 1988; Pasquino, 1980:20–21; Taylor et al., 1973:2–3).

than in terms of its actual discursive features. However, I do not thereby dispute the momentous practical effects exerted by Beccaria's text, the extent of which is indicated in Durkheim's (1901:113) confident assessment "it is incontestably the case that it was . . . *Of Crimes and Punishments* which delivered the mortal blow to the old and hateful routines of the criminal law."[3] Nor do I suggest that *Dei delitti* is to the history of criminology what the Piltdown Man hoax is to the history of physical anthropology. Instead I argue, second, that the persistent misrepresentation of the arguments of *Dei delitti* is actively encouraged by the ambiguity of many of Beccaria's own positions and by the obscure and secretive style of much of his prose—common enough textual practices in the dangerous publishing conditions that existed during much of the Enlightenment. Only with considerable difficulty, therefore, can the nature and intended objects of Beccaria's discourse be discerned. Third, I demonstrate that the chief object of *Dei delitti* is the application to crime and penality of the "science of man," a deterministic discourse implicitly at odds with conventional assumptions about the exclusively humanist and volitional bases of "classical criminology." In making this claim, I fundamentally challenge the existing interpretations of the context and object of Beccaria's book. In so doing, finally, I cast doubt on the very existence of a distinctive "classical criminology." It is a corollary of my argument that those modern-day criminologists who adhere to models of human agency based on "free will" and "rational choice" must look to some discourse other than Beccaria's to discover their intellectual ancestry.

IMAGES OF *DEI DELITTI*

The first copies of *Dei delitti* were printed in Livorno, Italy, and circulated anonymously in the summer of 1764.[4] Beccaria's short treatise of 104 pages was an instant and dazzling success. The first Italian edition was quickly followed by two others and then in 1765, through the intercession of the *philosophes* d'Alembert, Malesherbes, Voltaire, and the Abbé Morellet, a widely read French translation (*Traité des délits et des peines*). By 1800 there had

---

3. See also Maestro (1942:124–151; Paolucci (1963); C. Phillipson (1923:89–106); Venturi (1971:100–116; and Young (1984, 1986).

4. Although he had received a law degree from the University of Pavia in 1758, Beccaria knew very little about criminal law and punishment when he began to write *Dei delitti* in March 1763, and the project itself actually was first suggested to him by Pietro Verri and then developed through discussion with fellow *illuministi* in the *Accademià dei pugni*. Beccaria completed his treatise in January 1764, after working on it for only 10 months. Biographical details of Beccaria's career can be found in Cantù (1862), Landry (1910:7–46), Maestro (1942:51–55, 1973:5–12), Paolucci (1963:ix–xxiii), and C. Phillipson (1923:26).

been no less than 23 Italian editions, 14 French editions, and 11 English editions (3 printed in the United States).[5] Clearly, Beccaria's proposals for the reform of criminal law appealed to a large cross-section of educated society. His disciples included such benevolent and not-so-benevolent despots as Gustavus III of Sweden, Catherine II of Russia, and Empress Maria Theresa of Austria; lawyers and legal philosophers in England like William Blackstone[6] and Jeremy Bentham;[7] republican revolutionaries in colonial America such as

---

5. Which of the several editions of *Dei delitti* represents Beccaria's intended text is not entirely clear. The first Italian edition of 1764 arguably contains the text closest to Beccaria's initial thinking, but it was published only after extensive editing by his friend Pietro Verri. The first French edition of 1765 certainly made the greatest impact on intellectual circles outside Italy, and of the early editions it had by far the largest circulation. However, its translator, the famous Abbé Morellet, made a variety of changes to Beccaria's manuscript without his permission, ostensibly for the sake of clarity of presentation but which perhaps resulted in an undue emphasis on its utilitarian features; for this, Morellet's translation was castigated by the *philosophe* Melchior Grimm (1765a:424–425) and scorned as a perversion of the author's meaning by the anonymous translator of the first English edition of 1767. Yet no compelling evidence (*pace* Venturi, 1971:106–108; Young, 1984:164–165) exists that Beccaria himself was overly concerned either with Morellet's rearrangement of the text or with the effects of the translation. In one of his letters to Morellet, Beccaria (1766:862–863) commented on this very issue in the following terms:

> My work has lost none of its force in your translation, except in those places where the essential character of one or the other language has imparted some difference between your expression and mine . . . I find quite without foundation the objection that your changing the order of my text resulted in a loss of its force. The force consists in the choice of expressions and the *rapprochement* of ideas, neither of which has been harmed.

Nevertheless, the edition of *Dei delitti* used here is the sixth Italian edition of 1766. This is so because all its major arguments are faithful to the original edition, because it appeared not long after the original, and because it was the final edition personally supervised by Beccaria himself. This choice is also favored by the Italian Enlightenment specialist Franco Venturi (1965); fortunately, it has recently been made available in an excellent English translation by Young, and on which I largely depend here.

6. In his *Commentaries on the Law of England*, Blackstone (1769:Vol. 4, ch. 1:3, 4–18) referred to Beccaria as "an ingenious writer," and he praised Beccaria's humanism and his specific recommendations for rules of evidence, for deterrence ("certainty" rather than "severity" of punishment) and a "proportionate scale" of punishments. On the timeliness of Beccaria's ideas for English reformers, and on Blackstone's indebtedness to them, see Beattie (1986:555–557) and Lieberman (1989:209–209). Beccaria's influence on other English reformers, such as William Eden, Henry Dagge, and Manasseh Dawes, is discussed in Green (1985:290–303).

7. Upon reading *Dei delitti*, Bentham exclaimed: "Oh! my master, first evangelist of Reason, you who have raised your Italy so far above England, and I would add above France . . . you who have made so many useful excursions into the path of utility, what is there left for us to do?—Never to turn aside from that path" (cited in Halévy, 1928:21; see also Hart, 1982:40–52). Elsewhere, Bentham wrote of Beccaria that "he was received by the intelligent as an Angel from heaven would be by the faithful. He may be styled the father of *Censorial Jurisprudence*" (1776:14).

Thomas Jefferson and John Adams;[8] and most important, the *philosophes* in France. Among the *philosophes*, Beccaria's ideas were highly esteemed by such luminaries as d'Alembert, Diderot, Helvétius, Buffon, and Voltaire. D'Alembert (1765:313), for example, thought that Beccaria had successfully combined "philosophy, truth, logic, and precision with sentiments of humanity" for which he would gain an "immortal reputation." An astonishing accolade was bestowed on *Dei delitti* when in 1766, and in many subsequent editions, Voltaire's glowing *Commentaire sur le livre des délits et des peines* was appended to Beccaria's text.

Although *Dei delitti* was received with rapture by a large majority of the *philosophes*, some among them greeted it with cautious criticism. While they unanimously endorsed Beccaria's humanitarianism, some disagreed with either the direction or the extent of his specific proposals for reform of the criminal law. Against Beccaria's reticence about the legality of suicide, for example, Voltaire explicitly denied that it was a crime. Against Beccaria's complete opposition to torture, Diderot and others argued that it was justified for the discovery of a guilty party's accomplices. Others protested Beccaria's absolute opposition to capital punishment. Moreover, according to the dour Melchior Grimm (1765:424), Beccaria's proposals were "too geometrical," a vague and overused term that implied a narrow emphasis on probabilism and mathematics. A similar accusation was leveled at Beccaria's work by the Scottish Enlightenment painter Allan Ramsay, who complained that "it is useless to treat penal questions abstractly, as if they were questions of geometry and arithmetic" (n.d.:55).

Worse still, among many jurists in Italy and France, *Dei delitti* immediately became an object of derision and scorn. Beccaria's novel ideas about torture, capital punishment, and equality before the law were condemned as highly dangerous, for example, by Muyart de Vouglans, Daniel Jousse, and the French attorney general Louis Séguier (Maestro, 1942:64–67).[9] Powerful elements in Roman Catholicism also opposed Beccaria's proposals. Thus, in

---

8. Thomas Jefferson, for example, "copied long passages from it in his *Commonplace Book* and used it as his principal modern authority for revising the laws of Virginia" (Wills, 1978:94). In 1770, during his speech in defense of the British soldiers implicated in The Boston Masacre, John Adams pleaded "I am for the prisoners at the bar, and shall apologize for it only in the words of the Marquis Beccaria: 'If I can but be the instrument of preserving one life, his blessing and tears of transport, shall be a sufficient consolation to me, for the contempt of all mankind' " (quoted in Kidder, 1870:232).

9. Maestro (1973:38–39) has outlined the attack made on Beccaria in 1771 by the French jurist Daniel Jousse, in the latter's *Traité de la justice criminelle de France*. Maestro asks, "Why these attacks on Beccaria on the part of the jurists?" and responds "[because] the men who had built their lives, their fortunes, and their reputations on the old customs could not bear to see this young idealist suddenly ruin their edifice." This answer, while correct, fails to specify the precise terms in which the jurists of the *ancien régime* recognized Beccaria's book as such a dangerous threat.

early 1765 the Dominican friar Ferdinando Facchinei—a cantankerous mouthpiece of the Inquisitorial Council of Ten in Venice—published a tract that accused Beccaria of sedition, impiety, and a new heresy, which he termed "socialism"; Facchinei derided Beccaria as "the Rousseau of the Italians" (1765:173; see also Maestro, 1973:35–37). The next year, Beccaria's book was condemned for its extreme rationalism and placed on the papal *Index Prohibitorum*, where it remained for almost two centuries.

Notwithstanding some later retributivist objections to Beccaria's utilitarianism voiced in Germany, the initial furor over *Dei delitti* gradually gave way to a stock of complacent assumptions about the intentions of its author.[10] Chief among them has been the view that the key ideas in *Dei delitti* can be apprehended in terms of their practical effects. An unmediated and necessary association is held typically to exist between Beccaria's intentions, as they were formulated in his text, in other words, and their more or less successful appropriation for the practice of criminal law and criminal justice in the eighteenth century. Since then, most, if not all, sociologists and historians of penology (e.g., Gorecki, 1985:67–68; Jones, 1986:33–57; Mueller, 1990) have read backwards from the effects of the written word to Beccaria's intentions and have thereby made two assumptions about *Dei delitti*. First, they assumed it was primarily a humanist project, inspired by the tradition of the French *philosophes* and motivated by the author's humanitarian opposition to the arbitrariness and barbaric cruelty of European criminal justice in the mid-eighteenth century. Second, they assumed it had as its chief objects the reform of judicial irrationality (including judicial torture and capital punishment) and the institution of a utilitarian approach to punishment based on a calculus of pleasure and pain. In concert, these assumptions have retrospectively led to another, namely, that Beccaria was the founder of classical criminology (e.g., Matza, 1964:3, 13), marked as it is by a penal calculus based on the doctrine of the social contract and couched in the rhetoric of the free legal subject.

This Whiggish consensus has been challenged by recent studies that have attempted to scrutinize the ideological content of *Dei delitti*. In particular, Foucault (1979:73–103, 1988) has argued that neither Beccaria's classical criminology nor its effects were the projects of genuinely enlightened or humanitarian reform. Instead, he has claimed, they were but two among many artifacts peculiar to a new disciplinary power. Following Foucault, a number of other critical assessments of *Dei delitti* have been voiced. The radical pioneering role usually assigned Beccaria within classical criminology has been contradicted, for example, and he has been viewed as allegedly far more conservative than other Enlightenment theorists because he deliberately

---

10. See especially, Kant's (1979:102–107) *Metaphysical Elements of Justice* and Hegel's (1821:70–71) *Philosophy of Right*.

equivocated on such dangerous issues as materialism and spiritualism (Jenkins, 1984; see also Roshier, 1989:16–18). Beccaria is held to have been a champion of aristocratic values that, in his native Lombardy, had been deeply penetrated by the ideology and interests of capitalist agriculture and the new bourgeoisie (Humphries and Greenberg, 1981:224). Beccaria's liberalism, it is claimed, responded to a fundamental difficulty of post-feudal societies: how to prevent the criminality of the masses while masking the fact that the criminal law preserved a class system based on social inequality? Beccaria's solution to this problem is portrayed as a popularization of the legal doctrine "equality before the law," a bourgeois fiction that, simply by doctrinal fiat, lodges criminal responsibility at the level of the individual (Weisser, 1979:133–138). Even Beccaria's intervention in judicial history has been dismissed as a fairy tale, his humanism ridiculed because he did not know that the process of abolishing judicial torture had already been initiated through a decisive transformation of the medieval law of proof (Chadwick, 1981:98; Langbein, 1976:67–68). His attempts to reform the criminal law have therefore been described as fundamental only to the myth of rational sentencing replacing arbitrary injustice (Hirst, 1986:152–155; see also Newman and Marongiu, 1990; Young, 1983).

Many of these assessments of the discourse in *Dei delitti* assume that Beccaria's arguments and ideological presuppositions can be understood more or less exclusively in terms of their manifest effects. Beccaria's intervention in criminal jurisprudence, for example, continues to be regarded as (1) "humanist" because it opposed the barbaric practices of the *ancien régime*, (2) as "revolutionary" because it was in the vanguard of the Italian Enlightenment in exposing religious intolerance, or (3) as "conservative" because it did not travel as far down the road of materialism as others undoubtedly did at that time.

Dei delitti, however, shares with many Enlightenment treatises the fact that the meaning of the author's arguments do not always strike with immediate clarity. To a certain extent, I will suggest, the vivid humanism in the 47 rambling chapters of *Dei delitti* is a mask behind which some of Beccaria's other arguments lie hidden, arguments that can only be discerned with some difficulty and not a little speculation. Accordingly, neither the structure nor the content of Beccaria's discourse should be taken at face value. To understand how and why this is so, something must be known of the conditions of production of *Dei delitti* as a text of the Enlightenment.

READING *DEI DELITTI* AS A TEXT OF ENLIGHTENMENT

A key feature of Italy's Enlightenment was how backward its practitioners believed it to be compared with that of other countries in Europe. "This backwardness was ascribed," Woolf (1979:75) has recorded, "to the stifling effects of the 'official' counter-reformist culture in Italy, to a conformist mentality which led to acquiescence in the teachings of churchmen and lawyers, an acceptance of scholasticism, superstition and curialism" (see also Gross, 1990:258). In matters of religion, science, politics, and economics, the intellectual universe of the *illuministi* was one in which transgressions of the permitted bounds of discourse invited more or less severe censure either from the papacy or from the tiny political cliques that ruled each state.

During the first half of the eighteenth century, in the decade or two prior to the publication of *Dei delitti*, the degree of publicity and openness attending Enlightenment discussion of such matters as religious doctrine, scientific development, and the relationship between them, was largely dictated by the ebb and flow of the political interests of the papacy. Concern about the political divisions of Italy, for example, naturally led to a fierce and threatening debate about the sovereign powers of Church and State, which raised questions about authority over the clergy, the limitation of mortmain, customs duties, and restraint of trade. In the first decade of Benedict XIV's pontificate (1740–1750), Rome opened itself up somewhat to the new culture of science, especially physics and chemistry, in the expectation that science could be applied to the alleviation of chronic economic and social problems in the papal states. Then, during the 1750s, the religious and scientific communities engaged in a heated debate on the nature of faith, the existence of magic, and the remedies for witchcraft. This debate was led by Muratori, the first Italian advocate of scientific history, and it encompassed both the attack on miracles in the *Encyclopédie* by d'Alembert and Diderot and also the discussion between La Mettrie and Maupertuis on the scientific calculation of pleasure and pain. Initially, these and other scientific arguments were couched in the rhetoric of religious doctrine. Rapidly, however, the antagonists in this debate discovered discursive weapons that were even more potent than religion: first Cartesian rationalism, then enlightenment, and finally "reason" (Venturi, 1972:103–129; Woolf, 1979:83–84).

In Beccaria's Milan, the state of Lombardy was subject to the political and economic dominance of the enlightened Austro-Hapsburg ruler Maria Theresa. Under Austrian rule, various aspects of social life in Lombardy were somewhat more liberal than elsewhere in Italy. For example, Maria Theresa had loosened the influence of the Church with the *Giunta economale* and the 1762 Pragmatic Sanction, which required royal consent before papal letters and papal bulls could be entered and published (Roberts, 1960:38). In addition, her representative in Lombardy, Count Firmian—to whom Beccaria would later be indebted for warding off attempts to prosecute him for his book—had enacted a variety of liberal inroads into social and intellectual life, including toleration of debate and discussion by reform-minded *illuministi*.

Beccaria himself was a member of the Milanese *illuministi*. These were typically government officials who sought to create a model bourgeois society that combined spiritual and moral regeneration with and through the materialist advantages of economic growth. However, far from being simple "thermometers of bourgeois opinion," these Milanese reformers envisioned a well-ordered, hierarchical society whose reconstruction would emanate from an enlightened state administration that, although working in alliance with such other powers as the papal administration, could dominate all other power blocs and would include all men of property and education (Klang, 1984:41–46). For the *illuministi*, the problem, both intellectual and organization, was how this collective dream could be implemented.

This problem was the chief focus of the group of Milanese reformers with whom Beccaria mixed in the literary club *Accademià dei pugni* (Academy of Fisticuffs), whose members included the Verri brothers Pietro and Allesandro, the economist Gian Rinaldo Carli, the ecclesiastical law expert Alfonso Longo, and the mathematicians Paolo Frisi and Luigi Lambertenghi. In 1762 the ideas of the *Accademià* began to be published in its critical literary journal *Il Caffè* which, Beccaria (1766:866) later confided, imitated Joseph Addison's *Spectator* in England. Beccaria himself was undoubtedly motivated to join the *Accademià*, and then to compose *Dei delitti*, by his discomfort with the lack of reforms in Lombardy in the domain of criminal law and the administration of justice and also with the continued burden of censorship of the written word. Throughout the Enlightenment, in Italy especially but also elsewhere and with varying degrees of necessity, its practitioners employed ubiquitous trickery to defeat the censor and the police and, in Beccaria's Lombardy, to avoid the prying eyes of the Inquisitorial Council of Ten.[11] Everyday ruses were devised simply to allow heretical, seditious, or egalitarian ideas to be transmitted to the reading public. As with *Dei delitti*, these included anonymous authorship, frontispieces with phoney places of publication, secret printing presses, and an underground network for the distribution and sale of books and pamphlets. Numerous other ploys were designed to cover the truth with a thin veil that would protect a text from hostile eyes. These included the publication of the diaries of imaginary travelers abroad, the translation of imaginary foreign books, and pervasive use of double entendre, which would allow only the *cogniscenti* the pleasure of piercing its message (Darnton, 1979, 1982).

Few works of Italian *illuminism* were able to escape such textual deformities, and the style and the content of the arguments in *Dei delitti* suffered from

---

11. Beccaria himself was painfully aware of the fates of Machiavelli, Galileo, and the historian Giannone (see Beccaria, 1766:863). They published *and* perished! Thus, Pietro Verri wrote in 1765 that for his friend Beccaria the major difficulty in preparing his book was how to publish "such delicate matters without having trouble" (cited in Maestro, 1942:54–55).

BEIRNE

them. As a result, a serious difficulty in understanding the arguments of *Dei delitti* is that, like many other Enlightenment texts, it employed an array of devious textual practices, which relied on the cautious dictum that it is better to be a secret witness of Enlightenment than a posthumously acknowledged martyr. Thus, the stated objects of Beccaria's protestations in *Dei delitti* were not the despotic monarchies of contemporary Italy but those of the "state of nature" and classical Rome and Greece (1764:15, 45, 49, 53), and his angry remarks on religious intolerance are utterly devoid of clear temporal and empirical referents. Moreover, in what was more than simply a casual failure to document his sources, Beccaria's text is virtually bereft of intellectual bearings, which, had he openly pointed to them, would have allowed his readers ("the few sages scattered across the face of the earth"—pp. 52–53) the privilege of observing more clearly the precise mast to which he chose to nail his colors. Thus, Beccaria referred to no contemporary sources other than the standard Enlightenment fare of Hobbes (p. 5) and Montesquieu (pp. 4, 5, 28), and even then, no specific reference is made to any particular work.

The lack of formal acknowledgment to other authors creates an immediate hardship for anyone attempting to trace a genealogy of Beccaria's ideas. The voluminous secondary literature on *Dei delitti* has attempted to solve this thorny problem by declaring that it is not in fact a problem at all. Was not Beccaria casually indulging in the free trade of current ideas so prevalent among Enlightenment authors in his day? Can one not read into Beccaria's text the popular views held, if not by all, then by most members of the Enlightenment, and especially by the French *philosophes*?

ENLIGHTENMENT AND ENLIGHTENMENTS

It is not easy to generalize about the eclectic ideas of that period from the middle of the seventeenth century to the last quarter of the eighteenth century that the *philosophes* joyously referred to as "*l'éclairecissement*" and that the taciturn English ironically dubbed "the Age of Enlightenment." It can perhaps be said that all members of the Enlightenment affirmed their belief in the principles of reason, the precision of the scientific method, and the authority of nature; but because there was enormous disagreement about each one of these beliefs, this says little of real substance.[12] Moreover, there was

---

12. In response to religious intolerance, for example, Helvétius, d'Holbach and La Mettrie professed atheism; Condillac, Catholicism; and Diderot alternately embraced both, "according to the state of his nerves" (Knight, 1968:5). Some *philosophes* were ardent materialists; others subscribed to spiritualism. Some were Cartesians, others Newtonians. Some looked to the anthropological state of nature with a romantic nostaligia; others detected in it the sorry aftermath of mankind's fall from grace and the onset of original sin. Some, like Diderot, assented to a limited use of judicial torture. Some opposed capital punishment, but others, like Voltaire and Montesquieu, believed that on certain occasions it was an appropriate device.

not just one Enlightenment but several, and in France, Italy, Holland, Germany, Sweden, Russia, England, Scotland, colonial America, and elsewhere, there existed diverse and sometimes quite incompatible notions of the content and direction of enlightenment.

The objects in Beccaria's text naturally reflected this diversity of opinion, and it is unwise to assume that they had some unitary source. As Beccaria himself suggested, it was in "the choice of expressions and the rapprochement of ideas" (1766:863) that the power of his text resided. His attempted rapprochement occurred with respect to two chief ideas, each of which exerted different effects on his text, and with varying degrees of impact. In concert, both testified to the salient fact that the Italian Enlightenment, which set in relatively late, was unusually under the influence of foreign authors. One was the humanism of the French *philosophes*; the other was the largely unacknowledged influence of the embryonic "science of man" in Scotland.

THE HUMANISM OF THE FRENCH PHILOSOPHES

On more than one occasion, Beccaria openly ackowledged his profound indebtedness to the humanist writings of the French *philosophes*. For example, in a letter to Abbé André Morellet, the translator of the first French edition of his book, Beccaria gushed that "I myself owe everything to French books" (1766:862).[13] Here, he specifically referred to the influence of d'Alembert, Diderot, Helvétius, Buffon, and Hume (p. 864).[14] Among the *philosophes*, it was Montesquieu who exerted the greatest influence on Beccaria's thinking prior to the publication of *Dei delitti*. Thus, Beccaria (1766:865) declared that he had first been converted to the study of philosophy by Montesquieu's *Lettres persanes* of 1721. Moreover, it was on Montesquieu that the only significant textual acknowledgment was bestowed in *Dei delitti*: "invisible truth has compelled me to follow the shining footsteps of this great man" (Beccaria, 1764:4).[15]

---

13. Beccaria at once continued that "they [i.e., French books] developed in my soul feelings of humanity that have been stifled by eight years of a fanatical education" (1766:862). It is significant that Beccaria received from those schoolmasters of Europe, the Jesuits, training in arithmetic, algebra, and geometry, "a fanatical education" as he described it, and one that he shared with anti-Jesuit intellectuals in France, such as Descartes, Montesquieu, Fontenelle, Voltaire, Diderot, Buffon, Condorcet, and possibly, Condillac. See further, Beccaria's comments to d'Alembert on the Jesuits (1765a:860).

14. Beccaria added that he derived many of his ideas from Helvétius's *l'Esprit*, which had alerted him to the misfortunes of humanity (see also note 37); from Buffon, who opened up for him the *"sanctuaire"* of nature; and from d'Alembert: "I know enough about mathematics to appreciate the great discoveries of this celebrated man, and to regard him as the greatest geometer of our century" (1766:865–866). After reading *Dei delitti*, Melchior Grimm thus aptly observed that "M. Beccaria writes in French with Italian words" (1765:330–331). See further, note 20.

15. Significantly, Montesquieu's (1748) *De l'ésprit des lois* is full of misgivings and

Although these few observations are far from conclusive, the influence of the *philosophes* can with reasonable confidence be discerned in the spacious antechamber to Beccaria's edifice, and it is lavishly decorated with their humanist rhetoric. It is demonstrated in two ways. First, Beccaria inherited from Montesquieu—and through Montesquieu, ultimately from the secular law tradition of Grotius and Pufendorf—a desire to disentangle and then sever criminal law and justice from religion. In arguing for the supremacy of the rule of law in human affairs, Beccaria thus rejected any claim that the laws that regulate social relationships derive from Divine Will. For him, it was imperative that sin be demarcated from crime, spiritual powers from temporal powers, and ecclesiastical bodies from secular courts. The Supreme Being who politely haunts the pages of *Dei delitti* is not therefore the omnipotent God the Father of Roman Catholicism but a depersonalized god who has been cast into the nether regions where all other spirits dwell. This god was merely another benevolent despot who could be contemplated "with respect untempered with fear or adoration" (Becker, 1932:50) and whose jurisdiction, for Beccaria, encompassed sins ("offenses between men and God") rather than crimes ("offenses between men and men"). For Beccaria, then, crime— "I do not address myself to sins (1764:73)—is not a theological concept but a social one. Thus, he wrote,

> the true measure of crimes is . . . *the harm done to society*. This is one of the palpable truths which one needs neither quadrants nor telescopes to discover (p. 17).

A second way in which French humanism was manifest in Beccaria's text lay in his rejection of the cruel physical pain inflicted by the judiciary on suspects and on convicted felons. At one point, for example, he drew a stark contrast between "the indolence of the judge and the anguish of someone accused of a crime—between the comforts and pleasures of the unfeeling magistrate . . . and the tears and squalid condition of a prisoner" (p. 36). His strictures in this regard were directed almost exclusively, however, at the practices of judicial torture and capital punishment. Thus, "the torture of the accused while his trial is still in progress is a cruel practice sanctioned by the usage of most nations" (p. 29). More dramatic still, in what was likely a macabre comment on the popular and crowd-pleasing manner of disposing of

---

uncertainties about the thorny problem of free will and determinism. It is instructive, for example, to juxtapose the sort of persistent claim Montesquieu made at the very beginning of his book that "it is absurd to say that "*a blind determinism [fatalité] has produced all the effects that we see in the world*: what could be more absurd than to say that a blind determinism seems to have produced intelligent beings?" (Bk. I:7; emphasis in original) with his materialist analysis of the geographical distribution of various social events in Book XVI. There, Montesquieu actually claimed that such factors as climate and soil influence even sexual inequality and the type and content of laws (1748, Bk. XVI:280–294).

witches and heretics, Beccaria declared that "rational men" object to the distasteful spectacle of "the muffled, confused groans of poor wretches issuing out of vortices of black smoke—the smoke of human limbs—amid the crackling of charred bones and the sizzling of still palpitating entrails" (p. 72).[16] Elsewhere Beccaria confessed (p. 23, and see pp. 4, 29) that he would deem himself fortunate if,

> in the course of upholding the rights of men and invincible truth, I should contribute to saving an unhappy victim of tyranny or of equally pernicious ignorance from suffering and from the anguish of death, then the blessings and tears of that one person overcome with joy would console me for the contempt of all humanity.

Although it was a major impetus to the aims in Beccaria's text, the humanism of the *philosophes* was not at all the sole feature of its discourse. Indeed, at times Beccaria's humanism seems only an incidental feature that was grafted almost in *ad hoc* fashion to other, more significant arguments in *Dei delitti*.[17] Although humanism asserted itself in elegant passages that disavow the physical brutality of criminal law and that adopt a charitable position bent on ameliorating economic inequality, the depth of its textual penetration must not be exaggerated. This is unremarkable, though, if only because the *philosophes* themselves did not often address in their own writings the issues of penality raised in *Dei delitti*. Even in the case of those *philosophes* who did address issues of criminal law and punishment, such as Montesquieu and the Chevalier de Jaucourt (1751), the textual structure of their works resembled unkempt mazes rather than the systematicity to which Beccaria's treatise aspired.

To uncover the principal discursive inspiration behind Beccaria's treatise, one therefore must look elsewhere. It is to be found, I suggest, in the ideas of Enlightenment authors in Britain, especially as they were developed in Scotland.

THE "SCIENCE OF MAN" IN SCOTLAND

I have suggested that, because the publishing conditons in Lombardy were so fraught with danger, Beccaria was forced to conceal some of the intellectual influences on *Dei delitti* and, moreover, some of the arguments within it. Nevertheless, with typical Enlightenment flourish, Beccaria attached to his

---

16. In *Dei delitti*, Beccaria (1764:48–49) argued that capital punishment is justified if (1) an incarcerated citizen is still a threat to society, (2) a citizen's mere existence could produce a revolution dangerous to the state, or (3) a citizen's execution deterred others from committing crimes.

17. Contemporary interest in the humanist aspects of Beccaria's text were probably stimulated by a propaganda campaign mounted by Voltaire (1762a; 1762b; 1763; see also, Maugham, 1928) on behalf of the unfortunate Jean Calas.

text a deliberate clue of extraordinary significance for unlocking the aims of his work. Preceding the text, and prominently displayed on the frontispiece of each of the six editions of *Dei delitti* personally authorized by Beccaria, is an epigram (originally in Latin) from one of the first purveyors of Enlightenment ideas, Francis Bacon (1561–1626): "In all Negociations of Difficulty, a Man may not look to sow and reap at once; But must Prepare Business, and so Ripen it by Degrees" (1632:283).

It is interesting to speculate why Bacon's advice was so highly esteemed by Beccaria that he actually introduced his text with it. An obvious but perhaps superficial explanation is that Beccaria was declaring his intention to practise a virtue that was decidely lacking in other *illuministi*, namely, patience. In other words, although fearing that his proposals in *Dei delitti* might arouse stiff opposition from Church and State, Beccaria nevertheless was secure in the knowledge that they would eventually see the light of day, ripen, and bear fruit, and he was hereby stating as much. Still, an intriguing question remains. If Beccaria chose to introduce his text with a message for the faithful, why did he do so with an epigram from Bacon rather than, say, Montesquieu or Helvétius or Voltaire? Is it only that Beccaria had enormous admiration for Bacon?[18] One of Beccaria's (n.d.1:459–470) unpublished manuscripts, indeed, reveals that with marginal lines and copious notes he devoured several of Bacon's treatises, including *Sermones Fideles, De Dignitate, De Augmentis Scientiarum*, and the *Novum Organum*. Or is it more likely that Beccaria wished to invite his readers to draw a favorable parallel between what Bacon had attempted to do to English law in Elizabethan times and what it was that he intended to do to Italian criminal law in his day? Indeed, to his eighteenth-century Enlightenment disciples, Bacon was admired not only because he was the founder of empiricism and a great philosopher and scientist; to would-be legal reformers, like Beccaria in Italy and William Blackstone in England, Bacon was also revered for his legal theorizing, for his statute consolidation, and for the attempt in his *Digests* to give the law "light" (Lieberman, 1989:181–186). These very purposes were among Beccaria's own, as well, with respect to Italian criminal law. Beccaria

---

18. Beccaria shared his neglected Baconian heritage with the anti-Cartesian humanist Giambattista Vico (1668–1744), the professor of Latin Eloquence at the University of Naples and one of the most creative social theorists in the entire Enlightenment. In his books *On the Study Methods of Our Time* (1709) and *The New Science* (1725), Vico audaciously applied Bacon's evolutionary and inductivist analysis of nature of natural law, jurisprudence, and history. Vico anticipated the *philosophes* in arguing that, through the judicious use of rewards and punishments, aristocratic laws can turn private vices into public virtues, and thus ensure civil happiness. Moreover, in *The New Science*, his expansive historical analyses suggested that on the "concrete and complex order of human civil institutions, we may superimpose the order of numbers" (1725:339–340; see also, Berlin, 1960). However, few of the *philosophes* themselves bothered to pierce Vico's obscure, convoluted, and tormented style, and in his lifetime he exerted almost no influence.

thus had good reason to pay homage to Chancellor Bacon and to England, "a nation whose literary glory, whose superiority in commerce and wealth (and hence in power), and whose examples of virtue and courage leave no doubt as to the excellence of its laws" (1764:31–32).[19]

The placement of Bacon's epigram must be mentioned not least because of Beccaria's use of it as an introduction to his text. As an introduction, it directs the reader to another dimension of Enlightenment thinking, the powerful presence of which in *Dei delitti* has largely been overlooked (*pace* Wills, 1978:149–151) but which was, I suggest, its central thrust and one that Beccaria had very good reason to hide from Catholic censors. This is the drift toward a science of man that had been inaugurated by enlightenment English philosophers such as Bacon himself, and by Newton and Shaftesbury, and after them by Locke. Later, it was developed even more forcefully in the civic tradition of Scottish authors such as Hutcheson, Hume, John Millar, Adam Ferguson, and Adam Smith.[20] Indeed, in a letter of April 6, 1762, Pietro Verri described his young friend Beccaria as "a profound mathematician . . .

---

19. Beyond the explanations given above, the remote possibility exists that there is even more to Beccaria's prominent placement of Bacon's epigram than meets the eye. Perhaps Beccaria was indulging in another Enlightenment game with his readers, designed not so much to stimulate his readers to seek its textual meaning *between* the lines but *before* them. Perhaps it was not to this particular Baconian passage that Beccaria wished to alert his fellow *philosophes*, but to the one preceding it, which states: "In Dealing with Cunning Persons, we must ever Consider their Ends, to interpret their Speeches; And it is good, to say little to them, and that which they least look for" (quoting Bacon, 1632:282–283). If Beccaria was inviting his readers to "interpret" his own argument, then, given that his opposition to judicial arbitrariness was not hidden in his text, but quite exposed, it is possible that there was some other important, though hidden, feature of his text, to which Beccaria wanted to alert his readers.

20. In Maestro's (1942) *Voltaire and Beccaria as Reformers of Criminal Law*, for example, there is no mention of either Bacon or Francis Hutcheson (1694–1746), and neither John Locke (1632–1704) nor David Hume (1711–1776) merit more than passing mention, although Hutcheson merits a brief comment in his (Maestro, 1973:21) authoritative *Cesare Beccaria and the Origins of Penal Reform*. Similarly, Chadwick (1981:96) writes regarding the Milanese Enlightenment that "Paris loomed much closer. The English and Scottish writers were less important." Venturi (1983) has noticed several fortuitous "parallels" between Beccaria's text and Scottish authors, but he identifies Henry Home, Lord Kames, Ferguson, and Smith rather than Hutcheson.

This is not to suggest that it was only the Scottish philosophers who were concerned to develop a scientific account of society. Far from it. Beccaria's French colleague Jean d'Alembert, for example, typically believed that only his Baconian-inspired "geometry," or "science of man," could unravel intricate religious doctrine, and when he (e.g., d'Alembert, n.d. 1:571–572; n.d. 2:99–114) addressed issues of human rights and duties he did so with the rhetoric of *esprit géométrique* and the methods of the exact sciences. On one occasion, he even argued that "mathematics should be used to subvert the Inquisition. Infiltrate enough geometers into the citizenry of a country oppressed by the Church, and Enlightenment would follow inevitably" (d'Alembert, quoted in Hankins, 1970:14).

with a mind apt to try new roads if laziness and discouragement do not suffo-
cate him" (cited in Maestro, 1942:53). Given the virulent Anglomania that
gripped the Italian devotees of the Enlightenment, it is only to be expected
that Beccaria should have been compared with some English theorist. But it
is most interesting that the comparison was not with a legal reformer, such as
William Blackstone, but with the great scientist Isaac Newton; the most affectionate and admiring nickname given Beccaria by his friends was
"Newtoncino"—little Newton (Gay, 1966:12).

Before I try to demonstrate the influence of certain British authors on Beccaria's arguments in *Dei delitti*, let me offer some anticipatory evidence of this
connection from the period just prior to and contemporaneous with its publication in 1764. To begin with, it must be stressed how unexceptional it is that
Beccaria's discourse drew so heavily on the ideas of Enlightenment authors in
England and Scotland. Among the Italian *illuministi*, they, of all the authors,
exercised enormous influence, the peak of which they enjoyed from the late
1750s to the early 1770s. In much of Italy there was widespread feeling that
the economic and political progress of countries like England, France, and
Holland, was directly linked to the scientific rationalism embedded in the
empiricist discourse of the Enlightenment triumvirate of Bacon, Newton, and
Locke. Although some key works in this tradition had been banned in Italy
by state authorities, the papacy, or both,[21] they were nevertheless widely
available—Bacon and Newton could easily be found in Latin, and French
translations of Locke's *Essay Concerning Human Understanding* and
Voltaire's *Eléments de la philosophie de Newton* appeared in 1700 and 1738,
respectively. Indeed, the work of British authors dominated the conversations and the literary discourse of Beccaria's *Accademià* meetings.
Accademià members regularly read and discussed works by Bacon, Shake-
speare, Swift, Addison, Pope, Dryden, and Locke (Landry, 1910:13–14), and
also by the Scottish philosophers, among whom certainly were Hutcheson
and Hume (Shackleton, 1972:1470–1471).

The subtle complexity of *Dei delitti* cannot be comprehended in all its rich-
ness without recognizing the effects on his text of Beccaria's thoroughgoing
admiration for enlightened British writings, especially those in the Scottish
"civic tradition." Beginning with the writings of Andrew Fletcher in the late
seventeenth century, this tradition was concerned above all, and to a degree
that existed in no other country, with the multifaceted relationship between
political institutions and economic progress (Robertson, 1983). This concern,
heightened at the turn of the century by the possibility of enforced union with
England, was directed to a variety of issues, many of which naturally excited

---

21. Locke's *Essay Concerning Human Understanding*, for example, was placed on the
Index in 1734 by Pope Clement XII explicitly because its empiricism threatened religious
belief.

the reformist yearnings of the Italian *illuministi* as well in the middle of the eighteenth century. Chief among these topics were religious toleration, property and industry, the rule of law, constitutional government, justice, and the conditions of social order. Moreover, from about 1750 to 1770 the Scottish civic tradition was pivotal in the rise of a presociological discourse about society, and within that discourse a central place was occupied by the attempt to construct a science of man (Phillipson, 1981; Swingewood, 1970).

It is instructive now to consider Beccaria's other early writings, which, against *Dei delitti*'s bright reception, have generally been ignored. This is unfortunate because, although Beccaria's other writings did not exert much influence, they provide a broader view of his concerns at the time he wrote *Dei delitti*. Prior to the publication of *Dei delitti*, Beccaria published two short tracts, each of which yields some details as to the direction of his thought. In his first work, he (Beccaria, 1762a) addressed the economic problems of the Milanese currency. This essay drew its inspiration from Hume, Sir William Petty (Schumpeter, 1954:298), and especially, he (Beccaria, 1762a:8) admitted, from Locke; here Beccaria (1762a:8) specifically referred to the influence of Locke's *Nuove considerazioni* on his monetary analysis.[22] In another *Il Caffè* essay, Beccaria (1762a) creatively used algebraic formulae to analyze the costs and benefits of the crime of smuggling; here his main question was "given that a certain proportion of smuggled goods will be seized by the authorities, what is the total quantity that smugglers must move to be left with neither gain nor loss?"[23] His answer to this

---

22. "*Nuove considerazioni* . . ." was doubtless Locke's *Further Considerations Concerning Raising the Value of Money* (1695; see also Hutcheson, 1755, Bk.II, Ch. 12). Locke's book had been translated into Italian in 1749 by the Tuscan Abbés Pagnini and Tavanti, although its publication was delayed until 1751, probably because the translators feared that there must have been "some hidden mystery, as for instance that it might not be to the liking of certain important persons" (Venturi, 1963:783; see also Venturi, 1972:230–231). Moreover, it is no small coincidence that in his *Essay Concerning Human Understanding*—available throughout Europe in Latin since the 1690s, Locke had argued, in the context of equating the growth of crime with the rise of money as a universal form of exchange, that those who committed crime did so because they were trying either to assuage an immediate pain or to satisfy an absent pleasure (1689, 1:97–122); see further Schumpeter (1954:297–299) and especially Caffentzis (1989:61–68).

23. Beccaria's algebraic response to this question perhaps inaugurated the idea of indifference theory in modern economics (Schumpeter, 1954:179; see also Beccaria, 1804:551–562). For present purposes, it is fair to say that this idea anticipates Beccaria's attempt in *Dei delitti* to calculate the precise amount of pain needed to deter the pleasure gained from committing a crime. Thus, "the prison sentence of a tobacco smuggler should not be the same as that of a cutthroat or a thief, and the smuggler's labor, if confined to the work and service of the royal revenue administration that he had meant to defraud, will be the most suitable type of punishment" (Beccaria, 1764:64).

In 1765 Beccaria (1765b:858) confessed to Archduke Ferdinand, the Austrian governor of Lombardy, that he had never enjoyed the study of law and that, rather than don the judicial robe, he wanted to serve his country by engaging in sciences more relevant to the

question was probably influenced by his reading of Jonathan Swift's satirical *Gulliver's Travels* (1762b:164).

It has never been properly acknowledged that, like several other continental adherents of Enlightenment (e.g., Helvétius, 1758; Jaucourt, 1751; see also Wood, 1989), Beccaria was inspired by the ideas of the founder of the Scottish Enlightenment, the Glaswegian philosopher Francis Hutcheson, and by Hutcheson's pupil Hume (whose "profound metaphysics" he praised generously: Beccaria, 1766:865). One of Beccaria's (1765c:169) early essays, for example, shows the unmistakable influence of Hutcheson's (1725a:48–51) idea of the beauty of theorems.[24] The influence of Hutcheson on Beccaria's *Dei delitti* far transcends the communality of discursive practices often engaged in by Enlightenment writers. When Beccaria introduced *Dei delitti* with the enigmatic sentence "Mankind owes a debt of gratitude to the philosopher who, from the despised obscurity of his study, had the courage to cast the first and long fruitless seeds of useful truths among the multitude!" (1764:3; see also Scott, 1900:273–274),[25] he was undoubtedly referring to Hutcheson, who had explicitly termed himself "an obscure Philosopher" (Hutcheson, 1725b:vii).

Nearly every page of *Dei delitti* is marked, I suggest, by Hutcheson's towering influence on Beccaria's thinking. It is found in the common metaphors of expression used in *Dei delitti* and in Hutcheson's (1755) *System of Moral Philosophy*;[26] these metaphors are taken from such diverse fields as theology, law, architecture, Newtonian mechanics, and geometry. Hutcheson's influence is also found in the extraordinary correspondence between key recommendations in Beccaria's *Dei delitti* and those in Hutcheson's *System*. Careful comparison reveals that whole sections of *Dei delitti* either restate or develop the proposals for law and criminal justice in Hutcheson's *System*.

---

economic regulation of a state. Thus, from 1769 to 1773 he lectured on political economy at the Palatinate, at the same time beginning a career in government administration in Lombardy, until his death in 1794 (see further Canetta, 1985; Maestro, 1973:81–150).

24.   The same mathematical heresies that led to the condemnation and avoidance for two decades of Hutcheson's work in France at once endeared it to various scholars in Italy. However, in the middle of the century the *philosophes* revived interest in Hutcheson's mathematical approach to utilitarianism: Lévesque de Pouilly, Maupertuis, and Duclos wrote of happiness in Hutchesonian terms, Marc Antoine Eidous published a French translation of Hutcheson's *Inquiry*, and Diderot described his aesthetic ideas in the *Encyclopédie* (Shackleton, 1972:1468–1470). It is almost certain that Beccaria had read Hutcheson's (1725b) *Inquiry into the Original of our Ideas of Beauty and Virtue*, probably in a French translation of 1749 (Scott, 1900:273; see also Robbins, 1968:195).

25.   In the introduction to *Dei delitti*, this exclamation comes on the heels of Beccaria's statement of belief in the utilitarian formula; see further Scott (1900:273–274).

26.   In 1738 Hutcheson had circulated the manuscript of his *System of Moral Philosophy* in Scotland, Ireland, England, and Holland. It had therefore been known on the continent considerably before its actual date of publication in 1755; nowhere was it more popular than in Italy, especially in Lombardy.

Among the most important of these are those that refer to property as the basis of the social contracts (see Hutcheson, 1755:Bk. II, ch. 6:319–322; Beccaria, p. 7); the definition of crime (Hutcheson, Bk. II; ch. 15:86–87, "injury"; Beccaria, p. 17, "harm"; the uniformity of laws (Hutcheson, Bk. II; ch. 15:101–102; Beccaria, pp. 11–12); the simplicity of laws (Hutcheson, Bk. III; ch. 9:322–323; Beccaria, pp. 12–13, 75); the harm inflicted by corrupt public servants and magistrates (Hutcheson, Bk. II; ch. 15:88–89; Beccaria, p. 78); the compensatory use of fines (Hutcheson, Bk. II; ch. 15:88–91; Beccaria, pp. 39–40, but see pp. 34–45); the deterrent nature of punishment (Hutcheson, Bk. II; ch. 15:87, 93–94; Bk. III; ch. 9:333; Beccaria, pp. 23, 33, 47, 50, 74–75); the proportionality of punishment to crime (Hutcheson, Bk. III; ch. 9:331–338; Beccaria, pp. 14–16, 23, 46–47, 55, 64); and opposition to judicial torture (Hutcheson, Bk. II; ch. 15:97; Bk. III; ch. 9:337–338); Beccaria, pp. 29–33, 70–72).

But my chief intention here is not to document in detail the remarkable identity in the respective penal recommendations of Hutcheson's *System* and those of Beccaria's *Dei delitti*. Rather, it is to show that just as much of the specific content of Beccaria's famous treatise is taken from Hutcheson's (1755) *System* so, too, is much of the structure of its argumentation. As discussed below, Beccaria's treatise must thus be placed in a trajectory radically different from the "classical" one conventionally accorded it. In the same way that Hutcheson's *System* contained a progeny of useful truths otherwise known to Beccaria as the new "science of man" so, too, did Beccaria aspire in *Dei delitti* to apply this science to the field of crime and punishment.

THE SCIENCE OF MAN IN *DEI DELITTI*

Some of the arguments of *Dei delitti* embodied a deterministic discourse that, if not for their author then in retrospect, seem decidedly at odds with the classic dependence on free will that is commonly attributed to *Dei delitti*. Among Enlightenment thinkers this discourse was denominated loosely and was signified by such terms as Pascal's *esprit géométrique*[27] and, after mid-century, the Scottish civic tradition's "science of man." Beccaria himself variously referred to it as "geometry," "moral geography," "political arithmetic," "number," and the "science of man." Woven within Beccaria's stylistic eloquence and his passionate humanism is a strong reliance on the discursive use of determinist principles derived from the science of man.

Several key features of the science of man are plainly recognizable in *Dei*

---

27. By the middle of the eighteenth century the term *"esprit géométrique"* had lost much of its original meaning as a mathematical antonym for "the philosophical spirit"; it had become, according to Knight (1968:18–19), "a kind of ritual invocation of a whole cluster of virtues associated with science of all kinds, including the anti-mathematical science of the empirical tradition."

delitti. Chief among them are the doctrines of utilitarianism, probabilism, associationism, and sensationalism. The doctine of utilitarianism operated for Beccaria as a core justificatory argument for establishing "the right to punish," and it is positioned prominently at the very beginning of the text. With it Beccaria attempted to forge linkages, as had Hutcheson before him, among the rule of law, justice, and the economic marketplace. Beccaria employed probabilism, associationism, and sensationalism throughout *Dei delitti*, and he wielded the three doctrines in concert as mechanisms with which to advance various technico-administrative aspects of his chosen penal strategies (or "how to punish").

THE RIGHT TO PUNISH

The point of entry into Beccaria's discourse about penal strategies is provided by his subscription to an economistic form of social contract theory based on utilitarianism and secured through the rule of law.[28] *Dei delitti* begins with a utilitarian argument for "the greatest happiness" cast in the specific context of a plea for the supremacy of the rule of law. Whereas in the past, according to Beccaria, law had most commonly been the instrument of the passions of a few persons, "the impartial observer of human nature [would] grasp the actions of a multitude of men and consider them from this point of view: *the greatest happiness shared among the majority of people*" [*la massima felicità divisa nel maggior numero*] (1764:3).[29] The happiness of "a

---

28. It is reasonable to suppose that Beccaria derived this—the foundation of *Dei delitti*—from the algebraic formulations in Hutcheson's (1725b) *Inquiry into the Original of our Ideas of Beauty and Virtue* (see also Scott, 1900:273–274; Shackleton, 1972:1466–1472). In the first edition of his *Inquiry*, Hutcheson had written "that action is best, which procures the greatest happiness for the greatest numbers; and that worst, which in like manner, occasions misery" (1725b:177–178). In the fourth and final edition, although much else in it had been considerably modified, Hutcheson argued that "the most perfectly virtuous actions" are those "as appear to have the most universal unlimited Tendency to the greatest and most extensive Happiness of all the rational agents, to whom an Influence can reach" (1738:184).
I do not mean to suggest that the utilitarian principle originated in the work of Hutcheson; see, for example, the even earlier formulation by Locke (1689, 1:112)—"the highest Perfection of intellectual Nature lies in a careful and constant Pursuit of true and solid Happiness." Indeed, its roots can be discovered in the works of Cicero (wishing his friend "bonis affici quam maximis" in *De Finibus*) and in that of late Stoics such as Antoninus (see also Scott, 1900:275–277). Alternative contemporary candidates, albeit with far weaker claims than Hutcheson's, were Pietro Verri "[là] felicità pubblica o sia la maggior felicità possibile divisa colla maggiore uguaglianza possibile," 1763:84) and Helvétius ("l'utilité du public, c'est-à-dire, du plus grand nombre d'hommes soumis à la même forme de gouvernement," 1758:Discourse 2, Ch. 17:175). See further the speculations about alternative candidates by Gianni Francioni in *Cesare Beccaria: Opere* (Firpo, 1984, 1:23).
29. Beccaria's wording of this utilitarian slogan differed slightly (*contra* Young's translation of it) both from Hutcheson's original statement and from the version of it later popularized by Bentham, a fact due to its frequent translation from one language to

few illustrious persons" is therefore something Beccaria derided as tyranny (p. 43). To whatever he intended as the content of the otherwise empty utilitarian objective *felicità*,[30] Beccaria attached the condition that if all individual members are bound to society then—as opposed to the original, warlike state of nature—society is likewise bound to all of them by a binding contract of mutual obligation.

> This obligation, which reaches from the throne to the hovel and which is equally binding on the greatest and the most wretched of men, means nothing other than that it is in everybody's interest that the contracts useful to the greatest number should be observed. Their violation, even by one person, opens the door to anarchy (p. 9).

Beccaria harnessed his declared utilitarianism to two mechanisms, which he tended to elevate to the status of ends. The first is the rule of law: "the true foundations of the happiness I mentioned here are security and freedom limited only by law" (p. 62). For Beccaria, law is the condition by which "independent and isolated men, tired of living in a constant state of war and of enjoying a freedom made useless by the uncertainty of keeping it, unite in society" (p. 7). As will be discussed in some detail, Beccaria urged that criminal law especially have various features of formal and substantive rationality, including clarity, logical inclusiveness, and predictability. Beccaria's plea for the rule of law emerged largely *via negativa,* as a result of his disenchantment with the theocentrism of Rome, with its ecclesiastical courts and its inquisitorial practices. Law and justice must develop apart from the activities of religious policing:

> It is the task of theologians to establish the limits of justice and injustice regarding the intrinsic goodness or wickedness of an act; it is the task of the observer of public life to establish the relationships of political justice and injustice, that is, of what is useful or harmful to society (p. 5).[31]

Moreover, Beccaria asserted that those who believe that the intention of the criminal is the true measure of crime are in error because crime can only be measured by "the harm done to the nation" (p. 16) or "to the public good" (p. 15):

---

another—beginning in English (1725, Hutcheson), then to French (1749, Marc Antoine Eidous), to Italian (1764, Beccaria), to French (1765, Morellet), and finally back to English (1768, Priestly). See further Shackleton (1972).

30. In Beccaria's discourse the content of the relationship between the state and its citizenry is never properly spelled out in words like *"felicità."* To him "happiness" seems to have meant both the warm mental sensations associated with individualism—where the public good is the aggregate of individually pursued self-interest—and also such virtues as courage, liberty, justice, and honor.

31. Unfortunately, except for the crime of suicide, Beccaria was otherwise quite circumspect on this issue. About suicide, he argued that "it is a crime which God punishes (since He alone can punish even after death)" (Beccaria, 1764:63).

> Given the necessity of men uniting together, and given the compacts
> which necessarily result from the very clash of private interests, one may
> discern a scale of misdeeds wherein the highest degree consists of acts
> that are directly destructive of society and the lowest of the least possible
> injustice against one of its members. Between these extremes lie all
> actions contrary to the public good, which are called crimes . . . (pp.
> 14–15).

For the achievement of his declared utilitarian objective, Beccaria envis-
aged a second mechanism, namely, the economic marketplace. In this
respect, he believed that the juridico-political basis of the modern state should
be secured, not through such feudal relics as theocentrism and the divine
right of kings, but through the utilitarian principles of large-scale, bourgeois
commodity exchange. The free economic agent and the subject of law are,
indeed, one and the same individual; the atomized individual who "thinks of
himself as the center of all the world's affairs" (p. 8) is an economic agent
simply reconstituted in juridical terms. Thus, Beccaria argued that although
"commerce and the ownership of goods" are not the goal of the social contract, they can be a means of achieving it (p. 66); "*common utility*," in other
words, is "the basis of human justice" (p. 16). Beccaria was enthusiastic
about the "quiet war of industry [that] has broken out among great nations,
the most humane sort of war and the kind most worthy of reasonable men"
(p. 3), and he praised "easy, simple, and great laws . . . that require only a nod
from the legislator to spread wealth and vigor" (p. 66). Indeed, the surest
way of securing the compliance of individuals with the law of their nation is
to

> improve the relative well-being of each of them. Just as every effort
> ought to be made to turn the balance of the trade in our favor, so it is in
> the greatest interests of the sovereign and of the nation that the sum total
> of happiness . . . should be greater than elsewhere (p. 62).

Given this relationship, Beccaria's concept of crime as "what is harmful to
society" is likewise intimately linked to the economic marketplace (see also
Wills, 1978:153–154; Zeman, 1981:20). For Beccaria, the social contract
entails that all citizens surrender a portion of their liberty to the state, in
return for which the state protects their right to security and tranquility;
"there is no enlightened man who does not love the open, clear, and useful
contracts of public security when he compares the slight portion of useful
liberty that he has sacrificed to the total sum of all the liberty sacrificed by
other men" (Beccaria, 1764:76). The sum of all these portions of liberty is
thus a "deposit" that no citizen can ever "withdraw" from the "common
store" or from the "public treasury" (pp. 7, 34), and therein lies the basis of
the state's right to punish its subjects:

> The mere formation of this deposit, however, [is] not sufficient; it [has] to

be defended against the private usurpations of each particular individual
. . . Tangible motives [are] required sufficient to dissuade the despotic
spirit of each man from plunging the laws of society back into the original chaos (p. 7).

Crime is thus an offense against both law and economic intercourse.
Accordingly, when in *Dei delitti* Beccaria referred to particular crimes, he
only emphasized crimes against property, including theft, counterfeiting,
bankruptcy, smuggling, and indolence. He especially condemned political
indolence (which "contributes to society neither with work nor with wealth"
pp. 41–42) and "timid prudence" (which "sees only the present moment" p.
66). At several points in his discussion of punishment, moreover, he invoked
a symmetry between the aims and conditions of penal servitude and those of
the marketplace. One feature of this symmetry is described as "the faint and
prolonged example of a man who, deprived of his liberty, has become a beast
of burden, repaying the society he has offended with his labors" (p. 49). Elsewhere he urged that "the most fitting punishment [for theft] . . . is the only
sort of slavery that can be deemed just: the temporary subjugation to society
of the labor and the person of criminal" (p. 40).

HOW TO PUNISH

It is not my concern here to outline each of Beccaria's chosen penal strategies but to show how his argumentation regarding them again demonstrates
his adherence to various aspects of the new science of man. Chief among
those aspects were the loosely defined doctrines of probabilism, sensationalism, and associationism.

PROBABILISM

Beccaria's attempt to apply "probability" and "number" to matters of punishment derives from his dependence on the ideas of wise governance held by
British authors such as Locke[32] and Hutcheson[33] rather than by the French

---

32. Locke himself attached great importance to the roles of number, probability, and
mathematics in the analysis of human affairs. "In all sorts of Reasoning," he argued,
"every single Argument should be manag'd as a Mathematical Demonstration" (Locke,
1689, 3:397; see also 1:85, 308–309). It is tempting to suggest that Beccaria also drew
inspiration from the writings of one of Hutcheson's mentors, the English statistician and
physician Sir William Petty (1623–1687). Besides his noted contribution to the development of statistics, Petty was a staunch critic of physical punishments. In Chapter 10 of his
Treatise of Taxes & Contributions, he urged that pecuniary "mulcts" (i.e., fines), made over
to the Commonwealth as "reparations," were far better than physical punishments, which
benefit no one, and actually deprive the state of useful labor. Thus, "Here we are to
remember in consequence of our opinion [that 'Labour is the Father and active principle of
Wealth, as Lands are the Mother'], that the State by killing, mutilating, or imprisoning
their members, do withall punish themselves; wherefore such punishments ought (as much

philosophes.

Near the beginning of *Dei delitti*, Beccaria asserted his intention of "going back to general principles" (pp. 3–4) to uncover the rampant political and judicial errors "accumulated" over several centuries. In a sense, his search for these principles reflected an abhorrence of uncertainty. Thus, he objected to "arbitrary notions of vice and virtue" (p. 4). Sometimes, he complained, "despotic impatience" and "effiminate timidity" transform "serious trials into a kind of game in which chance and subterfuge are the main elements" (p. 24), and he derided "the errors and passions that have successively dominated various legislators" (p. 15). Such errors included the useless tortures "multiplied" with prodigious and useless severity; the punishment of crimes that are "unproven"; and the horrors of a prison, "augumented" by "uncertainty" ("that most cruel tormentor of the wretched" (p. 4). Simultaneously, Beccaria bemoaned the unhappy fact that, unlike "the symmetry and order that is the lot of brute, inanimate matter" (p. 74), "turbulent human activity" and "the infinitely complicated relationships and mutations of social arrangements" are impossible to reduce to a "geometric order devoid of irregularity and confusion" (pp. 74–75; see also p. 5):

> It is impossible to prevent all disorders in the universal strife of human passions. They increase at the compound rate of population growth and the intertwining of public interests, which cannot be directed toward the public welfare with geometric precision. In political arithmetic, one must substitute the calculation of probability for mathematical exactitude (p. 14).

Beccaria's advocacy of probability extended as well to each stage of the criminal justice system, including the clarity of the law itself, judicial torture, witnesses and evidence, jurors, and sentencing practices. In this regard, his remarks were addressed not only to the *illuministi* and *philosophes* but also, especially, to enlightened lawmakers, to "the legislator [who] acts like the good architect, whose role is to oppose the ruinous course of gravity and to bring to bear everything that contributes to the strength of his building" (p. 15). A brief outline of these remarks is now in order.

Beccaria urged that only a fixed and predictable law could provide citizens

---

as possible) to be avoided and commuted for pecuniary mulcts, which will encrease labour and publick wealth" (Petty, 1662:68; cf. Hutcheson, 1755, Bk. II:318–319, 341).

    33. Unlike that of the philosophes, Hutcheson's utilitarianism was explicitly formulated in mathematical and economic terms. Thus, when Hutcheson wrote "that action is best, which procures the greatest happiness *for the greatest numbers*" [emphasis added], he meant it literally and mathematically; when he attempted to calculate the precise incidence of "perfect virtue" and "moral evil," he did so strictly in terms of algebraic equations (1725b:187–193). Indeed, the original title of Hutcheson's *Inquiry* contained the words *"with an attempt to introduce a mathematical calculation in subjects of morality."* This inclination was shared by Beccaria.

with personal security and liberate them from judicial arbitrariness. Thus, "the greater the number of people who understand the sacred law code and who have it in their hands, the less frequent crimes will be, for there is no doubt that ignorance and uncertainty concerning punishments aid the eloquence of the passions" (p. 13). The law itself must be unambiguous because only with "fixed" and "immutable" laws can citizens acquire personal "security": "this is just because it is the goal of society, and it is useful because it enables [citizens] to calculate precisely the ill consequences of a misdeed" (p. 12). Moreover,

> when a fixed legal code that must be observed to the letter leaves the judge no other task than to examine a citizen's actions and to determine whether or not they conform to the written law, when the standard of justice and injustice that must guide the actions of the ignorant as well as the philosophic citizen is not a matter of philosophic controversy but of fact, then subjects are not exposed to the petty tyranies of many men (p. 12).

For minor and less heinous crimes, moreover, there should be a statute of limitations that relieves citizens of "uncertainty" regarding their fate (p. 56); but such time limits "ought not to increase in exact proportion to the atrocity of the crime, for the liklihood of crimes is inversely proportional to their barbarity" (p. 56).

Beccaria's subscription to the doctrine of probabilism throws more light on the question of how *Dei delitti* viewed judicial torture. As discussed above, it was on humanist grounds that Beccaria opposed the practice of interrogating an accused with methods of torture.[34] If in this specific context "humanism" simply connotes a condemnaton of the infliction of physical pain on others, then one is left with some difficulty because Beccaria vigorously supported noncapital corporal punishment (*pene corporali*) "without exception" for crimes against persons and for crimes of theft accompanied by violence (pp.

---

34. Beccaria's arguments on torture were greatly influenced by the counsel of his friend Pietro Verri, whose book *Osservazioni sulla tortura* was only published posthumously in 1804. Whether Beccaria was correct in his assumption that judicial torture was still a widespread practice in mid-eighteenth-century Europe is an interesting question, but one that will not be addressed here. In his provocative book *Torture and the Law of Proof*, Langbein (1976; see also Hirst, 1986:152–154) has fundamentally reinterpreted the history of the transformation of judicial torture in Europe. He claims that the conventional account of the demise of torture through the Enlightenment efforts of Beccaria and others is a fairy tale. His thesis is that there is an unmistakable causal relationship between the abolition of judicial torture and a contemporaneous revolution in the law of proof. He suggests that a fundamental reason why historians have written hardly anything on the importance of changes in the law of proof is that they have uncritically accepted the critical explanations of the eighteenth-century abolitionist writers, who themselves knew very little about these changes or, if they did, did not understand their significance.

37, 40).[35] Yet this apparent paradox can be resolved by stressing that, besides his humanism, Beccaria articulated his opposition to judicial torture in another, even more insistent way. Here he claimed that judicial torture is an inefficient method of establishing the "probability" or the "certainty" of the guilt or innocence of the accused. Accordingly, "the problems of whether torture and death are either just or useful deserve a mathematically precise solution" (p. 23). Elsewhere, Beccaria added that it is "a remarkable contradiction in the laws that they authorize torture, yet what sort of interrogation could be more *suggestive* than pain?" (p. 71):

> The outcome of torture, then, is a matter of temperament and calculation that varies with each man in proportion to his hardiness and his sensitivity, so that, by means of this method, a mathematician could solve the following problem better than a judge could: given the strength of an innocent person's muscles and the sensitivity of his fibers, find the degree of pain that will make him confess himself guilty of a given crime (p. 31).

In place of judicial torture, Beccaria recommended "the real trial, the 'informative' one, that is, the impartial investigation of facts which reason demands" (p. 34).

In respect to witnesses and evidence, Beccaria argued that to determine the guilt or innocence of a defendant more than one witness is necessary because, if one witness affirms the guilt and another denies its, "there is no certainty" (p. 24; see also Locke, 1689, 1:309).[36] A witness is credible if he is "a rational man" and his credibility increases if his reason is undisturbed by a prior relationship with either the defendant or the victim. "The credibility of a witness, therefore, must diminish in proportion to the hatred or friendship or close relationship between himself and the accused" (Beccaria, 1764:24). The credibility of a witness also diminishes significantly as the gravity of the alleged crime increases or as its circumstances become more "improbable" (pp. 24–25). The credibility of a witness is virtually nil in cases that involve making words a crime: "[it is] far easier to slander someone's words than to slander his actions, for, in the latter case, the greater the number of circumstances adduced as evidence, the greater are the means available to the

---

35. Moreover, Beccaria urged that among the serious crimes, those such as infamy, which "are founded on pride, and [which] draw glory and nourishment from pain itself" (1764:41), did not warrant the use of painful corporal punishments.

36. Elsewhere in *Dei delitti*, Beccaria extended to magistrates his idea of the relation between the number of concurring witnesses and the certainty of a verdict. Thus, he wrote about the "corps of those charged with executing the law that "the greater the number of men who constitute such a body, the less the danger of encroachments on the law will be" (1764:78). It should be noted that Beccaria's observations on witnesses, juries, and magistrates were instrumental in the development of a *"science sociale"* by Condorcet (1795b:62–63) and Laplace (1814).

accused to clear himself" (p. 25). Somewhat inconsistently, Beccaria also held that to the degree that "punishments become moderate, that squalor and hunger are banished from prisons, and that compassion and humanity pass through the iron gates . . . the law may be content with weaker and weaker evidence to imprison someone" (p. 54).

For Beccaria, there exists a "general theorem" that is most useful in calculating with certainty the facts of a crime, namely, the "weight of evidence." In unfolding the aspects of this theorem, he argued that (1) when different pieces of factual evidence are substantiated only by each other, the less certain is any one fact; (2) when all the proofs of a fact depend on one piece of evidence, the number of proofs neither augments nor diminishes the probability of the fact; and (3) when proofs are independent of each other, then the probability of the fact increases with each new witness (p. 25). Moreover, Beccaria deemed it ironic that the most atrocious and obscure crimes—that is, "those that are most unlikely"—are the hardest to prove. Such crimes are typically proved by conjecture and by the weakest and most equivocal evidence; it is as though "the danger of condemning an innocent man were not all the greater as the probability of his innocence surpasses the liklihood of his guilt" (p. 58). That is not to say that there are not some crimes that are both frequent in society and difficult to prove—such as "adultery" and "pederasty"—and, in these cases, "the difficulty of establishing guilt takes the place of the probability of innocence" (p. 58). Finally, because the respective probabilities of "atrocious" crimes and of lesser offenses differ greatly, they must be adjudicated differently: for atrocious crimes the period of judicial examination "should decrease in view of the greater liklihood of the innocence of the accused . . . but with minor crimes, given the lesser liklihood of the innocence of the accused, the period of judicial investigation should be extended, and, as the pernicious consequences of impunity decline, the delay in granting immunity from further prosecution should be shortened" (p. 57).

Finally, Beccaria offered some brief comments on jurors and on sentencing practices from the perspective of probabilism. About jurors, he recommended, without explanation, that when a crime has been committed against a third party "half the jurors should be the equals of the accused and half the peers of the victim" (p. 27). About sentencing practices, he warned that "certainty" ought to be required for convictions in criminal cases and that if geometry "were adaptable to the infinite and obscure arrangements of human activity, there ought to be a corresponding scale of punishments, descending from the most rigorous to the slightest" (p. 15).

Many of the strategies in Beccaria's penal calculus, including his key concept of deterrence, are derived not from geometry or probabilism, as such, but from the doctrines of associationism and sensationalism. To these related doctrines in the science of man we now turn.

ASSOCIATIONISM

Beccaria's penal calculus rested on the view that it is better to prevent crimes than to punish them. This can only occur if the law forces potential criminals to make an accurate "association" of ideas between crime and punishment. "It is well established," Beccaria claimed, along with Hume and Helvétius, "that the association of ideas is the cement that shapes the whole structure of the human intellect; without it, pleasure and pain would be isolated feelings with no consequences" (p. 36).[37] Following Hume, Beccaria urged that associated ideas must be in a position of constant conjunction and that they must comprise a relation of cause and effect. Beccaria characterized the nexus of the desired association between crime and punishment in many ways, such as "deterrence" (p. 33), "intimidation" (pp. 23, 29), and "dissuasion" (p. 23).[38] The key properties of the association between crime and punishment are condensed in the following formula, which is the concluding sentence of *Dei delitti,* now appropriately enshrined as the original statement of the principle of deterrence:

> *in order that any punishment should not be an act of violence committed by one person or many against a private citizen, it is essential that it should be public, prompt, necessary, the minimum possible under the given circumstances, [and] proportionate to the crimes"* (p. 81).

Elsewhere in his text, yet still within an associationist framework, Beccaria expanded on several items in this formula, most notably on the need for prompt, mild, and proportionate punishment. About the promptness of punishment, first, Beccaria believed that the shorter the time period between a crime and chastisement for the crime "the stronger and more permanent is the human mind's association of the two ideas of crime and punishment, so that imperceptibly the one will come to be considered as the cause and the other as the necessary and inevitable result" (p. 36). Delay thus serves only

---

37. The philosophical writings of Hume and Helvétius (both followers of Hutcheson) were among the "French books" to which Beccaria admitted "I myself owe everything" (1766:862; see also 1764:19). About Hume's general influence on *Dei delitti* see, for example, his *Treatise of Human Nature* (1739, especially Bk. 1, Pt. 1 and Pt. 3); specifically, compare Beccaria (1764:19) with Hume (1739, Bk. 1, Pt. 1, s. 4, p. 10). See also Beccaria (1762a, 1766:865), where he praised Hume's "profound metaphysics." Helvétius contributed little that was original to the principle of associationism, although Beccaria's (1766:862) generous comment about Helvétius's influence on *Dei delitti* probably refers to Helvétius's *De l'esprit* (1758:Discourse I, Chs. 1–2; Discourse II, Ch. 15).

38. This is not to suggest that Beccaria's recommendations for penal strategies were based exclusively on an intended purpose of deterrence. At certain points in *Dei delitti,* his equation of crime with social harms also led Beccaria to a posture of retributivism toward criminals. However, given his overwhelming concern with deterrence, Beccaria's retributivism was not and could not have been an important feature of his text (*pace* Young, 1983).

to sever the association between the two ideas. Moreover, the temporal proximity of crime and punishment is of paramount importance if one desires to
arouse in "crude and uneducated minds the idea of punishment in association
with the seductive image of a certain advantageous crime" (p. 37). About the
mildness of punishment, second, Beccaria argued that to achieve its intended
effect the intensity of a punishment should exceed the benefit resulting from
the crime and that in its application punishment should be "inexorable,"
"inevitable," and "certain" (pp. 46–47). Cruel punishments, insofar as they
destroy the association between law and justice, therefore undermine the aim
of deterrence. Finally, about the required proportion between punishment
and crime, Beccaria warned that "the obstacles that restrain men from committing crimes should be stronger according to the degree that such misdeeds
are contrary to the public good and according to the motives that lead people
to crimes" (p. 14; see also p. 15). This is so because, if two unequally harmful
crimes are each awarded the same punishment, then would-be miscreants will
tend to commit the more serious crime if it holds greater advantage for them.
If punishments are disproportionate to crime by being tyrannical (i.e., excessive), then popular dissatisfaction will be directed at the law itself—"punishments will punish the crimes that they themselves have caused" (p. 16).[39]
Further, in arguing that "punishment . . . should conform as closely as possible to the nature of the crime" (p. 37), Beccaria implicitly attempted to link
the argument about the proportionality of crime and punishment with
the desired association among ideas about the type of crime (e.g., theft), form
of punishment (penal servitude with forced labor), and virtue of
industriousness.[40]

In the context of Beccaria's use of the doctrine of associationism, it is
worth returning briefly to his opposition to capital punishment. It is fair to
suggest that Beccaria opposed capital punishment not because he thought it
cruel, which he did, but because it did not serve the new penal objective of
deterrence.[41] He argued instead that a life sentence is a sufficiently intense

---

39. For this reason, Beccaria therefore suggested that some punishments might even
be considered as crimes (1764:17); for example, "it appears absurd to me that the laws . . .
commit murder themselves . . . [and] command public assassination" (1764:51).

40. Interestingly, appearing in a frontispiece engraving in a 1765 edition of *Dei delitti*
is the figure of Justice, who is portrayed as combining law and wisdom in the features of
Minerva. Justice herself recoils from the executioner's offering of three decapitated heads
and instead gazes approvingly at various instruments of labor, of measurement, and of
detention. The engraving of Justice was incised for the third edition of *Dei delitti* (1765,
Lausanne) and, according to Venturi (1971:105), the sketch for the engraving was completed by Beccaria himself.

41. Only much later did Beccaria (1792:739–740) argue that the rights of an accused
are violated by the death penalty because, once an execution had been carried out, there is
no "possibility" of reversal even after proof of innocence.

substitute for the death penalty and that it includes all the necessary ingredients needed to deter the most hardened criminal. "Neither fanaticism nor vanity survives among fetters and chains, under the prod or the yoke, or in an iron cage . . . a lifetime at hard labor" (p. 50). It is thus not the severity of punishment that, for Beccaria, has the greatest impact on a would-be criminal but, albeit in addition to its other characteristics, its duration:

> If someone were to say that life at hard labor is as painful as death and therefore equally cruel, I should reply that, taking all the unhappy moments of perpetual slavery together, it is perhaps even more painful, but these moments are spread out over a lifetime, and capital punishment exercises all its power in an instant. And this is the advantage of life at hard labor; it frightens the spectator more than the victim (p. 50).

SENSATIONALISM

A third hallmark of the science of man engraved in *Dei delitti* is the doctrine of sensationalism. In Beccaria's discussion of the nature of honor, for example, the presence of this doctrine is indicated by a Newtonian metaphor:

> How miserable is the condition of the human mind! It has a better grasp of the most remote and least important ideas about the revolutions of the heavenly bodies than of the most immediate and important moral concepts, which are always fluctuating and confused as they are driven by the winds of passion and guided by the ignorance that receives and transmits them! (p. 19; see also Halévy, 1928:57).

This "ostensible paradox" will disappear, Beccaria (1764:19) continued, only when one considers that

> just as objects too close to one's eyes are blurred, so the excessive proximity of moral ideas makes it easy to confuse the large number of simple ideas that go to form them. Wishing to measure the phenomena of human sensibility, the geometric spirit needs dividing lines. When these are clearly drawn, the impartial observer of human affairs will be less astonished, and he will suspect that there is perhaps no need for so great a moral apparatus or for so many bonds in order to make men happy and secure.

These two passages betray the influence on *Dei delitti* of the doctrine of sensationalism, which, in the course of his unheralded book on aesthetics, Beccaria (1770:81–93; see also Beccaria, 1766:866) explicitly acknowledged having taken from works by Locke and Condillac.[42] Besides the humanism inherent in his widely circulated condemnation of religious persecution and

---

42. Beccaria's (1770) unfinished book *Ricerche intorno alla natura dello stile* was condemned in its French translation by Diderot (1771:60), who politely discounted it as "an obscure work based on a subtle metaphysic."

superstition in *Letters Concerning Toleration*, Locke's sensationalism tended to suggest that all things painful are by definition bad and all things pleasurable, good. Interestingly, his original discussion of the doctrine of hedonism—the pleasure/pain principle as outlined in chapter 20 of his *Essay Concerning Human Understanding*—occurred within the framework of sensationalism; when Locke discussed the status of hedonism in human affairs, he did so in a radically materialistic way, arguing that "pleasure and pain, and that which causes them, Good and Evil, are the hinges on which our *passions* turn" (1689,1:95). Among the *philosophes*, Condillac (1715–1780) was the most ardent champion of the antimetaphysical, empirical tradition of Bacon, Newton, and Locke (Knight, 1968). In his preparatory *Essai sur l'origin des connaissances humaines* (1746), in *Traité des systèmes* (1749), and then in *Traité des sensations* (1754), Condillac developed Locke's doctrine of sensationalism, positing that the human mind is at birth a *tabula rasa*, which operates through sensations. Like Locke, Condillac (1754:338) championed the rigidly materialistic conclusion that "man" is simply what he has acquired through his sensations:

> It is pleasures and pains compared, that is to say, our needs which exercise our faculties. As a result, it is to them that we owe the happiness that is ours to enjoy. We have as many needs as different kinds of enjoyment; as many degrees of need as degrees of enjoyment. And there you have the germ of everything that we are, the source of our unhappiness or of our happiness. To observe the influence of this principle is thus the sole means to study ourselves.

It is difficult to imagine a doctrine more hostile to the doctrine of free will than sensationalism. When Beccaria applied it to criminal justice, sensationalism effectively displaced the volitional subject of Catholic theology and, thereby, denied any active role in human society for the Supreme Being. Beccaria was so fearful of the censor precisely because his text implied that human agents are no more than the products of their sensory reactions to external stimuli. His text, replete as it is with probabilism, associationism, and sensationalism—all directed to the new objective of deterrence—is resolutely opposed to any notion of free will. *Dei delitti* contains a concept of volition, it is true, but it is a determined will rather than a free will: "sentiment is always proportional to the result of the impressions made on the senses" (p. 25). The penal recommendations of *Dei delitti* are not at all predicated, therefore, on the notion of a rational calculating subject who, when faced with inexorable punishment, will weigh the costs and benefits and choose to desist from crime. In this discourse, punishments ("tangible motives") have "a direct impact on the senses and appear continually to the mind to counterbalance the strong impressions of individual passions opposed to the general good" (p. 7).

51

Sensationalism intersects concretely with Beccaria's chosen penal strategies in three ways. First, it is an extra ground on which judicial torture must be rejected. Beccaria insisted that, in terms of their respective results, the only difference between judicial torture and other ordeals, such as fire and boiling water, is that the former appears to depend on the will of the accused and the latter on a purely physical act. To this he responded that

> speaking the truth amid convulsions and torments is no more a free act than staving off the effects of fire and boiling water except by fraud. Every act of our will is always proportional to the strength of the sense impressions from which it springs. . ." (p. 31).

Sensationalist claims are also inserted into Beccaria's arguments about the nature of deterrence. During his discussion of the appropriateness of prompt punishment, for example, he argued that "that gravity-like force that impels us to seek our own well-being can be restrained only to the degree that obstacles are established in opposition to it" and that "remote consequences make a very weak impression" (pp. 14, 64). Effecting a link with probabilism, he argued that "experience and reason have shown us that the probability and certainty of human traditions decline the farther removed they are from their source" (p. 13). Effecting yet another link, this time with associationist claims, he reflected that

> the magnitude of punishment ought to be relative to the condition of the nation itself. Stronger and more obvious impressions are required for the hardened spirits of a people who have scarcely emerged from a savage state. A thunderbolt is needed to fell a ferocious lion who is merely angered by a gun shot. But to the extent that human spirits are made gentle by the social state, sensibility increases; as it increases, the severity of punishment must diminish if one wishes to maintain a constant relation between object and feeling (p. 81).

Finally, Beccaria attached his belief in sensationalism to a variety of non-penal strategies designed to manipulate and channel sense impressions into law-abiding actions. While penal strategies tend to operate swiftly and dramatically on their subjects, non-penal strategies are designed as positive mental inducements that operate slowly and calmly at the level of custom and habit, or at what is nowadays known as the domain of "socialization." Thus, Beccaria suggested that in order to prevent crimes, "enlightenment should accompany liberty" (p. 76). What precisely he meant by this recommendation is not very clear, but perhaps it was "education," an instrument whose importance he also stressed (pp. 76–79), as did such thinkers as Montesquieu, d'Alembert, Helvétius, Rousseau, and Charles Pinot Duclos. He warned that "the most certain but most difficult way to prevent crimes is to perfect education" (p. 79). By "education," a vague term with no clear institutional or empirical referent in *Dei delitti*, Beccaria likely intended a process whose outcome, at least, was the gradual inculcation in the citizenry of such attributes as virtue, courage, and liberty—for the encouragement of which he recommended the distribution of prizes (p. 79).

FROM THE SCIENCE OF MAN TO *HOMO CRIMINALIS*

> Morality, politics, and the fine arts, which are respectively the sciences of virtue, of utility, and of beauty, have a greater identity of principles than can be imagined: these sciences all derive from one primary science, the science of man; it is hopeless to think that we will ever make rapid progress in fathoming the depths of these secondary sciences without first immersing ourselves in the science of man (Beccaria, 1770:71).[43]

In addition to the contemporary protestations of certain luminaries, such as Grimm (1765a, 1765b) and Ramsay (n.d.), that Beccaria's treatment of penal questions in *Dei delitti* was "too geometrical," other legal scholars and social reformers of the period more or less clearly understood the proto-scientific intentions of *Dei delitti* and valued it for that very direction.[44] To the French mathematician and *philosophe* Condorcet, for example, Beccaria was one of a select group of scholars—that included the Scottish political economists, Rousseau and Montesquieu—whose works, since the time of Locke, had advanced the moral sciences, or *"mathématique sociale"* and *"science sociale"* as he termed the application of "the calculus of . . . probabilities" to the understanding of human societies (1795b:178; see also Baker, 1975:193).[45] The influential English legal scholar Blackstone observed in his *Commentaries on the Laws of England* that Beccaria "seems to have well studied the springs of human action" (1769:4:17), and he emphatically placed Beccaria's

---

43.   In his *Elementi di economia pubblica*, a series of lectures completed at the Palatine School in 1771, Beccaria displayed a keen interest in various aspects of the new statistics of populations that had become a key factor in the development of the science of man. These included statistical tables and comparative evidence on births, marriages, education, and life expectancy (1804:401–433). On the uncanny similarities between Beccaria's *Elementi* and the *Wealth of Nations* by Hutcheson's pupil, the Scottish political economist Adam Smith, see Schumpeter (1954:179–183).

44.   Besides Beccaria, Melchior Grimm also attacked Beccaria's mentor Condillac for being "too geometrical" (see Knight, 1968:2–3, 235; and Becker, 1932:83–84).

45.   In letters to Beccaria of 1771, Condorcet condemned the injustices of existing criminal jurisprudence and he expressed his desire to follow Beccaria's lead in using mathematics to search for rationality in judicial decision making (cited in Baker, 1975:231–232). Later, he (Condorcet, 1785) recommended to Frederick II of Prussia the application of the "calculus of probabilities" to Beccaria's ideas on capital punishment and on wise legislation. Moreover, although it was perhaps first used in late 1791 by his friend Dominique-Joseph Garat, it was Condorcet who in 1795 popularized the term *"science sociale"* in his *Tableau historique des progrès de l'ésprit humain* (see also Baker, 1975:391). In the *Tableau*, Condorcet (1795b:177–178) referred to *"l'art social"* as one of the sciences.

"humane" reform proposals within the rubric of a new discourse of crime and penality that emerged in Britain in the 1760s and that stressed investigation of the "causes of crime," deterrence, and the correction of offenders.

Indeed, attached to Beccaria's discourse on penal strategies, there is present in *Dei delitti* a very rudimentary attempt to forge some key concepts of an embryonic criminology. Those concepts include "crime," "criminal," and "causes of crime." Quite apart from his innovative approach to the understanding of crime ("the harm done to society"),[46] Beccaria also attempted to identify the criminal as something other than a mere bundle of illegalities. This concept of a criminal operates in concert with and is burdened by Beccaria's humanism and his advocacy of legal rationality, yet it marks, one might say, a movement away from a single-minded focus with how to punish *homo penalis* to a wider "criminological" concern with understanding the situation of *homo criminalis*. An example of this movement occurs when, during an impassioned tirade against unjust laws, Beccaria (1764:51) inserted the following words into the mouth of "a scoundrel":

> What are these laws that I must respect and that leave such a great distance between me and the rich man? . . . Who made these laws? Rich and powerful men who have never deigned to visit the squalid hovels of the poor, who have never broken a moldy crust of bread among the innocent cries of their famished children and the tears of their wives. Let us break these bonds that are so ruinous for the majority and useful to a handful of indolent tyrants; let us attack injustice at its source.

At several other points in his text, as well, Beccaria indicated that criminals and criminal behavior should be understood causally, in material and social terms rather than purely individualistic ones. He suggested, for example, that "theft is only the crime of misery and desperation; it is the crime of that unhappy portion of humanity to whom the right of property . . . has left only a bare existence" (p. 39). It is difficult to know how much to invest in Beccaria's reasoning in passages such as these, other than to say that he seems keen to position illegalities in a quasi-social context. Similarly suggestive reasoning is directed to the crimes of adultery (pp. 58–59), pederasty (p. 60), and infanticide (*infanticidio*) "by a woman" (p. 60).[47]

It must also be said that *Dei delitti* even contains an adumbration of a

---

46. See further *supra*: 22, 33–34, 39–40.

47. *Dei delitti* provides no real clues as to Beccaria's understanding of the gendered position of women before law, although in the chapter on "The Spirit of the Family" Beccaria (1764:43–45) seems to oppose authoritarian (i.e., male-dominated) families ("little monarchies"). Nowhere in his text does Beccaria indulge in the antifeminism of those such as Rousseau and Buffon, although its publication date precludes his participation in the progressive ideas of feminist *philosophes* like Condorcet. On the periodicity of Enlightenment feminism, see generally Clinton (1975).

"dangerous class."[48] This is visible at several points. Thus, Beccaria spoke philosophically of wanting to disabuse those "who, from a poorly understood love of liberty, would desire to establish anarchy" (p. 18) and who are inclined toward "a desperate return to the original state of nature" (p. 47). These unfortunates he described as "the credulous and admiring crowd" (p. 39), "a fanatical crowd" (p. 47), "a blind and fanatical crowd, pushing and jostling one another in a closed labyrinth" (p. 77) that "does not adopt stable principles of conduct" (p. 7). In crowds there resides a "dangerous concentration of popular passions" (p. 22) that is akin to the sentiments in "the state of nature . . . the savage" (p. 74).[49] Its actions include "concealed despotism . . . turbulent mob anarchy" (p. 57) and those events especially

> that disturb the public tranquility and the peace of citizens: matters such as tumults and carousing in public thoroughfares meant for business and for traffic, or such as fanatical sermons that excite the fickle passions of the curious crowd. These passions gather strength from the great number of the audience; they owe more to the effects of a murky and mysterious rapture than to clear and calm reason, which never has any effect on a large mass of men (p. 22).[50]

Ultimately, *Dei delitti* teases its audience with a presociological view of the relation between crime and social organization:

> Most men lack that vigor which is equally necessary for great crimes and great virtues; thus, it seems that the former always coexist with the latter in those nations that sustain themselves by the activity of their governments and by passions working together for the public good, rather than in countries that depend on their size or the invariable excellence of their laws. In the latter sort of nation, weakened passions seem better suited

---

48. The term "dangerous classes" first appeared in France during the Restoration and was popularized by Frégier's (1840) classic study. See further Tombs (1980) and Beirne (1987a:1144–1148).

49. From Beccaria's vague references to social life in the "state of nature," it is very difficult to know whether he appropriated this term from Hobbes's "*bellum omnium contra omnes*," from *philosophes* such as Montesquieu and Rousseau, or even from the Hutchesonian "mutual offices of good will," all of which are very different notions from Beccaria's.

50. In the following passage Beccaria even indicated a stark contrast between an embryonic dangerous class and the law-abiding citizenry:

> Enslaved men are more sensual, more debauched, and more cruel than free men. The latter think about the sciences; they think about the interests of the nation; they see great examples, and they imitate them. The former, on the other hand, content with the present moment, seek a distraction for the emptiness of their lives in the tumult of debauchery. Accustomed to uncertain results in everything, the doubts they have about the outcome of their crimes strengthens the passions by which crimes are determined (1764:75).

to the maintenance rather than to the improvement of the form of government. From this, one can draw an important conclusion: that great crimes in a nation are not always proof of its decline (p. 58).

CONCLUSION: WHITHER CLASSICAL CRIMINOLOGY?

Less by way of conclusion to this paper than as an invitation for further exploration, several implications must now be drawn about the place of *Dei delitti* in the intellectual history of criminology.

First, I have not disputed the conventional view that Beccaria's advocacy of humanism and legal rationality are important features of his treatise. Rather, I claim that neither the method of *Dei delitti* nor its object can be understood in terms of those tendencies alone. An altogether different tendency, veiled and incompletely developed, actually comprised the kernel of Beccaria's discourse—the application to crime and penality of key principles in the science of man. It is in the framework of that new science that the two major themes of *Dei delitti* (the "right to punish" and "how to punish") are couched as, too, are Beccaria's advocacy of deterrence and his opposition to capital punishment and judicial torture.

Second, contrary to prevailing opinion, the discourse of *Dei delitti* was not erected on the volitional subject of classical jurisprudence, or "free will" as it is often termed. Although Beccaria's view of volitional conduct is not clear in *Dei delitti*, it is possible that, like many of his contemporaries in the eighteenth-century Enlightenment who saw in this no contradiction, he subscribed to a notion of human agency simultaneously involving "free" rational calculation *and* "determined" action. But the concept of an unfettered free will must be relegated along with humanism to the margins of *Dei delitti*. The warriors and wretches who inhabit its pages are not volitional agents but creatures trapped in a web of determinism. The potential criminals in Beccaria's schema "act" like automata; in effect, they are recalcitrant objects who must be angled, steered, and forced into appropriate and law-abiding behavior.[51] But this is only to be expected of a discourse that relies on rigidly deterministic principles concretely manifest in the specific doctrines of probabilism, associationism, and sensationalism. As such, at the very least, the position of *Dei delitti* in intellectual history does not and cannot lie at the center of classical criminology as it is conventionally understood. Nor, however, despite the temptation of focusing on Beccaria's predeliction for the science of man, should it be placed, however precariously, at the beginning of the tradition to which it is commonly opposed, namely, positivist criminology. Beccaria's utterances on crime and penality were never intended—nor

---

51. See also Beccaria's deterministic account of sexual attraction and adultery, which, like gravity, "diminishes with distance" but, unlike gravity, "gathers strength and vigor with the growth of the very obstacles opposed to it" (1764:59).

could they have been—to inhabit the same positivist terrain as that so eagerly tenanted a century later by his compatriot Cesare Lombroso.[52]

Finally, the very category of a distinct "classical" period in criminology must be reconsidered. "Classical criminology" was not the creation of Beccaria, Bentham, and others, but the retrospective product of scholarly self-aggrandizement. As an identifiable set of assumptions about crime and punishment, classical criminology was not actually denominated as such until the 1870s, and then by another generation of Italian theorists—positivist criminologists such as Lombroso, Garofalo, and Ferri. These thinkers were keen to distance their invention of a scientific criminology from that of Beccaria's "outmoded discourse of free will," either because they failed properly to understand the arguments of *Dei delitti* or, more likely, because it did not suit their own interests to do so. Yet if the discourse of *Dei delitti* is not couched in the rhetoric of classical jurisprudence, if its chief object (the construction of a rational and efficient penal calculus) is not directed to the actions of volitional subjects but to those of automata given by the science of man, and if humanism is a minor rather than a major feature of this discourse, then what is left of the classical edifice? Perhaps very little.

REFERENCES

Alembert, Jean Lerond d'
   n.d.1   De l'abus de la critique en matière de religion. Vol. 1:547–572 in *Oeuvres complètes de d'Alembert*. 1821–1822. 5 vols. Paris: A. Belin.
   n.d.2   Explication détaillée du Système des Connaissances humaines. Vol. 1:99–114 in *Oeuvres complètes de d'Alembert*. 1821–1822. 5 vols. Paris: A. Belin.
   1765   Lettera a Paolo Frisi. 312–314 in Venturi (ed.), *Cesare Beccaria, Dei delitti e delle pene*. 1965. Turin: Giulio Einaudi.

Bacon, Francis
   1632   *The Essayes or Counsels Civill and Morall, of Francis Lo[rd] Verulam*. London: John Haviland.

Baker, Keith Michael
   1975   *Condorcet: From Natural Philosophy to Social Mathematics*. Chicago: University of Chicago Press.

Beattie, J.M.
   1986   *Crime and the Courts in England 1550–1800*. Princeton: Princeton University Press.

---

52. So also must I resist the intriguing temptation of arguing—even in the relative safety of a footnote—that *Dei delitti* should be seen as the first link in a chain that proceeds to Condorcet's obscure *Essai sur l'application de l'analyse à la probabilité des décisions rendues à la pluralité des voix* (1785) and his *Tableau général de la science* (1795a; see also Baker, 1975:227–242; Condorcet, 1785; Hankins, 1985:182–183; Lottin, 1912:362) and concludes with the rise of well-formed, presociological analyses of crime as found in the 1830s in the discourse of moral statistics.

Beccaria, Cesare

n.d.   Estratti da Bacone: Nota al testo, materiali non pubblicati. Vol. 2:457–473 in Luigi Firpo (ed.), *Cesare Beccaria: Opere.* 1984. Milan: Medio banca.

1762a   *Del disordine e de'rimedi delle monete nello stato di Milano nell'anno 1762.* Vol. 1:7–34 in Sergio Romagnoli (ed.), *Cesare Beccaria: Opere.* 1958. Florence: Sansoni.

1762b   Tentativo analitico su i contrabbandi. Vol. 1:164–166 in Sergio Romagnoli (ed.), *Cesare Beccaria: Opere.* 1958. Florence: Sansoni.

1764   *On Crimes and Punishments*, trans. David Young. 1986. Indianapolis: Hackett.

1765a   A Jean-Baptiste Le Rond D'Alembert. Vol. 2:859–861 in Sergio Romagnoli (ed.), *Cesare Beccaria: Opere.* 1958. Florence: Sansoni.

1765b   All'arciduca Ferdinando d'Austria, duca di Modena, governatore della Lombardia. Vol. 2:858–859 in Sergio Romagnoli (ed.), *Cesare Beccaria: Opere.* 1958. Florence: Sansoni.

1765c   Frammento sullo stile. Vol. 1:167–174 in Sergio Romagnoli (ed.), *Cesare Beccaria: Opere.* 1958. Florence: Sansoni.

1766   Ad André Morellet, le 26 janvier. Vol. 2:862–870 in Sergio Romagnoli (ed.), *Cesare Beccaria: Opere.* 1958. Florence: Sansoni.

1770   *Ricercne intorno alla natura dello stile.* Vol. 2:63–206 in Luigi Firpo (ed.), *Cesare Beccaria: Opere.* 1984. Milan: Mediobanca.

1792   Voto per la riforma del sistema criminale nella Lombardia Austriaca riguargante la pena di morte. Vol. 2:735–741 in Sergio Romagnoli (ed.), *Cesare Beccaria: Opere.* 1958. Florence: Sansoni.

1804   *Elemti di economia pubblica.* Vol. 1:379–649 in Sergio Romagnoli (ed.), *Cesare Beccaria: Opere.* 1958. Florence: Sansoni.

Becker, Carl L.

1932   *The Heavenly City of the Eighteenth-Century Philosophers.* New Haven: Yale University Press.

Beirne, Piers

1987a   Adolphe Quetelet and the origins of positivist criminology. *American Journal of Sociology* 92(5):1140–1169.

1987b   Between classicism and positivism: Crime and penality in the writings of Gabriel Tarde. *Criminology* 25(4):785–819.

1988   Heredity versus environment: A reconsideration of Charles Goring's *The English Convict* (1913). *British Journal of Criminology* 28(3):315–339.

Beirne, Piers and Alan Hunt

1990   Lenin, crime, and penal politics, 1917–1924. Pp. 99–135 in Piers Beirne (ed.), *Revolution in Law: Contributions to Soviet Legal Theory, 1917–1938.* Armonk, N.Y.: M.E. Sharpe.

Bentham, Jeremy

1776   *A Fragment on Government.* 1988. New York: Cambridge University Press.

Berlin, Isaiah

1960   The philosophical ideas of Giambattista Vico. Pp. 156–236 in Harold Acton et al., *Art and Ideas in Eighteenth-Century Italy.* Rome: The Italian Institute of London.

Blackstone, Sir William

1769   *Commentaries on the Laws of England* (1783, 9th ed.). 1978. 4 vols. London: Garland.

Caffentzis, Constantine George
1989   *Clipped Coins, Abused Words, and Civil Government: John Locke's Philosophy of Money.* New York: Autonomedia.

Canetta, Rosalba
1985   Beccaria economista e gli atti di governo. Pp. 11–27 in *Cesare Beccaria: Atti di governo.* Milan: Mediobanca.

Cantu, Cesare
1862   *Beccaria e il diritto penale.* Florence: Barbera.

Chadwick, Owen
1981   The Italian Enlightenment. Pp. 90–105 in Roy Potter and Mikulás Teich (eds.), *The Enlightenment in National Context.* New York: Cambridge University Press.

Clinton, Katherine B.
1975   *Femme et philosophe*: Enlightenment origins of feminism. *Eighteenth-Century Studies* 8(3):283–299.

Condillac, Etienne Bonnot, Abbé de
17754   *A Treatise on the Sensations.* Pp. 175–339 of *Philosophical Writings of Etienne Bonnot, Abbé de Condillac,* trans. Franklin Philip, with the collaboration of Harlan Lane. 1982. Hillsdale, N.J.: Lawrence Erlbaum.

Condorcet, Marie–Jean–Antoine Nicolas Caritat
1782   Discours prononcé dans l'Académie française le jeudi 21 février 1782. Vol. 1:389–415 in A. Condorcet–O'Connor and M.F. Arago (eds.), *Oeuvres de Condorcet.* 1847. Paris:
1785   Letter to King Frederick II of Prussia, 2 May 1785. Vol. 13:268–273 in *Oeuvres posthumes de Fréderic II, roi de Prusse.* 1788. 15 vols. Berlin: Voss.
1795a   Tableau général de la science qui a pour objet l'application au calcul aux sciences politiques et morales. Vol. 1:539–573 in A. Condorcet–O'Connor and M.F. Arago (eds.), *Oeuvres de Condorcet.* Paris: Firmin Didot.
1795b   *Tableau historique des progrés de l'ésprit humain.* 1990. Paris: G. Steinheil.

Darnton, Robert
1979   *The Business of Enlightenment: A Publishing History of the Encyclopédie, 1775–1800.* Cambridge, Mass.: Harvard University Press.
1982   *The Literary Underground of the Old Regime.* Cambridge, Mass.: Harvard University Press.

Diderot, Dennis
1771   Des recherches sur le style par Beccaria. Vol. 4:60–63 in *Diderot: Oeuvres complétes.* Paris: Garnier.

Durkheim, Emile
1901   Two laws of penal evolution. Pp. 102–132 in Steven Lukes and Andrew Scull (eds.), *Durkheim and the Law.* 1983. New York: St. Martin's Press.

Facchinei, Ferdinando
1765   Note ed osservazioni sul libro intitolato "Dei delitti e delle pene." Pp. 164–177 in Franco Venturi (ed.), *Cesare Beccaria, Dei delitti e delle pene.* Turin: Giulio Einaudi.

Firpo, Luigi (ed.)
1984   *Cesare Beccaria: Opere.* 6 vols. Milan: Mediobanca.

Foucault, Michel
  1979   *Discipline & Punish: The Birth of the Prison*, trans. Alan Sheridan. New
          York: Vintage.
  1988   The dangerous individual. Pp. 125–156 in Lawrence D. Kritzman (ed.),
          *Foucault: Politics, Philosophy, Culture (Interviews and Other Writings
          1977–1984)*, trans. Alain Baudot and Jane Couchman. London: Routledge.

Garland, David
  1985   *Punishment and Welfare: A History of Penal Strategies*. Brookfield, Vt.:
          Gower.

Gay, Peter
  1966   *The Enlightenment: An Interpretation*. New York: Alfred A. Knopf.

Gorecki, Jan
  1985   *A Theory of Criminal Justice*. New York: Columbia University Press.

Green, Thomas Andrew
  1985   *Verdict According to Conscience: Perspectives on the English Criminal Trial
          Jury 1200–1800*. Chicago: University of Chicago Press.

Grimm, Melchior
  1765a   Examen de la traduction du *Traité des Délits et des Peines de Beccaria par
          Morellet*. Vol. 6:422–429 in *Correspondance littéraire, philosophique et
          critique*. 1878. 6 vols. Paris: Garnier.
  1765b   Sur le traité des *Délits et des Peines, par Beccaria*. Vol. 6:329–338 in
          Correspondance littéraire, philosophique et critique. 1878. 6 vols. Paris:
          Garnier.

Gross, Hanns
  1990   *Rome in the Age of Enlightenment*. New York: Cambridge University Press.

Halévy, Elie
  1928   *The Growth of Philosophical Radicalism*. London: Faber & Gwyer.

Hankins, Thomas L.
  1970   *Jean d'Alembert: Science and the Enlightenment*. Oxford: Clarendon Press.
  1985   *Science and the Enlightenment*. New York: Cambridge University Press.

Hart, H.L.A.
  1982   *Essays on Bentham*. Oxford: Clarendon Press.

Hegel, G.W.
  1821   *The Philosophy of Right*, trans. T.M. Knox. 1967. London: Oxford
          University Press.

Helvétius, Claude–Adrien
  1758   *De l'ésprit*. Paris: Durand.

Hirst, Paul Q.
  1986   *Law, Socialism and Democracy*. London: Allen & Unwin.

Hume, David
  1739   *A Treatise of Human Nature*. 1967. Oxford: Clarendon Press.

Humphries, Drew and David F. Greenberg
  1981   The dialectics of crime control. Pp. 209–254 in David F. Greenberg (ed.),
          Crime & Capitalism: Readings in Marxist Criminology. Palo Alto, Calif.:
          Mayfield.

Hutcheson, Francis
1725a   *An Inquiry Concerning, Beauty, Order, Harmony, Design.* 1973. The Hague:
         Martinus Nijhoff.
1725b   *An Inquiry into the Original of our Ideas of Beauty and Virtue. In Two
         Treatises.* 1738. London: printed for D. Midwinter, A. Bettesworth, and C.
         Hitch.
1755   *A System of Moral Philosophy.* London: A. Millar and T. Longman.

Jaucourt, Chevalier de
1751   Crime (faute, péché, délit, forfait). Vol. 1:466–470 in Diderot and
         d'Alembert (eds.), *Encyclopédie, ou dictionnaire raisonné des sciences, des arts
         et des métiers.* 1969. 6 vols. New York: Pergamon.

Jenkins, Philip
1984   Varieties of Enlightenment criminology. *British Journal of Criminology*
         24(2):112–130.

Jones, David A.
1986   *History of Criminology: A Philosophical Perspective.* New York: Greenwood
         Press.

Kant, Immanuel
1797   *The Metaphysical Elements of Justice.* Part I of *The Metaphysics of Morals,*
         trans. John Ladd. 1965. Indianapolis: Bobbs–Merrill.

Kidder, Frederic
1870   *History of the Boston Massacre.* Albany: Joel Munsell.

Klang, Daniel M.
1984   Reform and enlightenment in eighteenth-century Lombardy. *Canadian
         Journal of History/Annales Canadiennes d'Histoire* 19(April):39–70.

Knight, Isabel F.
1968   *The Geometric Spirit: The Abbé de Condillac and the French Enlightenment.*
         New Haven: Yale University Press.

Landry, Eugenio
1910   *Cesare Beccaria: Scritti e lettere inediti.* Milan: Ulrico Hoepli.

Langbein, John H.
1976   *Torture and the Law of Proof: Europe and England in the Ancien Régime.*
         Chicago: University of Chicago Press.

Laplace, Pierre Simon de
1814   *A Philosophical Essay on Probabilities,* trans. F.W. Truscott and F.L. Emory.
         1951. New York: Dover.

Lieberman, David
1989   *The Province of Legislation Determined.* New York: Cambridge University
         Press.

Locke, John
1689   *Essay Concerning Human Understanding,* and Of the Conduct of the
         Understanding. Vol. 1:1–342 and vol. 3:389–428 in *The Works of John
         Locke.* 1727. London, printed for Arthur Bettesworth.
1695   *Further Considerations Concerning Raising the Value of Money.* London:
         printed for A. and J. Churchill.

Lottin, Joseph
  1912   *Quetelet: Statisticien et sociologue.* 1967. New York: Franklin.

Maestro, Marcello T.
  1942   *Voltaire and Beccaria as Reformers of Criminal Law.* New York: Columbia University Press.
  1973   *Cesare Beccaria and the Origins of Penal Reform.* Philadelphia: Temple University Press.

Matza, David
  1964   *Delinquency and Drift.* New York: John Wiley & Sons.

Maugham, Frederic Herbert
  1928   *The Case of Jean Calas.* London: William Heinemann.

Montesquieu, Charles Louis de Secondat
  1721   *Lettres persanes.* 1960. Paris: Garnier.
  1748   *De l'ésprit des lois.* 1973. 2 vols. Paris: Garnier.

Mueller, G.O.W.
  1990   Whose prophet is Cesare Beccaria? An essay on the origins of criminological theory. Vol. 2:1–14 in William S. Laufer and Freda Adler, eds., *Advances in Criminological Theory.* New Brunswick, N.J.: Transaction Publishers.

Newman, Graeme and Pietro Marongiu
  1990   Penological reform and the myth of Beccaria. *Criminology* 28(2):325–346.

Paolucci, Henry
  1963   Translator's introduction. Pp. ix–xxiii in Beccaria, *On Crimes and Punishments.* Indianapolis: Bobbs–Merrill.

Pasquino, Pasquale
  1980   Criminology: The birth of a special savior. *Ideology and Consciousnness* 7:17–32.

Petty, William
  1662   A treatise of taxes & contributions. Pp. 1–97 in Charles H. Hull (ed.), *The Economic Writings of Sir William Petty.* 1899. New York: Cambridge University Press.

Phillipson, Coleman
  1923   *Three Criminal Law Reformers: Beccaria/Bentham/Romilly.* 1975. Montclair, N.J.: Patterson Smith.

Phillipson, Nicholas
  1981   The Scottish Enlightenment. Pp. 19–40 in Roy Porter and Mikulás Teich (eds.), *The Enlightenment in National Context.* New York: Cambridge University Press.

Ramsay, Allan
  n.d.   Lettre à A.M. Diderot Vol. 4:56–60 in *Diderot: Oeuvres complètes.* Paris: Garnier.

Robbins, Caroline
  1968   *The Eighteenth-Century Commonwealthman.* New York: Atheneum.

Roberts, John M.
  1960   Enlightened despotism in Italy. Pp. 25–44 in Harold Acton et al., *Art and Ideas in Eighteenth-Century Italy.* Rome: The Italian Institute of London.

Robertson, John
    1983   The Scottish Enlightenment at the limits of the civic tradition. Pp. 137–178 in Istvan Hont and Michael Ignatieff (eds.), *Wealth and Virtue: The Shaping of Political Economy in the Scottish Enlightenment*. New York: Cambridge University Press.

Roshier, Bob
    1989   *Controlling Crime: The Classical Perspective in Criminology.* Chicago: Lyceum Books.

Schumpeter, Joseph A.
    1954   *History of Economic Analysis.* New York: Oxford University Press.

Scott, William Robert
    1900   *Francis Hutcheson.* New York: Cambridge University Press.

Servin, Antoine Nicholas
    1782   *De la législation criminelle.* Basel: Schweigenhauser.

Shackleton, Robert
    1972   The greatest happiness of the greatest number: The history of Bentham's phrase. Vol. 90:1461–1482 in *Studies on Voltaire and the Eighteenth Century*.

Swingewood, Alan
    1970   Origins of sociology: The case of the Scottish Enlightenment. *British Journal of Sociology* 21(2):164–180.

Taylor, Ian, Paul Walton, and Jock Young
    1973   *The New Criminology.* London: Routledge & Kegan Paul.

Tombs, Robert
    1980   Crime and the security of the state: The "dangerous classes" and insurrection in nineteenth-century Paris. Pp. 214–237 in V.A.C. Gatrell, Bruce Lenman, and Geoffrey Parker (eds.), *Crime and the Law: The Social History of Crime in Western Europe since 1500*. London: Europa.

Venturi, Franco
    1963   Elementi e tentativi di riforme nello Stato Pontificio del Settecento. *Rivista Storica Italiana* 25:778–817.
    1971   *Utopia and Reform in the Enlightenment.* New York: Cambridge University Press.
    1972   *Italy and the Enlightenment,* trans. Susan Corsi. New York: New York University Press.
    1983   Scottish echoes in eighteenth-century Italy. Pp. 345–362 in Istvan Hont and Michael Ignatieff (eds.), *Wealth and Virtue: The Shaping of Political Economy in the Scottish Enlightenment*. New York: Cambridge University Press.

Venturi, Franco (ed.)
    1965   *Cesare Beccaria, dei delitti e delle pene. Con una raccolta di lettere e documenti relativi alla nascita dell'opera e alla sua fortuna nell'Europa del Settecento.* Turin: Giulio Einaudi.

Verri, Pietro
    1763   *Meditazioni sulla felicità.* Milan: Galeazzi.

Vico, Giambattista
    1709   *On the Study Methods of Our Time*, trans Elio Gianturco. 1965.
            Indianapolis: Bobbs–Merrill.
    1725   *The New Science*, trans. T.G. Bergin and M.H. Fisch. 1970. Ithaca, N.Y.:
            Cornell University Press.

Vold, George B. and Thomas J. Bernard
    1986   *Theoretical Criminology*. New York: Oxford University Press.

Voltaire, François–Marie Arouet de
    1762a   Lettre à M. d'Alembert. Vol. 42:78–79 in *Oeuvres complètes de Voltaire*.
            Paris: Garnier.
    1762   Lettre à M. d'Alembert. Vol. 42:167–168 in *Oeuvres complètes de Voltaire*.
            Paris: Garnier.
    1763   Traité sur la tolérance à l'occasion de la mort de Jean Calas. Vol. 25:18–118
            in *Oeuvres complètes de Voltaire*. 1879. Paris: Garnier.

Weisser, Michael R.
    1979   *Crime and Punishment in Early Modern Europe*. Atlantic Highlands, N.J.:
            Humanities Press.

Wills, Garry
    1978   *Inventing America: Jefferson's Declaration of Independence*. Garden City,
            N.Y.: Doubleday.

Wood, P.B.
    1989   The natural history of man in the Scottish Enlightenment. *History of
            Science* 28(1):89–123.

Woolf, Stuart
    1979   *A History of Italy, 1700–1860*. London: Methuen.

Young, David
    1983   Cesare Beccaria: Utilitarian or retributivist? *Journal of Criminal Justice*
            11(4):317–326.
    1984   "Let Us Content Ourselves with Praising the Work While Drawing a Veil
            Over Its Principles": Eighteenth-century reactions to Beccaria's *On Crimes
            and Punishments*. *Justice Quarterly* 1:155–169.
    1986   Property and punishment in the eighteenth century: Beccaria and his critics.
            American Journal of Jurisprudence 31:121–135.

Zeman, Thomas Edward
    1981   Order, crime and punishment: The American criminological tradition.
            Unpublished Ph.D. dissertation in the History of Consciousness (Political
            and Social Thought), University of California at Santa Cruz.

Piers Beirne is Professor of Sociology and Legal Studies at the University of Southern Maine. He recently edited *Revolution in Law: Contributions to the Development of Soviet Legal Theory, 1917–1936*, and is author of the forthcoming *Inventing Criminology: The Rise of 'Homo Criminalis', 1750–1915*. With Jim Messerschmidt, he is the author of the textbook *Criminology* (1991). His current research is on abolitionism.

POVERTY, POWER, WHITE-COLLAR CRIME AND THE PARADOXES OF CRIMINOLOGICAL THEORY*

John Braithwaite†

Sutherland's aspiration for a general theory of both white-collar and common crime can be pursued by focusing on inequality as an explanatory variable. Powerlessness and poverty increase the chances that needs are so little satisfied that crime is an irresistible temptation to actors alienated from the social order and that punishment is non-credible to actors who have nothing to lose. It may be theoretically fruitful to move away from a positivist conception of need to needs socially constructed as wants that can be satisfied (contrasted with greed — socially constructed as insatiable wants). When needs are satisfied, further power and wealth enables crime motivated by greed. New types of criminal opportunities and new paths to immunity from accountability are constituted by concentrations of wealth and power. Inequality thus worsens both crimes of poverty motivated by need for goods for use and crimes of wealth motivated by greed enabled by goods for exchange. Furthermore, much crime, particularly violent crime, is motivated by the humiliation of the offender and the offender's perceived right to humiliate the victim. Inegalitarian societies, it is argued, are more structurally humiliating. Dimensions of inequality relevant to the explanation of both white-collar and common crime are economic inequality, inequality in political power (slavery, totalitarianism), racism, ageism and patriarchy. Neither of these lines of explanation is advanced as the whole story on crimes of the powerless or crimes of the powerful; but they may be a theoretically interesting and politically important part of the whole story.

Unlike many contemporary criminologists, I continue to be motivated by the goal that Edwin Sutherland set for us of developing criminological theory of maximum possible generality. Like most contemporary criminologists, I accept that Sutherland's revelation of the nature and extent of white-collar crime creates some acute problems for traditional criminological theories. And as Sutherland so convincingly argued, the dominant tradition of criminological theory that excises white-collar crime from its explanatory scope lays the foundations for a class-biased criminology and criminal justice policy.

Having accepted all this, in this article I want to reject Sutherland's view that the widespread reality of white-collar crime means that poverty and inequality cannot be important variables in a general theory of crime. Sutherland is provocative on this point: 'If it can be shown that white collar crimes are frequent, a general theory that crime is due to poverty and its related pathologies is shown to be invalid' (Sutherland, 1983:7). Sutherland did show that white-collar crime is frequent, when white-collar crime is defined as 'a crime committed by a person of respectability and high social status in the course of his occupation' (Sutherland, 1983: 7). Indeed, work since Sutherland leaves little doubt that more of the most serious crimes that cause the greatest property loss and the greatest physical injury are perpetrated by the rich than by the poor (eg, Cullen, Maakestaad and Cavender, 1987; Clinard and Yeager, 1980; Pepinsky and Jesilow, 1984; Geis, 1973; Pearce, 1976).

My contention is that inequality is relevant to the explanation of both crime in the streets and crime in the suites. I will seek to argue that this is true of various forms of inequality — based on class, race, age and gender. Yet how do issues of inequality of wealth and power connect with my explanatory theory of crime in *Crime, Shame and Reintegration*? In a sense, what I do in this article is couple the work in that book to

---

* This article is a revised version of a paper presented to the Edwin Sutherland Conference on White-Collar Crime, 12-15 May 1990, Indiana University.
† Australian National University and American Bar Association.

my 1979 book, *Inequality, Crime and Public Policy*. This first attempt to make sense of the connection between the analysis of inequality and crime and the analysis of shaming and crime has only become possible thanks to a number of recent and exciting contributions to the criminological literature. These are Jack Katz's (1988) *Seductions of Crime,* the work of Scheff and Benson on humiliation and rage, and Cohen and Machalek's (1988) 'General Theory of Expropriative Crime'.

In this article I will not summarise the evidence for the inequality-crime association compiled in *Inequality, Crime and Public Policy,* nor the evidence accumulated since. The purpose of the article is simply to advance a theoretical solution to a problem left with us by Sutherland. It is to show that the claim that poverty is causally implicated in crime can in fact be reconciled with the widespread reality of white-collar crime documented by Sutherland. While the reconciliation is theoretically interesting, whether it is empirically right is something which I simply leave on criminology's research agenda. Even if it is right, inequality is advanced only as a partial explanation of crime of modest explanatory power. More impressive explanatory capacity is only likely when inequality is integrated with other explanatory variables, perhaps in the way I suggested in *Crime, Shame and Reintegration,* perhaps in some other way.

I regard the theoretical work in this article as relevant to explaining crime conceived in either of two ways. First, as in *Crime, Shame and Reintegration,* it can be read as an attempt at explaining what Glaser (1978: 31-2) conceived as predatory crime (crime where an offender preys on others). What is advanced does not seem to me a very good theory of nonpredatory crimes such as drug use.

Alternatively, it can be read as theory concerning that domain of crimes which republicans ought to regard as crimes. Republican normative theory contends that acts ought only to criminalised when they threaten the dominion of citizens, and when there is no less intrusive way of protecting that dominion than criminalisation (Braithwaite and Pettit, 1990). Dominion includes the sphere of control citizens properly enjoy over their persons, their property and their province. To enjoy dominion, a citizen must live in a social world where other citizens respect their liberty and where this mutual respect is socially assured and generally recognised. An attraction of the republican definition for our present purposes is that it connects with a key empirical claim I will advance: when inequality of wealth and power is structurally humiliating, this undermines respect for the dominion of others. And a society where respect for dominion is lost will be a society riddled with crime.

Republican normative commitments direct us to take both political and economic inequality (Montesquieu, 1977: Chs 3-4; Pettit, 1990) and community disapproval (Pocock, 1977; Braithwaite and Pettit, 1990) seriously as issues. Sunstein (1988) advances 4 commitments as basic to republicanism: (1) deliberation in government which shapes as well as balances interests (as opposed to simply doing deals between pre-political interests); (2) political equality; (3) universality, or debate to reconcile competing views, as a regulative ideal; and (4) citizenship, community participation in public life.

Opportunity Theory

In this section, I argue:
    (1) that crime is motivated in part by needs;
    (2) that needs are more likely to be satisfied as we move up the class structure; and

(3) that redistributive policies will do more to increase the need satisfaction of the poor than to decrease the need satisfaction of the rich.

Notwithstanding these 3 hypotheses, greed motivates crime even after need is satisfied. More importantly, wealthly actors who have their needs satisfied will want to accumulate goods for exchange rather than use. Accumulations of goods for exchange enable the constitution of illegitimate opportunities for the rich that cannot be constituted for the poor. Hence, I will argue that inequality causes crime by:

(i) decreasing the goods available for *use* by the poor to satisfy needs; and
(ii) increasing the goods available to rich people (and organisations) who have needs satisfied, but whose accumulation of goods for *exchange* constitute criminal opportunities to indulge greed.

Inequality therefore at the same time causes:

crimes of *poverty*	Crimes of *wealth*
motivated by *need*	motivated by *greed*
for goods for *use*	enabled by goods for
	exchange (that are surplus
	to those required for use).

Inequality, Crime and Public Policy began to explore the theory and empirical evidence in support of the proposition that societies with more unequal distributions of wealth and power will have deeper crime problems. An account was advanced as to why inequality will often worsen both crime in the streets and crime in the suites. Through building on Cohen and Machalek (1988), I believe we can more clearly theorise the dynamics of this proposition than I was able to manage in *Inequality, Crime and Public Policy*.

The traditional account of opportunity theory as an explanation for crimes of the powerless continues to hold great attraction. This starts with Merton's (1957) observation that in any society there are a number of widely shared goals which provide an aspirational frame of reference. The most important of these in capitalist societies is material success. In addition to cultural goals held up as worth striving for, there are defined legitimate institutionalised means for achieving the cultural goals. When these are blocked, crime is more likely. Elaborating on Merton, Cloward and Ohlin (1960) maintained that if delinquency is to result from blockage of legitimate means to achieving a cultural goal, then there is a second requirement: illegitimate means for achieving the goal must be open.

The problem is reconciling white-collar crime within this framework. White-collar crime highlights the fact that illegitimate opportunities are grasped not only to satisfy need but also to gratify greed. In a sense, what I will set up here is explication of a transition as we move up the class structure from crime motivated by beliefs about the importance of satisfying needs to crime motivated by greed — even by the belief, in the immortal words of Michael Douglas from the movie 'Wall Street', that 'greed is good'.

But first things first — crime motivated by beliefs about needs. I am not interested in a positivist definition of need. I am interested in the phenomenon of need being socially constructed in culturally contingent ways that motivate crime. So we have criminals who act on a subsistence model of need, as in the classic case of English slum dwellers transported to Australia for stealing a loaf of bread to feed their family. There are criminals who act on models of need represented at every point of Maslow's (1954) hierarchy of needs. There are criminals motivated by the need for a decent standard of living, where 'decent' can mean what they perceive most people in their community to enjoy, what whites but not blacks enjoy, what they used to enjoy before they lost their job, what they were led to expect to enjoy by the advertising and dramatisation of bourgeois lifestyles on television. In short, the social construction of needs which motivate crime is culturally relative.

However relative they are, I advance one claim about them of general import. This claim is that as we become wealthier, it becomes more likely that any and all conceptions of need will be satisfied. If my income doubles, irrespective of whether my needs are framed in terms of subsistence, the average standard of living, or unrealistic expectations or aspirations, it is likely that I will view those needs as better met than they were before. The general claim is that as we move up the class structure, people are more likely to view their needs as satisfied. This, of course, is an empirically rebuttable claim.

Substituting the term needs in Cloward and Ohlin's (1960) formulation, the theory becomes that when legitimate means for satisfying needs are blocked and illegitimate means are open, crime is more likely. Controlling for aggregate national wealth, let us then compare a society with an equal distribution of wealth and one with an unequal distribution. It follows that because the poor will be poorer in the unequal case, those toward the bottom of the class structure will be less likely to perceive their needs as met (whether those needs are of a subsistence, absolute or relative sort). Because they view so few of their needs as met, the poor are also more likely to take the view that they have little to lose through a criminal conviction. More polemically, the more unequal the class structure, the more of scarce national wealth is devoted to gratifying greed among people whose needs are satisfied, the less is devoted to satisfying unmet need.

Consider a socially defined need for housing. The more unequal the class structure, the greater the proportion of housing expenditure that will be devoted to building bigger and bigger mansions for the rich, the greater the number of homeless, and the more the poor will turn to crime in preference to being put on the street. A more equal class structure may reduce the incidence of crimes of the poor connected to the need for housing.

Because wealthier people are more likely in a position where most of their needs are met, they are less likely to steal for this reason. As in standard welfare economics, let us assume that as we get richer we progressively work down our needs, starting with those that are most important to us. The wealthier we are, the lower the marginal returns to need satisfaction from acquiring a dollar of extra wealth through crime. Our first dollar is worth more to us than our ten millionth dollar. Hence, the crime-preventive effects of redistributing wealth from rich to poor to satisfy the needs of the poor will not be fully counterbalanced by crime-instigating effects on wealthy people who suffer reduced satisfaction of their needs.

Yet we know that even when wealthy people have all of their self-defined personal needs fully met, the extra dollar is not valueless to them. Even though a dollar has less value to a person whose needs are mostly satisfied than to one whose needs are not, the dollar will mostly continue to have some value to people with satisfied needs. Such people can continue to be motivated to pursue wealth for many other reasons — to signify their worth by conspicuous consumption, to prove success to themselves, to build an empire, to leave an inheritance.

For this reason, it is sensible to also apply a Mertonian framework to the economic aspirations of the upper class. We can readily conceive of the blocked aspirations of the already wealthy man to become a millionaire. We might understand his behaviour in paying a bribe in these terms: legitimate means for securing a contract are blocked at the time and an illegitimate opportunity to do so corruptly is open. Vaughan (1983: 59) suggests that a cultural emphasis on economic success motivates the setting of a new goal whenever the old one is attained. While needs are socially constructed as wants that can be satisfied, greed is distinguished as a want that can never be satisfied: success is ever-receding; having more leads to wanting more again.

> While it is meaningless to accumulate certain sensual use-values indefinitely, since their worth is limited by their usefulness, the accretion of exchange-value, being merely quantitative, suffers no such constraints. (Haug, 1986: 18)

Wheeler's (1991) paper directs us to the motivational importance of fear of falling as well as greed for gain in white-collar crime. There is no problem in accommodating this within the theoretical framework of the present analysis. Crime can be motivated by: (a) a desire for goods for use; (b) a fear of losing goods for use; (c) a desire for goods for exchange; or (d) a fear of losing goods for exchange. My proposition is that (a) and (b) are more relevant to motivating the crimes of poor people; (c) and (d) are more relevant to motivating the crimes of wealthy people and organisations. These distributional tendencies can hold even though (a) to (d) might all be involved in the mixed motives driving say a single corporate crime. Some individuals who play a part in the crime may be motivated by (a), others by (b), others (c) and others (d). Indeed, within some individuals there may be mixed motives that range across the four categories. This does not change the distributional hypothesis that use-motivations will more often be involved in the criminal choices of the poor, exchange-motivations more often involved in the criminal choices of the rich.

I will now argue that just as the poverty of the poor in unequal societies contributes to crime, so does the wealth of the wealthy. We have established that the latter cannot be true because of a purely Mertonian analysis of legitimate opportunities to satisfy needs because the rich have more of their needs satisfied by ready access to legitimate means of need satisfaction.

One line of argument here is that conspicuous concentrations of wealth increase the illegitimate opportunities available to the poor (and indeed the non-poor). Being a car thief is more remunerative when there are many $50,000 cars available to be stolen than when $20,000 cars are the best one can find. Evidence that wealthy neighbourhoods located near slums are especially likely to be victimised by property offenders supports this line of analysis (Boggs, 1965). But it is not a theoretical path I wish to pursue here.

The theoretically important criminogenic effect of increasing concentrations of wealth is in enabling the constitution of new forms of illegitimate opportunity that are not available to the poor or the average income earner, opportunities that can be extremely lucrative. It is important to understand here that increasing wealth for the poor or the average income earner does not constitute new illegitimate opportunities in the way I will discuss.

Marx's distinction of value for use and value for exchange is helpful here. In his 'Economic and Philosophical Manuscripts', use is associated with need: 'every real and possible need is a weakness which will tempt the fly to the gluepot' (Marx, 1973: 148). Also every product that can be used 'is a bait with which to seduce away the other's very being, his money'. Up to the point where legitimate work generates for the worker only value for use (in meeting needs), she has no surplus. Up to this point, extra income is used instead of invested in the constitution of illegitimate opportunities. But when surplus is acquired (value for exchange rather than for use), it can be invested in the constitution of illegitimate opportunities.

A limitation of Cloward and Ohlin's (1960) analysis is that it tends to view illegitimate opportunities as a fact of society independent of the agency of the criminal actor — ready and waiting for the criminal actor to seize. This conception forgets the point that, if they are powerful enough, criminals can actively constitute illegitimate opportunities. This power is not totally explained by control of surplus value — the working class juvenile can constitute a gang as a vehicle for collective criminal enterprises that would be beyond her grasp as an individual. But surplus value can be used to constitute criminal opportunities of an order that is not available to the poor. As Weisburd et al (1989: 79) found in their systematic study of white-collar criminals in New York: 'The most consequential white-collar crimes — in terms of their scope, impact and cost in dollars — appear to require for their commission, that their perpetrators operate in an environment that provides access to both money and the organisation through which money moves.'

Persons with some spare capital can start up a company; the company can be used as a vehicle to defraud consumers or investors; the principal can siphon off funds into a personal account, bankrupting the company and leaving creditors stranded. They can set up a Swiss bank account and a shell company in a tax haven. But to launder dirty money, to employ the lawyers and accountants to evade taxes, they must have some surplus to start with. And the more they have, the more grand the illegitimate opportunities they can constitute. When they become big enough, shares in their company can be traded publicly. They can then indulge in some very lucrative forms of insider trading and share ramping. If they become billionaires like Nelson Bunker Hunt and W Herbert Hunt, they can even try to manipulate the entire market for a commodity like silver (Abolafia, 1985). If they become an oligopolist in a market, they can work with the other oligopolists to fix prices and breach other trade practice laws. If they become a monopolist, a further array of illegal predatory practices become available. The proposition is that capital can be used to constitute illegitimate opportunities, and the more capital the bigger the opportunities. And obversely to our analysis of need, an egalitarian redistribution of wealth away from surplus for the rich in favour of increased wealth for the poor will not correspondingly expand illegitimate opportunities for the poor. This is because in the hands of the poor, income is for use; it is not available as surplus for constituting illegitimate opportunities.

Other things being equal, the rich will prefer to stay out of trouble by investing in legitimate rather than illegitimate opportunities. But when goals are set with the expectation that they will be secured legitimately, environmental contingencies frequently intervene to block legitimate goal attainment. Powerful actors regularly have the opportunity in these circumstances to achieve the goal illegitimately. The production target cannot be achieved because the effluent treatment plant has broken down. So it is achieved by allowing untreated effluent to flow into the river late at night. Most capital investment simultaneously constitutes a range of both legitimate and illegitimate means of further increasing the wealth of the capitalist. The wealth that creates legal opportunities at the same time brings illegal opportunities for achieving the same result into existence. In this additional sense, investment creates criminal opportunities in a way that use does not. It is just that there is a difference in the way we evaluate illegitimate opportunities that are inherent in any legitimate investment compared with illegitimate opportunities that are created intentionally. The former are unfortunate side-effects of mostly desirable processes of creating wealth. The latter are the main and intended effects of a mostly undesirable process of criminal exploitation. Whatever the mix of desirable and undesirable effects of shifting wealth from the poor to the rich, the only effect we are theoretically interested in here is the creation of more illegitimate opportunities for the rich. My main point is that surplus can be used intentionally to constitute illegitimate opportunities — whether by setting up an illegal traffic in arms or drugs or by setting up a tax evasion scheme — in a way that income for use cannot.

Here it is useful to think of the implications of Cohen and Machalek's (1988) evolutionary ecological approach to expropriative crime. The first point in this analysis is that the returns to an expropriative strategy vary inversely with the number of others who are engaging in the same strategy. In nature, a behavioral strategy of predation is more likely to persist if it is different from that used by other predators. There is no 'best' strategy that will be adopted by every predator because it is the best; for a predator to opt for a strategy, it must be one that is not crowded out by others using a similar strategy. Minority strategies can flourish.

Extreme wealth fosters extraordinarily lucrative minority strategies. The wealthy can pursue illegitimate strategies that are novel and that excel because they cannot be contemplated by those who are not wealthy. Where there is no limit on what can be spent on an expropriative strategy, it can be designed to beat all alternative less adequately funded strategies against which it must compete. This is why the most damaging and most lucrative expropriative strategies are white-collar crimes. Those who have no inhibitions against duck-shooting out of season, who need spare no expense on their artillery, for whom no strategy is too novel (even shooting other hunters), are likely to get the best haul of ducks.

Anyone can stage a bank robbery. But bank robbery is not a particularly cost-effective form of illegitimate work. Very few people can buy a bank. Yet as Pontell and Calavita (1990) quote in their paper on Savings and Loans fraud, 'The best way to rob a bank is to own one'.

Cohen and Machalek (1988) suggest that the 'resource holding potential' (RHP) of the poor means they will commit crimes that amount to 'making the best of a bad job'. The RHP of the rich, in contrast, allows them to 'take advantage of a good job'. The rich will rarely resort to the illegitimate means which are criminal staples among the poor because they can secure much higher returns by pursuing either legitimate or illegitimate means to which the poor have no access. There will be little direct competition between the powerful and the powerless criminal. Instead, they will develop different minority strategies that reflect their different RHPs. Where there is direct competition, it is fragile. The small drug dealer can be crushed by the powerful organised criminal unless she finds a way of complementing him, picking up his crumbs or operating outside his area instead of competing with him.

The other peculiar advantage that powerful criminals have is in the domain that the evolutionary ecologists call counter-strategy dynamics. Fast predators activate a selective force favouring faster prey and vice versa (Cohen and Machalek, 1988). The expropriative strategy of conning consumers into buying dangerous or ineffective patent medicines was countered by the strategy of regulatory agencies seizing drugs which had not been through a pre-Marketing clearance process. The most ruthless participants in the industry used their considerable resources to short-circuit such counter-strategies, however. They bribed those responsible for pre-marketing clearance decisions; they paid unethical researchers to produce fraudulent evidence that their products were safe and efficacious (Braithwaite, 1984). To indulge this kind of thwarting of the counter-strategy process requires abundant resources of a sort unavailable to indigent criminals. Box (1983: 59) has written at length on how the greatest comparative advantage of corporate criminals 'lies in their ability to prevent their actions from becoming subject to criminal sanctions in the first place'. Again Pontell and Calavita's (1990) case study of the Savings and Loans crisis illustrates: the counter-strategy relevant there was the deregulatory reforms that the financial sector extracted from the Congress and the Executive in the early 80s, thus rendering their power less accountable.

In *Inequality, Crime and Public Policy,* I developed in some detail the proposition that it is the unaccountable power that accrues to the most wealthy that explains why they can get away with crimes of extreme seriousness. It was argued there that power corrupts and unaccountable power corrupts with impunity.[1] The upper class use their resources to ensure that their power is unaccountable; they benefit from a hegemony that renders their power corrupting. At its most basic level, only people in positions of power have the opportunity to commit crimes that involve the abuse of power, and the more power they have, the more abusive those crimes can be. As Taylor, Walton and Young (1973: 30) put it:

> ... radical deviancy theory has the task of demonstrating analytically that such rule-breaking is institutionalized, regular and widespread among the powerful, that it is a given result of the structural position enjoyed by powerful men — whether they be Cabinet ministers, judges, captains of industry or policemen.

In this analysis, power as well as money is conceived as something that can be exchanged, invested to generate more power. Hence, the crimes of a J Edgar Hoover (Geis and Goff, 1990) can be interpreted as motivated by an insatiable desire to accumulate more power for exchange. The extreme manifestation of this problem is seen in a Marcos or Ceausescu, whose power is inestimable, whose immunity from accountability is total, whose capacity for crime knows no bounds. In contrast to the insatiable demands of a totalitarian ruler to control more totally more and more people, the criminogenic powerlessness of the poor is bounded. It is bounded by the need to assert control over the life of just one person — their own person.

Inequality, Crime and Public Policy argued that if crime in the suites arises from the fact that certain people have great wealth and power, and if crime in the streets arises from the fact that certain other people have very little wealth or power, then policies to redistribute wealth and power may simultaneously relieve both types of crime problems.

I have been led to the same conclusion by the considerations in this article. If it is wealth and power that enable a range of extremely harmful expropriative strategies that are distinctive to those at the top of the class structure, then redistribution of wealth and power in favour of the upper class will increase that which enables their crimes. Redistribution of wealth and power away from the poor will worsen the 'bad lot' of which the best they can make is crime. It will further exacerbate the blockage of legitimate means, thereby increasing the attraction of illegitimate means for satisfying needs. And it will increase the alienation, the hopelessness, the live-for-the-moment desperation of those who feel that they do not have power over their own future.

Moreover, it may be that extremes of wealth and power mean that the rich justify their exploitative class position with exploitative and criminogenic ideologies not so unlike the caricature, 'greed is good'. It may be that just as the criminality of the rich is accounted for in terms of the fact that they exploit, the criminality of the poor is accounted for by the fact that they are exploited. While the forms of crime that predominate at the two ends of the class spectrum are sharply distinguishable minority strategies, they may be different sides of the same coin, both products of the same inequality, of the exploitation perceived by those who are exploited and of the exploiting legitimated for those who exploit.

At both ends, criminal subcultures develop to communicate symbolic reassurance to those who decide to prey on others, to sustain techniques for neutralising the evil of crime (Sykes and Matza, 1957) and to communicate knowledge about how to do it. Black criminal subcultures in America collect, dramatise and transmit the injustices of a society dominated by whites and ruled by an oppressive Anglo-Saxon criminal justice system. The subcultures of Wall Street rationalise exploitative behaviour as that which made America great. Business subcultures of tax evasion are memory files that collect the injustices of the Internal Revenue Service (cf Matza, 1964:102) and communicate resentment over the disproportionate tax burden shouldered by the rich. An oligopolistic price fixing subculture under the auspices of an industry association communicates the social benefits of 'orderly marketing'; it constitutes and reproduces an illegitimate opportunity structure.

The focus of the discussion so far has been excessively on property crime. But it need not have been. A business subculture of resistance to an occupational health and safety agency can foster methods of legal defiance, circumvention and counter-attack that kill. The unaccountable power of a Marcos or a Ceausescu can be used to kill. A wealthy person can use their capital to establish a toxic waste disposal company that directs the violence of cancer against an unsuspecting community by illegal dumping of toxins. The resentment of a black person who feels powerless and exploited because of his race can be manifested by violent as well as acquisitive crime. There are, however, some arguments about inequality that may have some special force in the domain of violent crime. To these I now turn.

The Social Structure of Humiliation

A stunning recent contribution to criminology is Jack Katz's (1988) *The Seductions of Crime*. On the central issue of this paper, Katz stands with Sutherland: 'Because of its insistence on attributing causation to material conditions in personal and social backgrounds, modern social thought has been unable either to acknowledge the embrace of evil by common or street criminals, or, and for the same reason, develop empirical bite and intellectual depth in the study of criminality by the wealthy and powerful' (Katz, 1988:10).

The importance of Katz's work resides in his analysis of violence or rage as 'livid with the awareness of humiliation' (Katz, 1988: 23). Rage both recalls and transforms the experience of humiliation. The experience of a sense of righteousness is the stepping stone from humiliation to rage; the embrace of righteous violence resolves humiliation 'through the overwhelming sensuality of rage' (Katz, 1988: 24; see also Marongiu and Newman, 1987). For Katz it is not coincidental that spouse assault is so often associated with taunting about sexual performance or innuendo of sexual infidelity. Domestic homicide transforms such sexual degradation 'in a last violent stand in defence of his basic worth' (p 26). Rage transcends the offender's humiliation by taking him to dominance over the situation.

Katz's analysis of righteous slaughter is a useful complement to the rather instrumental analysis of opportunity and strategy in the first part of this paper precisely because it is such a non-instrumental analysis. Katz notes the frequency with which murderers cease an attack long before death and indeed in the midst of evidence of persistent life such as screams and pleas for mercy (p 32). The inference that rage is not instrumentally concerned with causing death is also warranted in cases where death is not a *sufficient* concern:

> In a 'stomping', the attacker may announce to his victim the objective of 'kicking your eyes out of your head'. The specific practical objective — to remove precisely the condition of

the attacker's humiliation, the victim's offending gaze — is more imaginatively related to the project of transcending humiliation than would be the victim's death. (p 33)

Violence transcends humiliation by casting the person who degraded the offender into an ontologically lower status. Mounted in a flurry of curses, the attack 'will be against some morally lower, polluted, corrupted, profanized form of life, and hence in honor of a morally higher, more sacred, and — this bears special emphasis — an eternally respectable realm of being' (p 36). The claim that rage is about asserting respect, I will argue, is fundamental to distinguishing forms of shaming that provoke crime and forms that prevent it. Shame and respect are the key concepts for understanding crime. Far from being a self-interested instrumental evildoer, the attacker is immersed in a frenzy of upholding the decent and respectable. Just as humiliation of the *offender* is implicated in the onset of his rage, so the need to humiliate the *victim* enables her victimisation.

Katz reached these conclusions from an analysis of several hundred criminal acts quite independently of similar conclusions reached by psychiatric scholars. Kohut (1972), a psychoanalyst, identified 'narcissistic rage' as a compound of shame and rage. Lewis's (1971) cases led her to conclude that unacknowledged shame and anger causes a feeling trap, alternation between shame and anger that can produce explosive violence she calls humiliated fury. The work of Lansky (1984, 1987) and Scheff et al (1989) similarly emphasises the importance of humiliation that is unacknowledged. Innuendo, underhanded disrespect more than overt insult, opens up a cycle of humiliation, revenge, counter-revenge, ultimately to violence. Scheff (1987) identified two ways of reacting to scorn — shame or anger. But sometimes humiliated actors alternate between the two in what Scheff calls a shame-rage spiral.

Katz denies that material circumstances have anything to do with his conclusions about humiliation and rage. Here I believe he is wrong. Some societies and institutions are structurally more humiliating than others. For a black, living in South Africa is structurally more humiliating than living in Tanzania. Living in a prison is structurally more humiliating than living in a nursing home and the latter is more humiliating than dwelling in a luxury apartment. Slavery is structurally more humiliating than freedom.

School systems such as I experienced as a child, where children are linearly ordered in their classroom according to their rank, 'dunces' sitting at the front, are structurally humiliating for those who fail. These are school systems where dunces are regularly afflicted with degradation ceremonies. And there are alternative structures which are less humiliating, less the mouse race that caricatures the rat race for which children are prepared. An example is Knight's (1985: 266) conception of redemptive schooling:

> A redemptive schooling practice would aim to integrate students into all aspects of school learning and not build fences around students through bureaucratic rituals or prior assumptions concerning student ability. A clear expectation from teachers must be that all students can be taught, and in turn an expectation on the part of students that they can learn. A school succeeds democratically when everyone's competence is valued and is put to use in a variety of socially desirable projects. Indeed, the same may be said to hold for a good society.

More generally, *inegalitarian societies are structurally humiliating.* When parents cannot supply the most basic needs of their children, while at the same time they are assailed by the ostentatious consumption of the affluent, this is structurally humiliating for the poor. Where inequality is great, the rich humiliate the poor through conspicuous consumption and the poor are humiliated as failures for being poor. Both sides of this equation are important. The propensity to feel powerless and exploited among the poor and the propensity of the rich to see exploiting as legitimate both, as we have seen, enable crime.

Racist societies are structurally humiliating: These are societies where the despised racial group is viewed as unworthy of respect, where the superordinate group humiliates the subordinate group, where the subordinate group feels daily humiliation. Such racist oppression can be criminogenic.

Patriarchy is structurally humiliating: Patriarchy is a condition where women enjoy limited dominion, where men do not respect the dominion of women, where women are humiliated by men. However, it is common in patriarchal societies for women not to feel humiliated. Similarly, it is not uncommon for oppressed racial minorities and for the poor *not* to feel humiliated in racist and inegalitarian societies. Here the Gramscian (1971) concept of hegemony is useful. It often happens that part of the success of the domination by the superordinate group is in persuading the subordinate group that they should accept the ideology of superordination; they identify their own interests with those of their rulers.[2] Their subordination is regarded as something natural rather than something to resent (see also Scheff, 1990).

But hegemony never works perfectly. A substantial fraction of the oppressed group is always humiliated by their oppression. It is just that historically, hegemony has tended to work better with the oppression of women than it has with the oppression of racial minorities. In the US or Australia, for example, even though there are many more women than blacks, there are more cases of blacks than of women who feel humiliated to the point of daily seething rage which explodes into violence.

To understand why women commit less crime than men, in spite of their oppression, we need to understand why it is that women, instead of feeling humiliation and rage, feel shame and guilt. I have begun to address this in *Crime, Shame and Reintegration,* and will return to the issue later in this article. For the moment, I note only how I would propose to deal with the critical issue of the operationalisation problem with the infamously vague concept of hegemony. It is through measuring the things to which the theory proposes hegemony leads — shame and guilt when it is present, humiliation and anger when it is not (see further Scheff, 1990).

The fact that patriarchy does not engender feelings of humiliation and rage among most women does not absolve patriarchy of criminogenesis. Remember, there are two sides to our story. The hypothesis is that humiliation both motivates violence among those humiliated and enables violence among those who humiliate. Hence, the degradation of women countenanced by men who do not grant women dominion enables rape and violence against women on a massive scale in patriarchal societies, not to mention commercial exploitation of the bodies of women by actors who might ambiguously be labelled white-collar criminals. Empirical work on homicides by men against women confirms that homicide can be viewed as an attempt by the male to assert '. . . their power and control over their wifes' (Wallace, 1986: 126; Polk and Ranson, 1991). In passing, it is important to note that the willingness to humiliate women should, according to the theory, be more profound among men who see themselves as having been humiliated — as a black humiliated by whites, as an American soldier in Vietnam humiliated by protesters back home, by 'Gooks' who defeat him militarily, and by an authoritarian military.

Ageist societies are structurally humiliating: Where the very young or the very old are not worthy of respect, where they do not enjoy the dominion accorded human beings at the peak of their powers, the young and the old will be abused, including physically abused — both in the home and in institutions specialising in their care (schools and nursing homes). While the very old rarely have the physical power to transcend their humiliation with violent rage, the young do, especially as they become older, stronger young males. The physical powerlessness of the very old makes their abuse the most invisible and insidious in complex societies. As Joel Handler (1989: 5) points out, even prisoners can riot, but the frail aged have neither muscle nor voice. The very young, and particularly the very old (Fattah and Sacco, 1989:174-7), are also vulnerable and attractive targets for consumer fraud.

Ageist and gendered exploitation interact in important ways. Contemporarily we see this in many studies of elder abuse which report over 70%, and sometimes over 80%, of victims of elderly abuse to be female (Hudson, 1986; Wolf and Pillemer 1989:33).[3] Historically, we see it in the victimisation of older women labelled as witches in the 16th and 17th centuries in many parts of the western world (Stearns, 1986: 7).

Totalitarian societies are structurally humiliating: Totalitarian societies are, by definition, disrespectful of the dominion of ordinary citizens. They are societies that trample on the dominion of individual citizens to serve the interests of the ruling party. Atrocities by the state are enabled by disrespect for its citizens. The disrespect that degraded citizens in turn accord to the laws of the totalitarian state is also criminogenic.

Retributive societies are structurally humiliating[4]: These are societies where evildoers are viewed as unworthy of respect, as enjoying no right to have their dominion protected, as worthy of humiliation. The degraded status of prisoners in retributive societies frees those responsible for their daily degradation from restraints to respect the dominion of prisoners. The result can be the systematic violence directed against prisoners that we saw documented in the Royal Commission into New South Wales Prisons (Jewson, 1978) and which was a central cultural fact of the first 100 years of our colonial history. We can see this in Stotland's interpretation of the slaughter of prisoners at Attica: 'For both troopers and guards, sense of competence, violence and self-esteem . . . are linked' (Stotland, 1976: 88). 'A person's self-esteem can be threatened by failure [and] insults' (p 86) (see also, Scheff, 1989: 187; McKay Commission 1972). In another study of the 1970 killings by National Guardsmen at Kent State University, Stotland and Martinez (1976: 12) reached the same conclusion:

> The events . . . leading up to the killings were a series of inept, ineffectual, almost humiliating moves by the Guardsmen against the 'enemy' . . . The answer to these threats to their self-esteem, to their sense of competence, was violence . . . Another aspect . . . which added to the threat to the self-esteem of the Guardsmen [was that] during their presence on . . . campus . . . the students insulted Guardsmen. . . [and the Guardsmen] were not in a position to answer back. Their relative silence was another humiliation for them.

Scheff et al (1989) have discussed both of these cases of collective violence. They focused on the 'brutality and humiliation of the inmates' (such as forcing prisoners to crawl through mud) documented in the McKay Commission (1972) report. But the prison officers were also humiliated by the assertion of inmate power, the mistreatment of hostages and the recognition their superiors in the prison administration gave to prisoner demands (treating them 'as if they were equals'), and their denunciation by the prisoners on television. Scheff et al (1989: 193) interpreted this as a triple shame/rage spiral:

The guards were shamed by the behaviour of the administration and the inmates, were powerless to confront the administration, and became hostile toward the inmates, who in turn were shamed by the guards' lack of respect and reacted with an angry lack of respect towards the guards.

When two parties are each stigmatising the other, on both sides stigmatisation enables one's own violence and provokes the violence of the other.

In *Crime, Shame and Reintegration,* I have developed in more detail the criminogenic consequences of stigmatisation. Because I mainly talk of stigmatisation there rather than humiliation, it is important to clarify the difference between the two terms. Humiliation means disrespectful disapproval. Stigmatisation is humiliation that is sustained over an indefinitely long period. In *Crime, Shame and Reintegration* I partitioned shaming into reintegrative shaming (which prevents crime) and stigmatisation (which encourages it).[5] Reintegrative shaming is disapproval extended while a relationship of respect is sustained with the offender. Stigmatisation is disrespectful, humiliating shaming where degradation ceremonies are never terminated by gestures of reacceptance of the offender. The offender is branded an evil person and cast out in a permanent, open-ended way. Reintegrative shaming, in contrast, might vigorously shame an evil deed, but the offender is cast as a respected person rather than an evil person. Even the shaming of the deed is finite in duration, terminated by ceremonies of forgiveness-apology-repentance. The preventive effect of reintegratively shaming criminals occurs when the offender recognises the wrongdoing and shames himself. This distinction also appears in the work of Katz (1988: 26-7): 'Thus I may "become ashamed of myself" but I do not become humiliated of myself'.

The case is made in *Crime, Shame and Reintegration* that stigmatisation fosters crime by increasing the attraction of criminal subcultures to the stigmatised; we have also in this article seen that humiliation directly provokes violence. Here we have sought to suggest that stigmatisation not only encourages crime *by* those stigmatised; it also enables crime to be targeted *against* those stigmatised. For example, carers for the aged who have stigmatised images of the elderly are more likely to be found among those who abuse their old folk (Phillips, 1983).

The empirical claims derived from the theory in this chapter can be simply summarised. Nations will have more crime the more they are unequal in wealth and power, racist, patriarchal, ageist, totalitarian and retributive. To the extent that hegemony works to convince the subordinate fractions of the population that their oppression is natural rather than humiliating, these effects will be attenuated — we will see evidence of feeling ashamed rather than feeling humiliated, perhaps of more inwardly-directed rather than other-directed violence. The prediction of the theory, nevertheless, is that even where hegemony is strong, inequality will still have some effect on the crime rate because: (a) hegemony will never be total, and (b) because hegemony undermines feelings of being exploited without undermining the ideology of exploitation that enables the victimisation of the exploited. These hypotheses are not banal; they cut against the grain of some popular alternative accounts of crime — for example, the account of Sutherland, Katz and others that materialist explanation does not work, the account that a high crime rate is a price we pay for freedom, the account that retributive crime control policies will have crime-reducing deterrent effects. In the years ahead, I will be doing my best to apply some international comparative data to crude preliminary tests of these propositions.

It may be that when humiliation is deeply structured into a social system, it is not only the subordinate who suffer frequent humiliation. In a class system where the motivation to conspicuously flaunt superior wealth is profound, in a school system motivated by ranking in the class, dropping from number one to number two can be humiliating. Merton saw this point, quoting a well-to-do Hollywood resident of the 30s: 'In this town, I'm snubbed socially because I only get a thousand a week. That hurts.' (Merton, 1968: 190). We also saw this in the case of the Attica riot: in a social system where the prisoners were totally subordinated, the very willingness of the administration to negotiate with the prisoners was humiliating to the prison officers.

This two-way street is perhaps most vivid in the domain of gender and sexuality. Patriarchy is often manifested as measuring the worth of women against a yardstick of youthful physical beauty, while machismo is about male domination of women by sexual virility — the revered male is he who conquers the largest number of beautiful women. Needless to say, societies where success is so measured are structurally humiliating for women who inevitably lose their youth and who resent being used as a score. But when resentment and humiliation is structured into sexuality, the male is also at risk. Katz's (1988) work shows how women taunt men for their poor sexual performance and how violence can be unleashed when they do so.

The key to a feminist criminology of some explanatory power, I submit, is to understand the relationship between gender and my two types of shaming. The sexually stratified structure of shame is why women kill less than men (Braithwaite, 1989). The sexually stratified structure of humiliation is why when women do kill, it is rarely other women (Zahn, 1980: 125; Katz, 1988; Polk and Ranson, 1991).

Just as in the first half of this article the disproportionate emphasis was on property offences, in the second half we have been developing an approach which seems most powerful in the domain of traditional violent offences. However, the analysis is by no means without relevance to the explanation of property and white-collar offences as well.

Katz (1988) makes much of the 'badass' who takes pride in a defiant reputation as bad:

> The badass, with searing purposiveness, tries to scare humiliation off; as one ex-punk explained to me, after years of adolescent anxiety about the ugliness of his complexion and the stupidity of his every word, he found a wonderful calm in making 'them' anxious about *his* perceptions and understandings. (Katz, 1988: 312-3)

The point here is that pride in a badness that transcends humiliation might just as well be the badness of vandalism or theft as the badness of violence. This has been a repeated theme in street-corner criminological research. It is most strongly expressed in Albert Cohen's (1955) notion of reaction formation. Humiliation at school brings about a status problem for the children who fail in a competitive school system. This status problem is solved collectively with other students who have been similarly humiliated by the school. The outcasts set up their own status system with values which are the exact inverse of those of the school — contempt for property and authority instead of respect for property and authority, immediate impulse gratification instead of impulse control, toughness instead of control of aggression. This inverted status system is one in which the delinquent is guaranteed some success. It is clear that many non-violent forms of delinquency will do for dealing with humiliation by rejecting one's rejectors.

Benson (1990) has shown the importance of humiliation and rage among 30 convicted white-collar property offenders. Adjudication of their cases engendered anger and rage as well as shame and embarrassment. The way humiliation unfolded meant that anger usually won out over shame as a way of dealing with the situation. The likely result of feeling unfairly stigmatised, according to Benson, is reduced commitment to the legitimacy of the law. In this sense, Benson argues, a criminal justice system based on reintegrative shaming is less likely to be counter-productive than one based on stigmatisation.

It would be perverse indeed to interpret the second half of this article as only a story about the explanation of common violence in the streets. In the same year that Edwin Sutherland introduced white-collar crime into our lexicon, the greatest white-collar criminal of our century set the world alight. His name was Adolf Hitler. Thomas Scheff points out that 'Every page of Hitler's Mein Kamp bristles with shame and rage' (Scheff, 1987: 147). Indeed Hitler's appeal was the appeal of humiliated fury, an appeal which struck a responsive chord with many German people who felt they had been tricked and humiliated at Versailles[6], defeated by 'traitors, Communists and Jews'. War crimes are partly about blocked legitimate opportunities to achieve national economic objectives. But they are also about being humiliated, wanting to humiliate, and fear of being humiliated on both sides of a conflict.

> There is fear of defeat and fear of humiliation. There is the great fear of being seen to be a loser. It could be argued that the reason the British war fleet was sent to the Falklands was really the fear of humiliation. The preservation of a self-image on a personal or national level is extremely important and fear of losing that image is a strong motivator. Indeed, Enoch Powell goaded Mrs Thatcher in the House of Commons with exactly this approach: how could she, of all people stand for this Argentine insult. (de Bono, 1985:145).

When Saddam Hussein broadcast his appeal of 10 August 1990 to all Arabs, humiliation was a key repetitive element of his text: 'Rise up, so that the voice of right can be heard in the Arab nation. Rebel against all attempts to humiliate Mecca. Make it clear to your rulers, the emirs of oil, as they serve the foreigner; tell them the traitors there is no place for them on Arab soil after they have humiliated Arab honour and dignity.' (*The Times,* 11 August 1990, p1)

Criminology as a Model of how to do Social Theory?

In all of these recent developments in criminological theory, it seems to me that we can do more than satisfy Sutherland's ideal of criminological theory which brings in white-collar crime, which is maximally general in its scope. We can bring class back in (in a way that Sutherland would not approve) and gender, race, age and politics as well. We can call on normative theory which is articulated to explanatory theory to define objects of explanation that are not trivial to the human condition. Philip Pettit and my republican theory (Braithwaite and Pettit, 1990) is, we hope, the most comprehensively developed such normative theory of criminal justice. But there are Marxist, socialist realist, liberal and retributivist models available which are also specified with increasing coherence.

Nevertheless, the most important accomplishment which might be within our grasp is at a more meta-theoretical level. This is to integrate theoretically four ideas:
   (1) the reasoning individual (the strategist) and the reasoning collectivity (the corporate strategist);
   (2) the somatic, the body, emotions (humiliation, rage, shame, forgiveness, love, respect);
   (3) the micro interaction (the degradation ceremony, the assault, the proffering of forgiveness, apology, the ceremony to decertify deviance);
   (4) the macro, the structural (relations of production, patriarchy, communitarianism, age structure, urbanisation).
Each of these four levels can be shown to be actively shaping, enabling and constraining each of the others. In *Crime, Shame and Reintegration,* I made much of

the reasoning individual acting in ways enabled and constrained by structural factors, but exercising agency in micro encounters that both reproduce and transform those very structures.

Where I did not go far enough was in playing up a similar recursiveness among the somatic, the micro and the macro. Yet we should be emboldened by the work of Scheff and Katz to take this extra step. As Barbalet and Lyon (1989) have pointed out, we have Foucault more than anyone to thank for bringing the body back in to social theory. But for Foucault the body is little more than a text on which is inscribed disciplinary practices, relations of power. Agency is rarely conceded to the somatic. Yet the non-trivial role of Hitler's humiliation and sustained rage in events which transformed the world shows that social theory which writes out somatic agency will have truncated explanatory power.

Katz failed to go beyond the interface between the compelling force of emotions and individual reasoning in the micro encounter. It is the failure for which an earlier generation of micro-sociologists was so eloquently condemned by Taylor, Walton and Young (1973). Why can we not put all of these newer elements together with the legacy of Sutherland to make criminology one of the best exemplars we have in the social sciences of how to do social theory and praxis? It is within our grasp to constructively bring together normative and explanatory theory. And explanatory theory is possible which illuminates the mutual shaping that occurs among reason, emotion, micro-process and macro-structure.

NOTES

1 Sorokin and Lunden (1959: 37) make essentially the same point: 'The greater, more absolute, and coercive the power of rulers, political leaders, and big executives of business, labor and other organisations, and the less freely this power is approved by the ruled population, the more corrupt and criminal such ruling groups and executives tend to be ... With a progressive limitation of their power, criminality of rulers and executives tends to decrease qualitatively (by becoming less grave and murderous) and quantitatively (by decreasing the rate of criminal actions)'.

2 Merton was not unaware of this issue. He conceded that where the poor do not aspire to the same material success goals held out as important for the upper classes, where there are 'differential class symbols of success', they will not suffer the same frustration from blocked legitimate opportunities (Merton, 1968: 201).

3 The exception to this finding is the victim survey of Pillemer and Finkelhor (1988). In this study elderly males were significantly more likely to be abused than elderly females, though the female victims suffered more severe victimisations than the males.

4 Retributiveness may not seem to be a dimension of inequality. But I have argued elsewhere (Braithwaite, 1982; Braithwaite and Pettit, 1990) that under retributive policies 'just deserts' tends to be imposed successfully on the poor and unsuccessfully on the rich. Retributivism exacerbates important inqualities under any feasible programe of implementation.

5 Stigmatisation at least encourages crime among those who are stigmatised, though it will discourage crime among others who witness the stigmatisation (see Braithwaite, 1989:Ch 5).

6 Certainly the emotions attributed to the Germans at the time were in the vocabulary of humiliation. The Australian press observer at Versailles described the arrival of the German foreign minister thus: 'Count von Brockdorff-Rantzau appeared to feel the humiliation of his position, and stood bareheaded ...' (*Sydney Morning Herald,* 3 May, 1919).

REFERENCES

Abolafia, Mitchel Y (1985) 'Self-Regulation as Market Maintenance: An Organization Perspective; in R G Noll (ed) *Regulatory Policy and the Social Sciences*. Berkeley: University of California Press.

Barbalet, Jack and Margot Lyon (1989) unpublished paper presented to Sociology Department Seminar, Australian National University.

Benson, Michael (1990) 'Emotions and Adjudication: A Study of Status Degradation Among White-Collar Criminals' unpublished Paper. Department of Sociology, University of Tennessee.

Boggs, S L (1965) 'Urban Crime patterns' *American Sociological Review* 30: 899-908.

Box, Steven (1983) *Power, Crime and Mystification*. London: Tavistock.

Braithwaite, John (1979) *Inequality, Crime and Public Policy*. London: Routledge and Kegan Paul.

— (1982) 'Challenging Just Deserts: Punishing White-Collar Criminals' *Journal of Criminal Law and Criminology* 73: 723-60.

— (1984) *Corporate Crime in the Pharmaceutical Industry*. London: Routledge and Kegan Paul.

— (1989) *Crime, Shame and Reintegration*. Melbourne: Cambridge University Press.

Braithwaite, John and Philip Pettit (1990) *Not Just Deserts: A Republican Theory of Criminal Justice*. Oxford: Oxford University Press.

Clinard, Marshall and Peter C Yeager (1980) *Corporate Crime*. New York: Free Press.

Cloward, Richard A and Lloyd E Ohlin (1960) *Delinquency and Opportunity: A Theory of Delinquent Gangs*. Glencoe, Ill: Free Press.

Cohen Albert K (1955) *Delinquent Boys: The Culture of the Gang*. Glencoe, Ill: Free Press.

Cohen, Lawrence E and Richard Machalek (1988) 'A General Theory of Expropriative Crime: An Evolutionary Ecological Approach' *American Journal of Sociology* 94: 465-501.

Cullen, Francis T, William J Maakestaad, and Gray Cavender (1987) *Corporate Crime Under Attack: The Ford Pinto Case and Beyond*. Cincinnati: Anderson.

de Bono, Edward (1985) *Conflicts: A Better way to Resolve them*. London: Harrap.

Fattah, E A and V F Sacco (1989) *Crime and Victimization of the Elderly*. New York: Springer-Verlag.

Geis, Gilbert (1973) 'Victimization Patterns in White-Collar Crime' in I Drapkin and E Viano (eds) *Victimology: A New Focus*, vol V. Lexington, Mass: Lexington Books.

Geis, Gilbert and Colin Goff (1990) 'Edwin Sutherland and the FBI: The Evil of Banality' paper to Edwin Sutherland Conference on: White-Collar Crime, Indiana University.

Glaser, Daniel (1978) *Crime in Our Changing Society*. New York: Holt, Rinehart and Winston.

Gramsci, Antoniono (1971) *Selections from the Prison Notebooks of A. Gramsci*, ed and Trans, Q Hoare and G Nowell-Smith. London: Lawrence and Wishart.

Handler, Joel F (1989) 'Community Care for the Frail Elderly: A Theory of Empowerment' unpublished Paper.

Haug, W F (1986) *Critique of Commodity Aesthetics: Appearance, Sexuality and Advertising in Capitalist Society*, Trans Robert Bock. Cambridge: Polity Press.

Hudson, Margaret (1986) 'Elder Mistreatment: Current Research' in Karl A Pillemer and Rosalie S Wolf (eds) *Elder Abuse: Conflict in the Family*. Dover, Mass: Auburn House.

Jewson, Bob (1978) 'The Prisoners' Action Group's Summary of the Royal Commission into NSW Prisons Following the Hearing of Evidence" in P R Wilson and J Braithwaite (eds) *Two Faces of Deviance: Crimes of the Powerless and Powerful*. Brisbane: University of Queensland Press.

Katz, Jack (1988) *Seductions of Crime: Moral and Sensual Attractions of Doing Evil*. New York: Basic Books.

Knight, Tony (1985) 'Schools and Delinquency' in A Borowski and J M Murray (eds) *Juvenile Delinquency in Australia*. Melbourne: Methuen.

Kohut, H (1972)'Thoughts on Narcissism and Narcissistic Rage' *The Psychoanalytic Study of the Child* 27: 360-400.

Lansky, M (1984) 'Violence, Shame and the Family' *International Journal of Family Psychiatry* 5:21-40.

— (1987) 'Shame and Domestic Violence' in D Nathanson (ed), *The Many Faces of Shame*. New York: Guilford.

Lewis, Helen (1971) *Shame and Guilt in Neurosis*. New York: International Universities Press.

McKay Commission (New York State Special Commission on Attica) (1972) Attica: A Report. New York: Praeger.

Marangiu, Pietro and Graeme Newman (1987) *Vengeance: The Fight Against Injustice*. Totowa, New Jersey: Rowan & Littlefield.

Marx, Karl (1973) *Ecomonic and Philosophic Manuscripts of 1844*. Trans M Milligan. London: Lawrence and Wishart.

Maslow, Abraham H (1954) *Motivation and Personality*. New York: Harper and Row.

Matza, David (1964) *Delinquency and Drift*. New York: Wiley.

Merton, Robert K (1968) *Social Theory and Social Structure*. Glencoe, Ill: Free press.

Montesquieu, Barron De (1977) *The Spirit of Laws*, Abr and ed by D W Carrithers, Berkeley, California: University of California Press.

Pearce, Frank (1976) *Crimes of the Powerful: Marxism, Crime and Deviance*. London: Pluto Press.

Pepinsky, Harold E and Paul Jesilow (1984) *Myths That Cause Crime*. Washington DC: Seven Locks Press.

Pettit, Philip (1989) 'Liberty in the Republic' *John Curtin Memorial Lecture*, Research School of Social Sciences, Australian National University.

Phillips, L R (1983) 'Abuse and Neglect of the Frail Elderly at Home: An Exploration of Theoretical Relationships' *Journal of Advanced Nursing* 8: 379-92.

Pillemer, Karl and David Finkelhor (1988) 'The Prevalence of Elder Abuse: A Random Sample Survey' *The Gerontologist* 28: 51-7.

Pocock, J G A (ed) (1977) *The Political Works of James Harrington*. New York: Cambridge University Press.

Polk, Ken and Ranson, D L (1991) 'Homicide in Victoria' in D Chappell, P Grabosky and H Strang (eds) *Australian Violence: Contemporary Perspectives*. Canberra: Australian Institute of Criminology.

Pontell, Henry and Kitty Calavita (1990) 'Bilking Bankers and Bad Debts: White-Collar Crime and the Savings and Loan Crisis' paper to Edwin Sutherland Conference on White-Collar Crime, Indiana University.

Scheff, Thomas J (1990) *Microsociology*. Chicago: University of Chicago Press.

— (1988) 'Shame and Conformity: The Deference-Emotion System'. *American Sociological Review* 53: 395-406.

—(1987) 'The Shame-Rage Spiral: A Case Study of an Interminable Quarrel' in H B Lewis (ed) *The Role of Shame in Symptom Formation*. Hillsdale, NJ: LEA.

Scheff, Thomas J, Suzanne M Retzinger and Michael T Ryan (1989) 'Crime, Violence and Self-Esteem: Review and Proposals' in A Mecca, N Smelser and J Vasconcellos (eds) *The Social Importance of Self-Esteem*. Berkeley: University of California Press.

Sorokin, P A and W A Lunden (1959) *Power and Morality*. Boston: Porter Sargent.

Stearns, Peter N (1986) 'Old Age Family Conflict: The Perspective of the past' in Karl A Pillemer and Rosalie S Wolf (eds) *Elder Abuse: Conflict in the Family*. Dover, Mass: Auburn House.

Stotland, Ezra (1976) 'Self-Esteem and Violence by Guards and Troopers at Attica' *Criminal Justice and Behavior* 3: 85-96.

Stotland, Ezra and J Martinez (1976) 'Self-Esteem and Mass Violence at Kent State' *International Journal of Group Tensions* 6: 85-96.

Sundstein, Cass (1988) 'Beyond the Republican Revival' *Yale Law Journal*, 97: 1539-90.

Sutherland, Edwin H (1983) *White Collar Crime: The Uncut Version*. New Haven: Yale University Press.

Sykes, Gresham and David Matza (1957) 'Techniques of Neutralization: A Theory of Delinquency' *American Sociological Review* 22: 664-70.

Taylor, Ian, Paul Walton and Jock Young (1973) *The New Criminology: For a Social Theory of Deviance.* London: Routledge and Kegan Paul.

Vaughan, Diane (1983) *Controlling Unlawful Organizational Behaviour: Social Structure and Corporate Misconduct.* Chicago: University of Chicago Press.

Wallace, A (1986) *Homicide: The Social Reality.* Sydney: New South Wales Bureau of Crime Statistics and Research.

Weisburd, David, Stanton Wheeler, Elin Warning and Nancy Bode (1989) *Crimes of the Middle Classes,* unpublished manuscript.

Wheeler, Stanton (1990) 'White-Collar Crime: Some Reflections on a Socio-Legal Research Program' paper to Edwin Sutherland Conference on White-Collar Crime, Indiana University.

Wolf, Rosalie S and Karl A Pillemer (1989) *Helping Elderly Victims: The Reality of Elder Abuse.* New York: Columbia University Press.

Zahn, Margaret A (1980) 'Homicide in the Twentieth Century United States' in James A Inciardi and Charles E Faupel (eds) *History and Crime.* Beverley Hills: Sage.

Journal of Quantitative Criminology, Vol. 10, No. 3, 1994

Reconsidering Strain Theory: Operationalization, Rival Theories, and Adult Criminality[1]

Velmer S. Burton, Jr.,[2] Francis T. Cullen,[3] T. David Evans,[4] and R. Gregory Dunaway[5]

Recently a revisionist view of strain theory's empirical adequacy has emerged which holds that the theory's explanatory power depends on how it is operationalized. With an adult community sample, we empirically assess three separate measures of strain to explain self-reported crime: the gap between aspirations and expectations, blocked opportunities, and relative deprivation. The findings reveal that the aspirations–expectations measure is not related to criminal involvement, while perceived blocked opportunities and feelings of relative deprivation significantly affect adult offending. These relationships, however, fail to persist after measures from competing theories (i.e., low self-control, differential association, and social bond) are introduced as controls in the regression equations. Thus, measures from rival theories offer a more fruitful approach to explaining self-reported adult offending.

KEY WORDS: strain theory; adult criminality; self-control; social bond; differential association.

1. INTRODUCTION

Although strain theory has been a long-standing criminological paradigm (Cole, 1975), many commentators have argued that the theory has little empirical support and have called for its abandonment as a causal

---

[1]A version of this paper was presented at the 1993 American Society of Criminology meetings, Phoenix, Arizona.
[2]Criminal Justice Program, Department of Political Science, Washington State University, Pullman, Washington 99164.
[3]Department of Criminal Justice, University of Cincinnati, Mail Location 389, Cincinnati, Ohio 45221-0389.
[4]Department of Sociology and Anthropology, University of North Carolina—Wilmington, Wilmington, North Carolina 28403-3297.
[5]Department of Sociology and Anthropology, P.O. Drawer C, Mississippi State University, Mississippi State, Mississippi 37962.

0748-4518/94/0900-0213$07.00/0 © 1994 Plenum Publishing Corporation

explanation of crime (Hirschi, 1969; Kornhauser, 1978). As Agnew (1994) suggests, strain theory's ostensible empirical weakness has contributed to its decline as a dominant theory (cf. Cole, 1975).

A revisionist view on strain theory's empirical adequacy, however, has emerged (see Agnew, 1984; Burton and Cullen, 1992; Farnworth and Leiber, 1989; Jensen, 1994). This perspective argues that support for strain theory depends on its operationalization and that the concept of strain has been inadequately measured in previous research. Thus, it is suggested that empirical support for strain has less to do with its explanatory power as a causal model of crime and delinquency and more to do with the way in which it is measured by researchers.

To date, there have been relatively few studies that have tested the relative explanatory power of competing measures of strain (Burton, 1991; Quicker, 1974). Building on the literature covering previous tests of strain theory, this study employs an adult sample to assess empirically three operationalizations of strain and their relationship with self-reported criminal involvement. These strain measures will then be assessed in conjunction with primary measures from competing theoretical paradigms (i.e., social bond, low self-control, and differential association) to explain several forms of self-reported offending. First, however, an assessment of the previous literature and various measures of strain is presented.

2. OPERATIONALIZING STRAIN

The core assumption of traditional strain theories is that crime or "delinquency results when [people] are unable to achieve their goals through legitimate channels" (Agnew, 1984, p. 425). The works of Merton (1938, 1968), Cohen (1955), and Cloward and Ohlin (1960), which have dominated the strain paradigm, put forth the thesis that blocked opportunity or status frustration is a powerful source of criminality (Agnew, 1987). While several theorists have argued that strain should be interpreted from a structural perspective (Bernard, 1987; Messner, 1985, 1988), the most popular approach to measuring strain is as an individual-level theory: the strain of being denied access to desired goals leads people to break the law (Agnew, 1984, 1992; Burton and Cullen, 1992; Quicker, 1974).

The issue, however, is how to operationalize this concept of "strain." Most often, researchers have measured strain either as the gap between aspirations and expectations or as perceived blocked opportunities (Agnew, 1987; Burton and Cullen, 1992), though other scholars have suggested that strain in the Mertonian tradition might be assessed as relative deprivation. Our research examines these three operationalizations of strain.

2.1. The Aspirations–Expectations "Gap"

In *Causes of Delinquency*, Travis Hirschi (1969, pp. 171–173) assumed that the locus of strain rested within "frustrated educational aspirations." Thus, to measure strain, Hirschi conceptualized a variable assessing the "gap" or discrepancy between educational aspirations and expectations.[6] He asked youths "How much schooling would you like to get eventually?" against the question of "How much education do you expect to get?" (Hirschi, 1969, pp. 171–177). Since Hirschi's (1969) aspirations–expectations operationalization of strain, a number of researchers have employed this measure, or similar measures, in an attempt to explain delinquency (see, e.g., Akers and Cochran, 1985; Cheung and Ng, 1988; Eve, 1978; Johnson 1979; Paternoster and Triplett, 1988). Research using this operationalization, however, has failed to provide empirical support for strain theory (Burton and Cullen, 1992; Farnworth and Leiber, 1989; Elliott *et al.*, 1985; Elliott and Voss, 1974; Kethenini, 1990; Paternoster and Triplett, 1988).

Given the majority of previous tests' emphasis on operationalizing strain as the "gap" between educational aspirations and expectations, this study will include an aspirations–expectations variable. Although the majority of studies has examined "educational" aspirations, the use of an adult sample necessitates modifying the terminology of the measure for several reasons. First, most adults are beyond the stage in the life cycle in which they are involved in formal schooling. Second, the emphasis on "economic" aspirations is closer to Merton's original thesis that economic success is the dominant cultural goal (Farnworth and Leiber, 1989). Third, given that Merton (1938) and Cloward and Ohlin (1960) were most concerned with the emphasis placed on economic (financial) goals—and most empirical tests of strain have assessed juvenile delinquency—economic goals should take on added salience as an explanation of adult criminality.

Accordingly, for this study, we assess the "gap" between *economic* aspirations and expectations.[7] Consistent with the operationalizations from the Hirschi (1969) tradition, we assume that strain exists when individuals with high economic aspirations have low expectations to make money in the future.

2.2. Blocked Opportunities

Because strain theory assumes that structural constraints generate frustration and crime by blocking access to opportunities for achieving desired

---

[6]It should be noted that while Hirschi (1969) also examined the gap between occupational aspirations and expectations, he did not find support for this operationalization of strain. Moreover, Akers and Cochran (1985) also failed to find a significant effect for this measure of strain and delinquency.

[7]Unfortunately, our data set does not contain items to also assess the gap between "occupational" aspirations and expectations.

success goals (Merton, 1938, 1968), researchers have operationalized strain as "perceived blocked opportunities." Studies have indicated that delinquency is related to various kinds of perceived blocked opportunities: occupational opportunities (Aultman and Wellford, 1979; Datesman *et al.*, 1975; Rivera and Short, 1967; Seagrave and Halstead, 1983; Short *et al.*, 1965), educational opportunities (Cernkovich, 1978; Cernkovich and Giordano, 1979), and economic opportunities (Burton, 1991; Landis and Scarpitti, 1965). Thus, given the consistent support for the perceived blocked opportunities measure of strain in previous studies (see Burton and Cullen, 1992, pp 14–16), we include a variable of perceived blocked "economic" opportunities in our analyses.

2.3. Relative Deprivation

Although strain theory has been operationalized most often as either the gap between aspirations and expectations or blocked opportunities (Burton and Cullen, 1992), several scholars have suggested that Merton's paradigm might be conceived as arguing that crime is rooted in "relative deprivation"; at the very least it is argued that the paradigm might be extended profitably in that direction (Blau and Blau, 1982; Currie, 1985; Passas, 1987; Rosenfeld, 1989; Thio, 1975). As Thio (1975) has pointed out, despite writings on reference group processes (Merton, 1957; Merton and Rossi, 1968), Merton did not explicitly link relative deprivation to his social structure and anomie paradigm. Even so, scholars have asserted that the essence of the Merton–Cohen–Cloward and Ohlin perspective is that crime is prompted not by the strain of absolute deprivation brought on by blocked opportunities but from being deprived of what others in society have the opportunity to obtain. Referring to Merton and his fellow strain theorists, for example, Currie (1985, p. 161) notes that their work "suggested that more important than the sheer material impact of absolute deprivation was the social—psychological wound of relative deprivation—of being hindered from attaining what others were able to attain."

In his "general strain theory," Agnew (1992; with White, 1992) has similarly suggested that the "classic strain theories" in the Mertonian tradition, which see strain as derived from the failure to achieve positively valued goals, might be extended by incorporating notions of "justice/equity." Agnew argues that criminogenic strain arises not only from unfulfilled aspirations, but also—and perhaps more powerfully—from whether people see their inability to achieve valued goals as equitable or fair (cf. Wilson and Herrnstein, 1985, pp. 56–59). Although equity–fairness is a complex concept and could involve various operationalizations, relative deprivation would seem to fall under this theoretical umbrella.

Recently, moreover, Burton and Dunaway (1994) examined empirically the relationship of relative deprivation to delinquency. Drawing on the literature of "reference groups" (Cohen, 1965; Merton, 1957; Merton and Rossi, 1968), a measure was developed to assess feelings of strain generated from youths' negative comparisons of themselves to others in their immediate reference (i.e., peer) group. That is, feelings of strain may arise when individuals compare their "relative . . . attainments [against] others [within their reference group] who serve as reference objects" (see Cohen, 1965, p. 5). Burton and Dunaway's (1994) analyses indicate that this measure of relative deprivation significantly affected increased delinquent involvement.

In sum, relative deprivation may be seen as capturing the essence of classic Mertonian strain theory or as a form of strain that is a close kin to the strain depicted by those writing in the Mertonian tradition. In either case, there is sufficient conceptual reason, and beginning empirical evidence, to suggest that relative deprivation should be considered in attempts to operationalize strain theory. Accordingly, we incorporated into our analysis a measure of relative deprivation.

3. METHODS

3.1. Sample

Because virtually all researchers have tested strain theory with samples composed only of juveniles (see Burton and Cullen, 1992), empirical analysis of strain theory with adult populations has yet to be systematically undertaken. A central thesis of Merton's (1938, 1968) work is that success goals are *financial* in nature; thus his strain theory is meant as much, if not more so, for adults. Accordingly, this study investigates the relationship to crime of strain measures with a community sample of adults.

Data on adult criminality were gathered through a self-report survey of the general population, age 18 and older, residing in a midwestern, urban area. Questionnaires were randomly sent to 1500 individuals within our sampling frame. Following Dillman's (1978) total design method, sampled individuals were sent a reminder letter shortly after the anticipated arrival date of the initial questionnaire mailing. Subsequently, two additional mailings of questionnaires were sent to those who had not responded. On the final mailing, we included a pen as an incentive to completing the survey. Finally, a private firm was hired to call each nonrespondent to solicit their participation. Another questionnaire was mailed to those individuals who agreed to participate in the survey.

For various reasons (e.g., change of address, death), 303 questionnaires could not be delivered. Of the 1197 delivered surveys, 555 completed surveys were returned, a response rate of 46.6%. The response rate for white subjects, however, appears to exceed 60%, and thus our analysis is confined to whites. We return to this issue below.

The sample generally represents the community from which it was drawn from on a number of key attributes. The median age for the populations under analysis (individuals 18 years of age and older) is 40.5 years of age, while the median sample age is 41 years of age (see U.S. Bureau of Census, 1992). Moreover, males over age 17 comprise 45% of the population, whereas for our sample they are 42%. Our sample's economic characteristics approximate those among the population. The sample's personal median income is nearly $23,000, while the population's personal median income is $21,006. With family income, the sample median is $30,000 and the population median family income is $26,774. Finally, 56.8% of the sample are not married.

The sample's main limitation, however, is that it underrepresents racial minorities: Nonwhites comprise 35.3% of the community but only 14.1% of the sample. Accordingly, we decided to restrict the analysis reported here to whites (in footnote 15, however, we do note the results for nonwhites).

It is possible to estimate the approximate response rate for whites in our sample based on the "number of deliverable surveys" (see Babbie, 1990, p. 183). According to the U.S. Census data, the community is 64.7% white and 35.3% nonwhite. Of the 1197 possible respondents, we would expect that there would be 778 whites (64.7%) and 419 nonwhites (35.3%). We received 477 surveys from whites for a response rate of 61.3% and 78 surveys from nonwhites (18.6%). As a result, we confined the analysis to white respondents.[8]

3.2. Dependent Variables

Crime measures for the analysis were selected and modified from the National Youth Survey (NYS) delinquency scale (see Elliott and Ageton, 1980). Modifications to items from the NYS delinquency scale consisted primarily of making items appropriate for adults instead of youths, such as replacing school-related items with workplace–crime items. In addition, newly developed items assessing adult participation in insurance fraud and tax cheating were included in the survey. Individual crime items in this crime scale are presented in Appendix 1.

---

[8]The response rate for whites is, as noted, an estimate. If nonwhites were more likely to have moved and thus been a disproportionate percentage of the 303 respondents to which a survey was nondeliverable, then the base of eligible white respondents would have been larger than 778; if so, the response rate reported here would be a high estimate. In any case, however, the response rate for whites is reasonably high.

Respondents were asked how many times during the past 12 months they had committed 49 various criminal acts (see Appendix 1). Each item was recoded so that respondents received a value of 1 if they had committed a specific criminal act in the past 12 months or 0 if they answered no to an item. Recoded items were then summed, so that scores could vary from 0 to 49. This scale measures the *prevalence* of committing crime. The reliability coefficient for this scale is 0.80.[9]

Since theoretical measures may have differential impacts depending on the type of crime, we attempted to develop measures for traditional offense categories (e.g., violent, property, public disorder). Similar to other self-report studies (cf. Gottfredson and Hirschi, 1990), the reliabilities for these offense categories were not consistently high enough to allow for analysis. As an alternative, we employed two strategies.

First, following Farnworth and Leiber (1989), we were able to divide items into two crime types: utilitarian and nonutilitarian. In the strain paradigm, crimes are "utilitarian" to the extent that they address directly the source of strain—economic deprivation—by providing economic gain. In effect, these offenses involve "innovation" or the use of illegitimate means to gain material rewards. In contrast, nonutilitarian offenses, while perhaps providing psychic rewards, do not provide economic resources.

In the strain paradigm, theorists have suggested that strain can lead to nonutilitarian and utilitarian crimes (see e.g., Agnew, 1992; Cloward and Ohlin, 1960; Cohen, 1955; Merton, 1938). In their empirical study of juveniles, Farnworth and Leiber (1989) found that, depending on the crime measure used, their aspirations–expectations variable had significant relationships with both utilitarian and nonutilitarian offenses. This finding must be viewed as tentative, however, because their analysis failed to include controls for competing theories or for demographic variables (cf. Jensen, 1994).

To compose the utilitarian crime scale, 12 items were drawn from the overall crime scale. The measure included items such as theft at work, burglary, holding stolen property, and selling drugs (see Appendix 2). The utilitarian offense scale has a reliability of 0.51. In contrast, the nonutilitarian scale, composed of 18 items, included offenses such as vandalism of automobiles and property, assaultive behaviors, gang fights, driving drunk, speeding in a vehicle, and being loud and rowdy in public (see Appendix 2). The reliability coefficient for the nonutilitarian crime scale is 0.76.

The utilitarian and nonutilitarian crime scales are prevalence measures. Each item was recoded so that respondents received a value of 1 if they

[9]We attempted also to measure the *incidence* of crime—a measure which sums all 49 crime items. This crime measure is excluded from the analysis due to a low reliability level ($a = 0.27$).

committed a specific criminal act in the past 12 months or 0 if they answered no to an item. For the 12-item utilitarian crime measure, summed scores range from 0 to 12, while nonutilitarian crime scale scores range from 0 to 18.

Second, strain theorists, including those focusing on relative deprivation (Agnew, 1987, 1992; Blau and Blau, 1982; Cloward and Ohlin, 1960; Currie 1985), see strain as possibly engendering violence against nonintimates. To assess this possibility, we employ a prevalence measure (coded 0 for no and 1 for yes) of "assault" against strangers.[10] The item "assault of others" was used; note that this item specifically examines assaults of people other than family members and co-workers. Arguably, assault against strangers is an act of bold aggression involving risk of injury to both the offender and the victim (see Luckenbill, 1977).

3.3. Independent Variables

We rely on previous research to operationalize strain three ways: the gap between economic aspirations and expectations, perceptions of blocked economic opportunities, and relative deprivation. For each item, respondents were instructed to respond by using a Likert scale that ranged from 1 = strongly agree to 6 = strongly disagree. When necessary, responses were recoded so that a high score on an item indicated the presence of strain, social bonding, low self-control, or differential association.

In addition to assessing the effects of strain variables on self-reported crime, this analysis controls for adults' level of social bonds, low self-control, and differential association for two reasons. First, since Hirschi's (1969) empirical investigation of strain, social bond, and differential association theories, numerous studies have followed his approach of pitting these rival theories against each other in a single analysis to explain delinquent involvement (for a review of empirical literature, see Burton, 1991; Burton and Cullen, 1992). Second, and relatedly, without controls for differential association and social control theory, findings regarding strain theory will be open to the charge that the effects are misspecified. In contrast, if significant effects are found with measures of the rival perspectives in the model, this will increase confidence in the results.

3.4. Strain Variables

3.4.1. Economic Aspirations–Expectations

Economic aspirations are conceptualized as the "overall or general" desire individuals feel about "making money" in the future. Conversely,

---

[10]While we attempted to create a multi-item assault crime subscale, a low reliability level resulted in our employing a single-item measure of assault.

expectations are the actual chances the individual believes he or she has to "make a lot of money" in the future. According to the assumptions of strain theory, the greater the *gap* between economic aspirations and expectations, the greater the feelings of strain experienced by the individual.

We take the suggestion of Farnworth and Leiber (1989) and measure the *economic* dimension of aspirations versus expectations. Thus, for economic aspirations, respondents were asked their opinion to the statement, "I'd like to make a lot of money in my life." To measure expectations, respondents were asked the question "Realistically, I don't think I'll make as much money as I'd like."

To measure the degree of strain an individual is experiencing, both items were recoded: All "agree" responses were coded as 1, while all "disagree" responses were coded as 0. Only those individuals scoring a 1 on *both* items are treated as feeling strain. That is, these respondents hold high aspirations of making a great deal of money yet have low expectations of ever making much money; as such, they experience a *gap* between economic aspirations and expectations. All other respondents are not considered to have a means-goal gap. Individuals possessing a high level of aspirations to make a lot of money, while expecting actually to make the money, are not considered to be experiencing strain. Similarly, those with low aspirations, regardless of their expectations, would not, according to strain theory, face "pressures" to commit criminal acts. In our analysis, the aspiration–expectations "gap" is treated as a dummy variable (1 = yes, 0 = no).

We employ this measure of strain because, since Hirschi's (1969) study, the majority of empirical tests measuring strain theory has continued to measure strain as the *gap* between aspirations and expectations (see Cheung and Ng, 1988; Eve, 1978; Figueira-McDonough, 1983; Paternoster and Triplett, 1988; Shue, 1988; Smith and Paternoster, 1987).

Additionally, the analysis will employ a single-item measure of expectations: "Realistically, I don't think I'll make as much money as I'd like." Within the expectation item, the reference to "as much as I'd like" may invoke the respondent's aspirations. Perhaps the item, as worded, might actually be conceptualized as an indicator of a discrepancy between aspirations and expectations in and of itself. Thus, this additional measure is included in the analysis to measure both aspirations and expectations, within the aspiration/expectation conception of strain.[11]

3.4.2. Perceptions of Blocked Economic Opportunities

Strain also has been operationalized as perceptions of blocked economic opportunities in an individual's life. This conception of strain derives from

[11]Including the single-item expectation measure was suggested by an anonymous reviewer.

the work of Cloward and Ohlin (1960) and Stinchcombe (1964), which postulates that blocked opportunities—particularly blocked occupational opportunities—are a primary source of strain in an individual's life. Moreover, this operationalization of strain has demonstrated the greatest empirical support among strain variables in explaining criminal and delinquent involvement (Burton and Cullen, 1992).[12]

A three-item scale was used to measure perceptions of blocked economic opportunities. One item was borrowed from Coleman (1966) and Eve (1978) and asks, "Every time I try to get ahead, something or someone stops me." Derived from the work of Short *et al.* (1965) and Rivera and Short (1967), we employ an item to assess the perception that having "connections" is required to be successful. Thus, respondents were asked, "If I had connections, I would have been more successful." Finally, to capture or identify feelings of frustration deriving from blocked opportunities, the following item was created: "I've often been frustrated in my efforts to get ahead in life." While this item has not been used in previous research testing strain theory, the aspect of "frustration" is central to the work of Cohen (1955) and Cloward and Ohlin (1960). The blocked economic opportunities scale had an α of 0.59.

3.4.3. Relative Deprivation

To assess feelings of deprivation, a three-item scale was included in the survey instrument. Drawing from the work of Landis and Scarpitti (1965), respondents were asked to rate the question, "It bothers me that most people have more money to live on than I do." Two additional items were borrowed from Burton and Dunaway (1994) to assess feelings of deprivation based on individuals' relative comparison of themselves against others. Accordingly, subjects were asked to react to the following statements: "It's frustrating to see people driving nicer cars and living in nicer homes than I do," and "I get angry when I see people having a lot more money than I do spend their money on foolish things." The reliability coefficient for this scale is 0.75.

3.5. Social Bond Measures

Social bond theory asserts that individuals with strong ties to institutions such as marriage, family, and work will be insulated from criminal involvement (Covington, 1985; Laub and Sampson, 1993; Lasley, 1988;

---

[12]Unfortunately, this data set contains only measures of blocked economic opportunities. While the wording of scale items does not address specific occupational opportunities, the items do imply that blocked occupational opportunities are being assessed. That is, for adults, meeting success goals will occur through one's occupational standing or lack thereof.

Sampson and Laub, 1990, 1993). Thus, we employ the adult social bond measure of marital status and the measure of attachment to family as controls in the analysis.

3.5.1. Marital Status

Although control theory has been most often used to explain juvenile delinquency, recent research has begun to apply this perspective to adult criminality. In these studies, marriage is seen as a social bond that, by providing informal social control, insulates individuals from criminal participation (Laub and Sampson, 1993; Sampson and Laub, 1990, 1993; see also Knight *et al.*, 1977; Rand, 1987). Accordingly, in our analysis, we are able to use marital status as a measure of an adult social bond (1 = married, 0 = unmarried). The limit of this measure, however, must be noted: We are able to assess only marital status, and not the quality of the marital relationship (see Sampson and Laub, 1990, 1993).

3.5.2. Attachment to Family

In previous research assessing control theory, and building on Hirschi's (1969) initial investigation, attachment to family (parents) is often used as a social bond measure. In fact, studies indicate that the effects of attachment on crime are more pronounced than other elements of the social bond identified by Hirschi. Accordingly, we include a measure of attachment to family of origin (or parents).

This measure allows us to assess whether long-standing attachments to parents insulate against crime in adulthood. Thus, drawing on research by LaGrange and White (1985) and Rosenbaum (1987), adults were asked to rate the level of "respect" for their mother and father. The second item is modified from previous tests of social control (Eve, 1978; Simons *et al.*, 1980) and asks whether subjects have "gotten along" well with their parents. The level of reliability for the attachment to family scale is 0.86.

One potential limitation of using a family of origin measure with adults is that Hirschi's original theory was intended for youths and not adults. At the same time, Hirschi (1969) did not argue that parental attachments lose effects over time; in fact, in recent writings, he suggests that early family relations have life-long consequences (Gottfredson and Hirschi, 1990). In any case, it remains a largely unexplored empirical issue whether continuing parental attachments affect criminal involvement in adulthood.

3.6. Low Self-Control Measure

In their recent, but widely read, general theory of crime, Gottfredson and Hirschi (1990) assert that individuals with low "self-control" are predisposed to increased criminal and delinquent involvement. That is, "people who lack self-control will tend to be impulsive, insensitive, physical (as opposed to mental), risk-taking, short-sighted, and nonverbal, and they will tend therefore to engage in criminal and analogous acts . . . [which] . . . persist through life" (Gottfredson and Hirschi, 1990, pp. 90–91). Recent research, moreover, has demonstrated that low self-control is positively related to drunken driving, criminal and delinquent involvement, and imprudent behaviors (see, e.g., Arneklev *et al.*, 1994; Brownfield and Sorenson, 1993; Grasmick *et al.*, 1993; Keane *et al.*, 1993; Mak, 1990; Nagin and Paternoster, 1993; Wood *et al.*, 1993). Accordingly, we have included self-control as a rival theory in the analysis.

We measure self-control with a 12-item scale ($\alpha = 0.64$) which is listed in Appendix 3. The items have been recoded so that high scores indicate low self-control. The items were developed to assess the description of self-control provided by Gottfredson and Hirschi (1990, pp. 90–91). Because their "general theory of crime" treats self-control as a unitary concept—that is, they do not suggest that different aspects of self-control have differential effects—we use a composite measure (see also Nagin and Paternoster, 1993, p. 478). Use of a composite measure also allows for a more parsimonious analysis of the data.

3.7. Differential Association Measures

The core thesis of differential association theory is that individuals' exposure to procriminal values and interaction with criminal associates (criminal friends) increases the likelihood of criminal involvement (Matsueda, 1982; Matsueda and Heimer, 1987). Thus, in the analysis, we control for three differential association variables: individual definitions toward the law, others' definitions toward the law, and number of criminal friends. These variables assess not only internalized values toward criminal involvement but also exposure to others' criminality.

3.7.1. Individual Definitions Toward the Law

The individual definitions toward crime scale is composed of four items and has a reliability of 0.71. To measure individual definitions toward crime, items were created that assessed the degree of tolerance for criminal behavior, the moral validity of violating the law, and the level of agreement with committing criminal acts. We use these operationalizations of individual definitions toward crime since a core assumption of Sutherland's (1949) work is that individuals develop internalized definitions favorable or nonfavorable toward violating the law. Thus, items for this measure ranged from nonfavorable to favorable definitions toward criminal involvement.

To measure absolute disapproval toward violating the law, an item was adapted from previous research (Akers *et al.*, 1989; Jackson *et al.*, 1986; Short, 1960): "No matter how small the crime, breaking the law is a serious matter." A second item, "It is morally wrong to break the law," also assessed anticriminal definitions (see Jackson *et al.*, 1986; Matsueda, 1989; Silberman, 1976; Tittle *et al.*, 1986). In contrast, to measure adults' "willingness" to violate the law, a third item was included: "Sometimes you just don't have any choice but to break the law." Similarly, drawing from previous research (Krohn *et al.*, 1984; Short, 1960), adults were asked, "If breaking the law really doesn't hurt anyone, and you can make a quick buck doing it, then it's really not all that wrong."

3.7.2. Others' Definitions Toward the Law

This scale has three items and a reliability of 0.65. According to Sutherland (1949), criminal behavior occurs primarily through exposure to others holding definitions favorable toward violating the law. Relying on previous tests of differential association (Akers *et al.*, 1979; Cressey, 1953; Dull, 1983; Griffin and Griffin, 1978; Jaquith, 1981; Johnson *et al.*, 1987; Short, 1960; Tittle *et al.*, 1986), we included the item, "Many of the people I associate with think it's okay to break the law if you can get away with it." The second item is designed to determine the type of people (criminal or noncriminal) with whom an individual associates. Thus, subjects were presented with the question, "Most of the people I associate with would never break the law." In previous research, items similar to this have been related to delinquent involvement (Akers *et al.*, 1989; Kethenini, 1990; Krohn *et al.*, 1984; Jackson *et al.*, 1986; Orcutt, 1987). Finally, the third item assesses the extent to which individuals are "often in situations where people encourage [them] to do something illegal."

3.7.3. Criminal Friends

Numerous empirical tests of differential association theory have relied on measures of criminal friends as evidence of interaction with criminal members within an individual's primary group (see, e.g., Akers *et al.*, 1979; Dull, 1983; Johnson *et al.*, 1987; Matseuda, 1982; Matseuda and Heimer, 1987; Orcutt, 1987; Warr and Stafford, 1993; Winfree *et al.*, 1989). Thus, we employ a measure of the number of criminal friends as a control in our model. That is, to assess the number of criminal friends, respondents were asked the following question: "In the last 12 months, how many of your five closest friends have done something they could have gotten arrested for?"[13]

3.8. Control Variables

The variables of age, gender, and income are employed as control variables in the analyses. Gender is a dummy variable and coded accordingly: male = 1 and female = 0. Age is measured as years of age, while income is the annual household income.

4. RESULTS

Zero-order correlations for the four strain measures and the overall self-reported crime measure reveal all strain variables are significantly related with the crime measure. The relative deprivation measure produced the greatest correlation ($r = 0.24$), followed by blocked opportunites ($r = 0.19$), aspiration–expectation ($r = 0.18$), and the aspiration/expectation "gap" measure ($r = -0.10$). Thus, initial analyses indicate that strain measures, when examined independently, exhibit significant relationships with self-reported criminality.

Table I reports the results of the four strain variables and demographic controls regressed separately against the overall self-reported criminality measure. The equation in the first column in Table I indicates that the measure of aspiration–expectations "gap" is not significantly related with the crime scale. Moreover, the aspirations–expectations single-item measure (expectations only) also failed to affect adult criminal involvement significantly.[14]

The findings reveal, however, that perceived blocked opportunities and feelings of relative deprivation significantly affect self-reported offending

---

[13]The criminal friends measure was utilized for several reasons. First, we sought to determine the proportion of close friends to capture the "intensity" of interaction inherent in the process of differential association. Second, we "bounded" the question to five closest friends since respondents may interpret types of friends differently. Third, we focused on behavior of friends which could have resulted in arrest since that behavior is criminal.

[14]The single-item aspiration measure was also employed in the analysis as suggested by an anonymous reviewer. The intent of inclusion was to assess level of commitment and determine whether less committed adults were more involved in criminal activity as argued by social control theorists (Hirschi, 1969; Liska, 1971; see also Farnworth and Leiber, 1989). The analysis did not result in any significant effects on self-reported offending. Thus, the results are not reported in the text or tables.

Table I. The Impact of Measures of Strain on Crime (β Values)

	Adult crime	Adult crime	Adult crime	Adult crime
Strain				
Aspiration/expectation "gap"	−0.02			
Aspiration–expectation single item	X^a	−0.04		
Blocked opportunities	X	X	0.13*	
Relative deprivation	X	X	X	0.12*
Control variables				
Age	−0.50*	−0.49*	−0.48*	−0.47*
Sex (0 = female)	0.20*	0.20*	0.19*	0.20*
Income	−0.04	−0.05	−0.02	−0.04
R^2	0.281	0.283	0.297	0.303

$^a X$ = variables not included in equation. Number of cases = 477.
*$P < 0.001$.

among the adult sample (see third and fourth columns in Table I). In all four equations, age and gender have significant effects, with younger and male respondents having a higher involvement in crime.[15]

The findings in Table I indicate that the control variables age and sex produce effects greater than any strain measure in the four equations. As an additional analysis, the control variables only were regressed against the crime measure without strain measures and produced an R^2 of 28%. Thus, even among the significant strain variables of blocked opportunities and relative deprivation, less than 2% of the variation in adult offending was explained beyond that of the control variables of age, sex, and income. Accordingly, strain variables for this sample of adults, while statistically signficant, have only a marginal effect on crime.

Given the significant effects of blocked opportunities and relative deprivation measures on crime, and to avoid the possibility that the results found in Table I are spurious, regression analyses were undertaken with equations containing measures from the competing theories. Table II reports the results of the four strain measures, in addition to social bond, low self-control, differential association, and demographic control variables, regressed separately against the overall crime measure.

Again, the findings in Table II indicate that both the aspiration-expectations "gap" measure and the aspiration–expectation "single-item"

[15]Regression analyses were undertaken with the 78 nonwhites in the sample. The results indicate that no strain variable significantly affected nonwhites' self-reported offending. These results, however, should be interpreted with caution due to the low response rate of nonwhite respondents.

Table II. The Impact of Strain, Social Control, and Differential Association Measures on
Crime (β Values)

	Adult crime	Adult crime	Adult crime	Adult crime
Strain				
Aspiration/expectation				
"gap"	−0.02			
Aspiration–expectation	X^a	0.06		
Blocked opportunities	X	X	−0.01	
Relative deprivation	X	X	X	0.01
Social control				
Marital status				
(0 = not married)	−0.10**	−0.09**	−0.10**	−0.10**
Attachment to family	0.03	0.03	0.03	0.03
Low self-control	0.32*	0.32*	0.32*	0.31*
Differential association				
Individual definitions				
toward law	0.16*	0.15*	0.16*	0.15*
Others' definitions				
toward law	0.03	0.03	0.03	0.03
Criminal friends	0.22*	0.22*	0.23*	0.23*
Control variables				
Age	−0.25*	−0.25*	−0.26*	−0.26*
Sex (0 = female)	0.06	0.05	0.06	0.06
Income	−0.01	−0.01	−0.01	−0.01
R^2	0.529	0.533	0.530	0.530

$^a X$ = variables not included in equation. Number of cases = 477.
*$P < 0.01$.
**$P < 0.05$.

measure failed significantly to explain adult offending. Additionally, neither
blocked opportunities or relative deprivation significantly affected adult criminal participation (see Table II).

A closer examination of Table II reveals that the greatest effect among
theoretical variables in the model was produced by the low self-control
measure, which was significant and positively related to self-reported adult
offending. Additionally, the differential association measures of criminal
friends and individual definitions toward crime generated significant effects
on adult crime. Also, the social bond measure of marital status (nonmarried)
was significant and inversely related to adult offending. Again, age (younger)
was significantly related with the crime scale.

As noted earlier, both utilitarian and nonutilitarian crime scales were
developed for analysis. Tables III and IV report results from separate regression analyses with models containing each strain measure, social bond, low

Table III. The Impact of Measures of Strain, Social Control, Differential Association, and Age, Sex, and Income Regressed Separately on Utilitarian Crime Measures (β Values)

	Utilitarian	Utilitarian	Utilitarian	Utilitarian
Strain				
Aspiration/expectation				
"gap"	−0.04			
Aspiration–expectation	X	0.09		
Blocked opportunities	X	X	−0.04	
Relative deprivation	X	X	X	0.00
Social control				
Marital status				
(0 = not married)	−0.02	−0.01	−0.02	−0.02
Attachment to family	−0.05	−0.04	−0.05	−0.05
Low self-control	0.15**	0.16*	0.16*	0.15**
Differential association				
Individual definitions				
toward law	0.16*	0.16*	0.16*	0.16*
Others' definitions				
toward law	0.06	0.06	0.06	0.06
Criminal friends	0.09	0.09	0.10	0.10
Control variables				
Age	−0.08	−0.08	−0.09	−0.09
Sex (0 = female)	0.01	0.00	0.01	0.01
Income	−0.04	−0.04	−0.04	−0.03
R^2	0.182	0.189	0.181	0.180

$^a X$ = variables not included in equation. Number of cases = 477.
*$P < 0.01$.
**$P < 0.05$.

self-control, differential association, and demographic control variables against both utilitarian and nonutilitarian crime measures.

Table III reveals that no strain measure significantly affected adults' self-reported utilitarian offending behavior. Again, however, only the measures of low self-control and individual definitions toward the law were significantly related to criminal participation.

Moreover, when regression analyses were conducted with the nonutilitarian crime measure, no strain measure was significantly related to self-reported offending (see Table IV). Of the remaining theoretical variables, low self-control and differential association measures demonstrated the greatest effects on nonutilitarian crime. Additionally, the social bond measure of marital status (nonmarried) produced a significant and inverse relationship with nonutilitarian offending for the four models. Age (younger) was significantly related to nonutilitarian criminal behavior.

Table IV. The Impact of Measures of Strain, Social Control, Differential Association, Age, Sex, and Income Regressed Separately on Nonutilitarian Crime Measures (β Values)

	Nonutilitarian crime	Nonutilitarian crime	Nonutilitarian crime	Nonutilitarian crime
Strain				
Aspiration/expectation "gap"	−0.03			
Aspiration–expectation	X^a	0.06		
Blocked opportunities	X	X	−0.00	
Relative deprivation	X	X	X	0.01
Social control				
Marital status (0 = not married)	−0.14*	−0.13*	−0.14*	−0.14*
Attachment to family	0.05	0.06	0.05	0.05
Low self-control	0.31*	0.31*	0.31*	0.30*
Differential association				
Individual definitions toward law	0.14*	0.13*	0.14*	0.14*
Others' definitions toward law	0.03	0.03	0.03	0.05
Criminal friends	0.20*	0.20*	0.21*	0.21*
Control variables				
Age	−0.26*	−0.25*	−0.26*	−0.26*
Sex	0.05	0.04	0.05	0.05
Income	−0.01	−0.01	−0.01	−0.01
R^2	0.429	0.496	0.490	0.492

$^a X$ = variables not included in equation. Number of cases = 477.
*$P < 0.01$.
**$P < 0.05$.

    As a final analysis, each strain measure (and all controls) were regressed against the measure of assaultive behavior against strangers.[16] The analysis reveals that among the four strain measures, no variable was significantly related to adults' assaultive behavior. Instead, only low self-control approached significance among the theoretical variables. As might be expected, however, gender (male) produced the greatest single effect among the models explaining assault.

[16]Only the measure of low self-control approached a significant relationship with self-reported assaultive behavior ($P = 0.07$). Thus, a table was not included in the text. However, this table is available upon request. Also, the R^2 for these analyses explaining assaultive behavior ranged from 8 to 9%.

5. DISCUSSION

Researchers have raised the issue of whether varying operationalizations of strain differentially explain criminal offending (Burton and Cullen, 1992; Farnworth and Leiber, 1989; Quicker, 1974). The primary purpose of this paper was to assess empirically three distinct concepts of strain theory employed in previous investigations: the "gap" between aspirations/expectations (in addition to a single-item measuring aspiration–expectations), perceptions of blocked opportunity, and relative deprivation. Through empirical analyses we attempted to determine which strain measures significantly explain differing forms of adult criminal involvement.

Initially, zero-order correlations among strain measures and crime revealed significant relationships. Moreover, regression models assessing separately each strain variable and control variables of age, sex, and income indicated that measures of relative deprivation and blocked opportunities significantly affected adults criminal involvement. These variables, however, contributed less than 2% of the explained variation in the models, thus indicating that while strain variables were significant, the magnitude of their effect on crime was minimal.

As an additional analysis, strain, differential association, social bond, low self-control, sex, age, and income were regressed on self-reported crime measures. The findings indicated that the effects of strain variables were "washed out" and nonsignificant (c.f. Akers and Cochran, 1985; Jensen, 1994). That is, no strain variable significantly affected any form of criminal involvement, including overall self-reported crime, utilitarian, nonutilitarian, or assaultive behavior. The analysis revealed, however, that low self-control, marriage, and the differential association measures of criminal friends and individual definitions toward the law significantly affected adult criminal participation.

Overall, then, this study found strain theory is less fruitful than rival theories in explaining criminal involvement. Some caution should be exercised, however, before dismissing strain as a cause of crime. First, it should be recalled that this study assessed the conception of strain, drawn from the Mertonian tradition, that has dominated criminological theorizing: what Agnew (1992) calls "the denial of positively valued goals." In his general strain theory, Agnew (1992, 1994) argues that other types of strain may prove criminogenic; thus he identifies two additional categories of strain (i.e., "removal of positively valued stimuli" and "presentation of noxious or negative stimuli"). Agnew's research also provides beginning evidence that these alternative types of strain increase criminal involvement (Agnew, 1985, 1989; Agnew and White, 1992).

Second and relatedly, strain may prove criminogenic only when social deprivation is harsh and immediately felt (see Bernard, 1990). Support for this view comes from McCarthy and Hagan's (1992) study of delinquency among youths living on the "mean streets" of Toronto. They found that youths experiencing the adverse situations of hunger, unemployment, and lack of shelter were more likely to steal food and to obtain money by pilfering property and by prostitution.[17]

In contrast to strain theory's weak performance in the analysis, the data provided support for rival theoretical perspectives. First, the differential association theory measures of individual definitions toward the law and criminal friends significantly affected several forms of adult offending. Thus, consistent with past research based primarily on studies of delinquency, criminal involvement in our adult sample was more likely among those who internalized pro-criminal definitions and associated with criminal friends (see, e.g., Akers *et al.*, 1979; Burkett and Jensen, 1975; LaGrange and White, 1985; Marcos *et al.*, 1986; Matseuda, 1982; Matsueda and Heimer, 1987; Orcutt, 1987; Warr and Stafford, 1993; Winfree *et al.*, 1989).

Second, another variable significantly related to adult offending was the social bond of marriage. Consistent with previous findings by Sampson and Laub (1990, 1993) and Laub and Sampson (1993), the lack of marital attachment among adults increased criminal involvement.

Third and perhaps most noteworthy, the data provide support for Gottfredson and Hirschi's (1990) general theory of crime: the measure of low self-control was the most powerful predictor of criminal involvement. This finding is consistent with the emerging literature, which suggests that low self-control increases criminal, delinquent, and "imprudent" behaviors (Arneklev *et al.*, Brownfield and Sorenson, 1993; Grasmick *et al.*, 1993; Keane *et al.*, 1993; Nagin and Paternoster, 1993; Wood *et al.*, 1993). Accordingly, Gottfredson and Hirschi's (1990) self-control perspective may offer special promise as an explanation of adult and juvenile criminality.

[17]Other criminologists believe that strain theory's strength is not in linking stressful situations to individuals' criminal conduct but as a macrolevel theory explaining differential rates of crime across societies and within different sectors of any given society. See, e.g., Messner and Rosenfeld (1994).

APPENDIX 1

Individual Crime Items Measuring Crime Scale

1. Been drunk in public
2. Avoided paying for small things such as food or movies

3. Filed false insurance claims
4. Parked your car illegally
5. Provided liquor to a minor
6. Involved in public disorder or unruly behavior
7. Hitchhiked illegally
8. Speeding in vehicle
9. Begged or panhandled
10. Hit and run from auto accident
11. Claimed false deduction on tax return you knew was false
12. Did not report all income on tax return
13. Gambled illegally
14. Paid someone to have sex with you
15. Driven auto when drunk
16. Made obscene telephone calls
17. Urinated in public
18. Been involved in gang fights
19. Sold marijuana
20. Sold hard drugs
21. Bought, sold, or held stolen goods
22. Taken a vehicle for a ride without owner's permission
23. Thrown objects at cars or people
24. Stole things less than $5 at work
25. Stole things at work valued between $5 and $50
26. Stole things at work worth more than $50
27. Stole things less than $5 at places other than work
28. Stole things worth between $5 and $50 at places other than work
29. Stole things worth more than $50 at places other than work
30. Carried hidden weapon other than pocket knife
31. Damaged property belonging to family member
32. Damaged property belonging to employer
33. Damaged property belonging to others
34. Committed burglarly
35. Motor vehicle theft
36. Robbed family members
37. Robbed co-workers
38. Robbed others
39. Assaulted co-workers
40. Assaulted family members
41. Assaulted others
42. Committed sexual assault
43. Committed felonious assault with intent to kill or seriously injure
44. Used marijuana

45. Used hallucinogens
46. Used amphetamines
47. Used barbiturates
48. Used heroin
49. Used cocaine

APPENDIX 2

Utilitarian Crime Scale Items

1. Filed false insurance claim
2. Bought, sold, or held something stolen
3. Stole things less than $5 at work
4. Stole things at work between $5 and $50
5. Stole things at work more than $50
6. Claimed false deduction on tax return you knew was false
7. Did not report all income on tax return
8. Stole things less than $5 at places other than work
9. Stole things worth between $5 and $50 at places other than work
10. Stole things worth more than $50 at places other than work
11. Committed burglary
12. Avoided paying for small things such as food and movies

Nonutilitarian Crime Scale Items

1. Been drunk in public
2. Provided liquor to a minor
3. Involved in public disorder or unruly behavior
4. Speeding in vehicle
5. Hit and run from auto accident
6. Driven auto when drunk
7. Made obscene telephone calls
8. Urinated in public
9. Been involved in gang fights
10. Taken vehicle for ride without owner's permission
11. Thrown objects at cars or people
12. Carried a hidden weapon other than pocket knife
13. Damaged property belonging to others
14. Assaulted others
15. Committed sexual assault
16. Committed felonious assault with intent to kill or seriously injure

17. Used marijuana
18. Used cocaine

APPENDIX 3

Self-Control Scale Items

If I see something in a store that I want, I just buy it.
I'd rather spend my money on something I wanted now than to put it in the bank.
I don't deal well with anything that frustrates me.
I really get angry when I ride behind a slow driver.
If someone insulted me, I would be likely to hit or slap them.
I enjoy activities where there is a lot of physical contact.
I like to read books.
The best way to solve an argument is to sit down and talk things out, even if it takes an hour or so.
I enjoy roller coaster rides.
Even when I'm not in a hurry, I like to drive at high speeds.
I like to take chances.
The things I like to do best are dangerous.

ACKNOWLEDGMENTS

This study was supported by a grant from the University Research Council at the University of Cincinnati and by funding from the Departments of Criminal Justice and Sociology, University of Cincinnati.

REFERENCES

Agnew, R. (1984). Goal achievement and delinquency. *Sociol. Soc. Res.* 68: 435–499
Agnew, R. (1985). A revised strain theory of delinquency. *Soc. Forces* 64: 151–164.
Agnew, R. (1987). Testing structural strain theories. *J. Res. Crime Delinq.* 24: 281–286.
Agnew, R. (1989). A longitudinal test on the revised strain theory. *J. Quant. Criminol.* 5: 373–388.
Agnew, R. (1992). Foundation for a general strain theory of crime and delinquency. *Criminology* 30: 47–87.
Agnew, R. (1994). The contribution of social-psychological strain theory to the explanation of crime and delinquency. In Adler, F. (ed.) *Advances in Criminological Theory: Legacy of Anomie, Vol. 6,* Transaction Press, New Brunswick, NJ.
Agnew, R., and White, H. (1992). An empirical test of general strain theory. *Criminology* 30: 475–499.
Akers, R., and Cochran, J. (1985). Adolescent marijuana use: A test of three theories of deviant behavior. *Deviant Behav.* 6: 323–346.

Akers, R., Krohn, M., Lanza-Kaduce, L., and Radosevich, M. (1979). Social learning and deviant behavior: A specific test of a general theory. *Am. Sociol. Rev.* 44: 298–310.

Akers, R., LaGreca, A., Cochran, J., and Sellers, C. (1989). Social learning and alcohol behavior among the elderly. *Sociol. Q.* 30: 625–638.

Arneklev, B., Grasmick, H., Tittle, C., and Bursik, R. (1994). Self-control theory and imprudent behavior. *J. Quant. Criminol.* 9: 225–247.

Aultman, M., and Wellford, C. (1979). Towards an integrated model of delinquency causation: An empirical analysis. *Sociol. Soc. Res.* 63: 316–327.

Babbie, E. (1990). *Survey Research Methods*, 2nd ed., Wadsworth, Belmont, CA.

Bernard, T. (1987). Testing structural strain theories. *J. Res. Crime Delinq.* 24: 262–80.

Bernard, T. (1990). Angry aggression among the "truly disadvantaged." *Criminology* 28: 73–96.

Babbie, E. (1990). *Survey Research Methods*, 2nd ed., Wadsworth, Belmont, CA.

Blau, J., and Blau, P. (1982). The cost of inequality: Metropolitan structure and violent crime. *Am. Sociol. Rev.* 47: 114–129.

Brownfield, D., and Sorenson, A. (1993). Self-control and juvenile delinquency: Theoretical issues and an empirical assessment of selected elements of a general theory of crime. *Deviant Behav.* 14: 243–264.

Burke, H. S., and Jensen, E. (1975). Conventional ties, peer influence, and the fear of apprehension: A study of adolescent marijuana use. *Sociological Quarterly* 16: 522–533.

Burton, V., Jr. (1991). *Explaining Adult Criminality: Testing Strain, Differential Association, and Control Theories*, Unpublished Ph.D. dissertation, University of Cincinnati, University Microfilms International, Ann Arbor, MI.

Burton, V., Jr., and Cullen, F. (1992). The empirical status of strain theory. *Crime and Justice* 15: 1–30.

Burton, V., Jr., and Dunaway, R. G. (1994). The importance of relative deprivation theory on middle-class delinquency. In Barak, G. (ed.), *Varieties of Criminology: Readings from a Dynamic Discipline,* Preager, New York.

Cernkovich, S. (1978). Evaluating two models of delinquency causation: Structural theory and control theory. *Criminology* 16: 335–352.

Cernkovich, S., and Giordano, P. (1979). Delinquency, opportunity, and gender. *J. Crim. Law Criminol.* 70: 145–151.

Cheung, Y., and Ng, A. (1988). Social factors in adolescent deviant behavior in Hong Kong: An integrated theoretical approach. *Int. J. Comp. Appl. Crim. Just.* (Spring) 12: 27–46.

Cloward, R., and Ohlin, L. (1960). *Delinquency and Opportunity: A Theory of Delinquent Gangs,* Free Press, New York.

Cohen, A. (1955). *Delinquent Boys: The Culture of the Gang.* Free Press, New York.

Cohen, A. (1965). The sociology of the deviant act: Anomie theory and beyond. *Am. Sociol. Rev.* 30: 5–14.

Cole, S. (1975). The growth of scientific knowledge: Theories of deviance as a case study. In Coser, L. (ed.), *The Idea of Social Structure: Papers in Honor of Robert K. Merton,* Harcourt Brace Jovanovich, New York.

Coleman, J. (1966). *Equality of Educational Opportunity,* Government Printing Office, Washington, DC.

Covington, J. (1985). Gender differences in criminality among heroin users. *J. Res. Crime Delinq.* 22: 329–353.

Cressey, D. (1953). *Other People's Money,* Free Press, Glencoe, IL.

Currie, E. (1985). *Confronting Crime: An American Challenge,* Pantheon, New York.

Datesman, S., Scarpitti, F., and Stephensen, R. (1975). Female delinquency: An application of self and opportunity theories. *J. Res. Crime Delinq.* 12: 107–122.

Dillman, D. (1978). *Mail and Telephone Surveys: The Total Design Method,* John Wiley and Sons, New York.

Dull, T. (1983). Friend's drug use and adult drug and drinking behavior: A further test of differential association theory. *J. Crim. Law Criminol.* 4: 608–619.

Elliott, D., and Ageton, S. (1980). Reconciling race and class differences in self-reported and official estimates of delinquency. *Am. Sociol. Rev.* 45: 95–110.

Elliott, D., and Voss, H. (1974). *Delinquency and Drop-Out.* D. C. Heath, Lexington, MA.

Elliott, D., Huizinga, D., and Ageton, S. (1985). *Explaining Delinquency and Drug Use.* Sage, Beverly Hills, CA.

Eve, R. (1978). A study of the efficacy of interactions of several theories of explaining rebelliousness among high school students. *J. Crim. Law Criminol.* 49: 115–125.

Farnworth, M., and Leiber, M. (1989). Strain theory revisited: Economic goals, educational means, and delinquency. *Am. Sociol. Rev.* 54: 262–274.

Figueira-McDonough, J. (1983). On the usefulness of Merton's anomie theory: Academic failure and deviance among high school students. *Youth Society* 14: 259–279.

Gottfredson, M., and Hirschi, T. (1990). *A General Theory of Crime,* Stanford University Press, Stanford, CA.

Grasmick, H., Tittle, C., Bursik, R., and Arneklev, B. (1993). Testing the core empirical implications of Gottfredson and Hirschi's general theory of crime. *J. Res. Crime Delinq.* 30: 5–29.

Griffin, B., and Griffin, C. (1978). Marijuana use among students and peers. *Drug Forum* 7: 155–165.

Hirschi, T. (1969). *Causes of Delinquency,* University of California Press, Berkeley.

Jackson, E., Tittle, C., and Burke, M. (1986). Offense specific models of the differential association process. *Soc. Problems* 33: 335–356.

Jaquith, S. (1981). Adolescent marijuana and alcohol use: An empirical test of differential association theory. *Criminology* 19: 271–280.

Jensen, G. (1994). Salvaging structure through strain: A theoretical and empirical critique. *Advances in Criminological Theory, Vol. 6,* Transaction Press, New Brunswick, NJ.

Johnson, R. (1979). *Juvenile Delinquency and Its Origins: An Integrated Approach,* Cambridge University Press, Cambridge.

Johnson, R., Marcos, A., and Bahr, B. (1987). The role of peers in the complex etiology of adolescent drug use. *Criminology* 25: 323–340.

Keane, C., Maxim, P., and Teevan, J. (1993). Drinking and driving, self-control, and gender: Testing a general theory of crime. *J. Res. Crime Delinq.* 30: 3–46.

Kethenini, S. (1990). *Adolescent Drug Use in India,* Unpublished Dissertation, Rutgers University, University Microfilms International, Ann Arbor, MI.

Knight, B., Osborn, G., and West, D. (1977). Early marriage and criminal tendency in males. *Br. J. Criminol.* 17: 348–360.

Kornhauser, R. (1978). *Social Sources of Delinquency: An Appraisal of Analytical Models,* University of Chicago Press, Chicago, IL.

Khron, M., Lanza-Kaduce L., and Akers, R. (1984). Community context and theories of deviant behavior: An examination of social learning and social bonding theories. *Sociol. Q.* 25: 353–371.

LaGrange, R., and White, H. (1985). Age differences in delinquency: A test theory. *Criminology* 23: 19–45.

Landis, J., and Scarpitti, F. (1965). Perception regarding value orientation and legitimate opportunity: Delinquents and nondelinquents. *Soc. Forces* 44: 83–91.

Lasley, J. (1988). Toward a central theory of white-collar offending. *Journal of Quant, Crim.* 4: 347–362.

Laub, J., and Sampson, R. (1993). Turning points in the life course: Why change matters to the study of crime. *Criminology* 31: 301–325.

Liska, A. (1971). Aspirations, expectations, and delinquency: Stress and additive models. *Sociol. Q.* 12: 99–107.

Luckenbill, D. (1977). Criminal homicide as a situated transaction. *Soc. Problems* 25: 176–186.

Mak, A. (1990). Testing a pyschosocial control theory of delinquency. *Crim. Just. Behav.* 17: 215–30.

Marcos, A., Bahr, S., and Johnson, S. (1986). Test of a bonding/association theory of adolescent drug use. *Soc. Forces* 65: 135–161.

Matsueda, R. (1982). Testing control and differential association theories: A causal modeling approach. *Am. Sociol. Rev.* 47: 489–504.

Matsueda, R. (1989). The dynamics of moral beliefs and minor deviance. *Soc. Forces* 68: 428–457.

Matsueda, R., and Heimer, K. (1987). Race, family structure, and delinquency: A test of differential association and social control theories. *Am. Sociol. Rev.* 52: 826–40.

McCarthy, B., and Hagan, J. (1992). Mean streets: The theoretical significance of situation delinquency among homeless youth. *Am. J. Sociol.* 98: 597–627.

Merton, R. (1938). Social structure and anomie. *Am. Sociol. Rev.* 3: 672–682.

Merton, R. (1957). *On Theoretical Sociology*, Free Press, New York.

Merton, R. (1968). *Social Theory and Social Structure*, 2nd ed., Free Press, New York.

Merton, R., and Rossi, A. (1968). Contributions to the theory of reference group behavior. In Merton, R. (ed.), *Social Theory and Social Structure*, enlarged ed., Free Press, New York.

Messner, S. (1985). Sex differences in arrest rates for homicide: An application of general theory of structural strain. *Comp. Soc. Res.* 8: 187–201.

Messner, S. (1988). Merton's "social structure and anomie": the road not taken. *Deviant Behav.* 9: 33–53.

Messner, S., and Rosenfeld, R. (1994). *Crime and the American Dream*, Wadsworth, Belmont, CA.

Nagin, D., and Paternoster, R. (1993). Enduring individual differences and rational choice theories of crime. *Law Soc. Rev.* 27: 467–496.

Orcutt, J. (1987). Differences association and marijuana use: A closer look at Sutherland (with a little help from Becker). *Criminology* 25: 342–358.

Passas, N. (1987). Anomie and relative deprivation. Paper presented at the annual meeting of the Eastern Sociological Society.

Passas, N. (1990). Anomie and corporate deviance. *Contemp. Crises.* 14: 157–178.

Paternoster, R., and Triplett, R. (1988). Disaggregating self-reported delinquency and its implications for theory. *Criminology* 26: 591–615.

Quicker, J. (1974). The effect of goal discrepancy on delinquency. *Soc. Problems* 22: 76–86.

Rand, A. (1987). Transitional life events and desistence from delinquency and crime. In Wolfgang, M., Thornberry, T., and Figlio, R. (eds.), *From Boy to Man: From Delinquency to Crime*, University of Chicago Press, Chicago, pp. 134–164.

Rivera, R., and Short, J. (1967). Significant adults, caretakers, and structures of opportunity: An exploratory study. *J. Res. Crime Delinq.* 4: 76–97.

Rosenbaum, J. (1987). Social control, gender, and delinquency: An analysis of drug, property, and violent offenders. *Just. Q.* 4: 117–132.

Rosenfeld, R. (1989). Robert Merton's contributions to the sociology of deviance. *Sociol. Inq.* 59: 453–466.

Sampson, R., and Laub, J. (1990). Crime and deviance over the life course: The salience of adult social bonds. *Am. Sociol. Rev.* 55: 609–627.

Sampson, R., and Laub, J. (1993). *Crime in the Making: Pathways and Turning Points Through Life,* Harvard University Press, Cambridge, MA.

Seagrave, J., and Halstad, D. (1983). Evaluating structural and control models of delinquency causation: A replication and extension. *Youth Society* 14: 437–456.

Short, J. (1960). Differential association as a hypothesis: Problems of empirical testing. *Soc. Problems* 8: 14–24.

Short, J., Rivera, R., and Tennyson, R. (1965). Perceived opportunities, gang membership, and delinquency. *Am. Sociol. Rev.* 30: 56–67.

Shue, J. (1988). Juvenile delinquency in the Republic of China. *Int. J. Comp. Appl. Crim. Just.* 12 (Spring): 59–72.

Silberman, M. (1976). Toward a theory of deterrence. *Am. Sociol. Rev.* 41: 442–461.

Simons, R., Miller, M. and Aignor, S. (1980). Contemporary theories of deviance and female delinquency. *J. Res. Crime Delinq.* 17: 42–57.

Smith, D., and Paternoster, R. (1987). The gender gap in theories of deviance: Issues and evidence. *Criminology* 24: 140–172.

Stinchcombe, A. (1964). *Rebellion in a High School,* Quadrangle Press, Chicago, IL.

Sutherland, E. (1949). *White-Collar Crime,* Holt, Rinehart, and Winston, New York.

Thio, A. (1975). A critical look at Merton's anomie theory. *Pacific Sociol. Rev.* 18: 139–158.

Tittle, C., Burke, M., and Jackson, E. (1986). Modeling Sutherland's theory of differential association: Toward an empirical clarification. *Soc. Forces* 65: 405–432.

U.S. Bureau of the Census (1992). *Census of Population and Housing, 1990: Summary Tape File III (Ohio)* (machine readable data files), Washington, DC.

Warr, M., and Stafford, M. (1993). Age, peers, and delinquency. *Criminology* 31: 17–40.

Wilson, J. Q., and Herrnstein, R. (1985). *Crime and Human Nature,* Simon and Schuster, New York.

Winfree, L., Griffiths, C., and Sellers, C. (1989). Social learning theory, drug use, and American Indian youths: A cross-cultural test. *Just. Q.* 6: 395–418.

Wood, P., Pfefferbaum, B., and Arneklev, B. (1993). Risk-taking and self-control: Social psychological correlates of delinquency. *J. Crime Just.* 16: 111–130.

A troublesome but generally ignored paradox characterizes contemporary sociological expla-nations of crime causation. Although many sociologists interpret crime as if it were pathological or aberrant and thus "abnormal" behavior, most simultaneously embrace Durkheim's famous dictum of crime as "normal" behavior. A review of Durkheim's theory of crime causation reveals that it is burdened by several serious logical flaws. And ironically, despite his reputation for propagating a purely sociological explanation of crime, Durkheim resorts ultimately to individ-ual characteristics, rather than social facts, in order to identify the root causes of crime. Contemporary evolutionary game theory affords an alternative explanation of the normalcy of much crime without suffering the deficiencies of the classical Durkheimian approach. The authors' evolutionary ecological-based theory explains the incidence of "expropriative" crime as a by-product of normal patterns of social organization and processes of social interaction. Furthermore, this alternative perspective successfully explains, within one theoretical frame-work, the link between key macro- and microlevel forces responsible for patterns of expropriative crime.

The Normalcy of Crime

FROM DURKHEIM TO EVOLUTIONARY ECOLOGY

LAWRENCE E. COHEN
University of California, Davis

RICHARD MACHALEK
University of Wyoming

The current state of theoretical criminology features a bewildering but generally ignored paradox. On the one hand, many social scientists have long viewed crime as if it were pathological or aberrant behavior. Indeed, the criminological literature is replete with attempts to explain the root causes of crime by invoking such "abnormal" states as social disorganization, anomie, malfunctioning cultural systems, malintegrated cultures, ineffective sociali-

Authors' Note: *The authors are especially grateful to Mary Jackman, who read and gave many useful comments on earlier drafts of this article. Peter Richerson, Brian Vila, John R. Hall, and Burke Grandjean also contributed critical comments on an earlier version of this article, and we are most grateful for their help.*

RATIONALITY AND SOCIETY, Vol. 6 No. 2, April 1994 286-308
© 1994 Sage Publications, Inc.

zation, various forms of psychopathy and sociopathy, and constitutional excesses, deficiencies, or abnormalities, both psychological and biological (for an excellent summary of this literature, see Vold and Bernard 1986). On the other hand, however, such explanations appear to contradict the frequently cited and well accepted dictum of the venerated sociologist Emile Durkheim (1893, 1895) that crime is "normal" behavior performed by normal individuals living in unexceptional social systems. Against the current trend in criminological theorizing, we too propose that much crime is best understood as normal behavior. Our purpose is to reexamine Durkheim's thesis within an evolutionary ecological framework in order to refine, develop, and extend his insights regarding the normalcy of crime.

We note that although Durkheim is considered to be one of the founding fathers of sociology, his reasoning about the nature and causes of human behavior is often surprisingly naturalistic in tone. Although Durkheim was quite explicit that the subject matter of sociology was distinct from the subject matters of other disciplines, he was equally explicit in the claim that the methods of sociology must be the same as those of the natural sciences. For example, he often viewed societal problems such as suicide and crime as measures of the health of a society, and it is no wonder that his analyses of society are frequently suffused with expressions such as "health and disease," "social morbidity," "social species," "social pathology," "the social organism," and other such terms that he borrows from the life sciences to describe and discuss social phenomena (e.g., Durkheim 1964, 47-75). His use of such concepts, however, was only by way of didactic analogy, and therein lies a weakness in his approach. That is, although he frequently used biologically inspired concepts, Durkheim never adequately developed and exploited them for a compelling "naturalistic" explanation of human social behavior in general, and criminal behavior in particular. A more thoroughly naturalistic approach has great potential, but such a perspective for explaining crime has yet to be developed fully.[1] This can be attributed largely to sociology's neglect of recent developments in evolutionary and ecological theories of social behavior that could help explain the incidence of much crime as a by-product of normal patterns of social organization and processes of social interaction. It is certainly true that some biologically based reductionistic approaches to the study of crime often suffer serious deficiencies precisely because they fail to acknowledge how emergent properties of social systems contribute to the incidence of crime (e.g., Wilson and Herrnstein 1985). By contrast, an evolutionary ecological approach can inform our understanding of the normal emergent social dynamics that are implicated in crime causation without necessarily implying that crime is biologically determined, and without committing several logical errors that are commonly attributed to Durkheim's general theoretical approach.

In essence, here we argue for a naturalistic approach that explains social facts such as crime in terms of individual behavior, but relies on the mechanisms of cultural rather than genetic evolution. We contend that repetitive involvement in certain forms of expropriative criminal behavior can be derived from models of evolutionary strategy selection in which individuals try to increase their probability of acquiring resources. Such an approach suggests a possible solution to the following analytical questions that have both intrigued and frustrated social scientists since Durkheim: What is the relation between the behavior of individual human beings and the organized aggregates in which they live? Should individuals or social aggregates be regarded as the appropriate focus of analysis, and how are the two linked?

THE NORMALCY OF CRIME RECONSIDERED

On the one hand, sociologists have long appreciated Durkheim for having helped to establish sociology as a science, and many have shared his enthusiasm for viewing social phenomena as ultimately no less tractable to scientific explanation than the rest of nature. On the other hand, even some of Durkheim's most ardent admirers have cautioned against a social science that is naturalistic in approach: "The fact that biological theories have started coming back today is probably more of an indication of how the political tides are turning rather than of any advance in sociological research" (Collins 1982, 89). Yet, confusion prevails on this point. Although Collins lauds Durkheim's explanation of crime as sociologically superior to biological approaches, he fails altogether to recognize the potential of an indisputably naturalistic extension of Durkheim's approach for a viable explanation of how macro- and microlevel social processes interact to generate criminal behavior.

Granted, there is good reason to regard with suspicion those theories of crime that rely heavily on identifying physiological or morphological "traits" said to predispose certain types of individuals to committing crimes (e.g., see Wilson and Herrnstein 1985). Until recently, however, sociologists have seriously misconstrued the status of theoretical explanation in contemporary evolutionary ecology by drawing a false opposition between sociological and evolutionary explanation (for a notable exception, see Lenski and Lenski 1970). Both sociologists and evolutionary ecologists share the notion that characteristics, including behavior, of organisms are not randomly distributed across time and space, and that such organisms frequently interact within a

114

web of dynamic interdependent relationships that helps influence the nature, distribution, and abundance of these characteristics. These characteristics (e.g., behaviors) and the dynamic relationships among them can best be understood when framed in terms of evolutionary ecological theory. Instead of implying a biologically naive, reductionistic or "genetic deterministic" explanation of crime, however, evolutionary ecological theory can be used to advance our understanding of the contextual factors that influence criminal behavior. This is precisely because evolutionary ecological theory affords fundamental new insights about how the emergent properties of social organization and social interaction contribute to the genesis of crime.

We begin our discussion of Durkheim's theory with the assertion that his use of organismic analogy, and his account of crime as normal behavior suffer from certain basic flaws: First, his explanation of the essentially social nature and origins of crime is tautological. Second, his explanation of the universality of crime and punishment is teleological. Third, his analysis hinges on a reified view of society that erroneously identifies society, rather than individuals, as the ultimate beneficiaries of crime and punishment. And finally, despite its reputation as a purely "sociological" explanation of crime, the evidence suggests that Durkheim himself resorted ultimately to individual characteristics in order to identify the root causes of crime. Although the criticisms of illegitimate teleology and reification have been raised previously, no alternative explanation of the normalcy of crime has been offered that avoids these logical flaws. The following discussion will demonstrate how adopting a theoretical framework informed by evolutionary ecological theory provides an explanation for the normalcy of crime that avoids these logical traps.

DURKHEIM'S THEORY OF CRIME

In his determination to establish the normalcy of crime, Durkheim (1964) defines crime as a constitutive component of all societies. Stated succinctly, by his reasoning, a phenomenon should be understood as normal if it is "generally distributed" throughout a society and is "bound up with the fundamental conditions of all social life" (pp. 55, 60, 70). For Durkheim, the normalcy of crime is thereby established: "There is, then, no phenomenon that presents more indisputably [than crime] all the symptoms of normality, since it appears closely connected with the conditions of social life" (p. 66). Yet, Durkheim never specifies those "fundamental conditions" or exactly how crime is "bound up" with them. Instead, he argues, albeit persuasively, that crime and punishment confer benefits on the societies in which they occur. Because crime can be shown to be indirectly beneficial to society,

Durkheim concludes that it is a normal and unavoidably universal feature of social life (pp. 70-72). He reasoned therefore that a certain level of crime is both necessary and beneficial to society because (1) individual deviation from the social norm is a primary source of innovative social change; (2) increases in crime rates can warn or alert officials to damaging problems existing within social systems that give rise to such crimes; (3) crime enforcement helps to establish and to maintain behavioral boundaries within communities; and finally, (4) crime provokes punishment that in turn enhances solidarity within communities.

The gist of Durkheim's (1964) logic is that if a phenomenon is common and beneficial, it must be normal. Without belaboring the criticism, we contend that *defining* as normal any component of society that is merely *declared* to be constitutive of social organization, and then *asserting* that crime is such a component does not comprise a causally adequate explanation of the normalcy of crime. Instead, it seeks to accomplish explanation by definitional fiat. If one assumes as a premise for an argument the very conclusion that it is intended to prove, the fallacy committed is that of tautological reasoning. In his explanation of the normalcy of crime, Durkheim concludes only that which has already been asserted in the premise, thus he fails to establish the truth of the conclusion of his argument.

Second, despite his warnings about confusing cause and function, Durkheim (1964) essentially contends that crime exists because societies *need* it: "Crime is, then, necessary; it is bound up with the fundamental conditions of all social life, and by that very fact, it is useful, because these conditions of which it is a part are themselves indispensable to the normal evolution of morality and law" (p. 70). Reifying society with the notion that societies, like organisms, can be healthy, he contends further that crime is "an integral part of all healthy societies" (p. 67). An adequate explanation of how beneficial traits "evolve," however, requires one to identify the specific processes and mechanisms of variation and selection by means of which the beneficial trait, such as the crime-punishment complex, is generated. Yet, Durkheim's explanation fails this test of explanatory adequacy, because he neglects altogether to specify such processes and their "phylogenetic" history. Disappointingly, his account merely implies the necessary evolution of the crime-punishment complex because it is needed to generate and reaffirm the collective conscience upon which society depends (p. 64). Again, this account can only be interpreted as a subtle but no less disturbing instance of illegitimate teleology (for more on this point see Machalek and Cohen 1991).

Third, critics have long accused Durkheim and his successors, the structural-functional theorists, of subscribing to an overly reified view of society. As noted earlier, Durkheim (1964) promoted such an outlook by society as a "social organism" that can either enjoy "health" or suffer "disease" (pp. 49-53). In his view, crime is not a disease but, rather, a social trait that contributes to the overall health of a society. Although the individual victims of crime may suffer serious costs associated with their victimization, society *as a whole* will likely benefit, because the punishment of such crimes reaffirms the collective conscience upon which social order depends. Consequently, Durkheim's reified view of society causes him to neglect completely the fact that crimes do impose costs upon their victims, even if other members of the population derive some sort of associated benefits. Had he subscribed to a less reified view of society, he would have been able to conceptualize the possibility that any crime could be assessed for its net balance of consequences (Merton 1968) by contrasting the benefits it confers to collectivities to the costs that it imposes on the individuals it victimizes. This would have enabled Durkheim to refine his thesis so as to acknowledge *both* benefits and costs associated with crime events and crime patterns (see, also, Liska and Warner 1991). As is, Durkheim's theory is constructed upon a highly reified view of society that causes him to overlook completely the fact that "flesh and blood" individuals often suffer debilitating costs imposed by those crimes, the punishment of which is said to benefit society as a whole.

Durkheim's reified view of society also tends to obscure genuine social conflicts of interest that are the foundation of both evolutionary theory and many sociological theories of social behavior. Thus, by emphasizing exclusively the societal benefits of punishment, Durkheim fails to acknowledge sufficiently that many crimes represent contests of sorts, in which one's gains represent another's losses. In his zeal to establish the normalcy of crime, Durkheim (1964) appears at one point to dismiss any possible connection between pathology and crime: "From this point of view, the fundamental facts of criminality present themselves to us in an entirely different light. Contrary to current ideas, the criminal no longer seems a totally inassimilable body, introduced into the midst of society. On the contrary, he plays a definite role in social life" (p. 72). The Durkheimian theory transforms the criminal from an exploiter into an inadvertent benefactor of the social organism. Durkheim's explanation of crime and punishment presumes, rather than proves, that the collective benefits of crime (via punishment) outweigh any costs incurred by victims. Accordingly, the crime-punishment complex is seen as a necessary and ineradicable feature of any society. Despite the individual costs of crime suffered by victims, the collective benefits of punishment will assure the universality and persistence of crime (and punishment) in human societies. Thus, Durkheim's reification of society unrealistically portrays human social life as devoid of serious conflicts of interest and, instead, as organized for the collective well-being of the system as a whole.

Finally, problems inhere in Durkheim's (1964) claims about the "fundamental" cause of crime. Among students of deviance and crime, Durkheim is credited with establishing the essentially social nature of crime by virtue of the functions it performs for maintaining the social order. Ironically, an often overlooked and somewhat mysterious passage from one of his most frequently cited books indicates clearly that Durkheim himself is on record as having attributed the fundamental causes of criminal behavior not to social organization or social processes, but ultimately to the characteristics of individuals:

> Thus, since there cannot be a society in which the individuals do not differ more or less from the collective type, it is also inevitable that, among these divergences, there are some with a *criminal character* [emphasis ours]. What confers this character upon them is not the intrinsic quality of a given act but the definition which the collective conscience gives them. (p. 70)

Some might object that it is unfair to accuse Durkheim, on the mere basis of these two sentences, of having betrayed his explanatory commitment to social facts, versus individual character traits, as the primary causes of crime. Could Durkheim, the inveterate "social realist," really have meant to reduce the fundamental causes of crime to individual character? How much should be made of these two sentences? Despite the discomfort that this passage from Durkheim may cause his devotees, we believe that he meant just what he said. The meaning of this statement is quite clear and deliberate. Somewhat surprisingly, Durkheim, the champion of the explanatory power of social facts as causes of social behavior, undeniably submits to the thesis that the fundamental causes of crime are the individual characteristics of those who commit crimes. Although his reduction of crime's ultimate causes to individual traits rather than social facts does not seem to square with his reputation for insisting that social facts must be explained in terms of other social facts, this statement, unfortunately, represents his only attempt to specify the root causes (vs. functions) of criminal behavior. Although he is clear in disavowing the notion that some individuals are inherently criminal, he indisputably claims that the "character" of certain individuals compels them to behave in ways that society *defines* as criminal. Therefore, even if it is society that labels certain classes of behavior as criminal, Durkheim explains clearly that the root causes of the behaviors that societies label as crime are characterological or perhaps even constitutional in nature.

Again, the subtlety of this distinction could elude a reader who is strongly predisposed to think of Durkheim as an unstinting social realist in his explanations of human behavior. We are confident, however, in our interpretation of the meaning of Durkheim's statement. According to the passage cited above, individuals differ in character (individual traits), and these "character divergences" result in behavioral differences. No such behaviors, however, are *intrinsically* criminal. Instead, the criminal character of these behaviors is a matter of labeling. Thus, although the definition of a behavior as criminal is strictly a matter of social labeling, the *root causes of the behavior itself* are to be traced to individual character traits. Somewhat paradoxically, then, Durkheim here clearly reduces the root causes of behavior to individual traits while, at the same time, insisting that such behavior comes to be regarded as criminal only by the social labeling processes.

It is not that trying to reduce the root causes of crime to individual traits is a scientifically indefensible position (e.g., see Wilson and Herrnstein 1985). Rather, it is curious to find Durkheim, the uncompromising social realist, relying ultimately upon individual traits to account for the universality and persistence of behaviors that some societies label as crime. As we shall demonstrate, evolutionary ecological theory enables us to locate the roots of crime in patterns and processes of social organization without *necessarily* having to rely on any notion of a criminal character or type.

Having identified and discussed what we see as several disturbing flaws in Durkheim's reasoning regarding the normalcy of crime, we submit an alternative, more naturalistic thesis that we believe to be free of these limitations. The approach developed herein builds on and expands the general theory of expropriative crime explicated recently by Cohen and Machalek (1988).

EVOLUTIONARY ECOLOGICAL THEORY AND CRIME

Evolutionary ecological theory characterizes individuals as "strategists." This simply means that individuals have evolved generally to pursue actions that tend to be beneficial to them. As we shall explain later, however, this does not mean that all strategic actions are necessarily guided by rational choice in the economist's narrow sense that the strategists always pursue their ends as effectively as possible, or that they do not commit logical errors in ordering their preferences. Adopted strategies do not have to represent informed choices or attempts at expected utility maximization. Indeed, evolutionary theory has been used to predict when it might be useful to violate the canons of rationality and engage in actions produced by altruistic or malevolent emotions. In contrast to the position held by sociobiologists, however, we argue that the preferences that guide these actions are largely the product of cultural rather than genetic evolution. In our approach the primary causal forces of behavior are determined by social selection out of which individual decision-making (strategy selection) evolves.

A *strategy* is conceived broadly as a behavioral policy, one of a set of possible alternative behaviors by means of which individuals or groups achieve ends, whether these ends are intended and consciously recognized or not. Alternatively, a strategy may be thought of as a "decision rule," a specification of what to do in different situations that might arise (Axelrod 1984, 14). Through the use of evolutionary reasoning, we explain how culturally mediated behaviors, such as "expropriative crime," evolve and prolif- erate within societies. This is accomplished by reformulating Durkheim's important insights through an admixture of both evolutionary theory and evolutionary game theory (see Boyd and Richerson, 1985; Axelrod 1984; Dawkins 1980, 1982; Maynard Smith 1974, 1979, 1982).[2]

Our central thesis with respect to the analysis of the evoltion and ecology of crime is that the social organization of productive activity creates an opportunity structure that invites invasion by various strategies of expropria- tion. Expropriation describes a process whereby actors use coercion, decep- tion or stealth to usurp a valued resource from producers. Alternatively, resources may be acquired by production, the process of employing technol- ogy, energy, and raw materials to create goods and services. For example, the establishment of trade among societies that transported commodities by sea-going vessels created opportunities for the evolution of piracy. Hence, although individuals can benefit from mutual cooperation in productive activities, they may often do as well, or even better, by exploiting the productive activities of others. When the expropriative act entails the viola- tion of a criminal law, the behavior is described as an expropriative crime (see Cohen and Machalek 1988). Thus understood, expropriative crime is a predictable by-product of normal patterns of social organization and conduct.

Furthermore, a behavioral system in which a large proportion of individu- als are actively engaged in productive activities is likely to be inherently unstable, because it is highly susceptible to invasion by self-enhancing alternative strategists that we call expropriators. In short, the social organi- zation of production invites the evolution of expropriation, including expro- priative crime. Production and expropriation are conceptualized as behav- ioral strategies within a context of interaction that is described as a "game (Axelrod 1984; Dawkins 1980; Maynard Smith 1982). Within a population of individuals, strategies "compete" among themselves, with the result that the more "successful" strategies are those that confer more benefits to the individuals who adopt and execute them rather than other, alternative strate- gies. Furthermore, some strategies can be viewed as more successful than others to the extent that they proliferate more rapidly and thoroughly throughout populations and across generations. Evolutionary game theory attempts to specify the factors responsible for the variable success of alternative behavioral strategies competing within a population. As such, it affords new fundamental insights about the dynamic relationships between production and expropriative crime.

In evolutionary ecological theory, strategies are selectively retained and transmitted consciously or unconsciously because of their consequences, and the processes involved comprise "strategy evolution" as discussed by Axelrod (1984). Any given strategy, and its potential for success, depends strongly on the kinds of strategies adopted by others within the population and the relative frequencies with which these strategies are employed. A fundamental premise of evolutionary game theory is that populations in which everyone pursues the same strategy are often highly susceptible to invasion by alternative strategies. This is because alternative strategies face less competition, because they are, by definition, rarer. Consequently, alternative strategies often enjoy a competitive advantage over the more commonly employed strategies. When the average payoff for a strategy varies inversely with the number of others who are employing the same strategy, the success of the strategy is said to be "frequency dependent" (Fisher 1930). Hence a population of productive strategists is an open invitation to invasion by any innovative expropriative strategy. For example, a population of "honest reciprocators" (those who always pay back others from whom they received a resource) is vulnerable to invasion by an innovative "cheater," or nonreciprocator. This helps explain why confidence game artists thrive among populations of honest reciprocators. As the proportion of cheaters in a population increases, however, competition among cheaters increases and the average payoff to each cheater may decline. For, as the notion of frequency-dependent selection implies, an inverse relationship typically obtains between the proportion of individuals adopting a strategy and the rate of average returns yielded by that strategy.

These population-level dynamics could yield any of four hypothetical outcomes. Two logically possible, but theoretically implausible outcomes involve one population composed entirely of "saints" (pure producers), and a second consisting entirely of "sinners" (pure expropriators). In reality, however, two other possibilities commonly emerge: (1) either the expropriator/ producer strategy ratio will oscillate indefinitely within populations at some nonzero level; or (2) a stable proportion of expropriative criminal to productive strategies will evolve. In any case, the resulting ratio of criminal to noncriminal behaviors within populations reflects the advantages of certain *strategy proportions*, not *necessarily* a mix of different types of *individuals*.

121

This introduces an explicitly sociological dimension to the evolution of expropriative criminal strategies. It means that the population-level dynamics of social interaction among strategists become a crucial force shaping emergent patterns of behavioral diversity, including the relative incidence of criminal and noncriminal behaviors in populations.

At the individual-level of analysis, events such as expropriative crime can be viewed in game-theoretic terms as zero-sum "contests" over resources between potential offenders and their victims. In this context, the outcomes of criminal events are not solely dependent on the combination of strategies that happen to meet. In fact, the strategy itself is most predictive of contest outcome in cases where opponents are relatively evenly matched. Often, however, contestants are unequal in ways (other than strategy) that are related to the outcome of criminal expropriative events. Thus, in addition to considering the tactics employed by competitors, the nature of these contests and their outcomes often vary because of two additional basic factors: (1) differences in individual traits and access to resources among individual competitors themselves, and (2) differences in the value that individual participants assign to the contested resource.

For example, individual contestants often differ in traits relevant to contest outcomes such as size, strength, intelligence, experience, possession of technology, and so on. The complete ensemble of traits employed by an individual in an attempt to win such a contest is described as the contestant's "resource holding potential (RHP)" (Parker 1974). In addition, RHP differences may be balanced or even offset by the respective value that each contestant assigns to the contested resource—its "resource value (RV)" (Parker 1974). That is, RHP deficiencies can sometimes be overcome in criminal encounters when the trait-deficient participant assigns a greater value to the contested resource than does his or her more advantaged opponent. The RHP-superior opponent may be unwilling to assume the cost required for acquiring or holding on to a resource that he or she values less than his or her more highly motivated, but less advantaged opponent (for more details on RHP and RV factors and their relevance to the outcome of competitions, see Cohen and Machalek 1988, 471-72).

Within different social contexts, then, asymmetries of individual ability and/or need can themselves be important determinants of contest outcomes and strategy evolution. From an evolutionary ecological perspective, resource niches are exploited and diverse behavioral strategies evolve that individuals use to gain and exploit opportunities for acquiring valued resources. Within any particular social context, the ability of individuals to execute successfully certain strategies varies both directly and indirectly with a wide range of sociocultural, physiological, psychological, and developmental factors (that is, individual traits, structural, and historical characteristics). These traits will thus necessarily affect one's ability to compete strategically (both legally and illegally) for valued resources within diverse social environments. It is in this sense that individual and social traits can be said to influence strategy evolution within populations. Given this interpretation, an evolutionary ecological view of crime can be said to accommodate both the individual and social correlates of expropriative crime, while at the same time emphasizing the importance of a previously neglected sociological element of the criminal event—the influences of strategy mix within populations.

Importantly, we emphasize that expropriative criminal strategies are *not* solely the properties of individuals or groups as such, but rather, behavioral options, the expression of which can, and often does, vary *independently* of the social characteristics or individual traits of the persons who adopt them. By identifying behavioral strategies (rather than individuals and their traits) as the focus of analysis for the study of crime, and by viewing behavioral strategies (both criminal and noncriminal) to be competing entities in their own right, we are able to explain how the characteristics of the strategies themselves can contribute to their proliferation throughout populations.

The main point to be emphasized here is that to many psychologists and economists who study crime, large-scale criminal patterns are seen as the aggregate result of individual behaviors. To the macrolevel-oriented theorists who follow Durkheim's stated position, the explanation of large-scale crime patterns is to be found among causal processes acting on the scale of whole societies that, in turn, influence individual behavior. Evolutionary ecological theory, on the other hand, demonstrates that the two levels of analysis are reciprocally linked (Boyd and Richerson 1985). We take as our fundamental unit of analysis the population of *behavioral strategies* that are expressed by a population of individuals. These behavioral strategies are distributed variably throughout a population of individuals because of the forces of cultural evolution. Some of these forces originate in individual learning and "rational calculation" and express themselves as what Boyd and Richerson have called "guided variation" and "biased cultural transmissions." Other forces result from large-scale population-level social processes, such as frequency dependent selection (Fisher 1930). In this connection, an important point deserving emphasis is that it is more useful to focus on the success of any given strategy averaged over all individuals using it, rather than the success of any individual actor employing this strategy. Such an approach is at once both decisively sociological and consistent with the undeniable fact that it is always individuals who commit criminal acts. Our focus on crime as strategic activity provides a means of linking within one theoretical framework key macro- and microlevel forces that drive expropriative crime rates. Evolutionary theory acknowledges that social system properties are rooted ultimately in the characteristics of individuals, in the sense that population-level inter-actions among strategies ultimately derive from and change individual-level characteristics. For example, individual characteristics can create population compositions that drive populations toward one equilibrium or another (Maynard Smith, 1982). At the same time, however, we suggest here that by treating behavioral strategies as the focus of analysis, the incidence and expansion of expropriative crime within a population can be explained without having to focus solely or ultimately on the individual characteristics of the criminals themselves, an approach that is strongly advocated by Wilson and Herrnstein (1985) and, as we have shown, even Durkheim himself.

Microlevel-oriented theorists such as Wilson and Herrnstein (1985) be-lieve we can understand the general processes that affect criminal behavior only if we can identify the individual traits that lead people to incur risks in choosing behaviors. We suggest that, to the surprise of those who fear reductionism in naturalistic approaches to the study of human behavior, the sociological influences on crime patterns become even more apparent when they are examined in evolutionary ecological terms. This is because an evolutionary ecological approach to interpreting patterns of behavioral strate-gies enacted in a population allows us to explain how patterns of normal production and activity give rise to patterns of illegal expropriation, or crime. Thus we are able to locate the social roots of crime in both population-level forces that give rise to patterns of behavioral strategies *and* in the individual characteristics of persons who are the most highly motivated and suitably equipped to execute these strategies. Because a population of productive strategies does not, by definition, include expropriative behaviors, our expla-nation of the relationship between social organization and crime is not tautological, as is Durkheim's. That is to say, our conceptualization of society does not include, by definition, crime as a constitutive component, as does Durkheim's. Instead, our conception of social organization emphasizes that it is at least *logically* possible (although highly improbable) to have a crime free social system of mutually cooperative producers.

What is distinct about this perspective is that it is advantageous to conceive of alternative strategies, not just individuals, as competing against one another in the population, with cultural selection (or other evolutionary forces) acting directly on the pool of alternative strategies: thus we treat individuals simply as the temporary executors of these alternative strategies (Dawkins 1980; Boyd and Richerson 1985). When this perspective is adopted, an added dimension to conventional crime analysis is gained. It can now be shown that expropriative crime can occur normally within popula-tions simply because of expropriative opportunities created by patterns of productive strategies within a population. That is, the rarer criminal strategy for acquiring a resource may be selected over more common productive strategies simply because it affords a relatively greater chance of success or a greater average payoff (for those individuals with the appropriate combination of RHP and RV), due to less intense competition.

Such reasoning, by offering an account of the specific processes constituting the sociogenesis of crime, is free of the problem of teleology that plagues Durkheim's analysis. In addition, a focus on the evolution of behavioral strategies does not require us to assume, as did Durkheim, and more recently Wilson and Herrnstein (1985), that crime derives ultimately from individual "characterological" differences. Although individual traits in the form of RHP and RV differences may very well influence the probability that one will adopt an expropriative criminal strategy within a particular social context, the incidence of crime and the proliferation (or demise) of criminal strategies within populations cannot be reduced to such individual differences alone. Instead, as evolutionary ecological theory makes clear, the incidence of expropriative crime within a population is largely a by-product of opportunities created by the evolution of patterns of productive activity, not simply the result of "deviant" behaviors that somehow necessarily derive from traits possessed by certain individuals.

In fact, evolutionary ecological theory discourages facile generalizations that concentrate on establishing direct links between individual traits and the likelihood that any self-interested person will commit a crime. Consider, for example, questions about the role of socioeconomic status in predisposing crime. For different (but related) reasons, both those who enjoy superior RHP profiles (for example, those with power, wealth, and prestige) and those who suffer RHP deficiencies (those lacking power, wealth, or prestige), but who assign disproportionately high value to a resource (RV), may, on occasion, adopt expropriative criminal strategies. Individuals suffering RHP deficiencies (i.e., many street criminals) may acquire and employ relatively rare and unconventional behavioral strategies, such as criminal expropriation, as a way of "making the best of a bad job." On the other hand, individuals with advantaged RHP profiles (i.e., white-collar criminals and elites) may employ expropriative strategies to "take advantage of a good job" through greater access to opportunities and technology with minimal risk. Indeed, in some cases, elites, through the use of political power, may be able to prescribe and interpret normative codes in their favor so as to avoid prosecution for their expropriative activity. Thus, whereas RHP deficiencies may occasion petty theft, RHP prowess may encourage higher yield forms of expropriative crime, such as insider-trading or savings and loan frauds. Therefore, ceteris paribus, illegal expropriative behavioral strategies will proliferate when frequency-dependent payoffs tend to make such rare strategies successful for those who adopt them, regardless of the individual traits of the strategy executors. Thus the specific form of expropriation varies according to RHP, RV, and opportunities in the strategic environment.

HOW CRIMINAL STRATEGIES ARISE AND SPREAD

Expropriative criminal strategies arise and spread by means of culturally mediated processes that are akin to natural selection in that the more successful strategies have consequences that contribute to their proliferation. The characterization of these processes as "natural selection" is not merely analogical. Evolutionary reasoning is appropriate, because natural selection can operate on both genetic and nongenetic informational media. Hence a Darwinian approach can be used to describe the growth or decline over time of learned behavioral strategies based on media such as language or other forms of symbolic expression—so long as the media-specific differences in the constituent processes and mechanisms of evolution by natural selection (replication, variation, selection, transmission) are taken into account (Boyd and Richerson 1985; Cohen and Machalek 1988). Thus, because expropriative crime strategies are transmitted primarily by culture, and culture is a system of inheritance, expropriative crime is tractable to evolutionary analysis. If cultural traits such as expropriative criminal strategies are inherited by learning, and if the more successful strategies have different likelihoods of being transmitted than do less successful ones, then a Darwinian model of criminal strategy evolution is applicable, even though this inheritance is not mediated by DNA. Consequently, expropriative crime is to be interpreted as a form of strategic activity that is influenced significantly by processes of sociocultural evolution.[3]

Humans, however, are not simply passive imitators. They actively learn for themselves, and often select what to imitate from others. Individuals modify the culture they receive by conscious and unconscious decisions influenced by a number of nonrandom forces. Boyd and Richerson (1985), for example, argue that these forces (which they term "guided variation" and "biased transmissions") act as proximal agents in selection through imitation and learning, and predispose persons to select certain cultural variants over others. Guided variation involves individual trial-and-error learning or deliberate invention that generates nonrandom behavioral variation. Biased transmissions that generate behavioral variations involve imitation. They are usually more powerful than guided variation and occur at a more rapid rate. Boyd and Richerson identify three distinctive types of biased transmission forces: (1) behavior that is imitated because it reflects a preference that has direct personal consequences for the actor; (2) behavior that is common in the general population, and is imitated because the actor wishes to be in fashion with what the majority in society are doing; and (3) behavior that is imitated because it is attractive due to the fact that it is displayed by other individuals to whom the actor assigns high prestige and wishes to emulate. Types 1 and 3 above are the variants most commonly identified in the criminology literature to account for the learning and imitating of criminal behavior (see, for example, Vold and Bernard 1986).

EVOLUTIONARY ECOLOGICAL THEORY: PRECURSORS AND COMPETITORS

Societies in which a sizable proportion of individuals are engaged in routine productive activities are highly susceptible to invasion by expropriative criminal strategies. In such societies, unconventional behaviors (including expropriative crime) often emerge in response to opportunities created by a pattern of normal productive activity. This interpretation has also been advanced by criminal opportunity theorists who maintain that a certain level of criminal activity is enabled simply by opportunities created by routine production activities.

For example, Cohen and Felson (1979) have shown that the rise in the rates of expropriative crime (which they call "predatory crime") in the United States since the end of World War II has been facilitated by increases in criminal opportunities that have created a "target rich" environment for criminals, particularly in urban areas. They explain that the expropriative crime rate in any area is largely a function of the convergence in space and time of three elements: (1) motivated offenders, (2) suitable targets available to expropriate, and (3) the absence of guardians capable of preventing the expropriation from occurring. Cohen and Felson (1979, 589) suggest that the convergence in space and time of the pool of suitable targets in the absence of capable guardians may lead to significant variation in crime rates without any necessity for change in the pool of motivated offenders within populations. That is, if the pool of motivated offenders, or even the pool of suitable targets in a given population were to remain constant, other changes in routine production and social activities could still alter guardianship patterns in a community, thereby creating more opportunities for crime and increasing the crime rate.

Cohen and Felson (1979) present data from 1947-74 to demonstrate that changes in routine production and social activities in the United States appear indeed to have influenced significantly expropriative crime rates. For exam-

127

ple, they report evidence that increases in the female labor force participation rate (i.e., productive activity) appear to have decreased home guardianship during the day, making these households more vulnerable to burglary. Also, increases in the frequency of leisure activity outside the home appear to have eroded guardianship capabilities by exposing these homes to greater risk while family members are away. Additionally, the growth of suburban neighborhoods and increased residential mobility have led to a further decline in effective guardianship. These trends have had an impact on traditional neighborhood cohesiveness relative to earlier time periods, because families in these "newer neighborhoods" often find themselves with fewer intimate neighbors on whom they may depend to help look after their own property while they are away from home. Finally, and of greatest importance to the present discussion, Cohen and Felson have shown that recent changes in routine production activities (e.g., use of transistors, plastics, etc.) have led to the greater availability of portable and increasingly valuable goods, thus creating a greater number of targets suitable for theft.

Such approaches to crime are frequently classified (or perhaps misclassified) as "rational choice" theories of crime (Siegel 1989, 114). Both the motivation to commit crime and the supply of criminal offenders are assumed under these rational choice theories to be relatively constant, with changes in crime rates seen mainly as a function of criminal opportunities available within a society (Cornish and Clarke 1986; Siegel 1989; Gottfredson and Hirschi 1990). Such theories, however, have been criticized for not attending to individual differences in offender motivation (e.g., LaFree and Birkbeck 1991, 92).

Like these rational choice theories of crime, our evolutionary game-theoretic approach acknowledges the importance of the creation of criminal opportunities by productive populations, but it features certain added advantages over the less comprehensive approaches such as the opportunity theory and rational choice explanations from microeconomics. First, our evolutionary game-theoretic approach makes apparent the importance of the frequency dependence dynamics inherent in expropriative crime that have been neglected by opportunity theorists. For example, when criminal behavior is rare, society's investment in guardianship need not be very high, yet this is the very situation that will strongly favor the rare criminal strategy. At the same time, when guardianship is high, criminal strategies may have negative payoffs, but guardianship may be high only because it was elevated by a previous period of high criminal activity. Because evolutionary ecological theory can explain crime patterns at the population-level, it has the advantage over the static optimizing and individually oriented rational choice explanations in that the former easily account for lags and oscillations whereas the latter predict that rational strategies should lead to instant equilibria.

Second, not only does an evolutionary ecological approach subsume opportunity theory, it also addresses the most frequent criticism leveled against this perspective—that it ignores individual and group differences in the propensity to engage in crime. Unlike most opportunity theories, evolutionary ecology attempts to integrate population with individual-level explanations and does not ignore the potential role of individual and group differences in the differential propensity to engage in crime. While identifying the mediating (rather than casual) role of such factors, we submit that the approach outlined herein can explain individual or social correlates of expropriative crime at least as well, if not better, than any other extant criminological theory. For example, evolutionary ecological theory can easily incorporate extant empirical findings on individual and group variations in the reported correlates of expropriative crime through use of the concepts of RHP and RV differences and asymmetries through their interaction with productive and expropriative opportunities in populations (Cohen and Machalek 1988, 479-90). We stress again, however, our insistence that the incidence and expansion of expropriative crime within a population cannot be explained fully without an account of how diverse behavioral strategies derive from normal patterns of population-level social organization and interaction. On this point, the advantage of an evolutionary ecological approach over its theoretical competition is clear. This novel approach identifies two additional sets of causes that are omitted from competing explanations: (1) properties of expropriative crime strategies themselves that affect the rate of occurrence and successful completion of these behaviors (e.g., some techniques for embezzling funds are simply superior to others), and (2) the incidence of multiple kinds of strategies, with varying frequencies in a population that contributes independently to the rate of expropriative crime.

Third, many criminologists have great difficulty interpreting certain criminal acts as rational behaviors. While acknowledging that individuals may very well choose strategies consciously and purposively, evolutionary ecological theory does not *require* us to embrace the assumption that people engage in conscious, rational calculations in order to select the best strategy from among a range of behavioral options. That is, many rational choice theories generally assume that people act rationally insofar as they select their actions from a range of alternatives that best serve their ends, given the beliefs that they hold about available options and their probable consequences (Little 1991, 39-67; Moser 1990, 11-16). We propose, instead, that strategies can be transmitted through normal processes of socialization and social learning, and that people commonly acquire and execute such behavioral strategies *without any conscious awareness* of the expected costs and benefits that may derive from these strategies. Hence evolutionary ecological theory does not require us to assume that criminal strategies, however successful they may be, are chosen as a result of cost-benefit calculations conducted by individuals (see also, Axelrod 1984, 18). Nor, however, does this theory preclude this possibility. For example, cultural traditions of "cooperation" or "thievery" might generate lags or cycles within populations. At some points in the cycle, many people may be behaving "irrationally" such that the burglary may have been a more rational strategy in 1980 than in 1990, when judged against their current potential to earn legitimate income, and the certainty and/or severity of the punishments meted out during these two different time points.

Thus an evolutionary ecological theory of crime identifies a new prerequisite for such behaviors not previously acknowledged by opportunity theories. In addition to the three components previously specified by opportunity theorists (motivated offenders, suitable targets, absence of capable guardianship), evolutionary ecological theory demonstrates the importance of *effective strategies* in the successful completion of the criminal event. For a more complete discussion of the various means by which humans might gain information on such strategies, the reader is urged to consult Boyd and Richerson (1985) and Cohen and Machalek (1988, 488-91).

CONCLUSIONS

The theoretical approach proferred herein combines both ecological and evolutionary principles. Ecological factors include variables such as competition, the availability and distribution of resources to be expropriated, and patterns of production. The evolutionary dynamics among strategies themselves deserve additional comment. Strictly speaking, organic evolution involves changes in gene frequencies across generations. In the context of this discussion of culturally mediated behaviors, evolution refers similarly to variation in the proportions of various culturally acquired strategies within populations across time. Strategy evolution implies that, over time, new successful strategies will emerge and proliferate throughout populations whereas other strategies will decline or even vanish (Axelrod 1984). Population-level patterns of social behavior evolve as some strategies prosper whereas others become extinct.

Among the various processes characterizing strategy evolution, one of the most interesting and pertinent to crime is *coevolution*. Coevolution describes a process whereby strategies being enacted within a population exert reciprocal influences on their evolution. In the context of biological evolution, for example, the evolution of more effective predators creates selection pressures favoring the evolution of more evasive prey which, in turn, favors the evolution of even more effective predators. This positive feedback system is commonly described by evolutionary biologists as an "arms race" (Dawkins 1980).

Within human populations, the evolution of expropriative crime strategies commonly gives rise to deterrent counterstrategies that may reduce potential victims' vulnerability to subsequent expropriative crimes. For example, the manufacture and sale of commercial computer software invites the expropriation of this product by illegal duplication. This imposes constraints favoring the introduction of various protective mechanisms that will inhibit duplication. This, in turn, favors the evolution of even more innovative strategies for expropriating "copy protected" software. This constitutes an arms race between computer software producers and software "pirates," or expropriators. Consequently, the behaviors exhibited by the strategies themselves exert a reciprocal influence on their evolution. Such producer/expropriator coevolutionary dynamics constitute a major force in the evolution of crime patterns within populations, and evolutionary ecological theory makes vividly apparent the normalcy of such patterns of social behavior. Until the development of evolutionary ecological theory, even scholars predisposed to see crime as normal, such as Durkheim, were unable to specify the population-level processes and mechanisms actually responsible for generating crime in virtually all societies. The evolutionary ecological theory of crime uncovers the fundamental processes involved.

Evolutionary ecological theory advances our theoretical understanding of expropriative crime on several fronts. To begin, we can now explain better that which Durkheim largely intuited: that indeed, crime is normal. Unlike Durkheim, however, we are compelled neither to reify society nor to employ teleological reasoning to reach the conclusion that crime is normal. Instead, we use elementary principles derived from evolutionary ecology to develop a truly naturalistic account of the normalcy of crime. Because Durkheim based his concept of normalcy on the two conditions of universality and necessity, he assumed that society is always better off for the existence of crime. By default, what is normal must be for the good of society. An evolutionary game-theoretic approach, however, does not require any such claim.

Our conception of normalcy does not require us to assert that crime evolves for the collective good. Instead, we explain that the normalcy of crime derives from opportunities created by productive strategies within the population. In a population comprised solely of producers, the average payoff for a given strategy could be greater than that which exists in one comprised of both producers and expropriators. Clearly, in this case one could argue that a society without crime would be better for *all* concerned than would a society with crime. But a society without crime would be an unstable equilibrium, because any rare invading criminal strategy should typically have a relatively high payoff. Thus such utopias, or "Societies of Saints," are unstable because they are vulnerable to invasion (see Machalek and Cohen 1991). This example conveys a fundamental disagreement with Durkheim's, and other "group-selectionist" viewpoints, and suggests that interactions among individual-level payoffs can typically lead to something less than the "best of all worlds."

Another advantage of the evolutionary ecological approach over that of its theoretical competition concerns the proper unit of analysis from which best to explain crime. Unlike scholars such as Wilson and Herrnstein (1985), we do not see crime as rooted *primarily* in individual traits. Instead, we emphasize that patterns of expropriative crime represent *emergent* properties created by the evolution of population-level interactions among behavioral strategies. Individual traits influence strategy evolution primarily because RHP and RV asymmetries interact with the availability of opportunities created by the frequency of alternative strategies in the population. Thus we identify a crucial but previously neglected dimension of crime causation: the contribution of expropriative strategies, rather than individuals or groups, to the production of crime. The extant configuration of strategies in a population itself powerfully determines the type and frequency of expropriative criminal behaviors that will evolve in that population. The incorporation of strategy evolution introduces an entirely new dimension to the theoretical explanation of crime, one that is not limited to any particular historical period or cultural setting (Cohen and Machalek 1988, 498-99). This emphasis leads to a number of novel hypotheses that are not derivable from alternative theories of crime (for a list and discussion of these hypotheses, see Cohen and Machalek 1988, 496-98). Initial efforts to model six of these hypotheses using mathematical analysis and numerical simulation experiments find strong confirmatory evidence in support of the theory (Vila and Cohen 1993).

Finally, this approach simplifies and unifies many previously disconnected interdisciplinary theoretical arguments on expropriative crime, especially those that argue that different individual traits and structural properties are the causes of crime (Cohen and Machalek 1988, 475-94). One characteristic of a good theory is parsimony—the ability to unite many disparate data and perspectives into an integrated whole by means of a simple theory. This theoretical perspective allows us to synthesize key elements and major empirical findings from sociology, psychology, political science, economics, and the biological sciences while providing a logically consistent and dynamic account of the role of both micro- and macrolevel factors in the social production of crime.

Although we have chosen here to focus explicitly on the topic of crime, it is obvious that an evolutionary ecological analysis could be applied fruitfully to other more general classes of expropriation, such as various forms of class, race, and gender inequality and exploitation, traditional topics of study among sociologists. As we have argued, expropriation is a normal outgrowth of routine productive activities within societies. Expropriation in the form of crime persists, not because of "social benefits" as argued by Durkheim, but due to frequency-dependent payoffs to individuals and to RHP and RV asymmetries that affect the competition for resources within populations. Individuals often take advantage of the opportunities created by the dynamic interaction of these factors. In this way, they negotiate, however unwittingly, their everyday activities so as to realize their interests.

NOTES

1. By naturalistic we do not mean to imply biological reductionism or a vulgar genetic determinism. Instead, we mean an approach that emphasizes the application of general ecological and evolutionary principles to the analysis of social behavior, and at the same time acknowledges the unique character of the species in question. When studying humans, for example, the naturalist is required to take into account the unique human capacities for symbolic communication, language, and culture as they impinge on social behavior.

2. Clearly written and easily accessible introductions to evolutionary game theory are available in Barash (1982) and Dawkins (1980). More sophisticated theoretical treatments can be found in Axelrod (1984) and Maynard Smith (1982).

3. This is not to say that the ways in which natural selection works in human societies are identical to that in the rest of the biological world. Sociocultural variations, for example, differ from their purely genetic counterparts in that they occur at an extraordinarily fast pace, often arise nonrandomly, and frequently result from social diffusion, which may have no close parallel in the biological world. Nevertheless, Boyd and Richerson (1985) present a powerful and convincing argument for the similarities in selection processes between biological and cultural evolution. In so doing, they offer a cogent explanation of how natural selection can act directly and indirectly on culturally transmitted information. In addition, they offer formal mathematical models to determine the circumstances under which natural selection might favor modes of cultural transmission observed in contemporary human societies.

REFERENCES

Axelrod, R. 1984. *The evolution of cooperation*. New York: Basic Books.
Barash, D. P. 1982. *Sociobiology and behavior*, 2d ed. New York: Elsevier.

Boyd, R., and P. J. Richerson. 1985. *Culture and the evolutionary process*. Chicago: University of Chicago Press.

Cohen, L. E., and M. Felson. 1979. Social change and crime rate trends: A routine activity approach. *American Sociological Review* 44:588-608.

Cohen, L. E., and R. Machalek. 1988. A general theory of expropriative crime: An evolutionary ecological approach. *American Journal of Sociology* 94:465-501.

Collins, R. 1982. *Sociological insight: An introduction to nonobvious sociology*. New York: Oxford University Press.

Cornish, D. B., and R. Clarke. 1986. *The reasoning criminal: Rational choice perspectives on offending*. New York: Springer-Verlag.

Dawkins, R. 1980. Good strategy or evolutionary stable strategy? In *Beyond nature/nurture*, edited by G. W. Barlow and J. Silverberg, 331-67. Boulder, CO: Westview.

——. 1982. *The extended phenotype: The gene as the unit of selection*. San Francisco: Freeman.

Durkheim, E. 1893. *De La Division Du Travail Social: Etude Sur L'Organisation Des Societies Superieures*. Paris: Felix Alcan.

——. 1895. *Les Regles De La Methode Sociologique*. Paris: Felix Alcan.

——. 1964. *The rules of sociological method*. New York: Free Press.

Fisher, R. A. 1930. *The genetical theory of natural selection*. Oxford: Clarendon.

Gottfredson, M. R., and T. Hirschi. 1990. *A general theory of crime*. Stanford: Stanford University Press.

LaFree, G., and C. Birkbeck. 1991. The neglected situation: A cross-national study of the situational characteristics of crime. *Criminology* 29:73-98.

Lenski, Gerhard, and J. Lenski. 1970. *Human societies: A macrolevel introduction to sociology*. New York: McGraw-Hill.

Liska, A. E., and B. D. Warner. 1991. Functions of crime: A paradoxical process. *American Journal of Sociology* 96:1441-63.

Little, D. 1991. *Varieties of social explanation*. Boulder, CO: Westview.

Machalek, R., and L. E. Cohen. 1991. The nature of crime: Is cheating necessary for cooperation? *Human Nature* 2:215-33.

Maynard Smith, J. 1974. The theory of games and the evolution of animal conflicts. *Journal of Theoretical Biology* 497:209-21.

——. 1979. Game theory and the evolution of behavior. *Proceedings of the Royal Society of London* B205:475-88.

——. 1982. *Evolution and the theory of games*. Cambridge: Cambridge University Press.

Merton, R. K. 1968. *Social theory and social structure*. Glencoe, IL: Free Press.

Moser, P. K. ed. 1990. *Rationality in action: Contemporary approaches*. Cambridge: Cambridge University Press.

Parker, G. A. 1974. Assessment strategy and the evolution of animal conflicts. *Journal of Theoretical Biology* 47:223- 43.

Siegel, L. J. 1989. *Criminology*, 3d ed. St. Paul, MN: West.

Vila, B. J., and L. E. Cohen. 1992. Crime as strategy: A preliminary test of an evolutionary ecological theory of expropriative crime. Unpublished manuscript, University of California at Davis, Sociology Department.

Vold, G. B., and T. J. Bernard. 1986. *Theoretical criminology*, 3d ed. New York: Oxford.

Wilson, J. Q., and R. J. Herrnstein. 1985. *Crime and human nature*. New York: Simon & Schuster.

TALKING ABOUT CRIME: OBSERVATIONS ON THE PROSPECTS FOR CAUSAL THEORY IN CRIMINOLOGY*

Don C. Gibbons
Department of Sociology
Portland State University

INTRODUCTION

Over the past 35 years of involvement in the criminological enterprise, I have been engaged in a variety of activities. Many of them have centered on the query "What does it all mean?" In other words, I have concentrated on causal analysis, attempting to make sense of current theoretical directions and research evidence. I have authored a number of books as well as a collection of essays that take stock of the existing theory and empirical findings. Indeed, it might be said that I have been a criminological parasite, filching bits and pieces from a host of persons and assembling them in one book or another! *The Criminological Enterprise* was my effort to make sense of theoretical endeavors up to the end of the 1970s.[1]

All of this is by way of saying that I am currently writing a new book which is to some degree the continuation of *The Criminological Enterprise*. The earlier book, however, was mainly a history of ideas, largely restricted to sociological criminology; the new book will be concerned more with a critique of theories, including emphasis on formalization of arguments and the defects of discursive theorizing. It will also be concerned with key theoretical issues. For example, Kathryn Ann Farr and I (Farr and Gibbons 1990) authored a paper that discusses the need for a taxonomic system for making sense of the disparate forms of lawbreaking. That paper ultimately will find its way into the new book.

Today I single out a segment of this project for comment. More specifically, I ask whether the development of integrated and/or general theories is a viable goal for criminology.

---

*An earlier version of this text was delivered during Professor Gibbons' tenure as Beto Chair Professor in the College of Criminal Justice, in the spring semester of 1992.

135

THEORETICAL WORK IN CONTEMPORARY CRIMINOLOGY

In recent years, a number of persons have bemoaned the stagnation of criminological theory. For example, Meier (1980) argued that few new theoretical leads have been produced since the 1960s. A similar claim has been made by Australian criminologist John Braithwaite. In a particularly dismal summary of the current state of affairs, he asserted that

the present state of criminology is one of abject failure in its own terms. We cannot say anything convincing to the community about crime; we cannot prescribe policies that will work to reduce crime; we cannot in all honesty say that societies spending more on criminological research get better criminal justice policies than those that spend little or nothing on criminology (1989a:133).

Braithwaite attributed this sorry situation in part to the tendency of individual criminologists to engage in savaging the arguments of other scholars rather than attempting to build upon their efforts. He ended his essay with a call for work directed at the development of "clear, manipulable formulations that make for testable prediction" (133).

Braithwaite was born in the year I entered graduate school. From my longer time perspective, our situation seems less dismal than he describes. Criminologists currently display a good deal of interest in "Theory Work"--that is, construction and research scrutiny of causal arguments. Our stockpile of theoretical claims and research evidence has grown markedly since the 1950s, when Sutherland's theory of differential association was virtually the only game in town and when criminology textbooks were long on opinions and short on facts. In the 1950s we had no routine activities theorizing or research, no evidence on income inequality and crime, no substantial body of data on unemployment and crime, no sophisticated theories to account for state-by-state variations in rates of forcible rape, very few detailed analyses of white-collar crime, and no large literature on homicide. This list could be expanded considerably. In short, in comparison with the 1950s, we enjoy a surfeit of theoretical arguments and research evidence on which further work might proceed. Calls for theoretical integration and/or general theories have arisen because we have a large and bewildering collection, rather than a shortage, of criminological materials.

Why are some criminologists currently attempting to create general or integrated theories? In the case of general arguments, a number of scholars appear to believe that greater criminological progress is likely to occur if we develop a "central notion" to provide coherence to our endeavors. This view parallels Gibbs's (1989) advocacy of "control" as a central notion around which sociological inquiry might be structured. Criminology is not now guided by a central notion or organizing paradigm that is embraced by most scholars in the field.

The major argument in favor of theoretical integration is that a larger "bang for the buck" might come from an integrated causal theory than from various individual formulations, each of which accounts for only part of the variance in lawbreaking and conforming conduct. For example, this argument underpinned Johnson's (1979) integrated theory of delinquency.

Are general and/or integrated theories of criminality possible?[2] The answer depends in considerable measure on the standards by which theories are to be judged. If one is unconcerned about the *structural* and/or *empirical* adequacy of formulations, the response is obviously "yes." If one takes the position, however, that criminologists must endeavor to develop conceptually and structurally rigorous theories, the task may be considerably more difficult.

Let me comment further on the structural forms of criminological theorizing. In an earlier paper (Gibbons 1991) I drew on Gibbs's (1972) discussions of discursive and formal theory, arguing (as he did) that sociologists and criminologists ought to strive to construct formalized and rigorous theoretical statements to replace the fuzzy and ambiguous arguments that often pass for theory in our field. That paper also sorted a number of existing arguments in criminology into four broad categories along the dimension of discursiveness: general perspectives, discursive theories, semiformal theories, and formal theories (although the last category contains no entries!).

The idea of general theory is not entirely new. Criminology has long included a number of discursive, broad-ranging formulations that some persons have labeled as theories. Merton's (1938) "anomie" perspective was general, as were "social disorganization" views that were popular in the 1950s (e.g., Faris 1955). Carr's (1950) delinquency argument, Reckless's (1973) "containment theory," and Sutherland': (1947) differential association perspective are examples of somewhat better structured formulations.[3]

Some of the ventures toward general and/or integrated theories, such as those of Braithwaite (1989b) and Gottfredson and Hirschi (1990), are more tightly structured than the earlier statements of Merton, Sutherland, and others. As we shall see, however, criminologists have not managed to articulate a large collection of relatively formalized arguments in a general or integrated form.

To this point I have spoken of general and/or integrated theories as though criminologists agree on the meaning of these terms. In point of fact, however, considerable disagreement exists. Let us examine the lay of the land regarding these terms.

SOME DEFINITIONAL OBSERVATIONS

The basic idea of theoretical integration is straightforward; it concerns the combination of single theories or elements of those theories into a more comprehensive argument. At the same time, it would be well to note that in practice, integration is a matter of degree: some theorists have combined or integrated more concepts or theoretical elements than have others. Also, biological or psychological factors rarely have appeared in integrative expositions by sociological criminologists.

In addition, some integrated theories have been centered on a single form of criminality such as forcible rape. Others, according to their authors, apply equally well to a relatively broad collection of crime forms or patterns of criminality.

2

Consider the expositions by Braithwaite (1989b) and by Gottfredson and Hirschi (1990). Braithwaite declared that his book presents a general theory, and he also indicated his intent to integrate elements from a number of existing theoretical traditions with his own ideas about the role of shaming and reintegrative efforts in shaping criminal pathways. Although he did not specify the elements that identify theories as general, he apparently had in mind some kind of multivariate formulation that applies to a "significant portion" of the offender population, but not necessarily to all of it. In other words, Braithwaite apparently would argue that generality is a matter of degree. If an argument applies to a significant chunk of the lawbreaker population, it is general; if it applies only to rapists, murderers, or some other small subgroup, it is low on generality.

Gottfredson and Hirschi's *A General Theory of Crime* (1990) also lacked any explicit discussion of the identifying marks of a general theory. On the other hand, they asserted in various places that most (how many?) crimes require little skill and are mundane, rational, deliberate acts. They also devoted considerable space (1990:1-44) to the characteristics of "ordinary crime(s)," asserting that white-collar offenses, homicides, burglaries, and various other offenses are all relatively similar. That is, they have features in common; moreover, the persons who carry out these acts exhibit a good many common characteristics. The Gottfredson and Hirschi general theory runs as follows:

[C]rime involves the pursuit of immediate pleasure. It follows that people lacking self-control will also tend to pursue immediate pleasures that are not criminal: they will tend to smoke, drink, use drugs, gamble, have children out of wedlock, and engage in illicit sex (90).

This kind of general theory is different from Braithwaite's. It is general in that it asserts that various forms of deviant conduct have much in common and that persons who lack self-control are most likely to engage in deviance, but it lacks any appreciation of other causal factors such as Braithwaite's theory contains.

If we were to pursue these distinctions further, we could produce a fourfold table of theory types, or an n by n one if we made finer distinctions along two classificatory dimensions. This fourfold table would sort theories as specific or general and as integrated or unintegrated. Braithwaite's (1989b) theory is both general and integrated, whereas Gottfredson and Hirschi's (1990) is a general theory that emphasizes lack of self-control to the exclusion of other variables; thus it is not an integrated argument. Baron and Straus's (1990) theory of variations in forcible rape rates, which combines gender inequality, pornography readership, social disorganization, and "cultural spillover" arguments, is a specific, integrated argument; so is Ellis's (1989) controversial "synthesized theory of rape," in which one of the factors to which rape is linked is high levels of androgen (male hormone) among forcible rapists.[4] Finally, the income inequality explanation of predatory crime is an entry in the nongeneral (specific) and nonintegrated cell.

Other distinctions among theories also ought to be noted. Theorists have produced a wide array of accounts dealing with causal processes; thus some system for ordering these viewpoints is needed. Often they have been sorted in terms of their major explanatory variables: biogenic, psychogenic, and sociogenic, with perhaps a residual category for approaches such as rational choice, which is favored by economists and some other investigators.

Particularly important is the distinction made many years ago by Cressey (1960) between causal accounts focused on epidemiology and those focused on individual conduct. I have borrowed this distinction (Gibbons 1991, 1992) and have renamed the two problems as those of social structure and crime and the "Why do they do it?" question. When Cressey spoke of epidemiology, he meant explanations of crime in the aggregate: that is, rural-urban distributions, relationships between social class and crime, variations in male and female crime rates, and the like. By contrast, theories centered on individual conduct point to factors that determine whether specific individuals engage in crime or refrain from it. Differential association theory is a prominent example of this second category.

Some theoretical statements have paid attention jointly to social-structural factors that appear to explain crime rates and to the processes by which individuals become engaged in lawbreaking. Many formulations, however, including general and integrated ones, have focused mainly on one or the other, of these matters but not on both.[5] Accordingly it makes considerable sense to sort theories in terms of the explanatory level at which they are pitched.

THE LOGIC OF INTEGRATED AND GENERAL THEORIES

The basic argument for theoretical integration seems reasonable: namely that it will give us a "bigger bang for the buck" in the way of explanatory prowess than will a narrower formulation which includes only a portion of the relevant independent variables (Elliott 1985). This thesis runs through a number of recent statements on theoretical integration, including the volume that resulted from a conference on theoretical integration held at SUNY-Albany in 1988 (Messner, Krohn, and Liska 1989). Yet although this argument seems commonsensically plausible, more than meets the eye may be involved here. Hirschi (1979) has been a particularly vigorous critic of the idea of integration. He notes that it may be impossible to merge concepts drawn from theories which are based on differing underlying "domain assumptions" without creating a theoretical "stew" which does violence to these assumptions. In his view, we would do better to devote our energies to the development of specific lines of theorizing and to research testing of competing theories.

As for general theory, its underlying premise seems counterintuitive to many persons. Scholars often have contended that the forms of criminal conduct or the types of persons who engage in these disparate acts cannot possibly be explained by a single, overarching theory.

There is no logical principle, however, that can be invoked in order to deny the idea of general theory. On the contrary, Braithwaite (1989a) argues that in order for a general theory of crime to be developed, it is necessary only that instances of it have *some* characteristics in common; They need not be homogeneous on all dimensions. The task of the theorist is to identify those commonalities which justify treating some congeries of activity as a single category or form. As Braithwaite put it: "In advance, giraffes, clover and newts might seem a hopelessly heterogeneous class, yet the theory of evolution shows how the proof of the pudding is in the eating (1989a:130)."

The most detailed discussion of general theory in criminology was provided by Tittle (1985). After establishing some metes and bounds around this notion, he reviewed five forms of what he termed "futilitarianism"--that is, objections to the goal of general theory. One of these is that the subject matter of criminology is ambiguous because of the relativity of laws over time and from place to place. A second objection concerns the alleged heterogeneity of our subject matter, which requires separate explanations for different crimes or criminals.

Tittle's third contention regarding the futility of general theory efforts is in the ethnomethodology genre: to wit, crime-related social processes are situationally problematic rather than recurrent, orderly, and concrete. As a result, we cannot generalize about them within the framework of a general theory based on assumptions that criminal acts, causes of lawbreaking, and responses to criminality are objective and predictable social facts. A fourth argument is that crime-related phenomena are produced by myriad and diverse factors; thus broad causal generalizations cannot be constructed. Finally, Tittle noted the claim that past efforts at general theory have failed; thus there is little reason to suppose that such endeavors will pay off in the future.

After presenting these negative views, Tittle challenged them effectively. I do not have time to review his counterarguments, but I concede that he, and Braithwaite as well, have provided convincing rebuttals to "futilitarianism" views which deny, in principle, the possibility of general theory. To echo "the proof is in the pudding": general and/or integrated theories may be achievable in principle but not in fact.

Let us examine the results of efforts that have been made in these directions. In the comments below, I include formulations dealing with delinquency within the category of criminological theory.

THEORETICAL INTEGRATION IN CRIMINOLOGY

INTEGRATED THEORIES OF DELINQUENCY

Attempts to account for juvenile delinquency have taken a number of directions, including various biogenic and psychogenic formulations, social disorganization and social control perspectives, social status and opportunity arguments, and theories of cultural values and social learning. Each of these may contribute to explaining delinquency (Empey 1982; Gibbons and Krohn 1991; Quay 1987); thus some scholars have concluded that a theory which combines elements of these viewpoints may do a better job of accounting for delinquency than will any single one.

One of the most ambitious integrative efforts was made by Colvin and Pauly (1983). They described it as a structural Marxist theory centered around the following proposition: "This entire process of delinquency production is comprehended as a latent outcome of the reproduction of capitalist relations of production and the class structure" (515).

This theory was painted in broad strokes and involved several claims of debatable accuracy. For example, one major contention centered on the harmful effects of tracking experiences on schoolchildren, but the evidence on this negative impact is not entirely clear. In addition, the theory was discursive; it was relatively rich in texture and was filled with details from other lines of discursive theory on which it drew, such as compliance theory, structural Marxism, and the like. Although the argument was provocative and insightful, it leaves a good bit to be desired if judged by the criterion of theoretical rigor.

Johnson's (1979) less global integration of delinquency theories involved several broad groups of factors: social class, family experiences, perceptions of future opportunities, delinquent associates, delinquent values, and deterrence (perceptions of the risks of being apprehended for delinquent acts). Johnson brought together these factors into a path-analytic model, which identified a number of independent "paths" or causal sequences that he hypothesized to be linked to delinquent conduct. His research provided mixed support for this model.

The third integrative effort, by Elliott, Ageton, and Canter (1979), linked social learning/differential association, control theory, and strain arguments into a single, relatively complex formulation. Elliott and his associates also conducted a large-scale study of delinquency and drug use which employed this integrated theory as its theoretical framework (Elliott, Huizinga, and Ageton 1983). Hirschi (1987), however, reviewed the Elliott, Huizinga, and Ageton findings and concluded that they did not provide much empirical support for the theory that governed the study.

INTEGRATED THEORIES OF ADULT CRIMINALITY

The preceding remarks suggest that the integration of delinquency theories is no small task. If this is so, one might wonder whether such formulations about adult criminality are possible at all, in that juvenile lawbreaking is considerably more homogeneous than adult criminality. Scholars, however, have made attempts at conceptual and theoretical integration regarding adult crime, including one by Pearson and Weiner (1985).

Pearson and Weiner began by surveying a number of criminology journals in order to identify the most frequently mentioned theories in the literature. They generated a curious list of explanatory perspectives that differ widely as to the scope of what they endeavor to explain. For example, the routine activities approach is concerned mainly with predatory property crimes, whereas differential association is meant to explain all forms of criminal behavior. Also, Pearson and Weiner made no attempt to evaluate the degrees of empirical support for the various theories that were to be integrated; as a

4

result, one might wonder about the quality of the product when empirically shaky arguments are merged with others that have considerable empirical support.

Pearson and Weiner's integration translated concepts from various theories into a common vocabulary rather than combining different propositions into a single theory. For example, they asserted that many of the terms used in differential association theory are analogous to those in other formulations.

Pearson and Weiner's conceptual integration involved a set of concepts with which others were to be "integrated." The authors used an operant conditioning framework involving such terms as *behavior, utilities, utility demand,* and *discriminative stimuli*; this framework also included a place for rule-governed behavior that had been formed by earlier contingency-shaped learning.

This social learning argument contains little that is novel, but the plot thickened in Pearson and Weiner's elaboration. They presented a graphic version labeled as a dynamic model of micro-level factors influencing the probability of criminal behavior, complete with pseudomathematical notation and narrative statements such as "the probability of apprehension and processing by the cjs (criminal justice system) (K2) is denoted by Qj, while the probability of not being apprehended by the cjc is 1 - Qj" (1985:123). Big deal!

Because their social learning framework was psychological and social psychological, and focused on the individual level of explanation, Pearson and Weiner added constructs of "*social structural production and distribution of* (1) utilities, (2) opportunities, (3) rules of morality and expedience, and (4) beliefs about sanctioning practices" (emphasis in the original) in order to account for macro-level causal theories. They also put forth a number of pedestrian observations such as the following: "Behavior is partly dependent upon the legitimate role and status *opportunities* available to the individual. These opportunities are not distributed equally across all structural locations" (1985:126; emphasis in the original).

Pearson and Weiner's conceptual integration consisted, in part, of a table in which their "integrative concepts" were arranged along one axis and the various criminological theories that were to be integrated were listed along the other. The cells were filled with check marks showing where various concepts from differential association or other theories were "mapped into" (their term) the integrative concepts.

"Mapping" refers to a relatively arbitrary process of shoehorning concepts into spaces in a summary table. For example, consider the treatment of Sutherland's assertions that: "the process of learning criminal behavior involves all of the mechanisms that are involved in any other learning" and that "criminal behavior is an expression of general needs and values" (Sutherland and Cressey 1978:82). Pearson and Weiner (1985:130-33) concluded that these statements were alternative ways of speaking of utility demand; they overlooked the fact that the former were disclaimers about factors that Sutherland viewed as *peripheral* rather than as core ingredients of the theory. Along the same line, they contended that "definitions favorable to the violation of legal codes" is another way of speaking of rationalizations, or what they also called "rules of expedience." Sutherland, however, argued that

definitions *precede* criminal acts, whereas "rationalizations" are exculpatory defenses of one's conduct invoked *after the fact.* Then, too, Pearson and Weiner did not mention the crucial dimensions along which differential associations vary, namely intensity, frequency, duration, and priority. Similar problems are found throughout this entire "mapping" exercise.

What should be said about this conceptual integration? In my opinion, there is little to be gained from exercises that merely attempt to reconcile a number of mushy and poorly defined concepts from one perspective with those from another.

Another integrated (and general) theory can be found in Wilson and Herrnstein's *Crime and Human Nature* (1985), in which the authors articulated a "comprehensive theory of crime" and reviewed the related evidence. Their title implies that the book contains a theory of lawbreaking in all of its forms, but in fact it is restricted to persons who engage in "aggressive, violent, or larcenous behavior" or to individuals who "hit, rape, murder, steal, and threaten" (22). It makes no mention of inside traders, violators of occupational safety regulations, plunderers of savings and loans, or other kinds of criminality and criminals. Further, the authors' claim that offenders exhibit mesomorphic bodily structure, somewhat lower intelligence than their noncriminal peers, and impulsivity and other psychological traits that free them from restraint against lawbreaking seems (at least to me) to have little applicability to Ivan Boesky, Don Dixon, Charles Keating, and other criminals of that ilk.

The core of Wilson and Herrnstein's (1985:41-66) "theory" of criminal behavior was an eclectic, social learning-behavioral choice formulation. The chapter in which they outlined this theory included a number of pseudomathematical formulas; the appendix (531-35) presented what they referred to as the full "mathematical" version of the theory. No *values*, however, were assigned to any of the symbols or equations; thus the argument has the appearance but not the substance of precision.

As Gibbs (1985) noted, Wilson and Herrnstein stated discursively most of their claims about the link between criminality and impulsivity, low intelligence, hereditary factors, family and school experiences, the effects of the mass media, and other variables. In view of the imprecision of their argument, as well as the equivocal or incomplete nature of much of the criminological evidence, it is little wonder that reviewers have produced widely varying assessments of this book (Cohen 1987; Gibbons 1987; Gibbs 1985; Kamin 1986; Sarri 1987; Schrag 1987). Some have praised it, but others have claimed that the authors either unwittingly or deliberately misinterpreted or distorted many of the findings upon which they drew, while ignoring a body of other research results that ran counter to their position.[7]

The Wilson and Herrnstein book appeared in 1985, accompanied by dust-jacket puffery that described it as "a major contribution to criminology" and as "a magisterial survey of the now very extensive literature." It passed from the scene rather quickly, however, in considerable part because of the flaws it contains which were reported by the critics. Like a number of other "blockbuster" books in sociology and criminology, it had a relatively short shelf life.

5

This review suggests that integrative efforts have not been entirely successful. Colvin and Pauly's (1983) global and discursive argument consists of an amalgam of claims, some of which lack empirical support. The integrations of Johnson and of Elliott et al. are more narrowly focused, being largely developmental and social psychological. Efforts to test these arguments have led to equivocal results. The conceptual integration by Pearson and Weiner is unimpressive at best. Finally, the comprehensive theory proposed by Wilson and Herrnstein is less precise and less rigorous than claimed by the authors. Moreover, the evidence that they adduce for it is less than convincing.

GENERAL THEORY: TWO RECENT CASES

BRAITHWAITE'S THEORY OF REINTEGRATIVE SHAMING

One of the more significant theoretical expositions to appear in the last few years is Braithwaite's *Crime, Shame, and Reintegration* (1989b). As I noted earlier, this book advanced an integrated and general theory.[8] After grappling with the question of whether crime is sufficiently homogeneous to justify the articulation of a general theory, Braithwaite reviewed a number of existing arguments about lawbreaking: labeling, subcultural claims, control theory, opportunity formulations, and learning theories. He concluded that these viewpoints offer much of value, but also that they do not account for many of the facts of crime that must be explained.[9] His general and integrated theory added another element to the mix, namely *reintegrative shaming*, which concerns positive and negative *reactions* to lawbreakers. Some sense of his theory is captured in the following passage:

> Let us simplify the relevance of this chapter by imagining Fagin's lair as something of a caricature of a criminal subculture. We need control theory to bring young offenders to the doorstep of the criminal subculture (primary deviance); stigmatization (labeling theory) to open the door; subcultural and learning theory to maintain the lair as a rewarding place for secondary deviants to stay in; and opportunity theory to explain how such criminal subcultures come to exist in the first place. This is the scheme supplied by the theory of reintegrative shaming to synthesizing the dominant theoretical traditions (1989b).

The unique ingredient in Braithwaite's integrated argument, reintegrative shaming, involves "expressions of community disapproval, which may range from mild rebuke to degradation ceremonies, which are followed by gestures of reacceptance into the community of law-abiding citizens" (55). Stigmatizing forms of social disapproval frequently drive lawbreakers into further acts of misbehavior, whereas reintegrative shaming often works to bring them back into line.

A large part of Braithwaite's analysis centered on the personal characteristics and societal conditions that encourage or discourage reintegrative shaming. In particular, persons who are cut off from intensive social ties with others are least likely to be influenced by shaming; conversely, socially bonded persons are amenable to the positive influences of shaming. Societies low on "communitarianism" are not likely to be highly successful at reintegrative shaming. It is most effective in communitarian societies, of which Japan is a notable example.

Braithwaite's elaboration of this argument was similar to much other criminological theorizing. Much of it was discursive: concepts were introduced and were mixed in with illustrative material intended to illuminate the conceptual notions.

Braithwaite's book is highly provocative; I have provided only a very brief outline here. Although the book is pregnant with stimulating ideas, it is also true that the author experienced some of the same difficulties as the rest of us who try to commit our thoughts to paper. His narrative contains soft spots and unclear passages.

On page 1 in his book, Braithwaite asserted that the key to crime control is reintegrative shaming; on the same page, however, he spoke of the types of shaming which *cause* rather than prevent crime. He also contended that "individuals who resort to crime are those insulated from shame over their wrongdoing." It is not entirely clear whether his argument focuses mainly on influences that succeed or fail in deterring "primary deviants" from further misbehavior or whether it also asks why people flirt with lawbreaking in the first place.

My own interpretation is that persons who are unbonded or lacking in interdependence become involved initially in acts of lawbreaking because the bite of conscience is lacking in their cases. They feel no *anticipatory shame* (my term) when they contemplate embarking upon misdeeds; thus they fail to police themselves by directing shame at themselves. In addition, persons who engage in initial acts of lawbreaking or flirtations with misconduct are less susceptible to *reactive shaming by others* and thus are likely to continue to engage in misbehavior.

Another unclear line of analysis pertains to white-collar crime. White-collar criminality did not appear in the inventory of basic facts about lawbreaking enumerated early in the book. Also, it seems doubtful that these offenders are low on interdependency in the same way as the unskilled street criminals who commit crude predatory offenses and who are at the center of much of Braithwaite's argument.

Although Braithwaite's book has rough spots, it is an important contribution to theory. One reviewer (Scheff 1990) likened Braithwaite to a "new Durkheim," and concluded that "[The book] will, I believe, generate new ideas and research into the foreseeable future." That forecast, however, may be overoptimistic.

GOTTFREDSON AND HIRSCHI'S GENERAL THEORY

Let me turn to Gottfredson and Hirschi's (1990) *A General Theory of Crime*, which might be titled more accurately *A General Theory of Some Instances of Some Forms of Crime*.

Much of the content of this relatively small volume is drawn from various published works by the authors, dealing with crime and age relationships, social control, and other

6

matters. The book reprises a number of pithy observations made earlier by these authors. For example, Gottfredson and Hirschi zap those criminologists who have oversold longitudinal cohort studies as the way to criminological salvation, as well as those who have contributed heavily to criminological confusion with the notion of "criminal careers." Also, their remarks about biological positivism, particularly the shortcomings of twin studies, are revealing. Ultimately, however, the book will be judged on the basis of whether the authors have made a persuasive case for their general theory.

Although this book is complex, provocative, and controversial, its central theme is straightforward: criminals and other deviants exhibit low self-control. Most of the other causal influences that loom large in the thinking of many criminologists are dismissed as secondary or unimportant influences at best or as wrongheaded at worst.

Another key claim in this book is that most lawbreaking is "ordinary crime" which consists of trivial and mundane criminal acts (16). For example, the authors describe "the standard or ordinary embezzlement" (39) as follows: "In the ordinary embezzlement a young man recently steals money from his employer's cash register or goods from his store." They say that embezzlement of large amounts of money by older employees in positions of trust is a "rarity." Many criminologists are likely to be troubled by these observations and will be moved to ask: "How trivial? How ordinary? How rare?" Then, too, the evidence does not support the authors' frequent assertion that most offenders who engage in repeated offenses commit a wide range of crimes. Rather, the available data suggest that although repeat offenders do not usually specialize in a single form of crime, their "careers" are not entirely unpatterned.

Polk and Ranson (1991) take issue with Gottfredson and Hirschi's contentions about "the typical homicide," arguing that few of the Australian homicide cases they studied fit their characterization. Other critics suggest that the book contains a highly distorted picture of white-collar crime. For one thing, embezzlements frequently are carried out by older persons, and they often involve relatively large amounts of money. Even more to the point, Gottfredson and Hirschi perform some verbal legerdemain on the notion of white-collar crime: They acknowledge no savings and loan plunderers, corporate miscreants, or other upper-world lawbreakers.

Gottfredson and Hirschi's theory is more than a little circular. The authors describe the dependent variable, deviance and criminality, as trivial and mundane behavior, requiring little or no planning or skill for commission. If they are correct in this description, surely it would not come as much of a surprise if we were to discover that lawbreakers and deviants are low on social control, lack long-term goals, and are not overbright. But as I have stated, it is by no means clear that the "facts" marshaled by Gottfredson and Hirschi in their book demonstrate the validity of this thesis.

SOME OTHER CONSIDERATIONS

A number of other issues regarding integrated and general theories ought to receive attention, but I can only mention them here. One nagging issue is most criminologists' inattention to the possibility that biological factors are involved in criminality. In my opinion, criminologists ultimately must come to grips with biological hypotheses and findings. Several recent reviews of the evidence have strengthened the view that "there may be something there" (Ellis and Hoffman 1990; Fishbein 1990; Gibbons 1992:138-69; Trasler 1987).

An equally thorny issue that sociological criminologists have not addressed adequately is the role of psychological factors in criminality. Who would be so bold as to deny the existence of "monsters" among the offender population--that is, individuals who are "socialization failures" and who, by any reasonable definition, are markedly abnormal persons? Who would endeavor to account for such persons as Ted Bundy, John Gacy, Richard Speck, or Jeffrey Dahmer through the principles of differential association or by invoking Gottfredson and Hirschi's notion of low social control? Put another way, some offenders are truly aberrant persons whose personality patterns mark them off from garden-variety violators.

One possible response to this claim about "monsters" is that it is relevant to only a small part of the offender population; thus socialization failure and aberrant personality patterns are relatively infrequent factors in lawbreaking.

Some persons, however, contend that involvement in criminality and avoidance of lawbreaking conduct are nearly always due, at least in part, to individual differences in psychological characteristics. Andrews and Wormith (1989) asserted that many sociological criminologists have engaged in "knowledge destruction," denying the evidence of the role of psychological patterns in criminality. In my rejoinder to their paper (Gibbons 1989) I suggested that Andrews and Wormith had constructed a "straw person": individual differences in personality characteristics may well make a difference, as far as involvement in criminality is concerned. For example, persons with a taste for living on the edge may be more likely to engage in various kinds of criminal "risk-taking" than individuals of a more conservative disposition. Indeed, Katz (1988) authored a provocative, although somewhat murky, treatise that draws attention to the "moral and sensual attractions of doing evil." It is also clear, however, that criminologists have given relatively little attention to spelling out how individual psychological differences are implicated in various forms of criminality. The task of integrating sociological with psychological lines of argument has scarcely begun.

CONCLUDING REMARKS

In this paper I have taken note of the various meanings of notions such as "general theory" and "integrated theory." I also examined efforts that have been made to date to articulate general and/or integrated theoretical arguments. Two concluding observations about these efforts are in order.

First, these products vary widely. Thus some are broader and more general than others, and some endeavor to merge more factors or variables than do others. Second, all of the formulations considered here are relatively discursive. For example, some are less than clear about the dependent variable that they endeavor to explain; others contain murky concepts and fuzzy propositions.

7

Some critics believe that efforts directed at general or integrated theories have not succeeded and that further ventures of this sort inevitably will fail, largely because of the heterogeneity involved in criminality. According to the pessimists, specific theories are required for the various forms of lawbreaking.

Although this contention of heterogeneity is plausible, it is not logically compelling. Braithwaite (1989b) and Gottfredson and Hirschi (1990) may turn out to be correct in their claim that certain common threads run throughout a host of seemingly unlike forms of criminal conduct.

I suspect, however, that the pessimists are correct. The compass of the criminal law in contemporary societies is extremely broad; it covers myriad acts that have little in common with each other except that they have been proscribed or prescribed by some legislative body.

Although criminologists have made relatively little progress on developing an agreed-upon taxonomic system for sorting forms of crime into theoretically meaningful groups (Farr and Gibbons 1990), my guess is that progress lies in the direction of theories focused on specific forms of lawbreaking. Much of the evidence reviewed in my criminology text (Gibbons 1992) appears to me to support this proposition. Recent studies such as the Weisburd, Wheeler, Waring, and Bode (1991) investigation of white-collar federal offenders point in the same direction. These researchers identified four relatively distinct groups among the offenders they studied. In summary, the relatively modest goal of developing a "family of theories" may make the greatest sense for the criminological enterprise.[10]

NOTES

[1]My delinquency text (Gibbons and Krohn 1991) and my criminology book (Gibbons 1992) are also efforts at stocktaking.

[2]Throughout this paper I have tried to refrain from speaking of general theories of *crime*, even though some of the major theoretical works that are discussed here were described by their authors as presenting such theories (Braithwaite 1989b; Gottfredson and Hirschi 1990). Instead I have identified the arguments discussed here as theories dealing with criminality, criminal behavior, delinquency, and delinquent behavior. It seems preferable to reserve the term *theories of crime* for those efforts which have been made to account for the creation, by legislatures and other lawmaking bodies, of criminal statutes, delinquency codes, and the like. Put another way, the general theories discussed in this paper center on the law-violating behavior of persons, rather than on the social forces that led initially to the creation of legal norms.

[3]For more detailed comments on the flaws of anomie theory, see Gibbons and Jones (1975:88-97). For a discussion of the development of differential association theory, see Gibbons (1979:48-61). The nature of containment theory and its strengths and weaknesses are discussed in Gibbons and Krohn (1991:107-109).

[4]Ellis's arguments have received vigorous criticism from Barth (1991) and from Fish (1990).

[5]Two theories that have attended to both of these causal questions are those of Johnson (1979) and Colvin and Pauly (1983).

[6]The end product of this part of Pearson and Weiner's (1985:128) conceptual integration is a figure labeled "Dynamic Model of the Probability of Criminal Behavior," involving a flow diagram which vaguely resembles a path diagram and to which a variety of pseudomathematical notations are attached. Yet, it is difficult to see how this presentation is an advance over a more discursive version of the same argument, because it only appears to be precise, but is not.

[7]These remarks about quarrels over the meaning and significance of empirical findings assume that all of the disputants are devotees of scientific method and practitioners of scientific standards; therefore, they disagree because of flaws or gaps in the data. Yet there is more than a little reason to suspect that some of these quarrels are between criminologists who knowingly play fast and loose with the evidence and criminologists who follow the rules of proper inference and the like. In particular, a number of Herrnstein and Wilson's (1985) conclusions appear to constitute stretching of the data well beyond anything that can reasonably be concluded from those data.

[8]Braithwaite's book was the 1991 winner of the Michael J. Hindelang Award of the American Society of Criminology, given to the book judged to have made the greatest contribution during the preceding three years. (Also see note 2.) Technically speaking, Braithwaite presented a general theory of criminality (behavior) rather than of crime (the nature and origins of legal rules). In my discussion of his book, I follow him in speaking of "crime," but readers should interpret these comments as pertaining to "criminal behavior."

[9]Braithwaite contended that those formulations which he reviewed do not explain adequately the basic facts of crime. What are those facts? He asserted that the major ones are as follows:

1. *Crime is committed disproportionately by males.*
2. *Crime is committed disproportionately by 15- to 25-year-olds.*
3. *Crime is committed disproportionately by unmarried people.*
4. *Crime is committed disproportionately by people living in large cities.*
5. *Crime is committed disproportionately by people who have experienced high residential mobility and who live in areas characterized by high residential mobility.*
6. *Young people who are strongly attached to their school are less likely to engage in crime.*
7. *Young people who have high educational and occupational aspirations are less likely to engage in crime.*
8. *Young people who do poorly in school are more likely to engage in crime.*

8

9. *Young people who are strongly attached to their parents are less likely to engage in crime.*

10. *Young people who have friendships with criminals are more likely to engage in crime themselves.*

11. *People who believe strongly in the importance of complying with the law are less likely to violate the law.*

12. *For both women and men, being at the bottom of the class structure, whether measured by socioeconomic status, socioeconomic status of the area in which the person lives, being unemployed, or being a member of an oppressed racial minority (e.g., blacks in the U.S.), increases rates of offending for all types of crime apart from those for which opportunities are systematically less available to the poor (e.g., white-collar crime).*

13. *Crime rates have been increased since World War II in most countries, both developed and developing. Japan is the only country which has been clearly shown to have a falling crime rate in this period* (1989b:44-50; emphasis in the original)

[10]By a family of theories, I mean formulations which are specific to or focused on particular forms of crime but which may have some concepts or other ingredients in common. For example, income inequality may be an important factor both in predatory crime and in violence, but additional variables may be specific to predatory crime or to violence. Also, I do *not* refer to very narrowly defined "crime patterns" such as vandalism on public transit vehicles in Portland, Oregon or public intoxication in Huntsville, Texas. For one indication of the type of crime categories I have in mind, see Farr and Gibbons (1990).

REFERENCES

Andrews, D.A. and J. Stephen Wormith (1989) "Personality and Crime: Knowledge Destruction and Construction in Criminology." *Justice Quarterly* 6:289-309.

Baron, Larry and Murray A. Straus (1990) *Four Theories of Rape.* New Haven: Yale University Press.

Barth, Pauline (1991) "Review." *Contemporary Sociology* 20:268-70.

Braithwaite, John (1989a) "The State of Criminology: Theoretical Decay or Renaissance." *Australian and New Zealand Journal of Criminology* 22:129-35.

_____ (1989b) *Crime, Shame, and Reintegration* Cambridge: Cambridge University Press.

Cohen, Lawrence E. (1987) "Review: Throwing Down the Gauntlet: A Challenge to the Relevance of Sociology for the Etiology of Criminal Behavior." *Contemporary Sociology* 16:202-205.

Colvin, Mark and John Pauly (1983) "A Critique of Criminology: Toward an Integrated Structural-Marxist Theory of Delinquency Production." *American Journal of Sociology* 89:513-51.

Cressey, Donald Roy (1960) "Epidemiology and Individual Conduct: A Case from Criminology." *Pacific Sociological Review* 3:47-58.

Elliott, Delbert S. (1985) "The Assumption That Theories Can Be Combined with Increased Explanatory Power: Theoretical Integrations." In Robert F. Meier (ed.) *Theoretical Methods in Criminology,* pp. 123-49. Beverly Hills: Sage.

Elliott, Delbert S., Suzanne S. Ageton, and Rachelle J. Canter (1979) "An Integrated Theoretical Perspective on Delinquent Behavior." *Journal of Research in Crime and Delinquency* 16:3-27.

Elliott, Delbert S., David Huizinga, and Suzanne S. Ageton (1985) *Explaining Delinquency and Drug Use.* Beverly Hills: Sage.

Ellis, Lee (1989) *Theories of Rape.* New York: Hemisphere.

Empey, LaMar T. (1982) *American Delinquency.* Revised ed. Homewood, IL: Dorsey.

Faris, Robert E.L. (1955) *Social Disorganization.* 2nd ed. New York: Ronald.

Farr, Kathryn Ann and Don C. Gibbons (1990) "Observations on the Development of Crime Categories." *International Journal of Offender Therapy and Comparative Criminology* 34:1223-38.

Fish, Virginia Kemp (1990) "Review." *Deviant Behavior* 11:99-102.

Fishbein, Diana H. (1990) "Biological Perspectives in Criminology." *Criminology* 28:27-72.

Gibbons, Don C. (1979) *The Criminological Enterprise.* Englewood Cliffs, NJ: Prentice-Hall.

_____ (1987) "Review." *Society* 24:92-93.

_____ (1989) "Comments--Personality and Crime: Non-Issues, Real Issues, and a Theory and Research Agenda." *Justice Quarterly* 6:311-23.

_____ (1991) "Talking about Crime and Criminals: Some Comments on the Structure of Criminological Theories." Paper presented at meetings of the Pacific Sociological Association.

_____ (1992) *Society, Crime, and Criminal Behavior.* 6th ed. Englewood Cliffs, NJ: Prentice-Hall.

Gibbons, Don C. and Joseph F. Jones (1975) *The Study of Deviance.* Englewood Cliffs, NJ: Prentice-Hall.

Gibbons, Don C. and Marvin D. Krohn (1991) *Delinquent Behavior.* 5th ed. Englewood Cliffs, NJ: Prentice-Hall.

Gibbs, Jack P. (1972) *Sociological Theory Construction.* Hinsdale, IL: Dryden.

_____ (1985) "Review Essay." *Criminology* 23:381-88.

_____ (1989) *Control: Sociology's Central Notion.* Urbana, IL: University of Illinois Press.

Gottfredson, Michael R. and Travis Hirschi (1990) *A General Theory of Crime.* Stanford, CA: Stanford University Press.

Hirschi, Travis (1969) *Causes of Delinquency.* Berkeley: University of California Press.

_____ (1987) "Review." *Criminology* 25:193-201.

_____ (1979) "Separate and Equal Is Better." *Journal of Research in Crime and Delinquency* 16:34-38.

Johnson, Richard E. (1979) *Delinquency and its Origins.* New York: Cambridge University Press.

9

Kamin, Leon J. (1986) "Is Crime in the Genes? The Answer May Depend on Who Chooses What Evidence." *Scientific American* 254:22-27.

Katz, Jack (1988) *Seductions of Crime.* New York: Basic Books.

Meier, Robert F. (1980) "Review Essay: The Arrested Development of Criminological Theory." *Contemporary Sociology* 9:374-76.

Merton, Robert K. (1938) "Social Structure and Anomie." *American Sociological Review* 3:672-82.

Messner, Steven F., Marvin D. Krohn, and Alan E. Liska, eds. (1989) *Theoretical Integration in the Study of Deviance and Crime.* Albany, NY: SUNY Press.

Pearson, Frank and Neil Alan Weiner (1985) "Toward an Integration of Criminological Theories." *Journal of Criminal Law and Criminology* 76:116-50.

Polk, Kenneth and David Ranson (1991) "Patterns of Homicide in Victoria." In Duncan Chappell, Peter Grabosky, and Heather Strang (eds.), *Australian Violence,* pp. 53-118. Canberra: Australian Institute of Criminology.

Quay, Herbert C., ed. (1987) *Handbook of Juvenile Delinquency.* New York: Wiley.

Reckless, Walter C. (1973) *The Crime Problem.* 5th ed. Santa Monica: Goodyear.

Sarri, Rosemary (1987) "Review." *Social Work* 32:259.

Scheff, Thomas J. (1990) "Review Essay: A New Durkheim." *American Journal of Sociology* 96:741-46.

Schrag, Clarence C. (1987) "Review." *Crime and Delinquency* 33:155-60.

Sutherland, Edwin (1947) Principles of Criminology. 4th ed. Philadelphia: Lippincott.

Sutherland, Edwin H. and Donald R. Cressey (1978) *Criminology.* 10th ed. Philadelphia: Lippincott.

Tittle, Charles R. (1985) "The Assumption That General Theories Are Not Possible." In Robert F. Meier (ed.) *Theoretical Methods in Criminology,* pp. 93-121. Beverly Hills: Sage.

Trasler, Gordon (1987) "Biogenetic Factors in Crime." In Herbert C. Quay (ed.) *Handbook of Juvenile Delinquency,* pp. 184-215. New York: Wiley.

Weisburd, David, Stanton Wheeler, Elin Waring, and Nancy Bode (1991) *Crimes of the Middle Class.* New Haven: Yale University Press.

Wilson, James Q. and Richard J. Herrnstein (1985) *Crime and Human Nature.* New York: Simon and Schuster.

ABOUT THE AUTHOR

Don C. Gibbons is Emeritus Professor of Urban Studies and Sociology at Portland State University. He is the author of a number of papers and books in criminology, including *Changing the Lawbreaker* and *Society, Crime, and Criminal Behavior.* He is a fellow of the American Society of Criminology and Editor of *Crime and Delinquency.* His latest book, *Talking About Crime,* which contains an expanded version of this paper, will be published by Prentice-Hall in 1993.

10

144

SOCIAL AREA INFLUENCES ON DELINQUENCY: A MULTILEVEL ANALYSIS

DENISE C. GOTTFREDSON
RICHARD J. McNEIL III
GARY D. GOTTFREDSON

One research tradition in criminology has focused on the distribution of crime rates among social areas, and a second tradition has examined the distribution of crime among individuals. Rarely are both traditions combined in a single study. This study explores social area influences on the delinquent behavior of 3,729 adolescents who are clustered within diverse social areas. The research examines mechanisms through which the characteristics of social areas —measured independently of the characteristics of the individuals—contribute to the explanation of individual delinquent conduct. Results imply that social areas have a small effect on individual delinquent behavior. Individuals living in areas characterized by weakened family units and social disorganization report more negative peer influence and less attachment and commitment to school than do individuals living in more organized areas. Results imply that these intermediary effects produce more male aggressive crime. Females in disorganized areas also report more aggressive crimes, but the effect is only partially mediated by the theoretical intervening variables in the model. On the other hand, males living in more affluent areas report more property crimes. This area effect is present regardless of the age, race, or socioeconomic status of the respondents and is not mediated by social bonding or delinquent associates.

Crime rates are generally higher in densely populated inner city areas than in other areas. Several theories attempt to explain why individuals living in

Based on papers presented at the Annual Meeting of the American Society of Criminology, Montreal, November 1987. Preparation of the article was supported in part by grant no. 85-IJ-CX-0059 from the National Institute of Justice, U.S. Department of Justice. The opinions expressed in this article are those of the authors and do not necessarily reflect the position or policy of the Department. Some of the census data used in the study were made available by the Interuniversity Consortium for Political and Social Research, University of Michigan. We are grateful for the help of Renee Castañeda who mapped street addresses to census areas, Charles Fox who made the maps available, Douglas Smith and Charles Wellford who offered helpful comments, and Renee Castañeda, Lois Hybl, and Mark Melia who provided office assistance.

JOURNAL OF RESEARCH IN CRIME AND DELINQUENCY, Vol. 28 No. 2, May 1991 197-226
© 1991 Sage Publications, Inc.

high crime areas commit more crime than do people in low crime areas. Some theories (e.g. Cloward and Ohlin 1960; Miller 1958; Shaw and McKay 1942; Sutherland 1942) suggest mechanisms through which communities affect their inhabitants' criminal behavior. In contrast, Wilson and Herrnstein (1985) have suggested that high crime areas may simply be places that attract and concentrate persons predisposed to crime, and that community disorganization has no causal status.

In this article, we explicate two distinct traditions in criminology — individual-level and ecological research — and the few studies that have combined the two traditions.[1] We then present the results of a multilevel study of the effect of area characteristics on individual delinquency.

Individual-Level Research

One research tradition has focused on the individual-level correlates of adult crime or delinquent behavior. For example, Hirschi (1969) has provided evidence that bonds to the social order (such as attachment to conventional others or institutions, belief in the validity of social rules, and commitment to conventional goals) restrain people from engaging in delinquent behavior.

Others (Akers, Krohn, Lanza-Kaduce, and Rodesvich 1979) assume that peers may exert causal influence through a social learning or differential association mechanism and have provided evidence consistent with this assumption. Wilson and Herrnstein (1985) have reviewed evidence that individuals differ in personality or other enduring characteristics related to criminal behavior. Many personal characteristics are known to be statistically associated with delinquent behavior. These include school competency (–), impulsiveness or daring (+), belief in conventional rules (–), commitment to conventional goals (–), attachment to institutions and adults (–), being male and adolescent (+), association with delinquent peers (+), and exposure to harsh or erratic discipline in the family (+) (for evidence or reviews see G. Gottfredson 1981, 1987; West and Farrington 1975; Wilson and Herrnstein 1985).

Ecological Research

Shaw and McKay (1942) demonstrated systematic relations between social areas and crime rates and showed how crime rates often decline in concentric zones away from a central — high crime rate — area in cities. Similar patterns were found in many cities and for several different kinds of misconduct.

Subsequent research has usually provided evidence of strong associations between area characteristics and crime or victimization rates (Block 1979; Harries 1976; Pope 1978). Block, for example, reported high correlations at the census-tract level between log robbery rates and percentage high school graduates (−.54), percentage of families at 75% of the poverty level or below (.46), and percentage of families headed by females (.53). Researchers in the human ecological tradition (Shaw and McKay 1942; White 1932; Lander 1954; Bordua 1958-1959; Gordon 1967; Chilton and Dussich 1974; Gottfredson and Gottfredson 1985) and social geographers (Jonassen and Peres 1960; Hadden and Borgatta 1965; Smith 1973) have adduced evidence that crime, delinquency, or victimization rates vary in regular ways across social areas.

Bursik (1986), Shannon (1984), and Schuerman and Kobrin (1986) have contributed evidence about the evolution of high crime areas over time. For example, Shannon showed continuities in relationships between area characteristics and crime rates over time in Racine, and Schuerman and Kobrin attempted to identify changes in area characteristics associated with changes in crime rates in Los Angeles County. This work suggests that crime is perpetuated over time in certain areas, and it suggests a focus on activities that might make social areas less conducive to crime.

Shaw and McKay (1942, and others following in their tradition) demonstrated that crime rates vary systematically across social areas. Shaw and McKay also formulated a theory to explain how structural characteristics of the community contribute to crime rates. Low economic status, ethnic heterogeneity, and residential mobility are said to increase crime by decreasing community social organization. As Sampson and Groves (1989) pointed out, much of the research linking crime rates to area characteristics has focused on establishing the predicted association between the exogenous structural community and crime rates. Sampson and Groves (1989), in more explicit tests of Shaw and McKay's theory, demonstrated that much of the effect of exogenous structural characteristics of the community (low economic status, ethnic heterogeneity, residential mobility, family disruption, and urbanicity) on community crime and victimization rates are mediated by more proximate measures of community social disorganization according to a statistical model derived from Shaw and McKay's theory.

A Multilevel Approach

Research on individual criminal behavior makes scant use of environmental formulations. Despite growing recognition of the importance of environments, situations, and person-environment interactions (e.g., Barker 1968; Epstein and O'Brien 1985; Holland and Gottfredson 1976; Houts, Cook, and Shadish 1986; Magnusson and Endler 1977), and despite repeated calls for greater attention to environmental and situational influences on criminal behavior (Martin, Sechrest, and Redner 1981; Monahan 1981; Reiss 1986; Shah 1978), little research has empirically investigated the influence of the environment on individual criminal behavior.[2]

Hypotheses about the mechanisms through which the environment might influence individual criminal behavior pervade accounts of delinquency from the social disorganization tradition. Reiss (1986) suggested that delinquent peer groups in disorganized areas socialize children into a criminal subculture. He also suggested that, in communities characterized by high proportions of children being raised by other than intact natural family units, crime may be more prevalent because the children are less well supervised or because social bonds to parents or school are not so readily developed. In such circumstances, Reiss reasons, "parental authority and control is replaced by that of peers. . . . The effect of weakened family control is heightened when a strong peer-control system forms an antisocial subculture" (p. 15). This perspective is fueled primarily by ecological research which has demonstrated strong associations between area social and demographic characteristics and crime rates. The contextual effect of the community on individual behavior implied by this perspective has not been established.

Robinson's (1950) clear account of the "ecological fallacy" warns that an association discovered in data pertaining to social areas may be misleading if interpreted as if it applied to individuals. Individual-level correlations can be zero or opposite in sign of the corresponding ecological correlations. More specifically, a grouping effect occurs when the membership of the ecological unit (e.g., neighborhood or school) is statistically linked with one or both of the variables involved in the correlation. For example, segregation by socioeconomic level among schools produces a larger correlation between socioeconomic status (SES) and academic achievement test means at the school level than is observed at the individual student level. Whereas individual-level correlations between SES and achievement tests are typically around .3, averages for schools in a district may correlate .8 or higher (Cooley, Bond, and Mao 1981). It is possible that a similar process produces the high and often reproduced correlations between area characteristics and crime rates. Because there is usually considerable homogeneity within areas and substantial heterogeneity between areas on inhabitant characteristics that are at least modestly correlated with criminal behavior, aggregation would tend to produce high correlations.

Variations in crime rates across social areas might be generated by either a *contextual* or a *compositional* mechanism, or both. A contextual explanation involves the proposition that the social organization of an area influences the individuals who inhabit it, such as might occur if a community loses control over its inhabitants. A compositional explanation involves the proposition that the differences in crime rates in different areas are a result of the aggregate characteristics of the individuals who inhabit the areas such as might occur if a community recruits crime-prone people. In Wilson and Herrnstein's (1985) words, "A neighborhood may have more crime because conditions there cause it or because *certain kinds of neighborhoods attract persons predisposed to criminality*" (p. 291, emphasis added). Direct attempts to determine whether community characteristics exert contextual influence on individual criminality (whether community conditions cause crime) are rare.

In this article we test the hypothesis that in disorganized and poor areas, individuals will experience less supervision from adults, feel less attached to school and committed to education, associate more with delinquent peers who exercise weak or no control, and believe less in conventional proscriptions against misconduct. In other words, these areas fail to control the behavior of their inhabitants by failing to provide these sources of social control. One aim of our research is to learn whether social areas exert a contextual effect on the behavior of their inhabitants.

Previous Multilevel Studies

We know of only three multilevel studies of the effect of area characteristics on individual criminal involvement. The first (Reiss and Rhodes 1961) examined official delinquency status for more than 9,000 White boys who were enrolled in one of the 39 public, private, or parochial schools in Nashville, Tennessee during the 1957 school year. The researchers cross-tabulated official delinquency status with a 7-category measure of the SES of the school ("social status structure") and a 3-category measure of the SES of the boys' fathers ("ascribed social status"). They found that official delinquency was related both to ascribed social class and to the average social class of the school, but that "the status structure of the school exercises a greater effect on delinquent behavior than does ascribed status." This conclusion was based on the observation that the range of variation in delinquency rates related to ascribed status was less than that related to the status structure of schools: The overall delinquency rate for lower class individuals was 7.6%, compared with 3.0% for higher class individuals; the rate for individuals from upper and upper middle class schools was .5% compared with 15.6% from lower class schools.

Reiss and Rhodes' crosstabular analyses do not provide a ready estimate of the relative importance of school and individual social status in their model of delinquency. Our reanalysis of their published data using multiple regression reveals that delinquency *is* more a function of school social status than individual social status in their data. The standardized regression coefficients of delinquency on the two status measures are $-.02$ (not significant) for the individual and $-.08$ ($p < .01$) for the school measure.[3] The reanalysis also reveals that *neither* status variable accounts for much variance in individual delinquency, and that the extreme categories of the school status variables account for the association between school status and delinquency in the Reiss and Rhodes data.

Johnstone (1978) studied aggressive, property, drug-related, and status offenses in a sample of 1,237 14- to 18-year-old males and females living in 221 census tracts in Chicago. He reported the mean level of each kind of delinquency for individuals in each cell defined by the crosstabulation of a census measure of area SES with family SES. The results imply that different models fit the data for different kinds of offenses. For serious property offenses (burglary, larceny, and robbery) and self-reported arrest, the best-fitting model assumed that family socioeconomic status, but not community status, determines delinquency. For aggressive offenses, the best-fitting model assumed that the effects of family and community status are cumulative. For status offenses and drug-related offenses, the best-fitting model was a "relative deprivation" model which assumed that the greatest amount of delinquency occurs in situations in which the individual experiences the greatest amount of socioeconomic disadvantage. In this model, lower class individuals in higher class areas engage in the most delinquency, and higher status individuals in lower status areas the least.

The results of the Johnstone study do not accord with the Reiss and Rhodes study in suggesting that the lower SES areas produce more individual delinquency and that area SES is more important than family SES in explaining delinquency. Instead, the results raise interesting questions about interactions between individual and area status and about the possibility that different models fit different crime types.

Although suggestive, the results of these multilevel studies cannot be interpreted as providing unequivocal evidence for a community contextual effect on criminal behavior. Methodologists have debated about the techniques appropriate for establishing contextual effects (Alwin 1976; Barton 1970; Burstein, Linn, and Capell 1978; Farkas 1974; Hauser 1970a, 1970b).

The methods employed by Reiss and Rhodes and by Johnstone may be subject to what Hauser (1970a) calls the "contextual fallacy," that is, the interpretation of residual differences among social groupings after one or more individual attributes have been partialed out as "contextual effects." To the extent that important individual-level predictors of the outcome of interest which are excluded from the model are correlated with the aggregate-level measure, the contextual effect is overestimated.

Johnstone controlled only for individual SES. Race, gender, and age were not controlled in the analyses. The Reiss and Rhodes study controlled for race and gender by virtue of its sample, and for individual SES, but it omitted another relevant individual characteristic — the age of the student. Age is usually correlated with delinquency status, and is also very likely correlated with school SES — the contextual measure used in the study. Schools differ in their rates of grade retention. Schools that retain large proportions of their students each year have students who are considerably older than those that retain small proportions of students. It is not uncommon for retention rates, and hence the age of the students in the school, to vary with the SES of the school. In one southern school district, for example, the correlation of average age of the eighth grade population and the percentage of eighth grade students eligible for free lunch (a frequently used indicator of the socioeconomic level of the population) was .78.[4] Clearly, the individual-level models used in these early multilevel studies are incomplete. Compositional rather than contextual explanations may account for their results.

Simcha-Fagan and Schwartz (1986) examined community effects in a more complete model of individual delinquency among 553 adolescent males from randomly selected households in 12 New York City communities. The communities were selected to maximize variation on two area dimensions — family disorganization (measured by the percentage of married-couple families, divorce rate, percentage of children living in 2-parent families, etc.) and economic level (measured by family income, percentage of persons employed in professional and managerial occupations, etc.). Simcha-Fagan and Schwartz predicted delinquent behavior — both self-reported and official — from a model including these census-based measures and additional predictors: community aggregate measures of formal and informal community structure, the extent of the deviant-criminal subculture in the neighborhood derived from interviews with community residents, household-level measures corresponding to the community-level interview measures, and the age of the adolescent. They also examined effects of the community measures on interview-based measures of the intervening theoretical variables through which area influences may operate, such as attachment and commitment to school and association with delinquent peers. In this study, the measure of *community disorganization* remained significantly related to severe self-reported delinquency and officially recorded delinquency in the multivariate equation which controlled for individual- and family-level measures, but the effect was for the most part not mediated through school attachment or association with delinquent peers.[5] In contrast to the Reiss and Rhodes and Johnstone studies, this study found no independent effect of area economic level on official or severe self-reported delinquency.

Prior multilevel studies of area effects on delinquency, although provocative, have failed to produce consistent evidence of an area effect on individual delinquency. The studies leave open the questions of *which* area characteristics (disorganization or economic level) might influence delinquency, what might be the form of the effect (i.e., linear or nonlinear), and whether the area effect (if present) is due solely to the compositional characteristics of the area's inhabitants. The present study addresses these questions by estimating the effects of area disorganization and economic level in a model similar to that used in the Simcha-Fagan and Schwartz study in a sample of individuals from a larger and more diverse sample of social areas.

METHOD

Data

Individuals. Data were collected as part of the national evaluation of the Office for Juvenile Justice and Delinquency Prevention's Alternative Education Initiative—the School Action Effectiveness Study (SAES; Gottfredson 1982; Gottfredson, Gottfredson, and Cook 1983) and from the evaluation of a similar school-based delinquency prevention project operating in two Baltimore city schools—the Effective School Project (D. Gottfredson 1987). Questionnaires asking students to report on their own delinquent activities and on a number of characteristics, attitudes, and behaviors related to delinquency were administered to students in 10 middle or junior high schools located in four cities. Five of the schools in the sample are located in the urban centers of Charleston and Baltimore. Three are located in suburban communities in Charleston and Kalamazoo, Michigan, 1 in a rural farming community in Charleston, and 1 in Christiansted, St. Croix.

TABLE 1:   Students' Ethnicity and Parental Education by City and School (in percentages)

| City/School | Black | Hispanic | Parents Completed | |
			High School	College
Charleston	76	01	81	21
	31	01	89	30
	87	02	86	23
	89	01	82	18
	94	00	79	18
	67	01	70	18
Kalamazoo	25	02	78	26
	20	02	78	27
	35	02	78	22
Christiansted	54	26	62	13
Baltimore	88	01	68	12
	85	01	71	16
	90	00	65	09
Total	71	02	74	18

NOTE: Italicized table entries show citywide percentages.

Surveys were completed in Spring of 1982 for the SAES schools and in the Spring of 1984 for the Baltimore schools. A random sample of approximately 200 students was drawn from a current school roster for each participating school, except for 3 schools which elected to survey the entire student population. Each school's sample is representative of youths attending that school. Survey response rates averaged .82 in Charleston, .81 in Kalamazoo, .79 in Christiansted, and .72 in Baltimore. The overall survey response rate for all 10 schools was .80.

Student demographic characteristics, shown in Table 1, indicate that the study sample is predominantly minority — 71% Black. The percentage of parents completing high school and college in our sample is 74% and 18% respectively, figures which are similar to corresponding figures reported from national samples (Bachman, Johnson, and O'Malley 1980).

Neither the schools nor their student populations are representative of the nation. The sample is best described as a convenient sample of youths enrolled in middle or junior high schools in diverse locations. Previous multilevel studies have examined areas within single cities — Nashville, Chicago, and New York.

Only students for whom we obtained both a completed survey and a usable address are included in the study sample. For purposes of this study, a "usable

153

TABLE 2:   Number of Individuals and Social Areas by City

City	Individuals	Social Areas	Individuals per Social Area	
			Average	Range
Baltimore	1,761	132	13.3	1 - 67
Charleston	1,112	88	12.6	1 - 59
Kalamazoo	748	81	9.2	1 - 35
Christiansted	108	20	5.4	1 - 15

NOTE: Social areas are census block groups, except for nine of the areas in Charleston and all of the areas in the Virgin Islands, which are census enumeration districts.

address" is an address for which we were able to locate a census geographical code at the block group or enumeration district level. The proportion of students with surveys who also had a usable address was high in those cities for which the Census Bureau produces Geographic Base Files. For addresses outside of metropolitan areas we used street maps, tax maps showing the location of each house number on each street, and census maps showing the boundaries of each census block or enumeration district to link street addresses to census areas. For Kalamazoo and Baltimore virtually all addresses were usable. For Charleston and Christiansted the percentage usable addresses were 82% and 86%, respectively. The overall percentage usable addresses was 93%.

Social areas. In this study a social area is defined as a census block group or enumeration district. Blocks usually contain about 100 persons (but range from 0 to 1,000 persons), and are bounded on all sides by a visible physical feature such as a street, railroad track or stream. Much of the information collected by the Census Bureau is censored at the block level to protect the confidentiality of individual responses. But most information collected in the decennial census is available at the next level of aggregation — the block group. A block group is composed of approximately 10 city blocks and contains between 1,000 and 1,200 persons. Most of the individuals in our sample live in blocked areas. Christiansted and two complete and one partial school catchment area in our Charleston sample are not blocked. For these areas, our social areas are what the Census Bureau calls "enumeration districts," the smallest unit of census geography for which statistics are prepared in areas without blocks. Enumeration districts contain 500 to 600 people.

Table 2 shows the number of individuals and social areas in each of the four cities, as well as the average number of individuals per area. The 3,729 individuals live in 321 different block groups or enumeration districts. The number of individuals in the sample from a given area depends on the population density, the percentage of the population attending the public school, and on our sampling techniques and response rates. For example, our strategy of sampling the entire student population rather than a random sample in the Baltimore schools results in a higher number of individuals per area in Baltimore. Small numbers of individuals in social areas are not a problem in this study because measures of the area are derived from Census records — not from aggregated survey responses.

Measures

All measures of individual characteristics are developed from the surveys described earlier. A brief description of each measure follows. Alpha reliabilities appear in parentheses after each entry.

DELINQUENT BEHAVIOR

Three self-report delinquency scales are used. Responses are combined to produce last-year variety scales for three types of criminal activity. These scales are sums of the number of different delinquent activities admitted by the individual. Variety scales containing broad samples of types of delinquent acts typically outperform alternative scaling procedures using more restricted content (Hindelang, Hirschi, and Weis 1981).

Interpersonal aggression. This scale is composed of items about five specific offenses against persons. Items range in seriousness from hitting or threatening to hit another student to carrying a concealed weapon (.64).

Theft and vandalism. This scale is composed of items about seven specific property offenses that range in seriousness from joyriding to breaking and entering (.73).

Drug Involvement. This is a scale composed of seven items about the use of certain drugs in the last year. It includes items asking about the use of cigarettes, alcohol, marijuana, glue, and "other" drugs. It also includes items asking if the student has gone to school "high" or sold drugs. In our data as in Hindelang, Hirschi, and Weis's (1981) data, the inclusion of items measuring relatively minor forms of drug involvement (e.g., cigarettes) improved the reliability of the drug involvement scale (.69).

BACKGROUND MEASURES

Parental education. This 2-item scale is the average of students' reports of the mothers' and fathers' educations (.67).

Student age and race (dummy variables for Black and Hispanic) are single-item self-reports.

DELINQUENT ASSOCIATES

Negative peer influence. Items asked students to describe their friends. Items include "most of my friends think getting good grades is important" (–) and "how many of your friends have been picked up by the police?" (+) (.58).

SOCIAL BONDING

These measures are designed to assess elements of social bonding as described by Hirschi (1969).

Parental attachment/supervision. This 10-item scale includes items such as "how much do want to be like the kind of person your mother is?" and "how close do you feel towards your father?" as well as items asking students to report about how closely parents watch for student misbehavior and how they react when it occurs. Such items include "my parents know where I am and what I am doing" and "I would be punished if my parents knew that I broke a school rule." Attachment and supervision items were combined into a single scale because separate scales were highly correlated in this sample (.65).

School attachment/commitment. This 18-item scale includes items such as "I like this school" and "I have lots of respect for my teachers" as well as questions about educational and occupational aspirations, perceived parental pressure to go to college, and effort expended on school work. Attachment and commitment items were pooled in a common scale because separate scales were highly correlated in this sample (.74).

Involvement. Students used a 12-item checklist to report whether or not they spent time on activities including athletic teams, various kinds of school clubs, community organizations such as scouts and the YMCA, and helping out as a library assistant or office helper at school (.61).

Belief in conventional rules. This 6-item scale includes items such as "it is all right to get around the law if you can" and "taking things from stores doesn't hurt anyone" (.48).

MEASURES OF SOCIAL AREAS

Because our sample of individuals is not representative of the social areas from which they are drawn, it is not possible to derive area measures by aggregating the responses of all individuals from a given social area—a

TABLE 3: Varimax Rotated Principal Factor Analysis of Census Variables

Census Variable	Factor I	II	h^2
Female-headed households	.86	.09	.75
Welfare	.81	-.11	.67
Poverty	.75	-.32	.66
Divorced	.65	-.04	.42
Male unemployment	.53	-.19	.32
Female unemployment	.46	-.24	.27
Male employment	-.60	.30	.45
Female employment	-.24	.46	.27
Professional/managerial employment	-.26	.61	.44
Family income	-.51	.61	.63
Education	-.53	.56	.59
Farm income	-.25	-.45	.26
Nonpublic school enrollment	-.03	.38	.14

NOTE: The factor analysis is based on a random sample of 1,224 Illinois block groups.

common practice in the study of school effects on individuals (Alexander and Eckland 1975; Alwin 1976; Firebaugh 1979). Instead, our measures of social areas are derived from aggregations of variables from the 1980 Census of Population and Housing (U.S. Bureau of the Census 1982) for each area's inhabitants.

Previous work on the dimensions of social areas implies that much of the variance in measures of areas can be explained by two underlying factors. The first of these is defined by a high proportion of families headed by females in the community, high rates of divorce and separation, high unemployment, and relatively many families on welfare. This dimension has been observed in several studies undertaken in different cities, at different times, and using different geographical units (e.g., Smith's [1973] social problems and social deprivation factors derived from a study of census tracts in Tampa; Gottfredson and Gottfredson's [1985] poverty and disorganization factor found in a national study of school catchment areas; Simcha-Fagan and Schwartz's [1986] family disorganization factor found in a study of New York City communities; Hadden and Borgatta's [1965] non-White factor; and Ross, Bluestone, and Hine's [1979] family status factor). The second factor is defined by communities with high income and education, little poverty, and relatively many professional and managerial workers. This factor has also been found in previous work (e.g., Smith's socioeconomic status factor; Gottfredson and Gottfredson's affluence and education factor; and Simcha-Fagan and Schwartz's social rank factor).

157

The development of our area measures was guided by this previous work. We first attempted to replicate the often-observed factor structure in an independent sample of 1980 census block groups. We performed these analyses in a different sample than the one we used for subsequent analyses because we wanted to identify and measure general dimensions of typical areas rather than dimensions that might have been peculiar to the areas included in our study, and we wanted to compare variation in the area dimensions for the areas included in our sample with variation for a random sample of areas so that we would know to what extent our sample restricted the range of variation. Hence we created a construction sample of randomly selected block groups from the 1980 Census of Illinois — a state which we reasoned contained a wide range of different types of areas.

Earlier work on the dimensions of social areas (summarized above) guided our selection of 13 items from the census counts. These items — listed in Appendix A — were expected to measure the two dimensions of social areas found in these earlier works. A principal factor analysis of these 13 items for Illinois produced the varimax-rotated structure shown in Table 3. The 2-factor solution explained 45.3% of the common variance in the 13 census variables. The first factor is defined by a high proportion of families headed by females, high proportions of families on welfare and with incomes below the poverty level, a high divorce rate, and a low level of male employment. This factor closely resembled the first factor found in previous work; we call this factor *disorganization*.

The second factor is defined by a high proportion families with incomes above the national median income, a high proportion persons employed in professional and managerial occupations, a high proportion persons who completed high school, a high proportion employed females, and a low ratio of families with farm income to families with earnings from wages and salaries. It is a SES dimension, closely resembling the second dimension found in previous work. We call this factor *affluence and education*.

We used the solution from the factor analysis just described to compute factor scores for all census block groups and enumeration districts containing at least one individual in our sample and merged these factor scores with the individual records. Table 4 shows the means, standard deviations, and ranges of factor scores for individuals in the four cities included in the study. By comparing these figures with the same statistics for the construction sample we can gain insight into the degree of variation in the area factors in our sample. Individuals in our sample live in relatively disorganized and poor areas compared to the construction sample — a random sample of Illinois block groups. The means for disorganization for individuals in our sample is

TABLE 4: Means, Standard Deviations, and Ranges for Area Scales by City

	Disorganization				Affluence and Education			
City	M	SD	Range	N	M	SD	Range	N
Kalamazoo	0.68	1.14	-0.96 to 3.38	742	0.20	0.64	-1.41 to 1.58	742
Charleston	0.58	0.74	-0.83 to 3.74	1,094	-0.33	0.58	-2.13 to 1.45	1,094
Christiansted	0.74	0.66	-0.24 to 2.33	108	-0.32	0.64	-1.24 to 1.66	108
Baltimore	1.76	0.80	-0.18 to 4.84	1,743	-0.14	0.44	-1.09 to 1.40	1,743
Construction sample	-0.02	0.90	-1.29 to 8.10	1,166	0.02	0.83	-2.55 to 2.92	1,166

greater than the construction sample mean for all four cities, and it is two standard deviations above the construction sample mean for one city. The range of areas included in our study sample is great: The least disorganized area is about one standard deviation lower on the disorganization scale than the average construction sample area, and the most disorganized area is about five standard deviations higher.

The distribution of the affluence and education factor more closely resembles the Illinois construction sample distribution. Most individuals in our sample live in areas whose mean affluence level is within two standard deviations of the construction sample mean, and the city averages are all within one half of one standard deviation of the construction sample mean. The range of affluence across areas included in our study sample is great. The two community factors are correlated in the study sample ($r = -.152$ and $-.232$ for females and males, respectively.

Means, standard deviations, and individual-level correlations among all measures used in this study are available from the authors.

Analytic Strategy

We used the "contextual variables" method[6] (Alwin 1976) for estimating the effects of area variables on individual outcome variables. This method uses multiple regression to estimate the effects of the area variable in a model which controls for relevant individual-level variables. These multiple regression analyses were performed separately for males and females because tests for interactions implied that the regressions differed by gender.[7] We first regressed each of the three delinquency measures on the area factors and the individual background measures. Then we added the measures of the theoretical intervening variables to the model and decomposed the total effect of the community measures into direct and indirect effects via the theoretical measures according to the method described by Alwin and Hauser (1975).

~ *RESULTS*

Tables 5 and 6 show the correlations, standardized and unstandardized regression coefficients from the regression of delinquency on the two community factors and the individual background measures (the second column under each outcome measure titled "Total"), and on all independent measures (the third column under each outcome measure titled "Direct").

The tables show that the level of delinquency to which an individual admits on a self-report instrument and the level of disorganization or affluence of

TABLE 5: Regression Coefficients Relating Three Measures of Delinquency to Area Factors, Individual Background Measures, and Theoretical Predictors —Males (N = 1,858)

	Theft and Vandalism			Interpersonal Aggression			Drug Involvement		
	r	Total	Direct	r	Total	Direct	r	Total	Direct
Disorganization	.037	.057 (.011)	.015 (.003)	.083**	.064 (.016)	.021 (.005)	-.020	-.030 (-.007)	-.076** (-.017)
Affluence and education	.075*	.075* (.026)	.092** (.032)	.001	.020 (.009)	.033 (.015)	.061	.045 (.018)	.050 (.020)
Hispanic	.026	.007 (.010)	.004 (.006)	-.002	-.008 (-.016)	-.008 (-.014)	.022	.001 (.002)	.000 (.000)
Black	-.079*	-.087** (-.038)	-.033 (-.015)	.002	-.028 (-.016)	.028 (.016)	-.095**	-.082** (-.041)	-.022 (-.011)
Parental education	-.058	-.063* (-.012)	.004 (.000)	-.084**	-.068* (-.016)	.002 (.000)	-.077*	-.089** (-.019)	-.007 (-.002)
Age	.110**	.093** (.015)	.031 (.005)	.117**	.099** (.021)	.037 (.008)	.177**	.175** (.032)	.100** (.018)
Negative peer influence	.389**		.230** (.216)	.402**		.258** (.310)	.413**		.259** (.276)
Parental attachment/supervision	-.298**		-.090** (-.039)	-.283**		-.074** (-.040)	-.340**		-.134** (-.065)
School attachment/commitment	-.397**		-.209** (-.091)	-.381**		-.184** (-.102)	-.408**		-.172** (-.085)
Involvement	.028		.080** (.092)	-.005		.037 (.053)	-.083**		-.027 (-.035)
Belief	-.277**		-.123** (-.010)	-.272**		-.120** (-.124)	-.260**		-.098** (-.090)
R^2		.029	.249		.022	.233		.049	.276

NOTE: Tests of significance for area measures are based on the number of individuals. See note 3. Unstandardized regression coefficients are in parentheses.

*$p < .05$; **$p < .01$.

TABLE 6: Regression Coefficients Relating Three Measures of Delinquency to Area Factors, Individual Background Measures, and Theoretical Predictors —Females (N = 1,841)

	Theft and Vandalism			Interpersonal Aggression			Drug Involvement		
	r	Total	Direct	r	Total	Direct	r	Total	Direct
Disorganization	-.045	-.009 (-.001)	-.034 (-.004)	.098**	.086** (.016)	.057* (.011)	.006	.029 (.006)	-.002 (.000)
Affluence and education	.028	-.012 (-.002)	.010 (.002)	-.038	-.034 (-.012)	-.011 (-.004)	.047	.000 (.000)	.007 (.003)
Hispanic	.021	-.017 (-.014)	-.022 (-.018)	.018	-.007 (-.010)	-.010 (-.015)	-.021	-.080** (-.131)	-.079** (-.130)
Black	-.146**	-.151** (-.038)	-.099** (-.025)	-.029	-.078** (-.034)	-.012 (-.005)	-.186**	-.222** (-.109)	-.153** (-.075)
Parental education	-.036	-.040 (-.004)	.028 (.003)	-.123**	-.096** (-.017)	-.014 (-.002)	-.127**	-.123** (-.025)	-.024 (-.005)
Age	.071*	.067* (.006)	.006 (.000)	.136**	.111** (.017)	.037 (.006)	.225**	.204* (.036)	.124** (.022)
Negative peer influence	.305**		.189** (.114)	.382**		.237** (.251)	.352**		.184** (.220)
Parental attachment/supervision	-.240**		-.097** (-.023)	-.315**		-.156** (-.064)	-.374**		-.194** (-.090)
School attachment/commitment	-.304**		-.157** (-.041)	-.367**		-.168** (-.077)	-.385**		-.135** (-.070)
Involvement	.018		.096** (.061)	.006		.116** (.129)	-.137**		-.012 (-.015)
Belief	-.234**		-.108** (-.056)	-.265**		-.092** (-.082)	-.231**		-.077** (-.078)
R^2		.028	.171		.039	.239		.105	.270

NOTE: Tests of significance for area measures are based on the number of individuals. See note 3. Unstandardized regression coefficients are in parentheses.
*$p < .05$; **$p < .01$.

the community in which the individual lives are associated, but that the association varies somewhat by gender and type of delinquency.

For males (Table 5), disorganization is positively related to interpersonal aggressive crimes. This association is reduced to nonsignificance[8] when individual background measures are included in the model and further reduced when measures of the theoretical intervening variables are added. Disorganization has no total effect on males' theft and vandalism or drug involvement. The significant negative coefficient relating disorganization to drug involvement in the full model is offset in the reduced form equation by an unmeasured positive indirect effect which operates primarily via negative peer influence.

Area affluence and education is significantly related to males' reports of theft and vandalism. These effects are not mediated through other variables included in the model. Males living in more affluent communities report *more* theft and vandalism. This negative effect of community affluence was also found in Johnstone's earlier work (1978). The signs of the individual and community measures of SES are opposite for males: Higher SES males engage in slightly *less* crime than do their lower SES counterparts, but males living in high SES areas engage in slightly *more* criminal behavior than their counterparts in lower SES areas.

We attempted to replicate the interaction effect of area characteristics with individual SES found by Johnstone. Recall that in Johnstone's study, lower class individuals in higher class areas engaged in more of certain types of crime than did individuals of different social class backgrounds living in the same areas. Our tests for interaction of area effect with individual social class implied no interaction for males. Only for females did we find that the area effects varied significantly by individual SES, and these interaction effects were small despite their statistical significance (the largest increment to variance in the outcome variable explained by any of the interaction terms was .008).[9]

Table 6 shows the regressions corresponding to those in Table 5 for females. As for males, the less social organization in the area, the more interpersonal aggressive crimes are admitted. But unlike the males, females from disorganized areas report more interpersonal aggressive crimes regardless of their race, social class or age, and the effect is only partially mediated by measures of the theoretical variables. Disorganization is not significantly related to other kinds of self-reported crime for females, and affluence and education is not related to female delinquency.

The area effects shown in Tables 5 and 6 are small. Each area measure accounts for less than 1% of variance in the delinquency outcomes. In only one of the six equations (males' theft and vandalism) is the total effect of an area variable larger than that of our measure of individual social class, a variable which is not generally highly related to delinquency (Tittle, Villemez, and Smith 1978).

Table 7 shows the effects of the area variables on the theoretical variables. The table entries are standardized and unstandardized (in parentheses) regression coefficients in regressions of the theoretical variables on the area factors and the background variables. The area factors have small effects on some of the measures of the theoretical variables. Males and females in disorganized areas report more negative peer influence and less school attachment and commitment. These effects of area disorganization on the theoretical variables increase the delinquency of youths in these areas, according to the model. Parental attachment and supervision, involvement in conventional activities and belief are not significantly related to disorganization.

Consistent with the results reported in previous tables, effects of affluence and education on the theoretical variables are weaker than those of disorganization. Females and males in more affluent communities are less involved in school and community activities.

SUMMARY AND DISCUSSION

Our results suggest that two dimensions of area — socioeconomic status and social disorganization — are slightly related to individual delinquency, but the mechanisms relating each to delinquency are different. This study provides some evidence that areas characterized by weak family and other social structures do, as Shaw and McKay suggested, lose control over their children. Children in these areas report less bonding to potentially controlling institutions, more negative peer influence, and more delinquency of the interpersonal aggressive type.

The level of affluence and education (i.e., SES) of the area's population has no effect on social bonding or association with deviant peers according to our results. Our study shows no effect of area affluence on interpersonal aggression, and the only other study which examined individual aggressive acts separately from property and drug-related crimes (Johnstone) showed that a model which gave priority to family status (rather than community status) better explained violent crime. The best evidence now implies that area affluence is not much related to individual differences in participation in crimes involving aggression.

Theft and vandalism among males are higher in more affluent areas. Both Johnstone's study and ours found this to be true. But these effects are not

TABLE 7: Regression Coefficients Relating Theoretical Variables to Area Factors, by Gender

Community Factor	Negative Peer Influence	Belief	School Attachment/Commitment	Involvement	Parental Attachment/Supervision
Males					
Disorganization	.114**	.016	-.069*	-.013	-.050
	(.024)	(.004)	(-.031)	(-.002)	(-.023)
Affluence and education	-.007	.028	.021	-.100**	-.010
	(-.003)	(.012)	(.017)	(-.031)	(-.008)
R^2	.059	.005	.079	.032	.047
Females					
Disorganization	.068*	-.032	-.066*	-.052	-.032
	(.012)	(-.007)	(-.028)	(-.009)	(-.015)
Affluence and education	-.041	.045	.023	-.078**	-.026
	(-.014)	(.018)	(.017)	(-.025)	(-.022)
R^2	.067	.024	.109	.076	.065

NOTE: Tests of significance for area measures are based on the number of individuals. See note 3. Unstandardized regression coefficients are in parentheses. Each equation includes measures of race, parental education level, and age as well as the two area factors.
*$p < .05$; **$p < .01$.

straightforward. Johnstone offered guarded support for a relative deprivation explanation: The social class of the individual and the community
interact such that persons in positions of greatest status discrepancy engage
in the most delinquency. Our results do not support this interpretation. Males
and females from lower status families are no more likely to engage in crime
if they live in more affluent than less affluent areas. These individuals are
slightly more likely to engage in crime than others regardless of where they
live.

Our results are more consistent with an availability speculation: Targets
for theft may be more attractive in more affluent areas. Individuals (at least
males) from these areas may engage in theft and vandalism more not because
they are less bonded to society, not because they are more influenced by
delinquent associates, not because they are more likely to believe it is
acceptable to steal and take drugs, but simply because targets are attractive
(Felson 1986). We have no measure of perceived attractiveness of targets in
the social areas, but this speculation seems a plausible explanation of the
direct effect of the affluence of the area observed in our data.

Caveats

The generalizability of our results requires further exploration. The sample used in the study is not representative of any clearly defined population.
It is instead a mixture of youths from a variety of areas, with a large proportion
of the youths in the sample being minority youths who live in areas characterized by higher than average levels of disorganization. But the results
regarding the magnitude of the effect of area effects on delinquency accord
well with the results of previous studies.

Readers of earlier versions of this report have questioned the wisdom of
pooling social areas in places as diverse as Christiansted, Baltimore and rural
areas in South Carolina. Because previous multilevel studies have been
limited to studies of a single city, we thought that a study of many different
types of areas would add more to the literature than another study of a single
city. We, too, wondered about the possibility of heterogeneity of regression
across these different kinds of areas. Tests for homogeneity of regression
across area types indicated no significant differences between Christiansted
and the mainland areas, or between urban and suburban areas.

The measurement of area characteristics is another concern. Studies
whose area measures are derived from census data are frequently criticized
because these measures are not designed to measure the relevant theoretical
constructs thought to mediate the effect of community structural character-

istics on crime rates (Sampson and Groves 1989). Perhaps more direct measures of the level of social disorganization of the area would yield higher associations with the delinquency outcomes than were observed in our study. But the validity of census data for measuring the exogenous structural characteristics theorized by Shaw and McKay to increase crime rates has not been questioned. Indeed, Sampson and Groves' (1989) recent test of social disorganization theory demonstrated that the structural characteristics included in our study (affluence and disorganization) exert indirect effects on offending rates via their influence on unsupervised peer groups. Their measures of family disruption (similar to our disorganization factor) also exerted a strong direct effect on property crime rates.

Simcha-Fagan and Schwartz (1986) provided evidence in support of census-based measures of area characteristics in their study which used both area census measures and measures of areas from interviews with community residents. Their study showed that (a) the census measures correlate highly and in the expected direction with the interview measures (for example, an interview-derived measure of "Community Disorder" correlated .85 with a census measure of the percentage of children in single parent households), (b) the magnitude of the association between the interview-derived measures and delinquency is always roughly the same as the magnitude of association between the census-derived measures and delinquency (the largest difference between correlation coefficients for interview and census measures with delinquency is .06), and (c) the causal modeling analyses including the interview-derived measures produced community effects of roughly the same magnitude as those reported in our study. In the Simcha-Fagan and Schwartz study, the percentage of variance in the delinquency outcome measures explained by any one of the area measures, interview-derived or census-derived, did not exceed 2.2%. These findings, when added to the large body of research connecting census-derived area characteristics to crime rates, support the use of census-derived measures as measures of theoretically interesting structural characteristics of the area.

The estimates of area effects in this and other studies depend on the models employed. One reader of an earlier version of this report was concerned that estimating "total" effects of community variables in a model that included individual demographic variables underestimates the community effects. Inspection of the zero-order correlations reveals, however, that even with no other variable in the model, the total effects — which would equal the zero-order correlation with the criterion — would be small. A related worry is that, to the extent that important area variables that are independent of those in the model are excluded from our models, the area effects are underestimated in our study. Similarly, to the extent that individual characteristics known to be related to involvement in delinquent behavior are excluded from our models, the effects of individual characteristics are underestimated. Furthermore, if individuals are grouped in social areas on the basis of these important omitted characteristics, models (like ours) which exclude these characteristics will produce erroneous "direct" area effects (Hauser 1970a).

One reviewer was particularly concerned about the omission of school measures from the model. Ecological studies of school disorder show that the level of victimization reported by teachers and students in a school is related to measures of the social and educational climate in the school and the way the school is governed. These characteristics of the school are highly related to the level of disorganization and affluence in the community, but they nevertheless make a unique contribution to the explanation of victimization rates (Gottfredson and Gottfredson 1985). If characteristics of the school environment also have a direct effect on individual offending behavior, their omission from the model would result in overestimating the direct effect of area affluence and disorganization to the extent that the school characteristics are related to our area measures. Their omission would underestimate the total effect of area measures to the extent that these school environment measures were interpreted as area measures.

We added to the models estimated for Tables 5 and 6 nine dummy variables representing the schools included in our study. Adding the dummies to the full model (which includes intervening variables, individual background and area measures) resulted in less than 1% additional variance explained in any of the delinquency outcomes. F tests for the significance of the increment to explained variance failed to reach significance in any of the six equations. The regression coefficients for the area measures became smaller with the addition of the dummy variable and the previously significant direct effect of area disorganization on male drug involvement was reduced to nonsignificance.

Adding the dummy variable to the equation including only individual background measures and area measures increased the variance explained in individual delinquency by 1.1% to 1.8%, depending on the equation. These increments to variance explained were significant in three of the six equations (interpersonal aggression, males and females; drug involvement, males). As in the full-model equations, the regression coefficients for the area measures changed slightly when the dummies were entered. The total effect of affluence and education was reduced to nonsignificance in the male theft and vandalism equation and became barely significant in the female interpersonal aggression equation. The previously significant total effect of area disorganization on female interpersonal aggression became nonsignificant.

These analyses suggest that school characteristics may affect individual offending behavior via the intervening variables included in the model. Further studies are required to specify and measure the relevant school variables and to demonstrate that the effects observed in our study using dummy variables are not spuriously due to omitted individual or area measures.

These analyses demonstrate that the inclusion of variables measuring school environments would not change the interpretation of the area effect as "small." Nevertheless, specification concerns in general temper our conclusions about the size of the area effects observed in our study and in previous studies.

All these limitations notwithstanding, the assumption that community characteristics explain much of the differences among individuals in criminal behavior no longer seems tenable. A maximum of 2% of the variance in individual delinquency is accounted for by area factors in any of the multilevel studies examined — and a more reasonable estimate is less than 1%. The results of every multilevel study relating individual delinquency to measures of area characteristics imply that most of the variability among individuals must have sources other than differences in the communities they inhabit.

APPENDIX A: Items used in Factor Analysis of Social Area Characteristics

Female-headed households. Ratio of female-headed households with children under 16 years of age to husband-wife-headed households with children under 16 years of age.

Welfare. Proportion of families with income from public assistance or welfare.

Poverty. Proportion of families with incomes 1.24 times the poverty level or below.

Divorced. Proportion of persons aged 14 and over who are married with spouse absent, separated, or divorced.

Male unemployment. Proportion of males aged 16 or over and in the labor force who are unemployed.

Female unemployment. Proportion of females aged 16 or over in the labor force and who are unemployed.

Male employment. Proportion of males aged 16 or over who are employed or in the armed forces.

Female employment. Proportion of females aged 16 or over who are employed or in the armed forces.

Professional/managerial employment. Proportion of employed persons aged 16 and over employed in professional or managerial occupations.

Family income. Proportion of families with income of $12,000 or above.

Education. The proportion of population 25 years of age or older who completed 4 years of high school or more.

Farm income. Ratio of families with income from farm self-employment to families with wage and salary income.

Nonpublic school enrollment. Ratio of nonpublic to public school enrollment.

NOTES

1. A third tradition, sometimes identified by the label "environmental criminology" involves the study of the *locations* where crime occurs. This research tradition is illustrated by the work of Brantingham and Brantingham (1981), Jeffrey (1971), and Newman (1972). This tradition contrasts with our focus on the distribution of *people* who engage in offenses, wherever those offenses are committed. The environmental perspective is relevant in the sense that people who reside in and primarily experience well-defended environments may learn to avoid crime, but when restricted to this sense the environmental perspective seems to merge with the social disorganization perspective — the primary remaining distinction being the focus on offense location rather than offender residence data. The distribution of offense locations is beyond the scope of our investigation. We are concerned with the socialization of individuals.

2. For exceptions see Glaser (1969), Gottfredson and Taylor (1986), Reitzes (1955-1956), and Monahan and Klassen (1982).

3. These significance tests use the number of individuals in the analysis as the number of independent observations. The significance of the school-level variables may be overestimated because the number of independent observations for the school variables is much smaller ($n =$

39) than the number of individuals. The standard error of the estimate used in the calculation of statistical significance is underestimated.

4. This correlation is based on all eighth graders in the district's 15 schools containing an eighth grade.

5. The significance tests in the study use the number of individuals rather than the number of communities (n = 12) as the number of independent observations. See note 3.

6. An alternative method for analyzing area effects on delinquency is the analysis of covariance (ANCOVA) method recommended by Hauser (1968, 1971). This method uses measures of the area computed by aggregating the individual-level predictor variables to decompose the area effect into two components — one reflecting the compositional effect of the area mean on individual delinquency, that is, the portion of the effect due only to the aggregation of individuals in the community, and another residual term which might be interpreted as a true contextual effect. This ANCOVA framework and the regression approach employed in our study produce equivalent estimates of the contextual effect when aggregated measures of the variables in the individual-level model are used as area measures (Alwin 1976). We did not use the aggregated individual measures as our area measures because we had independent measures of social areas. We have too few observations per area to allow for reliable estimates of area means.

7. When we estimated the alpha reliability of coefficients separately for males and females we found differences of .13 and .08 in the estimates for theft and vandalism and interpersonal aggression, respectively. Because the measurement models may differ somewhat for males and females, the meaning of differences in the regression coefficients is ambiguous. Such differences might reflect either structural or measurement differences. Because gender differences in the explanation of delinquency are outside the focus of the present study, we decided not to pursue this question further (see Smith and Paternoster 1986).

8. The significance tests in the study use the number of individuals rather than the number of communities (n = 321) as the number of independent observations. See note 3.

9. For females, the social class of the individual is more highly related to interpersonal aggression in the least disorganized areas than in other areas. Low status females in these areas report having committed more than twice as many such crimes as high status females. This relationship is observed only for females in the least disorganized areas, and results in a high level of crime among low status females who reside in highly organized areas — an observation which tends to support the relative deprivation perspective.

REFERENCES

Akers, Ronald L., Marvin D. Krohn, Lonn Lanza-Kaduce, and Marcia Rodesevich. 1979. "Social Learning and Deviant Behavior: A Specific Test of a General Theory." *American Sociological Review* 44:636-55.

Alexander, Karl L. and Bruce K. Eckland. 1975. "Contextual Effects in the High School Attainment Process." *American Sociological Review* 40:402-16.

Alwin, Duane F. and Robert M. Hauser. 1975. "The Decomposition of Effects in Path Analysis." *American Sociological Review* 40:37-47.

Alwin, Duane F. 1976. "Assessing School Effects: Some Identities." *Sociology of Education* 49:294-303.

Bachman, Jerald G., Lloyd D. Johnson, and Patrick M. O'Malley. 1980. *Monitoring the Future. Questionnaire Responses from the Nation's High School Seniors.* Ann Arbor: University of Michigan Institute for Social Research.

Barker, Roger. 1968. *Ecological Psychology*. Stanford, CA: Stanford University Press.

Barton, Allen H. 1970. "Allen Barton Comments on Hauser's 'Context and Consex.'" *American Journal of Sociology* 76:514-17.

Block, Richard. 1979. "Community, Environment, and Violent Crime." *Criminology* 17:46-57.

Bordua, David J. 1958-1959. "Juvenile Delinquency and 'Anomie': An Attempt at Replication." *Social Problems* 6:230-38.

Brantingham, Paul J. and Patricia L. Brantingham (eds.). 1981. *Environmental Criminology*. Beverly Hills, CA: Sage.

Bursik, Robert J., Jr. 1986. "Ecological Stability and the Dynamics of Delinquency." Pp. 35-66 in *Communities and Crime* edited by A. J. Reiss, Jr. and M. Tonry. Chicago: University of Chicago Press.

Burstein, Leigh, Robert L. Linn, and Frank J. Capell. 1978. "Analyzing Multilevel Data in the Presence of Heterogeneous Within-Class Regressions." *Journal of Educational Statistics* 3(4):347-83.

Chilton, Richard J. and John P. J. Dussich. 1974. "Methodological Issues in Delinquency Research: Some Alternative Analyses of Geographically Distributed Data." *Social Forces* 53:73-82.

Cloward, Richard A. and Lloyd E. Ohlin. 1960. *Delinquency and Opportunity*. New York: Free Press.

Cooley, William W., Lloyd Bond, and Bor-Jiin Mao. 1981. "Analyzing Multilevel Data." Pp. 64-83 in *Educational Evaluation Methodology: The State of the Art*, edited by Ronald A. Berk. Baltimore, MD: Johns Hopkins University Press.

Epstein, Seymour and Edward J. O'Brien. 1985. "The Person-Situation Debate in Historical and Current Perspective." *Psychological Bulletin* 3:513-17.

Farkas, George. 1974. "Specification Residuals and Contextual Effects." *Sociological Methods and Research* 2:333-63.

Felson, Marcus. 1986. "Linking Criminal Choices, Routine Activities, Informal Control, and Criminal Outcomes." In *The Reasoning Criminal: Rational Choice Perspectives on Offending*, edited by Derek B. Cornish, and Ronald V. Clarke. New York: Springer-Verlag.

Firebaugh, Glen L. 1979. "A Comparison of Two Methods." *Sociological Methods and Research* 7(4):384-95.

Glaser, Daniel. 1969. *The Effectiveness of a Prison and Parole System*. Indianapolis: Bobbs-Merrill.

Gordon, Robert A. 1967. "Issues in the Ecological Study of Delinquency." *American Sociological Review* 32:927-44.

Gottfredson, Denise C. 1987. "An Evaluation of an Organization Development Approach to Reducing School Disorder." *Evaluation Review* 11:739-63.

Gottfredson, Gary D. 1981. "Schooling and Delinquency." In *New Directions in the Rehabilitation of Criminal Offenders*, edited by S. E. Martin, L. B. Sechrest, and R. Redner. Washington, DC: National Academy Press.

———, ed. 1982. *The School Action Effectiveness Study: I*. Report No. 325. Center for Social Organization of Schools. Baltimore, MD: Johns Hopkins University. ERIC Document Reproduction Service No. ED 222 835.

———. 1987. "American Education — American Delinquency." *Today's Delinquent* 6:1-65.

Gottfredson, Gary D. and Denise C. Gottfredson. 1985. *Victimization in Schools*. New York: Plenum.

Gottfredson, Gary D., Denise C. Gottfredson, and Michael S. Cook. 1983. *The School Action Effectiveness Study: II*. Report No. 342. Center for Social Organization of Schools. Baltimore, MD: Johns Hopkins University. (ERIC Document Reproduction Service No. ED 237 892).

Gottfredson, Stephen D. and Ralph B. Taylor. 1986. "Person-Environment Interactions in the Prediction of Recidivism." In *The Social Ecology of Crime*, edited by James M. Byrne and Robert J. Sampson. New York: Springer-Verlag.

Hadden, Jeffrey K. and Edgar F. Borgatta. 1965. *American Cities: Their Social Characteristics*. Chicago: Rand McNally.

Harries, Keith D. 1976. "Cities and Crime: A Geographic Model." *Criminology* 14:369-386.

Hauser, Robert M. 1968. "Family, School and Neighborhood Factors in Educational Performances in a Metropolitan School System." Unpublished doctoral dissertation, University of Michigan, Department of Sociology, Ann Arbor.

——. 1970a. "Context and Consex: A Cautionary Tale." *American Journal of Sociology* 75:645-664.

——. 1970b. "Hauser Replies." *American Journal of Sociology* 76:517-520.

——. 1971. Socioeconomic Background and Educational Performance. *Rose Monograph Series*. Washington, DC: American Sociological Association.

Hindelang, Michael J., Travis Hirschi, and Joseph G. Weis. 1981. *Measuring Delinquency*. Beverly Hills, CA: Sage.

Hirschi, Travis. 1969. *Causes of Delinquency*. Berkeley: University of California Press.

Holland, John L. and Gary D. Gottfredson. 1976. Using a Typology of Persons and Environments to Explain Careers: Some Extensions and Clarifications. *Counseling Psychologist* 6:20-29.

Houts, Arthur C., Thomas D. Cook, and William R. Shadish, Jr. 1986. "The Person-Situation Debate: A Critical Multiplist Perspective." *Journal of Personality* 54:52-105.

Jeffrey, Clarence R. 1971. *Crime and Prevention Through Environmental Design*. Beverly Hills, CA: Sage.

Johnstone, John W. C. 1978. "Social Class, Social Areas and Delinquency." *Sociology and Social Research* 63:49-77.

Jonassen, Christen T. and Sherwood H. Peres. 1960. *Interrelationships of Dimensions of Community Systems: A Factor Analysis of Eighty-two Variables*. Columbus: Ohio State University Press.

Lander, Bernard. 1954. *Toward an Understanding of Juvenile Disruption*. New York: Columbia University Press.

Magnusson, David and Norman S. Endler, eds. 1977. *Personality at the Crossroads: Current Issues in Interactional Psychology*. Hillsdale, NJ: Lawrence Erlbaum.

Martin, Susan E., Leo B. Sechrest, and Robin Redner, eds. 1981. *New Directions in the Rehabilitation of Criminal Offenders*. Washington, DC: National Academy Press.

Miller, Walter B. 1958. "Lower Class Culture as a Generating Milieu of Gang Delinquency." *Journal of Social Issues* 14:5-19.

Monahan, John. 1981. *Predicting Violent Behavior: An Assessment of Clinical Techniques*. Beverly Hills, CA: Sage.

Monahan, John and Deidre Klassen. 1982. "Situational Approaches to Understanding and Predicting Individual Violent Behavior." In *Criminal Violence*, edited by M. Wolfgang and N. Weiner. Beverly Hills, CA: Sage.

Newman, Oscar. 1972. *Defensible Space*. New York: Macmillan.

Pope, Carl E. 1978. "Victimization Rates and Neighborhood Characteristics: Some Preliminary Findings." Paper presented at the meeting of the American Society of Criminology, Dallas.

Reiss, Albert J., Jr. 1986. "Why Are Communities Important In Understanding Crime?" Pp. 1-33 in *Communities and Crime*, edited by A. J. Reiss, Jr. and M. Tonry.

Reiss, Albert J., Jr. and Albert L. Rhodes. 1961. "The Distribution of Juvenile Delinquency In the Social Class Structure." *American Sociological Review* 26:720-32.

Reitzes, Dietrich C. 1955-1956. "The Effect of Social Environment Upon Former Felons." *Journal of Criminal Law, Criminology, and Police Science* 46:226-31.

Robinson, William S. 1950. "Ecological Correlations and the Behavior of Individuals." *American Sociological Review* 15:351-57.

Ross, P. J., H. Bluestone, and F. K. Heinz. 1979. *Indicators of Social Well-being for U.S. Counties.* Rural Development Research Report No. 10. Washington, DC: U.S. Department of Agriculture.

Sampson, Robert J. and W. Byron Groves. 1989. "Community Structure and Crime: Testing Social-Disorganization Theory." *American Journal of Sociology.* 94:774-802.

Schuerman, Leo and Solomon Kobrin. 1986. Community Careers in Crime. Pp. 67-100 in *Communities and Crime*, edited by A. J. Reiss, Jr. and M. Tonry. Chicago: University of Chicago Press.

Shah, Saleem A. 1978. "Dangerousness: A Paradigm for Exploring Some Issues in Law and Psychology." *American Psychologist* 33:224-38.

Shannon, Lyle W. 1984. *The Relationship of Juvenile Delinquency and Adult Crime to the Changing Ecological Structure of the City.* Iowa City: Iowa Urban Community Research Center.

Shaw, Clifford R. and Henry D. McKay. 1942. *Juvenile Delinquency and Urban Areas.* Chicago: University of Chicago Press.

Simcha-Fagan, Ora and Joseph E. Schwartz. 1986. "Neighborhood and Delinquency: An Assessment of Contextual Effects." *Criminology* 24:667-703.

Smith, David M. 1973. *The Geography of Social Well-being in the United States.* New York: McGraw-Hill.

Smith, Douglas A. and Ray Paternoster. 1987. "The Gender Gap in Theories of Deviants: Issues and Evidence." *Journal of Research in Crime and Delinquency* 24:140-72.

Sutherland, Edwin H. 1942. "Development of the Theory." In *The Sutherland Papers*, edited by A. Cohen, A. Lindesmith, and K. Schuessler. Bloomington: Indiana University Press.

Tittle, Charles R., Wayne J. Villemez, and Douglas A. Smith. 1978. "The Myth of Social Class and Criminality: An Empirical Assessment of the Empirical Evidence." *American Sociological Review* 43:643-56.

U.S. Bureau of the Census. 1982. *Census of the Population and Housing.* Summary Tape 3. Washington, DC: U.S. Government Printing Office.

West, Donald J. and David P. Farrington. 1975. *Who Becomes Delinquent?* London: Heinemann.

White, R. Clyde. 1932. "The Relation of Felonies to Environmental Factors in Indianapolis." *Social Forces* 10:498-509.

Wilson, James Q. and Richard J. Herrnstein. 1985. *Crime and Human Nature.* New York: Simon & Schuster.

TESTING THE CORE EMPIRICAL IMPLICATIONS OF GOTTFREDSON AND HIRSCHI'S GENERAL THEORY OF CRIME

HAROLD G. GRASMICK
CHARLES R. TITTLE
ROBERT J. BURSIK, Jr.
BRUCE J. ARNEKLEV

In A General Theory of Crime, *Gottfredson and Hirschi propose that low self-control, in interaction with criminal opportunity, is the major cause of crime. The research reported in this article attempts to test this argument while closely following the nominal definitions presented by Gottfredson and Hirschi. A factor analysis of items designed to measure low self-control is consistent with their contention that the trait is unidimensional. Further, the proposed interaction effect is found for self-reported acts of both fraud and force (their definition of crime). Inconsistent with the theory are (a) the finding that criminal opportunity has a significant main effect, beyond its interaction with low self-control, on self-reported crime and (b) the substantial proportion of variance in crime left unexplained by the theoretical variables. Suggestions are offered for modifying and expanding the theory.*

Gottfredson and Hirschi's (1990) *A General Theory of Crime* is sure to generate important theoretical debates and research. The theory is part of a trend in criminology that pushes the causes of crime further back in the life course into the family (e.g., Cernkovich and Giordano 1987; Hagan, Simpson, and Gillis 1987; Hill and Atkinson 1988; Laub and Sampson 1988; Larzelere and Patterson 1990; McCord 1979, 1991a, 1991b, 1991c; Loeber and Southamer-Loeber 1986; Patterson and Dishion 1985; Rankin and Wells 1990; Straus 1991; Thornberry, Lizotte, Krohn, Farnworth, and Jang 1991; Wells and Rankin 1986, 1988, 1991; Widom 1989). In this respect, it is a return to an emphasis found in the works of Sheldon and Eleanor Glueck

We wish to thank the College of Arts and Sciences, University of Oklahoma, for providing funds for this research as part of the annual Oklahoma City Survey. An earlier version of this article was presented at the 1991 Annual Meeting of the American Society of Criminology, San Francisco.

JOURNAL OF RESEARCH IN CRIME AND DELINQUENCY, Vol. 30 No. 1, February 1993 5-29
© 1993 Sage Publications, Inc.

(1937, 1950; see also McCord and McCord, 1959; Nye 1958) and also resembles in some ways important themes in the more recent work of Wilson and Herrnstein (1985). But unlike the Gluecks and unlike Wilson and Herrnstein (see also Ellis 1991; Eysenck 1989; Fishbein 1990; Fishbein and Thatcher 1986; Gove and Wilmoth 1990; Herrnstein 1983; Rowe 1986), Gottfredson and Hirschi stop short of proposing a genetic or other biological explanation of crime. Instead, their focus is on early childhood socialization in the family, which can produce an enduring criminal predisposition called low self-control.

The emphasis on early childhood socialization as the cause of crime is a departure from the emphasis on more proximate causes of crime initiated by Sutherland's (1947) theory of differential association (see Laub and Sampson 1991) and manifested most recently in such perspectives as labeling theory (Lemert 1972), routine activity theory (e.g., Felson and Cohen 1980; Miethe and Meier 1990) and some versions of rational choice theory (e.g., Cornish and Clarke 1986).[1] Further, the importance that Gottfredson and Hirschi attach to the single, unidimensional enduring trait of low self-control is at odds with the criminal career perspective (see Blumstein, Cohen, Roth, and Visher 1986), which argues that different independent variables probably will be necessary to explain participation in, frequency of, and persistence in crime (see also Nagin and Smith 1990; Smith, Visher, and Jarjoura 1991).

The research to be reported assesses the core empirical implications of Gottfredson and Hirschi's theory. The first concerns measurement. Their argument implies that low self-control is a unidimensional trait consisting of impulsivity, a preference for simple rather than complex tasks, risk seeking, a preference for physical rather than cerebral activities, a self-centered orientation, and a volatile temper.

The second implication is explanatory — that low self-control in combination with opportunity to commit crime is a (perhaps *the*) primary cause of criminal behavior, which Gottfredson and Hirschi define as acts of force or fraud in pursuit of one's self-interest. As in Hirschi's (1969) earlier influential work, motivation to commit crime is not a variable; rather, all actors are rational and motivated to pursue their self-interest, including the commission of crime. What varies among individuals is their level of self-control *and* their access to opportunities to commit crimes. But neither low self-control nor the existence of crime opportunity by themselves are the primary determinants of crime. Instead, it is the combination of the two, or their interaction effect, that results in criminal behavior.

These two arguments from *A General Theory of Crime* are so central that support for them is an essential prerequisite for future consideration of Gottfredson and Hirschi's theory. For now, we forgo criticism of the theory

176

(for a critical review, see Barlow 1991). Rather, for purposes of this initial test, we accept the assumptions and guidelines offered by Gottfredson and Hirschi. In that spirit, we try to develop operational definitions of the concepts, including low self-control, that closely match the nominal definitions offered by Gottfredson and Hirschi, and we incorporate their somewhat unconventional definition of crime as well as their definition of crime opportunity. When necessary, we assume that certain assertions from the theory are true as we assess the empirical implications described above. In those instances, we note the assumptions being made.

NOMINAL DEFINITIONS

Much to their credit, Gottfredson and Hirschi usually are very explicit in defining the concepts in their theory. For our purposes, definitions of low self-control, crime, and crime opportunity are essential.

Low Self-Control

In a section titled "The Elements of Self-Control," Gottfredson and Hirschi (1990, pp. 89-91) describe the "nature" of low self-control. Their definition is closely linked to their descriptions of criminal acts; consequently, people who have low self-control have personalities predisposing them toward committing such acts. Although we are not testing this in the present research, Gottfredson and Hirschi propose that low self-control is established in early childhood in families in which parents do not closely monitor the child's behavior, do not recognize deviant behavior when it occurs, and do not punish such behavior (1990, p. 97). Once established in early childhood, individuals' levels of self-control remain stable over the life course and are relatively unaffected by other institutions (1990, pp. 107-8). Instead, self-control affects individuals' performances or outcomes in institutions such as school, the labor force, and marriage that they encounter later in life (1990, pp. 154-8). Those with low self-control not only are more likely to commit crime but also are more likely to be unsuccessful in school, the labor force, and marriage.

Our reading of Gottfredson and Hirschi's definition led to the identification of six components of the personality trait of low self-control, and, as described later, questionnaire items aimed at tapping each of these were developed. We were gratified several months later, after our data had been collected, that Barlow (1991) identified essentially the same components.

First, Gottfredson and Hirschi note that low self-control includes a "tendency to respond to tangible stimuli in the immediate environment, to have a concrete 'here and now' orientation," in contrast to high self-control which enables people to "defer gratification" (1990, p. 89). This component of low self-control appears to correspond to the notion of *impulsivity*, which is an important theme in Wilson and Herrnstein's (1985) *Crime and Human Nature*. (For a critique of the concept of impulsivity, see Malle and Neubauer 1991.)

Second, low self-control involves a tendency to "lack diligence, tenacity, or persistence in the course of action" so that people with low self-control prefer "easy or simple gratifications of desires" and try to avoid complex tasks (1990, p. 89). In our research, we label this component of low self-control preference for *simple tasks*.

A third characteristic of people with low self-control is a tendency to be "adventuresome" rather than "cautious" because criminal acts are "exciting, risky, or thrilling" (1990, p. 89). We refer to this element as *risk seeking*.

Fourth, low self-control embraces a preference for physical activity rather than "cognitive" or "mental" activity (1990, p. 89). We call this the *physical activity* component of low self-control.

Fifth, "people with low self-control tend to be self-centered, indifferent, or insensitive to the suffering and needs of others" (1990, p. 89). This trait we label *self-centered*.

Finally, "people with low self-control tend to have minimal tolerance for frustration and little ability to respond to conflict through verbal rather than physical means" (1990, p. 90). We refer to this as the *temper* component of low self-control.

Two points should be noted concerning our interpretation. First, we have omitted three statements from Gottfredson and Hirschi's definition that seem to refer to consequences of low self-control rather than definitional components of the personality trait established in early childhood. One is the statement that "people lacking self-control need not possess or value cognitive or academic skills" and "need not possess manual skills that require training or apprenticeship" (1990, p. 89). To us, the statement that people lacking self-control "need not" possess these traits suggests they are irrelevant to the definition of self-control. Gottfredson and Hirschi would maintain, however, that people whose early family experiences lead to low self-control will, as they age, tend to lack the future orientation, willingness to engage in complex tasks, tenacity, and so on, to achieve academic or manual skills. Also, Gottfredson and Hirschi state that people with low self-control "tend to have unstable marriages, friendships, and job profiles" (1990, p. 89) and "tend to pursue immediate pleasures that are *not* criminal:

178

they will tend to smoke, drink, use drugs, gamble, have children out of wedlock, and engage in illicit sex" (1990, p. 90; see also Arneklev et al. forthcoming). All three of these statements seem to describe predicted outcomes of low self-control rather than personality traits that comprise low self-control. Consequently, these characteristics of individuals are not incorporated into our measure. Rather, our interpretation is that they should be viewed as dependent variables in subsequent research on the consequences of low self-control.

Second, Gottfredson and Hirschi clearly assert that these six traits we have sketched are not alternative ways of having low self-control; rather, they form a single unidimensional latent trait. As they suggest, "There is considerable tendency for these traits to come together in the same people, and since the traits tend to persist through life, it seems reasonable to consider them as comprising a stable construct useful in the explanation of crime" (Gottfredson and Hirschi 1990, pp. 90-91). In other words, a factor analysis of valid and reliable indicators of the six components is expected to fit a one-factor model, justifying the creation of a single scale called low self-control. In effect, this is a very crucial premise in Gottfredson and Hirschi's theory. A single, unidimensional personality trait is expected to predict involvement in all varieties of crime as well as academic performance, labor force outcomes, success in marriage, various "imprudent" behaviors such as smoking and drinking, and even the likelihood of being involved in accidents. Evidence that such a trait exists is the most elementary step in a research agenda to test the wealth of hypotheses Gottfredson and Hirschi have presented.

Crime

In their theory, crime is not equated with criminality. Crimes are acts, whereas criminality is an individual predisposition to commit crimes. Criminality, therefore, is subsumed under the personality trait low self-control, but low self-control also predisposes people to engage in certain other kinds of irresponsible behavior, which are not necessarily crimes (Gottfredson and Hirschi 1990, p. 91-94).

Gottfredson and Hirschi define crime as an act "of force or fraud undertaken in pursuit of self-interest" (1990, p. 15). Self-interest is equivalent to the pursuit of pleasure. Drawing from the writings of Bentham, they note that the typical definition of crime as illegal behavior acknowledges only one of four sanctioning systems, the political, and ignores physical, moral, and religious sources of pleasure and pain (Gottfredson and Hirschi 1990, pp. 4-14). By shunning a definition of crime in terms of law, Gottfredson and

179

Hirschi avoid the problem that a particular behavior might be illegal in some societies but not in others and, within one society, might be illegal at some point in history but not at others. Thus the definition of crime as the use of force or fraud undertaken in the pursuit of self-interest is one reason Gottfredson and Hirschi (1990, pp. 175-77) can maintain that their theory is a "general" theory, not bound to a specific culture or historical period. The definition also enables them to insist that no special theory, beyond their own general theory, is necessary to explain white-collar crime, which is but one type of fraud (Gottfredson and Hirschi 1990, pp. 180-201). Further, although opportunities for specific kinds of force and fraud vary by age, delinquency and adult criminality stem from the same causal factor (Gottfredson and Hirschi 1990, pp. 124-44).

Although criminal behavior is not equated with illegal behavior, Gottfredson and Hirschi (1990, p. 175) do acknowledge that most acts defined as illegal will be consistent with their definition of crime. It is worth noting that in more conventional definitions of crime and delinquency, "force" and "fraud" parallel somewhat the distinction between violent personal crimes and property crimes. Their contention that low self-control is a determinant of both of these, and, consequently, that the distinction between them is of little theoretical importance, is an important one that is addressed in the present research.[2]

Crime Opportunity

According to Gottfredson and Hirschi's theory, low self-control by itself is not the primary determinant of crime. Instead, crime opportunity is a second key independent variable, that specifies the conditions under which low self-control most likely leads to crime. In the presence of an opportunity to commit a crime, individuals with low self-control are likely to commit it whereas individuals with high self-control are not. Crime, then, is an interactive function of self-control and crime opportunity. Fraud and force occur primarily when individuals with low self-control encounter opportunities to engage in fraud or force. Consequently, characteristics of crime opportunities are an important feature of the theory.

Unfortunately, compared to their discussion of self-control and its consequences, Gottfredson and Hirschi say relatively little about crime opportunity. Although, like levels of self-control, opportunity is expected to vary across individuals, possible sources of such variance are not described in detail. This is potentially a crucial omission because a likely possibility is that social structural factors affect individuals' degree of exposure to crime opportunity. By failing to address this issue, the theory can be interpreted as one that focuses on personality and neglects social structure as a determinant of crime (see Barlow 1991).

Despite the absence of consideration of sources of variation in exposure to crime opportunities, Gottfredson and Hirschi (1990, pp. 12-13) do describe characteristics of situations in which force or fraud are most likely to enhance an individual's self-interest (i.e., provide pleasure). The description relies on evidence about typical incidents of burglary, robbery, homicide, auto theft, rape, and embezzlement. The opportunity for crime is said to be maximum in situations where force or fraud can produce "immediate" rather than "delayed" pleasure (Gottfredson and Hirschi 1990, p. 12); where force or fraud would be "mentally and physically easy," not requiring "mental and physical exertion" (Gottfredson and Hirschi 1990, p. 12); and where there is "little risk of detection and little risk of resistance" (Gottfredson and Hirschi, 1990, p. 13). Our measure of exposure to crime opportunities incorporates reference to situations in which acts of force or fraud would be immediately gratifying, easy, and unlikely to be quickly detected. We would note, however, an apparent inconsistency between the "risk seeking" component of low self-control and the inclusion of "little risk of detection" in the definition of crime opportunity. Those with low self-control, by Gottfredson and Hirschi's definition, should not be attracted to situations involving little risk.

CAUSAL EMPIRICAL IMPLICATIONS

The primary theme of *A General Theory of Crime* is that low self-control, combined with crime opportunity, is a major determinant of crime. However, in our reading, the theory is unclear about how much, if any, of an independent effect low self-control should have on crime other than through interaction with crime opportunity. Gottfredson and Hirschi state in one place that high self-control should lead to lower levels of crime "under all circumstances" (1990, p. 118), but in various passages in their book they acknowledge that situational circumstances and other individual characteristics, which are not specifically identified and therefore are not included in our research, might affect the extent to which low self-control affects criminal behavior. Hence, although their formulation seems to allow low self-control to affect crime independently, whether the theory actually specifies a large main effect of low self-control beyond its interaction with crime opportunity is problematic. It is clear, however, that the key contention of their theory is contingent—that low self-control is the primary determinant of crime *through* its interaction with criminal opportunity, as they define it.

181

Although the status of the main effect of low self-control in the theory is somewhat ambiguous, it seems much more certain that the theory does not anticipate an independent main effect for crime opportunity beyond its interaction with low self-control. A crime opportunity has little bearing on criminal behavior unless the individual encountering it has low self-control. Persons with high self-control will resist the temptations of crime opportunities. Given the primacy of the self-control variable and its interaction with opportunity in the theory, evidence of a significant main effect of crime opportunity surely would require additional theoretical elaboration beyond the somewhat meager discussion it receives, especially in light of the extensive discussion of low self-control. A significant main effect for crime opportunity would suggest that even in the absence of low self-control, crime opportunity leads to crime. The current version of Gottfredson and Hirschi's theory seems not to account for such a possibility.

METHODOLOGY

Sample

Data to test the measurement and causal hypotheses were collected as part of the 13th annual Oklahoma City Survey conducted by the Department of Sociology, University of Oklahoma, in spring 1991. A simple random sample of 395 adults (18 and older) was drawn from the R. L. Polk Directory for the city. Initial contact was made with a letter indicating that a member of the research team would soon try to schedule an appointment for an interview. Attempts to schedule appointments were made in person by trained interviewers. Members of the target sample who refused to participate or could not be located were replaced by random selection until a total of 395 face-to-face interviews was conducted.[3]

Unfortunately, 1990 Census data are not yet available, so we compared the 1991 sample to the 1980 Census figures for the community. In the population data, 53.2% are women, nearly identical to the 54.3% in the sample. The difference is not significant. Likewise, the difference between percentage White in the population (83.7%) and in the sample (81.5%) is not significant. However, the mean age of the sample (46.5) is significantly ($p <$ .001) greater than the mean age of the adult population in the 1980 Census (42.7). We suspect, however, that this difference reflects an actual aging of the population, consistent with national trends, rather than sampling bias. In fact, the mean age of the annual Oklahoma City Survey samples has been increasing steadily over the years that the annual survey has been conducted.

A listwise deletion of missing cases resulted in an N of 389 for the analysis that follows. Although the interviews were face-to-face, respondents recorded information about their criminal behavior on a separate answer sheet, which the interviewer did not see. Most likely, this strategy is largely responsible for the fact that of the original 395 cases, only 6 were lost due to missing data.

Measures

LOW SELF-CONTROL

As noted earlier, six components of the personality trait Gottfredson and Hirschi call low self-control were identified: impulsivity, preference for simple rather than complex tasks, risk seeking, preference for physical rather than cerebral activities, self-centered orientation, and a volatile temper linked to a low tolerance for frustration. Initially, we considered the self-control subscale (Sc) of the California Psychology Inventory (Gough 1975) as a possible measure of this trait. The Sc subscale does include some of the themes in Gottfredson and Hirschi's definition. For example, the item "Sometimes I feel like smashing things" would seem to capture a volatile temper. "I would do almost anything on a dare" is a possible indicator of being risk seeking. "I like to be the center of attention" might tap a self-centered orientation. "I often act on the spur of the moment without stopping to think" could be an indicator of impulsivity. Thus, in general, Gottfredson and Hirschi's definition of low self-control overlaps considerably with the Sc subscale on the California Psychological Inventory.

However, the 38-item Sc subscale contains no items tapping either preference for simple rather than complex tasks or preference for physical rather than cerebral activities. Further, the Sc subscale contains many items that simply lack face validity in terms of Gottfredson and Hirschi's definition of low self-control (e.g., "Police cars should be specially marked so that you can always see them coming," "I have had very peculiar and strange experiences," and "My home life was always happy.") Consequently, we chose to develop our own measures of the six components, following as closely as possible Gottfredson and Hirschi's descriptions of them.

Various combinations of items were pretested on several samples of college students with the goal of selecting a total of 24 items — four for each of the six components — that had sufficient variances and that tended to be unidimensional in their factor structure.

From the pretests, we arrived at the 24 items presented in Table 1. Respondents in the Oklahoma City Survey were presented with these and

TABLE 1: Low Self-Control Scale Items (N = 389)

Item	Mean	SD	Factor Loading
Impulsivity			
I often act on the spur of the moment without stopping to think.	2.53	0.97	.470
I don't devote much thought and effort to preparing for the future.	1.80	0.84	.388
I often do whatever brings me pleasure here and now, even at the cost of some distant goal.	2.06	0.91	.616
I'm more concerned with what happens to me in the short run than in the long run.	1.92	0.94	.580
Simple Tasks			
I frequently try to avoid projects that I know will be difficult.	2.11	0.93	.415
When things get complicated, I tend to quit or withdraw.	1.69	0.78	.420
The things in life that are easiest to do bring me the most pleasure.	2.16	0.86	.397
I dislike really hard tasks that stretch my abilities to the limit.	1.93	0.87	.472
Risk Seeking			
I like to test myself every now and then by doing something a little risky.	2.88	0.97	.288
Sometimes I will take a risk just for the fun of it.	2.37	1.05	.429
I sometimes find it exciting to do things for which I might get in trouble.	1.80	0.99	.523
Excitement and adventure are more important to me than security.	1.63	0.83	.500
Physical Activities			
If I had a choice, I would almost always rather do something physical than something mental.	2.36	0.89	.341
I almost always feel better when I am on the move than when I am sitting and thinking.	2.89	0.91	.349
I like to get out and do things more than I like to read or contemplate ideas.	2.73	0.91	.361
I seem to have more energy and a greater need for activity than most other people my age.	2.74	0.89	—

184

Self-Centered

I try to look out for myself first, even if it means making things difficult for other people.	1.65	0.77	.602
I'm not very sympathetic to other people when they are having problems.	1.59	0.80	.392
If things I do upset people, it's their problem not mine.	1.74	0.85	.395
I will try to get the things I want even when I know it's causing problems for other people.	1.49	0.68	.489

Temper

I lose my temper pretty easily.	2.02	1.01	.418
Often, when I'm angry at people I feel more like hurting them than talking to them about why I am angry.	1.62	0.84	.498
When I'm really angry, other people better stay away from me.	2.16	1.12	.407
When I have a serious disagreement with someone, it's usually hard for me to talk calmly about it without getting upset.	2.35	1.00	.416

asked to respond using the categories (4) strongly agree, (3) agree somewhat, (2) disagree somewhat, or (1) strongly disagree. A high score, therefore, indicates low self-control. The means and standard deviations are included as part of Table 1. Only the very first item in the table was taken directly from the Sc subscale in the California Psychological Inventory, although several others are slight modifications of Sc subscale items.

Principal components analysis was applied to the 24 items to determine if the creation of a single scale can be justified, as proposed by Gottfredson and Hirschi. The results are somewhat ambiguous as indicated by the factor eigenvalues, the first 10 of which are reported below. The numbers in parentheses are the difference between the eigenvalue of that factor and the previous one.

Factor	1	4.66
Factor	2	2.34 (2.32)
Factor	3	2.07 (0.27)
Factor	4	1.81 (0.26)
Factor	5	1.78 (0.03)
Factor	6	1.11 (0.67)
Factor	7	0.94 (0.17)
Factor	8	0.77 (0.17)
Factor	9	0.74 (0.03)
Factor	10	0.70 (0.04)

Among the 24 factors necessary to perfectly reproduce the correlation matrix, 6 have eigenvalues greater than 1.0. According to the Kaiser Rule for determining the number of factors, therefore, a 6-factor solution would be appropriate (Nunnally 1967). Both an orthogonal and an oblique rotation of the 6 factors generally separate each of the six components as distinct factors.

However, in a principal components analysis, the number of factors with eigenvalues greater than 1.0 will, in part, be an increasing function of the number of items. With a large number of items, the Kaiser Rule most likely overestimates the number of significant factors, and the Scree Discontinuity Test has been proposed as a preferable strategy for determining the number of factors (Nunnally 1967). Following the logic of the Scree test, the most obvious break in eigenvalues is the difference of 2.32 between the first and second factor, compared to .27 between the second and third, strongly suggesting a one-factor model would be appropriate. But the difference between the fifth and sixth factor of .67 is another discontinuity in eigenvalues between pairs of adjacent factors, although much smaller than the first. Therefore, because valid measurement is so crucial, we examined a five-factor model in some detail.

The five-factor solution was examined using varimax, quartimax, and oblique rotations, leading to the same conclusion in all cases. In the five-factor model, regardless of rotation method, one factor *tends* to combine the impulsivity and simple tasks items, whereas the remaining four factors are unique to each of the four other groups of items. However, a few of the items have substantial loadings on more than one factor. Attempts to improve the five-factor model by deleting specific items eventually results in the elimination of the impulsivity items, leaving five relatively clean factors for each of the remaining five components. Thus, the five-factor model, with the elimination of items with poor factor discrimination, eventually becomes identical to the six-factor model but without the impulsivity factor.

In general, we cannot find *strong* evidence that combinations of items into subgroups produces readily interpretable multidimensionality. Instead, from an empirical perspective, the strongest case can be made for a one-factor unidimensional model, given the large difference in eigenvalues between the first and second factors. Our conclusion is that the six components we have identified as Gottfredson and Hirschi's definition of low self-control appear to coalesce into a single personality trait. We do not, however, wish to give the impression that we consider ours the definitive conclusion on this issue. We would encourage others to replicate our measure and develop other items, testing their unidimensionality with a wide variety of samples.

Under the assumption that low self-control is unidimensional, the next step in scale construction is identifying the linear composite of items that produces the most reliable unidimensional scale. Reliability analysis suggests that Cronbach's alpha could be increased from .805 to .812 by eliminating from the scale the last one of the four items in the Physical Activities component. In retrospect, it is apparent that the "activities" referred to in this particular item need not be interpreted as physical activities by respondents, perhaps explaining why the item detracts from the reliability of the composite scale.

Deletion of any of the other items would reduce the scale reliability. Consequently, the remaining 23 items were subjected to a principal components analysis with a forced one-factor solution. The resulting loadings are reported in the last column of Table 1. As a group, the physical activities items tend to have the lowest loadings, suggesting that this might be the weakest component of the scale. The very lowest loading occurs for the first item in the risk seeking component, suggesting the possible need to find an alternative to this item in subsequent research.

We chose to create the scale for low self-control as the linear composite of the z-score transformations of the items, thereby giving equal weight to each item's variance in the variance of the composite. The sum of raw scores would have given more weight to the items with the higher standard deviations. Another alternative would be to weight items according to their factor loadings from Table 1. Although such a strategy might be worth pursuing, one consequence would be that the physical activities items, because they have as a group lower loadings than the other components, would contribute less to the variance of the composite. There are no suggestions in Gottfredson and Hirschi's description of low self-control that some components merit more weight than others.

As a sum of z-score transformations, the variable low self-control has a mean of 0. The standard deviation is 10.20. The kurtosis of 3.37 is not significantly different from that of a normal distribution ($t = +1.48$). However, the median is $-.39$, reflecting the positive skewness of the distribution (.45) which is significantly greater ($t = +3.65$) than the skewness of 0 in a normal distribution. In other words, compared to the normal distribution, there are a few outliers at the high end of the Low Self-Control Scale.

CRIMES

As noted previously, Gottfredson and Hirschi define crime as "acts of force or fraud undertaken in pursuit of self-interest" (1990, p. 15). The definition intentionally avoids equating criminal behavior with illegal behavior. We directly implement their definition in this research. Respondents were asked how many times in the past 5 years they had (a) "distorted the truth or falsely represented something to get something you couldn't otherwise obtain" (fraud), and (b) "used or threatened to use force against an adult to accomplish your goals" (force). The mean is 1.44 for fraud and .64 for force. For both crimes, the distributions are strongly positively skewed, and the overwhelming majority of respondents are in the category 0 (87% for fraud and 91% for force).

Two issues become readily apparent. First is the problem of causal order. Low self-control is measured as a present trait of respondents, but criminal behavior is measured with self-reports over the past 5 years. In most theories of crime, this would be a serious problem. But, in Gottfredson and Hirschi's formulation, low self-control is a personality trait established early in life, which remains relatively stable over the life course. In particular, the rank order of a group of people in terms of their levels of self-control is not expected to change with increased age. Thus the present level of self-control, or at least the present rank order of respondents in terms of self-control, according to the theory, can reasonably be expected to reflect the respondents' relative levels of self-control during the past 5 years. Although critics of the theory might question the invariance of self-control over the life course, our task is not to be critical, but rather to accept some of Gottfredson and Hirschi's claims in order to test others. With this strategy, temporal order is not an issue, and cross-sectional analysis is appropriate (see Gottfredson and Hirschi 1990, pp. 223-40). Gottfredson and Hirschi's argument that, because levels of self-control remain stable during the life course, panel designs would provide results identical to cross-sectional designs is one that must be tested in future research. Such research is essential for the theory and must involve a panel that begins with children at a very young age, younger than those included in typical panel studies. Age appropriate measures of low self-control and of force and fraud will have to be developed.

Second, the distributions of the crime variables pose problems for analysis. The overwhelming majority of respondents are in the 0 category. Because those who are not in the 0 category express a wide range of answers, a few extremes produce a high positive skewness for each offense. Our analysis strategies are adapted to these distributions.

CRIME OPPORTUNITY

The key causal argument in Gottfredson and Hirschi's theory is that low self-control, in conjunction with crime opportunity, leads to criminal behavior. Neither low self-control nor the presence of crime opportunity by themselves are primary causes of crime. Rather, their effect is interactive.

Again, we followed the theorists closely in formulating items to tap crime opportunities: Our questions asked about exposure to situations in which committing an act of force or fraud would have been "possible to do easily," "gratifying at the moment," "without much chance that somebody who might do something about it would quickly find out." Such a definition of opportunity was presented to respondents as a preface to this section of the questionnaire and was repeated for each of the two crimes. Like the questions concerning crimes, these opportunity questions ask reports of the number of crime opportunities encountered over the past 5 years. The mean is 4.64 for fraud and 4.19 for force. Again, the univariate distributions show a high proportion of cases in the 0 category (71% for fraud and 87% for force). Among those reporting some opportunity, the range is considerable and there are positive outliers, producing a high degree of positive skewness.

CONTROL VARIABLES

The analysis reported below includes controls for possible sources of spuriousness using dummy variables for gender and race (White vs. non-

White) and the continuous range of ages. Gottfredson and Hirschi offer hypotheses concerning the links between such variables and self-control, crime opportunity, and crime,[4] but tests of these hypotheses are beyond the scope of the present article. We will note, however, that our conclusions are identical, whether or not the control variables are in the equation.

ANALYSIS

To test the interaction argument, we use a multiplicative term involving low self-control and crime opportunity. Examination of the SPSS diagnostics indicated that multicollinearity would not be a problem (Belsley 1982). The high positive skewness in the univariate distributions of both crime and crime opportunity create obstacles for straightforward OLS regression. A common adjustment for skewness is the log transformation of the variable. However, log transformations result in the estimation of nonlinear effects, although Gottfredson and Hirschi make no claims that the effects their theory predicts are nonlinear. Instead, the corrective strategy for positive skewness we employ, which has been suggested by Nagin and Smith (1990), is to recode all scores above the 90th percentile to the 90th percentile. However, for three of the four items, strict adherence to the procedure would have produced a dichotomy. For these, we decided to allow three categories. When the transformations were completed, the crime items for both fraud and force and the crime opportunity item for force had values from 0 to 2. The crime opportunity item for fraud ranged from 0 to 10.

If the theory is correct, we would expect evidence consistent with three predictions. First, the multiplicative term representing the interaction of low self-control and crime opportunity should have a large significant positive effect on the measures of fraud and force. This follows from the argument that low self-control permits the individual to respond to opportunities for criminal behavior. Thus as opportunity increases, so should the effect of low self-control on crime. Second, the magnitude of the effect of the interaction term should be greater than the main effect of low self-control. Our reading of Gottfredson and Hirschi's theory is that the primary channel through which low self-control leads to crime is in its interaction with crime opportunity. At best, their theory is ambiguous concerning whether low self-control should have any main effect at all; at a minimum, the theory appears to predict that the interaction effect will be greater than the main effect of low self-control alone. And third, crime opportunity should have no direct main effect on crime beyond its interaction with low self-control. The presence of a crime

TABLE 2:   OLS Regressions of Truncated Crime on Low Self-Control and Crime
Opportunity (N = 389)

	Fraud			Force		
	b	Beta	p	b	Beta	p
Low self-control	.007	.117	.023	.022	.035	.466
Crime opportunity	.040	.227	<.001	.312	.397	<.001
Low self-control x crime opportunity	.004	.235	<.001	.011	.156	.002
Intercept	3.870			2.577		
R^2	.222			.262		
p	<.001			<.001		

NOTE: Coefficients reported include controls for gender, race, and age. Tests of
significance are one-tailed.

opportunity results in a crime only when that opportunity is encountered by
a person with low self-control.

The results presented in Table 2 permit an evaluation of these predictions
concerning the prominence of a Low Self-Control × Crime Opportunity
interaction effect on criminal behavior. In the equations, gender, race, and
age are controlled, although their coefficients are not reported. Before considering specific regression coefficients, the ability of the model to account
for variance in criminal behavior should be noted. The R^2 is .222 for fraud
and .262 for force. These values are overwhelmingly attributable to the
theoretical variables because removal of the control variables from the
equations results in only slight reductions to .200 for fraud and .241 for force.
Even without the control variables, the overall F's for the two equations are
significant far beyond the .001 level.

The first prediction, that the multiplicative term for the interaction of low
self-control and crime opportunity will have a significant positive effect, is
upheld. The standardized coefficients for the product terms in both equations are positive and significant: .235 ($p < .001$) for fraud, and .156 ($p =
.002$) for force. The importance of this finding should not be overlooked.
Rarely do theories of crime predict interaction effects, and interaction effects
often are difficult to detect statistically because multiplicative terms are by
nature correlated with their components, which also are independent variables in the equation. Further, the fact that the product term is significant for
both fraud and force is important, providing evidence for Gottfredson and
Hirschi's view that these two kinds of behavior which differ in many ways
(see note 2) nevertheless are both a function of the interaction of low
self-control and crime opportunity.

191

Evidence for the second prediction is less definitive, but still generally supportive of the theory. For force, the prediction clearly is supported. While the Beta of .156 for the interaction term is significant, the Beta of only .035 for the main effect of low self-control is clearly insignificant. In other words, in the case of force, the *only* effect of low self-control on crime is through its interaction with crime opportunity. This finding is consistent with the importance Gottfredson and Hirschi attach to the Low Self-Control × Crime Opportunity interaction. The results for fraud, however, are less dramatic but still basically consistent with the prediction. Even with the multiplicative term in the equation, low self-control has a significant positive main effect on fraud. The Beta is significant at the .023 level. On the other hand, we suggested that the minimum expectation is that the effect of the product term be greater than the main effect of low self-control. In fact, this is the case (.235 vs. .117), although the difference between these two standardized coefficients is not significant. On balance, therefore, the findings concerning the second prediction generally favor the argument proposed by Gottfredson and Hirschi, but the significant main effect of low self-control on fraud would seem to require additional theoretical clarification.

The results in Table 2 for both force and fraud clearly fail to support the third prediction — that crime opportunity will not have a significant main effect. For fraud, the main effect of crime opportunity (Beta = .227) is nearly equal in magnitude to the interaction effect (Beta = .235), and the difference between the two is not significant. The findings for force are even more inconsistent with the prediction. The Beta of .397 for the main effect of crime opportunity is more than twice as large as the Beta of .156 for the multiplicative term, and the difference between the two coefficients is significant at the .003 level.[5] Not only does crime opportunity have a significant main effect on force, but that effect also is significantly greater than the interaction effect of low self-control and crime opportunity. Such a finding could not be predicted from Gottfredson and Hirschi's theory and is especially troublesome given the relative lack of attention they devote to this variable.

DISCUSSION

In this research we attempted to create a set of circumstances where Gottfredson and Hirschi's theory would have the greatest chance of success. Our measures of the variables followed closely their descriptions and guidelines; we adopted their definition of crime, and tried to measure it accordingly; we uncritically accepted their assumption of causal ordering; and we addressed what seem to us to be the central empirical implications of their argument. Our purpose has been to determine whether, under these favorable circumstances, the theory is promising enough to justify further attention by the criminological community.

Our overall answer is yes, the theory clearly merits serious consideration. The elements of low self-control they identify do appear to form a general unidimensional trait, although our findings on this issue certainly warrant further research. Moreover, just as the central argument of the theory suggests, and despite the statistical problems in detecting interaction effects, the interaction of low self-control and crime opportunity significantly predicts both fraud and force that the respondents reported committing during the previous 5 years. Finally, the effect that low self-control has on crime occurs primarily in interaction with crime opportunity.

However, some patterns in the data indicate that the theory is in need of modification and expansion. For one thing, in the context of our findings, Gottfredson and Hirschi have devoted insufficient attention to the criminal opportunity variable and the sources of its variation. Although they contend that the effect of low self-control is contingent on opportunity for crime, the main focus of their theory is low self-control. In fact, Akers' (1991) review of *A General Theory of Crime* does not even mention the opportunity variable.

One of the distinguishing features of Gottfredson and Hirschi's current formulation is its compatibility with a recently emerging line of theory and research challenging sociological arguments that give primacy to structural variables. Whether or not this is a fair assessment of the authors' intent, that is how the theory is likely to be interpreted in the absence of further consideration of crime opportunity and the sources of its variation (e.g., Barlow 1991; Nagin and Farrington 1991, 1992; for a critical assessment of this trend in criminology, see Krisberg 1991). In a brief section of the book, Gottfredson and Hirschi do suggest structural variables that affect the ability of families to instill self-control in their children (1990, pp. 102-5), but once the child's level of self-control is established in early childhood, it remains relatively stable throughout life as a predisposer toward crime. Sources of variation among individuals in exposure to criminal opportunities are essentially unexplored by Gottfredson and Hirschi. If crime opportunity is largely a consequence of social structure and process, Gottfredson and Hirschi's presentation, in its current form, can be said to give much greater weight to individualistic traits than to larger social organization characteristics.

Yet our data show crime opportunity, as Gottfredson and Hirschi define it, to be important not just in providing the condition under which low self-control has its primary effect on crime but also as a significant predictor of fraud and force independent of its interaction with low self-control. As a predictor of crime, crime opportunity in our data appears to be almost as strong as (in the case of fraud) or stronger than (in the case of force) the term representing the interaction of low self-control and crime opportunity. It appears that regardless of the level of self-control, the opportunity to commit crime predicts criminal behavior, at least to a modest degree. If our results can be believed and are sustained by additional research, they weaken considerably the appeal of Gottfredson and Hirschi's theory as presently formulated. It places too little emphasis on criminal opportunity, which most likely is linked to social structure (e.g., Cohen and Felson 1979) and focuses attention on the personality characteristic of low self-control. Our finding concerning the main effect of crime opportunity raises questions about the recent trend toward emphasis on individualistic variables linked to developmental and/or familistic process, a trend so elegantly and creatively epitomized in *A General Theory of Crime*. Indeed, our results direct attention back toward features of the social environment that influence the number and distribution of criminal opportunities. Hence, despite providing promising support for certain aspects of the theory, our data seem to weaken its structural challenge.[6]

Further, the variables drawn from the theory leave much of the variance in self-reported crime unexplained. Some surely is due to methodological weaknesses in our research. After all, the sample is restricted in size, age range, and locale. Although the theory presumably is applicable to all people under all circumstances, the possibility of some distortion from sample bias cannot be ignored. No doubt some of the unexplained variance is due to measurement error and can be reduced with further refinements in measurement. Inaccurate recall and other problems with self-reported data, as well as the skewed distributions of variables probably are other sources of unexplained variance. In addition, some might also stem from the apparent logical inconsistency between Gottfredson and Hirschi's definition of low self-control, which includes risk seeking, and their definition of criminal opportunity, which includes little risk of detection. To be true to the theory, this inconsistency was incorporated into our operational definitions.

But it is unlikely that such factors alone will account for all the unexplained variance. It seems highly likely that there are other variables not included within the theory, and therefore not in our equations, that are necessary for explaining crime. It appears that this theory, at best, has identified one mechanism that affects crime. By the usual criteria employed in evaluating theories, this alone is praiseworthy. In this case, however, it appears to fall short of the expectations generated by Gottfredson and Hirschi's presentation. Although they are careful to insert caveats disclaiming

194

the possibility of perfect prediction, acknowledging that "situational conditions" and "other properties of the individual" can counteract the causal effects of low self-control (Gottfredson and Hirschi 1990, pp. 89, 96), and specifically claiming only that "high self-control effectively reduces the possibility of crime" (p. 89) and that those with high self-control will be "less likely under all circumstances throughout life to commit crime" (p. 118), Gottfredson and Hirschi imply that their theory will explain the bulk of criminal behavior with a high degree of accuracy. This is clear from their contention that all important hereditary factors and components of personality in one way or another are incorporated within the self-control variable (p. 96, 110) and from their argument that situational and social structural variables are important only to the extent that they are linked to low self-control or expressed through the variable of opportunity, which interacts with low self-control (pp. 119, 123-214). Disclaimers notwithstanding, therefore, their overall portrayal suggests a powerful theory implying that the interaction of low self-control with criminal opportunity will predict criminal behavior with a high degree of accuracy without the help of other variables. Our results are inconsistent with such an expectation.

Our analysis suggests the need for additional variables. A good beginning point for expansion of the theory could be incorporation of variables that might affect motivation toward crime, variables that play a central role in "strain" theories. As did Hirschi (1969) in his earlier work, Gottfredson and Hirschi assume that everybody is equally motivated to commit acts of fraud and force, the differences in actual commission being due to variations in self-control and/or opportunity. There is good reason, however, to think that the things one can obtain by force and/or fraud carry different values for different individuals — that is, the motivation for crime is not equal for everybody (see Agnew 1992). Consequently, actual criminal behavior should vary to some extent independently of self-control or opportunity, and motivation for crime might influence the extent to which individuals' perceive situations as constituting criminal opportunity as well as the extent to which self-control produces crime, given opportunity. In the past, Hirschi (1979) has not been favorable toward calls for theoretical integration. Whether Gottfredson and Hirschi will maintain this posture for their present theory remains to be seen. In our opinion, the premise stated early in *A General Theory of Crime* that all individuals are equally motivated to commit crime, is not a necessary ingredient of the theory.

Second, Gottfredson and Hirschi often allude to situational circumstances and individual characteristics that might mute or counteract the effects of low self-control. To elaborate and improve the theory, they might systematically spell out what those circumstances or characteristics are. With those addi-

195

tional contingencies, the main hypothesis might be far more conditional than it presently appears to be, and as a result, prove far more accurate. At the very least, identifying and theoretically elaborating those contingent circumstances would enable researchers to measure and take them into account. The result should be far better prediction.

The supportive findings in our research certainly mandate serious further consideration of the theory, and they justify investigation of additional implications and hypotheses from it. At the same time, however, contrary results suggest that the theory needs expansion, refinement, and elaboration before it can explain crime to the degree Gottfredson and Hirschi imply. We conclude, therefore, that Gottfredson and Hirschi's formulation constitutes an important innovation, but that it requires additional theoretical work.

NOTES

1. Gottfredson and Hirschi consider their theory compatible with rational choice theory: Individuals with low self-control make different choices than individuals with high self-control (1990, pp. 64-84). Other developments in rational choice theory, however, focus on more immediate characteristics of the crime setting. They rely on advances in decision-making theory, especially discussions of decision-making heuristics, which propose that actors make choices that sometimes are less than optimal but nevertheless predictable (see Cornish and Clarke 1986).

2. See Loeber and Southamer-Loeber (1986, pp. 92-95) for a discussion of the possibility that family socialization experiences associated with subsequent fraud may not be the same as those associated with force.

3. We should note that our research is an application of Gottfredson and Hirschi's theory to *adults*. From their own perspective, however, this is not problematic. Although absolute levels of key variables such as criminal opportunity and criminal behavior might be different for adults than for adolescents, the patterns of relationships among low self-control, criminal opportunity, and criminal behavior are expected to be invariant across age levels (Gottfredson and Hirschi 1990, pp. 126-44).

4. In Gottfredson and Hirschi's (1990, pp. 154-68) formulation, adult respondents' years of education and other measures of socioeconomic status would not be potential sources of spuriousness because they are dependent on, rather than causes of, self-control. Thus, we have not included such variables as controls. Future research, however, might consider the extent to which the effects of self-control on crime are indirect *via* socioeconomic status as an intervening variable.

5. Given the different metrics in which the variables in the equations in Table 2 were measured, it was necessary to conduct tests for the equality of the standardized regression coefficients to compare the effect of the interaction term to the effects of low self-control and crime opportunity. We approached this through LISREL by first estimating the full model (which by definition has a chi-square value of 0) and then imposing a set of equality constraints on the standardized coefficients. If these restrictions do not result in a significant increase in the chi-square statistic, then the null hypothesis of equality cannot be rejected. In the fraud equation, the comparisons made indicate that the effect of the product term is not significantly different from the main effect of either low self-control or crime opportunity. However, this is not the

case for the force equation. Setting the coefficient for crime opportunity equal to that of the interaction effect results in an increase in the chi-square statistic that is significant at the .003 level. Thus the null hypothesis that these two coefficients are equal is rejected, and, given their relative magnitudes, the conclusion must be that the direct effect of crime opportunity is greater than the direct effect of the Low Self-Control × Crime Opportunity interaction.

6. For a similar view, see Barlow 1991, p. 237.

REFERENCES

Agnew, Robert. 1992. "Foundation for a General Strain Theory of Crime and Delinquency." *Criminology* 30:47-87.

Akers, Ronald L. 1991. "Self-Control as a General Theory of Crime." *Journal of Quantitative Criminology* 7:201-11.

Arneklev, Bruce J., Harold G. Grasmick, Charles R. Tittle, and Robert J. Bursik, Jr. Forthcoming. "Self-Control Theory and Imprudent Behavior." *Journal of Quantitative Criminology*.

Barlow, Hugh D. 1991. "Explaining Crimes and Analogous Acts, or the Unrestrained Will Grab at Pleasure Whenever They Can." *Journal of Criminal Law and Criminology* 82:229-42.

Belsley, David A. 1982. "Assessing the Presence of Harmful Collinearity and Other Forms of Weak Data Through a Test for Signal-to-Noise." *Journal of Econometrics* 20:211-53.

Blumstein, Alfred, Jacqueline Cohen, Jeffrey Roth, and Christy A. Visher, eds. 1986. *Criminal Careers and "Career Criminals,"* Vol. 1. *Report of the Panel on Research on Criminal Careers, National Research Council.* Washington, DC: National Academy Press.

Cernkovick, Stephen A. and Peggy C. Giordano. 1987. "Family Relationships and Delinquency." *Criminology* 25:295-321.

Cohen, Lawrence E. and Marcus Felson. 1979. "Social Change and Crime Rate Trends: A Routine Activities Approach." *American Sociological Review* 44:588-608.

Cornish, Derek B. and Ronald V. Clark, eds. 1986. *The Reasoning Criminal: Rational Choice Perspectives on Offending.* New York: Springer-Verlag.

Ellis, Lee. 1991. "Monoamine Oxidase and Criminality: Identifying an Apparent Biological Marker for Antisocial Behavior." *Journal of Research in Crime and Delinquency* 28:227-51.

Eysenck, Hans J. 1989. "Personality and Criminality: A Dispositional Analysis." Pp. 89-110 in *Advances in Criminological Theory, Volume One,* edited by William S. Laufer and Freda Adler. New Brunswick, NJ: Transaction Publishers.

Felson, Marcus and Lawrence E. Cohen. 1980. "Human Ecology and Crime: A Routine Activity Approach." *Human Ecology* 8:389-406.

Fishbein, Diana H. 1990. "Biological Perspectives in Criminology." *Criminology* 28:27-72.

Fishbein, Diana H. and Robert W. Thatcher. 1986. "New Diagnostic Methods in Criminology: Assessing Organic Sources of Behavioral Disorders." *Journal of Research in Crime and Delinquency* 23:240-67.

Glueck, Sheldon and Eleanor Glueck. 1937. *Later Criminal Careers.* New York: Commonwealth Fund.

———. 1950. *Unraveling Juvenile Delinquency.* New York: Commonwealth Fund.

Gottfredson, Michael R. and Travis Hirschi. 1990. *A General Theory of Crime.* Stanford, CA: Stanford University Press.

Gough, Harrison G. 1975. *California Psychological Inventory Manual.* Palo Alto, CA: Consulting Psychologists Press.

Gove, Walter R. and Charles Wilmoth. 1990. "Risk, Crime, and Neurophysiologic Highs: A Consideration of Brain Processes That May Reinforce Delinquent and Criminal Behavior."

Pp. 261-93 in *Crime in Biological, Social, and Moral Contexts*, edited by Lee Ellis and Harry Hoffman. New York: Praeger.

Hagan, John, John Simpson, and A. R. Gillis. 1987. "Class in the Household: A Power-Control Theory of Gender and Delinquency." *American Journal of Sociology* 92:788-816.

Herrnstein, Richard J. 1983. "Some Criminogenic Traits of Offenders." Pp. 31-46 in *Crime and Public Policy*, edited by James Q. Wilson. San Francisco, CA: Institute for Contemporary Studies.

Hill, Gary D. and Maxine P. Atkinson. 1988. "Gender, Familial Control, and Delinquency." *Criminology* 26:127-49.

Hirschi, Travis. 1969. *Causes of Delinquency*. Berkeley: University of California Press.

———. 1979. "Separate and Unequal Is Better." *Journal of Research in Crime and Delinquency* 16:34-38.

Krisberg, Barry. 1991. "Are You Now or Have You Ever Been a Sociologist?" *Journal of Criminal Law and Criminology* 82:141-55.

Larzelere, Robert E. and Gerald R. Patterson. 1990. "Parental Management: Mediator of the Effect of Socioeconomic Status on Early Delinquency." *Criminology* 28:301-24.

Laub, John H. and Robert J. Sampson. 1988. "Unraveling Families and Delinquency: A Reanalysis of the Gluecks' Data." *Criminology* 26:355-80.

———. 1991. "The Sutherland-Glueck Debate: On the Sociology of Criminological Knowledge." *American Journal of Sociology* 96:1402-40.

Lemert, Edwin M. 1972. *Human Deviance, Social Problems, and Social Control*. 2d ed. Englewood Cliffs, NJ: Prentice-Hall.

Loeber, Rolf and Magda Southamer-Loeber. 1986. "Family Factors as Correlates and Predictors of Juvenile Conduct Problems and Delinquency." Pp. 29-149 in *Crime and Justice: An Annual Review of Research, Vol. 7*, edited by Michael Tonry and Norval Morris. Chicago: University of Chicago Press.

Malle, Bertram F. and Aljoscha C. Neubauer. 1991. "Impulsivity, Reflection, and Questionnaire Response Latencies: No Evidence for a Broad Impulsivity Trait." *Personality and Individual Differences* 12:865-71.

McCord, Joan. 1979. "Some Child-Rearing Antecedents of Criminal Behavior in Adult Men." *Journal of Personality and Social Psychology* 37:1477-86.

———. 1991a. "The Cycle of Crime and Socialization Practices." *Journal of Criminal Law and Criminology* 82:211-28.

———. 1991b. "Questioning the Value of Punishment." *Social Problems* 38:167-79.

———. 1991c. "Family Relationships, Juvenile Delinquency, and Adult Criminality." *Criminology* 29:397-417.

McCord, William and Joan McCord. 1959. *Origins of Crime: A New Evaluation of the Cambridge-Somerville Study*. New York: Columbia University Press.

Miethe, Terance D. and Robert F. Meier. 1990. "Opportunity, Choice, and Criminal Victimization: A Test of a Theoretical Model." *Journal of Research in Crime and Delinquency* 27:243-66.

Nagin, Daniel S. and David P. Farrington. 1991. "On the Relationship of Past and Future Participation in Delinquency." *Criminology* 29:163-89.

———. 1992. "The Onset and Persistence of Offending." *Criminology* 30:501-23.

Nagin, Daniel S. and Douglas A. Smith. 1990. "Participation in and Frequency of Delinquent Behavior: A Test for Structural Differences." *Quantitative Criminology* 6:335-65.

Nunnally, Jum C. 1967. *Psychometric Theory*. New York: McGraw-Hill.

Nye, F. Ivan. 1958. *Family Relationships and Delinquent Behavior*. New York: Wiley.

Patterson, Gerald R. and Thomas J. Dishion. 1985. "Contributions of Families and Peers to Delinquency." *Criminology* 23:63-79.

Rankin, Joseph H. and L. Edward Wells. 1990. "The Effect of Parental Attachments and Direct Controls on Delinquency." *Journal of Research in Crime and Delinquency* 27:140-65.

Rowe, David C. 1986. "Genetic and Environmental Components of Antisocial Behavior: A Study of 265 Twin Pairs." *Criminology* 24:513-32.

Smith, Douglas A., Christy A. Visher, and G. Roger Jarjoura. 1991. "Dimensions of Delinquency: Exploring the Correlates of Participation, Frequency, and Persistence of Delinquent Behavior." *Journal of Research in Crime and Delinquency* 28:6-32.

Straus, Murray A. 1991. "Discipline and Deviance: Physical Punishment of Children and Violence and Other Crime in Adulthood." *Social Problems* 38:133-54.

Sutherland, Edwin H. 1947. *Principles of Criminology*. 4th ed. Philadelphia, PA: Lippincott.

Thornberry, Terence P., Alan J. Lizotte, Marvin D. Krohn, Margaret Farnworth, and Sung Joon Jang. 1991. "Testing Interactional Theory: An Examination of Reciprocal Causal Relationships Among Family, School, and Delinquency." *Journal of Criminal Law and Criminology* 82:3-35.

Wells, L. Edward and Joseph H. Rankin. 1986. "The Broken Homes Model of Delinquency: Analytic Issues." *Journal of Research in Crime and Delinquency* 23:68-93.

———. 1988. "Direct Parental Controls and Delinquency." *Criminology* 26:263-85.

———. 1991. "Families and Delinquency: A Meta-Analysis of the Impact of Broken Homes." *Social Problems* 38:71-93.

Widom, Cathy Spitz. 1989. "Child Abuse, Neglect, and Violent Criminal Behavior." *Criminology* 27:251-71.

Wilson, James Q. and Richard J. Herrnstein. 1985. *Crime and Human Nature*. New York: Simon & Schuster.

DESTINY AND DRIFT:
SUBCULTURAL PREFERENCES, STATUS ATTAINMENTS, AND THE RISKS AND REWARDS OF YOUTH*

JOHN HAGAN
University of Toronto

I combine the concept of drift, drawn from social control theory, and a life course conceptualization to elaborate a paradigmatic model to study cultural stratification. I apply this model in a thirteen-year panel study to examine the effects of adolescent subcultural preferences on later adult status attainments. Adolescents adrift from parental and educational control are more likely than those with more controls to develop mild or more seriously deviant subcultural preferences. I identify two distinct adolescent subcultural preferences: a subculture of delinquency and a party subculture. Among males with working-class origins, identification with the subculture of delinquency has a negative effect on trajectories of early adult status attainment. However, among males from non-working-class backgrounds, identification with a party subculture has a net positive effect when the negative effects of partying on educational performance are removed.

S ociological research on deviance and stratification is largely unintegrated.[1] This is understandable, since deviance research emphasizes descent into disrepute, while stratification research more often focuses on the attainment of prestige. The stages of the life course that each field emphasizes also differ: Crime peaks during adolescence, while occupational destinations crystallize in adulthood. Theoretical concerns also distinguish these fields: The dominant theory of deviance emphasizes breakdowns in social control; the dominant stratification theory focuses on the socialization of aspiration and achievement. In general, deviance research attends to the inauspicious circumstances that lead to disrepute, while stratification research explores the more hopeful determinants of durable, if not distinguished, occupational careers.

From a more general perspective, however, it is obvious that adolescent deviance and adult stratification outcomes should be linked in some way and that their respective subfields could benefit from some level of integration. Yet only a few studies to date have attended to this linkage. In this paper I use the concept of drift from the deviance literature (Matza 1964) and research on cultural stratification (DiMaggio 1982, 1987) and the life course (Elder 1985) to further this effort.

The concept of drift evolved in direct response to Cohen's (1955) *Delinquent Boys* and in indirect response to Coleman's (1961) *The Adolescent Society*. Cohen initiated research on subcultural delinquency that is still central to sociological criminology and that spawned a British subcultural sociology (e.g., Hall and Jefferson 1976; Willis 1977; Hebdige 1984), while Coleman established a lasting appreciation of the adolescent cultural underpinnings of adult social stratification. However, despite a common concern with adolescent culture, these sociological classics exemplify disconnection in deviance and stratification research. For example, although Coleman's research is seminal in its attention to the roles of athletic and academic values in adolescent society (see also Otto and Alwin 1977), it neglects the disreputable kinds of values embodied in the subculture of delinquency (see Campbell 1969; Short and Strodtbeck 1965; Schwendinger and Schwendinger 1985). Meanwhile, the criminological and British traditions treat subcultural in-

* Direct correspondence to John Hagan, Faculty of Law, University of Toronto, Toronto Canada, M5S 2C5. This research was supported by a grant from the Social Sciences and Humanities Research Council of Canada, a Killam Research Fellowship from the Canada Council, and by the Canadian Institute for Advanced Research.

[1] The terms "stratification" and "status attainment" are used somewhat interchangeably in this paper. Of course, status attainment is only one (albeit important) aspect of stratification. Another aspect, involving measures of class position, is introduced later in the paper. Nonetheless, I intend no claim to comprehensiveness.

American Sociological Review, 1991, Vol. 56 (October:567-582)

567

volvements as a dependent variable, neglecting the role that such involvements can play in influencing later status attainments.

ADOLESCENT DEVIANCE AND ADULT OUTCOMES

A few studies have considered the consequences of adolescent deviance for adult stratification outcomes (e.g., Sampson and Laub 1990), and it is generally well recognized that adolescence is a critical transitional period from childhood to adulthood (Elder 1980; Modell, Furstenberg, and Hershberg 1976; Hagan and Palloni 1990). But this research is more complicated and open-ended in the possibilities it raises than often is realized (Hagan and Palloni 1988).

Robins's (1966) study of adult outcomes, *Deviant Children Grown Up*, followed two groups into adulthood: a clinic-based sample of predominantly low-status "severely antisocial children" and a "control group" who were without adolescent behavior problems and were matched with the clinic sample on race, age, sex, IQ, and SES. As adults the clinic sample experienced more unemployment for longer spells and with more frequent job changes, fewer promotions, depressed earnings, more credit problems and greater reliance on public assistance than did the control group.

The Gluecks (1950, 1968) applied a similar matched group design to study white males from Boston who, because of their persistent delinquency, were committed to one of two correctional schools in Massachusetts. Sampson and Laub (1990) reanalyzed these data and reported that not only adult criminal behavior, but "seven adult behaviors spanning economic, educational, employment, and family domains are also strongly related to adolescent delinquency" (p. 616). These outcomes included greater adult unemployment and welfare dependency among the delinquent sample.

As Jessor, Donovan, and Costa (forthcoming) noted, however, recent research on adult consequences of adolescent deviance suggests more complicated and socially contingent adult possibilities. For example, while Ghodsian and Power (1987) observed continuity in drinking among a national sample of British youth followed from ages 16 to 23, a subsequent analysis of these data by Power and Estaugh (1990, p. 493) argued that teenage drinking was "generally unrelated to early adult experience of either obtaining or remaining in employment."

Mixed findings also emerged from a study by Newcomb and Bentler (1988), whose sample of Los Angeles high school students demonstrated continuities in drug use and problems of job instability in early adulthood. However, the authors also noted that "early drug use did not generate a pattern of irresponsibility, laziness, and work avoidance" (p. 169). In addition, their composite measure of "social conformity" in adolescence had no net effect on income, job instability, job satisfaction, collected public assistance, or amount worked in early adulthood.

The most compelling study, however, is one of Colorado high school and college students by Jessor et al. (forthcoming). Although the authors found continuity in problem behaviors from adolescence into adulthood, these behaviors did not affect work and status attainment. They argue that the latter unexpected findings are made plausible by three factors:

First, our research involved normal rather than clinical samples, and the extent of their adolescent/youth involvement in problem behavior—even at its greatest—has to be seen as moderate for the most part. Second, our samples were largely middle class in socioeconomic status, and the openness of the opportunity structure for them and their access to "second chances" have to be seen as far greater than might be the case for disadvantaged youth who had been involved in problem behavior. Third, . . . , even for samples such as ours, there can still be compromising outcomes [yet] to be manifested. (chap. 9, p. 19)

Jessor et al. combine these observations in an "interactionist perspective," asserting that the course of psychosocial development is not inexorable, that past actions do not necessarily foreclose future options, and that there can be resilience in growth and change: "at least in social contexts that are not entirely malignant, and at a time in history when the social setting itself is relatively open and undergoing change" (chap. 9, p. 20).

DRIFT, PREFERENCES AND ATTAINMENTS IN THE LIFE COURSE

The theoretical perspective for this analysis begins with the concept of drift, which David Matza (1964) introduced in order to soften an assumption of determinacy that characterizes much research in stratification (cf. Jencks et al. 1972) as well as in deviance. Matza wrote that "drift stands midway between freedom and control," and he defined drifters as "those who have been granted the potentiality for freedom through the loosening of social controls but who lack the position, capacity, or inclination to become agents in their behalf" (pp. 28-29). He emphasized that such individuals tend to drift between criminal and conventional involvements, and that the process of "maturational reform" associated with the transition to adulthood means that the direction of drift between adolescence and adulthood is mostly from crime to convention — that is, from experimentation with delinquency and related interests to conventional, even mundane, adult occupations. Beyond this, little is known about the directions that the lives of adolescent drifters take.

Elder's (1985) conceptualization of the life course in terms of trajectories and transitions provides a useful framework for studying drifting adolescents as well as adolescents who are more directed. Trajectories — pathways through the life course, including occupational careers, marital histories, and parenthood — encompass patterned and age-graded sequences or transitions that consist of events, experiences, or processes, such as first and succeeding jobs, marriages, and births. Adolescent subcultural preferences reflect transitional cultural experiences that in association with other background and foreground contingencies may establish longer-term life course trajectories for directed as well as drifting adolescents.

Adolescent subcultural preferences are partly adaptations to the pressures of the passage to adulthood. They include behaviors and values that are distinct from, if not opposed to, adult norms (Campbell 1969). However, having fun is also important, particularly with the opposite sex (Bordua 1961), and elements of risk and excitement also characterize these preferences (Katz 1989). These possibilities lure Matza's drifters, freed from institutional controls, into subcultural involvements.

So while Cohen's (1955) classic conceptualization emphasized the oppositional content of the "delinquent subculture," Matza (1964; also Sykes and Matza 1957, 1961) argued that a "subculture of delinquency" represents a more loosely determined "subterranean convergence" between adult and adolescent values.[2] Subterranean

values include a Veblenesque search for adventure, excitement, and thrills (Veblen 1934); and Matza (1964) therefore observes that "an apparently tenuous and precarious subculture delicately balanced between crime and convention . . . is itself a subterranean tradition in American life" (p. 63). This is a tradition, notes Matza, into which individuals are more likely to drift than be directed.

The view of adolescent subcultures as perched between crime and convention emerged early in Matza's work, and this view has been extended by recent British research. For example, Hebdige (1984) wrote that for typical members of a working-class youth culture in contemporary Great Britain "there is a substantial amount of shared ideological ground not only between them and the adult working-class culture . . . but also between them and the dominant culture" (p. 86). Hebdige analyzed a cult of David "Bowie-ites" that provoked questions about gender as well as class in order "to negotiate a meaningful intermediate space somewhere between the parent culture and the dominant ideology" (p. 88).

Another important idea suggested by Matza is that teenage culture may sometimes curb serious deviancy. Campbell (1969) cited Matza in suggesting that much teenage culture is actually a conventional version of delinquency, "conventional in that it strips away delinquency's most odious features" (p. 846). Campbell's point is that although teenage culture emphasizes fun and adventure, disdains scholastic effort, and flirts with the boundary areas between propriety and immorality (e.g., staying out late, drinking, sexual explorations, and "conning" parents), nonetheless this culture is more accurately seen as "playing at" deviance. Campbell added irony to Matza's notion of subterranean convergence when he concluded that the "great social virtue" of much teenage culture is that "it offers sufficient inherent satisfactions to attract and maintain . . . many adherents who otherwise would be vulnerable to the appeals of delinquency" (pp. 840-41).

Many teenage subcultures may exist, with varying meanings, both for adolescents and their status attainments in adulthood (see also Roe 1984). DiMaggio (1982) anticipated this possibility at the middle and higher ends of the adolescent cultural continuum when he distinguished between "middlebrow cultural activity" (e.g., drawing,

---

[2] Two classic usages of the term "subculture" were outlined by Yinger (1960). The first points to basic differences in norms and values between subordinate and dominant groups in society. The second usage adds to the first a social psychological sense of frustration that stimulates the development and maintenance of the conflicting norms and values. Matza's usage of "subculture" allows more convergence and

correspondence between subordinate and dominant group norms and values and does not assume the presence of a driving sense of frustration. I have adopted Matza's usage.

photography, crafts, woodworking, and sewing) and "cultural capital" (e.g., theater attendance, visits to museums and galleries). DiMaggio (1982) found that the former cultural involvements have little impact on educational attainment, while cultural capital enhances educational attainment apart from measured ability. Thus, different adolescent cultural involvements may have varied implications for adult status trajectories. Matza's conceptualization adds to this continuum the possibility that while adolescents sometimes may be driven or directed by parents and schools to acquire cultural capital or other forms of middlebrow culture, without parental and educational direction they are more likely to drift into less reputable subcultural pursuits. These pursuits may take their own directions, which are as yet little understood.

DiMaggio (1982; 1987; DiMaggio and Mohr 1985) built his work on Coleman's, as well as on work by Weber [1968] (1972), Bourdieu (1977), Collins (1975, 1979), Roe (1984), and Hebdige (1984). He established a paradigmatic model of the impact of adolescent culture on educational and, ultimately (although this has not yet been explored empirically), occupational attainments. This paradigm locates adolescent culture as an intervening variable between status origins and the abilities and efforts of adolescent children on the one hand, and educational and occupational attainments on the other (see Katsillis and Rubinson 1990). DiMaggio and Mohr (1985) encouraged the extension of this paradigm to the lower end of the cultural spectrum, noting that while they have paid attention to positively valued cultural resources, "it is possible that negatively valued cultural styles (e.g., punk lifestyles) influence the stratification process in comparable but opposite ways" (p. 1256).

OPERATIONAL ISSUES AND HYPOTHESES

Some fundamental issues are unresolved in research on cultural preferences and status attainment. For example, DiMaggio's use of "interest in," "familiarity with," and "taste for" high culture in his theoretical statements made it uncertain whether operationalizations of cultural capital should be attitudinal or behavioral. DiMaggio's (1982) initial measures of cultural capital mixed the two kinds of content, and the item that loaded most heavily in his factor analyses was an attitudinal measure of interest in attending symphony concerts (p. 193, Table 2). DiMaggio's use

of behavioral measures follows the early use of such measures by Bourdieu (1973); but more recently Bourdieu (1984) has used subjective indicators, especially "taste," which he defined as "an acquired disposition to 'differentiate' and 'appreciate'" (p. 466).

The challenge is to capture the range of these "tastes" or "styles." Roe (1984 pp. 137-38, see also Appendix 3) argued that by age 15 adolescents have developed "specific taste attitudes" that preference measures distinguish more finely. This view is consistent with the emphasis on symbolic communication and style in contemporary subcultural writings (e.g., Hebdige 1984). Cultural tastes, styles, and preferences can have a range and detail that behavioral reports overlook. Although I consider behavioral measures, my primary measurement strategy is built around the kinds of preference measures suggested by Roe.

Some tentative hypotheses build on DiMaggio's model by treating adolescent cultural preferences as reflective of transitional experiences in the life course, capable of creating cultural deficits as well as cultural capital and other kinds of cultural resources that may extend their influence into the occupational sphere. My focus is on the fun and thrill-seeking side of teenage culture, that I infer from Matza's work is multidimensional, and that leads me to expect that:

H_1: Activities that adolescents perceive to be fun form distinct and internally coherent sets of subcultural preferences, some of which are more seriously deviant than others.

This hypothesis grounds predictions (below) about differential effects of subcultural preferences.

The subcultural preferences considered here derive salience partly from their separateness from high culture (including education) and from adults (especially parents). Indeed, it is the freedom from the hold of these institutions that allows adolescents to drift into these cultural domains. So I further expect that:

H_2: These subcultural preferences are negatively related to measures of educational ability, effort, aspiration, and expectation, as well as to parental efforts to control their adolescent children.

This hypothesis is selective in drawing from the subcultural tradition. While Cohen (1955) assumed that working-class origins lead adolescents to participate in the delinquent subculture, Matza's (1964) assumption of subterranean convergence questioned this link and placed greater emphasis on the relaxation of institutional controls. My second hypothesis follows Matza in predicting that subcultural preferences are directly linked to weaknesses in the school and family ties that can limit the drift into less reputable subcultural domains. However, as I discuss below, this does not imply that class origins are of no significance.

Before pursuing the influence of these transitional subcultural preferences in establishing life course trajectories, I further note that effects of subcultural preferences may be mediated by societal reactions to them. Labelling theorists argue that delinquent and other subcultural involvements are shaped by the reactions of others. For example, Lemert (1951) argued that reactions by police and others highlight "the symbolic appurtenances of the new role, in clothes, speech, posture, and mannerisms, which in some cases heighten social visibility" (p. 76). If this is the case, then:

H₃: The cultural deficit of more seriously deviant subcultural preferences is mediated by police contacts.

This hypothesis brings me to more precise predictions about the cultural deficits I expect to be associated with the subcultural preferences of drifting adolescents. Since Jessor et al. (1991) found little evidence of adverse adult socioeconomic outcomes from adolescent deviance in general (unmatched) samples, adverse effects may be limited to more serious subcultural involvements and to adolescents from the underclass. Although this proposition has not been tested within a specific data set, it explains apparently contradictory findings and is anticipated in the stratification literature.

For example, Cohen (1955) acknowledged this link to stratification research and narrowed the focus further for male adolescents when he wrote in *Delinquent Boys* that "Hollingshead, in his *Elmtown's Youth*, stresses throughout the importance of parental status in obtaining special consideration in school activities and on the job through 'connections' and other means of exerting pressure" (p. 111). Hollingshead (1949) was indeed emphatic, observing that "class control tends to result in the manipulation of institutional functions in the interests of individuals and families who have wealth, prestige, and power" (p. 452). The continuity of these premises is reflected in Goode's (1978) more recent argument that "the relative resources of the individuals or groups in prestige processes may have consider-

able effect on who gets how much public praise or dispraise," so that "juvenile delinquents of upper middle-class families often avoid much loss in respect" (p. 252). This avoidance of consequences is the "openness of the opportunity structure" and the "access to second chances" that Jessor et al. associated with the disreputable involvements of middle class youth.

Meanwhile, DiMaggio (1982; DiMaggio and Mohr 1985) included gender with parental educational origins in specifying attainment models. Robins (1966) also emphasized that childhood deviance can influence male and female adult outcomes differently, and therefore that it is important to analyze these experiences separately by gender. Following such leads, I specify models by gender and parental class background, to predict conditions under which more serious subcultural preferences establish diminished trajectories of status attainment. I expect that:

H₄: Only the more seriously deviant subcultural preferences crystallize as cultural deficits; this is more likely to occur among the adolescent sons of working-class fathers.

In other words, drift into subcultural delinquency may be most consequential in working class families. But there may also be measurable benefits of less serious subcultural inclinations. Recall Matza's suggestion that less serious subcultural involvements may have the ironic virtue of curbing more deviant inclinations. Subcultural work also emphasizes that these involvements can play a part in adolescent male sex-role socialization; they may also anticipate activities that can consolidate and enhance adult network ties. For example, partying, drinking, and related pursuits, apart from the educational distractions and difficulties caused during adolescence, may ultimately yield tangible payoffs through adult work-related network-building activities involving these and other mildly disreputable pleasures. But I suspect such benefits may be restricted to non-working-class males, so that:

H₅: Less seriously deviant subcultural preferences are more likely to crystallize as a cultural resource for males of non-working-class origins.

DATA, MEASURES AND METHODS

The Sample

Two waves of panel data were collected in 1976 and 1989 in a suburb of about a half million peo-

Table 1. Factor Loadings: Principal Factor Analysis with Oblique Rotation of Subcultural Preferences, Male and Female Adolescents

	Males		Females	
Factor	Delinquency Subculture	Party Subculture	Delinquency Subculture	Party Subculture
Subculture of Delinquency				
Stealing expensive things (e.g., worth over $50)	.755	.154	.896	.080
Stealing little things (e.g. shoplifting)	.758	.161	.840	.072
Breaking into schools, breaking up school property	.803	.272	.788	-.075
Breaking streetlights, windows, etc.	.822	.240	.794	.098
Running from police	.755	.321	.728	.122
Fighting (in gangs)	.738	.266	.699	.034
Fighting (between individuals)	.663	.220	.676	.045
Eigenvalue	4.777		4.431	
% of total variance	36.7		34.1	
Party Subculture				
Going to parties	.204	.759	-.018	.806
Going to rock concerts and dances	.162	.792	-.009	.787
Picking up girls, meeting boys	.219	.709	.152	.752
Dating	.125	.706	-.089	.724
Driving around in car	.299	.605	.089	.669
Drinking alcohol	.408	.580	.358	.489
Eigenvalue		2.264		3.024
% of total variance		17.4		23.3

Note: The correlation between factors is .303 for males and .083 for females.

ple adjacent to Toronto (Canada). This suburb has grown dramatically in population over the last 25 years, with population growth concentrated around the intersection of two major highways that access the city. The sampling frame for wave 1 of the study in 1976 was the enrollment lists of all students in grades eight through twelve from all four secondary schools (including a vocational school) that serve the central area of this community. The vocational school students are not included in this analysis because they did not receive grades comparable to other students; this made it impossible to introduce essential controls for ability and effort (Katsillis and Rubinson

1990).[3]

The original sample was disproportionately stratified by housing type to increase class variation; I used addresses to sample respondents in equal numbers from single- and multiple-family dwelling units. Students sampled were personally invited and paid five dollars each to participate after school in the survey. The response rate was 83.5 percent, providing 693 regular secondary school students for the wave 1 of the panel.

Thirteen years later, telephone interviews were completed with 490 of the wave 1 regular secondary school students. Nine of the original respondents had died; the response rate was 71.6 percent. Given the interval between waves, this response was high and similar to the most comparable study I could locate (Otto and Featherman 1975). However, nonrandom sample attrition remains a concern.[4]

Sample Selection and Status Attainment

By 1989, the respondents in the sample were in their late twenties and early thirties. At this stage, 93.3 percent of the men (N = 250) and 81.1 percent of the women (N = 180) were employed; their reported occupations were ranked using Treiman's (1977) Standard International Occu-

[3] Vocational school students are different from other students in the sample in some significant ways. For example, male vocational school students score higher on the subculture of delinquency scale (x = 19.9 compared to 13.3 for other students) and their fathers have lower socioeconomic status (x = 39.5 compared to 46.7). It is unlikely that including these students would increase the generalizability of our findings, since they are drawn from a much larger catchment area than those drawn from the other more representative schools in our sample; vocational school students would be overrepresented if they were simply combined with the other students. In any case, this issue appears to be moot because when these students are included in the equations the pattern of results is not substantially altered.

[4] A bivariate and then multivariate search for factors that distinguished the selected from the attrited respondents in the 13-year recontact survey revealed that the latter were more often female (48.3% vs. 45.3%), were lower in self-evaluated school performance (x = 3.19 vs. 3.35), moved more often as children (x = 1.98 vs. 1.83), more often lived in multiple-family dwellings (77% vs. 66%), less often lived with both parents from age five (35% vs. 23%), and came more often from outside central Canada (15% vs. 10%). These differences were not dramatic, but they are nonetheless taken into account in the correction for selection bias reported below.

pational Prestige Scale.

Therefore, there were two potential sources of sample selection bias: attrition between waves of the survey and nonparticipation in the labor force. Information from wave 1 is available to model retention in the panel and additional information from wave 2 is used to model labor force participation, allowing correction for sample selection (Heckman 1979; Berk 1983). Gender-specific probit models for these corrections are presented in Appendix 1, and lambda values representing respective correction factors are reported below in regression models of status attainment.

Subcultural Preference Measures

The wave 1 survey used unique measures of the fun and the rebellion involved in adolescent subcultural experiences: the teenage respondents were asked to rank activities on a scale from one to ten in terms of "how much fun you think they are." To assess the different dimensions embodied in adolescent subcultures and their roles in establishing trajectories of adult attainment, I followed the lead of DiMaggio and factor analyzed the items separately for males and females using varimax and oblique solutions. The results are similar across solutions and genders. The oblique solution is summarized in Table 1.

As suggested in hypothesis 1, two distinct and internally coherent factors yield eigenvalues above 2.0 and explain a majority of the variance in rankings. One factor conforms to expectations of the criminological literature; I call it the "subculture of delinquency." The second factor involves a less rebellious set of interests, I call it the "party subculture." As Matza suggests, the second factor is more conventional. While the first factor (involving theft, vandalism, fighting, and running from police) is similar to scales of self-reported delinquency (from Porterfield 1943 to Hindelang, Hirschi, and Weis 1981), the second factor only edges into the illegal with alcohol consumption, and is more focused on the pursuit of fun and the opposite sex. Drinking is, perhaps predictably, the only item that loads substantially on both factors, and it loads more heavily on the party factor. Removing drinking from the factor analysis makes little difference; for example, its removal only reduces the correlation between factors among males to .28 from .3.

The party subculture may only be a subculture to the extent that it is a more distinct part of adolescent than of adult society. Nonetheless, this subculture reflects much of the subterranean convergence that Matza postulates between adolescent and adult society, and the focus on partying, rock concerts, and drinking gives this factor a contemporary and adolescent Veblenesque cast (Veblen 1934). The means and standard deviations reported in Table 2 indicate that on average boys rank the subculture of delinquency higher than do girls, and that boys and girls rank the party subculture about equally, both ranking it higher than delinquency. The mean scores for the subculture of delinquency scale are relatively low (especially among girls) and the standard deviations are substantial. This kind of skewness is common in delinquency measures. I standardized the distributions of these scores and increased comparability across scales and genders by converting the delinquency and party measures separately by gender to z-scores (DiMaggio 1982; DiMaggio and Mohr 1985). These conversions emphasize relative more than absolute variation from the norm in assessing effects of subcultural preferences. Relativity is, of course, a common concern in considerations of deviance.

One might wonder how the above measures of subcultural preference correspond to actual behaviors. I included no behavioral measures of partying in the initial survey, but did include a self-report behavior scale that closely parallels the preference measures of the subculture of delinquency (Hirschi 1969).[5] The correlation of the subculture of delinquency preference scale with the self-report behavior scale is greater than .6, and the two scales cannot be considered simultaneously without causing collinearity problems. But I can follow DiMaggio's early example and join attitudinal and behavioral measures to create a second-order factor that provides an alternative scale of the subculture of delinquency (see footnote 7). However, I do not expect behaviors per se to have the strongest long-term effects on adult status attainments, other than through the stigma of police contacts that I measure directly in my models. Rather, I see the cultural tastes and styles formed in adolescence as the strongest influence and expressed in more diverse and detailed preference measures.

---

[5] The self-report delinquent behavior scale contains items that ask how often in the last year the respondent has taken little things (worth less than $2), taken things of some value (between $2 and $50), taken things of large value (worth over $50), deliberately banged up something that belonged to someone else, deliberately banged up or damaged something that belonged to the school, beaten up on anyone or hurt anyone on purpose (not counting brothers or sisters).

Table 2.   Means and Standard Deviations by Gender for Adolescent and Early Adult Variables

Variable	Measure	Males (N = 250) Mean (s.d.)	Females (N = 180) Mean (s.d.)
Adult SES	Treiman scale	47.800 (10.487)	49.71 (10.659)
Subculture of delinquency	Summed factor scores (Before conversion to z-scores)	13.306 (10.758)	7.325 (7.994)
Party subculture	Summed factor scores (Before conversion to z-scores)	28.574 (7.592)	28.144 (6.969)
Ability	"Compared to other students in your school, how do you rate yourself in the school work you do?" *(From 1 = among the worst to 5 = among the best)*	3.316 (.750)	3.411 (.650)
Effort	"On the average, how much time do you spend doing homework outside school?" *(From 0 = no homework to 6 = 3+ hours)*	2.404 (1.371)	2.839 (1.325)
Father SES	Treiman Scale when respondent was 12	46.712 (11.575)	45.567 (11.304)
Mother SES	Treiman Scale when respondent was 12	41.836 (7.664)	41.378 (7.372)
Relational control	"Do you talk about your thoughts and feelings with your mother/father?" *(From 0 = never to 3 = always)* "Would you like to be the kind of person your mother/father is?" *(From 0 = not at all to 4 = in every way)* (Alpha = .606/.615)	5.568 (2.348)	5.378 (2.531)
Instrumental control	"Does your mother/father know where you are when you are away from home?" "Does your mother/father know who you are with when you are away from home?" *(From 0 = never to 3 = always)* (Alpha = .811/.782)	5.700 (2.243)	7.25 (2.377)
Police contact	"Have you ever been picked up by the police?" *(From 0 = never to 4 = four+)*	.904 (1.280)	.172 (.615)
Educational aspiration	"How much schooling would you like to get eventually?" "How much schooling do you actually expect to get eventually?" *(From 1 = no more to 7 = college graduation)* (Alpha = .858/.906)	11.548 (3.204)	11.906 (3.072)
English grade	Percentage score in spring	59.828 (12.351)	66.256 (12.755)
Math grade	Percentage score in spring	65.412 (15.646)	68.828 (16.438)
Educational attainments	Highest level education completed *(From 1 = some high school to 6 = university graduate)*	3.716 (1.740)	3.563 (1.618)

Other Independent Variables

Remaining independent variables are described in Table 2. The inclusion of occupational prestige variables for fathers and mothers reflects an assumption in cultural theories that parental class origins influence sons' and daughters' status attainments. I used Treiman's Standard International Occupational Prestige Scale to measure respondents' early adult status attainments. Respondents' reports of their mothers' and fathers' occupations when respondents were 12 years old were scaled using the same index.[6] Treiman (1977) demonstrated that this index is cross-culturally valid, representing a generic hierarchy of occupations across societies. A further specification of the analysis by father's class position using measures developed by Wright (1978) is introduced below.

Except where otherwise indicated, the remaining independent variables in Table 2 were measured in the wave 1 survey. The measures of ability and effort are central to the cultural stratification paradigm (Katsillis and Rubinson 1990) and have added relevance in operationalizing the weakness of school as an institutional constraint on drift. A self-rated comparison with other students on school performance measured ability, and a self-report of average time spent on homework measured effort. I also included measures of educational aspirations and expectations; this scale yielded substantial alpha scores for males (.858) and females (.906).

The introduction of social control premises into the cultural stratification paradigm also required that I consider parental constraints on adolescents. Again, the premise is that parental constraints decrease the likelihood of adolescent subcultural drift (see Nye 1958; Hirschi 1969). I included scales of parental relational and instrumental controls in this analysis. I operationalized relational controls through questions about interaction (talking about thoughts and feelings) and identification with (wanting to be like) parents, and measured instrumental controls with questions about supervision (knowing who with) and surveillance (knowing whereabouts) of adolescents. Mother and father scores were joined to avoid collinearity problems. Alpha scores reported in Table 2 and analyses presented elsewhere (Hagan, Gillis, and Simpson 1988; Hagan, Gillis, and Simpson 1990) indicate that these scales are reliable.

It is likely that the remaining variables in Table 2 exert their influence between adolescent

---

[6] I have retained separate mother and father socioeconomic status measures in order to explore whether these measures differentially affect daughter and son outcomes. There is some evidence they do. The correlation between these parental status measures is below .2 for daughters and sons. Meanwhile, there is no consensus on how to treat single-parent households in this kind of analysis. Absent parents may or may not exert influence. When single-parent households are removed from the estimation of the equations in Table 4, the effect of the subculture of delinquency scale is increased modestly in the first equation, while the overall pattern of results remains the same.

subcultures and adult status attainments, although assuming this causal sequence is not necessary to the conclusions I reach. The first of these variables, police contact, is the number of times respondents have been picked up by the police. I assume police contacts result from activities associated with subcultural preferences. The next variables are English and math grades recorded from school files the spring after the wave 1 survey. Finally, a six-level index of educational attainment is included from the wave 2 survey. These attainments follow variables measured in the wave 1 survey.

I assumed a causal ordering of variables that is conservative in treating parental SES, self-rated ability, effort, and aspirations and expectations as predeterminants of identification with the delinquency or party subcultures. Police contacts, subsequent English and math grades, and educational attainments were added in sequence, as variables intervening between adolescent subcultural preferences and adult status attainments. This sequence is consistent with the cultural stratification paradigm (DiMaggio 1982; DiMaggio and Mohr 1985; Katsillis and Rubinson 1990). However, my conclusions do not depend on this assumed sequence.

ANALYSIS

I examined the determinants of adolescent subcultural preferences in Table 3 by regressing the subculture of delinquency and party subculture z-scores separately for males and females on fathers' and mothers' occupational prestige, adolescents' self-rated ability and effort, their aspirations and expectations, and parental relational and instrumental control. Since all hypothesized relationships specify direction, one-tailed tests of significance are reported.

Notable findings in Table 3 include negative effects of parental instrumental and relational control on subcultural preferences. The strongest of these effects are of parental instrumental control on the subculture of delinquency. Parental relational control also has a significant negative effect on identification with the party subculture among females. So sons and daughters who perceive themselves as less controlled by their parents are, as expected, more likely to drift into the preferences of the subculture of delinquency and the party subculture, even with parental status origins and educational measures of ability, effort, and aspiration/expectation held constant.

Ability, effort, and aspiration/expectation tend

Table 3. Unstandardized OLS Coefficients: Determinants of Subcultural Preferences Among Adolescent Males and Females

Variables	Males (N = 250)		Females (N = 180)	
	Subculture of Delinquency	Party Sub-culture	Subculture of Delinquency	Party Sub-culture
Father SES	-.011*	-.004	.011*	-.005
	(.005)	(.005)	(.006)	(.006)
Mother SES	.007	-.004	.006	-.001
	(.008)	(.008)	(.010)	(.010)
Ability	-.002	-.146*	-.311*	.041
	(.092)	(.091)	(.175)	(.171)
Effort	-.121**	-.027	.040	-.093*
	(.047)	(.047)	(.054)	(.053)
Educational aspirations	-.075**	-.039*	-.035	-.003
	(.021)	(.021)	(.024)	(.024)
Relational control	.010	-.013	-.041	-.078**
	(.029)	(.029)	(.030)	(.030)
Instrumental control	-.092**	-.043	-.119**	-.048
	(.032)	(.031)	(.032)	(.031)
Lambda A	-.694	.292	-1.619*	.265
	(.468)	(.472)	(1.006)	(1.016)
Lambda B	.537	-.004	-.256	.031
	(.487)	(.519)	(.275)	(.271)
Intercept	2.667	1.495	2.516	1.055
R^2	.191	.089	.150	.123

* $p < .05$ (one-tailed)   ** $p < .01$ (one-tailed)

Note: Standard errors are in parentheses.

to be negatively related to subcultural preferences in the models for males and females, indicating that weak attachment to school goals also plays a significant role in forming these preferences. Six of these effects are significant, supporting the hypothesis that weak institutional controls make subcultural drift more likely.

Finally, effects of parental occupational prestige are inconsistent and isolated to the subculture of delinquency, with a negative effect for males and a positive effect for females. Overall, there is more consistent support for hypothesis 2 than there is for an assumed influence of parental prestige: Weak parental controls and lower academic ability, effort and aspirations/expectations are significant sources of subcultural drift. The less controlled by parents and involved or committed to school adolescents are, the more likely they are to drift into the subculture of delinquency and the party subculture.

I turn now to the determinants of adult occupational prestige to assess trajectories of subcultural drift and adult status attainment 13 years later.

Table 4 presents the results of estimating four models separately by gender. Model 1 includes subcultural preferences and their predeterminants. This model reveals four significant effects among young adult males: positive effects of fathers' occupational prestige, son's self-rated academic ability, his aspirations/expectations, and a negative effect of the subculture of delinquency. Among females, ability has a notable effect as does aspirations/expectations, while identification with the subculture of delinquency has no significant effect. The party subculture has no significant effect in the first model among either males or females.

These findings confirm that drifting into the more seriously deviant subculture of delinquency, but not into the less deviant party subculture, creates a lasting cultural deficit among males.[7] Model 2 introduces police contacts to see if this variable mediates the effect of the subculture of delinquency on adult occupational prestige, as predicted in hypothesis 3. The effect of police contacts is significant and it does account for the effect of the subculture of delinquency among males.

Models 3 and 4 introduce grades and educational attainment. The effect of math grades is significant for males but not for females, while the effect of educational attainment is strong for both sexes. The most interesting result in model 4, however, is the emergence of a significant positive effect of the party subculture. Net of the measure of educational attainment introduced in model 4, identification with the party subculture improves the status attainments of young adult men with no similar effect apparent for women. Thus the tendency of the party subculture to re-

---

[7] A modified version of Table 4 is available on request. The modification introduced in this table replaces the preference measure of the subculture of delinquency with a second-order factor on which preference and self-report behavior scales are loaded equally. The second-order subculture of delinquency factor scores were converted into z-scores to facilitate comparisons between Table 4 and the modified table. The modified table does not reveal substantially altered findings: The unstandardized coefficients for the subculture of delinquency scales are quite similar, whether the preference factor or the second order combined attitude and behavior factor is used in models 1 to 4. I retain the preference measure because it is consistent with the measurement strategy I derived from Roe and my own theoretical expectations, as well as from the more recent work of Bourdieu and DiMaggio.

Table 4. Unstandardized OLS Coefficients: Determinants of Occupational Prestige Among Young Adult Males and Females

Variables	Males (N = 250)				Females (N = 180)			
	Model 1	Model 2	Model 3	Model 4	Model 1	Model 2	Model 3	Model 4
Father SES	.086*	.088*	.074	.059	-.071	-.071	-.077	-.119
	(.053)	(.052)	(.052)	(.051)	(.071)	(.071)	(.072)	(.074)
Mother SES	.092	.094	.091	.063	.164	.165	.164	.150
	(.080)	(.079)	(.079)	(.077)	(.106)	(.107)	(.106)	(.104)
Ability	2.471**	2.389**	1.902*	1.411	3.570*	3.563*	2.854	3.138
	(.924)	(.918)	(.981)	(.960)	(1.947)	(1.951)	(2.020)	(2.010)
Effort	.490	.415	.394	.079	.166	.174	.182	.316
	(.481)	(.480)	(.475)	(.468)	(.601)	(.611)	(.609)	(.603)
Relational control	.273	.292	.275	.230	.446	.445	.441	.415
	(.284)	(.282)	(.279)	(.272)	(.339)	(.340)	(.339)	(.335)
Instrumental control	.463	.373	.307	.241	-.547	-.053	-.087	-.164
	(.322)	(.323)	(.323)	(.314)	(.364)	(.365)	(.365)	(.361)
Educational aspiration	.358*	.292	.326	.159	.530*	.534*	.504*	.336
	(.214)	(.216)	(.215)	(.214)	(.265)	(.268)	(.268)	(.266)
Subculture of delinquency	-1.123*	-.783	-.665	-.829	-.237	-.248	-.249	-.119
	(.643)	(.664)	(.659)	(.643)	(.856)	(.867)	(.866)	(.872)
Party subculture	.787	.877	.940	1.301*	.593	.590	.612	1.003
	(.657)	(.654)	(.647)	(.635)	(.841)	(.841)	(.841)	(.843)
Police contacts	—	-1.021*	-1.036*	-.869*	—	.107	.031	.451
		(.544)	(.545)	(.532)		(1.344)	(1.344)	(1.359)
English grade	—	—	-.050	-.070	—	—	.083	.072
			(.057)	(.056)			(.073)	(.072)
Math grade	—	—	.105**	.091*	—	—	.013	-.005
			(.044)	(.043)			(.055)	(.054)
Educational attainment	—	—	—	1.597**	—	—	—	1.479**
				(.414)				(.591)
Lambda A	-6.249	-5.253	-5.085	-2.864	15.988	15.993	16.631	20.976
	(4.698)	(4.709)	(4.660)	(4.589)	(11.240)	(11.249)	(11.190)	(11.010)
Lambda B	-11.682**	-12.125**	-11.977**	-11.082**	-3.832	-3.842	-3.401	-2.565
	(2.870)	(2.556)	(2.552)	(2.821)	(3.104)	(3.108)	(3.133)	(3.141)
Intercept	28.446	28.426	26.942	29.207	18.349	18.261	14.769	12.402
R^2	.201	.212	.230	.274	.090	.091	.100	.131

* $p < .05$ (one-tailed)   ** $p < .01$ (one-tailed)

Note: Standard errors are in parentheses.

sult in reduced educational attainment suppresses the subculture's effect, but the net effect of this form of subcultural drift is positive.

Hypotheses 4 and 5 specify parental-class-origin interactions that more precisely predict negative subculture of delinquency effects for sons of working-class fathers, and positive party subculture effects for sons of non-working-class fathers. In the wave 2 survey respondents were asked to provide the kind of information used by Wright (1978) to classify locations in the class structure. Using this information on self-employment, employees, and supervisory responsibilities of fathers (retrospectively reported for when the respondent was age 12), I divided the respondents into those from working- and non-working-class origins. Working-class fathers were not self-employed, had no employees and no supervisory responsibilities; non-working-class fathers had at least one of these characteristics.

Among males, I initially specified the interaction effects of class origin and subcultural preferences on status attainment by creating product terms and adding them (and class) separately to model 4 estimated in Table 4. Despite collinearity between the product terms and their subcul-

Table 5. Unstandardized OLS Coefficients: Total and Direct Effects of Adolescent Subcultural Preferences on Young Adult Occupational Prestige Among Sons and Daughters of Working- and Non-Working-Class Fathers

	Total Effect	Direct Effect
Sons of Working-Class Fathers (N = 116)		
Subculture of delinquency	-2.108**	-1.995*
	(.944)	(.987)
Party subculture	-.346	.244
	(.912)	(.896)
Sons of Non-Working-Class Fathers (N = 134)		
Subculture of delinquency	-.780	-.244
	(.937)	(.921)
Party subculture	2.318**	2.775**
	(.989)	(.957)
Daughters of Working-Class Fathers (N = 80)		
Subculture of delinquency	-.381	-.221
	(1.041)	(1.062)
Party subculture	.789	.884
	(1.111)	(1.085)
Daughters of Non-Working-Class Fathers (N = 100)		
Subculture of delinquency	-.541	-.647
	(1.390)	(1.465)
Party subculture	.402	.897
	(1.255)	(1.283)

* $p < .05$ (one-tailed)   ** $p < .01$ (one-tailed)

Note: Results are from regressions of young adult occupational prestige on variables included in models 1 and 4 of Table 4. Only subcultural effects are reported to conserve space.

tural components (the r's are about .7), the t-values for subculture of delinquency and party interactions with class on occupational prestige are respectively -1.38 ($p = .08$) and 1.90 ($p = .03$). Given subsamples of about 100 cases each, these levels of significance may seem satisfactory, but the collinearity involving the product terms biases downward the estimated significance of these interactions.

A more accurate picture of the distinct causal structures that operate within the male class groupings is provided by a Chow test of the results of separately regressing adult occupational prestige within male class groupings on the subcultural preference scales and the remaining variables considered in model 4 of Table 4 (Chow 1960; Kennedy 1985, pp. 87-88,186). This test produces a significant F score (2.06, $p < .05$) for the prediction of a difference, given the same model, in the causal structure that operates with-

in class groupings.[8] The contingent effects that reflect this distinctiveness are apparent in the subcultural coefficients from the within class regressions.

The coefficients presented in Table 5 reveal that the effects of subcultural drift in establishing adult status trajectories are contingent on class origins. The total effect of identification with the subculture of delinquency on early adult occupational prestige is only significant and substantial among sons of working- class fathers; the direct effect of identification with this subculture within this context (and only in this context) is also robust. Meanwhile, the effect of adolescent identification with the party subculture is only significant and substantial among sons of non-working-class fathers. This effect is suppressed by the same kinds of educational measures noted above, so that when they are held constant, the direct causal effect of identification with the party subculture is even more pronounced.

Panel A of Table 6 presents t-tests of significance of the direct effects of the subculture of delinquency on adult occupational prestige among sons of working-class fathers, compared to the direct effects of this subculture among sons and daughters in the other class contexts; Panel B of this table presents similar tests for the direct effects of the party subculture among sons of non-working-class fathers compared to among sons and daughters in the other class contexts. Five of the resulting six comparisons are significant at the .05 level or above, and the sixth is in the right direction and approaches significance. Both male comparisons are significant. Overall, there is considerable support for hypotheses 4 and 5, that the effects of subcultural drift are contingent on gender and class of origin.

---

[8] The equation for the Chow test is:

$$F(k, n-2k) = \frac{[SSEn - (SSE1 + SSE2)] / k}{(SSE1 + SSE2) / (n-2k)},$$

where SSEn is the residual sum of squares for the full sample (18,569), SSE1 is the residual sum of squares for the first subsample (6840.2), SSE2 is the residual sum of squares for the second subsample (9286.7), n is the full sample size (250), and k is the number of independent variables (16). In the current case, then, F is 2.06 and is statistically significant at the .05 level. This indicates that the causal structure of the models estimated is distinct within groupings. Pair-wise tests of significance are presented below for differences in specific coefficients.

Table 6. Gender-Specific and Class-Specific Direct Effects of Subcultural Preferences on Adult Status Attainment

		Sons of Working-Class Fathers Compared to:		
A. Subculture of Delinquency	Direct Effects	Sons of Non-Working-Class Fathers	Daughters of Working-Class Fathers	Daughters of Non-Working-Class Fathers
	Difference in b's	1.755	1.774	1.348
	t-value of difference	1.844*	2.002*	1.097

		Sons of Non-Working-Class Fathers Compared to:		
B. Party Subculture	Direct Effects	Sons of Working-Class Fathers	Daughters of Working-Class Fathers	Daughters of Non-Working-Class Fathers
	Difference in b's	2.531	1.891	1.878
	t-value of difference	2.724**	1.914*	1.700*

* $p < .05$ (one-tailed)   ** $p < .01$ (one-tailed)

DISCUSSION AND CONCLUSIONS

My findings encourage researchers of deviance and stratification to broaden their visions of their fields. For example, one of the established findings in sociological criminology is that crime peaks in adolescence (Hirschi and Gottfredson 1983). However, sociological criminologists too often regard this finding as the endpoint of their research. What becomes of the former delinquents? Almost all cease their criminal activity, but this does not mean that earlier delinquent experiences are of no significance. I have found that identification with the subculture of delinquency has negative effects on trajectories of early adult occupational attainment for males with working-class origins, while males with non-working-class origins who identify with the delinquent subculture are apparently shielded from its deleterious effects. This becomes apparent only when one extends the traditional focus of subcultural research to include both the causes of delinquency and a consideration of its consequences as well.

The benefits of integrating research on deviance and stratification are not one-sided. Stratification theory and research have been enriched in recent years by the incorporation of concepts as diverse as luck and cultural capital. Still, stratification research is usually characterized by the conception of well-socialized actors who tend to be directed, if not driven, to their status destinations. Control theory and Matza's concept of drift counter balance this conceptualization by broadening considerations of the family and school to include conditions of relative looseness as well

as constraint, and by noting ways that adolescents are set free to drift into a range of subcultural preferences that are as central to teenage life as middlebrow and higher cultural interests. Broadened in this way, the cultural stratification paradigm acknowledges the probable effects of a range of cultural experiences in the transition to adulthood.

Finally, my findings point to the role of a party subculture that may socialize non-working-class males to participate in the kinds of pursuits that are later a part of male-bounded social networks. Old- as well as new-boy networks incorporate in their leisure pursuits much of what Matza had in mind (e.g., gambling, drinking and other mildly disreputable pleasures) when he spoke of a subterranean convergence between the avocations of adolescent and adult males. Although the party subculture lowers educational attainment among adolescents, when the effects of this are removed among males of non-working-class origins the resulting effect of the party subculture is positive.[9] Only a minority of youth with a party orientation avoid correlated problems of lower educational performance, as shown by this

---

[9] Gender stratification and stereotyping of this kind of "party" activity is an explanation cited for why female lawyers, for example, are less successful than male lawyers in recruiting male clients and for what is often called the "rainmaking" function in law firms. Thus a respondent in Epstein's (1981) study of *Women in Law* says succinctly of the "drinking routine" for network building, "There are a lot of mechanisms one can use to be informal that simply don't work in heterosexual situations, although in all-male settings they work very well" (p. 287).

statistical control. Nonetheless, this is a particularly intriguing minority group, and the specificity and strength of this suppression effect deserves further study.

My findings support the thesis that adolescents form distinct and internally coherent subcultural preferences that have class-specific effects on their trajectories toward adult occupational prestige. Further exploration of these effects promises to illuminate new paths of influence in our understanding of status attainment.

JOHN HAGAN is Professor of Sociology and Law and a Killam Research Fellow at the University of Toronto. He is also current President of the American Society of Criminology. His current research focuses on the causes and consequences of delinquency and crime in the life course, and on the professional and personal lives of lawyers. His book, Structural Criminology (Polity and Rutgers University Press, 1989), received the Outstanding Scholarship Award from the Crime and Juvenile Delinquency Division of the Society for the Study of Social Problems, and the Distinguished Scholar Award from the Crime, Law and Deviance section of the American Sociological Association.

Appendix 1. Gender-Specific Probit Models for Panel Retention and Labor Force Participation

I estimated separate probit models for males and females for retention in the second wave survey and labor force participation. I reasoned that retention would be influenced by the kinds of social competency and stability that are involved in maintaining an updated driver's licence registration and telephone listing. Respondents overall were more likely to be retained in the second wave survey if in the first survey they rated their school performance more highly, lived with both parents, were from central Canada, moved less, and lived in a single detached home. When these variables were included in gender-specific probit equations for retention, living with both parents significantly influenced male retention, while self-rated ability significantly influenced female retention ($p < .01$).

I reasoned that institutional commitments to schooling, family and work might influence labor force participation, considering marriage, childbearing, school attendance, and work commitment. As expected, the probit results indicated that female respondents were less likely to work if they had children, and that both men and women were less likely to work if they were in school ($p < .01$).

All subcultural preference and status attainment equations estimated in this paper are corrected for selection bias resulting from retention and labor force participation. The most significant results of these corrections involve labor force participation and occur in the estimation of the male status attainment equations. These corrections do not notably influence the estimated coefficients, but they do increase our confidence in them.

Appendix Table 1. Probit Equations for Male and Female Retention in Second Wave of Panel

Variable	Description	Males (N = 373) Coeff.	t-value	Females (N = 320) Coeff.	t-value
Intercept		-.561	-1.511	-.306	-.572
Self-evaluated ability	See ability in Table 2	.149	1.689*	.251	1.948**
Lived with both parents	1 = both parents	.375	2.336**	.073	.423
From central Canada	1 = central Canada	.369	1.828*	.021	.087
Residential mobility	1-5 = number of moves	-.004	-.061	-.066	-1.030
Parents' home	1 = single detached	.268	1.632*	.147	.832
Log-likelihood		-212.73		-193.14	
χ^2		17.936		7.997	
p		.003		.156	

* $p < .05$ (one-tailed)   ** $p < .01$ (one-tailed)

Appendix Table 2. Probit Equations for Male and Female Participation in Labor Force in Second Wave of Panel

Variable	Description	Males (N = 268) Coeff.	t-value	Females (N = 222) Coeff.	t-value
Intercept		1.698	8.733**	1.670	4.457**
Married	1 = married	.456	1.434	-.340	-1.241
Children	1 = children	-.593	-1.837*	-1.242	-4.180**
In School	1 = school	-2.37	-4.492**	-1.969	-2.914**
Work commitment after children	1 = will work	—	—	.299	1.119
Log-likelihood		-53.935		-82.772	
χ^2		24.116		49.816	
p		.000		.000	

* $p < .05$ (one-tailed)   ** $p < .01$ (one-tailed)

REFERENCES

Berk, Richard. 1983. "An Introduction to Sample Selection Bias in Sociological Data." *American Sociological Review* 48:386-97.

Bourdieu, Pierre. 1973. "Cultural Reproduction and Social Reproduction." Pp. 71-112 in *Knowledge, Education and Cultural Change* edited by R. Brown. London: Tavistock.

————. 1977. *Reproduction in Education, Society and Culture.* Beverly Hills: Sage.

————. 1984. *Distinction: A Social Critique of the Judgment of Taste.* Cambridge: Harvard University Press.

Bordua, David. 1961. "Delinquent Subcultures: Sociological Interpretations of Gang Delinquency." *Annals of the American Academy of Political and Social Science* 338:119-36.

Campbell, Ernest. 1969. "Adolescent Socialization." Pp. 861-84 in *Handbook of Socialization Theory and Research*, edited by D. Goslin. Chicago: Rand McNally.

Chow, Gregory. 1960. "Tests of Equality Between Sets of Coefficients in two Linear Regressions." *Econometrica* 28:591-605.

Cohen, Albert. 1955. *Delinquent Boys.* New York: Free Press.

Coleman, James. 1961. *The Adolescent Society.* New York: Free Press.

Collins, Randall. 1975. *Conflict Sociology: Toward an Explanatory Science.* New York: Academic Press.

————. 1979. *The Credential Society: An Historical Sociology of Education and Stratification.* New York: Academic Press.

DiMaggio, Paul. 1982. "Cultural Capital and School Success: The Impact of Status Culture Participation on the Grades of U.S. High School Students." *American Sociological Review* 47:189-201.

————. 1987. "Classification in Art." *American Sociological Review* 52:440-55.

DiMaggio, Paul and John Mohr. 1985. "Cultural Capital, Educational Attainment and Marital Selection." *American Journal of Sociology* 90:1231-61.

Elder, Glen. 1980. "Adolescence in Historical Perspective." Pp. 3-46 in *Handbook of Adolescent Psychology*, edited by J. Adelson. New York: Wiley.

————. 1985. *Life Course Dynamics.* Ithaca: Cornell University Press.

Epstein, Cynthia. 1981. *Women in Law.* New York: Basic Books.

Ghodsian, M. and C. Power. 1987. "Alcohol Consumption Between the Ages of 16 and 23 in Britain: A Longitudinal Study." *British Journal of Addiction* 82:175-80.

Glueck, Sheldon and Eleanor Glueck. 1950. *Unraveling Juvenile Delinquency.* Cambridge: Harvard University Press.

————. 1968. *Delinquents and Nondelinquents in Perspective.* Cambridge: Harvard University Press.

Goode, William. 1978. *The Celebration of Heroes: Prestige as a Social Control System.* Berkeley: University of California Press.

Hagan, John, A. R. Gillis and John Simpson. 1988. "Feminist Scholarship, Relational and Instrumental Control and a Power-Control Theory of Gender and Delinquency." *British Journal of Sociology* 39:301-36.

————. 1990. "Clarifying and Extending Power-Control Theory." *American Journal of Sociology* 95:1024-37.

Hagan, John and Alberto Palloni. 1988. "Crimes as Social Events in the Life Course: Reconceiving a Criminological Controversy." *Criminology* 26:87-100.

————. 1990. "The Social Reproduction of a Criminal Class in Working Class London, Circa 1950-80." *American Journal of Sociology* 96:265-99.

Hall, Stuart and T. Jefferson. 1976. *Resistance Through Rituals.* London: Hutchinson University Library.

Hebdige, Dick. 1984. *Subculture: The Meaning of Style.* London: Methuen.

Heckman, James. 1979. "Sample Selection Bias as a Specification Error." *Econometrica* 45:153-61.

Hindelang, Michael, Travis Hirschi, and Joseph Weis. 1981. *Measuring Delinquency.* Beverly Hills:Sage.

Hirschi, Travis. 1969. *Causes of Delinquency.* Berkeley: University of California Press.

Hirschi, Travis and Michael Gottfredson. 1983. "Age and the Explanation of Crime." *American Journal of Sociology* 89:552-84.

Hollingshead, August. 1949. *Elmtown's Youth: The Impact of Social Classes on Adolescents.* New York: John Wiley & Sons.

Jencks, Christopher, Marshall Smith, Henry Acland, Mary Jo Bane, David Cohen, Herbert Gintis, Barbara Heyns and Stephen Michelson. 1972. *Inequality.* New York: Basic.

Jessor, Richard, John Donovan and Frances Costa. Forthcoming. *Beyond Adolescence: Problem Behavior and Young Adult Development.* New York: Cambridge University Press.

Katsillis, John and Richard Rubinson. 1990. "Cultural Capital, Student Achievement, and Educational Reproduction: The Case of Greece." *American Sociological Review* 55:270-79.

Katz, Jack. 1989. *Seductions of Crime.* New York: Basic Books.

Kennedy, Peter. 1985. *A Guide to Econometrics.* 2d ed. Oxford: Basil Blackwell.

Lemert, Edwin. 1951. *Social Pathology.* New York: McGraw-Hill.

Matza, David. 1964. *Delinquency and Drift.* New York: Wiley.

Modell, John, Frank Furstenberg, and Theodore Hershberg. 1976. "Social Change and the Transition to Adulthood in Historical Perspective." *Journal of Family History* 1:7-32.

Newcomb, M. D. and P. M. Bentler. 1988. *Conse-*

quences of Adolescent Drug Use: Impact on the Lives of Young Adults. Newbury Park: Sage.

Nye, F. Ivan. 1958. *Family Relationships and Delinquent Behavior*. New York: Wiley.

Otto, Luther and Duane Alwin. 1977. "Athletics, Aspirations and Attainments." *Sociology of Education* 42:102-13.

Otto, Luther and David Featherman. 1975. "Social Structural and Psychological Antecedents of Self-Estrangement and Powerlessness." *American Sociological Review* 40:701-19.

Porterfield, Austin. 1943. "Delinquency and Its Outcome in Court and College." *American Journal of Sociology* 49:199-208.

Power, C. and V. Estaugh. 1990. "Employment and Drinking in Early Adulthood: A Longitudinal Perspective." *British Journal of Addiction* 85:487-94.

Robins, Lee. 1966. *Deviant Children Grown Up*. Baltimore: Williams and Wilkins.

Roe, Keith. 1984. *Mass Media and Adolescent Schooling: Conflict or Co-existence?* Stockholm: Almquist & Wiksell International.

Sampson, Robert and John Laub. 1990. "Stability and Change in Crime and Deviance over the Life Course: The Salience of Adult Social Bonds." *American Sociological Review* 55:609-27.

Schwendinger, Herman and Julia Siegel Schwend-inger. 1985. *Adolescent Subcultures and Delinquency*. New York: Praeger.

Short, James and Fred Strodtbeck. 1965. *Group Process and Gang Delinquency*. Chicago: University of Chicago Press.

Sykes, Gresham and David Matza. 1957. "Techniques of Neutralization: A Theory of Delinquency." *American Sociological Review* 22:664-70.

————. 1961. "Juvenile Delinquency and Subterranean Values." *American Sociological Review* 26:712-19.

Treiman, Donald. 1977. *Occupational Prestige in Comparative Perspective*. New York: Academic Press.

Veblen, Thorsten. 1934. *The Theory of the Leisure Class*. New York: Viking Press.

Weber, Max. [1968] 1972. *Economy and Society* edited by G. Roth and C. Wittich. New York: Bedminster.

Willis, Paul. 1977. *Learning to Labour*. London: Saxon House.

Wright, Erik Olin. 1978. "Race, Class and Income Inequality." *American Journal of Sociology* 83:1368-97.

Yinger, J. M. 1960. "Contraculture and Subculture." *American Sociological Review* 25:625-35.

Urban Poverty and the Family Context of Delinquency: A New Look at Structure and Process in a Classic Study

Robert J. Sampson

University of Chicago

John H. Laub

Northeastern University and Henry A. Murray Research Center

SAMPSON, ROBERT J., and LAUB, JOHN H. *Urban Poverty and the Family Context of Delinquency: A New Look at Structure and Process in a Classic Study.* CHILD DEVELOPMENT, 1994, **65**, 523–540. This paper reanalyzes data from the Gluecks' classic study of 500 delinquents and 500 nondelinquents reared in low-income neighborhoods of central Boston. Based on a general theory of informal social control, we propose a 2-step hypothesis that links *structure* and *process:* family poverty inhibits family processes of informal social control, in turn increasing the likelihood of juvenile delinquency. The results support the theory by showing that (1) erratic, threatening, and harsh discipline, (2) low supervision, and (3) weak parent-child attachment mediate the effects of poverty and other structural factors on delinquency. We also address the potential confounding role of parental and childhood disposition. Although difficult children who display early antisocial tendencies do disrupt family management, as do antisocial and unstable parents, mediating processes of informal social control still explain a large share of variance in adolescent delinquency. Overall, the results underscore the indirect effects of structural contexts like family poverty on adolescent delinquency within disadvantaged populations. We note implications for current debates on race, crime, and the "underclass" in urban America.

In 1950, Sheldon and Eleanor Glueck published their now classic study, *Unraveling Juvenile Delinquency.* In one of the most frequently cited works in the history of delinquency research, the Gluecks sought to answer a basic and enduring question—what factors differentiate boys reared in poor neighborhoods who become serious and persistent delinquents from boys raised in the same neighborhoods who do not become delinquent or antisocial? To answer this question, the Gluecks studied in meticulous detail the lives of 500 delinquents and 500 nondelinquents who were raised in the same slum environments of central Boston during the Great Depression era.

The research design of the Gluecks' study provides a unique opportunity to address anew poverty and its sequelae in adolescence. Namely, what is the *process* by which family poverty leads to delinquency within structurally disadvantaged urban en-

vironments? It is our contention that sociological explanations of delinquency have too often focused on structural background (e.g., poverty) without an understanding of mediating family processes, especially informal social control. Competing explanations based on behavioral predispositions (e.g., early conduct disorder) have also been neglected in structural accounts of delinquency. On the other hand, developmental models in psychology tend to emphasize family process and early antisocial behavior to the neglect of structural context and social disadvantage.

Based on our reconstruction and reanalysis of the Gluecks' original data, this article rejects a bifurcated strategy by uniting structure and process in an integrated theoretical framework. Our major thesis is that poverty and structural disadvantage influence delinquency in large part by reducing the capacity of families to achieve effective informal

We thank three anonymous reviewers and the guest editor of *Child Development,* Vonnie C. McLoyd, for constructive criticisms of a previous draft. We also thank Sandra Gauvreau for research assistance. The data were derived from the Sheldon and Eleanor Glueck archives of the Harvard Law School Library, currently on long-term loan to the Henry A. Murray Research Center of Radcliffe College. Requests for reprints should be sent to: Robert J. Sampson, Department of Sociology, The University of Chicago, 1126 E. 59th St., Chicago, IL 60637.

social controls. In this sense, we argue that scholars of child and adolescent development must come to grips with structural contexts of disadvantage and not just focus on families "under the roof."

The historical context of the Gluecks' data also serves as a baseline for assessing current research on children and poverty. The boys in the Glueck sample were born in the Depression era and grew to young adulthood in the context of a rapidly changing economy after World War II (1945–1965). This context raises interesting questions relevant to an understanding of how poverty influences developmental patterns of delinquency. For example, are the risk factors associated with crime similar across different structural contexts? Were characteristics of today's "underclass" (e.g., chronic joblessness, poverty) found among these earlier Boston families? Current debates, especially in public policy circles, seem to imply that criminal behavior is inevitably linked to race and drugs. Yet the delinquency problem in the historical context we are analyzing was generated not by blacks, but by white ethnic groups in structurally disadvantaged positions. And though drugs were not pervasive, delinquency and antisocial behavior were. Indeed, the boys in the Gluecks' delinquent sample were persistent and serious offenders, many of whom can be labeled "career criminals" using contemporary language. By analyzing a white sample that is largely "underclass" by today's economic definition (see Jencks, 1992; Wilson, 1987), we provide an alternative perspective to current thinking about race, crime, and poverty.

Family Process and Informal Social Control

The hypotheses guiding our analysis are derived from a general theory of age-graded informal social control over the life course (see Sampson & Laub, 1993). Our general organizing principle is that the probability of deviance increases when an individual's bond to society is weak or broken (Hirschi, 1969). In other words, when ties that bind an individual to key societal institutions (e.g., attachment to family, school, work) are loosened, the risk of crime and delinquency is heightened. Unlike formal sanctions, which originate in purposeful efforts to control crime, informal social controls "emerge as by-products of role relationships established for other purposes and are components of role reciprocities" (Kornhauser, 1978, p. 24).

Our theoretical conceptualization on the family is drawn in part from "coercion theory" as formulated by Patterson (1980, 1982). Unlike most sociological theories, coercion theory places a prominent etiological role on direct parental controls in explaining delinquency. In particular, the coercion model assumes that less skilled parents inadvertently reinforce their children's antisocial behavior and fail to provide effective punishments for transgressions (Patterson, 1982; see also Gottfredson & Hirschi, 1990, p. 99). Based on research designed to assess this perspective, Patterson argues that "parents who cannot or will not employ family management skills are the prime determining variables. . . . Parents of stealers do not track; they do not punish; and they do not care" (1980, pp. 88–89).

The emphasis on parent-child interaction in coercion theory shares much in common with Hirschi's (1969) social control theory. The model of Patterson differs mainly in the mediating mechanisms it emphasizes—that is, direct parental controls as found in discipline and monitoring practices. By contrast, Hirschi's (1969) original formulation of control theory emphasized indirect controls in the form of the child's attachment to parents. On balance, however, Patterson's model is consistent with social control theory because direct parental controls are likely to be positively related to relational, indirect controls (Larzelere & Patterson, 1990, p. 305). Moreover, Gottfredson and Hirschi (1990) include direct parental controls in a recent statement of control theory that relies heavily on Patterson's coercion model. Their reformulated theory of effective parenting includes monitoring behavior of children, recognizing their misdeeds, and punishing (correcting) those misdeeds accordingly in a consistent and loving manner (Gottfredson & Hirschi, 1990, p. 97). In addition, Hirschi (1983) argues that parental affection and a willingness to invest in children are essential underlying conditions of good parenting, and hence, the prevention of misbehavior.

This view of families also corresponds to Braithwaite's (1989) notion of "reintegrative shaming," whereby parents punish in a consistent manner and within the context of love, respect, and acceptance of the child. The opposite of reintegrative shaming is stigmatization, where parents are cold, authoritarian, and enact a harsh, punitive, and often rejecting regime of punishment (1989, p. 56). When the bonds of respect are broken by parents in the process of punishment, successful child rearing is difficult to achieve.

Given their theoretical compatibility, we draw on the central ideas of social control and coercion theory along with the notion of reintegrative shaming to develop a model of informal family social control that focuses on three dimensions—*discipline, supervision,* and *attachment*. In our view, the key to all three dimensions of informal social control lies in the extent to which they facilitate linking the child to family, and ultimately society, through emotional bonds of attachment and direct yet socially integrative forms of control, monitoring, and punishment. These dimensions of informal family control have rarely been examined simultaneously in previous research. Hence our theoretical model permits assessment of the relative and cumulative contributions of family process to the explanation of delinquency.

Poverty and Family Process

The second part of our theory posits that structural background factors influence delinquency largely through the mediating dimensions of family process (see also Laub & Sampson, 1988). Our specific interest in this article is the indirect effect of family poverty on delinquency among those children living in disadvantaged communities. Although examined in the developmental psychology literature (for a recent review see McLoyd, 1990), it is ironic that sociological research on delinquency often fails to account for how structural disadvantage influences parenting behavior and other aspects of family life. As Rutter and Giller (1983, p. 185) have stated, "serious socio-economic disadvantage has an adverse effect on the parents, such that parental disorders and difficulties are more likely to develop and good parenting is impeded" (see also McLoyd, 1990, p. 312). Furthermore, Larzelere and Patterson (1990, p. 307) have argued that many lower-class families are marginally skilled as parents, in part because they experience more stress and fewer resources than do middle-class parents. McLoyd (1990, p. 312) has also expressed the view that "poverty and economic loss diminish the capacity for supportive, consistent, and involved parenting." In reviewing the extant literature, she found that economically disadvantaged parents and those parents who experience economic stress are more likely to use punitive, coercive parenting styles, that is, use of physical punishment, as opposed to reasoning and

negotiation. Low-income parents also face heightened risks of spousal violence, drug and alcohol abuse, and criminal involvement (McLoyd, 1990), behaviors that undermine socially integrative parent-child relationships and interactions.

Equally important and relevant here is the large body of literature establishing the effects of stressors such as economic crises and divorce on parenting behavior. For example, Patterson (1988) has shown that stressful experiences increase the likelihood of psychological distress, which in turn leads to changes in parent-child management practices. Specifically, Patterson (1988) found that distressed mothers are more likely to use coercive discipline, thereby contributing to the development of antisocial behavior in children (see also Patterson, DeBaryshe, & Ramsey, 1989, p. 332). Elder and Caspi (1988) examined the effects of stressful economic circumstances on parents and their children. They found that in times of economic difficulty, aversive interactions between parents and children increase while the ability of parents to manage their children diminishes. Using more recent data, Conger et al. (1992) confirmed that economic hardship was indirectly linked to adolescent development largely through its effect on parenting behavior.

It seems clear that poverty and the accompanying stresses resulting from economic deprivation influence parent-child relationships and interactions within the family. Integrating this viewpoint with our general theory of informal social control, we thus hypothesize that the effect of poverty and disadvantaged family status on delinquency is mediated in large part through parental discipline and monitoring practices.

Antisocial Children: Reconsidering Family Effects

Two research findings raise questions regarding unidirectional models that attribute the development of delinquency as flowing solely from parental influence. The first is empirical research establishing the early onset of many forms of childhood misbehavior (Robins, 1966; West & Farrington, 1973; White, Moffitt, Earls, Robins, & Silva, 1990). In one of the best studies to date, White et al. (1990) examined the predictive power of behavior measured as early as age 3 on antisocial outcomes at ages 11 and 13. They found that teacher and/or parent-reported behavioral measures of hyperactivity and restlessness as a young child (age 3), difficulty in management of the child at age 3, and early onset of problem behaviors at age 5 predicted later antisocial outcomes. White et al.'s (1990) research shows the extent to which later delinquency is foreshadowed by early misbehavior and general difficulty among children.

Second, there is evidence that styles of parenting are in part a reaction to these troublesome behaviors on the part of children. Lytton (1990) has written an excellent overview of this complex body of research, which he subsumes under the theoretical umbrella of "control systems theory." This theory argues that parent and child display reciprocal adaptation to each other's behavior level (see also Anderson, Lytton, & Romney, 1986), leading to what Lytton calls "child effects" on parents. One reason for these child effects is that reinforcement does not work in the usual way for conduct-disordered children. As Lytton (1990, p. 688) notes, conduct-disordered children "may be underresponsive to social reinforcement and punishment." Hence, normal routines of parental child rearing become subject to disruption based on early antisocial behavior—that is, children themselves differentially engender parenting styles likely to further exacerbate antisocial behavior.

The behavior that prompts parental frustration is not merely aggressiveness or delinquency, however. Lytton (1990, p. 690) reviews evidence showing a connection between a child being rated "difficult" in preschool (e.g., whining, restlessness, inadaptability to change, strong-willed resistance) and the child's delinquency as an adolescent—a relation that holds independent of the quality of parents' child-rearing practices. For example, Olweus (1980) showed by a longitudinal path analysis that mothers of boys who displayed a strong-willed and hot temper in infancy later became more permissive of aggression, which in turn led to greater aggressiveness in middle childhood. Moreover, there is intriguing experimental evidence that when children's inattentive and noncompliant behavior is improved by administering stimulant drugs (e.g., Ritalin), their mothers become less controlling and mother-child interaction patterns are nearly normalized (Lytton, 1990, p. 688). All of this suggests that parenting, at least in part, is a reaction to the temperament of children, especially difficult ones.

Further evidence in favor of "child ef-fects" from the criminological literature is found in West and Farrington's (1973) well-known longitudinal study. They showed that boys' "troublesomeness" assessed at ages 8 and 10 by teachers and peers was a significant predictor of later delinquency, independent of parental supervision, parental criminality, and family size. However, the reverse was not true—parental effects on delinquency disappeared once early troublesomeness was taken into account. As Lytton observes, this finding "suggests the primacy of child effects" (1990, p. 690).

In short, there is a sound theoretical and empirical basis for expanding our model by introducing early childhood effects. Lytton's review suggests a strategy to ascertain the relative importance of parent and child influences. Namely, one can test the effects of early childhood factors on later delinquency, with parent factors held constant, against the prediction of parents' effects on delinquency, with early childhood factors held constant. The relative strength of each set of variables would be an index of the importance of the main independent variables—child or parent (1990, p. 694). Put more simply, the key question is whether our family process model holds up after we consider early childhood difficulty and antisocial predispositions. If parenting or family effects on delinquency are spurious, then our model should collapse once childhood behaviors are controlled. On the other hand, if control systems theory is correct, we are liable to see both child and parent effects on the outcome of adolescent delinquency. We assess our theoretical model of structure and family process by employing this strategy.

Method

The present article is based on data from the first wave of the Gluecks' original study of juvenile delinquency and adult crime among 1,000 Boston males born between 1924 and 1935 (Glueck & Glueck, 1950, 1968). As part of a larger, long-term project we have reconstructed and computerized these data, a process that included the validation of key measures found in the original files. For a full description of these and other procedures taken to address prior criticisms of the Gluecks' study, see Sampson and Laub (1993).

The Gluecks' delinquent sample comprised 500 10–17-year-old white males from Boston who, because of their persistent delinquency, had been recently committed to one of two correctional schools in Massachusetts (Glueck & Glueck, 1950, p. 27). The nondelinquent or "control-group" sample was made up of 500 white males age 10–17 chosen from the Boston public schools. Nondelinquent status was determined on the basis of official record checks and interviews with parents, teachers, local police, social workers, recreational leaders, and the boys themselves. The Gluecks' sampling procedure was designed to maximize differences in delinquency, an objective that by all accounts succeeded (Glueck & Glueck, 1950, pp. 27–29).

A unique aspect of the *Unraveling* study was the matching design. The 500 officially defined delinquents and 500 nondelinquents were matched case-by-case on age, race/ethnicity (birthplace of both parents), measured intelligence, and neighborhood deprivation. The delinquents averaged 14 years, 8 months, and the nondelinquents 14 years, 6 months when the study began. As to ethnicity, 25% of both groups were of English background, another fourth Italian, a fifth Irish, less than a tenth old American, Slavic, or French, and the remaining were Near Eastern, Spanish, Scandinavian, German, or Jewish. As measured by the Wechsler-Bellevue Test, the delinquents had an average IQ of 92 and nondelinquents 94. The matching on neighborhood ensured that both delinquents and nondelinquents grew up in disadvantaged neighborhoods of central Boston. These areas were regions of poverty, economic dependency, and physical deterioration, and were usually adjacent to areas of industry and commerce (Glueck & Glueck, 1950, p. 29).

A wealth of information on social, psychological, and biological characteristics, family life, school performance, work experiences, and other life events was collected on the delinquents and controls in the period 1939–1948. These data were collected through an elaborate investigation process that involved interviews with the subjects themselves and their families as well as interviews with key informants such as social workers, settlement house workers, clergymen, schoolteachers, neighbors, and criminal justice and social welfare officials. The home-interview setting also provided an opportunity to observe home and family life (Glueck & Glueck, 1950, pp. 41–53).

Interview data and home investigations were supplemented by field investigations that meticulously culled information from the records of both public and private agencies that had any involvement with a subject or his family. These materials verified and amplified the materials of a particular case investigation. For example, a principal source of data was the Social Service Index, a clearinghouse that contained information on all dates of contact between a family and the various social agencies (e.g., child welfare) in Boston. Similar indexes from other cities and states were utilized where necessary. For *Unraveling*, the Gluecks employed two case collators to sift through the several thousand entries over the 7½-year project.

The Gluecks also searched the files of the Massachusetts Board of Probation, which maintained a central file of all court records from Boston courts since 1916 and from Massachusetts as a whole from 1924. These records were compared and supplemented with records from the Boys' Parole Division in Massachusetts. Out-of-state arrests, court appearances, and correctional experiences were gathered through correspondence from equivalent state depositories. Of equal importance was the Gluecks' collection of self-reported, parental-reported, and teacher-reported delinquency of the boy.

Measures

Descriptive statistics and intercorrelations for the full set of measures are displayed in Table 1. To tap the central concept of *family poverty*, we created a scale from information on the average weekly income of the family and the family's reliance on outside aid. The latter measures whether the family was living in comfortable circumstances (having enough savings to cover 4 months of financial stress), marginal circumstances (little or no savings but only occasional dependence on outside aid), or financially dependent (continuous receipt of outside aid for support). The resulting standardized scale of poverty was scored so that a high value represents the combination of low income and reliance on public assistance. Although the Gluecks' matching design controls for neighborhood deprivation, there is still considerable variation among families in poverty (see Table 1).

Five additional features of the structural background of families are introduced as control variables.[1] *Residential mobility* is an

---

[1] Controls were selected on both theoretical grounds (see also Sampson & Laub, 1993, chap. 4) and empirical significance in preliminary analysis.

TABLE 1

DESCRIPTIVE STATISTICS AND CORRELATIONS

Variable	Mean	SD	Minimum	Maximum	Valid N
Structural context:					
Family poverty[a]	.00	1.64	-3.64	3.45	998
Residential mobility	6.75	4.72	1	16	999
Family size	5.08	2.21	1	8	999
Family disruption	.47	.50	0	1	1,000
Maternal employment	.40	.49	0	1	993
Foreign born	.60	.49	0	1	987
Parent/child disposition:					
Parental deviance	1.45	1.27	0	4	1,000
Parental instability	.62	.72	0	2	972
Child difficult/antisocial	.72	.80	0	3	884
Family process:					
Erratic/harsh discipline[a]	-.02	1.73	-3.24	3.14	856
Maternal supervision	1.97	.86	1	3	989
Parental-child attachment	3.72	1.21	1	5	960
Adolescent delinquency:					
Official status	.50	.50	0	1	1,000
Self-parent-teacher reported	8.44	6.67	1	26	1,000

PAIRWISE PEARSON CORRELATION COEFFICIENTS

	2	3	4	5	6	7	8	9	10	11	12	13	14
1. Family poverty	.40	.26	.21	-.04	-.07	.38	.25	.20	.35	-.32	-.34	.34	.33
2. Residential mobility		.05	.40	.18	-.18	.50	.35	.27	.28	-.44	-.43	.41	.41
3. Family size			-.09	-.20	.13	.08	.02	.01	.23	-.11	-.02	.16	.17
4. Family disruption				.19	-.13	.38	.24	.15	.13	-.27	-.46	.26	.28
5. Mother's employment					-.02	.17	.16	.08	.10	-.28	-.16	.14	.16
6. Foreign born						-.21	-.10	-.03	.07	.05	.04	-.04	-.07
7. Parental deviance							.35	.22	.36	-.48	-.44	.41	.41
8. Parental instability								.25	.30	-.39	-.31	.36	.34
9. Child difficult/antisocial									.35	-.30	-.30	.45	.45
10. Erratic/harsh discipline										-.51	-.40	.52	.50
11. Maternal supervision											.49	-.63	-.62
12. Parent-child attachment												-.50	-.49
13. Official status													.86
14. Self-parent-teacher reported													

[a] Standardized scale based on z scores.

interval-based measure of the number of times the boy's family moved during his childhood and ranges from none or once to 16 or more times. *Family size* is the number of children in the boy's family and ranges from one to eight or more. *Family disruption* is coded one when the boy was reared in a home where one or both parents were absent because of divorce, separation, desertion, or death. *Maternal employment* is a dichotomous variable where housewives were coded 0 and working mothers (full time or part time) were coded 1. *Foreign-born* indexes whether one or both parents were born outside the United States.

It is possible, of course, that the poverty status and other structural characteristics of families resulted from prior differences among parents that are correlated with dysfunctional family management (Patterson & Capaldi, 1991). To address this possible confounding, we control for the criminality and drinking habits of mothers and fathers as determined from official statistics and interview data. Criminality refers to official records of arrest or conviction, excluding minor auto violations and violation of license laws. Alcoholism/drunkenness refers to intoxication and includes frequent, regular, or chronic addiction to alcohol, and not to very occasional episodes of overdrinking in an atmosphere of celebration. Not surprisingly, there were strong relations between crime and heavy drinking and between mother's and father's crime/drinking. Hence we formed a summary scale ranging from 0 to 4 that measures the extent of what we term *parental deviance* (see Table 1). For example, a subject whose mother and father both had a criminal record and a history of excessive drinking received a score of 4.

The Gluecks also collected data on each parent's mental condition and temperament from official diagnoses and medical reports from hospitals and clinics, and on occasion from unofficial observations made by social workers (Glueck & Glueck, 1950, p. 102). The ordinal variable labeled *parental instability* reflects whether none (0), one (1), or both (2) of the boy's parents were diagnosed with "severe mental disease or distortion" including "marked emotional instability," "pronounced temperamental deviation," or "extreme impulsiveness." Taken together,

the parental deviance and instability measures capture key dispositional characteristics that have been argued to underlie family poverty and other disadvantaged outcomes.[2]

Family process.—The three intervening dimensions of family process are style of discipline, supervision, and parent-child attachment. Parenting style was measured by summing three variables describing the discipline and punishment practices of mothers and fathers. The first constituent variable concerns the use of physical punishment and refers to rough handling, strappings, and beatings eliciting fear and resentment in the boy—not to casual or occasional slapping that was unaccompanied by rage or hostility. The second constituent variable measures threatening or scolding behavior by mothers or fathers that elicited fear in the boy. The third component taps erratic and negligent discipline, for example, if the parent vacillated between harshness and laxity and was not consistent in control, or if the parent was negligent or indifferent about disciplining the boy.

The summation of these constituent variables resulted in two ordinal measures tapping the extent to which parents used inconsistent disciplinary measures in conjunction with harsh physical punishment and/or threatening or scolding behavior. In Braithwaite's (1989) scheme, these measures tap the sort of punitive shaming and negative stigmatization by families that engender delinquency. The validity of measures is supported by the high concordance between mother's and father's use of erratic/harsh discipline (gamma = .60). For example, of fathers who employed harsh physical punishment, threatening behavior, and erratic discipline (code = 3), 44% of the mothers were also coded 3. By contrast, less than 1% of boys' fathers coded 0 on the erratic/harsh scale had mothers coded high (3) in erratic/harsh discipline. For reasons of both theoretical parsimony and increased reliability, we created standardized scales that combined mother and father's *erratic/harsh discipline*.

Maternal supervision is an ordinal variable coded 3 if the mother provided supervision over the boy's activities at home or in the neighborhood. If unable to supervise the boys themselves, mothers who made ar-

---

[2] Evidence of the validity of the instability measure is suggested by its significant positive correlation with parental deviance (.35, see Table 1) and also an indicator of low parental IQ (data not shown). By comparison, low IQ was weakly related to our family-process measures, and thus we control for the more direct indicator of volatile and impulsive parental temperament.

rangements for other adults to watch the boy's activities were also assigned a 3. A code of 2 was assigned to those mothers providing partial or fair supervision. Supervision was considered unsuitable (code = 1) if the mother left the boy on his own, without guidance, or in the care of an irresponsible person.[3]

As the Gluecks originally observed, attachment is a "two-way street"—parent to child and child to parent (Glueck & Glueck, 1950, p. 125). Accordingly, the Gluecks gathered interview-based information from both the parents and boys themselves on emotional attachment and rejection. For example, the Gluecks developed a three-point ordinal indicator of the extent to which the boy had a warm emotional bond to the father and/or mother as displayed in a close association with the parent and in expressions of admiration. Similarly, the Gluecks measured whether the parents were loving and accepting of the child or were rejecting in emotional attention—that is, whether parents were openly hostile or did not give the child much emotional attention. Because the parent-child and child-parent indicators of attachment were strongly related (gamma = .58), we combined them into a single ordinal scale labeled *parent-child attachment* that ranges from 1 (low) to 5 (high).

Child effects.—Although the *Unraveling* study was not longitudinal, there are retrospective data on three key dimensions of troublesome childhood behavior. From the parent's interview there is an indicator distinguishing those children who were overly restless and irritable from those who were not. A second measure reflects the extent to which a child engaged in violent temper tantrums and was predisposed to aggressiveness and fighting. The Gluecks' collected data only on habitual tantrums—when tantrums were "the predominant mode of response" by the child to difficult situations growing up (1950, p. 152). This measure corresponds closely to one validated by Caspi (1987).[4] The third variable is the boy's self-reported age of onset of misbehavior. We created a dichotomous variable where a 1 indexes an age of onset earlier than age 8.

Those who had a later age of onset *and* those who reported no delinquency (and hence no age of onset) were assigned a zero.

As expected, all three measures are significantly correlated. For example, of those children rated difficult in childhood, 34% exhibited tantrums, compared to 13% of those with no history of difficultness. Similarly, for those with an early onset of misbehavior, 47% were identified as having tantrums, compared to 20% of those with no early onset (all p's < .05). To achieve theoretical and empirical parsimony, we summed the three indicators to form an ordinal scale that measures *child difficult/antisocial behavior*. The scale ranges from 0, indicating no signs of early conduct disorder or difficulty in child rearing, to a score of 3, indicating that a child was difficult and irritable, threw violent temper tantrums, and engaged in antisocial behavior prior to age 8.

There is evidence of the predictive validity of our child-effects measure derived from self, parent, and teacher reports. Fully 100% of those scoring high on child antisocial behavior were arrested in adolescence, compared to 25% of those scoring low (gamma = .69). More importantly, the child-effects measure predicts criminal behavior well into adulthood. Using data on adult crime collected by the Gluecks as part of a follow-up study (Glueck & Glueck, 1968), 60% of those scoring high on childhood antisocial behavior were arrested at ages 25–32, compared to less than 25% with no signs of early disorder. Perhaps most striking, there is a rather strong monotonic relation between childhood antisocial disposition and arrests even at ages 32–45 (gamma = .37). Hence, although early antisocial behavior was determined by retrospective reports, the techniques used by the Gluecks appear valid (see also Sampson & Laub, 1993, pp. 47–63).

Delinquency.—The outcome of adolescent delinquency is measured using both the official criterion of the Gluecks' research design (1 = delinquent, 0 = control group) and "unofficial" delinquency derived by summing self, parent, and teacher reports.

---

[3] The Gluecks did not collect data on father's supervision. This focus reflects the era in which the Gluecks' study was conceived, wherein mothers assumed primary responsibility for the supervision of children.

[4] The tantrum measure is taken from a combined parent/teacher-reported interview. As Lytton (1990) notes, the fact that it is typical to derive ratings of a child's early temperament and of parental practices from the parent interview alone makes for methodological confounding. We avoid this through multiple sources of measurement (self, parent, and teacher).

In preliminary analysis we also examined measures for particular offenses (e.g., truancy as reported by parents, teachers, and self) and the total amount of delinquency for all crime types reported by a particular source (e.g., self-report total, parent-report total). Because the results were very similar, the present analysis is based on the sum of all delinquent behaviors that were measured consistently across reporters. That is, we eliminated incorrigibility (e.g., vile language, lying) and other behaviors that were only asked of one source (e.g., teacher reports of school vandalism). The unofficial measure thus reflects adolescent delinquency measured by parents, teachers, and the boys themselves.

Reliability and Validity

Because of their strategy of data collection, the Gluecks' measures pertain to multiple sources of information that were independently derived from several points of view and at separate times. The level of detail and the range of information collected by the Gluecks will likely never be repeated given contemporary research standards on the protection of human subjects. As Robins et al. (1985, p. 30) also point out in their analysis of social-science data from an earlier era analogous to the Gluecks: "In conformity with the precomputer era of data analysis, the coding was less atomized than it would have been today. Consequently, we have only the coders' overall assessment based on a variety of individual items."

This method of data collection limits the extent to which reliability can be determined by traditional criteria (e.g., intercoder reliability). As described above, however, our basic measurement strategy uses multiple indicators of key concepts and composite scales whenever possible and theoretically appropriate. Note also that the Glueck data are different in kind from survey research where measurement error, especially on attitudes, is large. That is, the Glueck data represent the comparison, reconciliation, and integration of multiple sources of information even for individual items (see Glueck & Glueck, 1950, pp. 70–72; 1968, pp. 205–255). Moreover, our measures refer to behavior (e.g., discipline, supervision) and objective structural conditions (e.g., poverty, broken homes)—not attitudes.

To verify the coding of the family-process variables, we also conducted a validation test for the purposes of this article. Selecting a 10% random sample of the delinquent subjects ($N = 50$), we coded from the original interview narratives the three key elements of family process—supervision, parenting style, and parental attachment—blind to the actual codes of the Gluecks. We then compared our scores with those of the Gluecks and in general found excellent correspondence. For example, the correlation (gamma) between our coding and the Gluecks for parental supervision, father's rejection, and mother's rejection was .87, .92, and .98, respectively. We found significant levels of agreement for other key indicators of family process as well, using both gamma and kappa statistics on percent agreement corrected for chance.

Finally, the correlations in Table 1 reveal that our key measures are related in a manner consistent with theory and past research. In particular, erratic/harsh discipline is negatively related to supervision and parent-child attachment ($-.51$ and $-.40$, respectively, $p < .05$), whereas maternal supervision is positively related to parent-child attachment (.49, $p < .05$). These and other significant correlations in the predicted and expected direction (see Table 1) support standard criteria for construct validation.

Results

Our analysis begins in Table 2 with an overview of the bivariate association between family process and delinquency as measured by official records and total unofficial delinquency. The magnitude and direction of relationships support the informal social-control model. All relationships are in the expected direction, quite large, and maintain whether one considers official or unofficial delinquency. For example, both official and unofficial delinquency increase monotonically as erratic/harsh discipline increases (gammas = .70 and .59., respectively). Delinquency also declines monotonically with increasing levels of supervision and attachment. In fact, 83% of those in the low supervision category were delinquent, compared to only 10% of those in the high category (gamma = $-.84$). The unofficial criterion shows an even greater differential. Parental attachment is similarly related to both official and unofficial delinquency.

We next consider the extent to which the three dimensions of informal social control potentially mediate the effect of more distal, structural factors. To accomplish this goal, Panel A of Table 3 displays the results

225

TABLE 2

BIVARIATE ASSOCIATION BETWEEN FAMILY PROCESS AND DELINQUENCY

	DISCIPLINE ERRATIC/HARSH			MATERNAL SUPERVISION			PARENT-CHILD ATTACHMENT		
	Low (288)	Medium (224)	High (334)	Low (382)	Medium (252)	High (355)	Low (414)	Medium (194)	High (352)
Officially delinquent (%)	18	51	74	83	58	10	77	47	21
Gamma		.70*			-.84*			-.73*	
Unofficially delinquent[a] (%)	10	39	53	60	39	5	57	32	13
Gamma		.59*			-.72*			-.62*	

[a] Percent unofficially delinquent refers to the trichotomized "high" category.
* $p < .05$.

TABLE 3

OLS Linear Regression Models of Family Process on Structural Context
and Parent/Child Disposition

	FAMILY PROCESS					
A. Structural Context and Parental Disposition (N = 800)	Erratic/Harsh Discipline		Maternal Supervision		Parent-Child Attachment	
	β	t ratio	β	t ratio	β	t ratio
Family poverty	.17	4.66*	−.09	−2.84*	−.15	−4.28*
Residential mobility	.07	1.81	−.21	−5.85*	−.17	−4.59*
Family size	.16	4.90*	−.13	−4.30*	−.01	.29
Family disruption	−.05	−1.35	−.04	−1.16	−.22	−6.75*
Maternal employment	.05	1.54	−.20	−7.04*	−.03	−1.04
Foreign born	.13	4.30*	−.07	−2.60*	−.11	−3.81*
Parental deviance	.23	6.01*	−.24	−7.12*	−.18	−4.86*
Parental instability	.17	4.96*	−.19	−6.26*	−.10	−3.21*
Adjusted R^2	.26		.41		.32	

	FAMILY PROCESS					
B. Adding Child Effects (N = 716)	Erratic/Harsh Discipline		Maternal Supervision		Parent-Child Attachment	
	β	t ratio	β	t ratio	β	t ratio
Family poverty	.16	4.38*	−.06	−1.64	−.17	−4.58*
Residential mobility	.03	.73	−.18	−5.06*	−.15	−3.94*
Family size	.18	5.41*	−.16	−5.26*	−.02	−.58
Family disruption	−.06	−1.56	−.01	−.42	−.19	−5.55*
Maternal employment	.07	2.12*	−.22	−7.29*	−.02	−.70
Foreign born	.13	4.09*	−.08	−2.70*	−.12	−3.77*
Parental deviance	.20	4.90*	−.24	−6.80*	−.19	−4.83*
Parental instability	.13	3.79*	−.16	−5.01*	−.05	−1.44
Child diff./antisocial	.22	6.67*	−.15	−4.94*	−.13	−3.96*
Adjusted R^2	.30		.43		.34	

* $p < .05$.

of ordinary-least-squares (OLS) models of family process variables regressed on structural background factors and parental disposition. The results support the theoretical prediction that structural poverty has significant effects on informal social control. For example, the data in columns 1 and 2 show that poverty, in addition to large families, parental deviance, parental instability, and foreign-born status, contributes significantly to erratic use of harsh/punitive discipline (β = .17, t ratio = 4.66).[5]

The results for maternal supervision are also consistent with our general social control framework—poverty significantly reduces effective monitoring (t ratio = −2.84). In addition to parental disposition, other features of structural context are salient too, especially residential mobility, family size, and employment by mothers. There has been much debate about the effect of mother's employment outside of the home on delinquency, but relatively little on how supervision might mediate this structural factor (see Hoffman, 1974; Laub & Sampson, 1988; Maccoby, 1958). In the Glueck data and time era (circa 1940), employment by

[5] Statistical significance tests—including the use of one-tailed hypothesis tests appropriate for theoretical predictions—are not strictly applicable given the Gluecks' nonprobability sampling scheme. As a general rule of thumb, we thus focus on coefficients that are greater than twice their standard errors, which approximates a .05 level of significance. Among "significant" coefficients, our interest is the relative magnitude of effects.

mothers outside of the home appears to have a significant negative effect on mother's supervision.[6] This is exactly the pattern supportive of a social control framework and confirmed by other empirical research (see Maccoby, 1958; Wilson, 1980). It remains to be seen whether employment outside of the home by mothers has any direct effect on delinquency. It is also worth noting that mother's employment has no discernible effect on erratic/harsh discipline and parent-child attachment.

In columns 5 and 6 we turn to the relational dimension of family social control—emotional attachment and bonding between parent and child. Substantively, the results suggest that in families experiencing marital disruption, frequent residential moves, disadvantaged financial/ethnic position, and a pattern of deviant or unstable parental conduct, parents and children are more likely to exhibit indifference or hostility toward each other. Interestingly, these effects are rather substantial and much larger than those associated with family size and maternal employment.

Panel B displays the replication models that add "child effects" to the explanation of family process.[7] The results suggest that difficult and antisocial childhood behavior disrupts effective parenting. Specifically, children who were rated difficult, habitually engaged in violent tantrums, and exhibited early misbehavior tended to generate lower levels of supervision by their mothers during adolescence. Consistent with a control-systems perspective, troublesome childhood behavior also significantly predicts the erratic/harsh use of discipline by parents and weakened attachment between parent and child. These results support Lytton's (1990) arguments regarding the endogeneity of parental styles of discipline and control of children, especially direct controls. Simply put, parents appear responsive to early behav-

ioral difficulties—angry temperamental children who misbehave provoke in their parents a disrupted style of parenting and control.

Considering the central role of childhood behavior, the finding that the effects of structural context remain largely intact becomes all the more impressive. Indeed, the rationale for introducing child effects was not to establish conclusively the validity of "control systems" theory, but rather to test the validity of our theoretical conceptions about the indirect effects of poverty on adolescent delinquency. In this regard, note that family poverty, independent of child disposition, continues to exert significant and relatively large effects on erratic/harsh discipline and parent-child attachment. Moreover, it is possible that the reduced effect of poverty on supervision in Panel B (t ratio = -1.64, $p < .10$) reflects in part an indirect effect whereby poverty increases early antisocial behavior, which further disrupts parenting. In any case, the data support a structure-process model—poverty and structural context explain informal social control by families, regardless of parental disposition and childhood antisocial behavior.

Explaining Delinquency

Panel A of Table 4 displays the effects of structural context, parental disposition, and family process on adolescent delinquency.[8] The first two columns of data list the ML logistic results for the official delinquency criterion. Columns 3 and 4 list the OLS results for the summary measure of unofficially reported delinquency. In general the results are invariant across method and measurement of delinquency. The majority of structural context and parental disposition factors have insignificant direct effects on delinquency, operating instead through the family process variables. The main exception is family size, which has a direct positive effect

[6] Bearing in mind this historical context, the Gluecks' concern with working mothers and single parents was that children would be deprived of maternal supervision (see Glueck & Glueck, 1950, p. 112). Again, such views reinforce traditional gender roles of women as housewives and mothers by defining their primary role as nurturing children.

[7] Because of missing data on child effects, there are almost 100 fewer cases available for analysis in Panel B. Changes in parameter estimates from Panel A may thus reflect in part a slightly different sample composition.

[8] The dichotomous nature of official delinquency violates the assumptions of OLS regression. Maximum-likelihood (ML) logistic regression is thus used, preserving the ordinal and interval-based nature of predictor variables. The unstandardized logistic coefficients in Table 4 represent the change in the log-odds of official delinquency associated with a unit change in the exogenous variable. Because the units of measurement of the independent variables are not uniform, we also present the ML t ratios of coefficients to standard errors. The self-parent-teacher summary index of delinquency ranges from 1 to 26, and is estimated with OLS regression.

TABLE 4

OLS Linear and ML Logistic Regression of Delinquency on Structural
Context, Family Process, and Parent/Child Disposition

	DELINQUENCY			
	Official Status		Self-Parent-Teacher Reported	
A. Structural Context and Parental Disposition ($N = 800$)	ML Logistic[a]		OLS Linear	
	b	t ratio	β	t ratio
Family poverty	.10	1.36	.04	1.46
Residential mobility	.03	1.20	.07	2.21*
Family size	.14	2.63*	.08	2.82*
Family disruption	.32	1.36	.06	2.10*
Maternal employment	−.14	−.62	−.02	−.64
Foreign born	.04	.18	−.03	−1.32
Parental deviance	−.00	−.04	.01	.23
Parental instability	.21	1.36	.05	1.60
Erratic/harsh discipline	.38	5.26*	.17	5.25*
Maternal supervision	−1.27	−8.15*	−.36	−9.89*
Parent-child attachment	−.47	−4.51*	−.15	−4.70*
	ML Model $\chi^2 =$ 485, 11 df		OLS $R^2 = .48$	

	DELINQUENCY			
	Official Status		Self-Parent-Teacher Reported	
B. Adding Child Effects ($N = 716$)	ML Logistic[a]		OLS Linear	
	b	t ratio	β	t ratio
Family poverty	.09	1.18	.02	.64
Residential mobility	.01	.33	.07	1.97*
Family size	.18	3.04*	.10	3.59*
Family disruption	.33	1.24	.07	2.23*
Maternal employment	−.00	−.00	.01	.26
Foreign born	.01	.04	−.03	−1.25
Erratic/harsh discipline	.35	4.22*	.13	3.87*
Maternal supervision	−1.21	−7.06*	−.33	−8.77*
Parent-child attachment	−.50	−4.24*	−.15	−4.54*
Parental deviance	.03	.25	.01	.28
Parental instability	.10	.61	.02	.76
Child difficult/antisocial	1.09	6.35*	.19	6.72*
	ML Model $\chi^2 =$ 475, 12 df		OLS $R^2 = .52$	

[a] Entries for ML Logistic "b" are the raw maximum-likelihood coefficients; "t ratios" are coefficients divided by SE.
* $p < .05$.

on both official and self-parent-teacher-reported delinquency. Residential mobility and family disruption also have small direct effects on unofficial delinquency.

On the other hand, the three family-process variables exhibit significant effects on delinquency in the predicted theoretical direction. Several of these effects are quite large, especially the negative effect of maternal supervision on delinquency (OLS β = −.36, ML t ratio = −8.15). At the same time, erratic/punitive discipline and parent-child attachment have independent effects on delinquency of similar magnitudes (β = .17 and −.15, respectively). Net of back-

229

ground variables and parental disposition, then, both direct family controls (discipline and monitoring) and indirect social control (affective bonding between child and parent) distinguish nondelinquents from serious, persistent delinquents.

The initial results support the predictions of our theoretical strategy—when an intervening variable mediates the effect of an exogenous variable, the direct effects of the latter should disappear. For the most part that is what Table 4 yields. Moreover, when OLS and ML logistic regression models are estimated without the hypothesized mediating variables, virtually all structural context factors have large, significant effects on delinquency in the expected manner. In particular, the reduced-form t ratio for the effect of poverty on unofficial delinquency is 4.96 (further underscoring the between-family variations in poverty). But, as seen in Table 4, the significant effect of poverty on delinquency is eliminated when discipline, supervision, and attachment are controlled. The calculation of indirect effect estimates reveals that of the total effect of all structural context and parental disposition factors on delinquency, approximately 67% is mediated by family process. The results thus demonstrate the importance of considering indirect effects of poverty and other dimensions of structural background.[9]

Panel B of Table 4 displays two replication models of structural background, parental disposition, family process, and child effects on delinquency. The results suggest three substantive conclusions. First, much like earlier models, family poverty and most other structural background factors influence delinquency largely through the mediating dimensions of family process. Second, the child-effects measure has a significant direct effect on delinquency that is unaccounted for by family process and structural context. Third, and most important from our perspective, are the robust results regarding family process. Despite controlling for child-

hood and parental disposition, the dimensions of parental discipline, attachment, and supervision all continue to influence delinquent conduct in the manner predicted by our informal social-control model. Mother's supervision has by far the largest effect on self-parent-teacher-reported delinquency, with a standardized coefficient almost double the child effect ($\beta = -.33$).

On balance, then, our theoretical model remains intact, surviving a test that controls for early childhood antisocial behavior. Hence one way of interpreting Table 4 is that variations in adolescent delinquency unexplained by early propensity to deviance are directly explained by informal processes of family social control in adolescence. The magnitude of the family-process effects is especially noteworthy—for example, independent of all other factors including childhood antisocial behavior, a one-unit increase in mother's supervision (on a three-point scale) is associated with over a 50% decrease in official delinquency. The magnitudes of the standardized effects on unofficial delinquency tell the same story.[10]

Structural Equation Models

To this point in the analysis it is clear that structural context, parental disposition, and child antisocial behavior have similar effects on supervision, attachment, and erratic/harsh discipline. This pattern suggests that the three family-process measures are tapping the same latent construct. Further evidence for this specification was seen earlier in Table 1—all three indicators are highly intercorrelated—in fact, the smallest correlation is −.40 between attachment and erratic/harsh discipline. Thus, even though supervision, attachment, and erratic/harsh discipline exhibited independent effects in the OLS regression models, there are both theoretical and empirical reasons to consider an alternative strategy that specifies all three measures as underlying a latent construct of informal social control.

[9] Even when the unofficial delinquency measure is broken down by reporter (self, parent, teacher) and offense types, the same general pattern emerges (data not shown). Consistent with Table 4, for example, mother's supervision has the largest effect on truancy, runaway, larceny, smoking/drinking, vandalism, and motor-vehicle theft.

[10] To assess the robustness of results, we introduced additional control variables and examined mean-substitution and pairwise-deletion models where we entered a dichotomous variable for missing cases. For example, we controlled for residual differences in the matching variables of age and IQ, along with mesomorphy and extroversion, two "constitutional" variables emphasized by the Gluecks. Family-process effects retained their significant predictive power. We also examined attachment to delinquent peers and ethnic group differences in family process (using dichotomous variables for Italian, English, and Irish background). Again, the major substantive results remained intact (see also Sampson & Laub, 1993, pp. 94–95, 118–121).

To estimate this alternative conception, we take advantage of recent advances in Jöreskog and Sörbom's (1989) LISREL 7.20 and PRELIS 1.20 programs for maximum-likelihood (ML) estimation of linear covariance-structure models with data that are non-normally distributed. The basic specification of our covariance structure model is shown in Figure 1 (for a similar specification see Larzelere & Patterson, 1990). Both delinquency and informal social control are specified as latent constructs. The former is measured with official delinquency and self-parent-teacher reports, whereas the latent construct of informal social control is hypothesized to generate the correlations among erratic/harsh discipline, parent-child attachment, and maternal supervision. The direction and magnitude of factor loadings support the validity of specified variables as indicators of the latent constructs. As before, structural context and child/parent disposition are treated as exogenous observed variables. However, family disruption was insignificant in the initial LISREL estimation, and was thus dropped to improve the model fit.

Figure 1 presents the ML weighted-least-squares LISREL estimates of all significant path coefficients. The model fits the data very well, yielding a chi-square of 30 with 28 degrees of freedom ($p = .35$). Indeed, as seen in the adjusted goodness-of-fit index (.99), there is an excellent match between the observed covariances and our theoretical specification of family process. Informal social control also has a large and significant negative effect on the latent construct of delinquency (t ratio = -4.06). Perhaps most striking, the latent family construct now mediates all prior effects of structural context and parent/child disposition. Calculating indirect effect estimates, we find that 68% of the total effect of exogenous factors on delinquency is mediated by informal social control. Note, for example, that poverty has a significant negative effect on informal social control (t ratio = -2.12) net of other context variables and parent/child disposition. This finding substantiates earlier OLS analyses. Similarly, both parental deviance and instability independently reduce informal social control, in turn increasing delinquency.

Interestingly, however, note that the child-disposition measure has a large negative effect (t ratio = -5.61) on informal social control but no direct effect on delinquency. This is the only major finding that does not comport with earlier regression analyses—once a family-process measurement model is specified, the influence of childhood antisocial behavior on delinquency works solely through attenuated informal social control. Although this finding needs to be replicated in future analysis, it

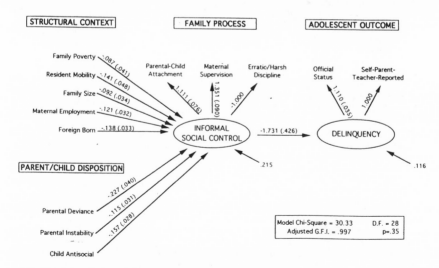

Note: All parameter estimates are significant at p<.05 (standard errors in parentheses)

FIG. 1.—ML weighted-least-squares covariance-structure model of structural context, parent/child disposition, informal social control, and delinquency ($N = 716$).

does support the control-systems hypothesis (Lytton, 1990) that child effects are important primarily for their influence on family management. Similarly, the lack of a direct effect on delinquency suggests that the correlation between childhood and adolescent delinquency is less an indication of a latent antisocial trait than a *developmental process* whereby delinquent children systematically undermine effective strategies of family social control, in turn increasing the odds of later delinquency. In any case, the more general message in Figure 1 is that the latent construct of informal social control is the primary factor in explaining adolescent delinquency.

Discussion

Our major finding is that family process mediated approximately two-thirds of the effect of poverty and other structural background factors on delinquency. Whether analyzed with standard regression techniques or covariance structure models, the data paint a consistent picture. Namely, poverty appears to inhibit the capacity of families to achieve informal social control, which in turn increases the likelihood of adolescent delinquency.

The data thus support the general theory of informal social control explicated at the outset. We believe that this theory has significance for future research by positing how it is that poverty and structural disadvantage influence delinquency in childhood and adolescence. A concern with only direct effects conceals mediating relations and may thus lead to misleading conclusions regarding the theoretical importance and policy relevance of more distal structural factors such as poverty (see also Conger et al., 1992; Larzelere & Patterson, 1990; McLoyd, 1990). More generally, families do not exist in isolation (or just "under the roof") but instead are systematically embedded in social-structural contexts—even taking into account parental predispositions toward deviance and impulsive temperament.

The data further point to the complex role of social selection and social causation in the genesis of delinquency. Although difficult children who display early antisocial tendencies do appear to self select or sort themselves into later states of delinquency, family processes of informal social control still explain a significant share of variance in adolescent delinquency. Moreover, the covariance structure analyses further suggest

that the effect of childhood antisocial/difficult behavior is mediated by family process. Although "child effects" are clearly present, a full understanding of delinquency thus requires that we also come to grips with the socializing influence of the family as reflected in disciplinary practices, supervision and direct parental controls, and bonds of attachment.

Not only do our results point to the indirect effects of poverty on adolescent delinquency, they simultaneously suggest that strong family social controls may serve as an important buffer against structural disadvantage in the larger community. Recall that all boys were reared in economically deprived neighborhoods of central Boston in the Great Depression era, conditions similar to disadvantaged "underclass" communities in many inner-city areas today (see Wilson, 1987). Yet there were marked variations in both family poverty and delinquency risk within these structurally deprived areas of Boston in the 1930s and 1940s, just as there are in the worst inner cities of today. Cohesive families characterized by consistent, loving, and reintegrative punishment, effective supervision, and close emotional ties appear to have overcome these disadvantaged conditions in producing a low risk of adolescent delinquency. In this sense it is mistaken to assume that residents of concentrated poverty areas (e.g., the "underclass") face homogeneous odds—whether it be for negative *or* positive outcomes.

Despite the consistency of results, we recognize that limitations of the data preclude definitive conclusions. Because the Gluecks used a sample of institutionalized delinquents and neighborhood socioeconomic status as one of the matching variables, our conclusions are limited to the relative effects of family poverty on serious and persistent delinquency within a disadvantaged sample (for a critique of this aspect of the Gluecks' research design, see Reiss, 1951). Whether our results hold for adolescents (including noninstitutionalized delinquents) drawn from a wider range of socioeconomic positions is an important issue for future research. Many of the measures we used in the present analysis were also retrospective in nature and may have been confounded by the original coders' global impressions. Issues of temporal order and discriminant validity thus cannot be resolved with certainty (see Bank, Dishion, Skinner, & Patterson, 1990). In particular, a richer set of prospective child-effects and parental-disposition measures is needed to assess more rigorously the role of individual differences. Whether child effects are fully mediated by family processes of informal social control (see Fig. 1) would seem to be an especially salient question for future work.

Nevertheless, it bears emphasis that our findings on family process are consistent with much previous research—including key observations of the Gluecks some 40 years ago. Note also the recent meta-analysis by Loeber and Stouthamer-Loeber (1986, p. 37) where they found that aspects of family functioning involving direct parent-child contacts are the most powerful predictors of delinquency and other juvenile conduct problems. Apparently, the fundamental causes of delinquency are consistent across time and rooted not in race (e.g., black inner-city culture) but generic family processes—such as *supervision, attachment,* and *discipline*—that are systematically influenced by family poverty and structural disadvantage. We hope that future research will address further the connections we have emphasized between poverty and mediating family processes, especially as they bear on both risk and avoidance of adolescent delinquency in disadvantaged communities.

References

Anderson, K., Lytton, H., & Romney, D. (1986). Mothers' interactions with normal and conduct-disordered boys: Who affects whom? *Developmental Psychology, 22,* 604–609.

Bank, L., Dishion, T., Skinner, M., & Patterson, G. (1990). Method variance in structural equation modeling: Living with "glop." In G. Patterson (Ed.), *Depression and aggression in family interaction* (pp. 248–279). Hillsdale, NJ: Erlbaum.

Braithwaite, J. (1989). *Crime, shame, and reintegration.* Cambridge: Cambridge University Press.

Caspi, A. (1987). Personality in the life course. *Journal of Personality and Social Psychology, 53,* 1203–1213.

Conger, R., Conger, K., Elder, G. H., Jr., Lorenz, F., Simons, R., & Whitbeck, L. B. (1992). A family process model of economic hardship and adjustment of early adolescent boys. *Developmental Psychology, 63,* 526–541.

Elder, G. H., & Caspi, A. (1988). Economic stress in lives: Developmental perspectives. *Journal of Social Issues, 44,* 25–45.

Glueck, S., & Glueck, E. (1950). *Unraveling juvenile delinquency.* New York: Commonwealth Fund.

Glueck, S., & Glueck, E. (1968). *Delinquents and nondelinquents in perspective.* Cambridge, MA: Harvard University Press.

Gottfredson, M., & Hirschi, T. (1990). *A general theory of crime.* Stanford, CA: Stanford University Press.

Hirschi, T. (1969). *Causes of delinquency.* Berkeley: University of California Press.

Hirschi, T. (1983). Crime and the family. In J. Wilson (Ed.), *Crime and public policy* (pp. 53–68). San Francisco: Institute for Contemporary Studies.

Hoffman, L. W. (1974). Effects of maternal employment on the child: A review of the research. *Developmental Psychology, 10,* 204–228.

Jencks, C. (1992). *Rethinking social policy: Race, poverty, and the underclass.* Cambridge, MA: Harvard University Press.

Jöreskog, K., & Sörbom, D. (1989). *LISREL VI: A guide to the program and applications.* Chicago, IL: Scientific Software.

Kornhauser, R. (1978). *Social sources of delinquency.* Chicago: University of Chicago Press.

Larzelere, R., & Patterson, G. (1990). Parental management: Mediator of the effect of socioeconomic status on early delinquency. *Criminology, 28,* 301–323.

Laub, J. H., & Sampson, R. J. (1988). Unraveling families and delinquency: A reanalysis of the Gluecks' data. *Criminology, 26,* 355–380.

Loeber, R., & Stouthamer-Loeber, M. (1986). Family factors as correlates and predictors of juvenile conduct problems and delinquency. In M. Tonry & N. Morris (Eds.), *Crime and justice* (Vol. 7, pp. 29–150). Chicago: University of Chicago Press.

Lytton, H. (1990). Child and parent effects in boys' conduct disorder: A reinterpretation. *Developmental Psychology, 26,* 683–697.

Maccoby, E. (1958). Children and working mothers. *Children, 5,* 83–89.

McLoyd, V. C. (1990). The impact of economic hardship on black families and children: Psychological distress, parenting, and socioemotional development. *Child Development, 61,* 311–346.

Olweus, D. (1980). Familial and temperamental determinants of aggressive behavior in adolescent boys: A causal analysis. *Developmental Psychology, 16,* 644–660.

Patterson, G. (1980). Children who steal. In T. Hirschi & M. Gottfredson (Eds.), *Understanding crime: Current theory and research* (pp. 73–90). Beverly Hills, CA: Sage.

Patterson, G. (1982). *Coercive family process.* Eugene, OR: Castalia.

Patterson, G. (1988). Stress: A change agent for family process. In N. Garmezy & M. Rutter

(Eds.), *Stress, coping, and development in children* (pp. 235–264). Baltimore: Johns Hopkins University Press.

Patterson, G., & Capaldi, D. (1991). Antisocial parents: Unskilled and vulnerable. In P. Cowan & M. Hetherington (Eds.), *Family transitions* (pp. 195–218). Hillsdale, NJ: Erlbaum.

Patterson, G., DeBaryshe, B., & Ramsey, E. (1989). A developmental perspective on antisocial behavior. *American Psychologist*, **44**, 329–335.

Reiss, A. J., Jr. (1951). Unraveling juvenile delinquency: II. An appraisal of the research methods. *American Journal of Sociology*, **57**, 115–120.

Robins, L. N. (1966). *Deviant children grown up.* Baltimore: Williams & Wilkins.

Robins, L. N., Schoenberg, S., Holmes, S., Ratcliff, K., Benham, A., & Works, J. (1985). Early home environment and retrospective recall: A test for concordance between siblings with and without psychiatric disorders. *American Journal of Orthopsychiatry*, **55**, 27–41.

Rutter, M., & Giller, H. (1983). *Juvenile delinquency: Trends and perspectives.* New York: Guilford.

Sampson, R. J., & Laub, J. H. (1993). *Crime in the making: Pathways and turning points through life.* Cambridge, MA: Harvard University Press.

West, D., & Farrington, D. P. (1973). *Who becomes delinquent?* London: Heinemann.

White, J., Moffitt, T., Earls, F., Robins, L., & Silva, P. (1990). How early can we tell? Predictors of childhood conduct disorder and adolescent delinquency. *Criminology*, **28**, 507–533.

Wilson, H. (1980). Parental supervision: A neglected aspect of delinquency. *British Journal of Criminology*, **20**, 203–235.

Wilson, W. J. (1987). *The truly disadvantaged: The inner city, the underclass, and public policy.* Chicago: University of Chicago Press.

0091-4169/91/8201-0211
THE JOURNAL OF CRIMINAL LAW & CRIMINOLOGY
Copyright © 1991 by Northwestern University, School of Law

Vol. 82, No. 1
Printed in U.S.A.

THE CYCLE OF CRIME AND SOCIALIZATION PRACTICES*

Joan McCord**

ABSTRACT

Crime appears to be transmitted through families. This article evaluates biogenetic and sociological interpretations in the light of evidence drawn from a prospective longitudinal study. Subjects for the study came from a larger investigation of males who had been in a program designed to prevent delinquency. At the time of their introduction to the prevention program, the boys ranged in age from five to thirteen. Although the treatment program failed to better the lives of its charges, it left a legacy of carefully documented case materials that are used here to examine interacting effects of biological and environmental conditions that appear to promote or retard transmission of aggressive antisocial behavior. The evidence suggests that aggressive models promote criminality and that maternal behavior can reduce the probability that a son will imitate a criminal father.

I. INTRODUCTION

Studies of delinquency are peppered with reports that crime runs in families. Aggressiveness and criminality among the parents of delinquents have been reported in Canada, the United States,

* This study was partially supported by United States Public Health Service Research Grant MH26779, National Institute of Mental Health (Center for Studies of Crime and Delinquency). The author wishes to express appreciation to the Department of Probation of the Commonwealth of Massachusetts, the Division of Criminal Justice Services of the State of New York, the Maine State Bureau of Identification, and the states of California, Florida, Michigan, New Jersey, Pennsylvania, Virginia, and Washington for supplemental data about the men. Only the author is responsible for the statistical analyses and for the conclusions drawn from this research. The author thanks Richard Parente, Robert Staib, Ellen Myers, and Ann Cronin for their work in tracing the men and their records and Joan Immel, Tom Smedile, Harriet Sayre, Mary Duell, Elise Goldman, Abby Brodkin, and Laura Otten for their careful coding.
** Professor of Criminal Justice at Temple University. Ph.D. in Sociology, Stanford University. She is a Fellow of the International Society for Research on Aggression and the American Society of Criminology, for which she served as President for 1988-89. Her prior publications include works on causes of crime, alcoholism, psychopathy, intervention programs, and theory.

235

Great Britain, and Finland.[1] Evidence from these studies suggests that criminality has both biological and social links. Both linkages also can be inferred from studies of domestic abuse that reveal that abused children have a relatively high probability of becoming violent adults.[2] Over the last two decades, studies of twins and of adoption have implicated genetic factors in the transmission of behaviors related to crime. For example, Goodman and Stevenson[3] found a considerable amount of heritability for hyperactivity among the twins they studied—whether hyperactivity was rated by fathers, by mothers, or by teachers. Several studies have also found evidence for heritability for such related concepts as activity level, impulsivity, and desire for excitement.[4]

Studies comparing biological with sociological father-son pairs in terms of crime show more similarities within the biological pairs.[5]

---

[1] *See, e.g.,* S. GLUECK & E. GLUECK, UNRAVELING JUVENILE DELINQUENCY (1950); L. ROBINS, DEVIANT CHILDREN GROWN UP (1966); Farrington, *Environmental Stress, Delinquent Behavior, and Convictions,* in 6 STRESS AND ANXIETY 93 (I. Sarason & C. Spielberger eds. 1979); Lewis, Pincus, Lovely, Spitzer & Moy, *Biopsychosocial Characteristics of Matched Samples of Delinquents and Nondelinquents,* 26 J. AM. ACAD. CHILD & ADOLESCENT PSYCHIATRY 744 (1987); McCord, *Some Child-Rearing Antecedents of Criminal Behavior in Adult Men,* 37 J. PERSONALITY & SOC. PSYCHOLOGY 1477 (1979); Offord, *Family Backgrounds of Male and Female Delinquents,* in ABNORMAL OFFENDERS, DELINQUENCY, AND THE CRIMINAL JUSTICE SYSTEM 129 (J. Gunn & D.P. Farrington eds. 1982); Pulkkinen, *Search for Alternatives to Aggression in Finland,* in AGGRESSION IN GLOBAL PERSPECTIVE 104 (A. Goldstein & M. Segall eds. 1983).

[2] Call, *Child Abuse and Neglect in Infancy: Sources of Hostility Within the Parent-Infant Dyad and Disorders of Attachment in Infancy,* 8 CHILD ABUSE & NEGLECT 185 (1984); Gelles, *Violence in the Family: A Review of Research in the Seventies,* 42 J. MARRIAGE & FAM. 873 (1980); Egeland & Sroufe, *Developmental Sequelae of Maltreatment in Infancy,* in DEVELOPMENTAL PERSPECTIVES ON CHILD MALTREATMENT 77 (R. Rizley & D. Cicchetti eds. 1981) [hereinafter DEVELOPMENTAL PERSPECTIVES]; Herrenkohl & Herrenkohl, *Some Antecedents and Developmental Consequences of Child Maltreatment,* in DEVELOPMENTAL PERSPECTIVES, this note, at 57; Jouriles, Barling & O'Leary, *Predicting Child Behavior Problems in Maritally Violent Families,* 15 J. ABNORMAL CHILD PSYCHOLOGY 165 (1987); Main & Goldwyn, *Predicting Rejection of Her Infant From Mother's Representation of Her Own Experience: Implications for the Abused-Abusing Intergenerational Cycle,* 8 CHILD ABUSE & NEGLECT 203 (1984); McCord, *A Forty-Year Perspective on Effects of Child Abuse and Neglect,* 7 CHILD ABUSE & NEGLECT 265 (1983); Widom, *Child Abuse, Neglect, and Violent Criminal Behavior,* 27 CRIMINOLOGY 251 (1989).

[3] Goodman & Stevenson, *A Twin Study of Hyperactivity. 1. An Examination of Hyperactivity Scores and Categories Derived from Rutter Teacher and Parent Questionnaires,* 30 J. CHILD PSYCHOLOGY, PSYCHIATRY & ALLIED DISCIPLINES 671 (1989).

[4] *See, e.g.,* Goldsmith & Gottesman, *Origins of Variation in Behavioral Style: A Longitudinal Study of Temperament in Young Twins,* 52 CHILD DEV. 91 (1981); Pedersen, Plomin, McClearn & Friberg, *Neuroticism, Extraversion, and Related Traits in Adult Twins Reared Apart and Reared Together,* 55 J. PERSONALITY & SOC. PSYCHOLOGY 950 (1988).

[5] Bohman, Cloninger, Sigvardsson & von Knorring, *Predisposition to Petty Criminality in Swedish Adoptees,* 39 ARCHIVES GEN. PSYCHIATRY 1233 (1982); Crowe, *An Adoptive Study of Psychopathy: Preliminary Results from Arrest Records and Psychiatric Hospital Records,* in GENETIC RESEARCH IN PSYCHIATRY 95 (R. Fieve, D. Rosenthal & H. Brill eds. 1975);

In addition, the longitudinal studies carried out by Eron and Huesmann have tied aggression at age eight to aggression in offspring twenty-two years later.[6]

Despite the wealth of evidence revealing continuities, biological explanations have moved little beyond the speculations of geneticists that gave rise to the Eugenics Movement during the first third of the twentieth century.[7] Suggestions about biological ties have focused on relationships between aggression and hormones,[8] criminality and low autonomic arousal,[9] prevalence of sinistrality among some types of criminals,[10] and difficulties in learning found among hyperactive and conduct disordered children.[11] Disconcertingly, ev-

---

Mednick, Gabrielli & Hutchings, *Genetic Factors in the Etiology of Criminal Behavior*, in THE CAUSES OF CRIME: NEW BIOLOGICAL APPROACHES 74 (S. Mednick, T. Moffitt & S. Stack eds. 1987) [hereinafter THE CAUSES OF CRIME]; Schulsinger, *Psychopathy: Heredity and Environment*, in BIOSOCIAL BASES OF CRIMINAL BEHAVIOR 109 (S. Mednick & K. Christiansen eds. 1977) [hereinafter BIOSOCIAL BASES].

[6] Huesmann & Eron, *Cognitive Processes and the Persistence of Aggressive Behavior*, 10 AGGRESSIVE BEHAV. 243 (1984); Eron, Huesmann, Dubow, Romanoff & Yarmel, *Aggression and Its Correlates Over 22 Years*, in CHILDHOOD AGGRESSION AND VIOLENCE: SOURCES OF INFLUENCE, PREVENTION, AND CONTROL 249 (D. Crowell, I. Evans & C. O'Donnell eds. 1987).

[7] H. EYSENCK & G. GUDJONSSON, THE CAUSES AND CURES OF CRIMINALITY (1989); M. HALLER, EUGENICS: HEREDITARIAN ATTITUDES IN AMERICAN THOUGHT (1963); id. (paperback ed. 1984).

[8] E. MACCOBY & C. JACKLIN, THE PSYCHOLOGY OF SEX DIFFERENCES (1974); Maccoby & Jacklin, *Sex Differences in Aggression: A Rejoinder and Reprise*, 51 CHILD DEV. 964 (1980); Mednick & Volavka, *Biology and Crime*, in 2 CRIME & JUST.: AN ANNUAL REVIEW OF RES. 85 (N. Morris & M. Tonry eds. 1980); Olweus, *Aggression and Hormones: Behavioral Relationship With Testosterone and Adrenaline*, in DEVELOPMENT OF ANTISOCIAL AND PROSOCIAL BEHAVIOR 51 (D. Olweus, J. Block & M. Yarrow eds. 1986); Olweus, *Testosterone and Adrenaline: Aggressive Antisocial Behavior in Normal Adolescent Males*, in THE CAUSES OF CRIME, *supra* note 5, at 263.

[9] Farrington, *Implications of Biological Findings for Criminological Research*, in THE CAUSES OF CRIME, *supra* note 5, at 42; Hare, *Electrodermal and Cardiovascular Correlates of Psychopathy*, in PSYCHOPATHIC BEHAVIOUR 107 (R. Hare & D. Schalling eds. 1978); Mednick, *A Bio-Social Theory of the Learning of Law-Abiding Behavior*, in BIOSOCIAL BASES, *supra* note 5, at 1; Satterfield, *Childhood Diagnostic and Neurophysiological Predictors of Teenage Arrest Rates: An Eight-Year Prospective Study*, in The CAUSES OF CRIME, *supra* note 5, at 146; Siddle, *Electrodermal Activity and Psychopathy*, in BIOSOCIAL BASES, *supra* note 5, at 199; Wadsworth, *Delinquency, Pulse Rates and Early Emotional Deprivation*, 16 BRIT. J. CRIMINOLOGY 245 (1976).

[10] Gabrielli & Mednick, *Sinistrality and Delinquency*, 89 J. ABNORMAL PSYCHOLOGY 654 (1980).

[11] Buikhuisen, *Cerebral Dysfunctions and Persistent Juvenile Delinquency*, in THE CAUSES OF CRIME, *supra* note 5, at 168; H. ELLIS, THE CRIMINAL (1890); id. (reprinted 1972); Goodman & Stevenson, *A Twin Study of Hyperactivity. 2. The Aetiological Role of Genes, Family Relationships and Perinatal Adversity*, 30 J. CHILD PSYCHOLOGY, PSYCHIATRY & ALLIED DISCIPLINES 691 (1989); Moffitt & Silva, *Self-Reported Delinquency, Neuropsychological Deficit, and History of Attention Deficit Disorder*, 16 J. ABNORMAL CHILD PSYCHOLOGY 553 (1988); Schalling, *Psychopathy-Related Personality Variables and the Psychophysiology of Socialization*, in PSYCHOPATHIC BEHAV. 85 (R. Hare & D. Schalling eds. 1978).

idence contradicting the suggested relationships as links appears as credible as supporting evidence.[12]

Unfortunately, efforts to understand how the environment interacts with biological differences in the production of crime have received little more than lip service.[13] Genetic studies rarely include direct measures of environmental effects. Furthermore, the most commonly used measure of heritability, h^2, devised by Falconer,[14] assumes the equivalence of environmental variance for monozygotic and dizygotic twins and additive effects. Both assumptions are dubious.

Several studies show that differential attractiveness influences interactions.[15] Dizygotic twins will be differently attractive in larger measure than are monozygotic twins and therefore, dizygotic twins are likely to be exposed to greater variation in environment.

A study of 300 children of unwed mothers[16] offers data suggesting an interactive effect between environment and heredity. In this study, the children were adopted within days of birth, and the adopting mothers did not know the psychological status of the biological mothers. The researchers correlated the scores for the biological mothers' emotional stability, based on an MMPI administered prior to giving birth, with the behavior evaluations of

[12] *See, e.g.*, Bohman, *Some Genetic Aspects of Alcoholism and Criminality: A Population of Adoptees*, 35 ARCHIVES GEN. PSYCHIATRY 269 (1978); Feehan, Stanton, McGee, Silva & Moffitt, *Is There an Association Between Lateral Preference and Delinquent Behavior?*, 99 J. ABNORMAL PSYCHOLOGY 198 (1990); Frost, Moffitt & McGee, *Neuropsychological Correlates of Psychopathology in an Unselected Cohort of Young Adolescents*, 98 J. ABNORMAL PSYCHOLOGY 307 (1989); Mawson & Mawson, *Psychopathy and Arousal: A New Interpretation of the Psychophysiological Literature*, 12 BIOLOGICAL PSYCHIATRY 49 (1977); Nachshon & Denno, *Violent Behavior and Cerebral Hemisphere Function*, in THE CAUSES OF CRIME, *supra* note 5, at 185; Plomin, Foch & Rowe, *Bobo Clown Aggression in Childhood: Environment, Not Genes*, 15 J. RESEARCH IN PERSONALITY 331 (1981); Riese, *Neonatal Temperament in Monozygotic and Dizygotic Twin Pairs*, 61 CHILD DEV. 1230 (1990); Schalling, *Personality Correlates of Plasma Testosterone Levels in Young Delinquents: An Example of Person-Situation Interaction?*, in THE CAUSES OF CRIME, *supra* note 5, at 283; Schmauk, *Punishment, Arousal, and Avoidance Learning in Sociopaths*, 76 J. ABNORMAL PSYCHOLOGY 325 (1970); Siddle & Trasler, *The Psychophysiology of Psychopathic Behaviour*, in FOUNDATIONS OF PSYCHOSOMATICS 283 (M. Christie & P. Mellett eds. 1981); Venables, *Autonomic Nervous System Factors in Criminal Behavior*, in THE CAUSES OF CRIME, *supra* note 5, at 110.

[13] For exceptions, see H. STÅTTIN & D. MAGNUSSON, PUBERTAL MATURATION IN FEMALE DEVELOPMENT (1990), and Udry, *Biological Predispositions and Social Control in Adolescent Sexual Behavior*, 53 AM. SOC. REV. 709 (1988), on the contribution of interaction between physical maturity and peers to adolescent deviant behavior among girls.

[14] D. FALCONER, INTRODUCTION TO QUANTITATIVE GENETICS (1960).

[15] For evidence and a review of such studies, see Webster & Driskell, *Beauty as Status*, 89 AM. J. SOC. 140 (1983).

[16] Loehlin, Willerman & Horn, *Personality Resemblances Between Unwed Mothers and Their Adopted-Away Offspring*, 42 J. PERSONALITY & SOC. PSYCHOLOGY 1089 (1982).

their children provided by their adopting mothers several years later.

Loehlin *et al.* found that the children of the least emotionally stable mothers were the most emotionally stable. Their explanation of the obtained negative correlations included biological-environmental interactions, suggesting that characteristics that would lead to poor mental health in one environment could promote good mental health in another.

Rather than address issues about how biological factors influence behavior, socio-biological research has typically attempted to answer the question "how much is inherited?" Answers to that quantitative question will vary under different circumstances. Understanding how the interactions occur, however, should transcend particular circumstances.

A common genetic approach to assessing environmental impact can be described (albeit crudely) as one which assigns to environment what remains after identifying biological impact. Such an approach, however, ignores the role of environment in realizing genetically determined characteristics. Thus, for example, the most elegant Rex Begonia will not grow without sufficient shade, warmth, and moisture. These environmental requirements for Rex Begonia, though critical, could not be detected through strategies based on "subtracting out" genetic effects from studies of healthy plants. Further, the genetic approach to assessing environmental impact overlooks the fact that some types of environments have more impact than others. For example, Peperomias are practically immune to differences in light but can be quickly killed through too much watering, whereas sunlight is crucial for the growth of Gladiolus. Hybridizers who popularized rhododendrons and azaleas in the United States combined manipulation of genetic differences with knowledge of appropriate environments to produce at least 1400 varieties of hardy blooming plants.[17] It seems unlikely that the interplay between genetics and environment would be less complex for human behavior.

Criminality within families could be a function of socialization practices more commonly found among families with a criminal heritage than among those without such heritage. Some differences in socialization practices could be produced through biological differences. Impatience, high activity level, and ready boredom are likely to have an impact on how a parent reacts to child rearing. Further-

---

[17] P. Livingston & F. West, Hybrids and Hybridizers: Rhododendrons and Azaleas for Eastern North America (1978).

more, no *a priori* grounds exist for assuming that similar socialization techniques will have similar results with children who have inherited different potentialities for aggressiveness. Regardless of the theoretical grounds for expecting differences, it would be wise to look for interactions between inherited and environmental conditions to understand the production of criminal behavior.

The present investigation assumes the possibility that some form of criminal diathesis can be genetically transmitted. As a preliminary approach to understanding the transmission, socialization practices of families in which fathers have criminal records are compared with families in which the fathers are not criminal. The analyses then turn to two questions: What child rearing characteristics—added to or interacting with a transmitted potentiality—promote the criminal behavior? And conversely, are there particular practices that serve as protective factors?

II. METHOD

Subjects for the study came from a larger longitudinal investigation of males who had been in a program designed to prevent delinquency. The delinquency prevention program included both "difficult" and "average" youngsters living in deteriorated urban areas of eastern Massachusetts. To permit evaluation of the program, boys in the treatment group had been matched to others from similar neighborhoods and families prior to intervention. At the time of their introduction to the prevention program, the boys ranged in age from five to thirteen (M = 10.5, S.D. = 1.6). Although the treatment program failed to better the lives of its charges, it left a legacy of carefully documented case materials.[18]

Approximately twice a month between 1939 and 1945, counselors visited the homes of 253 boys from 232 families. The counselors appeared at various times of day and throughout the week to help the boys and their families. After each encounter, the counselors filed a detailed report that included conversations and described behavior. Covering a span of more than five years, these running records reveal the texture of family life. To avoid counting particular constellations of families more than once, this study used only one child per family in the analyses. Additionally, 18 families in

---

[18] Results of the treatment program have been reported in McCord, *A Thirty-Year Follow-Up of Treatment Effects*, 33 AM. PSYCHOLOGIST 284 (1978); McCord, *Consideration of Some Effects of a Counseling Program*, in NEW DIRECTIONS IN THE REHABILITATION OF CRIMINAL OFFENDERS 394 (S. Martin, L. Sechrest & R. Redner eds. 1981); McCord, *Crime in Moral and Social Contexts*, 28 CRIMINOLOGY 1 (1990).

which the biological father could not be rated were dropped from the analyses.

In 1957, coders—who had no access to information about the subjects other than what was in the treatment records—transcribed information from the case records into categorical scales describing the parents, the boys, and family interaction.[19] The present study used these categorical scales, dichotomized, to investigate the impact of socialization practices.

To estimate reliability of the coding, a second rater independently read a 10% random sample of the cases. The Scott Interrater Reliability Coefficient, Pi,[20] was computed to indicate relative improvement over chance agreement between two raters.[21] Inter-rater agreement as reflected in Scott's estimate of improvement over chance ranged from 0.55 with 80% agreement on parental conflict to 0.92 with 96% agreement regarding family structure.

As part of the selection process in 1938, *neighborhoods* were rated in terms of delinquency rates, availability of recreational facilities, and proximity to bars, railroads, and junk yards. The variable describing neighborhood contexts was dichotomized to differentiate between those in the "worst" areas, those dominated by bars and debris, and the rest.

To identify *alcoholic fathers*, information from the case records was combined with information from the fathers' criminal records (which had been gathered in the late 1930's and again a decade later). A father was considered an alcoholic if he lost jobs because of drinking, had marital problems attributed primarily to excessive drinking, received treatment for alcoholism, had been convicted at least three times for public drunkenness, or if welfare agencies repeatedly noted that heavy drinking was the source of his problems. By these criteria, almost one-third of the fathers were alcoholics.

Fathers were coded as *absent* if for at least six months prior to the boy's seventeenth birthday, the boy's domicile was not the same as that of the father. This criterion resulted in identifying the fathers of 74 boys in the study as absent.

A rating of *parental conflict* was based on counselors' reports of disagreements about the child, values, money, alcohol, or religion. Ratings could be "no indication," "apparently none," "some," or

---

[19] *See* W. McCord & J. McCord, Origins of Alcoholism (1960).

[20] Scott, *Reliability of Content Analysis: The Case of Nominal Scale Coding*, 3 Pub. Opinion Q. 321 (1955).

[21] $Pi = (Po\text{-}Pe)/(1\text{-}Pe)$, where Po represents observed agreement between raters and Pe represents percent of agreement expected by chance, computed by summing the squared proportions of the cases in each category.

"considerable." Parents were classified as evidencing or not evidencing considerable conflict.

If frequent, noncritical interaction occurred between the mother and her son, then the *mother's attitude toward her son* was classified as "affectionate." Alternative classifications were "passively affectionate" (concerned for the boy's welfare, but little interaction); "passively rejecting" (unconcerned for the boy's welfare and interacted little); "actively rejecting" (almost constantly critical of the boy); "ambivalent" (marked alternation between affection and rejection of the child); and "no indication."

How a mother reacted when faced with problems determined the *mother's self-confidence* rating. If she showed signs of believing in her ability to handle the difficulties, then she was rated as self-confident. Alternative ratings were "no indication," "victim or pawn," and "neutral."

Maternal restrictiveness was rated as "subnormal" if a mother permitted her son to make virtually all his choices without her guidance. Alternative ratings were "no indication," "normal" and "overly restrictive."

Supervision described the degree to which a boy's activities after school were governed by an adult. Supervision could be rated "present," or alternatively, "sporadic," "absent," or "no information."

The mother's discipline was classified both by type and by consistency. *Punitive discipline* included very harsh verbal abuse as well as the use of physical force to control the boy. A parent was classified as punitive for either erratic or consistent use of such techniques. *Consistent, nonpunitive discipline* identified a parent who used praise, rewards, or reasoning to control the boy. Alternative categories were "inconsistent, non-punitive," "extremely lax, with almost no use of discipline," and "no information." Codes showing the mother's discipline as punitive and as consistent, nonpunitive were considered.[22]

The *aggressiveness of each parent* was rated as "unrestrained" if that parent regularly expressed anger by such activities as shouting abuses, yelling, throwing or breaking things, or hitting people. Alternative classifications were "no indication," "moderately aggressive," or "greatly inhibited." About 10% of the mothers were rated as highly aggressive and 16% of the fathers were so rated. In addition to the ratings of each parent separately, a combined rating

---

[22] These were not, of course, independent ratings.

identified a boy as exposed or not exposed to at least one highly aggressive parent.

Criminal records for fathers were gathered in 1948, when the fathers averaged fifty-two years in age (S.D. = 7.2 years). Criminal records for the sons were collected in 1978, when they averaged fifty years in age (S.D. = 1.6 years). Both fathers and sons were considered criminals if the record showed a conviction for a Type-1 Index crime: theft, breaking and entering, assault, murder, rape, attempted murder, or attempted rape.

Forty-nine fathers and 69 sons were criminals. Criminal sons constituted 45% of the 49 biological father-son pairs among which fathers were criminals, and 28% of the biological father-son pairs among which fathers were not criminals. Alternatively, of the 69 sons with criminal records, 32% had criminal fathers; of the 145 noncriminal sons, 18% had criminal fathers, $X^2_{(2)} = 4.659$, Phi = 0.148, p = 0.031.

III. RESULTS

Comparison between families in which fathers were criminals and those in which the fathers were not criminals revealed differences that might help to explain antisocial behavior among some sons of criminals. As compared with non-criminal fathers, those who had criminal records were more likely to be alcoholics and to be absent from the homes in which their sons were reared. The criminal fathers were also more likely to be highly aggressive and punitive. Parental conflict was more likely present in their families. Furthermore, the mothers of their sons were more likely to be aggressive (Table 1).

On the other hand, families of fathers with criminal records were not more likely than families of non-criminal fathers to live in the worst neighborhoods. Nor were their sons reliably less likely to have affectionate, self-confident mothers, to have consistent and nonpunitive discipline, to be supervised or to be subject to normal control (Table 2).

Collinearity among variables linked with a father's criminality may account for some of the cross-generational concordance in criminal behavior. For example, parental alcoholism and conflict are more prevalent among families in which fathers have been criminals; these variables, rather than paternal criminality, might cause delinquency. Possibly, however, parental alcoholism and conflict may be spuriously linked with delinquency; they are more prevalent among families in which fathers have been criminals, and

TABLE 1
DIFFERENCES BETWEEN CRIMINAL & NON-CRIMINAL FATHERS

(percent of each group)

Father:	Criminal (N =49)	Non-criminal (N =165)	p =
Father alcoholic	57	24	.000
Father absent	53	29	.002
Parental conflict	55	25	.000
Father aggressive	31	13	.003
Mother aggressive	20	7	.008
Either parent aggressive	45	20	.000

criminality might have heritable components. To account for such covariations, criminogenic and protective factors were assessed among families with criminal fathers and separately in families with-

TABLE 2
COMPARISONS BETWEEN CRIMINAL & NON-CRIMINAL FATHERS

(percent of each group)

Father	Criminal (N =49)	Non-criminal (N =165)	p
Worst neighborhoods	29	32	>.05
Mother affectionate to son	45	48	>.05
Mother self-confident	27	30	>.05
Mother not restrictive	43	33	>.05
Boy supervised	49	60	>.05
Mother's discipline punitive	43	48	>.05
Mother consistently nonpunitive	31	30	>.05

out them. In this manner, proclivities toward crime that might be transmitted biologically were controlled. Table 3 shows the relationships to criminality of the variables found more frequently in families with criminal than with noncriminal fathers.

Except through a relation to paternal criminality, neither paternal alcoholism nor a father's absence reliably increased the probability for the sons to be criminals. The top half of Table 3 compares sons who had criminal fathers. Among them, a majority of fathers of both criminal and non-criminal sons also were alcoholics. Viewed from the alternative perspective, 50% of the 28 sons whose fathers were both alcoholics and criminals had been convicted for Index crimes; 38% of the 21 sons whose fathers were criminals but not alcoholics had been convicted for Index crimes. Parallel differences appeared between sons of the non-criminals:

TABLE 3
DIFFERENCES BETWEEN CRIMINALS & NON-CRIMINALS
(percent of each group)

A. Criminal Fathers

Sons:	Criminal (N=22)	Non-criminal (N=27)	p=
Father alcoholic	64	52	NS
Father absent	50	56	NS
Parental conflict	77	37	.005
Father aggressive	45	19	.042
Mother aggressive	36	7	.012
Either parent aggressive	73	22	.000

B. Non-Criminal Fathers

Sons:	Criminal (N=47)	Non-criminal (N=118)	p=
Father alcoholic	34	20	NS
Father absent	34	27	NS
Parental conflict	36	21	.046
Father aggressive	19	10	NS
Mother aggressive	13	5	NS
Either parent aggressive	32	15	.016

40% of the sons of alcoholics (N=40) and 25% of the sons of nonalcoholics (N=125) were convicted.

The relationship between paternal criminality and paternal absence may account for an apparent relationship between paternal absence and criminal behavior. At least in this sample, a slightly higher proportion of non-criminals than of criminals came from homes without fathers. Viewing the proportions from the direction opposite to that shown in Table 3 indicates that sons of criminals who were present in the home were more, rather than less, likely to become criminals: 48% (N=23) versus 42% (N=26) for father being present or absent, respectively. Among the sons of non-criminals, 33% of the 48 sons whose fathers were absent and 27% of the 117 sons whose fathers were present became criminals.

The data suggest that aggressive parental models, however, are criminogenic above and beyond their relationship to paternal criminality. Table 3 shows that approximately three-out-of-four of the criminals who had criminal fathers also had been exposed to parental conflict and aggression. These proportions more than double those found among non-criminal sons of criminals and criminal sons of non-criminals. Computed in the opposite direction, the proportions evidence the degree to which parental conflict and aggressiveness increased probabilities that sons of criminals and of non-criminals would be criminals. In 27 families with criminal fathers, a considerable amount of parental conflict occurred, and 63% of their sons were convicted for Index crimes. In contrast, a significantly smaller proportion, 23% of sons from criminal but non-conflictful family backgrounds, were convicted, $X^2_{(1)} = 7.933$, p < 0.005. In 42 families with non-criminal fathers, a considerable amount of parental conflict also occurred, and 40% of their sons were convicted for Index crimes. In comparison, only 24% from non-conflictful backgrounds had been convicted, $X^2_{(1)} = 3.977$, p < 0.05. In families with criminal fathers, 22 contained at least one parent exhibiting unrestrained aggressiveness. More than two-thirds (73%) of their sons, compared with 22% of the remaining sons of criminal fathers, were convicted for Index crimes, $X^2_{(1)} = 12.499$, p < 0.000. Among the 33 sons of non-criminals having a parent who exhibited unrestrained aggressiveness, 45% were convicted for Index crimes; this proportion was reliably greater than the 24% of the remaining sons of non-criminal fathers who were convicted, $X^2_{(1)} = 5.831$, p < 0.016. The instigating impact of parental aggressiveness and conflict appears to accumulate. Table 4 shows the criminogenic effects of combining aggressive models with criminogenic heritage.

TABLE 4
INSTIGATING CONDITIONS AND CRIME

(percent of sons who were criminals)

Number of Instigating Conditions	Fathers:	
	Criminal	Non-criminal
none	(N: 18) 17	(N: 104) 21
one	(N: 13) 38	(N: 18) 38
two	(N: 18) 78	(N: 14) 50

$$X^2_{(6)} = 55.159, \text{ p} < .000$$

As Table 4 indicates, sons of criminal fathers were more likely to be exposed to socializing conditions conducive to crime. Furthermore, instigating conditions interact with criminogenic heritage in such a way as to increase the potentiality for crime when aggressive parents were in open conflict.

Although criminal fathers were not more likely than non-criminal fathers to live in the worst neighborhoods or to be married to women who showed signs of being poor mothers, effects of neighborhood or family socialization practices might depend on whether the child had inherited conditions that promote criminality. To inspect the possibility, criminality among sons of criminals and among sons of non-criminals were examined. Table 5 displays the results. Living in unstable neighborhoods appeared to have a criminogenic

TABLE 5

DIFFERENCES BETWEEN CRIMINALS & NON-CRIMINALS

(percent of each group)

A. Criminal Fathers

Sons:	Criminal (N=22)	Non-criminal (N=27)	p=
Worst neighborhoods	45	15	.018
Mother affectionate to son	23	63	.005
Mother self-confident	5	44	.002
Mother not restrictive	64	26	.008
Boy supervised	36	59	NS
Mother's discipline punitive	64	26	.008
Mother consistently nonpunitive	9	48	.003

B. Non-Criminal Fathers

Sons:	Criminal (N=47)	Non-criminal (N=118)	p=
Worst neighborhoods	34	31	NS
Mother affectionate to son	36	53	.046
Mother self-confident	17	35	.025
Mother not restrictive	43	29	NS
Boy supervised	45	66	.011
Mother's discipline punitive	53	46	NS
Mother consistently nonpunitive	21	33	NS

effect only on sons who had a criminogenic heritage. The relationship can be brought out by examining proportions from the alternative perspective. Fourteen of the families with criminal fathers lived in the worst neighborhoods, and 71% of the sons in these families were convicted for Index crimes. In comparison, 34% of the sons of criminals living in better neighborhoods were likewise convicted, $X^2_{(1)} = 5.576$, $p < 0.02$. Only 30% of the 53 sons from the worst neighborhoods whose fathers were not criminal were convicted, as were 28% of the sons of non-criminal fathers reared in better neighborhoods.

Reliably lower proportions of criminals than of non-criminals had mothers who were affectionate or self-confident. Mothers appeared to be particularly influential in determining whether sons of criminal men became criminal. Maternal affection, self-confidence, and consistently nonpunitive discipline or supervision apparently helped to protect their sons from criminogenic influences. These protective effects are brought out through examining the proportions who became criminals from various types of backgrounds.

Among the sons of criminals, for example, there were 22 men who had affectionate mothers. Although only 23% of these were convicted for Index crimes, 63% of the 27 sons of criminals whose mothers were not affectionate were convicted, $X^2_{(1)} = 7.933$, p < 0.005. Differences in crime rates related to maternal affection were less dramatic among sons of non-criminal fathers: 21% of the men with affectionate mothers (N=80) and 35% of the remaining men (N=85) were convicted, $X^2_{(1)} = 3.990$, p < 0.05.

Maternal self-confidence appeared to be an antidote to whatever criminogenic influences were transmitted from father to son. Only 1 of the 13 men who had criminal fathers and self-confident mothers was convicted for an Index crime; that 8% was reliably lower than the 58% who became criminals among the remaining 36 sons of criminals, $X^2_{(1)} = 9.901$, p < 0.002.

Among sons of non-criminals, those whose mothers were self-confident (N=49) were less likely to be convicted than those whose mothers were not self-confident (N=116): 16% versus 34%, $X^2_{(1)} = 5.058$, p < 0.03.

Among sons of criminals who had received little direction from their mothers (N=21), 67% became criminals; the proportion was reliably greater than the 29% (N=28) who became criminals despite more directive mothers, $X^2_{(1)} = 7.039$, p < 0.008. Differences related to maternal restrictions among sons of non-criminals were not reliable.

The mother's consistent, nonpunitive discipline seemed also to be protective. Although only 13% of the sons of criminals whose mothers used consistent, nonpunitive discipline (N=15) were convicted for Index crimes, 59% of the remaining sons of criminals (N=34) were convicted, $X^2_{(1)} = 8.706$, p < 0.003. On the other hand, 67% of the sons of criminals whose mothers used punitive discipline (N=21) were convicted for Index crimes, although only 29% of the remaining sons of criminal fathers (N=28) were convicted, $X^2_{(1)} = 7.039$, p < 0.008. Neither comparison among the sons of non-criminals yielded a statistically reliable difference.

Supervision had only a slight effect on sons of criminals. Among sons of non-criminals, however, supervision seemed to be protective. Only 21% of the 99 supervised sons compared with 39% of the 66 unsupervised sons were convicted, $X^2_{(1)} = 6.426$, p < 0.02.

Maternal affection, self-confidence, and consistently nonpuni-

tive discipline or supervision served as protections against criminogenic influences. The joint effects of these variables were
analyzed by defining a scale in which affection, self-confidence, and
having either consistently nonpunitive discipline (among sons of
criminals) or supervision (among sons of non-criminals) were given
equal weights. Table 6 shows the cumulative impact of protective
factors.

TABLE 6
PROTECTIVE FACTORS AND CRIME

(percent of sons who were criminals)

| | Fathers: | |
Number of Protective Factors	Criminal	Non-criminal
none	(N: 25) 64	(N: 39) 44
one	(N: 8) 50	(N: 46) 35
two	(N: 6) 33	(N: 58) 21
three	(N: 10) 0	(N: 22) 9

$$X^2_{(9)} = 47.060, p < .000$$

Stepwise discriminant analyses indicated that instigating and
protective factors contributed to criminal rates among sons both
with and without heritable risk for criminality. The instigating and
protective measures were more discriminating among the sons of
criminals, accounting for only 9% of the variance among sons of
non-criminals but accounting for 37.8% of the variance among sons
of criminals (Table 7).

TABLE 7
STEPWISE DISCRIMINANT ANALYSIS:

(criminals distinguished from non-criminals)

A. Sons of Criminals

	Partial R^2	Prob. > F	Mean R^2
Instigation	.277	.0001	.277
Protection	.140	.0088	.378

B. Sons of Non-Criminals

	Partial R^2	Prob. > F	Mean R^2
Protection	.066	.0008	.066
Instigation	.025	.0433	.090

Pairs of discriminant functions were built from the two scales
representing protective and instigating conditions. These functions

maximized discrimination between criminal and non-criminal sons. The functions correctly identified 18 of the 22 criminals (82%) and 21 of the 27 non-criminals (78%) whose fathers were criminals, together correctly discriminating 79.5% of the sons' of criminals. Among the sons of non-criminals, the functions correctly identified 26 of the 47 criminals (55%) and 82 of the 118 non-criminals (69%), together correctly identifying 65% of the sons of non-criminals. Knowledge about socialization practices clearly provided more accurate classification than would have knowledge of biological risk alone.

IV. SUMMARY AND DISCUSSION

A century ago, Havelock Ellis reminded his readers of two factors in criminal heredity: "There is the element of innate disposition, and there is the element of contagion from social environment . . . . Frequently the one element alone, whether the heredity or the contagion, is not sufficient to determine the child in the direction of crime."[23]

Nevertheless, during most of the twentieth century, social scientists have spent their energies disputing the case for nature *or* nurture, thus making little progress toward understanding how the interactions influence behavior. This study attempted to focus attention on how environmental conditions affect those who inherit different biologically-based predispositions toward crime.

This study controlled for unknown factors that can be attributed to heritage. Admittedly, the control was incomplete, because no convincing evidence exists that all criminals are criminals through heritable characteristics. By comparing effects of socialization among sons of men who were and who were not criminals, however, heritable qualities related to crime were included in the analyses.

To gain understanding of the processes accounting for intergenerational transmission of aggression, families in which fathers had been convicted for serious crimes were compared with families in which the fathers were not known to be criminals. This comparison suggests that criminal fathers had a greater likelihood of being alcoholic, aggressive, punitive, and absent. They were also more likely than their non-criminal counterparts to be in conflict with probably aggressive wives.

On the other hand, sons of criminals were not more likely than their peers to live in the worst neighborhoods, to be rejected or sub-

---

[23] H. ELLIS, THE CRIMINAL 92 (1890).

jected to maternal punitiveness, or to be deprived of competent maternal guidance.

Socialization variables fell into two sets. One set promoted crime. These "instigating conditions" were more common in families of criminal fathers than in families of non-criminal fathers. The set included parental conflict and aggression.

The second set was found with approximately equal frequency among families of both criminal and non-criminal fathers. These variables described socialization practices that seemed to reduce the likelihood of crime. The protective factors included having a self-confident mother and maternal affection. Effects of discipline as protection against criminogenic influences depended on whether the family was at genetic risk for criminality. In families having criminal fathers, nonpunitive and consistent discipline had beneficial effects. Although discipline made little difference in families without criminal fathers, supervision seemed beneficial. One may view these differences as indicating that genetically related potentialities require "fertilizer" to develop into antisocial behavior—fertilizer not available when parents provide the protections of affection and clearly specified directives.

Outcome of genetic risk depended on accompanying instigating conditions. That is, unless there was parental conflict and at least one aggressive parent, sons of criminals were not more likely to become criminals than were sons of non-criminals.

To examine joint effects of instigating and protecting factors, the scales measuring these influences were divided as close to the mean as possible. Crime rates within categories also were computed. Table 8 shows the results.

A categorical analysis of variance[24] evaluating the impact of paternal criminality, instigating conditions, protective factors, and their interactions indicated that each main effect was significant, and that the interaction between instigation and protection was also significant. None of the interactions with paternal criminality was significant, though the distributions show that heritable risk covaried with high instigating and low protective conditions.

Alternative explanations may account for these results. An emphasis on the social interpretation could call upon studies showing that children imitate aggression.[25] An emphasis on the biological

---

24 SAS, SAS User's Guide (1985).

25 Bandura & Huston, *Identification as a Process of Incidental Learning*, 63 J. Abnormal & Soc. Psychology 311 (1961); Bandura, Ross & Ross, *Transmission of Aggression Through Imitation of Aggressive Models*, 63 J. Abnormal & Soc. Psychology 575 (1961); Hall & Cairns, *Aggressive Behavior in Children: An Outcome of Modeling or Social Reciprocity?*, 20 De-

TABLE 8
HERITABLE RISK, INSTIGATING CONDITIONS, PROTECTIVE FACTORS AND CRIME

(percent criminal in each group)

Father	Criminal	Non-criminal
Instigation Low & Protection High	N: 10) 0	(N: 61) 11
Instigation Low & Protection Low	(N: 8) 38	(N: 43) 35
Instigation High & Protection High	(N: 6) 33	(N: 19) 37
Instigation High & Protection Low	(N: 25) 68	(N: 42) 43

Categorical Analysis of Variance Table

source	DF	Chi-Square	Prob
Father's Criminality	1	12.11	.0005
Instigation	1	11.24	.0008
Protection	1	5.39	.0203
Instigation × Protection	1	4.86	.0275

interpretation might suggest that parental aggressiveness signifies particularly strong genetic loading on criminogenic factors.

Rather than try to decide which is more cogent, it is worth noting that biological potentialities *must* provide necessary conditions for crime. These conditions may well vary according to dimensions of criminal acts, some requiring speed and some requiring brawn, for example. Beyond these essentials, the present study indicates that biological conditions may promote or retard criminal behavior. Perhaps more importantly, the data suggest that socialization practices have a considerable effect on how the biological potentialities develop into antisocial behavior.

Evidence from the present study indicates that the protective nature of maternal warmth and competence are particularly salient in reducing genetically transmitted characteristics that promote antisocial behavior. This discovery leads to a tentative conclusion that intervention techniques designed to develop competence among parents may be particularly effective when the targets are children at high genetic risk.

VELOPMENTAL PSYCHOLOGY 739 (1984); McCord, *Parental Behavior in the Cycle of Aggression,* 51 PSYCHIATRY 14 (1988).

RACIAL INEQUALITY AND RACIALLY DISAGGREGATED HOMICIDE RATES: AN ASSESSMENT OF ALTERNATIVE THEORETICAL EXPLANATIONS*

STEVEN F. MESSNER
University at Albany, SUNY
REID M. GOLDEN
Hartwick College

This research considers the relationship between levels of racial inequality and homicide rates for a sample of 154 U.S. cities. We identify four causal processes that have been cited in the theoretical literature to explain the link between racial inequality and criminal violence. These different causal explanations imply distinctive relationships between racial inequality and different types of homicide rates disaggregated by the racial characteristics of victims and offenders. Accordingly, we examine the effects of racial inequality on racially disaggregated homicide rates, as well as on total rates. We also introduce factor scales to alleviate the common problem of multicollinearity. Our results reveal significant, positive coefficients for racial inequality in equations predicting total homicide rates and race-specific offending rates. These results offer greatest support for theoretical arguments emphasizing a generalized effect of racial inequality on the offending behavior of residents of metropolitan communities.

In a recent analysis, Land et al. (1990) review the major macro-level studies of homicide that have been published during the past two decades. They discover that the findings in this literature are highly inconsistent across different time periods and units of analysis. They also demonstrate in a multilevel, multiyear analysis that the inconsistencies can be attributed, at least in part, to the problem of high levels of collinearity among some of the independent variables. After simplifying the dimensional structure of the covariates by principal components analysis, Land et al. are able to produce more consistent findings. Substantively, their models point to the importance of a "resource deprivation/affluence" component, population structure, and divorce rates as major determinants of levels of homicide for cities, standard metropolitan statistical areas (SMSAs), and states in the United States.

Land et al. do not consider explicitly the effects of racial inequality in socioeconomic status in their regression analyses because they limit attention

* We are grateful to Allen Liska, Scott South, and anonymous reviewers for comments on earlier drafts of this manuscript, to Peggy Plass for assistance in compiling the data from the Comparative Homicide File, and to Erika Von Schiller for collecting census data.

to variables for which data are available for three types of geographical units (states, cities, and SMSAs) over the 1960–1980 time period. They speculate, however, that measures of racial inequality would probably "cluster" along with the other variables that constitute the resource deprivation/affluence index (Land et al., 1990:944). If this is correct, efforts to assess the distinctive effects of racial inequality on homicide rates are likely to encounter problems of statistical estimation irrespective of any theoretical or substantive interest in the effects of this variable.

One purpose of our analysis is to attempt to construct a measure of racial inequality in socioeconomic status that is sufficiently distinct from other aspects of social structure to permit the reliable estimation of its effect on city homicide rates. We combine several indicators of relative disadvantages for blacks in income, education, employment, and housing with the measures of resource deprivation/affluence considered by Land et al. in a factor analysis.[1] Our results indicate that a racial inequality dimension can in fact be differentiated from the resource deprivation/affluence dimension and that meaningful factor scales can be computed to represent both of these aspects of social structure.

At least four causal processes linking racial inequality with criminal violence can be postulated on the basis of the theoretical literature. Moreover, the different processes imply distinctive effects of racial inequality on homicide rates disaggregated by racial characteristics of those involved. We accordingly examine the effects of racial inequality not only on total homicide rates but also on homicide rates disaggregated by race of offender and on rates disaggregated by both race of offender and race of victim. These analyses of total and racially disaggregated homicide rates thus facilitate an examination of the various ways in which racial inequality might exert causal effects on city homicide rates.

THEORY AND HYPOTHESES

The most influential statement of a theoretical link between racial socioeconomic inequality and violent crime has been formulated by Blau and colleagues (Blau and Blau, 1982; Blau and Schwartz, 1984). The arguments put forth by these researchers are actually rather complex, and different causal processes are suggested at different places. A common theme, however, is the emphasis on *ascriptive* forms of social differentiation. Blau et al. speculate

---

1. Land et al. (1990:942–943) use principal components analysis, rather than classical factor analysis, because they do not posit underlying dimensions but merely attempt to simplify the regressor space. Our analysis, in contrast, is informed by a theory that explicitly postulates a distinct dimension of urban social structure that can be conceptualized as reflecting racial inequality. Accordingly, we employ factor analytic techniques, as explained more fully below.

that inequality in any form is a potential source of conflict and violence, but "inborn" inequalities are especially conducive to such behaviors (Blau and Blau, 1982:118).

One of the ways in which ascriptive inequality allegedly generates conflict and violence is by its effect on the overall social climate of the community. Blau and Blau (1982) hypothesize that in a society with a formal commitment to democratic principles, inequality based on race interferes with social integration. The essence of the argument is that "inborn" inequalities generate hostile sentiments and at the same time weaken support for social norms that operate to restrain such sentiments. In their words,

> ascriptive socioeconomic inequalities undermine the social integration of a community by creating multiple parallel social differences which widen the separations between ethnic groups and between social classes, and it creates a situation characterized by much social disorganization and prevalent latent animosities (Blau and Blau, 1982:119).

Such a situation is "akin to Durkheim's concept of anomie," especially if the lack of regulation of passions is deemphasized in favor of "the prevalent disorganization, sense of injustice, discontent, and distrust generated by the apparent contradiction between proclaimed values and norms, on the one hand, and social experiences, on the other" (1982:119).[2]

This particular argument might be labeled a "social disorganization/anomie" explanation of the criminogenic effects of racial inequality. The primary causal mechanism leading to increased criminal violence is the poor integration and widespread anomie that accompany high levels of racial inequality. Insofar as this process does in fact operate, racial inequality should have a positive effect on the total homicide rate; it should also have positive effects on the offending behavior of racial subgroups. These predictions follow because social disorganization and anomie presumably have an impact on all segments of the population.

Another, slightly different, causal mechanism is suggested elsewhere in the theoretical arguments of Blau and colleagues. In particular, Blau and Schwartz (1984) focus attention more directly on the racial minority (see also Blau and Blau, 1982:119; Nettler, 1984:229–232). They emphasize the extent to which overt conflict over the distribution of resources requires an awareness of common economic interests. This awareness, they postulate, is more likely to emerge when inequalities are associated with group characteristics. Under such circumstances, the underprivileged are likely to become "aware of their collective interest in redistribution" (Blau and Schwartz, 1984:179).

---

2. This argument by Blau and Blau is reminiscent of Merton's (1968) theory of social structure and anomie. In essence, ascriptive inequality constitutes "disjuncture" between the cultural structure (i.e., democratic values) and the social structure (inborn obstacles to achievement). See Logan and Messner (1987:512–513).

The opportunity to pursue any such redistribution, however, may be blocked, with important consequences for the way in which conflict is expressed:

> If a minority's endeavors to obtain a fair share of resources are consistently frustrated, it means their attempts to give realistic expression to their conflict of interest are blocked. . . . The blocking of realistic conflict produces the pent-up aggression, which manifests itself in diffuse hostility and violence (Blau and Schwartz, 1984:180).

The most important feature of this argument for our purposes is the clear implication that racial inequality is problematic primarily for the racial minority. This is the group with an objective interest in redistribution but without resources to bring about such a redistribution. The racial minority presumably experiences relative deprivation, which engenders frustration leading ultimately to aggression. This explanation for the criminogenic effects of racial inequality can thus be called a "relative deprivation/frustration aggression" explanation. It implies that racial inequality should have a significant positive effect on the offending rates of the racially disadvantaged group, that is, blacks (cf. Harer and Steffensmeier, 1990; Sampson, 1985).

Although Blau et al. do not explicitly consider distinctive effects of racial inequality on the white population, the logic underlying their arguments for the racial minority suggests such a possibility. If it is in everybody's interest to maximize resources, as Blau and Schwartz argue (1984:176), then a condition of racial inequality is beneficial to the racial majority, at least when considered from the standpoint of immediate self-interest. Whites might, accordingly, derive certain benefits—both material and psychological—from being relatively advantaged vis-à-vis blacks, and this situation of advantage might reduce the frustrations that would otherwise promote aggressive impulses. In short, a "relative gratification/reduced aggression" explanation can be posed as an analogue to the relative deprivation explanation. The distinctive prediction here is that the level of racial inequality should be *inversely* related to the offending rate of whites.

A final prediction about the effects of racial inequality on levels of homicide can be derived from Blau's (1977) macrostructural theory of intergroup relations. Whereas the arguments presented above deal with the potential sources of *motivation* for homicide, Blau's theory of intergroup relations shifts attention to *opportunities* for intergroup contact. The fundamental premise of this theory is that an intergroup contact is required for the emergence of any meaningful intergroup association, and that basic structural features of communities influence the probability of intergroup contacts.

For our purposes, Blau's theorems about racial inequality are most relevant (1977:90–93, 101–125). Blau hypothesizes that racial inequality in various forms will reduce opportunities for fortuitous contacts between members of different races.[3] This, in turn, reduces the probability of interracial associations. Blau's theory thus implies an "opportunity" effect of racial inequality that is different from the motivational effects elaborated above. Racial inequality should be negatively related to rates of *interracial* homicide, that is, whites killing blacks and blacks killing whites.[4]

To summarize, various theoretical explanations of the link between racial inequality and criminal violence have either implicitly or explicitly invoked different causal mechanisms. These causal mechanisms imply, in turn, distinctive associations with homicide rates disaggregated by the race of the participants. The social disorganization/anomie explanation implies a positive effect of racial inequality on the total homicide rate and on racially disaggregated offending rates. The relative deprivation/frustration aggression explanation and the relative gratification/reduced aggression explanation suggest positive effects on black offending rates and negative effects on white offending rates, respectively. Finally, the macrostructural opportunity perspective predicts that racial inequality will exhibit a significant negative effect on rates of interracial homicide.

PREVIOUS RESEARCH

The work by Blau and associates on racial inequality and violent crime has stimulated two distinct bodies of literature. One set of studies involves attempts to replicate Blau and Blau's (1982) finding of a positive effect of racial inequality of violent crime rates. A second set of studies focuses on tests of Blau's (1977) theorems concerning the structural determinants of intergroup relations. Both research agendas are relevant to our analysis and warrant a brief review.

Research examining the relationship between racial inequality and the overall rate of violent crime has been inconsistent at best. In a study published prior to Blau and Blau's influential article, Braithwaite (1979) finds no

---

3. To simplify the theoretical discussion, we use the term "racial inequality" in a general sense to include both differentials in socioeconomic status (SES) and patterns of segregated housing. Previous research informed by Blau's theory (e.g., Messner and South, 1986; South and Messner, 1986) typically differentiates between residential segregation and racial inequality.

4. Strictly speaking, Blau's theory of intergroup relations attempts to explain how structural characteristics constrain the patterning of associations across groups, while the motivations for such associations are treated as exogenous to the model. Previous tests of the theory have thus typically examined "conditional probabilities," such as the proportion of marriages that are interracial (e.g., Blau et al., 1982) or the proportion of violent crimes that are interracial (Messner and South, 1992; Sampson, 1984; South and Messner, 1986). In our analysis of the rate of interracial homicide per population, we include those variables that have been identified in past research on homicide rates as the key etiological variables (Land et al., 1990). The hypothesized "opportunity effect" of racial inequality is therefore the effect ":et" of these other motivational factors.

relationship between racial inequality and crime rates for SMSAs, once over-all economic inequality is controlled. Blau and Blau note this discrepancy in their own discussion and attribute it to a probable strong correlation between Braithwaite's measure of racial inequality and overall inequality (Blau and Blau, 1982:119). Even at this early stage in the development of the literature, potential problems of multicollinearity are cited as an explanation for discrepant results.

The pattern of inconsistent findings becomes even more pronounced in efforts to test models quite similar to those of Blau and Blau. Balkwell (1983) adopts such a strategy in his analysis of 100 SMSAs. He is unable to replicate the Blau's findings and concludes that the effects of racial inequality are not very robust. Carroll and Jackson (1983), in their study of 93 nonsouthern cities, likewise find that a measure of racial inequality has negligible effects on crimes against the person. They also observe significant *negative* effects on rates of robbery and burglary. In a larger study based on 408 U.S. cities, Jackson (1984) finds that racial income inequality is not a significant predictor of crime rates when other city characteristics are taken into account.

Williams (1984) directly confronts the controversial conclusion of the Blau's that racial inequality rather than poverty promotes violent crime. He suggests that the Blaus' models are misspecified, failing to take into account nonlinear relationships. Reestimation of models that incorporate nonlinear relationships leads Williams to conclude that both poverty and racial inequality promote violent crime. In contrast, Blau and Schwartz (1984), employing logistic transformations to accommodate nonlinear relationships, find results consistent with the Blau's original thesis.

Simpson (1985) introduces an additional methodological refinement by considering logits for various "percentage-type" variables in the statistical models. He discovers powerful effects for regional culture, measured by Gastil's Southernness index, social disorganization, and sociodemographic factors. Racial inequality does not emerge as a significant predictor of violent crime in Simpson's analysis. Two additional studies further complicate the picture. Blau and Golden (1986) report that the effects of racial inequality are diminished but not eliminated if nonlinear relationships are taken into account and regional culture is measured by "percent Southern born." In contrast, Messner and Golden (1985) fail to find a significant relationship between racial inequality and homicide after increasing the sample size from 125 to 197 SMSAs, even though the models are similar to those of Blau and Golden.

Golden and Messner (1987) attempt to resolve some of these inconsistencies by examining systematically the effects of sample size, the measurement of racial inequality, and model specification on overall outcomes. They report that sample size has a negligible effect on the relationship between racial inequality and violent crime, whereas the measurement of racial inequality in terms of income versus socioeconomic status has a small effect. But, the key issue appears to be multicollinearity in the models. This makes the consistent estimation of equations highly problematic.

Balkwell (1990) has recently argued for a reorientation in studies of group inequality and levels of homicide. He criticizes past research for focusing solely on one racial minority—blacks, and he claims that previous macro-level studies have given insufficient attention to the micro-level processes that underlie the theoretical arguments. To remedy these deficiencies, he proposes a measure of inequality that incorporates information on multiple ethnic groups and that is weighted by the proportional representation of those groups.[5] His inequality measure emerges as the most powerful predictor of homicide rates in a regression analysis for a sample of SMSAs.

Balkwell also asserts that his models have fewer statistical problems than those employed in previous studies because his measure of ethnic inequality is more highly correlated with the dependent variable than with other predictors. But, this does not guarantee that his models are immune to problems of multicollinearity. Examination of the Spearman rank-order correlation matrix reported in his article strongly suggests that there are indeed serious problems of multicollinearity (e.g., the correlation between ethnic inequality and percent black is .792). Hence, his conclusions concerning the new measure of ethnic inequality are subject to the same ambiguities that have plagued previous research.

Finally, three additional studies are of particular interest because they include analyses of race-specific offending rates. Sampson reports contradictory results across two studies. In the first (1985), he finds a nonsignificant effect of racial inequality on overall homicide rates and a *negative* effect of racial inequality on black arrest rates. These findings, especially the latter, clearly run counter to the logic of the Blaus' theoretical arguments. In contrast, a second study by Sampson (1986a) based on a similar sample of cities reveals significant positive effects of racial inequality on total homicide rates and on white and black arrest rates.

Harer and Steffensmeier (1990) also analyze crime data disaggregated by race, and they use a within-race measure of income inequality as well as the

---

5. Balkwell's theoretical argument is highly similar to the relative deprivation/frustration aggression thesis explained above. Accordingly, we would argue that a more appropriate test of the theory can be made with race- (or group-) specific rates rather than with rates for the total population. When race-specific rates serve as the dependent variables, there is no need to employ Balkwell's weighting procedure (i.e., weighting the magnitude of group disadvantage by the relative size of the group) because these rates are standardized by the population size of the specified group. We do agree with Balkwell that it is important to consider inequality between ethnic groups as well as inequality between blacks and whites, although such analyses are beyond the scope of this paper.

between-race measure typically employed in previous research. They report that the effect of economic inequality on violent crime varies by race. Specifically, within-race income inequality is a poor predictor of offending rates for blacks but a robust one for whites. Between-race inequality is a weak predictor of all crime rates. They conclude that "the recent emphases on inequality as a criminogenic condition for black-white differences in crime provide an incomplete and inaccurate picture of the structural influences on exceptionally high rates of black violent crime" (1990:17).

The second, much more limited, body of literature relevant to our analysis is the set of studies that test Blau's (1977) macrostructural theory of intergroup relations. These studies consider the structural determinants of levels of interracial criminal incidents. In one such study, Sampson (1984) reports that levels of racial heterogeneity are positively associated with the likelihood of interracial victimization. In another study, Sampson (1986b) finds that the degree of urbanization has a strong positive effect on intergroup victimization. Both of these findings are consistent with Blau's theory.

South and Messner (1986) pursue similar objectives and report that racial composition and residential segregation are related in the theoretically expected manner to the probability of interracial violent crime as measured by National Crime Survey (NCS) data. In a second analysis focusing exclusively on robbery, Messner and South (1986) also find the hypothesized effects for racial composition and residential segregation. Interestingly, in neither of these analyses does racial income inequality emerge as a significant predictor of interracial crime. The generalizability of these results, however, is problematic because of the small sample of cities (26) available for analysis with the NCS data. In an analysis of a larger sample of U.S. cities, Messner and South (1992) report reasonably strong support for hypotheses derived from Blau's macrostructural theory. Specifically, residential segregation and racial socioeconomic inequality are inversely related to the probability that a homicide incident is interracial.

To summarize, studies that have examined the relationship between racial inequality and violent crime rates have yielded highly inconsistent results. The preponderance of evidence suggests that racial inequality does not have strong, positive effects on aggregate levels of criminal violence, but there are several studies with contrary findings. Research that examines racially disaggregated crime rates also offers mixed support for the hypothesis of an appreciable positive effect of racial inequality on black offending rates. However, the validity of this literature is suspect given the persistent problem of multicollinearity, a problem that is often acknowledged but rarely resolved. There is also some evidence suggesting that certain forms of racial inequality reduce levels of interracial crime, but this research is rather sparse. In the analyses to follow, we move beyond previous studies by systematically examining total and racially disaggregated homicide rates with models that are not flawed by high levels of multicollinearity.

DATA AND METHODS

DEPENDENT VARIABLES

The data for the dependent variables come from two sources. Total homicide rates are taken from the Federal Bureau of Investigation's Uniform Crime Reports (Federal Bureau of Investigation, 1980–1984). These rates refer to the number of murders and nonnegligent manslaughters per 100,000 resident population.

The other source for homicide data is the Comparative Homicide File (CHF).[6] The CHF is based on the annual Supplementary Homicide Reports collected as part of the FBI's Uniform Crime Reporting program. The CHF is particularly valuable for our purposes because it contains information on the race of the victim and the offender in homicide incidents. This permits the computation not only of race-specific offending rates, but also of rates of homicides defined in terms of the race of the victim and the offender.

Another useful feature of the CHF is that it provides "adjusted" counts of homicide incidents. Information on the race of offenders is missing in approximately one-quarter of the recorded homicides in the CHF. This implies that the "raw" estimates of homicide rates based on offender's race will certainly be underestimated and will perhaps be biased across cities. However, Williams and Flewelling (1987) have developed an imputation algorithm that "extrapolates the characteristics of the known cases to those with missing information" (Williams and Flewelling, 1988:426). This procedure, in essence, estimates the race of an offender (when unknown) on the basis of all recorded features of the incident and the racial patterning in a given city of similar incidents in which the race of the offender is known. Previous research on city homicide rates demonstrates the utility of these adjustments (Williams and Flewelling, 1988; see also Reidel, 1989:184–185).

We limit our analyses to murders and nonnegligent manslaughters with a single victim and single offender. This enhances comparability with previous research based on the CHF (Williams and Flewelling, 1987, 1988) and avoids ambiguities in the classification of incidents with multiple victims or offenders of different races.[7]

---

6. Professors Kirk Williams and Murray Straus created the CHF and kindly provided us with the requisite data for our analysis.

7. We have also computed additional race-specific rates with adjustments for multiple incidents for those homicides for which information is available on the race of all offenders. These adjustments are based on data reported in the FBI's Supplementary Homicide Reports (SHRs), in the tapes distributed by the Inter-university Consortium for

Our race-specific homicide rates include offending rates for whites and blacks, and an interracial rate based on the race of victims and offenders. The offending rates are computed by dividing the total number of incidents involving an offender of a given race by the total number of persons of that race and then multiplying by 100,000. The interracial rate is computed by first cross-tabulating incidents by race of victim and race of offender and then summing the cells involving an interracial incident (i.e., a black offender and a white victim, and a white offender and a black victim). The aggregate number of interracial incidents is standardized by total population and expressed per 100,000.

The complete city sample in the CHF includes the 168 cities with populations of 100,000 or more in 1980. Given our interest in computing race-specific measures of various variables, we follow the lead of previous researchers and impose a selection criterion of a minimum black population of 1,000 (cf. Sampson, 1987:360). This criterion, along with some missing data on independent variables, yields a sample of 154 cities. Finally, to minimize the impact of random year-to-year fluctuations, we aggregate the homicide data for the years 1980–1984. The selection of a five-year period, rather than the more customary three-year period, is dictated by our interest in estimating events that in some cities are likely to be highly infrequent.

MEASURES OF RACIAL INEQUALITY

Four indicators of racial inequality have been selected to reflect racial differentials in income, education, employment opportunities, and residential patterns. Racial inequality in income is operationalized by the ratio of white to black median family income. The income data are taken from the 1980 Census tapes (STF-3). Educational inequality is measured in a similar manner as the ratio of white to black median years of schooling attained by the population aged 25 and over (Bureau of the Census, 1982). Both measures indicate the *relative* position of the two racial groups and, more specifically, the extent to which whites enjoy advantages in comparison with blacks.

A third indicator of racial inequality is the ratio of unemployment levels. Unemployment is measured in the conventional way as the percentage of the civilian labor force that is officially unemployed (Bureau of the Census, 1982). To maintain consistency in the polarity of the indicators of racial inequality, the black unemployment rate is divided by the white rate. Thus, high values

---

Political and Social Research (ICPSR). The rates based on single-single incidents alone and those with adjustments for multiple incidents are very highly correlated. Of course, with the SHR data it is only possible to adjust for multiple incidents in which the racial characteristics of all offenders are known. However, because homicides involving multiple victims and offenders are relatively rare, the overall effect of excluding such incidents in the calculation of rates is likely to be minor.

represent greater relative disadvantage for blacks and greater advantage for whites.

The final indicator of racial inequality is residential segregation. Previous research indicates that segregation may be a particularly pernicious form of racial inequality, one that is highly resistant to change despite gains by blacks in other arenas (Massey and Denton, 1987; Massey and Eggers, 1990). Our measure of racial residential segregation is the index of dissimilarity, which is computed on the basis of block-level data from the 1980 Census.[8]

CONTROL VARIABLES

We employ as control variables 12 additional characteristics of cities. These variables include all 11 of the structural covariates used by Land et al. to estimate a baseline model for predicting homicide rates. In addition, we also consider the sex ratio (number of males per 100 females) as a control variable. Recent research (Messner and Sampson, 1991) indicates that this aspect of demographic structure is also a relevant predictor of city homicide rates.

We employ measures based on the total population in the analyses involving total and interracial homicide rates. In the analyses involving racially disaggregated offending rates, we use race-specific measures for percent ages 15–29, percent divorced, percent children living with two parents, median family income, percent poor, income inequality, unemployment, and the sex ratio. The specific measures and data sources are described in Appendix 1.

An examination of the univariate distributions for all variables reveals skewness for population size, population density, percent ages 15–29 for the black population, the sex ratio, and the homicide rates. Consistent with conventional practices (cf. Land et al., 1990:936–937), we have transformed the skewed measures by taking natural logarithms. We added a constant to the interracial homicide rate and the black offending rate, which have "0" values, to permit the log transformation (see Tufte, 1974:109).

A final word of caution is appropriate before turning to the results. Model misspecification is an inevitable danger in nonexperimental research. We have thus been careful to include as controls those variables that have consistently emerged as important ones in past studies of homicide. The inclusion of these variables can be justified by their relevance to the major theoretical perspectives on crime, such as subcultural approaches, social disorganization/social control perspectives, and opportunity perspectives (see Land et al., 1990:925–927 for a detailed discussion of the theoretical rationale for each of the individual predictors). Moreover, the list of control variables encompasses an extensive range of characteristics of cities that have been linked

---

8.   Professor Karl Taeuber and Dr. Franklin Monfort of the University of Wisconsin kindly provided the segregation scores in a personal correspondence.

theoretically with violent crime, including population structure, racial composition, age structure, family structure, socioeconomic status, sex ratio, and regional location.

It is still conceivable, of course, that significant correlates of homicide have been omitted from the model. However, the omission of such variables will bias the parameter estimates only if those variables are related to both the key independent variable of interest (racial inequality) and the homicide rate. Bias also will occur only if the omitted variables exhibit variance that is not captured by those controls that have been included in the model. Finally, it is important to remember that specification error can be induced by including irrelevant regressors, and thus risks are involved in simply "trying on" whatever variables are available in standard data sources (Wonnacott and Wonnacott, 1970:312). In sum, we are confident that our models are reasonable ones, given past theorizing and research on homicide, although the possibility of misspecification can never be entirely dismissed in this type of analysis.[9]

RESULTS

The first issue is the potential impact of restricting our analysis to only those cities with appreciable black populations. As Land et al. (1990:934) note, there is no theoretical basis in previous research for constraining samples to large communities. Accordingly, Land et al. include all cities with relevant data in their city-level analyses. We are forced to employ a more restricted sample given our special focus on racial inequality. Conceivably, the resulting "censoring" of cases could generate a sample that exhibits idiosyncratic patterns of the structural determinants of homicide rates.

To address this possibility, we first perform a principal components analysis for our sample using the same variables employed by Land et al. The

---

9.   An anonymous referee has suggested that the "household activity ratio" might be a relevant control variable in view of two studies by Jackson (1984, 1991) that have included this variable along with measures of racial inequality in analyses of homicide rates. However, in neither study does the household activity ratio exhibit appreciable associations with *both* racial inequality and homicide rates. In Jackson's earlier study (1984), the correlation between the household activity ratio and racial inequality is very small ($r = -.08$). In the latter study (1991), although racial inequality and the household activity ratio are moderately related ($r = -.25$), the household activity ratio yields very modest effects on homicide in regression equations with controls similar to those in our analyses (beta = .068). The empirical justification for including this variable as a control is thus somewhat problematic. Moreover, we know of no theoretical rationale for a causal link between racial inequality and the household activity ratio, either for the total population or for race-specific populations. Accordingly, we have decided to employ Land et al.'s baseline model (along with the sex ratio) in our analyses, recognizing that the list of "relevant" predictors will undoubtedly be modified on the basis of future research and theorizing.

results are reasonably similar to those reported previously. All variables identified by Land et al. as representing resource deprivation/affluence load highly on a single component in our analysis. Those variables are percent below poverty, percent children living with two parents, median family income, the Gini coefficient of income inequality, and percent black. In contrast with Land et al.'s results, the unemployment rate also yields a strong loading on this common dimension in our sample. We accordingly include the unemployment rate in the resource deprivation/affluence index rather than treat it as a separate predictor. The index is computed by summing variables weighted by the loadings from the principal components analysis.

Another slight difference between the structure of our data and that of Land et al. involves the population measures. Population size and density do not cluster together strongly in the principal components analyses. Preliminary regression analyses indicate that population density is generally unimportant in models that include population size. We consequently use population size as a single indicator of population structure, a procedure consistent with most previous research.

The results in Table 1 permit a comparison of similar regression models estimated for both Land et al.'s comprehensive sample and the sample restricted to cities with large black populations.[10] The similarities are quite striking. Coefficients for four of the predictors—population, resource deprivation/affluence, percent divorced, and percent ages 15 to 29—are in the same direction and achieve the same level of statistical significance. In addition, the adjusted R squares are similar: .547 for the Land et al. analysis and .632 for ours.

There is one noteworthy difference involving the regional variable. In the Land et al. analysis, the effect of being in the South is positive and significant at the .01 level; in our analysis, the effect is negative but nonsignificant. This sole discrepancy is most plausibly attributed to differing geographic distributions of the two samples. Overall, however, the two analyses yield very comparable results. There is thus no reason to suspect that the sample is a particularly peculiar one for the purposes at hand.

The next step in the analysis is to construct a measure of racial inequality. Here, we depart from the previous procedures of Land et al. As noted above (see footnote 1), Land et al. employ principal components analysis rather than a factor analytic technique because they intend merely to simplify the covariate space. Indeed, they stress that they make no assumptions about the underlying structure of the data. However, the theoretical arguments advanced by Blau and colleagues are clearly predicated on the premise that

---

10. To maintain consistency with Land et al.'s analysis, the homicide rate is not log transformed in the regression equations reported in Table 1, nor is the sex ratio included in the models.

Table 1. Comparison of Regression Results for Total
          Homicide Rates Across City Samples

Independent Variables	Land et al.'s Sample of 896 Cities (1980)	Present Sample of 154 Cities (1980–1984)
Population[a]	.192**	.162**
Resource Deprivation/ Affluence[b]	.528**	.636**
Percent Divorced	.121**	.275**
Percent Ages 15–29	−.107+	−.128+
Unemployment Rate[b]	.185	
South	.165**	−.097
Adjusted R^2	.547	.632

NOTE: Standardized regression coefficients are reported.
[a] In Land et al.'s analysis, a population structure index is employed that combines population size and density. The measure in the present sample is the natural logarithm of population size.
[b] In the present sample, the unemployment rate clusters on the resource deprivation/ affluence component and is included in the composite index for that variable.
*$p < .05$ (one-tailed test)
**$p < .01$ (one-tailed test)
+$p < .05$ (two-tailed test)

racial inequality is a dimension of social structure that is conceptually, and perhaps empirically, distinct from the general levels of poverty or deprivation.

We thus adopt a strategy of confirmatory factor analysis and hypothesize that an interpretable, two-factor solution will represent the intercorrelations among indicators of overall poverty and of racial inequality (see Kim and Mueller, 1978:55). Specifically, we combine the variables included in the resource deprivation/affluence index with the indicators of racial inequality in a single matrix and perform a maximum likelihood factor analysis specifying a two-factor solution. Moreover, because it seems unlikely that racial inequality and overall poverty will be statistically independent dimensions of social structure, we apply oblique rotation to the initial solution to allow for correlations between factors.

The results of the factor analysis generally support our hypotheses (see Table 2). The two factors extracted by the maximum likelihood procedure have eigenvalues greater than 1.000 for each of the three matrices—that is, for the total population, the white population, and the black population. For the total population and the black population, the two factors are moderately

Table 2.   Maximum Likelihood Factor Pattern Matrices After Oblique Rotation

	Matrix					
	Total Population		White Population		Black Population	
	1	2	1	2	1	2
Percent Poor	.965		.920		.916	
Kids Two Parents	−.879		−.762		−.774	
Median Income	−.847		−.700		−.768	
Income Inequality	.805		.758		.832	
Percent Black	.731					
Unemployment Rate	.671		.517		.542	
Racial Segregation				.594	.607	
Racial Income Inequality		.837		.819		.903
Racial Educational Inequality		.697		.686		.564
Racial Unemployment Inequality		.592		.569		
Eigenvalue	4.673	1.754	2.950	2.339	2.549	3.105

NOTE: Only factor loadings greater than or equal to .500 are reported.

correlated (r's = .21 and .29 respectively). The magnitude of these associations implies that although the two underlying dimensions are related, they are sufficiently distinct to permit an investigation of partial effects in regression analyses. For the white matrix, the two factors are completely independent of one another ($r = -.05$).

The factor loadings are also reasonably interpretable. For the total population matrix, the pattern of loadings shows that Land et al.'s indicators of resource deprivation/affluence all load highly on one dimension, whereas the three ratio measures of racial inequality load highly on the second dimension. Contrary to expectations, the measure of residential segregation does not load highly on either dimension for the total population matrix.

The general pattern is similar in the race-specific matrices, although the results are not quite as "clean." Consistent with the results for the total matrix, "percent poor" yields the highest loading on one factor, and racial income inequality on the other factor, for both the white and black matrices. But there are also some differences between results for the total matrix and those for the race-specific matrices. Racial composition no longer loads highly on either dimension, and racial segregation "switches" dimensions for whites versus blacks.[11] In addition, only two of the three racial inequality

---

11.   The differential loadings for racial composition across matrices are not surprising.

indicators yield high loadings on a common dimension for the black matrix. Overall, however, the patterns appear to be sufficiently similar across matrices to justify the construction of factor scales to represent two dimensions that can be conceptualized as representing resource deprivation/affluence and racial socioeconomic inequality. These scales have been constructed in the conventional manner using the factor score coefficients corresponding to the respective matrices. Although Table 2 reports only selected loadings to facilitate the interpretation of the factor structure, the scales are based on all variables included in the factor analysis and thus constitute "factor scales" rather than "factor-based" scales (see Kim and Mueller, 1978:70).

Before proceeding to our regressions, it is important to consider the extent of multicollinearity in the models. One sign of multicollinearity is strong bivariate correlations. A review of the correlations matrices (see Appendix 2) reveals that the theoretically strategic independent variable for the analysis— racial inequality—does not exhibit strong associations with any other predictor. There is no bivariate correlation larger than .310 between racial inequality and any other independent variable.

We have also computed variance inflation factors for the various sets of independent variables (Table 3). These statistics indicate the extent to which the standard errors of regression coefficients are likely to be inflated due to shared variance with other predictors (Fisher and Mason, 1981:190). The conventional criterion for severe multicollinearity is a value of 4 or higher on the variance inflation factor (cf. Sampson, 1987:361). The largest variance inflation factor in Table 3 is 2.29, which is well below the conventional threshold. The scaling procedures thus alleviate very effectively the statistical problem of multicollinearity that has plagued most previous analyses.

We can assess the various theoretical explanations for the potentially criminogenic effects of racial inequality with the regression results reported in Table 4.[12] The results clearly fail to support the predictions derived from the relative gratification/reduced aggression explanation or from macrostructural opportunity theory. The relative gratification account predicts a negative effect of racial inequality on the offending rate of the advantaged racial group

---

Blacks are more likely to be disadvantaged, and thus percent black can be expected to cluster with other indicators of disadvantage for the total population because of "compositional effects" (cf. Sampson, 1985:49). Such compositional effects do not apply to the racially disaggregated data. Reasons for the discrepant patterns for racial segregation are less obvious, although the high loading of this variable on the resource deprivation/affluence factor for blacks only might be interpreted with reference to Wilson's (1987) ideas about "concentration effects." For blacks, socioeconomic disadvantage and residential segregation are closely related.

12. We have computed measures of Cook's D for all cases in the equations in Table 4 to check for outliers (Cook and Weisberg, 1982). The results reveal that no city exerts a disproportionate influence on the parameter estimates. All values of D are below the conventional criterion of 1.0.

Table 3. Variance Inflation Factors for Matrices of
          Independent Variables: Total and Race-Specific
          Populations

Independent Variables	Matrix		
	Total Population	White Population	Black Population
Racial SES Inequality	1.10	1.13	1.20
Population	1.18	1.14	1.08
Resource Dep./Affluence	1.65	1.18	1.65
Percent Divorced	1.07	1.09	1.24
Percent Ages 15–29	1.35	1.29	2.29
South	1.09	1.08	1.06
Sex Ratio	1.96	1.50	2.09

(whites), while macrostructural opportunity theory implies a similarly negative effect of racial inequality on the interracial homicide rate. The significantly positive coefficient for racial inequality in Equation 2 and the
nonsignificant coefficient in Equation 4 are thus inconsistent with these two
theoretical accounts, respectively.

In contrast, the findings in Equation 3 are in accord with the relative depri-
vation/frustration aggression explanation. Racial inequality yields the predicted, positive effect on the black offending rate, although the magnitude of
the coefficient is rather modest. Frustration aggression theory does not, however, provide a complete explanation for the criminogenic consequences of
racial inequality. Racial inequality also exhibits significant, positive effects on
the white offending rate, and on the total homicide rate. The full range of
results for the racial inequality variable is most consistent with the causal
dynamics stipulated by the social disorganization/anomie explanation. Evidently, racial inequality affects the social order in some generalized way and
generates criminogenic pressures that bear on the entire population, not simply the disadvantaged racial minority.

Finally, the effects of the control variables in Table 4 are generally consistent with those of previous analyses. Both population size and "percent
divorced" have significantly positive effects on all four homicide rates. The
coefficients for age structure are consistently negative, which is counterintuitive but comparable to those in other macro-level studies (e.g., Land et al.,
1990; see also Messner and Sampson, 1991:707). The resource/deprivation
affluence measures and the sex ratio have significantly positive effects on three

Table 4. Regressions of Total Homicide Rate and Race-Specific Rates on Racial Socioeconomic Inequality Scale and Controls ($N = 154$)

	Dependent Variables			
Independent Variables	Total Homicide Rate (1)	White Offending Rate (2)	Black Offending Rate (3)	Interracial Homicide Rate (4)
Racial SES Inequality	.148**	.142**	.132*	.035
Population	.144**	.183**	.210*	.205**
Resource Deprivation/ Affluence	.754**	.522**	.026	.579**
Percent Divorced	.263**	.323**	.215**	.240**
Percent Ages 15–29	−.278+	−.317+	−.330+	−.220+
South	−.047	−.023	−.042	−.022
Sex Ratio	.254**	.341**	−.008	.215**
Adjusted R^2	.741	.552	.228	.478

NOTE: Standardized regression coefficients are reported. All homicide rates have been log (natural) transformed.

*$p < .05$ (one-tailed test)
**$p < .01$ (one-tailed test)
+$p < .05$ (two-tailed test)

of the four homicide rates.[13] Moreover, the nonsignificant coefficient for

---

13. The nonsignificant finding for the sex ratio in Equation 3 is contrary to results recently reported by Messner and Sampson (1991). The model estimated in the earlier study differs in several important respects from that estimated in our study, which reflects different theoretical purposes. Messner and Sampson measure the sex ratio with reference to the population at typical ages for marriage (i.e., ages 15–59) because of their interest in predicting not only crime rates but measures of family disruption (1991:699). Moreover, given their principal concern with family structure, Messner and Sampson include a measure of the "percentage of households headed by females" in their equations. The earlier study also operationalizes region in terms of location in the "West" rather than the "South" for similar reasons (see Messner and Sampson, 1991:702).

We have estimated a regression equation for the black offending rate that is more comparable to the model examined by Messner and Sampson. In this equation, we substitute an age-specific measure of the sex ratio (ages 15–59) for the unrestricted measure; we substitute a dummy variable for Western location for the Southern dummy variable, and we include a measure of the percent of black households headed by females. The results are very consistent with those reported above in Equation 3 of Table 4. The sex ratio still yields a nonsignificant effect. A possible, statistical explanation for the discrepant results for the sex ratio across these studies is that any model including both the sex ratio and resource deprivation in the equation predicting the black offending rate is consistent with previous research by Sampson (1986a:297), who also reports that racial inequality in SES, rather than the overall level of poverty or affluence, is the more relevant predictor of homicide offending for blacks (see also Huff-Corzine et al., 1986). Finally, regional location has been a rather inconsistent predictor of homicide rates; in our analyses, the effects of this variable are consistently nonsignificant.

SUMMARY AND CONCLUSIONS

Our findings indicate that, at least for certain samples of large cities in the United States, indicators of relative, racial disadvantage cluster together to form a dimension of social structure that can be conceptualized as distinct from a general resource deprivation dimension. Moreover, by employing factor analytic scaling techniques, it is possible to specify models that include measures of racial inequality and general socioeconomic disadvantage but that are not hampered by the confounding effects of multicollinearity. The partial effects of racial inequality on homicide rates in these samples thus can be assessed with conventional regression techniques.

The results of such an assessment lend differing support to four theoretical explanations for the link between racial inequality and violent crime. The hypothesis that racial inequality might actually decrease levels of offending for the racial majority is clearly disconfirmed. The effect of racial inequality on the white offending rate is significantly positive rather than negative. Accordingly, the notion that racial inequality might induce feelings of relative gratification among whites, feelings that might lessen aggressive impulses, is inconsistent with the data.

We also find no support for a prediction derived from macrostructural opportunity theory, namely, that racial inequality will reduce rates of *interracial* homicide because of reduced opportunities for contacts between members of the different racial groups. The coefficient for racial inequality in the equation predicting the interracial homicide rate is essentially zero. We can offer a speculative interpretation of this finding. Perhaps this null effect reflects countervailing processes. Racial inequality might indeed reduce opportunities for interracial contact, as postulated by macrostructural theory, but it might also increase the likelihood that the contacts that do occur will eventuate in a violent encounter. In other words, "motivational effects" of racial

---

female-headed households will inevitably exhibit high multicollinearity because of the causal connection between these two variables (see Messner and Sampson, 1991:709–710, fn 13). Parameter estimates will accordingly be unstable and sensitive to sample selection and model specification. In our sample, the age-specific sex ratio for blacks correlates with other predictors at levels in excess of .65, and a variance inflation factor for the equation exceeds 3.00. Interestingly, the coefficient for racial inequality is highly stable across these differing models.

inequality (which are reflected in our results for the total homicide rate and the race-specific rates) might conceivably counterbalance "opportunity effects," yielding no appreciable overall relationship on the interracial homicide rate.

We do find some support for the relative deprivation/frustration aggression explanation. As expected, racial inequality has the predicted, positive effect on the black offending rate. Interestingly, however, the effects of racial inequality on the white offending rate and the total rate are also significantly positive. The explanation that is most compatible with the full range of results is thus the social disorganization/anomie explanation. Racial inequality evidently affects the social order in some generalized way that increases criminogenic pressures on the entire population.

Several cautions are in order concerning these conclusions. First, the magnitude of the effects of racial inequality are modest at best. This may, of course, be due to random measurement error. Nevertheless, racial inequality does not emerge in our analysis as a particularly strong predictor of intermetropolitan variation in homicide rates.

Second, although our findings are most consistent with the social disorganization/anomie explanation, the precise processes linking racial inequality and homicide have not been fully explicated. Indeed, the social disorganization/anomie explanation advanced by Blau and Blau is probably the vaguest of the four explanations considered in the analysis. Blau and Blau have not explicitly defined their key concepts, and it is not clear that those concepts are being used in conventional ways. Is "social disorganization" being employed in the classical sense of "the inability of local communities to realize the common values of their residents or solve commonly experienced problems" (Bursik, 1988:521)? If so, precisely how does racial inequality impede this ability? Does "anomie" refer to the kind of normative situation depicted by Merton, that is, a situation wherein "the rules once governing conduct have lost their savor and their force" (Merton, 1964:226)? If so, what are the mechanisms through which racial inequality engenders this delegitimation of norms? In short, there is much theoretical work yet to be done to explain the observed generalized effect of racial inequality on homicide offending.

Third, there are limitations associated with our scaling procedures. The covariance structure of the independent variables yields some troubling ambiguities. This is particularly apparent in the analyses of the total and interracial homicide rates, analyses that use the total population matrix for estimating the effects of the predictor variables. The factor analysis for the total population matrix reveals that racial composition loads very highly on the dimension that has been labeled "resource deprivation/affluence." This creates obvious problems for the interpretation of the corresponding resource deprivation/affluence scale because economic aspects of social structure are confounded with purely demographic features (cf. Land et al., 1990:941–942).

A related ambiguity emerges in the analysis of black offending rates, although the problem is not as severe because the loading of racial composition on the resource deprivation/affluence dimension (.431) is not as strong.

In the prediction of white offending rates, these kinds of interpretive problems are more pronounced for the racial inequality scale than for the resource deprivation/affluence scale. The loading of racial composition on the racial inequality dimension for the white matrix (.496) is not extremely strong, but it is not trivial either. Accordingly, the observed effect of the racial inequality measure on white offending rates necessarily confounds aspects of racial composition with those of relative socioeconomic disadvantage. The requirements for statistical estimation unfortunately conflict with the objectives of theoretical interpretation in commonly used samples of population aggregates such as cities, and any solution to the statistical problem is likely to generate interpretive difficulties. Perhaps the only way to avoid this dilemma completely is to identify different types of data that are not characterized by such serious empirical overlap among theoretically strategic variables.

We also make no claim that our specific scaling procedure for racial inequality is *the* theoretically correct one; the theoretical arguments are too vague to provide unambiguous guidelines for the operationalization of relevant features of urban social structure. Nor do we assert that alternative procedures would necessarily yield comparable results. To the contrary, additional analyses (not reported) reveal that the use of different factor analytic algorithms can yield different results.[14] Our basic claim is simply that it is possible to generate meaningful scales that are relatively independent of one another in a statistical sense and that yield results compatible with theoretically derived predictions. Once again, however, definitive conclusions about the role of racial inequality as a structural determinant of levels of homicide must await the development of a more refined theoretical framework within which these empirical findings can be located.

We close with a final comment on the issue of "units of analysis." There has been a heated controversy in criminology about the appropriate type of population aggregate to employ in macro-level research on crime. The position that "smaller is better" seems to be gaining increasing support (see for example, Harries, 1990:101), although the work by Land et al. suggests that the choice among three common units—states, cities, and SMSAs—may be less critical than some have contended. In properly specified models, a

---

14. Ironically, the analysis contained in the original version of this manuscript when first submitted for review was based on different scaling procedures and produced substantively different results. The techniques employed in the current version were adopted in response to suggestions from an anonymous referee.

number of invariant relationships can in fact be observed across these different types of subnational entities.

When considering a phenomenon such as racial inequality, however, subnational units of any type may not be the most meaningful aggregates for research purposes. Race is such a highly salient characteristic in U.S. society that the criminogenic consequences associated with racial disadvantage might be diffused evenly throughout the nation. Accordingly, even if racial inequality proves to be a rather modest predictor of variation in homicide rates across jurisdictions within the United States, as suggested in this analysis, it might still be a major factor responsible for the high homicide rate of the United States when considered in international perspective (see Messner, 1989). This argument implies that, in addition to efforts to test more theoretically sophisticated models of the effects of racial inequality on homicide with data on jurisdictions within the United States, cross-national studies are needed to assess the criminogenic potential of this ascriptive form of social inequality.

REFERENCES

Balkwell, James W.
  1983   Metropolitan structure and violent crime: A further examination of the
            Blau and Blau relative deprivation thesis. Paper presented at the Thirty-
            fifth Annual Meeting of the American Society of Criminology, Denver,
            November 9–12.
  1990   Ethnic inequality and the rate of homicide. Social Forces 69:53–70.

Blau, Judith R. and Peter M. Blau
  1982   The cost of inequality: Metropolitan structure and criminal violence.
            American Sociological Review 47:114–129.

Blau, Peter M.
  1977   Inequality and Heterogeneity. New York: Free Press.

Blau, Peter M. and Reid M. Golden
  1986   Metropolitan structure and violent crime. Sociological Quarterly 7:15–26.

Blau, Peter M. and Joseph E. Schwartz
  1984   Crosscutting Social Circles. New York: Academic Press.

Blau, Peter M., Terry C. Blum, and Joseph E. Schwartz
  1982   Heterogeneity and intermarriage. American Sociological Review 47:45–62.

Braithwaite, John
  1979   Inequality, Crime and Public Policy. London: Routledge & Kegan Paul.

Bureau of the Census
  1982   U.S. Census of the Population, 1980. General Social and Economic
            Characteristics of the Population. Washington, D.C.: U.S. Government
            Printing Office.

Bureau of the Census
  1983   County and City Data Book. Washington, D.C.: U.S. Government
            Printing Office.

Bursik, Robert J., Jr.
1988   Social disorganization and theories of crime and delinquency: Problems
        and prospects. Criminology 26:519–551.

Carroll, Leo and Pamela Irving Jackson
1983   Inequality, opportunity and crime rates in central cities. Criminol-
        ogy:178–194.

Cook, R. Dennis and Sanford Weisberg
1982   Criticism and influence analysis in regression. In Samuel Leinhardt (ed.),
        Sociological Methodology, 1982. San Francisco: Jossey-Bass.

Federal Bureau of Investigation
1980–1984 Crime in the United States. Uniform Crime Reports. Washington, D.C.:
        Government Printing Office.

Fisher, Joseph C. and R. Mason
1981   The analysis of multicollinear data in criminology. In James R. Fox (ed.),
        Methods in Quantitative Criminology. New York: Academic Press.

Golden, Reid M. and Steven F. Messner
1987   Dimensions of racial inequality and rates of violent crime. Criminology
        25:525–541.

Harer, Miles D. and Darrell Steffensmeier
1990   The different effects of economic inequality on black and white rates of
        violence. Revised version of paper presented at the Fortieth Annual
        Meeting of the American Society of Criminology, Chicago, November
        9–12, 1988.

Harries, Keith D.
1990   Serious Violence: Patterns of Homicide and Assault in America. Spring-
        field, Ill.: Charles C Thomas.

Huff-Corzine, Lin, Jay Corzine, and David C. Moore
1986   Southern exposure: Deciphering the South's influence on homicide rates.
        Social Forces:64:906–924.

Jackson, Pamela Irving
1984   Opportunity and crime: A function of city size. Sociology and Social
        Research 68:172–193.
1991   Crime, youth gangs, and urban transition: The social dislocations of
        postindustrial economic development. Justice Quarterly 8:379–397.

Kim, Jae-On and Charles W. Mueller
1978   Factor Analysis: Statistical Methods and Practical Issues. Beverly Hills,
        Calif.: Sage.

Land, Kenneth C., Patricia L. McCall, and Lawrence E. Cohen
1990   Structural covariates of homicide rates. American Journal of Sociology
        95:922–963.

Logan, John R. and Steven F. Messner
1987   Racial residential segregation and suburban violent crime. Social Science
        Quarterly 68:922–963.

Massey, Douglas S. and Nancy A. Denton
1987   Trends in the residential segregation of blacks, Hispanics, and Asians:
        1970–1980. American Sociological Review 52:802–825.

Massey, Douglas S. and Mitchell L. Eggers
1990   The ecology of inequality: Minorities and the concentration of poverty, 1970-1980. Americal Journal of Sociology 95:1153-1188.

Merton, Robert K.
1964   Anomie, anomia, and social interaction: Contexts of deviant behavior. In Marshall B. Clinard (ed.), Anomie and Deviant Behavior: A Discussion and Critique. New York: Free Press.

Messner, Steven F.
1989   Economic discrimination and societal homicide rates: Further evidence on the cost of inequality. American Sociological Review 54:597-611.

Messner, Steven F. and Reid M. Golden
1985   Reconsidering the effects of poverty and inequality. Paper presented at the Eightieth Annual Meeting of the American Sociological Association, Washington, D.C., August 26-30.

Messner, Steven F. and Robert J. Sampson
1991   The sex ratio, family disruption, and rates of violent crime: The paradox of demographic structure. Social Forces 69:693-713.

Messner, Steven F. and Scott J. South
1986   Economic deprivation, opportunity structure, and robbery victimization. Social Forces 64:975-991.
1992   Determinants of interracial homicide: A macrostructural opportunity perspective. Sociological Forum (forthcoming).

Nettler, Gwynn
1984   Explaining Crime. 3rd ed. New York: McGraw-Hill.

Reidel, Marc
1989   Nationwide homicide datasets: An evaluation of UCR and NCHS data. In Doris L. Mackenzie, Phyllis J. Baunach, and Roy R. Robert (eds.), Measuring Crime: Large-Scale, Long-Range Efforts. Albany, New York: SUNY Press.

Sampson, Robert J.
1984   Group size, heterogeneity and intergroup conflict. Social Forces 62:618-639.
1985   Race and criminal violence: A demographically disaggregated analysis of urban homicide. Crime and Delinquency 31:47-82.
1986a   Crime in cities. In Albert J. Reiss, Jr., and Michael Tonry (eds.), Communities and Crime. Chicago: University of Chicago Press.
1986b   Effects of inequality, heterogeneity and urbanization on intergroup victimization. Social Science Quarterly 67:751-766.
1987   Urban black violence. American Journal of Sociology 93:348-382.

Simpson, Miles E.
1985   Inequality and regional culture: Another look. Sociological Focus 18:199-208.

South, Scott J. and Steven F. Messner
1986   Structural determinants of intergroup association. American Journal of Sociology 91:1409-1430.

Tufte, Edward R.
  1974   Data Analysis for Politics and Policy. Englewood Cliffs, N.J.: Prentice-
            Hall.

William, Kirk R.
  1984   Economic sources of homicide: Reestimating the effects of poverty and
            inequality. American Sociological Review 49:283–289.

Williams, Kirk R. and Robert L. Flewelling
  1987   Family, acquaintance, and stranger homicide: Alternative procedures for
            rate calculations. Criminology 25:543–560.
  1988   The social production of homicide: A comparative study of disaggregated
            rates in American cities. American Sociological Review 53:421–431.

Wilson, William Julius
  1987   The Truly Disadvantaged: The Inner City, the Underclass, and Public
            Policy. Chicago: University of Chicago Press.

Wonnacott, Ronald J. and Thomas H. Wonnacott
  1970   Econometrics. New York: John Wiley & Sons.

Steven F. Messner is Associate Professor of Sociology at the State University of New York at Albany. His research focuses on the effects of structural characteristics of population aggregates on levels of violent crime. He is currently studying the relationships between national homicide rates and indicators of various ascriptive forms of social inequality. He is also engaged in research on extensions and reformulations of anomie theory.

Reid M. Golden is an Assistant Professor at Hartwick College. He continues to explore the impact of racial inequality on such social problems as homicide and racial differences in infant mortality. He consults for various law enforcement agencies and is directing the building of a new 81 bed jail for the county in which he resides.

Dueling Paradigms:
Modernist versus Postmodernist Thought

Dragan Milovanovic
Northeastern Illinois University

REFLEXIVE STATEMENT

As is the case with many progressive scholars and activists of the 1990s, it is has become clear to me that the modernist framework in the social sciences has been supplanted by a framework that offers better tools for critical inquiry and for the development of visions for a more humanistic society. My own academic work has undergone a change in the last five or six years away from the modernist framework as it no longer offers the conceptual tools for moving on. Postmodernist thought, particularly viewpoints that have begun with Lacanian and critical thought, promises a paradigm for a better transpraxis. We must rise to the challenge of progressive humanistic scholarship and practice. We must go beyond the praxis of the past and begin to see the potentials of a transpraxis.

INTRODUCTION

Much, in recent days, has been said of a postmodernist analysis in the social sciences. Indeed, a number of comparisons occasionally arise in the literature between modernist and postmodernist analysis, usually as an introduction to some further study. Little, however, has appeared that takes as its primary goal a comparison of the two perspectives. Accordingly, this essay is more didactic and pedagogical in orientation. (In a forthcoming book, *Constitutive Criminology*, Henry and Milovanovic go beyond polarilizing the two paradigms in producing a post postmodern view they call a constitutive approach, 1995.) We have identified eight dimensions as a basis of comparison. Although presented as dichotomies, the differences often fall along a continuum; some tending toward further polarization; others becoming discontinuities, such as the differences between the centered and decentered subject, the privileging of disorder rather than order, the emphasis on Pathos rather than Logos, etc.

A considerable amount of literature from those who are committed to the modernist approach is of a defensive sort when confronted with the epistemological directions advocated by postmodernist analysis. The first tactic generally is to dismiss its claims as old wine in new bottles, followed by incorporating the postmodernist premises and concepts within the discourse of modernist thought. Much effort, then, is taken to undo the postmodernist's concepts by way of a discursive reorientation, at the conclusion of which modernist thinkers hope to say, "there, I told you so! Old wine in new bottles!" This attempt fails, however, even though it is the case that in some instances several modernist thinkers did in fact anticipate some aspects of the postmodern paradigm. What is necessary to recognize is that postmodernist analysis is indeed premised on radically new concepts, and discursive redefinitions will not help further progressive thought in the social sciences. What we do have are dueling paradigms: the modernist versus the postmodernist.

Modernist thought had its origins in the Enlightenment period. Here celebrated were the liberating potentials of the social sciences, the materialistic gains of capitalism, new forms of rational thought, due process safeguards, abstract rights applicable to all, and the individual – it was a time of great optimism (Milovanovic 1992a, 1994a; Dews 1987; Sarup 1989; Lyotard 1984; Baker 1993).

Postmodernists are fundamentally opposed to modernist thought. Sensitized by the insights of some of the classic thinkers, ranging from Marx, to Weber, to Durkheim, Freud, and the critical thought of the Frankfurt School, postmodernist thought emerged with a new intensity in the late 1980s and early 1990s. "Let us wage a war on totality" states one of its key exponents (Lyotard 1984, p. 82). Most of the key concepts of modernist thought were critically examined and found to be wanting. Entrenched bureaucratic powers, monopolies, the manipulative advertisement industry, dominant and totalizing discourses, and the ideology of the legal apparatus were seen as exerting repressive powers. In fact, the notion of the individual – free, self-determining, reflective, and the center of activity – was seen as an ideological construction, nowhere more apparent than in the notion of the juridic subject, the so-called "reasonable man in law." Rather than the notion of the individual, the centered subject, the postmodernists were to advocate the notion of the *decentered subject*.

Postmodernist analysis had its roots in French thought, particularly during the late 1960s and 1970s. Here, with the continued disillusionment with conventional critical thought, a transition from Hegelian to Nietzschean thought took place. Deleuze, Guattari, Derrida, Lyotard, Baudrillard, Foucault, Kristeva and many others were to emerge bearing the banner of postmodernist thinking. Feminists from the postmodern tradition were to become key thinkers. Such theorists as Irigaray, Moi, and Cixous were to apply much of this thought to gender construction. The central figure in developing alternative notions of the subject, the determining effects of discourse, and the nature of the symbolic order was Jacques Lacan.

New wave postmodernist thinkers are likely to draw from chaos theory, Godel's theorem, catastrophe theory, quantum mechanics and topology theory. Novel conceptions of space, time, causality, subjectivity, the role of discourse, desire, social structure, roles, social change, knowledge, and the nature of harm, justice and the law were developed and continue to be developed in postmodernist thought. The call is for the abandonment of a center, privileged reference points, fixed subjects, first principles, and an origin (Sarup 1989, p. 59).

This essay will outline the differences between the modernist and the postmodernist paradigm. As Thomas Kuhn has told us many years ago, paradigms tend to crystallize around key validity-claims that become premises for scientific thought. "Normal science" tends to work out the implications of this general body of knowledges through, for example, deductive logic. Occasionally, as in the case of postmodernist thought, a revolutionary new science with entirely new premises develops and becomes the body of knowledge from which new questions are asked and entirely new discoveries are made.

MODERNIST V. POSTMODERNIST THOUGHT

To clarify some of the more salient differences we have selected eight dimensions for comparison. These dimensions include the nature of: (1) society and social structure, (2) social roles, (3) subjectivity/agency, (4) discourse, (5) knowledge, (6) space/time, (7) causality, and (8) social change. This essay is more in the form of sensitization to the major differences that have emerged by the early 1990s. Accordingly, we will list the dimensions and comment briefly on each. We should add, whereas the modernist assumptions seem more descriptive, the postmodernist add a prescriptive dimension. Contrary to many modernist critics, postmodernism is not fatalistic, cynical, and non-visionary; rather, what the new paradigm offers is a more intense critique of what is and transformative visions of what could be.

1. Society and Social Structure

Key concepts:

Modernist	*Postmodernist*
Equilibrium; homeostasis; tension reduction; order; homogeneity; consensus; normativity; foundationalism; logocentricism; totality; transcendental signifiers.	*Far-from-equilibrium conditions; flux, change, chance, spontaneity, irony; orderly disorder; hetero-geneity; diversity; intensity; paralogism; toleration for the incommensurable; dissipative*

> *structures; anti-foundationalism;*
> *fragmentation; coupling;*
> *impossibility of formal closure;*
> *constitutive theory.*

Commentary:

a. Modernist thought. Much of the dominant literature of modernist thought can be traced to the work of structural functionalism or totalizing theory. Theorists such as Durkheim, Parsons, and Luhmann (1985) stand out as exemplary. A good part of this literature rests on an underlying homeostatic, tension-reduction, or equilibrium model. Freud, for example, rests his views on some conception of tension-reduction as the operative force in social structural development. Perhaps we can trace much of this to Newtonian physics and its influence. The central question is one of order. It is seen as desirable without further explanation. In fact, some, such as Parsons, define deviance in terms of distance from some assumed acceptable standard of normativity.

Modernist thought is focused on totalizing theory – the search for over-encompassing theories of society and social development. Some discoverable foundation was said to exist. At the center, a logos was said to be at play; whether, for example, as in Weber's forces of rationalization, Freud's homeostases, or as in Hegel's Absolute Spirit. These logics slumbered in anticipation of their correct articulation. These were the transcendental signifiers that were discoverable.

Much of the often-mentioned consensus paradigm in the social sciences, too, can be placed within the modernist paradigm. Thus meta-narratives are still replete with assumptions of homogeneity, desirability of consensus, order, etc.

b. Postmodernist thought. Postmodernist thought, although still emerging, and which initially found its basis in its critique of modernism, has found grounding in the insights of chaos theory, Godel's theorem, catastrophe theory, quantum mechanics, emerging cosmological insights, topology theory, and Lacanian thought – to name a few.

Postmodernists begin their analysis with privileging disorder rather than order. Their starting point is *paralogism*: privileging instabilities (Lyotard 1984). Accordingly, this model begins with far-from-equilibrium conditions as being the more "natural" state, and places a premium on flux, non-linear change, chance, spontaneity, intensity, indeterminacy, irony, and orderly disorder. No permanent stable order is possible or even desirable. No center, or foundation exists. Godel's theorem (1962), describing the impossibility of formal closure, dictates that the search for an overall, all-encompassing totalizing theory is an illusory exercise. In fact, as we shall show below, since no precise center exists, or since no possibility exists for precisely specifying initial conditions, then, the process of iteration will produce disproportional and unanticipated effects.

"Dissipative structures" are offered as relatively stable societal structures that remain sensitive and responsive to their environment (Baker 1993; see also Unger's suggestion for the establishment of criticizable institutions, 1987; see also Leifer on organizational transformations, 1989). This concept implies both relative stability as well as continuous change (i.e., order and disorder). Contrary to structural functionalism and its privileging of homeostasis, postmodernists see the desirability of ongoing flux and continuous change captured by the notion of far-from-equilibrium conditions. It is within these conditions that dissipative structures flourish.

Accordingly, some have offered the notion of *structural coupling* and *constitutive theory* to explain the movement of information between structure and environment (Luhmann 1992; Hunt 1993; Jessop 1990; Henry and Milovanovic 1991, 1995). Implied is the co-existence of multiple sites of determinants whose unique historical articulations are never precisely predictable. Due to inherent uncertainties in initial conditions, iterative practices produce the unpredictable. Here, the focal concern is on tolerance and support for the incommensurable. Assumed is the existence of perpetual fragmentation, deconstruction, and reconstruction. Advocated is the facilitation of the emergence of marginalized, disenfranchised, disempowered and other excluded voices.

Noteworthy in the analysis of societal structure by way of postmodernist analysis is Unger's work on an *empowered democracy* (1987), even if he didn't explicitly state his affinity with postmodernist thought. In his offerings, orderly disorder should be privileged. During the 1960s and 1970s, the development of the conflict paradigm in the social sciences marked some movement toward the postmodernist approach, but the promise fell short.

Chaos theory is increasingly becoming a key element in postmodern analysis. The founding figures include Ilya Prigogine, Henri Poincare, Mitchell Feigenbaum, Benoit Mandelbrot, and Edward Lorenz (see the overview by Briggs and Peat 1989; Gleick 1987; Stewart 1989). We find application of chaos theory to psychoanalysis (Deleuze and Guattari 1987; Milovanovic 1992a, 1993a); to literature (Serres 1992a, 1992b; Hayles 1990, 1991); to criminology (Young 1991a; Pepinsky 1991); to law (Brion 1991; Milovanovic 1993a); to psychology (Butz 1991, 1992, 1993); to sociology (Young 1991b, 1992; Baker 1993); to business and management (Leifer 1989); and to political science (Unger 1987). Others such as Charles Sanders Peirce anticipated some dimensions of this approach (see especially his essay on the doctrine of chance and necessity, 1940, pp. 157-73; and his notion of *Pure Play* or *musement*, 1934, pp. 313-16).

Nietzschean and Lacanian thought rather than Hegelain stand as inspirational for postmodernist thinkers. Feminist postmodernists traced to the former have perhaps contributed the most important insights. Julia Kristeva, Luce Irigaray, Helene Cixous and Toril Moi, to a considerable extent, have borrowed ideas from them in their elaboration of given phallocentric social structures and their possible alternatives (a useful overview is found in Sellers 1991; Grosz 1990; for an application in law, see Cornell 1991, 1993; Milovanovic 1994a, chapter 6; 1994b).

2. Roles

Key concepts:

Modernist	*Postmodernist*
Role-taking; socialization; integration; centripetal; closure; static; dichotomies; system serving;primacy to the "me" ; limit attractors;symphony orchestra player.	*Role-making; role-jumbling; variability; centrifugal; openness; porous boundaries; testing boundaries; primacy to the dialectic between "I-me" ; privileging the "I" ; strange attractors, torus; jazz player.*

Commentary:

a. Modernist thought. The modernist view tends to rely on a Parsonian construct of a role in which centripetal forces of society socialize the person into accepting the obligations and expectations that pertain to them. This, then, becomes the question of functional integration. Accordingly, roles tend to become dichotomized – male/female, employer/employee, good guy/bad guy, etc. In the specified balance of the I-me that many social theorists advocate (Durkheim, Mead, etc.), great weight is placed on the dominance of the "me," that part of the self which dresses itself up with the persona of the situation, struts upon the stage, and plays its part with various degree of success to various audiences. A person is relegated to role-taking. The operative metaphor we offer is a member of a symphony orchestra.

b. Postmodernist thought. Postmodernists see things differently. Roles are essentially unstable and are in a dialectical relationship between centrifugal and centripetal forces. And this is desirable. Whereas roles in the modernist view would be similar to what chaos theorists refer to as *limit attractors* (they tend toward stereotypical closure), roles in postmodernist analysis would be very much like *torus* or *strange attractors*. A strange attractor can appear as two butterfly wings where instances of behavior may occur in one (i.e., a person's conduct is situated in the illegal underworld), and in the other (i.e., a person's conduct is in the legitimate world). Where the two cross, maximal indeterminacy prevails. When instances of behavior are plotted in *phase space* (a diagrammatical depiction), what appears over time is some degree of global patterning (the distinct wings of the butterfly), but at any instance, that is at any specific location, variability and indeterminacy prevail (from quantum mechanics' uncertainty principle, one cannot at the same time, predict location and momentum). There exists, in other words, local indeterminacy but a relative global stability, an orderly disorder. A person's fate is relegated to role-making (Young 1994).

In George Herbert Mead's framework, role-making would indicate the active contribution of the "I." Unger's notion of *role-jumbling* would be another example (1987). Haraway's idea of a *postmodernist identity* would be another (1991). Others have advocated a simultaneous disidentification and identification with various discursive subject positions, a process by which re-identifications are produced (JanMohammed 1993; McLaren 1994). "It is ... a process of forming affiliations with other positions, of defining equivalences and constructing alliances" (JanMohammed 1993, p. 111). In fact, Lacan's view is that the person is decentered and is always subject to imaginary and symbolic play and therefore a stable *moi* is illusory and stability can only be maintained by the impositions of external forces (i.e., manipulative powers of the political and the advertisement industry; the violence of a phallocentric symbolic order, etc.). For the postmodernist view, the call is to be a jazz player and poet.

3. Subjectivity/Agency

Key concepts:
Modernist

Postmodernist

Centered; the individual;
transparent; reflective;
self-directing; whole;
positivistic; the "over-
socialized" conception;
juridic subject; homo-
duplex; homo-economicus;
homeostatic; passivity;
the good, interpellated,
spoken subjects; transcend-
ental self; cartesian;
Cogito, ergo sum; logos;
rational man; conscious,
autonomous being; desire
centered on lack.

Decentered; polyvocal; polyvalent;
parlêtre; l'être parlant; pathos;
subject-in-process; Schema L and
Schema R; subject of desire;
activity; subject of dis-identifi-
cation; assumption of one's
desire; effects of the uncon-
scious; positive/productive desire;
will to power.

Commentary

a. Modernist thought. Modernist thought has privileged the idea of the individual, a person that is assumed to be conscious, whole, self-directing, reflective, unitary, and transparent. In its extreme we have what had been characterized in the 1960s by Dennis Wrong and picked up in the critical literature as the "oversocialized conception of man." Other conceptions cling to a homo-duplex view in which human nature is said to be a balance of egoism and altruism. Here individual desires are said to be in need of synchronization with given socio-political systems. Alternatively we have *homo economicus.* The Enlightenment period was one in which the individual or the centered subject was discovered. This conception of the transcendental self, the cartesian subject, has been incorporated in the legal sphere as the juridic subject, the reasonable man/woman in law. Nowhere better has it been expressed than in *Cogito, ergo sum.*

Desire, for the modernists, is inscribed on the body; it is *territorialized* (Deleuze and Guattari 1987). As Foucault would point out, the desiring subject becomes a body of passivity and economic/political utility (1977). Desire must be tamed, captured within the coordinates of various dominant discourses. Here desire begins with a lack, the price it pays for its inauguration into the Symbolic Order, and the biography of the self is one in which repetition drives the organism in its attempt to fill the void (see also Dews 1987, pp. 132, 135). In the more passive form of adaptation, the person is driven toward homeostasis, tension-reduction, catharsis, etc. The subject is said to be interpellated into her/ his discursive subject-positions necessitated by the imperatives of a smoothly functioning socio-economic political order. Thus we have the *interpellated* (Althusser 1971), *spoken* (Silverman 1983) or the *good* subject (Pecheux 1982). In the more active form of adaptation, expressions of alienation, despair, resistance and opposition produce the oppositional subject caught within the *discourse of the hysteric* (Lacan 1991; Milovanovic 1993a).

b. Postmodernist thought. Postmodernist thought has offered the idea of the decentered subject. The subject is more determined than determining, is less internally unified than a desiring subject caught within the constraints of various discourses and their structuring properties. Kristeva has referred to the person as the subject-in-process; Lacan, *l'être parlant* or the *parlêtre* (the speaking being, or the speaking); and much African-American feminist analysis in law, for example, has argued for the polyvocal, polyvalent nature of consciousness (Harris 1991, pp. 235-62; Matsuda 1989; Williams 1987; Williams 1991; Bartlet 1991, pp. 387-89).

Perhaps the clearest exposition of the decentered subject has been provided by Lacan in his schema L (1977). This four-cornered schema proposes two diagonally intersecting axes: one represents an unconscious/symbolic axis, the other the imaginary axis. Here the subject is drawn over all four corners of this schema; s/he is simultaneously caught in the working of the symbolic and imaginary axes. The unconscious/symbolic axis has at one end of the pole the grammatical "I"; at the other end, the *Other*, the sphere of the unconscious structured like a language. The second axis, the imaginary axis, has one end the imaginary construction of the self (*moi*); the opposite end that of the *other*, the entity through whom the self establishes itself as a coherent (be it illusory), whole being. Lacan's more dynamic models of Schema L appear as the *graphs of desire* and Schema R (1977; see also Milovanovic's expose, 1992; on Schema R, see Milovanovic, 1994c).

The modernist's view of the subject often centers on the idea that desire emerges from "lack", and is predicated on the desirability of keeping desire in check – its free flowing expression being said to be inherently subversive or disruptive in ongoing social activity. The postmodernists add that the desiring subject is imprisoned within restrictive discourses; at one extreme in *discourses of the master*, where subjects enact key master signifiers producing and reproducing the dominant order; at the other, in the *discourses of the hysteric*, where despairing subjects find no adequate signifiers with which to embody their desire (Lacan 1991; Bracher 1988, 1993; Milovanovic 1993a, 1993b). Oppressive discursive structures interpellate subjects as supports of system needs (Althusser 1971; see also Silverman's analysis of the manipulative media effects, 1983). In either case hegemony is easily sustained.

Postmodernists offer both a more passive and a more active form of disruptions. In the more passive form we have the notion of disruptive voices, such as in the notion of *delire*, a disruptive language of the body (Lecercle 1985, 1990), or in *minor literature* and the *rhizome* (Deleuze and Guattari 1986, 1987), or in the notion of *noise* or the *parasite* (Serres 1982a, pp. 65-70; Hayles 1990, pp. 197-208), or in the non-linear discursive disruptions of the *enthymeme* that intrude on any linear discursive constructions (Knoespel 1991), or, finally, in Lacan's notion of an alternative form of *jouissance*, a jouissance of the body, a view that initiated much debate over the desirability of an *écriture féminine* (1985, p. 145). In the more active form, postmodernists offer a dialogically based pedagogy whereby the cultural revolutionary or revolutionary subject enters a dialogical encounter with the oppressed in co-producing key master signifiers and replacement discourses which more acurately reflect the given repressive order (see Lacan's discourse of the analyst in combination with the discourse of the hysteric, Milovanovic, 1993a; see also Freire 1985; McLaren 1994; Aronowitz and Giroux 1985).

For postmodernists, desire can "be conceived as a forward movement, a flight towards an object which always eludes our grasp, the attempt, never successful but never frustrating, to reach the unattainable by exploring the paths of the possible" (Lecercle 1985, p. 196). Here desire, contrary to merely responding to lack and being a negative, conservative force, is seen as equated with positive processes (Dews 1987, pp. 132, 135-36), a will to power, defined as "the principle of the synthesis of forces" (Deleuze 1983, p. 50). Nietzsche, not Hegel is the key figure. Deleuze and Guattari's notion of the *rhizome* brings out the non-linear paths taken by desire seeking expression at each level of semiotic production (Milovanovic 1992a, pp. 125-33).

For postmodernists, desire is liberating, joyous, ironic, playful and a positive force. Ultimately, the "hero" (or Nietzsche's *overman*) as opposed to the *common man* [woman], must avow her/his desire and act in conformity with it (Lacan 1992, pp. 309, 319-21; Lacan 1977, p. 275; Lee 1990, pp. 95-99, 168-70; Rajchman 1991, pp. 42-43).

4. Discourse

Key concepts:
Modernist   *Postmodernist*

Instrumental; uniaccentual;   *Multi-accentual; fractal signifiers;*
global; neutral; dominant;   *regime of signs; discourse of the*
master/university discourse;   *hysteric/analyst; linguistic coor-*
primacy to paradigm/syntagm;   *dinate systems; discursive forma-*
major literature; readerly   *ations; borromean knots;capitonnage;*
text; production/reproduction;   *symptoms; objet petit(a); primacy*
referential signifier and   *to other semiotic axes – metaphor/*
text; privileging of master   *metonymy, condensation/displace-*
signifiers and 'natural'   *ment; minor literature; writerly*
categories; privileging   *text; nonreferential text; hyper-*
noun forms.   *real; cyberspace; verb forms.*

Commentary:

a. Modernist thought. The Modernist paradigm assumes that discourse is neutral; it is but an instrument for use to express rationally developed projects of an inherently centered subject. In fact, some transcendental signifiers exist at the center of social structure and phenomena which are discoverable. Assumed, most often, is an ongoing dominant discourse that is seen as adequate for providing the medium for expression, whether for dominant or subordinate groups. The couplet, the signifier (the word), and the signified (that which it expresses) are said to stabilize and crystallize in conventional understandings (uniaccentuality). Signifiers are more often said to be referential: they point to something outside themselves - to some "concrete" reality (naturalism). Modernists are more likely to assume these natural categories rather than treating them as semiotically variable concepts (the Sapir-Whorf linguistic relativity principle anticipated many of the insights of postmodernist analysis).

Modernist discourse celebrates the noun rather than the verb forms (Bohm 1980). It is much more likely to make use of master signifiers such as prediction, falsification, replication, generalization, operationalization, objectivity, value freedom, etc.: these are "givens" in investigations (Young 1994).

Modernists are more likely to focus on the most conscious level of semiotic production. Consciously constructed discourses are coordinated by two axes: the paradigmatic axis which is a vertical structure, if you will, that provides word choices, a dictionary of sorts. The horizontal axis, the syntagmatic axis, stands for the grammatical and linear placement of signifiers. The two axes work together to produce meaning. Debates that do question the nature of dominant discourses often are centered on the differences between an oppressive master discourse versus an ostensibly liberating discourse of the university (on the nature of the four main discourses – *master, university, hysteric, and analyst*, see Lacan 1991; Bracher 1988, 1993; Milovanovic 1993a). The evolution of history, for the modernist thinker, is often seen as the progressive victory of the discourse of the university over the discourse of the master.

Discursive production, in modernist thought, is much more likely to produce the *readerly text* (Barthes 1974; Silverman 1983) and *major literature* (Deleuze and Guattari 1986). This text is a linear reading (or viewing) with the organizing principle of non-contradiction. Its goal is closure. Its effect is the production and reproduction of conventionality. Interpreters and viewers are encouraged to assume conventional discursive subject-positions and fill in gaps by use of dominant symbolic forms.

b. Postmodernist thought. Postmodernist thought does not assume a neutral discourse. There are many discourses reflective of local sites of production, each, in turn, existing with a potential for the embodiment of desire in signifiers and for the constructions of realities. The sign, composed of signifier and signified, finds its natural state as being in flux. The signified is multiaccentual, the site of diverse struggles (Volosinov 1986). The paradigm-syntagm semiotic axis is only the most manifest level of semiotic production, the most conscious. Two other levels have been identified and work at the unconscious level: the condensation-displacement semiotic axis, and the metaphoric-metonymic semiotic axis (Milovanovic 1992b, 1993b).

Desire, it is argued, begins at a deeper level of the psychic apparatus and undergoes embodiment – for Freud, "figuration"; for Lacan, essentially "fantasy," $\$ \Diamond a$ – by the contributory work ("overdetermination") of these two axes – they are the coordinating mechanisms which provide temporary anchorings to the floating signifiers found in the Other, the sphere of the unconscious –, finally reaching the level of a particular historically rooted and stabilized discourse or linguistic coordinate system. It is here where final embodiment must be completed in the paradigm-syntagm semiotic axis (i.e., a particular word or utterance is vocalized). It was Freud who began this analysis with his investigation of *dream work* as the "royal road to the unconscious." It was Lacan who added the metaphoric-metonymic semiotic axis. Much of the investigation of the effects of language by modernists is focused merely on the surface structure of paradigm-syntagm (in law, for example, see Greimas 1990; Jackson 1988; Landowski 1991).

Postmodernists identify the *violence of language* (Lecercle 1985, 1990). Linguistic repression and alienation are the results of historically situated hegemonic discourses (see also the notion of the *regime of signs* of Deleuze and Guattari 1987, and their notion of *minor* versus *major literature*, 1986; see also Foucault's notion of discursive formations and the *epistemes*, 1973; Milovanovic's notion of *linguistic coordinate systems*, 1992a, 1992b; Pecheux's notion of discursive formations, 1982).

Critically, as we have previously said, Lacan has offered four intersubjectively structured discourses (1991; Bracher 1988, 1993; Milovanovic 1993a; Arrigo 1992, 1993). Desire, it is argued, has various forms of embodiment in these structured discourses. Different discourses may, on the one hand, be manipulative and repressive in the expression of desire; and, on the other, offer greater possibilities of expression to these same desires.

Postmodernists would celebrate the *writerly text* (Barthes 1974; Silverman 1983). This text is seen as being more subversive than a readerly text. Encouraged in the viewer/interpreter is "an infinite play of signification; in it there can be no transcendental signified, only provisional ones which function in turn as signifiers" (Silverman 1983, p. 246). For the writerly form, deconstruction of the text is celebrated with the purpose of uncovering hidden or repressed voices (consider feminist's celebration of investigating her/story rather than history). This strategy, the postmodernists would say, is particularly important in a contemporary society characterized as producing the non-referential and autonomous *hyper-real* (Baudrillard 1981), and the new order of *cyberspace* (Gibson 1984).

Similarly, Deleuze and Guattari (1986) have offered the idea of *minor literature* which tends toward a deterritorialization, manifest in the carnivalesque genre or other forms expressive of *delire* (Lecercle 1985) such as in the writings of E.E.Cummings, Franz Kafka, and James Joyce. In this spirit, David Bohm (1980) has advocated the privileging and the further development of the verb over the noun form; this would allow us to transcend the limiting metaphysics and meta-narratives embedded in subject-verb-object discursive forms (consider, too, Benjamin Whorf's investigations of the Hopi language, 1956).

5. Knowledge

Key concepts:

Modernist	Postmodernist
Global; dominant; discourse of the master and university;	*Local; repressed voices; constitutive processes;*

| grand narrative; totalizing; binary (as in law); Logos; education as liberating; Truth; privileging scientific knowledge; Absolute postulates, axiomizability, deductive logic; banking education; closure. | meta-narratives; power/knowledge; fragmented; contingent and provisional truths;Pathos; discourse of hysteric and analyst; knowledge for sale; education as ideology and functional; narrative knowledge; noise, the parasite, enthymemes, the rhizome, delire; incompleteness; undecidability; dialogic pedagogy; abduction. |

Commentary:

a. Modernist thought. Enlightenment thought tended toward a totalizing Truth centered on an ostensibly discoverable Logos. Driven by formal rational methods, one inevitably dominant and globalizing thought would result. Lyotard, for example, has explained how *scientific knowledge* has usurped *narrative knowledge* (1984; see also Sarup 1989, pp. 120-21; Hayles 1990, pp. 209-210; see also Habermas' point concerning the establishment of new *steering mechanisms* based on power and money that fuel *purposive rational action*, 1987). Narrative knowledge, on the other hand, is based on myth, legend, tales, stories, etc., which provided the wherewithal of being in society (see also Habermas' idea of communicative or symbolic communication, 1987). Whereas scientific knowledge tends toward closure, narrative knowledge embraces imaginary free play.

Lacan has provided the mechanism for the production of knowledge and the reconstitution of Truths in his analysis of the *discourses of the master and university.* For the former, knowledge and ideology are embedded in dominant discourse. Since this discourse is the one which is seen as relevant and since subjects must situate themselves within it, they too are subject to its interpellative effects (Althusser 1971; Milovanovic 1988). Thus conventional knowledge is more likely to be reconstituted by way of the *readerly text, major literature,* or the *discourse of the master and university.*

The search for Truth by the modernists was inevitably guided by the ideal of establishing Absolute Postulates from which all other "facts" can be explained by linear, deductive logic. Efficiency and competency in the educative process is geared toward a *banking education* whereby conventional master signifiers or their derivatives are stored to be capitalized (Freire 1985).

b. Postmodernist thought. Postmodernists, on the other hand, view knowledge as always fragmented, partial, and contingent (see also, Sarup 1989; Dews 1987; Lyotard 1984). It always has multiple sites of production (Geertz 1983). It is derived from a dialogic pedagogy where novel signifiers are co-produced in the process of critique and the development of a *language of possibility* (Freire 1985). It is more likely to reflect Pathos, human suffering, than Logos. Since there are many truths and no over-encompassing Truth is possible (following Godel's undecidability theorem, 1962), knowledge defies closure or being stored passively as in a banking education. In fact, following chaos' idea of iteration, the unpredictable and unanticipated is likely to continuously appear.

Postmodernists celebrate local knowledge. Dominant and global knowledge always subverts voices that otherwise seek expression, either directly or indirectly; by the demand that all desire must be embodied within dominant concepts, signifiers, and linguistic coordinate systems, or by way of translation (intertextuality) from their more unique concrete form into abstract categories of law and bureaucracy. Postmodernists, however, view local knowledges as not necessarily subsumable under one grand narrative or logic (Godel's theorem).

Postmodernists view subjects within a social formation as thwarted in their attempts to be true to their desires. Even so, "space" does exist for possible articulation of desire. The destabilizing effects of *noise*, the *parasite*, the work of the *rhizome*, *minor literatures*, the non-linear disruptions of *enthymemes*, and the subversive *writerly* text always threaten dominant forms of knowledge. Denied subjects may be oppositional, as in the discourse of the hysteric; or revolutionary, as in the discourse of the analyst/hysteric (Milovanovic 1993a, 1993b).

For postmodernists, knowledge is always both relational and positional (Kerruish 1991). Accordingly, standpoints are always situated in social relations and within ideologies (p. 187). Power and knowledge are intricately connected and hierarchically arranged (see Dew's useful discussion of Foucault, Nietzsche, Lyotard, 1987). To enter a discursive formation (legal, medical, scientific, political, etc.) is to enter the logic and rationality embedded within it (Foucault 1973; Pitkin 1971); thus, truth is discourse-specific.

Feminist postmodernist analysis has been poignant as to the explanation of the construction of the phallic Symbolic order, gender roles, and possible alternative knowledges (see especially Cornell 1991, 1993; Brennan 1993). Investigations on the contribution of the imaginary sphere and its possible impact on reconstructing myths have been illuminating (Arrigo 1992, 1993). Constitutive theory has also offered the notion of replacement discourses (Henry and Milovanovic 1991; Milovanovic 1993a, 1993b). This new knowledge is based on contingent and provisional truths, subject to further reflection and historicity.

The notion of *abduction* offered by Charles S. Peirce is more accurately reflective of the postmodernist epistemology than deductive logic. Here, Absolute Postulates or major premises never achieve stability; rather, creative free play guides the formulation of tentative propositions. As Nancy Fraser and Linda Nicholson have said, postmodernist critique floats free of any universalist theoretical ground. No longer anchored philosophically, the very shape or character of social criticism changes; it becomes more pragmatic, ad hoc, contextual, and local ... [t]here are no special tribunals set apart from the sites where inquiry is practiced, [but only] ... the plural, local, and immanent (cited in Bartlett 1991, p. 388).

6. Space/Time

Key concepts:

Modernist	*Postmodernist*
3-dimensional space; integral; homogeneous; striated space; newtonian mechanics; euclidean geometry; cartesian coordinates; quantitative; differential equations and continuities; reversability of time.	*Multi-dimensional; smooth; fractal; imaginary; quantum mechanics/relativity; implicate (enfolded) order; non-euclidean geometry; holographic; topology theory; qualitative; twister space (imaginary); cyberspace; non-linear, non-reversable time.*

Commentary:

a. Modernist thought. Modernist thought rests on Newtonian mechanics. This classical view in physics rests on notions of absolute space and time. This in turn is connected with the existence of determinism within systems: if we know the positions, masses and velocities of a particle at one time we can accurately determine their positions and velocities at all later times (Bohm 1980, p. 121).

Newtonian physics and euclidean geometry with its use of Cartesian coordinates is the map or blueprint of space on which modernists construct the social world. It is what Deleuze and Guattari refer to as *striated space* (1987, p. 488): it consists of space with whole number dimensions where constant direction can be describable and end-states predictable. Drawing from Descartes' coordinate grid of an x-axis perpendicularly intersecting with a y-axis, a point could be located anywhere in two-dimensional space (similarly with 3-D space, with an added z-axis). Thus the equation, $y = 3x$, can be identified on this graph. At one stroke geometry and algebra is linked. And Newton refined this further with his calculus with its differential equations. Now a continuous change in one variable can be show to produce a calculable change in the other. And just as time flows forward, it can flow backward in a predictable way: the romantic past, the "good old days," can be recreated.

This model has been incorporated in the social sciences. A person's life course, for example, could be plotted with precision if we discover appropriate determinants. This is the basis of positivism. It is by a *striated space* (Deleuze and Guattari 1987) that science progresses and by which desire can be territorialized on the body (1986) by a political economy. But striated space needs its discrete variables with whole number dimensions.

b. Postmodernist thought. Postmodernists see things differently. Quantum mechanics, non-euclidean geometry, string theory, twister space, topology theory, and chaos theory, to name a few of the most prominent approaches, have offered alternative conceptions. The question of a dimension and prediction becomes problematic.

Nuclear physicists, for example, faced with trying to reconcile general relativity theory with quantum mechanics have come up with infinities. By adding space dimensions to their equations these begin to drop out of the equation. At 10-D in one model, and 26-D in another they disappear (Peat 1989; Kaku 1994). The 3-D model we see is perhaps just an explicate order with the rest of the dimensions rolled up tightly (compactified). This compactified order is the *enfolded* or *implicate order* (Bohm 1980), said to have its origins moments after the Big Bang.

Chaos theory has developed the idea of *fractal* dimensions. Rather than having whole dimensions we can refer to a space with 1 1/2 dimensions, 1 3/4, etc. (A point has a dimension of 0, a line a dimension of one; a plane, two; a volume, three.) A coastline, for example, can have a fractal dimension between one and two. So, for example, contrary to the boolean logic of doctrinal legal analysis, truths are always fractal in form. Deleuze and Guattari have developed the idea of a *smooth space* which is continuous, not discrete. The notion of fractals is in accord with smooth space (1987), and, as we shall show below, fields. It is within smooth space that becoming occurs; but progress and conventional science is done in striated space (p. 486; see also Bergson 1958; Serres 1982a, 1982b).

Yet others, such as the noted mathematician Penrose, have constructed a view of space in terms of imaginary numbers, a *twister space* (Peat 1988, chapter 8; Penrose 1989, pp. 87-98). Chaos theorists, such as Mandelbrot, made use of complex numbers in the form of $z = x + iy$, where i is an imaginary number (the square root of -1). By further plotting $z = z^2 + c$ and by taking the result and re-iterating by the use of the same formula they were to find enormously complex and esthetically appealing figures (see Penrose 1989, pp. 92-94). Yet others have relied on the hologram to indicate how inscriptions of phenomena are encoded and how they can be revealed with their multi-dimensional splendor (Bohm 1980 p. 150; Pribram 1973). Finally, we note the field of topology, the qualitative math which offers alternative ways of conceptualizing phenomena without the use of math. Here, in what is often called the "rubber math," figures are twisted, pulled, and reshaped in various ways. Breaking and gluing are not legitimate operations. Breaking produces entirely new forms. Much current thinking in nuclear- and astrophysics relies on topology theory (Peat 1988; Kaku 1994).

Lacan has made use of topology to explain such things as the structure of the psychic apparatus by using borromean knots, Mobius bands, the torus, and projective geometry (the cross-cap) (see also Milovanovic 1993b, 1994c; Granon-Lafont 1985, 1990; Vappereau 1988; for an introduction to topology theory, see Hilbert and Cohn-Vossen 1952; Weeks 1985; for non-euclidean geometry, see Russell 1956). In fact, in 4-D space the borromean knot of Lacan is no longer knotted. The cross-cap, which topologically portrays the working of schema R and how desire is embodied as a result of the effects of the Symbolic, Imaginary, and Real Orders, can also be presented in 3-D or 4-D space (Milovanovic 1994c; Hilbert and Cohn-Vossen 1952). It is not without effect when we move from 3-D to 4-D space (Rucker 1984; Banchoff 1990; for the contributions of non-euclidean geometry and 4-D space on cubism in art see Henderson, 1983). Much needs to be done in the analysis of the effects of these novel conceptions.

Thus, for the postmodernists, several notions of space are currently being explored and incorporated in their analysis of the subject, discourse, causality, and society: multiple dimensional (Peat 1989), fractal (Mandelbrot 1983), holographic (Talbot 1991; Bohm 1980: Pribram 1977), enfolded/implicate order (Bohm 1980; Bohm and Peat 1987), cyberspace (Gibson 1984), hyper-real (Baudrillard 1981), smooth space (Deleuze and Guattari 1987), twister space (Penrose 1989; see also Peat 1989), and topological (Lacan 1976, 1987; Peat 1989; Granon-Lafont 1985, 1990; Vappereau 1988; Milovanovic 1993b, 1994c; Lem 1984). Young has been succinct in indicating the relevance of these notions in that an alternative space is open for the development of conceptions of "human agency in ways not possible in those dynamics privileged by Newtonian physics, Aristotelian logic, Euclidian geometry and the linear causality they presume" (1992, p. 447). And there can be no return to the nostalgic "good old days": time is irreversible; since initial conditions are undecidable, then, with the passage of time and iteration, there can be no return to some decidable state.

7. Causality

Key concepts:

Modernist	*Postmodernist*
Linear; proportional effects; positivism; determinism; classical physics; I. Newton; "God does not play dice"; certainty; grand theorizing; predictability; future fixed by past; particle effects.	*Non-linear; disproportional effects; genealogy; rhizome; chance; contingency; quantum mechanics; uncertainty; iteration; catastrophe theory; paradoxical; discontinuities; singularities; field effects.*

Commentary:

a. Modernist thought. Modernist thought rests on the determinism of Newtonian physics. It appears most often in the form of positivism. Modernist thought would assume that given some incremental increase in some identified cause or determinant, a proportional and linear increase in the effect will result. The basic unit of analysis is the particle (i.e., assumed autonomous individuals, social "elements," and discrete categories) and their contributory effects. Cartesian coordinates, whole number dimensions, calculus, etc., in a few words, striated space is what makes possible a mathematics that has high predictive powers. Even Einstein refused to accept much of quantum mechanics that came after him, particularly the notion that God plays dice.

b. Postmodernist thought. Postmodernists see things differently. Chaos theory, Godel's theorem, and quantum mechanics stipulate that proportional effects do not necessarily follow some incremental increase of an input variable. Uncertainty, indeterminacy, and disproportional (non-linear) effects are all underlying assumptions and worthy of inquiry in explaining an event (genealogy). In the extreme, a butterfly flapping its wings in East Asia produces a hurricane in Warren, Ohio. Key thinkers here are Edward Lorenz, Benoit Mandelbrot, and Stephen Smale (see the excellent overview by Gleick 1988; Briggs and Peat 1989). In fact, in the extreme, something can emerge out of nothing at points identified as *singularities*; this is the sphere of order arising out of disorder.

Two current approaches within chaos theory are making their impact: one, focused more on order that exists in an otherwise apparently disorderly state of affairs (Hayles 1991, p. 12; see Feigenbaum 1980; Shaw 1981); the second, focused more on how in fact order arises out of chaotic systems – order out of disorder or self-organization (Hayles 1991, p. 12; 1990, pp. 1-28; see also Prigogine and Stengers 1984; Thom 1975). A growing number of applications is taking place. See particularly Unger's application in his prescription for an *empowered democracy* (1987).

The notion of iteration is a central concept of postmodernism. Simply, it means recomputing with answers obtained from some formula. Continuous feedback and iteration produces disproportional (not linear) effects. Derrida has applied it to how words obtain new meaning in new contexts (1976; see also Balkan 1987); in law, for example, the "original intent" of the "founding fathers" undergoes modification over time and can not be reconstructed. The point being made is that because of minute initial uncertainties – however small, consider Godel's theorem –, when iteration proceeds these are amplified producing indeterminacies (Hayles 1990, p. 183; Lyotard 1984, p. 55). Thus, rather than celebrating global theory, chaos theorists and postmodernists look to local knowledges where small changes can produce large effects (Hayles 1990, p. 211). In other words, postmodernists see otherwise small contributions as having profound possibilities. Yes, "small" person's actions can make a difference! One person's involvement in a demonstration, petition signature, act of civil disobedience, or "speaking up," can, in the long run, have greater effects than anticipated.

Causation can be attributed to field rather than particle effects (Bohm 1980; Bohm and Peat 1987). Borrowing from Bohm's insights concerning the *quantum potential* and the *enfolded order* where all is interconnected, rather than focusing, as the modernists do, on particles, points and point events, all of which are narrowly spatiotemporally defined (analogously, consider the subject in traditional positivistic sciences: an object, located socioeconomically, who has engaged in some act at a particular time and place), the unit of analysis, for postmodernists, should be a field with its moments, duration, intensities, flows, displacements of libidinal energy. Moments, unlike point events, have fluctuating time-space coordinates that defy precise measurement (Bohm 1980, p. 207). Within this field heterogeneous intensities can affect movement, even if they are not immediately discernible or linear and/or local. Nonlinear and nonlocal factors, therefore, even at a distance, can have a noticeable effect (Bohm and Peat 1987, pp. 88-93, 182-83). Research awaits in drawing out the implications of moving from 3-D to 4-D space, i.e., what is knotted in the former becomes unknotted in the latter (Rucker 1984; Kaku 1994; consider Lacan's borromean knot in 4-D space, Milovanovic 1993b).

In the postmodern view, certainties that do appear are often the creation of subjects: Nietzsche has shown, for example, how a subject in need of "horizons" finds *semiotic fictions* that produce the appearance of a centered subject; Peirce, anticipating chaos, has shown how free will is often created *after* the event as the "facts" are rearranged to fit a deterministic model and individual authorship (1923, p. 47); legal realists, in the early part of this century, have shown that what creates order in legal decision-making is not syllogistic reasoning and a formally rational legal system, but ex post facto constructions; and so forth. For postmodernists, especially Nietzsche and Foucault, it is the "fear of the chaotic and the unclassifiable" (Dews 1987, p. 186) that accounts for the order we attribute to nature.

8. Social change

Key concepts:
Modernist   *Postmodernist*

Evolutionary; Darwinian;   *Genealogy; transpraxis;*
rationalization; linear;   *standpoints epistemology(ies);*
Absolute Spirit; dialectical   *Pure Play/musement;*
materialism; praxis; Hegel;   *rhizome; dis-identifi-*
reaction and negation;   *cation; play of the imaginary;*

reversal of hierarchies;
reduction of complexity;
stable premises for action;
history as progress; variation,
selection, and transmission;
oppositional subject; discourse
of the hysteric.

dialectics of struggle;
affirmative action;
deconstruction and reconstr-
uction; proliferation of
complexity; premises of action
based on tolerability;
overcoming panopticism;
depense, mimeses; multiplici-
ties of resistance to power;
assuming one's desire; dialog-
ism, conscientization, langu-
age of possibility;revolution-
ary subject; discourse of the
hysteric/analyst.

Commentary:

a. Modernist thought. Modernist thought often sees change in terms of evolutionary theory, in various versions of Darwinian dynamics, particularly in terms of some "invisible hand" at work, or some working out of a logic as in the Absolute Spirit of Hegel, or in forces of rationalization as in Weber, or in dialectical materialism as in Marx. What often underlies these approaches is some linear conception of historical change. Perhaps praxis is the upper limit of modernist thought.

In the most liberal modernist view, Hegel's master-slave dialectic is a key parable of change. It is premised on reaction-negation dynamics. The slave (the oppressed) only creates value by a double negation. Nothing new is offered. The limits of an alternative vision remain tied to the initial logic of the major premise of the master-slave dialectic that falls on the side of the master. At best we have the oppositional subject who finds her/himself in the discourse of the hysteric, sometimes slipping into nihilistic and fatalist stances – in neither case offering anything new; at worst, a subject that inadvertently recreates the dominant repressive order (hegemony).

Modernist thought that often takes the form of evolutionary theory of change attempts to account for three phenomena: variation, selection, and transmission (Sinclair 1992, p. 95; Luhmann 1985, p. 249; see also Sinclair's critique of evolutionary theory of law, 1987). Luhmann's analysis is instructive. He tells us that the continuous differentiation of society tends to produce an *excess of possibilities* (1985, p. 237; see also Manning's application to police bureauc- racies and how diverse voices are channeled into "relevant" categories, 1988). Given this creation of excesses, law, Luhmann claims, functions to reduce complexity so that subjects may plan within certain discernible horizons which, in turn, produce predictability in social planning. Social change is therefore a linear affair with continuous adjustments of social institutions to continuous processes of differentiation.

b. Postmodernist thought. Postmodernist thought focuses more on non-linear conceptions of historical change, genealogical analysis, and transpraxis, a materialistically based politics that includes a language of critique and possibility (Freire 1985; McLaren 1994; Aronowitz and Giroux 1985). Postmodernists are in general agreement that, in studying historical change, much room must be made for the contributions of contingency, irony, the spontaneous, and the marginal. Nietzsche, once again, is the dominant thinker (1980; see also Love 1986; Deleuze 1983).

Nietzsche's version of the master-slave dialectic is key for postmodernists. Here, rather than reaction-negation dynamics as in Hegel, an inherently conservative approach, Nietzsche's position advocates active change. This includes deconstruction *and* reconstruction as inseparable elements. This has been captured by the idea of a transpraxis rather than a praxis (Henry and Milovanovic 1991; Henry and Milovanovic 1993; Milovanovic 1993b).

Most prominent in recent days are feminist postmodernist theorists who have built on various versions of Lacanian psychoanalytic semiotics as well as those who have developed a standpoint theory aided especially by numerous productive critiques. Accordingly, Cornell has identified the contributions of the imaginary and the rethinking of the myth (1991, 1993; Cixous 1986; Arrigo 1992); Cornell (1991, p. 147) and Grant (1993, p. 116) have noted that given ideologies "leave some critical space" or "slippage" (in this context Peirce's notion of *musement* or *Pure Play* is also relevant (1934, pp. 313-16); Kristeva has focused on the idea that semiotic processes that are situated in the form of the *readerly text* of Barthes are faced with semiotic overflow at privileged moments specified as the subversive triad: "madness, holiness and poetry" (cited in Grosz 1990, p. 153); Pecheux has focused on the notion of dis-identification (1982); Irigaray on *mimeses* (1985; see also Cornell's commentary, 1991, pp. 147-50); Lacan on the discourse of the analyst (1991; see also Bracher 1993); Milovanovic on the revolutionary subject (composite of the hysteric and analyst, 1993a) and on *knot-breaking* (1993b).

Some current trends in postmodernist analysis draw out the implications for social change from Freire (1985), whose work lies between modernist and postmodernist analysis. The wherewithal of the revolutionary and social change may be fruitfully situated in the integration of Lacan's work on the discourse of the hysteric/analyst with Freire's notion of *conscientization* rooted in social struggles over signification. In this integration, structure and subjectivity, material conditions and ideology, the macro and the microsociological, critique and visions for change, undecidability and decidability can be reconciled. The signifier can be rooted in the concrete, historical arena of struggles; it can attain provisional decidability and a *contingent universality* in producing utopian visions of what could be and contribute, by way of a dialogic pedagogy, to the subject-in-process (generally, see, McLaren 1994; Ebert 1991; Zavarzadeh and Morton 1990; Butler 1992).

Postmodernists, too, are concerned with the possible negative and unintended effects of struggles against oppression and hierarchy. Reaction-negation dynamics may at times lead to what Nietzsche referred to as *ressentiment* as well as to new master discourses, forms of political correctness, exorcism (Milovanovic 1991), and dogma. Transpraxis, however, has as a central element the privileging of reflexivity of thought and the specification of contingent and provisional foundational political positions for social change (i.e., *contingent universalities* can become the basis for political alliances and agendas for change, McLaren 1994).

Among ethical principle that may come into play, for the postmodernists, perhaps Lacan's idea of "assuming one's desire" will become a key one. Faced with the passivity of the *common man* [woman], Lacan advocates that the *hero* is the one who does not betray her/his desire; meaning, s/he will act in conformity with it and not embrace the offerings of manipulative powers that offer an abundance of substitute materials, or what Lacan referred to as *objets petit(a)* (Lacan 1992, pp. 309, 319-21; Lacan 1977, p. 275; Lee 1990, pp. 95-99, 168-70; Rajchman 1991, pp. 42-43). Here, the productive use of desire is advocated, not one based on lack, tension-reduction, and stasis. Thus a sociopolitical system that maximizes the opportunities for avowing one's desire is a good one; conversely, hierarchical systems, whether under the name of capitalism or socialism, that systematically disavow subjects' desire are bad ones. Elsewhere, a postmodernist definition of crime/harm has been offered (Henry and Milovanovic 1993).

Postmodernists faced with the question of variation, selection, and transmission, opt for the development of the greatest variation, the most expansive form of retaining local sites of production, and the most optimal mechanisms for transmission. Accordingly, faced with an increasingly differentiating society with "excesses in possibilities," and the modernist's call for ways of reducing complexity – the most extreme form being in *pastiche* (Jameson 1984; Sarup 1989, pp. 133, 145), an imitation of dead styles as models for action –, the central challenge of the postmodernist alternative is to create new cultural styles that privilege chance, spontaneity, irony, intensity, etc. while still providing some dissipative *horizons* within which the subject may situate her/himself.

CONCLUSION

This essay has presented some of the salient differences between modernist and postmodernist thought. Contrary to modernist critics, a new paradigm is upon us. And it is neither fatalistic or nihilistic; nor is it without visions of what could be. We were especially concerned with the possibilities of a new transpraxis and the development of replacement discourses. It might be argued that the postmodernist paradigm may take on the form of a *normal science* and tend toward closure. But, unlike the modernist enterprise, there are intrinsic forces that militate against closure and stasis.

Special thanks to T.R.Young, whose insights on the applicability of chaos theory to the social sciences have been inspirational. I have greatly benefited from his comments on this manuscript and from our on-going dialogue.

REFERENCES

Althusser, L. 1971. *Lenin and Philosophy*. New York: Monthly Review Press.

Aronowitz, S. and H.A. Giroux. 1985. *Education Under Siege*. South Hadley, MA: Bergin and Garvey.

Arrigo, B. 1992. "An Experientally-Informed Feminist Jurisprudence: Rape and the Move Toward Praxis." *Humanity and Society* 17(1): 28-47.

– 1993. *Madness, Language and the Law*. Albany, New York: Harrow and Heston.

Baker, P. 1993. "Chaos, Order, and Sociological Theory." *Sociological Inquiry* 63(2): 123-49.

Balkan, J.M. 1987. "Deconstructive Practice and Legal Theory." *Yale Law Journal* 96(4): 743-86.

Banchoff, T. 1990. *Beyond the Third Dimension*. New York: Scientific American Library.

Barthes, R. 1974. *S/Z*. New York: Hill and Wang.

Bartlett, K. 1991. "Feminist Legal Methods." Pp. 333-50 in K. Bartlett and R. Kennedy (eds.) *Feminist Legal Theory*. Oxford: Westview Press.

Baudrillard, J. 1981. *For a Critique of the Political Economy of the Sign*. St. Louis: Telos Press.

Bohm, D. 1980. *Wholeness and The Implicate Order*. New York: ARK Publisher.

Bohm, D. and F.D. Peat. 1987. *Science, Order, and Creativity*. New York: Bantam Books.

Bracher, M. 1988. "Lacan's Theory of the Four Discourses." *Prose Studies* 11: 32-49.

– 1993. *Lacan, Discourse, and Social Change*. Ithaca: Cornell University Press.

Brennan, T. 1993. *History After Lacan*. New York: Routledge.

Briggs, J. and F.D. Peat. 1989. *Turbulent Mirror*. New York: Harper and Row.

Brion, D. 1991. "The Chaotic Law of Tort: Legal Formalism and the Problem of Indeterminacy." Pp. 45-77 in R. Kevelson (ed.) *Peirce and Law*. New York: Peter Lang.

Butler, J. 1992. "Contingent Foundations: Feminism and the Question of `Postmodernism," in J. Butler and J.W. Scott (eds.) *Feminists Theorize the Political*. London: Routledge.

Butz, M.R. 1991. "Fractal Dimensionality and Paradigms." *The Social Dynamicist* 2(4): 4-7.

– 1992a. "The Fractal Nature of the Development of the Self." *Psychological Reports*, 71: 1043-63.

– 1992b. "Systematic Family Therapy and Symbolic Chaos." *Humanity and Society* 17(2): 200-22.

Cixous, H. 1986. *The Newly Born Woman*. Minneapolis, Minn.: University of Minnesota Press.

Cornell, D. 1991. *Beyond Accommodation: Ethical Feminism, Deconstruction and the Law*. New York: Routledge.

– 1993. *Transformations: Recollective Imagination and Sexual Difference*. New York: Routledge.

Deleuze, G. 1983. *Nietzsche and Philosophy*. New York: Columbia University Press.

Deleuze, G. and F. Guattari. 1986. *Kafka: Toward a Minor Literature*. Minneapolis: University of Minnesota Press.

– 1987. *A Thousand Plateaus*. Minneapolis: University of Minnesota Press.

Dews, P. 1987. *Logics of Disintegration: Post-Structuralist Thought and the Claims of Critical Theory*. New York: Verso.

Derrida, J. 1973. *Of Grammatology*. Baltimore: John Hopkins Press.

Ebert, T. 1991. "Writing in the Political: Resistance (Post)Modernism." *Legal Studies Forum* 15(4): 291-303.

Feigenbaum, M. 1980. "Universal Behavior in Nonlinear Systems." *Los Alamos Science* 1: 4-27.

Foucault, M. 1973. *The Order of Things*. New York: Vintage Books.

– 1977. *Discipline and Punish*. New York: Pantheon.

Freire, P. 1985. *The Politics of Education*. South Hadley, Mass.: Bergin and Garvey Publishers.

Geertz, C. 1983. *Local Knowledge: Further Essays in Interpretive Anthropology*. New York: Basic Books.

Gibson, W. 1984. *Neuromancer*. New York: Ace.

Gleick, J. 1987. *Chaos: Making a New Science*. New York: Viking.

Godel, K. 1962. *On Formally Undecidable Propositions in 'Principia Mathematica' and Related Systems*. Pp. 173-98 in R.B. Braitewaite (ed.). New York: Basic Books.

Granon-Lafont, J. 1985. *La Topologie Ordinaire De Jacaques Lacan*. Paris: Point Hors Ligne.

– 1990. *Topologie Lacanienne et Clinique Analytique*. Paris, France: Point Hors Ligne.

Grant, J. 1993. *Fundamental Feminism: Contesting the Core Concepts of Feminist Theory*. New York: Routledge.

Greimas, A. 1990. *The Social Sciences: A Semiotic View*. Minneapolis: University of Minnesota Press.

Grosz, E. 1990. *Jacques Lacan: A Feminist Introduction*. New York: Routledge.

Habermas, J. 1987. *The Theory of Communicative Action. Vol. Two*. Boston: Beacon Press.

Harraway, D. 1991. "Situated Knowledges." Pp. 183-201 in D. Harraway, *Simians, Cyborgs and Women*. New York: Routledge.

Harris, A. 1991. "Race and Essentialism in Feminist Legal Theory." Pp. 235-62 in K. Bartlett and R. Kennedy (eds.) *Feminist Legal Theory*. Oxford: Westview Press.

Hayles, K. 1990. *Chaos Bound*. New York: Cornell University Press.

– (ed.). 1991. *Chaos and Order: Complex Dynamics in Literature and Science*. Chicago: University of Chicago Press.

Henderson, L. 1983. *The Fourth Dimension and Non-Euclidean Geometry in Modern Art*. Princeton, N.J.: Princeton University Press.

Henry, S. and D. Milovanovic. 1991. "Constitutive Criminology." *Criminology* 29(2): 293-316.

– 1993. "Back to Basics: A Postmodern Redefinition of Crime." *The Critical Criminologist* 5(2/3): 1-2, 6, 12.

– 1995. *Constitutive Criminology* (in press, Sage Publications).

Hilbert, D. and S. Cohn-Vossen. 1952. *Geometry and the Imagination*. New York: Chelsea Publishing Company.

Hunt, A. 1993. *Explorations in Law and Society: Toward a Constitutive Theory of Law*. New York: Routledge.

Irigaray, L. 1985. *Speculum of the Other Woman*. Ithica: Cornell University Press.

Jackson, B. 1988. *Law, Fact and Narrative Coherence*. Merseyside, U.K.: Deborah Charles.

Jameson, F. 1984. "Postmodernism, or the Cultural Logic of Capital." *New Left Review* 146.

JanMohammed, A.R. 1993. "Some Implications of Paulo Freire's Border Pedagogy." *Cultural Studies* 7(1): 107-17.

Jessop, B. 1990. *State Theory: Putting the Capitalist State in its Place*. Cambridge: Polity Press.

Kaku, M. 1994. *Hyperspace*. New York: Oxford University Press.

Kerruish, V. 1991. *Jurisprudence as Ideology*. N.Y.: Routledge.

Knoespel, K. 1985. *Medieval Ovidian Commentary: Narcissus and the Invention of Personal History*. New York: Garland.

Lacan, J. 1977. *Ecrits*. New York: Norton.

– 1985. *Feminine Sexuality*. New York: W.W. Norton and Pantheon Books.

– 1991. *L'Envers de la Psychanalyse*. Paris, France: Editions du Seuil.

– 1992. *The Ethics of Pyschoanalysis*. New York: Norton.

Landowski, E. 1991. "A Note on Meaning, Interaction and Narrativity." *International Journal of the Semiotics of Law* 11: 151-61.

Lecercle, J.J. 1985. *Philosophy Through the Looking Glass: Language, Nonsense, Desire*. London: Hutchinson.

– 1990. *The Violence of Language*. New York: Routledge.

Lee, S. L. 1990. *Jacques Lacan*. Amherst: University of Massachusetts Press.

Leifer, R. 1989. "Understanding Organizational Transformation Using a Dissipative Structure Model." *Human Relations* 42: 899-916.

Lem, S. 1984. *Microworlds*. San Diego: Harcourt Brace, Jovanovich.

Love, N. 1986. *Marx, Nietzsche, and Modernity*. New York: Columbia University Press.

Luhmann, N. A. 1985. *Sociological Theory of Law*. Boston: Routledge and Kegan Paul.

– 1992. "Operational Closure and Structural Coupling: The Differentiation of the Legal System." *Cardozza Law Review* 13(5): 1419-41.

Lyotard, J-F. 1984. *The Postmodern Condition: A Report on Knowledge*. Minneapolis, Minn.: University of Minnesota Press.

McLaren, P. 1994. "Postmodernism and the Death of Politics: A Brazilian Reprieve." Pp. 193-215 in P. McLaren and C. Lankshear (eds.), *Politics of Liberation: Paths from Freire*. New York: Routledge.

Mandelbrot, B. 1983. *The Fractal Geometry of Nature*. New York: W.H. Freeman.

Manning, P. 1988. *Symbolic Communication*. Cambridge: The MIT Press.

Matsuda, M. 1989. "When the First Quail Calls: Multiple Consciousness as Jurisprudential Method." *Women's Rights Law Reporter* 11: 7, 9.

Milovanovic, D. 1988. "Jailhouse Lawyers and Jailhouse Lawyering." *International Journal of the Sociology of Law* 16: 455-75.

– 1991. "Schmarxism, Exorcism and Transpraxis." *The Critical Criminologist* 3(4): 5-6, 11-12.

– 1992a. *Postmodern Law and Disorder: Psychoanalytic Semiotics, Chaos and Juridic Exegeses*. Liverpool, U.K.: Deborah Charles Publications.

– 1992b. "Re-Thinking Subjectivity in Law and Ideology: A Semiotic Perspective." *Journal of Human Justice* 4(1): 31-54.

– 1993a. "Lacan's Four Discourses." *Studies in Psychoanalytic Theory* 2(1): 3-23.

– 1993b. "Borromean Knots and the Constitution of Sense in Juridico-Discursive Production." *Legal Studies Forum* 17(2): 171-92.

– 1994a. *Sociology of Law*. 2ed. Albany, New York: Harrow and Heston.

– 1994b. "The Postmodern Turn: Lacan, Psychoanalytic Semiotics, and the Construction of Subjectivity in Law." *Emory International Law Review* 8(1): 67-98.

– 1994c. "The Decentered Subject in Law: Contributions of Topology, Psychoanalytic Semiotics and Chaos Theory." *Studies in Psychoanalytic Theory* 3(1): 93-127.

– 1994d. "Postmodern Law and Subjectivity: Lacan and the Linguistic Turn." In D. Caudill and S. Gould (eds.) *Radical Philosophy of Law*. New York: Humanities Press, forthcoming.

Nietzsche, F. 1980. *On the Advantage and Disadvantage of History for Life*. Cambridge, Mass: Hackett Publishing Company, Inc.

Peat, D. 1989. *Superstrings and the Search for the The Theory of Everything*. Chicago: Contemporary Books.

Pecheux, M. 1982. *Language, Semantics and Ideology*. New York: St. Martin's Press.

Peirce, C.S. 1923. *Chance, Love, and Logic*. New York: Goerge Braziller, Inc.

– 1940. *The Philosophy of Peirce: Selected Writings*. J. Buchler (ed.). London: Routledge and Kegan Paul.

– 1934. *Pragmatism and Pragmaticism*. Cambridge, Massachusetts. Harvard University Press.

Penrose, R. 1989. *The Emperor's New Mind*. New York: Oxford University Press.

Pepinsky, H. 1991. *The Geometry of Violence and Democracy*. Bloomington: Indiana University Press.

Pitkin, H. 1971. *Wittgenstein and Justice*. Berkely: University of California Press.

Pribram, K. 1977. *Languages of the Brain*. Englewood Cliffs, New Jersey: Prentice-Hall.

Prigogine, I. and I. Stengers. 1984. *Order Out of Chaos*. New York: Bantam.

Rajchman, J. 1991. *Truth and Eros: Foucault, Lacan, and the Question of Ethics*. New York: Routledge.

Russell, F. 1956. *Foundations of Geometry*. New York: Dover Publications.

Rucker, R. 1984. *The Fourth Dimension*. Boston: Houghton Mifflin Company.

Sarup, M. 1989. *Post-Structuralism and Postmodernism*. Athens, Georgia: University of Georgia Press.

Schwartz, M. and D. O. Friedrichs. 1994. "Postmodern Thought and Criminological Discontent: New Metaphors for Understanding Violence." *Criminology* 32(2): 221-46.

Sellers, S. 1991. *Language and Sexual Difference: Feminist Writings in France*. New York: St. Martin's Press.

Serres, M. 1982a. *Hermes: Literature, Science, Philosophy*. Baltimore: Johns Hopkins.

– 1982b. *The Parasite*. Baltimore: Johns Hopkins.

Shaw, R. 1981. "Strange Attractors, Chaotic Behavior, and Information Flow." *Zeitschrift fur Naturforschung* 36: 79-112.

Silverman, K. 1983. *The Subject of Semiotics*. New York: Oxford University Press.

Sinclair, M.B.W. 1987. "The Use of Evolution Theory in Law." *University of Detroit Law Review* 64: 451.

– 1992. "Autopoiesis: Who Needs It?" *Legal Studies Forum* 16(1): 81-102.

Stewart, I. 1989. *Does God Play Dice?* New York: Basil Blackwell.

Talbot, M. 1991. *The Holographic Universe*. New York: Harper Collins.

Thom, R. 1975. *Structural Stability and Morphogenesis: An Outline of a General Theory of Models*. Reading, MA: W.A. Benjamin.

Unger, R. 1987. *False Necessity*. New York: Cambridge University Press.

Vappereau, J.M. 1988. *Etoffe: Les Surfaces Topologiques Intrinsiques*. Paris, France: Topolgie En Extension.

Volosinov, V. 1986. *Marxism and the Philosophy of Language*. Cambridge, Mass.: Harvard University Press.

Williams, J. 1991. "Deconstructing Gender." Pp. 95-123 in K. Barlett and R. Kennedy (eds.) *Feminist Legal Theory*. Oxford: Westview Press.

Williams, R. 1987. "Taking Rights Aggressively: The Perils and Promise of Critical Legal Theory for Peoples of Color." *Law and Inequality* 5: 103.

Whorf, B. 1956. *Language, Thought, and Reality*. J. Carrol (ed.). New York: John Wiley and Sons.

Young, T.R. 1991a. "Chaos and Crime: Nonlinear and Fractal Forms of Crime." *Critical Criminologist* 3(4): 3-4, 10-11.

– 1991b. "Change and Chaos Theory." *Social Science* 28(3).

– 1992. "Chaos Theory and Human Agency: Humanist Sociology in a Postmodern Era." *Humanity and Society* 16(4): 441-60.

– 11/29/94. Personal correspondence.

Zavarzadeh, M. and D. Morton. 1990. "Signs of Knowledge in the Contemporary Academy." *American Journal of Semiotics* 7(4): 149-60.

Enduring Individual Differences and Rational Choice Theories of Crime

Daniel S. Nagin   Raymond Paternoster

In explaining crime, some criminological theories emphasize time-stable individual differences in propensity to offend while others emphasize more proximate and situational factors. Using scenario data from a sample of college undergraduates we have found evidence to support both positions. A measure of criminal propensity (poor self-control) was found to be significantly related to self-reported decisions to commit three offenses (drunk driving, theft, and sexual assault). Even after considering differences in self-control, there was evidence to suggest that the attractiveness of the crime target, the ease of committing the crime with minimum risk, and perceptions of the costs and benefits of committing the crime were all significantly related to offending decisions. Our results suggest that theories of criminal offending should include notions pertaining to persistent individual differences in criminal propensity and choice-relevant variables.

Criminological theory has developed along two separate and distinct tracks. Theorists along one track have argued that time-stable individual differences distinguish offenders from nonoffenders. Such criminological theories have attributed crime to enduring individual characteristics like "willful antisocial proclivities" (Goring 1913:370), feeblemindedness (Goddard 1911), emotional instability (Abrahamsen 1960), physical and mental deficiency (Hooton 1939), and antisocial personality (Gough 1968). In one form or another such theories constitute "types of person" theories. While differing somewhat in their exact nomenclature, the theories share the common theme of explaining the distribution of criminal offending with reference to stable individual differences in something like "criminal disposition" or "criminal propensity."

The second track of criminological theory rejects the assumption that offenders dramatically differ from nonoffenders in terms of some time-stable personal characteristic. Instead, these theories attribute crime to circumstances and situations

This research was supported by the National Science Foundation under grant numbers SES-9122403 and SES-9023109. Address correspondence to Daniel S. Nagin, The Heinz School, Carnegie Mellon University, 5000 Forbes Ave.—HbH 2105, Pittsburgh, PA 15213.

Law & Society Review, Volume 27, Number 3 (1993)

in the social setting that are external and proximate to the offender. The early classical school of criminology, for example, attributed crime to the nexus of costs and benefits of offending. Economic theories of crime (Becker 1967) have elaborated this line of argument, and early social control/social learning theories brought nonlegal costs and benefits explicitly into considerations of the causes of crime (Toby 1957; Briar & Piliavin 1965; Reckless 1967; Hirschi 1969; Akers 1973).

On the surface, recent developments in criminological theory appear to sustain this trend of two separate theoretical tracks. The work of routine activities and lifestyle theorists such as Hindelang (Hindelang et al. 1978), Cohen & Felson (Cohen & Felson 1979; Cohen et al. 1980, 1981; Cohen & Land 1987; Maxfield 1987) and of rational choice theorists (Piliavin et al. 1986; Cornish & Clarke 1986; Clarke & Cornish 1985) focus on the role of situational factors and the perceived costs and benefits of crime as determinants of target selection and more broadly of the decision whether to offend. In contrast, work by Wilson and Herrnstein (1985) and Gottfredson and Hirschi (1991) continues the tradition of attributing persistent criminal offending to enduring differences in criminal propensity among persons; their work, however, radically departs from early "type of person" theories. While underappreciated, both sets of authors also incorporate key assumptions of rational choice theories.

We report here on an empirical study that combines considerations of stable criminal propensity with concepts that are central to utilitarian and social control theories of crime—the perceived costs and benefits of crime and the objective characteristics of an offending opportunity. We find substantial evidence that "lack of self-control," the central construct of the Gottfredson-Hirschi theory and implicitly of the Wilson-Herrnstein theory has a positive and highly significant association with intentions to commit several different types of crime. We also find that the perceived benefits and costs of crime have a comparably large impact on intentions. The latter finding supports the arguments of Sampson and Laub (1990, 1992, 1993) that the strength of social bonds materially influences propensity to engage in crime independent of enduring individual differences associated with life course antisocial behavior.

Contemporary Theories of Offending as a Reflection of Individual Differences and Rational Choice

Rational Choice Theories

At least two recent theoretical developments in criminology, routine activity/life style, and rational choice theories ignore or attach relatively little importance to notions of enduring individual differences in criminal propensity.[1] Routine activities/lifestyle theories (Hindelang et al. 1978; Cohen & Felson 1979; Cohen et al. 1980, 1981; Cohen & Land 1987; Maxfield 1987) are not theories of offending per se; rather they are theories of victimization risk. Notwithstanding, they have obvious implications for theories of offending (Hough 1987; Riley 1987; Tuck & Riley 1986). These theories, which presume a supply of motivated offenders, examine the effect of situational obstacles and attractions on their target selection. As such, routine activity/lifestyle theories focus on situational characteristics that vary across offense opportunities not offenders.[2]

The rational choice perspective shares the routine activity/lifestyle theory focus on situational inducements and impediments to offending but also places at least as much emphasis on would-be offenders' subjective estimates of expected rewards and costs (Cornish & Clarke 1986, 1987). From the rational choice perspective, costs and benefits of crime are not enduring characteristics of persons but vary from one potential crime situation to another, and comprise what Cornish and Clarke (1987:935) describe as the "choice-structuring properties" of offenses.

In sum, what is common to both the routine activities and rational choice theories is an inattention, in both the theoretical and empirical literature, to the possibility that persons may differ with respect to their initial propensity to offend. Theoretical writings provide virtually no discussion of time-stable individual variation in the motivation to offend, and empirical models fail to incorporate criminal propensity as one of their exogenous variables.[3]

Theories of Enduring Individual Differences

Early in their influential text, Wilson and Herrnstein (1985:25) make clear that the central theme of their theory of crime and human nature is enduring individual differences in

[1] Considerations of expected utility and rational choice have a long tradition in deterrence theory (see the articles in Cornish & Clarke 1986; Piliavin et al. 1986; Paternoster 1989; Grasmick & Bursik 1990). When referring to rational choice theory, then, we mean rational choice/deterrence theory.

[2] Another situational factor that affects criminal offending is the exposure of the crime target. Felson & Cohen 1981 define exposure as the accessibility or availability of potential victims to potential offenders. In our hypothetical scenarios, described below, the crime target and offender are brought together, making exposure nonproblematic. For this reason, we focus on what Cohen and Felson refer to as target attractiveness and guardianship.

[3] In fairness to routine activities/lifestyle theorists, the issue of enduring differences among would-be offenders is of only tangential relevance to the objective of their theories—explaining victimization. Our point, however, is that if such theories are recast as theories of target selection, the issue of enduring individual differences in criminal propensity is no longer tangential.

criminal propensity: "one can supply an explanation of criminality—and more important, of law abidingness—that begins with the individual *in, or even before, infancy*" (emphasis added). Quoting approvingly an earlier article by Gottfredson and Hirschi, Wilson and Herrnstein (p. 23) define criminality as reflecting "stable differences across individuals in the propensity to commit criminal (or equivalent) acts."

At the core of Wilson and Herrnstein's conception of criminal propensity is the idea that offenders possess certain enduring personality traits that include defiance, hostility, a weak conscience, and, in particular, an inability to plan for the future or defer gratification (impulsiveness). Wilson and Herrnstein further hypothesize that these characteristics, together with other equally stable individual characteristics such as low intelligence, incline persons to commit not only criminal offenses but a wide variety of legal but reckless behaviors—promiscuous sexual behavior, abuse of alcohol, job instability, and so on.

In *A General Theory of Crime* (1990), Gottfredson and Hirschi adopt a very comparable theory of individual differences in criminal propensity. The central theoretical concept in the Gottfredson-Hirschi scheme is self-control, the elements of which include (pp. 89–90) an inability to defer gratification, self-centeredness, a preference for risk taking, and little interest in long-term planning. Like Wilson and Herrnstein, Gottfredson and Hirschi argue that persons who lack self-control are likely to engage in both crime and legal but imprudent behaviors. Also, like Wilson and Herrnstein, Gottfredson and Hirschi are explicit in their belief that self-control is a time-stable personal attribute established early in life.

In summary, the recent work of both Wilson and Herrnstein and Gottfredson and Hirschi continues the track of criminological theory that emphasizes the influential role of time-stable individual differences in shaping population variation in offending through the life course. But neither of these two theories argues that persons who, in the parlance of Gottfredson and Hirschi, lack self-control are wholly unresponsive to incentives or devoid of a capacity to reason. Quite to the contrary; both theories treat individuals as rational decisionmakers who respond to perceived incentives. The Wilson-Herrnstein theory takes as given the central tenet of reinforcement theory—the influential role of rewards and penalties in shaping behavior. The Gottfredson-Hirschi theory adopts the key premise of routine activity theory—crime is the product of a motivated offender encountering an attractive opportunity. Gottfredson and Hirschi provide a theory of the "motivated" offender. Thus, neither theory argues that individuals who lack self-control are unresponsive to incentives or respond to different incentives than do individuals with greater levels of self-control.

The Role of Incentives

We raise the issue of rational choice in the Wilson-Herrnstein and Gottfredson-Hirschi theories because if incentives of the immediate situation are choice relevant, why are not other variables in the rational choice framework such as risk of damaged social bonds? Neither set of authors directly addresses this question, but their theories suggest at least two explanations of the limited impact of social bonds.

One is advanced by Hirschi (1986) in an article that anticipates some key aspects of the Gottfredson-Hirschi theory. He argues that individuals who commit crimes attend principally to the incentives of the moment and greatly discount uncertain and delayed consequences. Among these consequences are the threat of formal and informal forms of social censure. The threat of damaged social bonds is an ineffective deterrent not because social consequences are irrelevant per se but because offenders are so present oriented that the social censure that may ensue from crime receives little weight in their decision calculus.

For several reasons this present orientation argument is not persuasive. Both the Wilson-Herrnstein and Gottfredson-Hirschi theories share the premise that differences between persons who do and do not commit crimes are ones of degree, not kind. All individuals to some degree discount future consequences; individuals who engage in crime are just (on average) especially present oriented. They are not, however, incapable of foresight. If potential offenders (individuals with low self-control) are responsive to situational incentives affecting apprehension risk, it logically follows that they should to some degree be responsive to formal or informal forms of social control.

Now it may be the case that the *average* offender is so oriented to the present that as a practical matter future consequences have only a *de minimus* impact on their decision calculus. Even if this were the case, it does not follow that the *marginal* offender is completely indifferent to future consequences. The marginal offender is one who is on the boundary or margins of offending, neither strongly committed to crime nor unwaveringly conformist. In fact, the logic of the Gottfredson-Hirschi and Wilson-Herrnstein theories implies that the marginal offender will be more responsive to future consequences.

Both the Gottfredson-Hirschi and Wilson-Herrnstein theories posit a population distribution of self-control or its equivalent, with those persons most lacking in self-control being most crime prone. Thus, the average offender will be more lacking in self-control (and more present oriented) than the

marginal offender. Further, because the distribution of offending in the population is highly skewed, the distribution of self-
control must itself be comparably skewed. The skewed distribution of self-control implies that differences between the marginal offender and average offender may be especially large.
Stated differently, concluding from the behavior of the average
offender that future consequences have no material impact on
the decision to offend suffers from the same flaw as concluding
from the testimony of the average prisoner that the threat of
prison is not a deterrent.

A second and more substantial argument is that the
strength of social bonds are themselves determined by self-
control and have no *independent* influence on offending behavior. Weak social bonds are thus not a cause of crime but just
another manifestation of low self-control. Both Gottfredson
and Hirschi and Wilson and Herrnstein argue that the time-
stable attributes that give rise to a greater propensity to commit
crimes are also manifested in an inability to establish enduring
relationships and hold steady employment.

Space does not permit a lengthy response to this fundamental challenge, but we attempt a brief exposition of our argument. In an ongoing stream of research, Sampson and Laub
(1990, 1992, 1993) have attempted to reconcile three empirical
regularities: (1) individuals who do not display troublesome behaviors (e.g., fighting, defiance, impulsivity) as children rarely
become chronic offenders as adults, (2) virtually all chronic offenders displayed troublesome behaviors as children, but (3)
most individuals who were troublesome children do not become chronic offenders. Thus, most children who display tem-
peraments and behaviors that are the hallmarks of individuals
who become chronic offenders as adults do not themselves pursue careers of crime; something deflected their trajectory from
chronic antisocial behavior.

Sampson and Laub argue that this something is strong social bonds. They do not argue that enduring individual differences in predisposition to commit crime have no impact on the
development of social bonds, but they do argue that such individual differences are not the sole or necessarily even the most
important determinant of individual differences in the strength
of the social bond.

In a nutshell, our argument is twofold. First, we see no fundamental incompatibility between the theories of Wilson and
Herrnstein and Gottfredson and Hirschi that emphasize enduring individual differences and the rational choice, routine activities, and social control perspectives. Our argument is an extension of Hirschi's (1986) own position on the compatibility of
social control, routine activities, and rational choice theories.
Second, we share the view of Sampson and Laub that factors

310

emphasized in rational choice and social control theories are not necessarily of secondary importance compared to enduring individual differences in explaining criminal behavior.

In the analysis that follows, we provide an empirical test of a model that includes considerations of persistent individual differences in criminal offending, the situational elements of target vulnerability and attractiveness, and external and internal social control variables.

Methods

The Scenario Method

Data were assembled using a survey that presents respondents with a scenario describing in detail the conditions under which a crime is committed. Selected scenario conditions (described below) were experimentally varied across persons. Respondents were asked to estimate the probability that they would commit the act specified in the scenario, the chance that their commission of the offense would result in arrest and in exposure without arrest, and questions designed to measure their perceptions of the costs and benefits of committing the offense described in the scenario.[4] The survey also included a battery of questions to measure the extent of respondents' self-control.

The scenario method differs from conventional data collection approaches in perceptual deterrence research in only one important respect. Instead of using self-reports of one's own criminal involvement or alternatively self-reports of future criminal intentions as the response variable, the scenario method uses offending scenarios to elicit the response variable.

The principal weakness of this approach is that an expressed intention to offend is not synonymous with actual performance. Fishbein and Ajzen (1975:368–81), however, argue that under appropriate conditions, "there should be a high relation between a person's intention to perform a particular behavior and his actual performance of that behavior." They specify those conditions as (1) the degree to which the intention to behave is measured with the same specificity as the behavior that is being predicted, (2) the stability of the expressed

---

4 The strategy of using respondents' self-reported intention to offend, as opposed to self-reports of actual behavior, has been used successfully in much recent deterrence research (Grasmick et al. 1984; Tittle 1980; Murray & Erickson 1987; Klepper & Nagin, 1989a, 1989b; Bachman et al. 1992). Of these cited studies, however, only Klepper and Nagin and Bachman et al. use the scenario method as described below.

The use of behavioral intentions also has a rich and productive history in psychology (see Fishbein & Ajzen 1975). For example, elicitation of projected behavior has been extensively used by scholars of decisionmaking under uncertainty (Kahneman et al. 1982; Nisbett & Ross 1980).

intention, and (3) the degree to which the individual is able to willfully carry out the intention.

With these three criteria in mind we have attempted to construct the scenarios to maximize the correspondence between intention and actual behavior. Intentions to offend are measured under very specific conditions. Given the specificity of the scenarios and the fact that they involve situations that are not foreign to our respondents, there is no compelling reason to suspect instability in the expressed intentions. Finally, the behaviors in question are under the general volitional control of the respondents, and we measure the important impediments to behavior (e.g., moral inhibitions, social attachments, perceived opportunity).

Notwithstanding our efforts to maximize the link between intention and actual behavior, we acknowledge that this link is still problematic. In our judgment, however, certain advantages of the scenario method outweigh this weakness. These strengths stem from the specificity of the scenarios. First, it allows us to examine the effect of situational factors on intentions to offend and on perceptions of risks and rewards. Second, absent specificity about circumstances, respondents must necessarily impute their own. Imputed circumstances will undoubtedly vary across respondents and affect their responses to many variables of interest such as estimates of the risk of arrest and the social consequences of arrest. Third, for some offenses such as sexual assault, perceptions of what constitutes a breach of the legal prohibition will vary, perhaps considerably, across people. If differences in definition vary systematically with variables of interest (e.g., consequences of arrest or exposure), analyses relating self-reported offending to such variables may seriously misrepresent the relationship of the variables to actual behavior. Fourth, in both cross-sectional and panel studies using self-reports, questionable assumptions must be made about the appropriate lag interval between exogenous and endogenous (criminal offending) variables (Klepper & Nagin 1989a, 1989b; Grasmick & Bursik 1990). With scenario data, however, we are able to estimate what Grasmick and Bursik refer to as an "instantaneous" relationship between independent variables and self-reported intentions to offend.

The scenario methodology is a hybrid. It combines the use of hypothetical scenarios that provide respondents with a specific and detailed offense situation with traditional survey questions. We believe this hybrid approach is superior to past data collection methods used in perceptual deterrence research. The scenarios allow us to provide a specific situation to serve as a reference point for our inquiry into the perceived costs and benefits of the criminal behavior. Unlike traditional vignette research in this area (Rossi & Anderson 1981), we do not specify

312

beforehand the values of the risks and rewards but instead specify the circumstances of the offense and ask respondents to estimate their own values.

Sample

Respondents were undergraduates at the University of Maryland enrolled in several large introductory criminology and criminal justice courses. A total of 399 males and 300 females completed the questionnaire. Participation was voluntary but nobody refused to complete the survey.[5]

There has been a good deal of criticism of the use of convenience student samples in deterrence research (Jensen et al. 1978; Williams & Hawkins 1986). One of the major objections raised about such samples concerns their representativeness. While we acknowledge some element of truth to these criticisms, there are two reasons why we believe they pose less compelling arguments for the purposes of this study.

First, it should be understood that a sample of respondents from a large public university is likely to contain a moderate number of offenders, particularly for the kinds of offenses whose intentions to commit we are gauging (theft, drinking and driving, sexual assault). For example, from December 1991 to November 1992 the University of Maryland Police Department received 1,252 reports of theft. A spokesperson for the campus police relayed that the "overwhelming" proportion of these offenses involved student offenders. Although the number of thefts is small relative to the size of the university, this is the number of *reported* thefts. Alcohol use and drunk driving is undoubtedly even more pervasive. While campus police made only 19 arrests for drunk driving during the 1991–92 period, this official statistic vastly underestimates the prevalence of student drinking and driving. A survey of 1,287 University of Maryland students conducted in 1991 (Kuhn 1992) revealed

---

5 The respondents ranged in age from 17 to 32 with the mean and median age being about 20. About equal proportions of respondents were in their freshman, sophomore, junior, and senior years.

It might be argued that there may be some bias in our selection of introductory criminology courses since criminology students may respond to crime scenarios differently, and they may have some knowledge of deterrence from their course work. There are a number of reasons allaying our own concerns about this. First, according to the instructors' registration roles, fewer than 50% of the students enrolled in these classes were criminology majors. These criminology courses meet general university requirements for a social science course. As a result, about half of our respondents came from majors throughout the university (engineering, business, humanities, mathematics). Second, these were introductory courses with no prerequisite but were prerequisites for other, advanced criminology courses. It is quite unlikely, therefore, that any student had previously taken a criminology course before. Third, questionnaires were administered during the first week of classes before any lectures. There was no opportunity, therefore, for students to learn about deterrence or the criminal justice system. Fourth, class standing was unrelated to any of the outcome variables.

that almost one-half were regular users of alcohol and 45% of these reported drinking four or more drinks at a time. Of the drinking students, almost one-half reported vomiting, 30% reported experiencing memory loss, and over half reported driving within an hour after consuming their last drink.[6] Although the number of complaints to the police for sexual assault was low (fewer than 10 in a year), all campus officials indicated that this number grossly underestimates the number of actual sexual assaults occurring on campus. One rape counselor affiliated with the university but not the police reported to one of the authors that she had counseled about 20 victims of sexual assault in the past semester alone.[7] This is consistent with survey research in this area. Kanin and Parcell (1977) reported that nearly one-half of university women were victims of some form of unwanted sexual contact. In a recent survey involving 32 colleges and universities, Koss and her colleagues found that about one-third of university women were the victims of sexual aggression and this victimization most often came at the hands of a fellow student (Koss 1983; Koss & Oros 1982; Koss et al. 1987; see also Bourque 1989; Sanday 1990; Ward et al. 1991; Warshaw & Koss 1988). Collectively, this information leads to the conclusion that college students are frequent offenders in situations involving theft, drunk driving, and sexual assault.

Second, the kinds of research questions we are interested in ideally call for samples with a large proportion of marginal offenders. These marginal offenders are not persons whose self-control is so low that they would be unaffected by the delayed consequences of crime. For these more marginal offenders the commission of an offense is a matter of calculation and deliberation in which delayed consequences are of greater importance. Crime is neither precluded by strong compunctions nor is it compelled by strong motivation. This reason too makes a college sample particularly attractive.

Scenario Design

Respondents were presented with three scenarios, each involving a different offense: drunk driving, larceny, and sexual assault (males only). All were framed in settings familiar to our college student respondents.

---

[6] Further, a Bureau of Justice Statistics Report (Cohen 1992) reveals that the rate of arrest for driving while under the influence (DUI) is highest for those between the ages of 21 and 24. Those in the 18–20 age range had the second highest arrest rate for DUI. The college years (18–24), then, are a prime time for driving while drunk.

[7] The survey of Maryland students revealed that in a 12-month period nearly 10% of the sample reported being taken advantage of sexually while they had been drinking and an additional 10% reported that they had taken sexual advantage of another while drinking.

The following is an example scenario for the offense of drinking and driving:

> It's about two o'clock in the morning and George has spent most of Thursday night drinking with his friends at the "Vous" [a popular campus drinking spot]. He decides to leave the Vous and go home to his off-campus apartment which is about 10 miles away. George has had a great deal to drink. He feels drunk and wonders if he may be over the legal limit and that perhaps he should not drive himself home. To get home he knows that he must drive down Route 1 [a busy artery]. He also knows that his roommate is home and would be able to take him back to pick up his car the next day. He remembers hearing about a state police crackdown on drunk driving. George decides to drive himself home.

Comparable scenarios were created for theft and sexual assault. An example of each is provided in Appendix A. For female students scenario characters were women; otherwise the scenarios were identical across genders.

The scenarios were extensively pretested and reworked to insure their credibility with apparently good success. Across scenario types, from 95% to 99% of respondents reported that the vignette was "believable and realistic."

Measurement of Variables

Separate models were estimated for each scenario crime type. The dependent variable is the respondent's estimate of the probability they would do what the scenario character did. Responses were measured on a scale from 0 (no chance at all) to 10 (100% chance).

We next describe the independent variables included in the model:

Lack of Self-Control

Wilson and Herrnstein and Gottfredson and Hirschi are in general agreement on the distinguishing characteristics of chronic offenders. To be sure, they pointedly disagree on the cause of relevant individual differences, but this fundamental disagreement is not relevant for our purposes.[8] We thus use the label "lack of self-control" to reference the common cluster of personal characteristics that both sets of authors agree predispose individuals to crime.

In their discussion of the concept, Gottfredson and Hirschi (1990:89–90) provide a generally detailed description of the elements of self-control. Persons low in self-control have a

---

[8] Gottfredson and Hirschi argue that relevant individual differences are principally the result of early child-rearing practice, whereas Wilson and Herrnstein argue that the differences have a substantial constitutional, possibly genetic, basis.

315

"concrete 'here and now' orientation" (impulsiveness), "lack diligence, tenacity, or persistence in a course of action" (desire for simple tasks), are "adventuresome, active, and physical" (preference for both risk and physical activity), are "indifferent, or insensitive to the suffering and needs of others" (self-centered), and "tend to have minimal tolerance for frustration and little ability to respond to conflict through verbal rather than physical means" (quick temper).

Our measure of self-control comes from a 24-item instrument devised by Grasmick et al. (1993). This instrument is intended to measure the six elements of self-control discussed above; impulsiveness, desire for simple tasks, risk preference, preference for physical activity, self-centeredness, and temper. A composite measure of self-control was created by summing the responses across the 24 items (see Appendix B). High scores on the scale are indicative of low self-control.

Although the instrument measures six different elements or dimensions of self-control, the construct was intended to be unidimensional. In their original paper, Grasmick et al. conducted a series of factor analyses to examine its measurement properties and concluded that the 24 items do reasonably conform to a unidimensional scale. Factor analyses of our own data virtually duplicate Grasmick et al.'s results.[9]

Criminal Opportunity and Situational Factors

Routine activities and rational choice theory both suggest that persons are more likely to offend when the intended target is more accessible, vulnerable, and attractive. To examine the impact of objective features of the crime opportunity on intentions, scenario conditions were randomly varied across respondents.[10]

---

[9] A principal-components factor analysis extracted 6 factors from the 24 items, corresponding to the 6 dimensions. The first factor extracted, however, had an eigenvalue of 4.97 and explained 21% of the variance among the items. The eigenvalues of the other 5 factors were much smaller (2.49 for the second factor, 1.21 for the sixth), as was the amount of variance explained by each (10% for the second, 5% for the sixth). Following the Scree Test (Nunnally 1967), the greatest break between consecutive eigenvalues was between the first and second factor extracted, suggesting the appropriateness of a one-factor model. The factor loadings from this analysis were very comparable to those reported by Grasmick et al. (1993), as was the scale's reliability (Cronbach's alpha=.83).

We acknowledge that some might view the results of the factor analysis as suggesting that the self-control scale is multidimensional. Our purpose here, however, is not to untie the different dimensions of self-control, so the issue of the uni- or multidimensionality of self-control is not central to our work. We do believe, however, that we have found plausible evidence for the unidimensionality of the 24 items, and have, therefore, constructed a composite scale. Additional research on the psychometric properties of this scale and the utility of other self-control scales is needed.

[10] In deciding which conditions to manipulate, we were influenced by focus group sessions conducted at the University of Maryland. Undergraduate students from upper-level criminology and criminal justice courses were solicited to take part in these groups. Students were provided with a pretest version of each of the three scenarios

For example, in the drinking and driving scenario, four specific conditions were manipulated: (1) the distance traveled between the bar and George's home (ten miles or one mile), (2) the type of road George had to travel to get home (heavily traveled and patrolled Route 1 or back roads), (3) the inconvenience to George of returning to retrieve his car at the bar the next day (George's roommate was home and could take him or he had to catch a bus or walk), and (4) the vigilance of law enforcement (there was reduced surveillance because of state police budget cutbacks or a state police "crackdown" on drinking and driving).[11] Both routine activities and rational choice theory predict that these conditions would affect intentions either directly (e.g., convenience) or indirectly via risk perceptions (e.g., law enforcement vigilance). Table 1 reports the manipulated conditions for each of the three scenarios.

Perceived Utility—Costs and Benefits

Rational choice theorists have argued that the decision to commit an offense is negatively related to the perceived costs of crime and positively related to the perceived rewards of crime. We measured both dimensions of subjective utility in this research.

Our index of the perceived costs is constructed to capture theoretical arguments advanced by Williams and Hawkins (1986). Based on an appeal to ideas central to social control theory, they argue that such costs are triggered by others "discovering" the deviant behavior. Such discovery can result from arrest but can also occur even if the individual is not arrested. The offender may be exposed without arrest if the victim reports it to others but not to the police or if the offense is observed by others but not reported to the police. Respondents were thus asked to estimate the chances of arrest (p_a: discovery by arrest) and the chances of exposure without arrest (p_e: discovery by exposure).

To measure perceptions of the consequences of discovery by arrest and by exposure through informal social networks, respondents were asked to estimate the conditional probability that discovery by each of these two mechanisms would result in dismissal from the university ($p_{d/a}$, $p_{d/e}$), lost respect of close friends ($p_{fr/a}$, $p_{fr/e}$), lost respect of family ($p_{fa/a}$, $p_{fa/e}$), and diminished job prospects ($p_{j/a}$, $p_{j/e}$). Each of these conditional probabilities measures the risk conditional on discovery of

and were asked to talk about how realistic each was, and what factors would influence their decision to commit the offense. The results from these focus group discussions led us to select the particular situational elements contained in the scenarios and also influenced the design of the base scenario.

11 The reduced surveillance condition was not contrived; due to state budget problems, such cutbacks were in fact occurring at the time the survey was administered.

Table 1. Manipulated Scenario Conditions

Theft

1. How busy the room is:
   A. Lots of people are up and about
   B. Things are pretty quiet
2. Attractiveness of the victim:
   A. Bill does not recognize who is showering
   B. Rod is showering, Bill does not know him well
   C. Rod is showering, Bill thinks Rod is obnoxious
3. Amount of money stolen:
   A. $20
   B. $60

Drinking and driving

1. Distance to travel home:
   A. 10 miles
   B. 1 mile
2. Route traveled home:
   A. Down Route 1
   B. Mostly back roads
3. How to get the car the next day:
   A. Roommate is home and would take him
   B. Would have to take a bus or walk
4. State police activity:
   A. State police crackdown
   B. Cutbacks in state police patrols

Sexual assault

1. Prior relationship:
   A. Met for the first time
   B. Had been dating for several months
2. Drinking:
   A. Neither is drunk
   B. Both are quite drunk
3. Who the woman lives with:
   A. With roommates
   B. Lives alone
4. Kissing and fondling:
   A. She tells him to stop immediately
   B. She allows it for several minutes

either damaged attachments (i.e., relationships with significant others) or commitments (i.e, occupational prospects). As such, they measure risks of various types of informal sanctions. To measure perceived risk of formal sanctions, respondents were also asked to estimate the risk of jail $(p_{ja/a})$ and of losing their driver's license $(p_{1/a})$,[12] each contingent upon arrest.

Measures of the risk of the specified sanctions were created by multiplying each of these conditional probabilities by the

---

[12] This measure was only included in the drinking and driving analysis.

risk of the appropriate conditioning discovery event, arrest or exposure without arrest, and then additively combining them. For example, the perceived certainty of family disapproval was calculated by $p_{fa/e}\,p_e + p_{fa/a}\,p_a$. The first and second terms in this sum measure the risk of parental disapproval resulting, respectively, from exposure without arrest and from arrest; their sum measures the *ex ante* risk of parental disapproval if the offense is committed.

Even highly certain sanctions cannot be expected to affect decisions to offend unless they are also perceived to entail some cost (Andenaes 1974; Bailey & Lott 1975; Grasmick & Bryjak 1980; Grasmick & Bursik 1990). Thus, we asked respondents to estimate the perceived severity of each sanction. Using a measure much like one Grasmick and colleagues employed in their research, we asked each person to estimate "how much of a problem" each sanction would pose for them. Response options ranged on an 11-point continuum from "no problem at all" (coded 0) to "a very big problem" (coded 10). To create a sanction measure that reflected both the risk and cost of perceived punishment, we multiplied each certainty measure by its corresponding severity component.

In this research we are less interested in disentangling the independent effects of these different types of punishment than we are in considering the more general role of sanction threats themselves.[13] For this reason, a composite measure *total sanctions* was created by summing responses across each of the individual sanction threat items.[14]

In addition to the fear of externally imposed sanctions, tests of the rational choice perspective have recently included considerations of internally imposed punishments (Williams & Hawkins 1986; Grasmick & Bursik 1990; Grasmick et al. 1993). Grasmick and Bursik (1990) argue that persons who have internalized a moral prohibition against a particular deviant act contemplate the possibility and cost of guilt or shame for doing that act. These feelings of guilt—the "pangs of conscience" (Braithwaite 1989:74)—are experienced as "painful emotions" (Scheff 1988:396) and constitute another cost of crime.[15]

---

[13] Also, the large (positive) correlations across the specific types of sanctions generally makes it impossible to disentangle their independent effects.

[14] The index of total sanctions (TS) was created by the following composite index:

$$TS = P_e\,[(P_{d/e})\,(S_d) + (P_{fr/e})\,(S_{fr}) + (P_{fa/e})\,(S_{fa}) + (P_{j/e})\,(S_j)]$$
$$+ P_a\,[(P_{d/a})\,(S_d) + (P_{fr/a})\,(S_{fr}) + (P_{fa/a/})\,(S_{fa}) + (P_{j/a})(S_j)$$
$$+ (P_{l/a})\,(S_l) + (P_{ja/a})\,(S_a)],$$

where S_j is the perceived severity of sanction j and all other variables are as previously defined. The license revocation component was only included for drunk driving.

[15] Our definition of shame as a self-imposed punishment is comparable to Braithwaite's notion of conscience. Braithwaite's concept of shame or shaming consists of social expressions of disapproval and censure and is a component of our TS measure.

For these reasons, we included a measure of *shame* in the model that is constructed along the lines suggested by Grasmick and Bursik (1990). They argue that shame is a binary event; one either experiences it or not. Respondents were thus asked whether they would feel guilt or shame if they were discovered (either by arrest or exposure without arrest) committing the offense described in the scenario (yes/no). While the event of shame is assumed to be binary, the quantity or painfulness of the "pang" might very well vary across persons. To capture the intensity of guilt, respondents were asked to estimate how much of a problem guilt/shame would be for them if they were to commit the act in question. The shame index was constructed by multiplying the binary indicators of shame with the intensity of shame.

With a few exceptions (Carroll 1978; Tittle 1980; Scott & Grasmick 1981; Piliavin et al. 1986; Klepper & Nagin 1989a, 1989b), empirical tests of rational choice hypotheses have examined the cost but not the benefit dimension of offending. Available research generally finds that the perceived benefits of criminal offending are important considerations in would-be offenders' scheme of calculation and perhaps more important than the estimated costs (Carroll 1978; Piliavin et al. 1986). Any utility-based model of criminal offending that only includes the costs dimension is, thus, incompletely specified. A measure of the *perceived pleasure* of each scenario behavior was obtained by asking respondents to report "how much fun or a kick" it would be if they were to commit the offense under the scenario conditions. Response options varied on an 11-point continuum from 0 ("no fun or kick at all") to 10 ("a great deal of fun or kick").

In addition to the exogenous variables discussed above, two other variables were included in the model specification, *gender*[16] and *prior offending*[17] (number of times in the past year they had driven a car while drunk, stolen or shoplifted something, and used violence against another person for, respectively, the drunk driving, theft, and sexual assault model specifications).

---

[16] Since the sexual assault analysis involved only males, gender was excluded from this model. In the other models, gender is coded 0 for females and 1 for males.

[17] Stability in criminal offending over time may be due to persistent individual differences in some personality trait, such as self-control, or to some stable characteristic of a person's social environment, such as social class or neighborhood levels of crime. Our measure of self-control is designed to capture only the first of these reasons for persistent involvement in crime. Prior behavior is included to capture the influence of other sources of stable criminality. Nonetheless, prior offending may be viewed as still another indicator of lack of self-control. We note, however, that the results reported below are unaffected by the inclusion of prior offending in the specification. Thus, for the purposes of this study its interpretation is moot.

Analysis

The modal response category of the dependent variable was zero; 63% of the respondents reported that there was "no chance" that they would commit the specified theft, 33% reported "no chance" of drinking and driving under the scenario conditions, and 85% reported no chance of committing the specified sexual assault. Because the outcome variables are heavily censored at zero, the models were estimated using tobit regression. The results are reported in Table 2.

Consider first the coefficient estimates for self-control. In accord with the Gottfredson-Hirschi and Wilson-Herrnstein theories, for all three crime types lack of self-control has a direct, positive, and highly significant association with intentions to offend. Persons low in self-control are more likely to report that they would commit each offense (theft, drinking and driving, sexual assault) than those with greater self-control. This is true when other factors of the crime situation and the perceived costs and benefits are controlled. Consistent with these theories, then, self-control is related to diverse types of criminal offending. Our significant finding of a direct effect for self-control is consistent with the recent research of Grasmick and his colleagues (1993).[18]

Self-control is also indirectly related to intentions to offend in a way consistent with the Gottfredson-Hirschi and Wilson-Herrnstein theories. Two components of low self-control are a present orientation and a lack of regard for others. This would suggest that persons low in self-control would perceive a higher utility for crime since the rewards are immediate, would discount the costs since they are delayed, and would be insensitive to social censure. Wilson and Herrnstein's theory would further predict that those low in self-control would have less developed consciences, making self-censure less effective. To examine these expected effects, we regressed self-control on the measures of perceived utility, total sanctions, and shame. For each of the three offenses the results conformed to theoretical expectations. We found a significant positive relationship between self-control and perceived utility and significant inverse effects for self-control on both total sanctions and shame.[19] We have, then, clear evidence for several key hypotheses of the Gottfredson-Hirschi and Wilson-Herrnstein theo-

---

[18] Grasmick et al. (1993) tested an interactive model, examining among other things the interaction of self-control and criminal opportunity. They reported a main effect for self-control for offenses involving fraud but not for offenses involving force.

[19] This was true when self-control and a measure of prior offending were included in the model. The amount of variance explained in each case was not, however, substantial (less than 10%), suggesting that factors other than self-control are affecting these choice-relevant variables.

321

Table 2. Tobit Regression Coefficients, for Intentions to Commit Theft, Drinking and Driving, and Sexual Assault

Exogenous Variables	Theft		Drinking and Driving		Sexual Assault	
	b	(t)	b	(t)	b	(t)
Gender	.3967	(1.049)	−.6863	(−2.388)	b	
Prior behavior	2.2547	(5.637)	3.9375	(14.262)	.8292	(2.332)
Lack of self-control	.0807	(4.415)	.0570	(4.066)	.1126	(3.332)
Scenario conditions						
1st condition	.0547	(.147)	.1189	(.439)	−.1441	(−.226)
2d condition	.0890	(.688)	−.0108	(−.039)	.2582	(.407)
3d condition	.0594	(.173)	1.0053	(3.705)	−.3039	(−.486)
4th condition	a		.0401	(.148)	.8753	(1.391)
Total sanctions	−.0003	(−2.136)	−.0005	(−5.048)	−.0004	(−2.403)
Shame	−.0869	(−2.487)	−.0990	(−4.191)	−.0851	(−1.313)
Perceived utility	.6548	(7.960)	.4695	(5.646)	.3293	(2.990)
Constant	−6.223		−1.472		−9.296	
(n)	(643)		(661)		(365)	

a The theft scenario involved only three manipulated conditions (see Table 1).
b Only males are involved in this analysis.

ries. Persons low in self-control perceive the rewards of crime as more valuable and the costs of crime as less aversive, are less likely to feel the "pangs of conscience," and are more likely to report that they would commit crimes than those with more self-control.

Because the data are not longitudinal, however, we cannot test another important hypothesis, whether lack of self-control is time stable. Indirect evidence, however, suggests that it is. We regressed self-control on respondent self-reports of prior drunk driving, theft, and violence. In all three cases, the association was positive and highly significant, which indicates that current self-control is related to past behavior. We appreciate, of course, that this analysis does not resolve the issue of direction of causality, but the positive association is consistent with stability.

Both theories, as well as routine activity/rational choice theory, also predict that immediate characteristics of the criminal opportunity are choice relevant. Few of the manipulated scenario conditions had a significant direct effect on respondents' intentions to offend. None of the situational factors in the theft scenario were related to such intentions, and three out of four conditions in the drinking and driving and sexual assault scenarios were insignificant. For drinking and driving, only the inconvenience of the scenario character having to get his/her car the next day (condition 3) was related to the outcome variable; the association is positive as expected. For sexual assault, respondents receiving the scenario depicting some consensual sexual activity (the scenario female allowed the male to kiss and fondle her for a few minutes) reported higher intentions to commit the assault than respondents who received scenarios where there was no sexual activity prior to the assault (the female immediately told the male to stop kissing and fondling her).

While only limited evidence of scenario conditions having a direct effect on intentions was found, evidence of scenario conditions having an indirect effect via their impact on respondent perceptions of risks and benefits is more substantial. Regressions of scenario conditions on total sanctions, shame, and perceived pleasure reveal that several of these contextual factors did significantly affect respondents' perceptions of the costs and benefits of offending. For drinking and driving, sanction costs were significantly lower under the condition where the scenario character had a shorter distance to drive (1 vs. 10 miles, thereby reducing exposure time), could avoid surveillance by staying off heavily traveled streets ("back roads" vs. Route 1), and where the danger of detection by state police was lower (state police budget cutbacks vs. "crackdown" on drunk driving). The perceived reward of offending was also significantly higher under each of these conditions as well. For sexual assault, the likelihood of sanctions was perceived to be lower when both characters were described as being drunk and if the female lived alone. For theft, however, none of the scenario conditions were significantly related to total sanctions, shame, or perceived pleasure.

While the evidence of the objective crime circumstances directly affecting intention is less than compelling, evidence of perceived benefits and costs directly affecting intentions is very strong and in the theoretically expected direction: Perceived pleasure is positively related to intentions to offend and total sanctions and shame negatively related to intentions. With one exception, all such relationships are highly significant.[20] The findings of an inhibiting effect of external and internal control mechanisms, captured, respectively, by total sanctions and shame, is consistent with other recent deterrence and rational choice research (Klepper & Nagin 1989a, 1989b; Nagin & Paternoster 1991; Grasmick & Bursik 1990).

Further, the magnitudes of the associations of rewards and costs with intentions are quite large. Table 3 reports estimates of the percentage change in the dependent variable associated with a standard deviation increase in the specified independent

---

[20] The effect of shame on intentions to commit sexual assault was in the expected theoretical direction but not statistically significant ($t=-1.313$). It may be that shame had no effect on sexual assault because this offense only concerns males, and shame is more effective in inhibiting the conduct of females. Such was not the case, however. Separate analyses by gender were conducted on theft and drinking and driving. Shame had a significant inverse effect on intentions to drink and drive for females, but a nonsignificant effect for theft. For males, shame had a significant effect on both theft and drinking and driving.

variable holding all other independent variables in the model constant at their sample means.[21] A 1 standard deviation increase in total sanctions reduces intentions 17% for theft, 22% for drinking and driving, and 40% for sexual assault. The corresponding changes for shame are, respectively, −18%, −18%, and −20%. A 1 standard deviation increase in perceived pleasure increases intentions 67% for theft, 23% for drinking and driving, and 55% for sexual assault.[22] These changes are of comparable magnitude to those associated with self-control (39%, 17%, and 83%, respectively).

The lesson we deduce from Tables 2 and 3 is that while poor self-control plays a major role in explaining variation in intentions to offend, it is by no means the sole determinant of such intentions. Perceived risks and rewards play comparably important roles. In our judgment this is noteworthy because two of these variables, total sanctions and shame, are classical social control variables.[23] We interpret this evidence as indicating that independent of lack of self-control conventionally postulated mechanisms of social control are operating.

We acknowledge, however, that there are other interpreta-

[21] Unlike the coefficients of a least squares regression model, the coefficients of a tobit model cannot be directly used to compute magnitudes; the coefficient does not equal the change in the response variable associated with a 1-unit change in the coefficient's associated independent variable. The calculations reported in Table 3 were based on the following formula for computing the expected value of the response variable, $E(y)$, for given values of the exogenous variables, x:

$$E(y) = \phi(x\theta/\sigma) \; [x \; \theta + \sigma \; \Phi \; (x\theta/\sigma)/(1-\phi(x\theta/\sigma)],$$

where θ is a vector of estimated tobit coefficients, σ is the estimated standard deviation of the error term, ϵ, and $\phi(\bullet)$ and $\Phi(\bullet)$ are, respectively, the standardized cumulative normal distribution function and the standardized normal density function.

[22] The substantial association of perceived pleasure with intentions is not surprising, but we note that the two variables are not synonymous. In the rational choice framework, would-be offenders are assumed to balance the perceived benefits and costs of offending. Thus, a basic prediction of this framework is that an individual will not engage in a criminal act unless he or she perceives the act itself as producing benefits. To do otherwise would be irrational; the individual would risk punishment for no perceived gain. It does not follow, however, that just because the act is perceived as pleasurable the individual will necessarily commit it. If perceived risks outweigh perceived pleasures, the individual will be deterred.

[23] The model also includes two variables, prior offending and gender, that are not central to the investigation. They were merely included as "control" variables.

As expected, prior offending had a positive and significant association with intentions. Gottfredson and Hirschi argue that the positive association of past and future criminal involvement is a reflection of the time stability of lack of self-control. We note, however, that controlling for lack of self-control, prior behavior continues to have a highly significant positive relationship with intentions. While the magnitude of this association is mitigated modestly by the self-control index, it remains very large.

Our results concerning the gender effect are interesting and in some respects surprising. For both drunk driving and theft women reported significantly lower intentions of committing the act depicted in the scenario. However, with controls for other relevant variables the "male" effect in the larceny scenario, while positive, is statistically insignificant. Surprisingly, in the drunk-driving scenario, *ceteris paribus*, males were significantly *less* likely to drive while drunk than females. It is not clear what to make of this possible "female effect." It is very sensitive to model specification and becomes statistically insignificant if variables such as prior behavior or shame are deleted from the model.

Table 3. Expected Percentage in Offending

Scenario Type	% Change in Intentions
Theft:	
Self-control	39.3
Total sanctions	−17.4
Perceived pleasure	67.0
Shame	−17.9
Drinking and driving:	
Self-control	17.4
Total sanctions	−21.9
Perceived pleasure	23.2
Shame	−17.9
Sexual assault:	
Self-control	82.6
Total sanctions	−40.1
Perceived pleasure	55.5
Shame	−20.1

tions of the results. One is that responses to the survey items used to measure the social control variables may be a causal consequence of the intentions variable rather than the reverse. In an attempt to maintain internal consistency, respondents reporting a high (low) likelihood of engaging in the scenario act may have reported less (more) negative social repercussions. The fact that the randomly assigned scenario characteristics had little influence on reported intentions may give further credence to this interpretation.

While we cannot rule out this interpretation, we are skeptical of its plausibility. First, many of the experimental manipulations were designed to influence intentions indirectly through their impact on risk perceptions and subjective utility. As previously reported we did find more substantial evidence of scenario conditions affecting both these variables. Second, rank orderings of average responses across scenario crime types conform with research findings (Sellin & Wolfgang 1978; Rossi et al. 1974) that sexual assault is viewed as a more serious crime than drunk driving and larceny and that larceny, in turn, is a more serious crime than drunk driving. For example, the average reported likelihood of engaging in the scenario act is inversely related to crime seriousness and to virtually all of the social control measures. Such inverse associations across crime type could, of course, again be a reflection of the reverse-causality hypothesis, but in our judgment this interpretation strains credulity. Respondents would not only have to have the cognitive capacity to maintain internal consistency in their responses within crime type but also across crime type in a questionnaire of approximately 150 items.

A second interpretation of the results is that the seemingly

325

independent influence of the social control variables on intentions is an artifact of measurement error in the latent construct—lack of self-control. This interpretation harks back to our earlier discussion of the argument that strong social bonds are simply another manifestation of self-control and have no independent effect on the decision to offend. Because our index of self-control is an inexact measurement of the latent construct, the negative and significant associations of the social control variables with intentions are conceivably only a manifestation of the measurement error in self-control. Stated differently, the social control variables may be capturing the influence of that part of the latent construct, lack of self-control, that is not measured by our index of self-control.

We acknowledge that it is likely that to some extent the associations of the social control variables with intentions are inflated due to measurement error of the latent construct but we are skeptical that the associations are entirely or even predominately attributable to such error. Earlier we discussed the Sampson and Laub (1990, 1992, 1993) argument that social bonds affect criminal involvement independent of enduring personal characteristics related to lifelong patterns of antisocial behavior. They argue that events later in life, often fortuitous like meeting the "right" mate or employer, can and do have a pronounced impact on the strength of social bonds.

Our analysis here and findings reported in Nagin and Paternoster (1992) are consistent with the argument that self-control affects the strength of social bonds and the perceived pleasures of the criminal act. Variables such as total sanctions and shame are negatively and significantly related to lack of self-control and perceived utility is positively and significantly related. Notwithstanding, the associations only explain a small proportion of the variation in these choice relevant variables. This finding is consistent with Sampson and Laub's position. To be sure, this limited explanatory power may again be a reflection of large measurement error in our index of self-control. This interpretation, however, is inconsistent with the index's large and highly significant association with intentions. How, on one hand, can the index be a sufficiently reliable measurement of the latent construct to have a large and highly significant association with intentions but, on the other hand, be so poorly measured that other indicators of the latent construct are spuriously associated with intentions?

Discussion

We have examined the viability of two perspectives on criminal offending that have long traditions in criminology. One attributes crime to individual differences in criminal disposition that are established early in life, remain stable throughout the life course, and are related to a wide range of criminal and non-criminal but self-destructive behaviors. This tradition has recently been reasserted by Wilson and Herrnstein and Gottfredson and Hirschi. A second tradition sees crime as the result of proximate situational influences and the rewards and costs of offending. This branch of criminological thought has recently been advanced in the form of lifestyle/routine activities and rational choice perspectives. For the most part, these two traditions have worked apart from, if not in opposition to, one another.

Our research has found evidence in support of both traditions. Intentions to engage in three very distinctive offenses—drunk driving, theft, and sexual assault—are positively and very significantly related to lack of self-control. This relationship holds and remains sizable in magnitude even after prior behavior, situational characteristics of the offense, and the perceived rewards and costs of offending were controlled. We also found that self-control is indirectly related to intentions to offend through its influence on choice-relevant variables such as total sanctions, perceived utility, and shame. The findings support the conclusions of Nagin and Farrington (1992a, 1989b) and Sampson and Laub (1990, 1992, 1993) that criminological theory must include stable individual differences in propensity to offend as a central construct.

We also found substantial evidence in support of the tradition that attributes variations in criminal offending to variations in more proximate influences, such as the accessibility and vulnerability of the target and perceptions of the costs and pleasures of offending. While the analysis was not particularly successful in identifying many situational elements that directly affected would-be offenders' decisionmaking, it did reveal evidence of contextual factors indirectly affecting respondents' intentions to offend via perceptions of the risks and satisfactions of offending.

Consistent with recent research in deterrence and rational choice theory (Bursik & Grasmick 1990; Nagin & Paternoster 1991; Bachman et al. 1992), we found that perceptions of the certainty of formal and informal sanctions and self-imposed shame effectively controlled respondents' intentions to offend. Importantly, we also found that a variable often omitted from previous deterrence/rational' choice research—the perceived pleasure of offending—was significantly related to the expressed intention to offend. Moreover, the anticipated reward of offending generally had a greater impact on intentions than the perceived costs (Carroll 1978; Piliavin et al. 1986). As predicted by Gottfredson and Hirschi and by Wilson and Herrnstein, potential gains may be more important than potential losses to would-be offenders because the former are more immediate while the latter are both uncertain and in the future.

In the end, we do not 'believe that the two criminological traditions examined here should be viewed as competing explanations. Therefore, evidence in support of one theory should not be viewed as evidence in refutation of the other. Quite the contrary, we think that our empirical findings suggest that both must be included in a complete understanding of crime. We close by briefly outlining an approach to unify the two theoretical perspectives.

A belief that variation in offending is reflective of variations in criminal propensity or poor self-control does not preclude the possibility that would-be offenders are sensitive to the attractions and deterrents of crime. As already emphasized, neither Wilson and Herrnstein nor Gottfredson and Hirschi portray those with poor self-control as beings who are irrational or inexorably drawn to crime regardless of the quality of available criminal opportunities. Quite the opposite, in both theories people are presumed to respond to incentives in a way that does not fundamentally differ from the criminal actor portrayed in theories that emphasize more immediate and instrumental factors.

What is distinctive about those who are highly impulsive or with poor self-control, therefore, is not that they are unresponsive to incentives. Rather, because of their lack of self-control, such persons are less able to commit themselves to a line of conventional activity. A characteristic feature of Wilson and Herrnstein's and of Gottfredson and Hirschi's criminally predisposed persons is that they are excessively present oriented. Such persons require immediate gratification, are insensitive to others, and are unable to persevere in a planned course of action. Persons with low self-control, then, are unlikely to be able to establish long-term social relationships, persist in educational training, or commit themselves to a career. Stated differently, those with low self-control find it difficult to invest in conventionality because they discount future rewards in favor of immediate pleasures. Since they have fewer investments in the future, persons with low self-control have much less at risk than those with greater self-control. We believe that the reason persons with poor self-control commit crimes at a consistently higher rate than others is because they have less to lose.

In the language of labor economics, because of their present-orientation those with poor self-control have a high discount rate. Since they place less value on future consumption, they are unlikely to invest in a line of activity that sacrifices immediate for future gratification. Those with high discount rates, therefore, are less likely to invest in human capital—education, job training, or other activities that provide for future rather than current consumption. With less human capital accumulation than those with lower discount rates, those with poor self-control will have far less to lose by doing crime and fewer reasons to fear its consequences.

Rather than competing theories, then, we have found an important link between recent theories of time-stable criminal propensity and theories of criminal opportunity and rational choice. It is our intention to pursue this link in greater detail in subsequent research, and we encourage other researchers to do the same.

Appendix A. Scenarios

Sexual Assault Scenario

Susan and Josh have just returned to her apartment from a party. She and Josh have been dating each other for several months. Both of them had been drinking heavily at the party, and they are quite drunk. After they get to Susan's apartment, where she lives alone, they sit down on the couch and begin to listen to music. In a few moments Josh attempts to kiss and fondle Susan. She allows Josh to kiss and fondle her for several minutes. When Josh attempts to remove her clothes Susan says that she is not interested in having sex and tries to get off the couch. Josh then pins Susan to the couch so she cannot get up. He takes off her clothes and has sexual intercourse with her. Josh then leaves Susan's apartment.

Theft Scenario

Bill is a college sophmore and lives in the dorms. Bill wakes up and decides to take a shower. He goes to the shower room which consists of about a half dozen shower stalls and a separate changing room. It's about 8:00 A.M. on a Monday morning and a lot of people are up and about. He observes that three people are showering whom he does not recognize. As he starts to undress, Bill observes a $20 bill sticking out of the pocket of someone's jacket. He takes the $20 and leaves immediately.

Appendix B. Measures of Exogenous Variables

Self-Control

1. I devote time and effort to preparing for the future.
2. I act on the spur of the moment without stopping to think.
3. I do things that bring me pleasure here and now, even at the cost of some distant goal.
4. I base my decisions on what will happen to me in the short run rather than in the long run.
5. I try to avoid projects that I know will be difficult.
6. When things get complicated, I quit or withdraw.
7. I do the things in life which are easiest and bring me the most pleasure.
8. I avoid difficult tasks that stretch my abilities to the limit.
9. I test myself by doing things that are a little risky.
10. I take risks just for the fun of it.

11. I find it exciting to do things for which I might get in trouble.
12. Excitement and adventure are more important to me than security.
13. If I have a choice, I will do something physical rather than something mental.
14. I feel better when I am on the move than when I am sitting and thinking.
15. I'd rather get out and do things than read or contemplate ideas.
16. Compared to other people my age, I have a greater need for physical activity.
17. I look out for myself first, even if it means making things difficult for other people.
18. I'm not very sympathetic to other people when they are having problems.
19. I don't care if the things I do upset people.
20. I will try to get things I want even when I know it's causing problems for other people.
21. I lose my temper easily.
22. When I'm angry at people I feel more like hurting them than talking to them about why I am angry.
23. When I'm really angry, other people better stay away from me.
24. When I have a serious disagreement with someone, it's usually hard for me to talk calmly about it without getting upset.

Total Sanctions

Discovery Events

1. What is the chance you would be arrested by the police if you did what [the scenario character] did under these circumstances?
2. Suppose in fact you did what [the scenario character] did and *were not* arrested by the police. What is the chance that it would somehow become known that you had done this?

Consequences

1. What is the chance that you would be dismissed from the University of Maryland?
2. What is the chance that you would lose the respect and good opinion of your close friends?
3. What is the chance that you would lose the respect and good opinion of your parents and relatives?
4. What is the chance that you would jeopardize your job prospects?
5. What is the chance that you would go to jail?
6. What is the chance that you would lose your license?

Severity

1. How much of a problem would it create in your life if you were dismissed from the university for doing what [the scenario character] did?
2. How much of a problem would it create in your life if you lost the respect and good opinion of your close friends for doing what [the scenario character] did?
3. How much of a problem would it create in your life if you lost the respect and good opinion of your parents and relatives for doing what [the scenario character] did?
4. How much of a problem would it create in your life if you jeopardized you future job prospects for doing what [the scenario character] did?
5. How much of a problem would it create in your life if you lost your driver's license for doing what [the scenario character] did?

330

6. How much of a problem would it create in your life if you went to jail for doing what [the scenario character] did?

Shame

Discovery Events

1. What is the chance you would be arrested by the police if you did what [the scenario character] did under these circumstances?
2. Suppose in fact you did what [the scenario character] did and *were not* arrested by the police. What is the chance that it would somehow become known that you had done this?

Consequences

1. Would you feel a sense of guilt or shame if others knew that you had done this?
2. Would you feel a sense of guilt or shame if you were arrested for doing this?

Severity

1. How much of a problem would it create in your life if you felt a sense of shame and guilt for doing what [the scenario character] did?

Perceived Pleasure

1. How much fun or how much of a "kick" would it be for you if you did what [the scenario character] did under these circumstances?

References

Abrahamsen, David (1960) *The Psychology of Crime*. New York: Columbia Univ. Press.

Akers, Ronald L. (1973) *Deviant Behavior: A Social Learning Approach*. 2d ed. Belmont, CA: Wadsworth.

Andenaes, Johannes (1974) *Punishment and Deterrence*. Ann Arbor: Univ. of Michigan Press.

Bachman, Ronet, Raymond Paternoster, & Sally Ward (1992) "The Rationality of Sexual Offending: Testing a Deterrence/Rational Choice Conception of Sexual Assault," 26 *Law & Society Rev.* 401.

Bailey, William C., & Ruth P. Lott (1976) "Crime, Punishment and Personality: An Examination of the Deterrence Question," 67 *J. of Criminal Law & Criminology* 99.

Becker, Gary S. (1967) *Human Capital and the Personal Distribution of Income: An Analytical Approach*. Ann Arbor: Institute of Public Administration, Univ. of Michigan.

Bourque, Linda Brookover (1989) *Defining Rape*. Durham, NC: Duke Univ. Press.

Braithwaite, John (1989) *Crime, Shame and Reintegration*. New York: Cambridge Univ. Press.

Briar, Scott, & Irving Piliavin (1965) "Delinquency, Situational Inducements, and Commitments to Conformity," 13 *Social Problems* 516.

Carroll, John S. (1978) "A Psychological Approach to Deterrence: The Evaluation of Crime Opportunities," 36 *J. of Personality & Social Psychology* 1512.

Clarke, Ronald V., & Derek B. Cornish (1985) "Modeling Offenders' Decisions: A Framework for Research and Policy," in M. Tonry & N. Morris, eds., 6 *Crime and Justice: An Annual Review of Research*. Chicago: Univ. of Chicago Press.

Cohen, Lawrence E., and Marcus Felson (1979) "Social Change and Crime Rate Trends: A Routine Activity Approach," 44 *American Sociological Rev.* 588.

Cohen, Lawrence E., Marcus Felson, & Kenneth C. Land (1980) "Property Crime Rates in the United States: A Macrodynamic Analysis, 1947–1977, with Ex-Ante Forecasts for the Mid-1980's," 86 *American J. of Sociology* 90.

Cohen, Lawrence E., James R. Kluegel, & Kenneth C. Land (1981) "Social Inequality and Predatory Criminal Victimization: An Exposition and Test of a Formal Theory," 46 *American Sociological Rev.* 505.

Cohen, Lawrence E., & Kenneth C. Land (1987) "Age and Crime: Symmetry vs. Asymmetry, and the Projection of Crime Rates through the 1990's," 52 *American Sociological Rev.* 170.

Cohen, Robin L. (1992) "Drunk Driving." Washington, DC: Office of Justice Programs, Bureau of Justice Statistics, U.S. Department of Justice.

Cornish, Derek B., & Ronald V. Clarke, eds. (1986) *The Reasoning Criminal: Rational Choice Perspectives on Offending*. New York: Springer-Verlag.

——— (1987) "Understanding Crime Displacement: An Application of Rational Choice Theory," 25 *Criminology* 933.

Felson, Marcus, & Lawrence E. Cohen (1981) "Modeling Crime Trends: A Criminal Opportunity Perspective," 18 *J. of Research in Crime & Delinquency* 138.

Fishbein, Martin, & Icek Ajzen (1975) *Belief, Attitude, Intention, and Behavior*. Reading, MA: Addison-Wesley Publishing Co.

Goddard, Henry Herbert (1912) *The Kallikak Family: A Study in the Heredity of Feeblemindedness*. New York: Macmillan.

Goring, Charles (1913) *The English Convict: A Statistical Study*. London: HMSO.

Gottfredson, Michael R., & Travis Hirschi (1990) *A General Theory of Crime*. Stanford, CA: Stanford Univ. Press.

Gough, Harrison G. (1968) "An Interpreter's Syllabus for the California Psychological Inventory," in P. McReynolds, ed., 1 *Advances in Psychological Assessment.* Palo Alto, CA: Science & Behavior Books.

Grasmick, Harold G., & George J. Bryjak (1980) "The Deterrent Effect of Perceived Severity of Punishment," 59 *Social Forces* 471.

Grasmick, Harold G., & Robert J. Bursik, Jr. (1990) "Conscience, Significant Others, and Rational Choice: Extending the Deterrence Model," 24 *Law & Society Rev.* 837.

Grasmick, Harold G., Nancy J. Finley, & Deborah L. Glaser (1984) "Labor Force Participation, Sex Role Attitudes, and Female Crime," 65 *Social Science Q.* 703.

Grasmick, Harold G., Charles R. Tittle, Robert J. Bursik, Jr., & Bruce J. Arneklev (1993) "Testing the Core Implications of Gottfredson and Hirschi's General Theory of Crime," 30 *J. of Research in Crime & Delinquency* 5.

Hindelang, Michael J., Michael R. Gottfredson, & James Garofalo (1978) *Victims of Personal Crime: An Empirical Foundation for a Theory of Personal Victimization*. Cambridge, MA: Ballinger Publishers.

Hirschi, Travis (1969) *Causes of Delinquency*. Berkeley: Univ. of California Press.

——— (1986) "On the Compatibility of Rational Choice and Social Control Theories of Crime," in Cornish & Clarke 1986.

Hooton, Earnest Albert (1939) *Crime and the Man*. Cambridge: Harvard Univ. Press.

Hough, Mike (1987) "Offenders' Choice of Target: Findings from Victim Surveys," 3 *J. of Quantitative Criminology* 355.

Jensen, Gary F., Maynard L. Erickson, & Jack P. Gibbs (1978) "Perceived Risk of Punishment and Self-reported Delinquency," 57 *Social Forces* 57.

Kahneman, Daniel, Paul Slovic, & Amos Tversky (1982) *Judgment under Uncertainty: Heuristics and Biases*. Cambridge: Cambridge Univ. Press.

Kanin, Eugene J., & Stanley R. Parcell (1977) "Sexual Aggression: A Second Look at the Offended Female," 6 *Archives of Sexual Behavior* 67.

Klepper, Steven, & Daniel Nagin (1989a) "Tax Compliance and Perceptions of the Risks of Detection and Criminal Prosecution," 23 *Law & Society Rev.* 209.

——— (1989b) "The Deterrent Effect of Perceived Certainty and Severity of Punishment Revisited," 27 *Criminology* 721.

Koss, Mary P. (1983) "The Scope of Rape: Implications for the Clinical Treatment of Victims," 36 *Clinical Psychologist* 88.

Koss, Mary P., & Cheryl J. Oros (1987) "Sexual Experiences Survey: A Research Instrument Investigating Sexual Aggression and Victimization," 50 *J. of Consulting & Clinical Psychology* 455.

Koss, Mary P., Christine A. Gidycz, & Nadine Wisniewski (1987) "The Scope of Rape: Incidence and Prevalence of Sexual Aggression and Victimization in a National Sample of Higher Education Students," 55 *J. of Consulting & Clinical Psychology* 162.

Kuhn, Ralph (1992) "1991 Student Drug Survey" (unpublished report, President's Committee on Alcohol and Drug Policy). College Park: Univ. of Maryland.

Maxfield, Michael G. (1987) "Lifestyle and Routine Activity Theories of Crime: Empirical Studies of Victimization, Delinquency, and Offender Decision-making," 3 *J. of Quantitative Criminology* 275.

Murray, Glenn F., & Patricia G. Erickson (1987) "Cross-sectional versus Longitudinal Research: An Empirical Comparison of Projected and Subsequent Criminality," 16 *Social Science Research* 107.

Nagin, Daniel S., & David P. Farrington (1992a) "The Stability of Criminal Potential from Childhood to Adulthood," 30 *Criminology* 235.

——— (1992b) "The Onset and Persistence of Offending," 30 *Criminology* 501.

Nagin, Daniel S., & Raymond Paternoster (1991) "The Preventive Effects of the Perceived Risk of Arrest: Testing an Expanded Conception of Deterrence," 29 *Criminology* 561.

——— (1993) "Social Capital and Social Control: The Deterrence Implications of a Theory of Individual Differences in Criminal Offending" (unpublished, Carnegie Mellon Univ.).

Nisbett, Richard E., & Lee Ross (1980) *Human Inference: Strategies and Shortcomings of Social Judgment*. Englewood Cliffs, NJ: Prentice-Hall.

Nunnally, Jon C. (1967) *Psychometric Theory*. New York: McGraw-Hill.

Paternoster, Raymond (1989) "Decisions to Participate in and Desist from Four Types of Common Delinquency: Deterrence and the Rational Choice Perspective," 23 *Law & Society Rev.* 7.

Piliavin, Irving, Rosemary Gartner, Craig Thornton, & Ross L. Matsueda (196) "Crime, Deterrence, and Rational Choice," 51 *American Sociological Rev.* 101.

Reckless, Walter C. (1967) *The Crime Problem*. 4th ed. New York: Appleton-Century-Crofts.

Riley, David (1987) "Time and Crime: The Link between Teenager Lifestyle and Delinquency," 3 *J. of Quantitative Criminology* 339.

Rossi, Peter H., & Andy D. Anderson (1982) "The Factorial Survey Approach: An Introduction," in P. H. Rossi & S. L. Nock, eds., *Measuring Social Judgments*. Beverly Hills, CA: Sage Publications.

Rossi, Peter H., Emily Waite, Christine E. Bose, & Richard E. Berk (1974)

"The Seriousness of Crimes: Normative Structure and Individual Differences," 39 *American Sociological Rev.* 224.

Sampson, Robert J., & John H. Laub (1990) "Crime and Deviance over the Life Course: The Salience of Adult Social Bonds," 55 *American Sociological Rev.* 609.

——— (1992) "Crime and Deviance in the Life Course," 18 *Annual Rev. of Sociology* 84.

——— (1993) *Crime in the Making*. Cambridge: Harvard Univ. Press.

Sanday, Peggy Reeves (1990) *Fraternity Gang Rape: Sex, Brotherhood, and Privilege on Campus*. New York: NYU Press.

Scheff, Thomas J. (1988) "Shame and Conformity: The Deterrence-Emotion System," 53 *American Sociological Rev.* 395.

Scott, Wilbur J., & Harold G. Grasmick (1981) "Deterrence and Income Tax Cheating: Testing Interaction Hypotheses in Utilitarian Theories," 17 *J. of Applied Behavioral Sciences* 395.

Sellin, Thorsten, & Marvin E. Wolfgang (1978) *The Measurement of Delinquency*. Montclair, NJ: Patterson Smith.

Tittle, Charles R. (1980) *Sanctions and Social Deviance: The Question of Deterrence*. New York: Praeger.

Toby, Jackson (1957) "Social Disorganization and Stake in Conformity: Complementary Factors in the Predatory Behavior of Hoodlums," 48 *J. of Criminal Law, Criminology, & Police Science* 12.

Tuck, Mary, & David Riley (1986) "The Theory of Reasoned Action: A Decision Theory of Crime," in Cornish & Clarke 1986.

Ward, Sally K., Kathy Chapman, Ellen Cohn, Susan White, & Kirk Williams (1991) "Acquaintance Rape and the College Social Scene," 40 *Family Relations* 65.

Warshaw, Robin, & Mary P. Koss (1988) *I Never Called It Rape*. New York: Harper & Row.

Williams, Kirk R., & Richard Hawkins (1986) "Perceptual Research on General Deterrence: A Critical Overview," 20 *Law & Society Rev.* 545.

Wilson, James Q., & Richard J. Herrnstein (1985) *Crime and Human Nature*. New York: Simon & Schuster.

CASTE, CLASS, AND VIOLENT CRIME: EXPLAINING DIFFERENCE IN FEMALE OFFENDING*

SALLY S. SIMPSON
University of Maryland

During the past decade, criminological research has targeted gender as an important discriminator of criminal participation and persistence. Yet, the research question too often contrasts the criminality of males and females without taking into account key differences among female populations. In this paper, race and class combine to produce uniquely situated populations of females (e.g., "underclass" black females) who, when compared with their gender and racial counterparts, also appear to have unique patterns of criminality. Using the extant literature, black female violent crime is juxtaposed against that of white females and black males in order to show how crime varies across groups and the potential sources of those differences. Three theoretical perspectives (neo-Marxian, power-control, and socialist-feminist theory) are reviewed and evaluated for their intragender/racial inclusivity. Directions for further empirical research and theoretical development are suggested.

Class-oppressed men, whether they are white or black, have privileges afforded them as men in a sexist society. Similarly, class-oppressed whites, whether they are men or women, have privileges afforded them as whites in racist society. . . . Those who are poor, black, and female have all the forces of classism, racism, and sexism bearing down on them (Mantsios, 1988:66–67).

Violent criminality provokes an imagery that borders on caricature but one that is reinforced through official statistics and scholarly investigations. Serious street crime is a lower-class phenomenon (Elliott and Huizinga, 1983; Silberman, 1978; Wolfgang, 1958), disproportionately enacted by young (Greenberg, 1979), black (Hindelang, 1978; Tracy et al., 1991; Wolfgang et al., 1972), males (Hindelang, 1981; Tracy et al., 1991; Steffensmeier and Cobb, 1981). Studies and reports that support this portrait rely heavily on official arrest statistics, victimization surveys, and offender self-reports. With few exceptions, these data are not conducive to analyses of the often complex,

---

* An earlier version of this paper was presented at the 1988 annual meeting of the American Society of Criminology. I wish to thank the Center for the Study of Women and Society at the University of Oregon for its support of this project, along with Gary Hill, Dorie Klein, Coramae Richy Mann, Charles Wellford, and two anonymous reviewers for their helpful comments on earlier drafts.

CRIMINOLOGY VOLUME 29 NUMBER 1 1991 115

interactive effects of caste (gender and race) and class. Consequently, comparisons of violence within or between certain subgroups in the population, say lower-class white females versus lower-class black females, are typically neglected.

There has been intense debate among scholars regarding the "true" relationship between social class and crime (lucid summaries are provided by Braithwaite, 1981; Fagan et al., 1986; Hindelang et al., 1981; Tittle and Meier, 1990; see also Tittle et al., 1978), but there is little disagreement about the relationship between gender and violence. The violent female offender is an anomaly—both in the United States and cross-culturally (Harris, 1977; Weiner and Wolfgang, 1985). On those rare occasions when women are violent, their victims tend to be intimates (Bowker, 1981; Mann, 1987; Norland and Shover, 1977).

Recent evidence has done little to challenge this general truism; yet, there are unique patterns and trends in female criminal violence that bear investigation. Specifically, if females are not as a group violent, what accounts for variations in rates of criminal violence among them—particularly between blacks and whites (Hindelang, 1981; Laub and McDermott, 1985; Tracy et al., 1991)? As will be demonstrated, black females, especially those in the "underclass," engage in what might be considered anomalous behavior for their gender (i.e., violent crimes) but not for their race (Lewis, 1977). On the other hand, given the high level of violence among black males, black female rates of violent crime are relatively low.

Black females appear to respond differently to conditions of poverty, racism, and patriarchy than their class, gender, and racial counterparts. Race and gender merge into a theoretically interesting and important case, one that deserves more systematic inquiry (Hill and Crawford, 1990).

The purpose of this review is not to propose and develop a new theoretical perspective. My aims are more modest. Rather, violent crime among underclass black females is taken as illustrative of vertical (power) and horizontal (affiliative) differences between blacks and whites, males and females, and social classes (Hagan and Palloni, 1986). The degree to which extant theory can accommodate these caste and class differences in violent crime is assessed.[1] More specifically, three perspectives (neo-Marxian, power-control, and socialist-feminist theories of crime) are evaluated as to their sensitivity to intraracial and intragender variations in violent crime. To this end, the paper is divided into three parts: a review of the empirical literature on gender and

---

1. The focus on violent crime is justified on two counts. First, studies using self-report, victimization, and police reports suggest that gender and racial differences are most acute in personal crime categories (Ageton, 1983; Hindelang, 1981; Steffensmeier and Allen, 1988; Tracy et al., 1991). There are also reasons to suspect that violent crime emerges from different etiological processes than does more instrumental crime (Blau and Blau, 1982; Coser, 1968).

violent crime; a theoretical section in which each perspective is described and criticized; and finally, recommendations for theory modification, including cultural analysis.

THE VIOLENT FEMALE OFFENDER

MAKING AN EMPIRICAL CASE: PROBLEMS OF IDENTIFICATION

Distinguishing violent crime rates among females of different social classes and races is a difficult empirical task. Many studies employ noncomplimentary instruments and measures that preclude comparisons, or often, one or more of the key demographic variables is missing. For instance, Laub and McDermott (1985) and Laub (1983) compare racial and gender rates of offending, but class is ignored. Brownfield (1986) tests the relationship between several measures of social class and violent crime; yet, race and gender are not considered. Even the exceptions to this exclusionary rule (such as Ageton, 1983), test mostly for direct, not interactive effects; or when variable interactions are calculated, racial and class rather than racial and gender effects are the focus (Elliott and Huizinga, 1983).

In some cases, attempts to compare findings across the same variable are problematic. As Brownfield (1986) and others (Tittle and Meier, 1990) note, class may be calculated as relational (Colvin and Pauly, 1983; Hagan et al., 1985); common characteristics (Matza, 1966; Wilson, 1982); graduational (Elliott and Ageton, 1980; Hirschi, 1969; or social-ecological (Shaw and McKay, 1942). Race is typically dichotomized into white and black or the nonwhite category is broadened to include groups other than blacks (e.g., Hispanic and Asian). The only variable that seemingly defies this definitional drift is gender.

PATTERNS AND TRENDS

RACE

Clearly, extrapolation and interpretation from these data about violent female crime are speculative at best. But caveats aside, piecing together "apparent" patterns and trends from Uniform Crime Reports (UCRs) and victimization and self-report data does yield intriguing and remarkably consistent relationships. Black females have higher rates of homicide and aggravated assault than whites (Mann, 1987; McClain, 1982; Steffensmeier and Allen, 1988; Von Hentig, 1942). For certain types of personal crime victimizations, black female rates for both adults and juveniles are more similar to those for white males than those for white females (Hindelang, 1981; Laub and McDermott, 1985; Young, 1980).[2]

Among juveniles, black females are consistently more involved in assaultive crimes than whites (Ageton, 1983).[3] A recent cohort study (Tracy et al., 1991) found nonwhite female participation in UCR violent offenses to be 5.5 times that of white females. They are also more apt to be chronic offenders. Less dramatic, but similar patterns, were found by Sheldon (1987).

Black female participation in violent criminality does not compare with the high rates among their male counterparts; yet, "black women constitute well over half of all incarcerated women and are a higher proportion of all female offenders than are black men of all male offenders" (Lewis, 1981:69).[4] In light of these findings, gender alone does not account for the variation in criminal violence. Race as constitutive of structural and/or cultural difference demands greater conceptual and empirical attention (Chilton and Datesman, 1987; Hill and Crawford, 1990).[5]

RACE AND CLASS

Of the variables most often related to violent crime, class position is important for both blacks and whites (Elliott and Ageton, 1980; Tracy et al., 1991), but underclass status for blacks may be essential. A number of criminologists and sociologists (Blau and Blau, 1982; Currie, 1985; Silberman, 1978; Wilson, 1987) assert that economic inequality—especially the increasing marginalization and social isolation of underclass blacks—is correlated with high levels of criminal violence.

Changes in divorce laws, occupational segregation coupled with low pay for women, and the rise of single-parent mothers (Goldberg and Kremen, 1987; Norris, 1984; Weitzman, 1985) have significantly lowered the objective class position of many women. Since the 1960s, the major increase in poverty has occurred among those living in households headed by a single-parent mother (Goldberg and Kremen, 1987). Of these women, one-third are black

---

2. In the case of personal crimes (rape, robbery, assault, and larceny from the person), the black female rate of offending among 12- to 17-year olds exceeds that of their white male counterparts (Hindelang, 1981:465; see also Steffensmeier and Allen, 1988).

3. The sole exception is hitting parents. Here, white female participation exceeds that of blacks.

4. See French's discussion of the North Carolina female prison population (1977, 1978).

5. Crime data on other women of color (e.g., Chicanas, Indians, Asians, other Hispanics) are exceedingly difficult to come by. Therefore, in this review, "race" is operationalized as black and white. This does not, nor should it be interpreted to, imply that black female experiences somehow represent those of all women of color. More qualitative and historical studies (e.g., Campbell, 1984; Miller, 1986; Ross, 1988) offer evidence that different historical and cultural experiences of oppressed groups, intersecting with material conditions, influence whether, how, and to what degree group members are apt to act criminally.

(Norris, 1984). One out of three white children and three out of four black children can expect to spend some of their childhood in a single-parent family (New York Times, April 29, 1983). Like the crime statistics, black women and children are overrepresented.

The majority of single-parent mothers work, but most work within the pink-collar ghettos of clerical, service, and sales. Their average weekly earnings place them under the poverty level, which has earned them the title "the working poor" (Norris, 1984).

THE UNDERCLASS

The lower class, while disproportionately female and black, is relatively heterogeneous. Yet, the bottom of the lower class is more racially homogeneous. Wilson (1982:157) characterizes this population as *underclass*: "In underclass families, unlike other families in the black communities, the head of the household is almost invariably a woman. The distinctive make-up of the underclass is also reflected by the very large number of adult males with no fixed address."

The underclass is poorly educated, unskilled, and chronically under- or unemployed (Lichter, 1988; Wilson, 1987). Its single-parent mothers (often teenagers) are typically welfare dependent (Norris, 1984). The question of how an underclass is created and sustained is debatable. But whether its origins lie in large-scale, race-neutral structural change (Wilson, 1987) or in institutional racism (Duster, 1988; Lichter, 1988), its demographic characteristics are without refute. The face of the underclass is young and black; its geographical terrain is center-city urban.

VIOLENCE AND THE UNDERCLASS

Rates of violent crime vary significantly with the economic characteristics of communities. Some researchers suggest that violence is caused by relative economic deprivation (i.e., ascriptive inequality; Blau and Blau, 1982; Blau and Golden, 1984); others argue the violence is correlated with absolute poverty (Messner and Tardiff, 1986) or some interaction of class with race and urbanism (Blau and Blau, 1982; Laub, 1983; Wilson, 1987). Once again, causation is refutable but empirical patterns are more straightforward. Violent crime rates are highest in underclass communities—urban communities that are disproportionately black (Wilson, 1987).

In a recent study of underclass violence (Sampson, 1987), "disrupted" families (female-headed households) increase juvenile and adult robbery offending for both blacks and whites, but they have a greater effect on black homicide rates.[6] Although gender differences in the use of violence are not

6. Although it is important to note the relationship between family structure and crime, intrafamilial dynamics and female roles within particular family types are equally

taken into account, Sampson does suggest that underclass position, particularly labor marginality of black males and its accompanying economic marginalization, has profound negative consequences for black women with children.

In a similar vein, Matsueda and Heimer (1987) discover a positive relationship between broken homes and delinquency, an effect that is much stronger among blacks than whites. Moreover, black delinquency is more likely to be affected by "neighborhood trouble" than white. The authors conclude that "broad historical trends have led to different patterns of social organization among the urban underclass which influence rates of delinquency" (p. 837).

Given the significant impact of family structure on violent criminality among males, researchers must ask (1) whether this same pattern holds for females and (2) what it is about single-parent families that contributes to such a relationship. Both are empirical questions but neither, given the paucity of data, currently is within empirical grasp. Consequently, the answers offered here are necessarily speculative.

Two types of family structure emerge from poverty: (1) extended domestic networks (Stack, 1974; Valentine, 1978) and (2) isolated single-parent units (Miller, 1986). The structure of one's family of origin may influence whether females become involved in criminal activity and in what types of illegality they may engage. Miller's (1986) study of deviant street networks in Milwaukee found poorer women, especially blacks, to be members of shifting households composed of kin, nonkin, and pseudokin.

The extensive and shifting domestic networks in which black females are found are closely associated with criminal recruitment. According to Miller (1986:67),

> Because of the severe limitations that poverty places upon the control exercised by parents and guardians, young women from poor families are more likely to be recruited to deviant networks than those from families that are better off. Moreover, because of the greater frequency of highly developed and far reaching domestic networks among poor blacks than among poor whites, black girls appear to be differentially recruited to the fast life of the street.

The fast life described by Miller heightens female exposure to all types of crime, especially property, but personal offenses as well (e.g., robbery and assault). Yet, because much violent crime is irrational and noninstrumental, exposure to criminal opportunities through deviant street networks may only partially explain the violent crime gap between black and white females. And given that both males and females participate in deviant networks and share

---

important to study. As Brittan and Maynard (1984:120) remind us, "not only do . . . family forms differ in organization, . . . it cannot be assumed that women's involvement in them is everywhere the same.

similar class experiences, why is there not greater gender convergence in violent crime rates? Obviously, other elements are operative.

Feminists were among the first to call for greater sensitivity to class and racial differences among females, but feminist criminology has yet to produce a cohesive perspective that accounts for intragender racial differences in criminal offending (see, e.g., Messerschmidt, 1986). Similarly, most theories of crime are class (see Meier, 1985), but not gender and race, sensitive. In this next section, three criminological perspectives are assessed as to their ability to account for gender, class, and racial differences in violent offending. The three theories are examined precisely because they tie illegality to class and/ or gender *oppression*[7] and because feminist critics of androcentric criminological theory suggest that Marxian and control perspectives are, relative to others, more amenable to the "gender variable" (Leonard, 1982; Naffine, 1988).

THEORETICAL CONSIDERATIONS
NEO-MARXIAN THEORY

Neo-Marxian explanations formulate the crime problem by examining the objective class position of workers. Depending on the type of employment and employer (e.g., skilled worker/monopoly capitalist versus unskilled worker/competitive capitalist), workers will be disciplined differently and develop different bonds to authority (Colvin and Pauly, 1983). Parents who experience alienative bonding to authority in coercive work situations reproduce those relations with their children. Alienative bonding in juveniles is reinforced through the educational system (through such practices as tracking) and peer relations. The alienated youths who emerge from this process are more apt to be violently delinquent than youths who experience other types of discipline and bonding (e.g., remunerative/calculative or symbolic/ moral).

> The more coercive the control relations encountered in these various socialization contexts tend to be, the more negative or alienated will be the individual's ideological bond and the more likely is the individual to engage in serious, patterned delinquency (Colvin and Pauly, 1983:515).

Therefore, children whose parents are least skilled and subject to coercive discipline at work are more likely to act out in criminally violent ways.[8]

---

7. Oppression (as opposed to inequality or subordination) bases stratification in a complex combination of ideological, political, and economic forces (Phillips, 1987).

8. Some may raise concerns that Colvin and Pauly's (1983) neo-Marxian perspective is a theory of delinquency, not adult crime. However, the processes they identify as promoting delinquency (i.e., coercive discipline and alienative bonding to authority) begin in the workplace with adults. It is reasonable to assume that negative adult bonding to authority also may produce a criminal outcome, but how coercive discipline and alienative

This theory adds conceptual precision to the class-violent delinquency relationship, but it fails to account for gender differences among juveniles whose parents are similarly located. A recent empirical test of Colvin and Pauly's theory finds mixed support for both males and females, especially the class-delinquency relationships (Messner and Krohn, 1990). However, these findings may be due to questionable operationalization of concepts such as marxian class categories and serious patterned delinquency. Also, blacks are excluded from the analysis. Finally, if violence is highest among underclass populations who are increasingly isolated from the labor market, then the processes that are deemed essential to the production of violent crime (i.e., discipline and bonding in the workplace) are not in place. Recognizing some of these failures, John Hagan and his associates construct a theory that is class based, but also sensitive to how patriarchy may structure familial (1985, 1988) and workplace (1987) relations.

POWER-CONTROL THEORY

Power-control theory builds on the idea that workplace-family power relations affect how parental discipline operates (mother or father as instrument of control) as well as which child is most apt to be disciplined by which parent (male or female as object of control). According to this theory, delinquency will be gendered only under certain class and familial structures. Patriarchal families (which reflect the unequal authority positions of parents in the workplace) produce greater rates of "common" delinquency by sons than daughters, because within the family males are socialized to have a greater taste for risk than females. In more egalitarian families (i.e., both parents share similar work positions or households are female headed), delinquency is not patterned (or as patterned) by gender. "As Mothers gain power relative to husbands, daughters gain freedom relative to sons" (Hagan et al., 1987:792). Ostensibly, under these conditions, females become more risk prone and consequently more delinquent.

In framing power-control theory, Hagan and his associates (1979, 1985:1153–1154) clearly limit their focus to "common" forms of delinquency.[9] Yet, there is no reason that power-control theory cannot be modified to account for class and gender differences in violent crime. In fact, one permutation of power-control theory nestles the concept of power in the same neo-Marxian class categories that Colvin and Pauly (1983) theoretically link to "serious patterned delinquency." Additionally, the inclusion of personal

---

bonding are reproduced and reinforced through other relationships and organizations theoretically is unspecified.

9. They justify their choice by suggesting that crime seriousness may be a theoretical issue to be explained rather than assumed and that an exclusive focus on serious offending may limit theoretical development for other, less serious, crime types.

assaults in Hagan et al.'s (1985, 1988) measure of common delinquency raises the question of whether all juvenile assaults are benign enough to be viewed as not serious, or "common."

Appropriate modifications of the theory should focus on how violence is related to freedom to deviate, an absence of controls, and/or socialized risk preferences. For example, Colvin and Pauly (1983) and Hagan and colleagues (1985) claim that discipline and control within the family reproduce workplace authority structures. Common delinquency is expected to be positively related to class position (because freedom to deviate is associated with upperclass socialization and power position), but violent offending should vary negatively with class. Alienative bonding coupled with coercive discipline in the workplace will produce inconsistent bonding to authority and high levels of frustration and alienation in families. Following the original logic of power-control theory, one would expect greater gender differences in violent offending in patriarchal rather than in nonpatriarchal families. Patriarchal power within the family supports and reinforces traditional gender role socialization (i.e., male as aggressive/female as passive). Gender differences in violent offending should decrease with class position, partially because of the disproportionate representation of "egalitarian" single-parent mothers among lower-class families, but also as a result of the deteriorating authority of male and female workers, which is reproduced in parental relations with children.

Risk preference is expanded to include (a) the functionality of risk and (b) the perceived costs if one is caught. In employer classes, violence is apt to be dysfunctional for most males because it does not prepare them for careers nor, given the increased likelihood that this behavior is more apt to come to the attention of authorities than common delinquency, are the costs worth it.[10] For upper-class females, violence is neither functional nor legitimate. And, considering that countertype criminality by females (i.e., masculine crime) may be more harshly viewed by authorities (Bernstein et al., 1977; Schur, 1984; Visher, 1983), the costs of violence for this population of females may be especially high. As one moves down the class ladder, however, definitions of violence and its legitimacy may change. Violence as a means of achieving desired ends—whether pecuniary or interpersonal (power and dominance)—is apt to be more commonplace and less gender-role defined.

Power-control theory has been relatively unsuccessful in subsequent empirical tests (Singer and Levine, 1988),[11] perhaps because it fails to address how patriarchy varies across racial groups and social class lines. Male dominance

---

10. However, violence may prove functional for some upper-class males in order to maintain dominance and power within interpersonal relationships. Moreover, given that upper-class intimate violence is more hidden than its lower-class counterpart, its costs may be less.

11. Discrepant findings may be due to differences in sample populations, cohort or

and control do not necessarily operate similarly for black and white females, nor for racial groups across different classes. The relationship between black women and black men is not "the same or necessarily analogous to that which white women have to white men . . . these relationships are patriarchal and oppressive . . . [but] their form can be very different" (Brittan and Maynard, 1984:64). Consequently, power-control theory may offer insights into class and gendered delinquency, but as currently conceived its insensitivity to race is a major weakness.[12]

SOCIALIST-FEMINIST THEORY[13]

Socialist-feminist approaches to crime, although also unable to link race and racism systematically with class and patriarchy, are at least concerned with such conceptual failures. Messerschmidt (1986:xi) acknowledges that "racial oppression is as important as class and gender oppression, [but] socialist feminism has not linked it systematically with patriarchy and capitalism." Even with these confessed flaws, socialist-feminist approaches provide helpful ways in which to think about class and gender differences in crime.[14]

The strengths of socialist-feminism for this analysis are twofold. First, the criminality of males and females varies in frequency and type due to the gendered social organization of productive (class) and reproductive (family) spheres. Neither sphere is privileged over the other as a source of oppression; they are mutually reinforcing. Consequently, the economic base of capitalist society and its ideological superstructure (social institutions and culture) are seen as dynamic and dialectical. Second, personality and individual consciousness are seen to reflect the dominance/subordination relations found in production and reproduction (Messerschmidt, 1986:30–31).

Patriarchal capitalism creates two distinct groups: the powerful (males and

---

temporal effects, or to the addition of new variables (e.g., a measure of group risk taking is added to Singer and Levine's analysis).

12. Feminists note other weaknesses as well. Naffine (1988) argues that power-control theory stereotypically characterizes the process that keeps females from violating the law. Its image of a dependent, controlled, risk-avoiding, law-abiding female does not take into account the degree to which females are (1) tied to the conventional social order and (2) rational and calculating in their assessment of the personal costs of illegality. Further, power-control theory privileges the workplace over the family as the primary source of dominance. Although this approach may be applauded by Marxist-feminists, it is based on assumptions that are not shared by most feminists (c.f., Daly and Chesney-Lind, 1988; Messerschmidt, 1986; Simpson, 1989).

13. For this section, I rely almost exclusively on the work of Messerschmidt (1986). It is by far the most developed representation of this perspective.

14. Like power-control theory, socialist-feminist approaches typically ignore female participation in violent crime. For instance, Messerschmidt (1986:51–98) carefully distinguishes typical male from typical female crime types. In the case of conventional offending, powerless males commit violent crimes and powerless females engage in nonviolent offending.

capitalists) and the powerless (females and the working class). Opportunities to commit crime vary according to one's structural position. For the powerful, criminality is a means to maintain domination over the control of the powerless. Conversely, crimes by the powerless are interpreted as forms of resistance and accommodation to their structural position (Messerschmidt, 1986:42). From this perspective, the most costly and deleterious crimes are committed by capitalist males (e.g., corporate offenses). Lower-class and female crime reflects a powerless status, but because of gendered social organization (crime opportunities are distributed unequally and males are apt to resist while females accommodate their powerlessness), male and female criminality takes entirely different forms. Under patriarchal capitalism, powerless males commit violent street crime; powerless females engage mostly in nonviolent property and/or vice offending (primarily drugs and prostitution).

As noted earlier, one of the flaws of socialist-feminism is its neglect of how racial oppression and racism interact with other forms of oppression to produce distinct patterns of criminal offending. A related problem is its insensitivity to intragender variations in violent offending. To suggest that males are violent and females are not ignores the empirical reality of black female crime. In the next section, key concepts and theoretical insights from neo-Marxian, power-control, and socialist-feminist perspectives are used to address intraclass, gender, and racial differences in violent offending.

TOWARD THEORETICAL INCLUSIVITY

POWER

Class, gender, and race are best understood as intersecting systems of dominance and control. Power is ascribed and compliance determined by how these characteristics cluster across productive and reproductive spheres. Within the workplace, white females are less powerful than white males, but more powerful than black females. Bourgeois blacks are more powerful than lower-class blacks, but less powerful than bourgeois whites, and "white working class men are given at least a vicarious power over third-world peoples" (Silverstein, 1977:178).

In the family, it is less clear how class and race may affect gender relations. Some studies find greater middle-class attitudinal subscription to gender equality, but more equality in practice within working-class families (as measured by decision-making power, Blood and Wolfe, 1960).[15] Because there is greater economic parity between black males and females than there is

---

15. Blood and Wolfe's (1960) study is roundly criticized by feminist scholars, who argue that power in the family is not determined by different levels of economic resources brought into it by males and females. Rather, the marriage contract itself implicitly defines male and female roles; and beyond that, "we cannot ignore the sexism that characterizes heterosexual relations in general" (Johnson, 1988:251).

between whites (black female wage earnings are closer to those of black males than white female earnings are to those of white males; The Wall Street Journal, April 17, 1989), male economic power within black families is less. At the bottom end of the class structure, black males are often unavailable for family participation due to violent death, drug addiction, prison, or unemployment (Wilson, 1982). Here, interpersonal male power is negated by absence, but replaced with the patriarchal state (e.g., through female interactions with Aid for Dependent Children, children's services, the criminal justice system, and so on).

The shared experience of racism also can affect the intrafamilial operation of patriarchy. Although black women recognize their own subordination to men, they keenly feel the racism that keeps black males "in their place." Racism changes the features of male privilege and dominance within the black family.

CONTROL

On the control end, ideology (constraining belief systems that reflect the interests of the powerful)[16] and culture (the symbolic-expressive dimensions of human action; Wuthnow, 1987) determine who gets controlled and how. In traditional working- and upper-class families, control operates through patriarchal structures.

> Individuals are enmeshed in class and gender structures that organize the way people think about their circumstances and devise solutions to act upon them. Gender and class shape one's possibilities. The conditions individuals confront and the manner in which they choose to "handle" those conditions are socially regulated. Just as conforming behavior is socially regulated and intimately related to one's class/gender status, so is nonconforming behavior (Messerschmidt, 1986:41).

Yet, membership in the underclass is disruptive of this process. For blacks, social controls within the family (i.e., parental bonding and learning of "gender-appropriate" behaviors) are attenuated across extensive domestic networks.

The disruption of intrafamilial patriarchal reproduction occurs within a system stratified by racial privilege and framed by race-conscious ideologies. Underclass position, because of alienation and the breakdown of traditional social control in the family, should produce higher crime rates for both black and white females compared with other classes, but blacks—because they have little invested in a racist system or less to gain through conformity with that system—should be more criminal than similarly positioned white

---

16. As Thompson (1984) and Larrain (1977) use the concept, ideology retains its critical edge (i.e., tied to a critique of domination). In my case, ideology reflects the interests of upper-class white males.

women.[17]

White women are more apt to be deterred from crime because of its perceived consequences (e.g., loss of status, negative labeling, and rejection by a system that benefits whites). They will take fewer risks because they have more to lose in a system that accords privilege to whites. Moreover, they can mitigate their powerlessness by "attaching" themselves to a more powerful group in patriarchal racist society (e.g., white males).[18] As Lorde (1988:355) points out, "In a patriarchal power system where white skin privilege is a major prop, the entrapments used to neutralize black women and white women are not the same." White females, under the pretense of sharing power, may be seduced into joining the oppressor.[19]

For the white poor, racist ideology provides a psychologically nonthreatening explanation for their poverty and a language of collective resentment. MacLeod's (1987) study of working/lower-class boys in Clarendon Heights (a low-income housing development) describes how white boys believe blacks and the wealthy are favored at school and in employment. MacLeod notes that these boys exhibit dual contradictory consciousness, embodying "both progressive, counterhegemonic insights and reactionary, distorting beliefs" (p. 123). In a system in which failure is attributable to individual weakness and white skin confers greater value than black skin, it makes sense that white males and females do not reject the system but blame others' privileges for their failures. Psychologically, they cannot afford to do so. Moreover, family structure among impoverished whites is more likely either to be nuclear or isolated, single-parent units (Miller, 1986; Wilson, 1987). These structures are less conducive of breakdowns in patriarchal control, and violent crime opportunities are fewer than in the extended and integrative domestic networks of underclass blacks.

---

17.   Collins (1986:519) offers an important insight as to why black males in the underclass have higher rates of crime than black females. She argues that being poor, black, and female offers "a clearer view of oppression than other groups who occupy contradictory positions vis-à-vis white male power." Black males can always attempt to negate their oppression through a "questionable appeal to manhood." The source of this appeal is ideological. Patriarchy provides males (white and black) with a "manhood" typescript (Harris, 1977). This typescript defines male-appropriate reactions to stress and frustration (i.e., they act out against others). The dominant "womanhood" typescript is just the opposite. Stress and anger are internalized into self-destructive behaviors like suicide, depression, and other types of mental illness (Piven and Cloward, 1979).

18.   See Hook's discussion of white women's pragmatic use of their sex and race to "realize personal gains from the system" (1984:199).

19.   There is certainly historical precedent for these speculations. As black abolitionists and suffragists jointly struggled for civil rights in the middle 1800s, political expediency and racism drove many white middle-class feminists to side with their white male brethren against black enfranchisement (Hook, 1984).

CULTURE

Power and hierarchy determined by class, patriarchy, and race cannot be separated from horizontal relations of affiliation and solidarity (Hagan and Palloni, 1986). These relations are reciprocal and reinforcing. As structural conditions increasingly preclude mobility for the bottom of the surplus population, cultural redefinitions and adjustments may influence perceptions of, and beliefs about, the emergence and appropriateness of violence (Wilson, 1987).

Although power-control, neo-Marxian, and socialist-feminist perspectives link micro and macro factors to crime, none sufficiently develops the cultural processes that drive interpretation and social action. Most criminological theories that are attentive to cultural forces (e.g., Cloward and Ohlin, 1961; Miller, 1958; Wolfgang and Ferracuti, 1967) are primarily concerned with male criminality. Consequently, they fail to explain how culture either restricts or patterns female criminality (Leonard, 1982). They also tend to employ a narrow and static definition of culture—a system of norms, beliefs, and values that impose on individual actions. This conception divorces cultural production from its situated context and tends to see culture as a distinct and imposing force.

Yet, "culture is not composed of static, discrete traits moved from one locale to another. It is constantly changing and transformed, as new forms are created out of old ones" (Mullins, 1986:13). To understand the unique positioning of black women between two dominant groups in society (Lewis, 1977:343), it makes sense to discern how their material conditions affect how culture is created, interpreted, and reproduced, as well as culture's relation to power and hierarchy.

Collins (1986:524) calls attention to an essential relationship between structural/material conditions, black women's subjective consciousness, and social action:

> Oppressive structures create patterns of choices which are perceived in varying ways by black women. Depending on their consciousness of themselves and their relationship to these choices, black women may or may not develop black-female spheres of influence where they develop and validate what will be appropriate . . . sanctioned responses.

Although Collins is interested in explaining how black females politically mobilize, criminal behavior can be seen as emerging from similar cultural processes. Class is an oppressive structure for both black and white females, but black women's experiences of their material circumstances and their perceptions of self and choice vary qualitatively from those of whites.

The lives of black women and children are "stitched with violence and hatred . . . [and] violence weaves through the daily tissues of . . . living"

(Lorde, 1988:355). Living daily with the fact of violence leads to an incorporation of it into one's experiential self. Men, women, and children have to come to terms with, make sense of, and respond to violence as it penetrates their lives. As violence is added to the realm of appropriate and sanctioned responses to oppressive material conditions, it gains a sort of cultural legitimacy. But not for all. The observed gender differences in how violence is interpreted and incorporated into one's behavioral repertoire emerge from the contradictory cultural tendencies of caste (i.e., female = nonviolent, black = violent; Lewis, 1981). Black females, given their dedication to keeping home and community together (Joseph, 1981) are more apt than black males to delegitimate violence. However, given their racial oppression and differential experience of patriarchy in the family, black females are perhaps less apt to delegitimate violence than their white counterparts.

SUMMARY AND CONCLUSIONS

Criminologists have been mistaken to ignore important variations in criminal behavior among females. The simplistic assertion that males are violent and females are not contains a grain of truth, but it misses the complexity and texture of women's lives. A review of the empirical literature on violence reveals the confounding effects of gender, race, and class. Although their combined influences are difficult to tease out, a firm understanding of how they interact is fundamental for a more inclusive and elegant criminological theory. Neo-Marxian, power-control, and socialist-feminist perspectives offer some help in this regard.

Before criminologists launch into a major revision of current theory, however, further research is clearly necessary. Extant research yields only a murky picture of essential differences between and among males and females of different classes and races. Until large-scale quantitative designs can readily and meaningfully sort out differences in crime rates and qualitative research can offer subjective accounts of how violence is interpreted and understood by different subpopulations of interest, criminological theory will continue to be only vaguely relevant to the real world.

REFERENCES

Ageton, Suzanne S.
  1983   The dynamics of female delinquency, 1976–1980. Criminology 21:555–584.

Bernstein, Ilene, Edward Kick, Jan Leung, and Barbara Schultz
  1977   Charge reduction: An intermediary stage in the process of labeling criminal defendants. Social Forces 56:362–384.

Blau, Peter M. and Judith R. Blau
  1982   The cost of inequality: Metropolitan structure and violent crime. American Sociological Review 47:114–129.

Blau, Peter M. and Reid M. Golden
1984   Metropolitan structure and criminal violence. Paper presented at the annual meeting of the American Sociological Association, San Antonio, Texas.

Blood, Robert O and Donald M. Wolfe
1960   Husbands and Wives: The Dynamics of Married Living. Glencoe, N.Y. Free Press.

Bowker, Lee
1981   Women and Crime in America. New York: Macmillan.

Braithwaite, John
1981   The myth of social class and crime reconsidered. American Sociological Review 46:36–57.

Brittan, Arthur and Mary Maynard
1984   Sexism, Racism, and Oppression. Oxford: Basil Blackwell.

Brownfield, David
1986   Social class and violent behavior. Criminology 24:421–438.

Campbell, Anne
1984   The Girls in the Gang. New York: Basil Blackwell.

Chilton, Roland and Susan K. Datesman
1987   Gender, race, and crime: an analysis of urban arrest trends, 1960– 1980. Gender and Society 1:152–171.

Cloward, Richard A. and Lloyd E. Ohlin
1961   Delinquency and Opportunity. Glencoe, N.Y.: Free Press.

Cohen, Albert
1955   Delinquent Boys. Glencoe, N.Y.: Free Press.

Collins, Patricia Hill
1986   Learning from the outsider within: The sociological significance of black feminist thought. Social Problems 33:514–532.

Colvin, Mark and John Pauly
1983   A critique of criminology: Toward an integrated structural-Marxist theory of delinquency production. American Journal of Sociology 89:513–551.

Coser, Louis A.
1968   Conflict: Social aspects. In David L. Sills (ed.), International Encyclopedia of the Social Sciences. Vol. 3. New York: Macmillan.

Currie, Elliott
1985   Confronting Crime. New York: Pantheon.

Daly, Kathleen and Meda Chesney-Lind
1988   Feminism and criminology. Justice Quarterly 5:497–538.

Duster, Troy
1988   From structural analysis to public policy. A review of William J. Wilson's, The Truly Disadvantaged. Contemporary Sociology 17:287–290.

Elliott, Delbert S. and Suzanne S. Ageton
1980   Reconciling race and class differences in self-reported and official estimates of delinquency. American Sociological Review 45:95–110.

Elliott, Delbert S. and David Huizinga
  1983   Social class and delinquent behavior in a national youth panel. Criminology
          21:149–177.

Fagan, Jeffery, Elizabeth Piper, and Melinda Moore
  1986   Violent delinquents and urban youths. Criminology 24:439–471.

French, Lawrence
  1977   An assessment of the black female prisoner in the South. Signs 3:483–488.
  1978   The incarcerated black female: The case of social double jeopardy. Journal
          of Black Studies 8:321–335.

Goldberg, Gertrude S. and Eleanor Kremen
  1987   The feminization of poverty: Only in America? Social Policy 17:3–14.

Greenberg, David
  1979   Delinquency and Age Structure of Society. Pp. 586–620 in Sheldon L.
          Messinger and Egon Bittner (eds.) Criminology Review Yearbook. Beverly
          Hills, CA: SAGE.

Hagan, John and A. Palloni
  1986   Toward a structural criminology: Method and theory in criminological
          research. Annual Review of Sociology 12:431–449.

Hagan, John, A.R. Gillis, and John Simpson
  1985   The class structure of gender and delinquency: Toward a power-control
          theory of common delinquent behavior. American Journal of Sociology
          90:1151–1178.

Hagan, John, John Simpson, and A.R. Gillis
  1979   The Sexual Stratification of Social Control. British Journal of Sociology
          30:25–38.
  1987   Class in the household: A power-control theory of gender and delinquency.
          American Journal of Sociology 92:788–816.
  1988   Feminist scholarship, relational and instrumental control, and a power-
          control theory of gender and delinquency. British Journal of Sociology
          39:301–336.

Harris, Anthony R.
  1977   Sex and theories of deviance. American Sociological Review 42:3–16.

Hindelang, Michael
  1981   Variations in sex-race-age-specific incidence rates of offending. American
          Sociological Review, 46:461–474.
  1978   Race and involvement in common-law personal crimes. American Sociologi-
          cal Review 43:93–109.

Hindelang, Michael, Travis Hirschi and Joseph G. Weis
  1981   Measuring Delinquency. Beverly Hills, CA: SAGE.

Hill, Gary D. and Elizabeth M. Crawford
  1990   Women, race, and crime. Criminology 28:601–623.

Hirschi, Travis
  1969   Causes of Delinquency. Berkeley, CA: University of California Press.

Hook, Elizabeth F.
1984   Black women, white women: Separate paths to liberation. In Allison M. Jagger and Paula S. Rothenberg (eds.), Feminist Frameworks. 2nd ed. New York: McGraw-Hill.

Johnson, Miriam M.
1988   Strong Mothers, Weak Wives. Berkeley: University of California Press.

Joseph, Gloria I.
1981   Black mothers and daughters. In Gloria I. Joseph and Jill Lewis (eds.), Common Differences: Conflicts in Black and White Feminist Perspectives. Boston: South End Press.

Larrain, Jorge
1977   The Concept of Ideology. Athens: University of Georgia Press.

Laub, John
1983   Urbanism, race, and crime. Journal of Research in Crime and Delinquency 20:183–198.

Laub, John and M. Joan McDermott
1985   An analysis of serious crime by young black women. Criminology 23: 89–98.

Leonard, Eileen B.
1982   Women, Crime, and Society. New York: Longmans, Green.

Lewis, Diane
1977   A response to inequality: Black women, racism, and sexism. Signs 3:339–361.
1981   Black women offenders and criminal justice: Some theoretical considerations. In Marguerite Warren (ed.), Comparing Female and Male Offenders. Beverly Hills, Calif.: SAGE.

Lichtern, David T.
1988   Racial differences in underemployment in American cities. American Journal of Sociology 13:771–792.

Lorde, Audre
1988   Age, race, class, and sex: Women redefining difference. In Paul S. Rothenberg (ed.), Racism and Sexism: An Integrated Study. New York: St. Martin's Press.

MacLeod, Jay
1987   Ain't No Makin' It. Boulder, Colo.: Westview Press.

Mann, Coramae Richey
1987   Black female homicide in the United States. Paper presented at the Conference on Black Homicide and Public Health.

Mantsios, Gregory
1988   Class in America: Myths and realities. In Paula S. Rothenberg (ed.), Racism and Sexism: An Integrated Study. New York: St. Martin's Press.

Matsueda, Ross and Karen Heimer
1987   Race, family structure, and delinquency: A test of differential association and social control theories. American Sociological Review 52:826–840.

Matza, David
    1966   The disreputable poor. In Reinhard Bendix and Seymour M. Lipset (eds),
              Class, Status and Power. Glencoe, N.Y.: Free Press.

McClain, Paula D.
    1982   Black females and lethal violence: Has time changed the circumstances
              under which they kill? Omega 13:13–25.

Meier, Robert
    1985   Theoretical Methods in Criminology. Beverly Hills, CA: SAGE.

Messerschmidt, James W.
    1986   Capitalism, Patriarchy, and Crime. Totowa, N.J.: Rowman and Littlefield.

Messner, Steven F. and Marvin D. Krohn
    1990   Class compliance structures and delinquency: Assessing integrated Struc-
              tural-Marxist Theory. American Journal of Sociology 96:300-328.

Messner, Steven F. and Kenneth Tardiff
    1986   Economic inequality and levels of homicide: An analysis of neighborhoods.
              Criminology 24:297–316.

Miller, Eleanor M.
    1986   Street Woman. Philadelphia: Temple University Press.

Miller, Walter B.
    1958   Lower class culture as a generating milieu of gang delinquency. Journal of
              Social Issues 14:5–19.

Mullings, Leith
    1986   Anthropolitical perspectives on the Afro–American family. American
              Journal of Social Psychiatry 6:11–16.

Naffine, Ngaire
    1988   Female Crime: The Construction of Women in Criminology. Boston: Allen
              and Unwin.

Norland, Stephen and Neal Shover
    1977   Gender roles and female criminality. Criminology 15:87–104.

Norris, Pippa
    1984   Women in poverty: Britain and America. Social Policy 14:4–43.

Phillips, Anne
    1987   Feminism and Equality. Oxford: Basil Blackwell.

Piven, Frances Fox and Richard A. Cloward
    1979   Hidden protest: The channeling of female innovation and resistance. Signs
              4:461–470.

Ross, Luana K.
    1988   Toward an Indian Study of Indian deviance. Unpublished manuscript,
              Montana State University, Bozeman.

Sampson, Robert J.
    1987   Urban black violence: The effect of male joblessness and family disruption.
              American Journal of Sociology 93:348–382.

Schur, Edwin
    1984   Labeling Women Deviant. New York: Randon House.

Shaw, Clifford and Henry McKay
   1942   Juvenile Delinquency and Urban Areas. Chicago: University of Chicago
           Press.

Sheldon, Randall
   1987   The chronic delinquent: Gender and racial differences. Paper presented at
           the annual meeting of the American Society of Criminology. Montreal,
           Quebéc, Canada.

Silberman, Charles
   1978   Criminal Violence, Criminal Justice. New York: Random House.

Silverstein, M.
   1977   The history of a short, unsuccessful academic career. In J. Snodgrass (ed.),
           For Men Against Sexism. Albion, Calif.: Times Change Press.

Simpson, Sally S.
   1989   Feminist theory, crime , and justice. Criminology 27:607–631.

Singer, Simon I. and Murray Levine
   1988   Power-control theory, gender, and delinquency: A partial republication with
           additional evidence on the effects of peers. Criminology 26:627–647.

Stack, Carol B.
   1974   All Our Kin: Strategies for Survival in a Black Community. New York:
           Harper Colophon Books.

Steffensmeier, Darrell, T. and Emilie Anderson Allen
   1988   Sex disparities in arrest by residence, race, and age: An assessment of the
           gender convergence/crime hypothesis. Justice Quarterly 5:53–80.

Steffensmeier, Darrell J. and Michael J. Cobb
   1981   Sex differences in urban arrest patterns, 1934–1979. Social Problems
           28:37–50.

Thompson, John B.
   1984   Studies in the Theory of Ideology. Berkeley: University of California Press.

Tittle, Charles R., Wayne J. Villemez, and Douglas A. Smith
   1978   The myth of social class and criminality: An empirical assessment of the
           empirical evidence. American Sociological Review 43:643–656.

Tittle, Charles R. and Robert F. Meier
   1990   Specifying the SES delinquency relationship. Criminology 28:271–299.

Tracy, Paul E., Marvin E. Wolfgang, and Robert M. Figlio
   1991   Delinquency in Two Birth Cohorts. New York: Springer Press

Valentine, Bettylou
   1978   Hustling and Other Hard Work. Glencoe, N.Y.: Free Press.

Visher, Christy
   1983   Gender, police arrest decision, and notions of chivalry. Criminology
           21:5–28.

Von Hentig, Hans
   1942   The criminality of the colored woman. University of Colorado Studies
           (Series C1):231–260.

Weiner, Neil Alan and Marvin E. Wolfgang
   1985   The extent and character of violent crime in America. In Lynn A. Curtis
           (ed.), American Violence and Public Policy. New Haven: Yale University
           Press.

Weitzman, Lenore J.
   1985   The Divorce Revolution: The Unexpected Social and Economic Conse-
           quences for Women and Children in America. Glencoe, N.Y.: Free Press.

Wilson, William J.
   1982   The Declining Significance of Race. Chicago: University of Chicago Press.
   1987   The Truly Disadvantaged. Chicago: University of Chicago Press.

Wolfgang, Marvin
   1958   Patterns of Criminal Homicide. Philadelphia: University of Pennsylvania
           Press.

Wolfgang, Marvin and Franco Ferracuti
   1967   The Subculture of Violence. New York: Barnes and Noble.

Wolfgang, Marvin E., Robert M. Figlio, and Thorsten Sellin
   1972   Delinquency in a Birth Cohort. Chicago: University of Chicago Press.

Wuthnow, Robert
   1987   Meaning and Moral Order: Explorations in Cultural Analysis. Berkeley:
           University of California Press.

Young, Vernetta D.
   1980   Women, race, and crime. Criminology 18:26–34.

Sally S. Simpson is an assistant professor of Criminal Justice and Criminology at the University of Maryland, College Park. Her current research interests include testing neo-
marxian, power-control, and socialist-feminist perspectives for their gender-race inclusivity; corporate crime etiology and control; and female drug trafficking networks.

A RECONCEPTUALIZATION OF GENERAL AND SPECIFIC DETERRENCE

MARK C. STAFFORD
MARK WARR

The distinction between general and specific deterrence is widely recognized and accepted by deterrence researchers, and is used commonly to classify deterrence studies. However, the logical and empirical grounds for the distinction are not as clear as they might appear, and the conventional conception has done more to obfuscate than to clarify the deterrence process. Following a discussion of these issues, the authors propose a reconceptualization of general and specific deterrence, and apply it to several current controversies in the deterrence literature.

The deterrent effect of legal punishment has been one of the foremost topics of criminological research during the past three decades. In recent years, tests of the deterrence doctrine have become increasingly sophisticated as investigators have adopted panel designs, experimental and time-series techniques, and other methodological refinements. Nevertheless, the conception of deterrence that guides such research has remained largely unchanged.

A key element of that conception is the distinction between general and specific deterrence. Virtually all definitions of those phenomena point in one way or another to this distinction: Whereas general deterrence refers to the effects of legal punishment on the general public (i.e., potential offenders), specific deterrence pertains to the effects of legal punishment on those who have suffered it (i.e., punished offenders; for a review, see Gibbs 1975, pp. 32-39). For example, Nagin (1978) defines general deterrence as the "imposition of sanctions on one person [in order to] demonstrate to the rest of the public the expected costs of a criminal act, and thereby discourage criminal behavior in the general population" (p. 96). In contrast, Andenaes (1968) states that if persons are "deterred by the actual experience of punishment, we speak of *special* [specific] *deterrence*" (p. 78).

This is a revised version of a paper presented at the 1989 annual meetings of the American Society of Criminology in Reno.

JOURNAL OF RESEARCH IN CRIME AND DELINQUENCY, Vol. 30 No. 2, May 1993 123-135
© 1993 Sage Publications, Inc.

Both definitions recognize the importance of some kind of experience with legal punishment in deterring persons from committing crimes. But for members of the general public (general deterrence) it is indirect experience with punishment (observing or otherwise having knowledge of the punishment of others) that deters, whereas for punished offenders (specific deterrence) it is direct (personal) experience (Meier and Johnson 1977, pp. 294-95).

This conception of general and specific deterrence is widely recognized and accepted by criminologists, but it has serious shortcomings. Put briefly, we will argue that the conventional distinction between general and specific deterrence rests on faulty logic and that it has done little to clarify the deterrence process. After presenting these arguments, we propose a reconceptualization of general and specific deterrence, and apply it to some current controversies in the deterrence literature.

DISTINGUISHING GENERAL
AND SPECIFIC DETERRENCE

Deterrence studies are classified commonly as bearing on one type of deterrence or the other, with most purportedly involving general rather than specific deterrence (see reviews by Gibbs 1975, chap. 5; Tittle 1980, chap. 1; Zimring and Hawkins 1973, chap. 4). However, the rationale for such classification is not entirely clear.

Consider a hypothetical study of what is likely to be regarded as general deterrence. In such a case, investigators might focus on persons who have never suffered any legal punishment for any crime, on the grounds that such persons have knowledge of punishment, if at all, only indirectly from the experiences of others (Gibbs 1975, pp. 34, 37). However, there are two kinds of people who have never suffered a legal punishment: (a) those who have never committed any crime (ignoring the possibility that innocent persons can be punished) and (b) those who have committed crimes but have avoided punishment. Only the first kind of person can be said to have no direct experience with legal punishment. Although the second kind of person has not suffered a legal punishment, he or she has by definition acquired experience with *avoiding punishment*, and that experience is likely to affect the chances of committing crimes again. In particular, experience with avoiding punishment is likely to affect perceptions of the certainty and severity of punishment, the two principal variables in recent deterrence studies. Of these two variables, perceptions of certainty should be affected more strongly by punishment avoidance, because getting away with a crime provides little information about the legal consequences of being caught (Paternoster

1987, p. 189; Paternoster, Saltzman, Waldo, and Chiricos 1983a, p. 281, 1983b, p. 458).

Like the concept of deterrence, which involves the omission of legally proscribed acts (Gibbs 1975, p. 3; Meier and Johnson 1977), the notion of punishment avoidance may be somewhat difficult to imagine because it refers to events that did *not* happen. However, unlike deterrence, punishment avoidance is also contingent on events that did occur, that is, the commission of crimes. Hence, in contrast to deterrence, punishment avoidance is not inherently unobservable. For example, everyone who drives in urban America has observed another person driving in a reckless manner with no legal punishment, or has witnessed such criminal events as driving while intoxicated that did not even come to the attention of the police.

To some, the concept of punishment avoidance may appear to add little to deterrence theory, because punishment avoidance is simply the opposite of punishment itself. The distinction may be logically banal, but it is potentially critical for empirical reasons. To illustrate, it is possible that punishment avoidance does more to encourage crime than punishment does to discourage it. Offenders whose experience is limited largely to avoiding punishment may come to believe that they are immune from punishment, even in the face of occasional evidence to the contrary. Perhaps the greatest value of the concept is that it underscores the fundamental principle that no criminal act is without consequences. In the wake of a crime, offenders always will experience punishment or punishment avoidance, and it is dubious to argue that only the former impacts subsequent behavior.

The immediate point is that what usually is taken to be general deterrence is not limited necessarily to persons who have no direct experience with legal punishment. The point is crucial because, if self-report data are to be believed, there are few persons (at least among young males) who have never avoided punishment, especially for minor offenses (for a review, see Empey and Stafford 1991, chap. 6). Consequently, the conventional distinction between general and specific deterrence rests more on the *nature* of prior direct experience with legal punishment than on the mere presence of such experience.

Direct and Indirect Experience with Punishment

Now consider a related problem with specific deterrence. Studies of specific deterrence typically focus on punished offenders (or comparisons of punished and unpunished offenders) and examine the frequency of postpunishment offending for evidence of deterrence (e.g., Murray and Cox

1979; Schneider and Ervin 1990; Smith and Gartin 1989). There is nothing intrinsically wrong with this procedure, but investigators commonly assume that an offender's direct experience with suffering a punishment is the only operative variable when it comes to predicting future behavior. In addition to ignoring the offender's experience with avoiding punishment, such an assumption overlooks the possibility that one can suffer a legal punishment and at the same time have knowledge of punishment from the experiences of others (i.e., have indirect experience with punishment).

Suppose that an individual is caught and fined after shoplifting and that this is his or her first offense of any type. The direct experience of being fined is likely to be salient, but surely its deterrent efficacy will depend on whether the individual believes or knows that other persons (particularly others like him or her) have a similar certainty and severity of punishment, or whether he or she believes that in this particular instance the punishment was ill-fated and others would have gotten away with the crime, or that they would have received a less (or more) severe punishment (Ward, Menke, Gray, and Stafford 1986, pp. 502-3).

The point to be emphasized is that in most populations—whether members of the general public or punished offenders—people are likely to have a *mixture* of indirect and direct experience with punishment and punishment avoidance. That point is not lost on all deterrence researchers. For example, Lempert (1982, p. 532), in a study of enforcement of child-support orders, observes that men who have been jailed for nonpayment often meet or hear of others who are in jail for the same offense. Hence, these men gain both direct and indirect experience with legal punishment (p. 549). However, by adopting the conventional distinction between general and specific deterrence, investigators perpetuate the notion that the two forms of deterrence occur among distinct populations.

The problem with such a notion becomes clearer when one considers that offenders often commit more than one type of crime, and that they may or may not suffer a legal punishment for each type. Consider a person who is caught and punished after committing his or her first burglary, but who has also committed other crimes (e.g., drug use, robbery, auto theft) and avoided punishment in each case. To claim that the direct experience of being punished for the burglary is the only relevant consideration in predicting the offender's future behavior is to ignore what has been said about the potential effects of punishment avoidance, not to mention the potential effects of indirect experience with punishment. Putting it more carefully, there are four relevant considerations in the example at hand: (a) the direct experience with suffering the punishment for the burglary, (b) the direct experience with punishment avoidance for the other crimes, (c) indirect experience with punishment and punishment avoidance for the burglary, and (d) indirect experience with punishment and punishment avoidance for the other crimes.

One possibility is that the direct experience with punishment for the burglary could reduce the offender's likelihood of repeating the other crimes (e.g., by increasing the perceived certainty of punishment for these offenses). However, it could also work in the reverse—the direct experience of getting away with the other crimes could increase the chances of committing further burglaries. And when one considers *indirect* experience with punishment and punishment avoidance for all of the offenses, there are still other possibilities. For example, the arrest of fellow offenders for the same crime(s) might lead to the conclusion that the odds of arrest have increased substantially.

An underlying assumption in all such possibilities is that people may estimate the certainty and severity of punishment for a particular type of crime by reference to crimes in general or at least similar types of offenses (e.g., all property crimes) rather than from information that is "crime-specific" (Gibbs 1975, p. 35; Erickson and Gibbs 1975; Paternoster 1986). If so, it almost certainly will be true that a mixture of indirect and direct experiences with legal punishment and punishment avoidance will be relevant for most persons. Even if people estimate certainty and severity entirely from crime-specific information, a mixture of punishment experiences is likely to be relevant, and research is needed on such questions as whether direct experience with punishment and punishment avoidance affects the deterrent efficacy of indirect experience (Zimring and Hawkins 1973, pp. 224-29).

A RECONCEPTUALIZATION

The conceptual problems outlined above stem, we believe, from the manner in which general and specific deterrence commonly are defined. That is, the practice of distinguishing general and specific deterrence by reference to distinct populations (either the general public or punished offenders) tends to obfuscate critical issues. Instead, we propose that the distinction between the two types of deterrence be limited to contrasting kinds of experience with legal punishment. If deterrence is defined as the omission or curtailment of a criminal act out of fear of legal punishment (Gibbs 1975, p. 39), then general deterrence refers to the deterrent effect of *indirect experience with punishment and punishment avoidance* and specific deterrence refers to the deterrent effect of *direct experience with punishment and punishment avoidance*.

The proposed reconceptualization has several advantages over that currently in use. First, it recognizes the possibility that *both* general and specific deterrence can operate for any given person or in any population. Second, it treats punishment avoidance as analytically distinct from the experience of suffering a punishment.

A third advantage of the proposed reconceptualization of general and specific deterrence is its compatibility with contemporary learning theory, particularly the distinction between observational/vicarious learning and experiential learning (for discussions of the connection between deterrence concepts/principles and learning theory, see Akers 1990; Cavender 1979; Moffitt 1983). Bandura (1977), for example, argues that experiential learning

> results from the positive and negative effects that actions produce. When people deal with everyday events, some of their responses prove successful, while others have no effect or result in punishing outcomes. Through this process of differential reinforcement, successful forms of behavior are eventually selected and ineffectual ones are discarded. (p. 17)

As for observational or vicarious learning, Bandura (1977) notes that

> people can profit from the successes and mistakes of others as well as from their own experiences. In everyday situations numerous opportunities exist to observe the actions of others and the occasions on which they are rewarded, ignored, or punished. . . . Observed outcomes can alter behavior in their own right in much the same way as directly experienced consequences(p. 117)

Just as recent versions of learning theory suggest that any behavior is likely to be a consequence of both observational/vicarious learning and experiential learning (e.g., Akers, Krohn, Lanza-Kaduce, and Radosevich 1979, p. 638; Bandura 1977, chap. 2), the basic premise of the proposed reconceptualization is that the rate of crime in virtually any population will be a function of both general and specific deterrence. This is not to say that the two types of deterrence will be equally important from one population to the next (Gray, Ward, Stafford, and Menke 1985, pp. 83-84). Among persons with limited direct experience with punishment and/or punishment avoidance, the rate of crime is more likely to be a function of general deterrence (indirect experience with punishment and punishment avoidance). Indeed, in the special case of persons who have *no* direct experience with punishment or punishment avoidance—those who have never committed any crimes at all—the only possibly relevant consideration is general deterrence. However, among persons who have been punished many times and/or have avoided punishment repeatedly (i.e., habitual offenders), their criminal behavior should be largely a function of specific deterrence (direct experience with punishment and punishment avoidance). The implication is that individuals can be viewed as falling along a continuum characterized by general deterrence at one extreme and specific deterrence at the other.

The reconceptualization of general and specific deterrence proposed here is of little value unless it helps to clarify existing research and stimulates new theoretical questions. In the following section, we consider some applications of our reconceptualization.

APPLICATIONS OF RECONCEPTUALIZATION

The proposed reconceptualization has implications for a recent critique of deterrence research and logic. Put briefly, the criticism is that deterrence studies may have "reversed the causal ordering of key . . . variables" (Paternoster 1987, p. 174). Although deterrence researchers treat criminal behavior as a consequence of the perceived certainty of legal punishment, it is possible that criminal behavior may be the cause of such perceptions. As Paternoster (1987) puts it, negative associations between the perceived certainty of legal punishment and crime "may simply reflect the fact that most instances of rule breaking go undetected and that participants in crime eventually lower their initially unrealistically high estimates of the risks involved" (p. 180). The effects of criminal behavior on perceptions of the certainty of punishment are referred to as "experiential" effects to distinguish them from the reverse process—deterrence.

The notion of experiential effects is certainly plausible, and it is entirely consistent with what has been said about the possible effects of punishment avoidance. However, there are several problems with the logic and evidence for experiential effects. Studies that report stronger experiential than deterrent effects have tended to focus on minor crimes such as petty theft, shoplifting, vandalism, and marijuana use (e.g., Minor and Harry 1982; Paternoster et al. 1983a, 1983b; Saltzman, Paternoster, Waldo, and Chiricos 1982). Given the high incidence and low objective (i.e., actual) certainty of punishment for these crimes, offenders are in fact likely to have considerable direct experience with punishment avoidance, which is what proponents of experiential effects contend. However, what is to be said about infrequent offenders who have little or no direct experience with punishment avoidance, a situation that is more likely to characterize serious rather than minor crimes? For example, would a person who has committed one homicide, and who has avoided legal punishment for it, be expected to substantially lower his or her perception of the certainty of punishment for that crime? The answer is likely to depend on the person's indirect experience with punishment and punishment avoidance. If others also are perceived as having committed the crime with impunity, then there might be a substantial reduction in the person's perceived certainty of punishment for homicide. However, in the opposite and more likely case—where others are believed to have a high certainty of punishment—there should be little experiential effect.

To the extent that infrequent offenders (or nonoffenders) perceive a high certainty of legal punishment, proponents of experiential effects tend to attribute it to "naivete" (Paternoster 1987, p. 181). Such a characterization may appear warranted given the focus on minor crimes in experiential studies. However, this naivete may be just the stuff of which general deterrence is made. Presumably, persons with little or no direct experience with legal punishment and punishment avoidance form their perceptions of the certainty of punishment from other sources. The most likely candidate is indirect experience with punishment and punishment avoidance, that is, information obtained from friends, relatives, other offenders, or the media (Geerken and Gove 1975). Such information may be hopelessly incorrect and indeed might produce "naive" offenders, but surely the accuracy of the information does not determine its deterrent efficacy.

Granted that considerable direct experience with punishment avoidance could explain why frequent offenders have low perceptions of the certainty of punishment, a rejection of deterrence logic still is not necessarily warranted. In particular, the experiential argument overlooks the fact that direct experience with punishment and punishment avoidance (which are consequences of one's criminal behavior) may be difficult to separate empirically from the effects of indirect experience with punishment and punishment avoidance (consequences of the criminal behavior of others). In many situations, the direct experience of persons is likely to equal or match their indirect experience. For example, an offender may avoid punishment for a crime, and also observe or know that others have avoided punishment. Where such collinearity exists, positive evidence for an experiential effect cannot be construed automatically as negative evidence for a deterrent effect.

Aside from the experiential argument, another critique of deterrence research centers on the claim that the association between perceptions of certainty and crime is spurious. In a recent review of the perceptual deterrence literature, Paternoster (1987) states that

> support for the deterrent effect of perceived certainty is most likely to be found in those studies that are methodologically weakest. Such studies include those . . . with few controls for other exogenous variables, which allow estimated effects to be contaminated by excluded exogenous factors. (pp. 186-87)

Paternoster (1987, pp. 182-87) shows that, in studies that statistically control for nondeterrence variables, there is often little or no association between the perceived certainty of legal punishment and crime. One control variable frequently employed in these studies is extralegal punishments for crimes, including stigmatization and opportunity costs (see, e.g., Paternoster et al. 1983b; Paternoster and Iovanni 1986). However, Williams and Hawkins (1986, p. 558) argue convincingly that extralegal punishments may not operate independently of legal punishments. For example, "persons [may] anticipate that others will disapprove of their arrest for committing a certain act, and they [may] refrain from that activity because they fear the stigma of being caught" (Williams and Hawkins, pp. 562-63). In such cases, extralegal punishment is dependent on legal punishment. "By . . . controlling for this 'extralegal' influence, . . . part of the deterrence process . . . is lost" (Williams and Hawkins, p. 563). Hence, extralegal punishments actually may operate as deterrence variables, and if so, it is scarcely surprising that controlling for them tends to reduce or even eliminate the association between perceptions of certainty and crime (for a counterargument, see Paternoster 1987, pp. 209-13).

Another control variable that bears on the spuriousness issue, and one that is more relevant to our proposed reconceptualization of general and specific deterrence, is peer involvement in crime (Paternoster 1986, 1987, Table 3, 1988). Perhaps no other variable is more strongly associated with criminal behavior (e.g., Akers et al. 1979). However, like extralegal punishment, classification of peer involvement as a nondeterrence variable is questionable, especially considering how it is typically conceptualized and measured. In virtually all cases, investigators have simply asked respondents how many of their friends have committed particular types of crime, and responses to such questions usually are construed as measures of normative or situational pressures to violate the law.

But there is an alternative interpretation. If a person has friends who have committed crimes, then that person's behavior could reflect indirect experience with punishment and punishment avoidance (general deterrence) rather than peer pressure as conventionally interpreted (i.e., normative or situational pressures to violate the law). To disentangle these factors, questions about peer involvement must probe more deeply into what happens to friends who commit crimes—in particular, whether or not they have been caught and legally punished. Paternoster (1988, p. 138) agrees that peer involvement in crime may affect perceptions of the certainty of punishment by providing knowledge about the punishment experiences of others. Indeed, he repeatedly finds associations between the two variables (pp. 145, 157, 173). However, he persists in classifying peer involvement as a nondeterrence variable (p. 136) and, hence, seemingly denies that indirect experience with punishment and punishment avoidance has anything to do with the deterrence process.

The idea that peer involvement affects perceptions of the certainty and severity of punishment would appear to be consistent with Sutherland's (1947) theory of differential association (also see Matza 1964, pp. 186-88). Tittle, Burke, and Jackson (1986) indicate that "although neither Sutherland nor his interpreters did so, it seems reasonable to treat fear of legal sanctions as an aspect of criminal perspective possibly learned from association" (p. 413). However, there are other aspects of the "criminal perspective," perhaps the most important being normative evaluations about the rightness or wrongness of crimes (Tittle et al. 1986; Warr and Stafford 1991). Hence, although a connection between peer involvement and deterrence can be subsumed under Sutherland's theory (1947), the theory encompasses far more than just deterrence.

Setting aside the issue of spuriousness, a focus on peer involvement raises a critical point about indirect experience with legal punishment. Deterrence researchers—particularly those concerned with specific deterrence—frequently write as though offenders were limited to their own personal experience when it comes to judging the certainty and severity of punishment. However, in the case of delinquent behavior, that assumption is dubious at best. The reason is that delinquency is overwhelmingly a group phenomenon, a fact that has been demonstrated repeatedly for at least 60 years (for a review, see Reiss 1986). As such, delinquents are likely to have ready access to the *collective* experiences of their companions, meaning that their experiential base is likely to be much larger than their own personal experience. Indeed, an intelligent offender might be tempted to draw stronger conclusions about the certainty and severity of punishment from the cumulative experiences of friends than from his or her own relatively narrow life experiences.

Beyond this, deterrence researchers have been slow to recognize the possibility that the immediate presence of companions may alter situational perceptions of certainty and severity. As in other forms of collective behavior (e.g., Dipboye 1977; Mann, Newton, and Innes 1982), the presence of companions during delinquent episodes may produce a heightened sense of anonymity (one among many) as well as invulnerability among offenders, both of which may translate into perceptions of low certainty and severity. Such situational perceptions are probably very difficult to detect and measure, and are likely to be missed by the generalized measures of perceived certainty and severity conventionally used in deterrence research.

CONCLUSIONS

While no conception is right or wrong, some are more useful than others. For more than two decades, deterrence researchers have complained that there is no systematic theory of deterrence (e.g., Gibbs 1968, p. 530, 1975, p. 2; Tittle 1985, pp. 285-87; Zimring 1978, p. 172), which is a tacit admission that conventional conceptions of general and specific deterrence have provided little or no impetus to such theorizing. As Zimring and Hawkins (1973) observe, most researchers "who . . . draw this distinction [between general and specific deterrence] make no further use of it" (p. 73).

The proposed reconceptualization suggests that it is unnecessary to formulate separate theories of general and specific deterrence. Rather, a single theory is possible that centers on indirect experience with legal punishment and punishment avoidance and direct experience with legal punishment and punishment avoidance. Recognizing that people may think of punishment for crimes in general rather than in crime-specific terms, such a theory would need to consider indirect and direct experience with punishment and punishment avoidance for crimes other than those that individuals actually have committed.

Unfortunately, if the proposed reconceptualization is accepted, tests of the deterrence doctrine necessarily will become more complex. For example, tests based on survey data would need to include, at a minimum, measures of (a) persons' perceptions of their own certainty and severity of legal punishment for crimes, (b) persons' perceptions of the certainty and severity of legal punishment for others (presumably those within their immediate social network), (c) self-reported criminal behavior, including self-reports of direct experience with punishment and punishment avoidance, and (d) estimates of peers' criminal behavior, including their experiences with punishment and punishment avoidance.

Of course, there are alternatives to a survey methodology, such as an experimental design. Indeed, an experimental design might facilitate an assessment of the separate effects of indirect and direct experience with legal punishment and punishment avoidance on crime (see, e.g., Sherman and Berk 1984). However, only a very complex experimental design can facilitate an examination of the *relative* effects of indirect and direct experience with punishment and punishment avoidance, which may be the more important issue as far as a theory of deterrence is concerned.

REFERENCES

Akers, R. L. 1990. "Rational Choice, Deterrence, and Social Learning Theory in Criminology: The Path Not Taken." *Journal of Criminal Law and Criminology* 81:653-76.

Akers, R. L., M. D. Krohn, L. Lanza-Kaduce, and M. Radosevich. 1979. "Social Learning and Deviant Behavior: A Specific Test of a General Theory." *American Sociological Review* 44:636-55.

Andenaes, J. 1968. "Does Punishment Deter Crime?" *Criminal Law Quarterly* 11:76-93.

Bandura, A. 1977. *Social Learning Theory*. Englewood Cliffs, NJ: Prentice-Hall.

Cavender, G. 1979. "Special Deterrence: An Operant Learning Evaluation." *Law and Human Behavior* 3:203-15.

Dipboye, R. L. 1977. "Alternative Approaches to Deindividuation." *Psychological Bulletin* 84: 1057-75.

Empey, L. T. and M. C. Stafford. 1991. *American Delinquency: Its Meaning and Construction.* Belmont, CA: Wadsworth.

Erickson, M. L. and J. P. Gibbs. 1975. "Specific Versus General Properties of Legal Punishments and Deterrence." *Social Science Quarterly* 56:390-97.

Geerken, M. R. and W. R. Gove. 1975. "Deterrence: Some Theoretical Considerations." *Law and Society Review* 9:497-513.

Gibbs, J. P. 1968. "Crime, Punishment, and Deterrence." *Social Science Quarterly* 48:515-30.
———. 1975. *Crime, Punishment, and Deterrence*. New York: Elsevier.

Gray, L. N., D. A. Ward, M. C. Stafford, and B. A. Menke. 1985. "Observational and Experiential Effects in Probability Learning: The Case of a Deviant Behavior." *Social Psychology Quarterly* 48:78-85.

Lempert, R. 1982. "Organizing for Deterrence: Lessons From A Study of Child Support" *Law and Society Review* 16:513-68.

Mann, L., J. W. Newton, and J. M. Innes. 1982. "A Test Between Deindividuation and Emergent Norm Theories of Crowd Aggression." *Journal of Personality and Social Psychology* 42:260-72.

Matza, D. 1964. *Delinquency and Drift*. New York: Wiley.

Meier, R. F. and W. T. Johnson. 1977. "Deterrence as Social Control: The Legal and Extralegal Production of Conformity." *American Sociological Review* 42:292-304.

Minor, W. W. and J. Harry. 1982. "Deterrent and Experiential Effects in Perceptual Deterrence Research: A Replication and Extension." *Journal of Research in Crime and Delinquency* 19:190-203.

Moffitt, T. E. 1983. "The Learning Theory Model of Punishment: Implications for Delinquency Deterrence." *Criminal Justice and Behavior* 10:131-58.

Murray, C. A. and L. A. Cox, Jr. 1979. *Beyond Probation: Juvenile Corrections and the Chronic Delinquent*. Beverly Hills, CA: Sage.

Nagin, D. 1978. "General Deterrence: A Review of the Empirical Evidence." Pp. 95-139 in *Deterrence and Incapacitation: Estimating the Effects of Criminal Sanctions on Crime Rates*, edited by A. Blumstein, J. Cohen, and D. Nagin. Washington, DC: National Academy of Sciences.

Paternoster, R. 1986. "The Use of Composite Scales in Perceptual Deterrence Research: A Cautionary Note." *Journal of Research in Crime and Delinquency* 23:128-68.
———. 1987. "The Deterrent Effect of the Perceived Certainty and Severity of Punishment: A Review of the Evidence and Issues." *Justice Quarterly* 4:173-217.
———. 1988. "Examining Three-Wave Deterrence Models: A Question of Temporal Order and Specification." *Journal of Criminal Law and Criminology* 79:135-79.

Paternoster, R. and L. Iovanni. 1986. "The Deterrent Effect of Perceived Severity: A Reexamination." *Social Forces* 64:751-77.

Paternoster, R., L. E. Saltzman, G. P. Waldo, and T. G. Chiricos. 1983a. "Estimating Perceptual Stability and Deterrent Effects: The Role of Perceived Legal Punishment in the Inhibition of Criminal Involvement." *Journal of Criminal Law and Criminology* 74:270-97.

———. 1983b. "Perceived Risk and Social Control: Do Sanctions Really Deter?" *Law and Society Review* 17:457-79.

Reiss, A. J., Jr. 1986. "Co-Offender Influences on Criminal Careers." Pp. 121-60 in *Criminal Careers and "Career Criminals,"* edited by A. Blumstein, J. Cohen, J. A. Roth, and C. A. Visher. Washington, DC: National Academy Press.

Saltzman, L., R. Paternoster, G. P. Waldo, and T. G. Chiricos. 1982. "Deterrent and Experiential Effects: The Problem of Causal Order in Perceptual Deterrence Research." *Journal of Research in Crime and Delinquency* 19:172-89.

Schneider, A. L. and L. Ervin. 1990. "Specific Deterrence, Rational Choice, and Decision Heuristics: Applications in Juvenile Justice." *Social Science Quarterly* 71:585-601.

Sherman, L. W. and R. A. Berk. 1984. "The Specific Deterrent Effects of Arrest for Domestic Assault." *American Sociological Review* 49:261-72.

Smith, D. A. and P. R. Gartin. 1989, "Specifying Specific Deterrence: The Influence of Arrest on Future Criminal Activity." *American Sociological Review* 54:94-106.

Sutherland, E. H. 1947. *Criminology.* 4th ed. Philadelphia: Lippincott.

Tittle, C. R. 1980. *Sanctions and Social Deviance: The Question of Deterrence.* New York: Praeger.

———. 1985. "Can Social Science Answer Questions About Deterrence for Policy Use?" Pp. 265-94 in *Social Science and Social Policy,* edited by R. L. Shotland and M. M. Mark. Beverly Hills, CA: Sage.

Tittle, C. R., M. J. Burke, and E. F. Jackson. 1986. "Modeling Sutherland's Theory of Differential Association: Toward an Empirical Clarification." *Social Forces* 65:405-32.

Ward, D. A., B. A. Menke, L. N. Gray, and M. C. Stafford. 1986. "Sanctions, Modeling, and Deviant Behavior." *Journal of Criminal Justice* 14:501-8.

Warr, M. and M. Stafford. 1991. "The Influence of Delinquent Peers: What They Think or What They Do?" *Criminology* 29:851-66.

Williams, K. R. and R. Hawkins. 1986. "Perceptual Research on General Deterrence: A Critical Review." *Law and Society Review* 20:545-72.

Zimring, F. E. 1978. "Policy Experiments in General Deterrence: 1970-1975." Pp. 140-73 in *Deterrence and Incapacitation: Estimating the Effects of Criminal Sanctions on Crime Rates,* edited by A. Blumstein, J. Cohen, and D. Nagin. Washington, DC: National Academy of Sciences.

Zimring, F. E. and G. J. Hawkins. 1973. *Deterrence: The Legal Threat in Crime Control.* Chicago: University of Chicago Press.

0091-4169/91/8201-0003
THE JOURNAL OF CRIMINAL LAW & CRIMINOLOGY
Copyright © 1991 by Northwestern University, School of Law

Vol. 82, No. 1
Printed in U.S.A.

PRINCIPAL STUDIES

TESTING INTERACTIONAL THEORY: AN EXAMINATION OF RECIPROCAL CAUSAL RELATIONSHIPS AMONG FAMILY, SCHOOL, AND DELINQUENCY*

ROCHESTER YOUTH DEVELOPMENT STUDY**
TERENCE P. THORNBERRY
ALAN J. LIZOTTE
MARVIN D. KROHN
MARGARET FARNWORTH
SUNG JOON JANG

* Prepared under Grant No. 86-JN-CX-0007 (S-3) from the Office of Juvenile Justice and Delinquency Prevention, Office of Justice Programs, United States Department of Justice; Grant No. 5 R01 DA05512-02 from the National Institute on Drug Abuse; and Grant No. SES-8912274 from the National Science Foundation. Points of view or opinions in this document are those of the authors and do not necessarily represent the official position or policies of the funding agencies.

** Terence P. Thornberry is a professor, and former dean, of the School of Criminal Justice at The University at Albany. He received his Ph.D. in Sociology from the University of Pennsylvania. His major research interests are in developing and testing theories of delinquency and drug use, especially from a longitudinal perspective.

Alan J. Lizotte is an associate professor and associate dean of the School of Criminal Justice at The University at Albany. He received his Ph.D. in Sociology from the University of Illinois. He enjoys using quantitative research methods to analyze the development of delinquency, patterns of firearms ownership and use, and issues in victimization.

Marvin D. Krohn is a professor in the Department of Sociology at The University at Albany. He received his Ph.D. in Criminology from Florida State University. His research interests include the investigation of social psychological theories of adolescent substance abuse and delinquent behavior. He has recently presented a social network theory of adolescent deviant behavior and is currently involved in a panel study of inner-city youth designed to examine hypotheses derived from that perspective.

Margaret Farnworth is an associate professor in the College of Criminal Justice at Sam Houston State University. She received her Ph.D. in Sociology from the University of Georgia. Her major research interests are social stratification and crime and criminal court processing. Recent publications include the effects of strain on delinquency and felony processing in a Southwestern court.

Sung Joon Jang is a graduate student in the Department of Sociology at The Univer-

371

ABSTRACT

Attachment to parents and commitment to school are important buffers against delinquency. Adolescents who are emotionally bonded to their parents and who succeed at school are unlikely candidates for serious delinquency. These relationships have strong empirical support. In addition, however, it is possible that frequent involvement in delinquency can cause a substantial deterioration in the emotional bond between parent and child and in the adolescent's commitment to school. Indeed, an interactional perspective argues that bidirectional or reciprocal causal influences such as these are more accurate representations of how delinquency develops over the life-course. The present paper tests an interactional model for these variables using the first three waves of data from the Rochester Youth Development Study. Results strongly suggest that the causes of delinquency are more complex than originally thought. While weakened bonds to family and school do cause delinquency, delinquent behavior further attenuates the strength of the bonds to family and school, thereby establishing a behavioral trajectory towards increasing delinquency.

I. INTRODUCTION

Criminologists have long hypothesized that attachment to parents and commitment to school play a major role in reducing adolescent involvement in delinquent behavior; as such, they are prime candidates for manipulation in delinquency prevention programs. While many theoretical perspectives include these variables, attachment to parents and commitment to school are perhaps most central to social control theory, because they represent two of the major ways by which adolescents are "bonded" to society. According to this perspective, these variables exert a causal influence on delinquency, but are not influenced by delinquency.

Recent theories of delinquency—especially interactional theory[1]—have challenged this unidirectional causal order. Arguing that human behavior develops dynamically over time as people interact with one another and as the consequences of prior behavior are felt, interactional theory posits that delinquent behavior may also have reciprocal causal influences on such variables as attachment to parents and commitment to school. This article examines this hypothesis both theoretically and empirically. The article first reviews the basic premises of social control theory and various spec-

---

sity at Albany, where he received his M.A. His major research interests are in developing and testing theories on crime and delinquency, social deviance, and fear of crime, based on quantitative research methods. He has a special interest in the social dimensions of gender, age, and race in relation to crime, delinquency, and fear of crime.

[1] Thornberry, *Toward an Interactional Theory of Delinquency*, 25 CRIMINOLOGY 863 (1987).

ifications of the relationships among these bonding variables. It then examines empirically interactional theory's hypothesis that these variables are involved in reciprocal causal relationships that have the potential of propelling a person along an increasingly delinquent behavioral trajectory. Finally, it discusses the theoretical and policy implications of the empirical results.

II. Social Control Theory

The central thesis of social control theory is that people tightly bonded to conventional society are behaviorally constrained and therefore unlikely to violate society's rules and regulations. As an individual becomes more and more tightly ensnared in society's web, behavioral freedom diminishes and the chances of deviance dwindle. On the other hand, as society's grasp over the person weakens—as the web slackens and begins to tear—behavioral constraints also weaken and deviance becomes more likely. Thus, delinquency is a direct function of how tightly the person is bonded to conventional society.

As with most theoretical perspectives, proponents generally agree about social control theory's basic premises and claims, but exhibit lesser agreement about the structure of propositions used to explain a particular phenomenon. As a result, one can identify a number of versions of control theory. Among the more traditional versions there appear to be two major types, which we call classical control theory and integrated control theory.

A. CLASSICAL CONTROL THEORY

The classical version of control theory is represented in the writings of such theorists as Toby[2] and Nye[3] but is epitomized in Hirschi's *Causes of Delinquency*.[4] Hirschi argues that human nature contains a strong natural tendency towards deviance and, therefore, the motivation for delinquency is constant, or at least non-problematic. The theory does not have to account for why people deviate; deviance is part of our humanity. It does have to explain why people do *not* deviate; that is, it has to account for the forces that stem this natural tendency to be deviant.

Hirschi's explanation is that these natural tendencies are controlled to the extent that the person is bonded to society. The social

---

2 Toby, *Social Disorganization and Stake in Conformity: Complementary Factors in the Predatory Behavior of Hoodlums*, 48 J. Crim. L. & Criminology 12 (1957).

3 F. Nye, Family Relationships and Delinquent Behavior (1958).

4 T. Hirschi, Causes of Delinquency (1969).

order is the only force capable of preventing the enactment of self-interested, natural proclivities to deviate—this is the central, defining premise of all social control theories.

In Hirschi's version of the theory, four elements bond individuals to society, thereby reducing delinquency. The four elements are: *attachment* to others; *commitment* to conformity; *involvement* in conventional activities; and *belief* in the moral validity of conventional values. Attachment is the emotional or affective element of the bond. Adolescents attached to conventional others (*e.g.*, parents and teachers) are sensitive to their wishes and values and are, therefore, unlikely to engage in delinquency. Commitment is often referred to as the rational element of the bond. For people who have built up a stake in conformity, delinquent conduct places that investment in jeopardy and is, therefore, likely to be rejected. Involvement simply argues that adolescents heavily engrossed in conventional activities—family, school, sports and so forth—are too busy to be involved simultaneously in substantial amounts of delinquent conduct. Finally, belief is the moral element of the bond. People who believe strongly in the moral validity of society's norms are unlikely to violate those norms by engaging in delinquency. Thus, the behavior of people with high attachment, commitment, involvement, and belief is severely constrained and delinquency is unlikely. On the other hand, people with low attachment, commitment, involvement, and belief are not tightly ensnared in society's web and are much more likely to be delinquent.

The theoretical structure of Hirschi's control theory, as of most of the classical statements of control theory, is remarkably simple. The four elements of the bond appear as separate but equal factors, independently related to delinquency. Hirschi includes a brief but unsystematic discussion of how they might be interrelated,[5] but that is not pursued either theoretically or empirically.

In many ways, the great strength of classical control theory lies in its simplicity and resulting clarity. It identifies four of the core concepts that are causally related to delinquency and explicates how each operates to reduce delinquent behavior. That is a substantial contribution indeed.

Over the years, however, two major criticisms of the classical representation of control theory have emerged. First, it cannot easily account for the empirical importance of associations with delinquent peers in predicting delinquency; this limitation, in turn, has raised questions about classical control theory's amotivational as-

---

5 *Id.* at 27-30.

sumption. Second, both empirical observation and the logic of control theory suggest that the elements of the bond are interrelated and that their interrelationships might be helpful in explaining delinquency. These criticisms have given rise to integrated versions of control theory.

B. INTEGRATED CONTROL THEORIES

Integrated theories attempt to combine propositions from compatible theories to form a broader explanation of the phenomenon of interest.[6] Examples of efforts to expand the theoretical scope of classical control theory are those by Johnson,[7] Elliott et al.,[8] and Weis and Sederstrom.[9]

These theories share two general characteristics. First, they incorporate some elements of a social learning perspective into the explanation of delinquency, typically by including differential associations and deviant beliefs as important causal variables. As a result, classical control theory's assumption about the amotivational nature of deviance is weakened. Although some variation exists, integrated models assume that weakened bonds set the stage for delinquent behavior, but such behavior needs to be learned and reinforced before it is enacted. Thus, a weakened social bond is not, by itself, a sufficient explanation for delinquent behavior.

Second, these theories attempt to explicate the causal interrelationships among the elements of the bond. In general, the temporal and causal ordering starts with attachment to parents, is followed by commitment to and involvement in school, and is followed in turn by acceptance of conventional values. Also, all of the bonding variables precede the social learning variables. This approach provides a richer theoretical understanding of the causes of delinquency than is offered by classical versions. It begins to model the causal network that generates delinquent conduct; it assesses the impact of each element of the bond after the impact of the others is held constant; and, it estimates indirect as well as direct causal influences.

While the theoretical and empirical contributions of integrated

---

[6] *See* THEORETICAL INTEGRATION IN THE STUDY OF DEVIANCE AND CRIME: PROBLEMS AND PROSPECTS (S. Messner, M. Krohn & A. Liska eds. 1989) [hereinafter THEORETICAL INTEGRATION].

[7] R. JOHNSON, JUVENILE DELINQUENCY AND ITS ORIGINS (1979).

[8] Elliott, Ageton & Canter, *An Integrated Theoretical Perspective on Delinquent Behavior*, 16 J. RES. CRIME & DELINQ. 3 (1979); D. ELLIOTT, D. HUIZINGA & S. AGETON, EXPLAINING DELINQUENCY AND DRUG USE (1985).

[9] Weis & Sederstrom, *The Prevention of Serious Delinquency: What to Do?* (Reports of the National Juvenile Justice Assessment Centers, Department of Justice, OJJDP, Dec. 1981).

control theories are quite substantial, they too share a number of shortcomings. From the perspective of this paper, the most important shortcomings concern their static theoretical structure.

First, these models tend to ignore developmental issues. Despite the fact that criminal careers develop over time, a single and presumably invariant causal structure is offered. The same causal effects are presented for adolescents and young adults, for neophytes and experienced offenders. Such a view of human behavior does not accord very well with general observations, let alone with developmental psychology.

Second, these models generally do not allow for bidirectional causal influences either among the elements of the bond or between the elements and delinquency. Thus, if attachment to parents has a causal impact on commitment to school, commitment cannot influence attachment. Similarly, if commitment to school reduces delinquency, delinquency—no matter how serious or how prolonged— cannot influence commitment. Such a static view of the way in which social factors impinge upon human behavior is often quite implausible. For example, youngsters who join delinquent gangs and routinely use crack cocaine often find their commitment to school deteriorating as a result.

Thus, integrated control theories, like the more classical versions, offer implausibly static representations of the development of delinquency. Recognizing this limitation, recent theoretical models have attempted to incorporate a more developmental perspective[10] and a more dynamic causal structure[11] into the explanation of delinquency. In addition, longitudinal studies have begun to examine developmental and reciprocal issues empirically.[12] The present study examines one of these theoretical models—interactional the-

---

[10] 3 G. PATTERSON, A SOCIAL LEARNING APPROACH (1982); Loeber & Le Blanc, *Toward a Developmental Criminology*, in 12 CRIME & JUST.: A REVIEW OF RES. 375 (M. Tonry & N. Morris eds. 1990).

[11] Thornberry, *supra* note 1.

[12] *See, e.g.*, Agnew, *A Longitudinal Test of Social Control Theory and Delinquency*, 28 J. RES. CRIME & DELINQ. (1991) (forthcoming) [hereinafter Agnew, *A Longitudinal Test*]; Burkett & Warren, *Religiosity, Peer Influence, and Adolescent Marijuana Use: A Panel Study of Underlying Causal Structures*, 25 CRIMINOLOGY 109 (1987); Elliott, Huizinga & Morse, The Dynamics of Deviant Behavior: A National Survey (progress report submitted to the National Institute of Mental Health, Department of Health and Human Services 1985) [hereinafter Elliott, Dynamics of Deviant Behavior]; Liska & Reed, *Ties to Conventional Institutions and Delinquency: Estimating Reciprocal Effects*, 50 AM. SOC. REV. 547 (1985); Matsueda, *The Dynamics of Moral Beliefs and Minor Deviance*, 68 SOC. FORCES 428 (1989); Paternoster, *Examining Three-Wave Deterrence Models: A Question of Temporal Order and Specification*, 79 J. CRIM. L. & CRIMINOLOGY 135 (1988). For a review of these and related empirical studies, see Thornberry, *Empirical Support for Interactional Theory: A Review of the Literature*, in SOME CURRENT THEORIES OF CRIME AND DEVIANCE (D. Hawkins ed. 1991) (forthcoming).

ory—in more detail and tests empirically some of its core propositions.

III. INTERACTIONAL THEORY

Interactional theory proposes that the fundamental or primary cause of delinquent behavior is a weakening of bonds to conventional society. In this sense, it is a variant of social control theory that employs the basic argument that individuals who are attached to others, committed to conformity, and believe in conventional values are unlikely to engage in delinquent behavior.

When bonds to conventional society are weakened, however, a person acquires greater behavioral freedom. No longer bound to the straight and narrow, a number of alternatives become available to the individual, including the opportunity to engage in delinquent behavior. For that to occur, however, some mechanism that channels the behavioral freedom towards specifically delinquent conduct is required. This is especially so if one is concerned with explaining persistent and serious delinquency rather than isolated, nonpatterned acts of delinquency. Associations with delinquent peers and the learning environment they provide are the primary mechanisms for cultivating both delinquent beliefs and delinquent behavior. As delinquency is learned and reinforced, it is apt to become a stable part of the person's repertoire.

To this point, interactional theory is quite similar to the integrated control theories described earlier. It differs from those models in three fundamental respects, however.[13] First, it does not assume, as many control-based theories do, that variation in the strength of the bond just happens. This variation is systematically related to structural variables such as social class position and residential area. Second, it does not assume that causal models are stable over the life-course. Causal influences vary at different developmental stages and at different stages of criminal careers (*i.e.*, at initiation, maintenance, and termination). Third, it does not assume that causal influences are overwhelmingly unidirectional and that delinquency is merely an outcome variable. Many effects are bidirectional, and delinquency may contribute to the weakening of social bonds as well as being a consequence of weakened social bonds. Although interactional theory differs from other social control theories in these three respects, the present analysis is con-

---

[13] It also differs in that it is an elaborated, as opposed to an integrated, theory. *See* Thornberry, *Reflections on the Advantages and Disadvantages of Theoretical Integration*, in THEORETICAL INTEGRATION, *supra* note 6, at 51.

cerned almost exclusively with the third issue—whether social bonding variables and delinquency are better thought of as recursively or reciprocally related.

A.   RECIPROCAL RELATIONSHIPS

This article's empirical analysis focuses on two of the variables which bond a person to society; namely, attachment to parents and commitment to school. Interactional theory incorporates the element of involvement into a broadened concept of commitment, a view that has considerable theoretical and empirical support.[14] Also, interactional theory hypothesizes that at early adolescence, beliefs in conventional values should be relatively invariant and, therefore, add little to the explanation of delinquency.[15] The hypothesized invariance is observed in this data set, and conventional beliefs is dropped from the present analysis. The analysis thus focuses on the two elements of the bond generally thought to be most central to the explanation of delinquency during early adolescence—attachment to parents and commitment to school.

Classical versions of control theory view these variables as having independent, direct effects on delinquency (Figure 1a). For example, the most that Hirschi says about the interrelationships between these variables is that it is "safe to assume that attachment to conventional others and commitment to achievement tend to vary together."[16] In integrated versions of control theory (Figure 1b), the typical specification holds that attachment to parents directly affects commitment to school and delinquent behavior and that commitment to school also has a direct effect on delinquency.[17]

It is important to note in these models the effects that are presumed to play no causal role in the genesis of delinquency. First, attachment to parents is not influenced by either commitment to school or delinquent behavior. Thus, even if youngsters are doing very poorly in school and are heavily involved in delinquent behavior, these factors presumably have no negative impact on the affective bond between parent and child. Second, commitment to school is not influenced by delinquency. Delinquent behavior, no matter how persistent or serious, does not lead to a reduction in academic performance and commitment.

Interactional theory views both of these assertions as theoreti-

---

[14] Krohn & Massey, *Social Control and Delinquent Behavior: An Examination of the Elements of the Social Bond*, 21 SOCIOLOGICAL Q. 529 (1980).

[15] Thornberry, *supra* note 1, at 874.

[16] T. HIRSCHI, *supra* note 4, at 28.

[17] *See, e.g.*, R. JOHNSON, *supra* note 7, at 96.

FIGURE 1

**TYPICAL SPECIFICATIONS OF THEORETICAL RELATIONSHIPS AMONG
ATTACHMENT TO PARENTS, COMMITMENT TO SCHOOL, AND
DELINQUENT BEHAVIOR**

a. Classical Control Theory

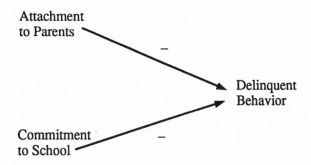

b. Integrated Control Theory

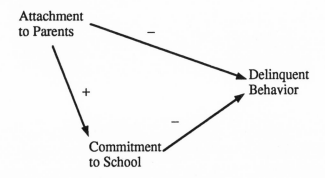

cally and empirically implausible. A mother's love may be undying, but it is not necessarily unbending. Precisely because of control theory's assumption that parents are monolithically conventional, extremely poor school performance and high involvement in delinquency on the part of the child should drive a wedge between parent and child, resulting in a weakening of attachment. Similarly, youngsters who become increasingly involved in delinquency are likely to experience a declining commitment to school. Having already jeopardized their stake in conformity by delinquent conduct, their commitment is likely to dwindle even further as delinquent conduct continues. Thus, interactional theory predicts more complex interrelationships among these variables than is found in either classical or integrated control theories. While weakened bonds to conventional society do tend to increase the chances of delinquency, delinquent behavior also reduces attachment to parents and commitment to school, further weakening the person's bond to society.

B. EMPIRICAL SUPPORT

Few empirical studies have examined reciprocal relationships for these three variables—attachment to parents, commitment to school, and delinquent behavior. The empirical studies that have done so suggest that reciprocal influences are indeed important, but the precise pattern of these relationships is not very consistent across studies. For example, Liska and Reed[18] reported a bidirectional relationship for school and delinquency while Agnew,[19] using the same data set, reported only an effect from delinquency to school attachment. On the other hand, Liska and Reed found a unidirectional effect from parental attachment to delinquency, while Agnew did not.[20] When social learning variables are added to the analysis, results also vary across studies. Using National Youth Survey data, both Elliott *et al.*[21] and Agnew[22] reported no significant relationships, either unidirectional or bidirectional, involving attachment, commitment, and delinquency. However, Paternoster,[23] using data from South Carolina, reported a consistent lagged reciprocal relationship for parental supervision and two separate forms of delinquency—marijuana use and petty theft.

These results suggest that additional research is needed to clarify the causal relationships among these variables. Findings of prior research demonstrate that some of the relationships involving attachment to parents, commitment to school, and delinquency are reciprocal, implying that the more traditional unidirectional specifications (see Figure 1) are erroneous. Nevertheless, research findings have yet to converge on a consistent pattern of bidirectional effects. Because of this divergence, priority is therefore given to establishing the nature of the reciprocal relationships between the

---

[18] Liska & Reed, *supra* note 12.

[19] Agnew, *Social Control Theory and Delinquency: A Longitudinal Test*, 23 CRIMINOLOGY 47 (1985).

[20] Agnew, *A Longitudinal Test, supra* note 12.

[21] Elliott, *Dynamics of Deviant Behavior, supra* note 12.

[22] Agnew, *A Longitudinal Test, supra* note 12.

[23] Paternoster, *supra* note 12.

bonding variables and delinquency before determining if those relationships vary in a broader theoretical context.

C. MODEL SPECIFICATION

Interactional theory's specification of the causal relationships for these variables during early adolescence is presented in Figure 2.[24] For reasons discussed earlier, strong reciprocal relationships among these variables are anticipated. That is, weakened bonds to conventional society should increase the chances of delinquency, and delinquent behavior should feed back upon and further attenuate the person's bond to society. A number of more specific points about the model in Figure 2 can also be made.

First, at Wave 1 the variables are treated as lagged endogenous variables and are allowed to be correlated with each other. Causal relationships among them are not modeled to improve the identification of the overall model.

Second, one-wave stability effects are predicted for each variable. More concretely, the person's current level on any variable is expected to be produced, to some sizeable extent, by the person's immediately prior level on the same variable. Including stability effects in all equations also allows lagged and instantaneous effects to be thought of as predicting change in the dependent variable.

Third, we include two types of reciprocal or bidirectional relationships in the model. The first are referred to either as instantaneous or contemporaneous relationships. These refer to a causal loop between two variables when both variables are measured at the same wave or time period. For example, a causal loop between two variables (X and Y) means that X_t has a direct effect on Y_t, and Y_t also has a direct effect on X_t. The second type are referred to as either lagged or cross-lagged relationships. These refer to mutual causal relationships between two variables that develop over time. For X and Y, this means that X_{t-1} has an effect on Y_t, and Y_{t-1} has an effect on X_t.

The theoretical model anticipates both lagged and instantaneous reciprocal effects for each of the dyadic relationships. One can illustrate these effects with commitment to school and delinquent behavior. Change in delinquency from one wave to the next is thought to be produced by both prior commitment (the lagged effect) and by current commitment (the instantaneous effect). Simi-

---

[24] The theoretical model is presented for early adolescence, since the data used in this study cover that developmental stage. Also, a three-wave panel model is presented to conform to the available data.

FIGURE 2

THEORETICAL MODEL OF CAUSAL RELATIONSHIPS AMONG ATTACHMENT TO PARENTS, COMMITMENT TO SCHOOL, AND DELINQUENT BEHAVIOR

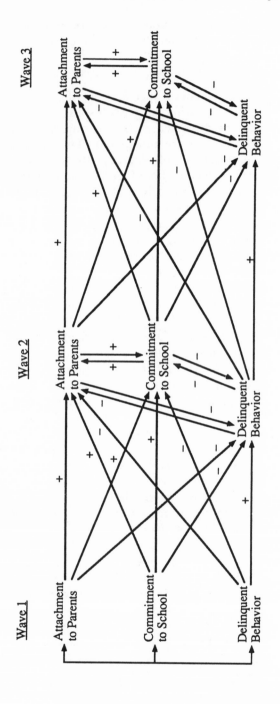

larly, change in commitment is thought to be produced by both prior delinquency (the lagged effect) and current delinquency (the instantaneous effect). The same pattern of relationships holds for the other variables in the model. Since the effects of these variables are expected to diminish over time, we include only lagged effects from the immediately prior wave.

Fourth, this model is derived from interactional theory's more general model and only refers to early adolescence.[25] As a result, major developmental hypotheses are not offered. One should note, however, that interactional theory posits that by middle adolescence, the causal impact of attachment to parents diminishes considerably, and no direct path from it to delinquency is predicted. Causal relationships among the other variables remain largely unchanged from early to mid-adolescence.

Theoretically, this model is more complex and less parsimonious than the versions presented in either classical or integrated control theories. Empirically, it requires more complicated statistical procedures for assessing its validity. Are these additional demands reasonable to place upon the theory? The remainder of this paper attempts to answer this question by analyzing data collected as part of the Rochester Youth Development Study.

IV. METHODS

The Rochester Youth Development Study (RYDS) is designed to examine the development of delinquent behavior and drug use in a predominantly high-risk, urban sample using a seven-wave panel design. Each adolescent respondent and his or her caretaker (in 95% of the cases this is the mother or stepmother) are interviewed at six-month intervals. Data are also collected from the Rochester schools, police, and other agencies that service youth.

A. SAMPLE

The total panel consists of 987 students who attended the seventh and eighth grades of the Rochester City public schools during the 1987-1988 academic year.[26] The present analysis is based on the first three waves of student interviews, which began in the spring

---

[25] Thornberry, *supra* note 1, at 870-76.

[26] A thorough description of the sampling strategy is provided in M. Farnworth, T. Thornberry, A. Lizotte & M. Krohn, Sampling Design and Implementation: Technical Report No. 1 (Aug. 1990) (available through Rochester Youth Development Study, School of Criminal Justice, The University at Albany).

semester of the adolescents' seventh or eighth grade and continued through the spring semester of their eighth or ninth grade.

To ensure that serious, chronic offenders are included in the study, the sample overrepresents high-risk youth in the following manner. Males are oversampled (75% versus 25%), because they are more likely to be chronic offenders and to engage in serious delinquent behavior than are females. In addition, students are selected proportionately to the resident arrest rates of the census tracts in which they live. These rates estimate the proportion of each tract's total population arrested in 1986. Students from tracts with the highest rates are proportionately overrepresented since they are at highest risk for serious delinquency; students from the lower rate tracts are proportionately underrepresented. Because the true probability of a youth living in a particular census tract is known, the sampling strategy provides the means to weight cases to represent the total seventh and eighth grade population. The sample is weighted in the analyses to follow.[27]

Current analysis is based on the 867 adolescents for whom Wave 1 through Wave 3 interviews are completed. The retention rate from Wave 1 to Wave 2 is 91%, while from Wave 1 to Wave 3 it is 88%.[28] Characteristics of students who remain in the study during all three waves compare favorably to those at the initial wave (see Table 1). There are only slight differences in terms of age, sex, ethnicity, and resident arrest rates of census tracts. At Wave 1, the unweighted sample was 69% Afro-American, 17% Hispanic, and 14% white; 74% male and 26% female; and ranged in age from eleven to fourteen, although 75% were thirteen or fourteen. These proportions are quite close to what was expected given the population characteristics of the Rochester Schools and the decision to oversample high-risk youth.

RYDS interviewers conducted interviews with students in private rooms at the schools. If the student could not be contacted in school, he or she was interviewed at home. Interviews lasted between forty-five minutes and one hour.

B.   MEASUREMENT OF VARIABLES

The model tested in this paper contains three variables: attachment to parents, commitment to school, and self-reported delin-

---

[27] For example, weighting the sample has the effect of equalizing the number of boys and girls in the sample.

[28] The total retention rate at Wave 3 is somewhat higher (92%). The 88% figure represents the percentage of subjects who completed all three interviews.

TABLE 1
CHARACTERISTICS OF THE UNWEIGHTED SAMPLE
AT WAVES 1, 2, AND 3

		Wave 1	Wave 2	Wave 3
Age at Wave 1				
	< 13	13.9	14.3	14.6
	13	37.5	38.1	39.0
	14	37.0	37.5	36.9
	> 14	11.6	10.1	9.5
Sex				
	Male	74.1	73.7	73.8
	Female	25.9	26.3	26.2
Ethnicity				
	Afro-American	68.7	69.2	69.6
	Hispanic	17.1	16.5	16.1
	White	14.2	14.3	14.3
Census Tracts Grouped By Resident Arrest Rates				
	1 = highest	33.1	32.8	33.7
	2	32.1	32.4	32.0
	3	18.1	18.2	17.9
	4	9.8	9.8	9.6
	5	5.2	5.1	5.0
	6 = lowest	1.7	1.7	1.8

quent behavior. Each variable is measured with identical items at all three waves.

1.   Attachment to Parents

An eleven-item scale adapted from Hudson's Child's Attitude Toward Mother Scale[29] is used to measure attachment to parents.[30] The scale measures adolescents' perceptions of warmth, liking, and the absence of hostility between themselves and their parent or primary caretaker.[31] Since the Hudson scale has been used previously and found to be reliable, we computed a confirmatory factor analysis for each wave of data collection to confirm that the items loaded on a single factor.[32] At all three waves, the items loaded on a single factor and the factor loadings are quite stable across waves. Coeffi-

---

[29] W. HUDSON, THE CLINICAL MEASUREMENT PACKAGE: A FIELD MANUAL (1982).

[30] Missing values never exceeded 10 respondents on individual items used to constitute the scales used in this study. Therefore, the mean on those items is substituted for missing values.

[31] In approximately 85% of the cases, the referent is the mother; in another 10% it is the stepmother; and the remaining cases refer to a variety of other caretakers (e.g., a father, grandparent, etc.).

[32] The individual items and their factor loadings appear in Appendix A.

cients of reliability (Chronbach's alpha) are quite high for all three waves (0.82, 0.87, and 0.87), and higher scale values indicate a closer relationship between child and parent.

2. *Commitment to School*

An exploratory factor analysis including the sixteen school-related items contained in the interview schedule generated two factors.[33] One factor includes items that asked respondents about their relationships to their teachers (eigenvalue = 1.24), while the other factor includes items that dealt with more general attitudes toward school (eigenvalue = 2.44). Because the teacher factor could be considered another measure of attachment to a conventional adult, only the ten-item scale measuring whether students like school, how well they do in school, and how hard they work on their schoolwork is retained. These items more clearly tap the concept of commitment. Scale reliabilities are high for all three waves (0.76, 0.80 and 0.83), and higher scores indicate that the student is more committed to school.

3. *Self-Reported Delinquency*

A total of forty-four types of delinquent behavior and drug use are included on the student interview schedule. These items are derived in large part from the National Youth Survey.[34] In the first interview, questions concerning delinquency were framed in terms of offenses that took place over the previous six months. In subsequent interviews the questions covered the period of time since respondents were last interviewed (which was also approximately six months).[35]

By excluding items that potentially double-count delinquencies,[36] a general delinquency scale comprised of 29 items ranging from running away from home to using a weapon to try to hurt someone is generated. In constructing this measure, responses are first screened to determine that they (a) fit the category of delin-

---

[33] We computed the factor analysis using a principle component analysis and a maximum likelihood estimation procedure.

[34] D. ELLIOTT, D. HUIZINGA & S. AGETON, EXPLAINING DELINQUENCY AND DRUG USE (1985).

[35] In order to assist respondents in focusing on the appropriate time period, interviewers show them a calendar, pointing out the date of their last interview and significant events (*e.g.*, holidays, the beginning and end of the school year, *etc.*) that occurred since then.

[36] For example, items about shoplifting and thefts of a certain value can potentially count the same event twice. In those instances, only one item is used to calculate the general delinquency score. The final items are listed in Appendix B.

quency being measured and (b) are "actionable" offenses. The latter criterion is intended to screen out trivial offenses (*e.g.*, pranks, sibling squabbles, and the like) that law enforcement officials would probably ignore.[37] If the subject's response meets these two criteria, it is included in the summated prevalence score. Since the scores on the delinquency scale are skewed toward the lower end, they are logged in subsequent analyses.

4.   *Other Variables*

In addition to the variables included in the theoretical model, sex, ethnicity, and age are included as control variables. Ethnicity is measured with two dummy variables representing Afro-Americans and Hispanics, with whites being the reference category. Sex is also a dummy variable with females as the reference category.

V.   ANALYSIS

Equations for this analysis are estimated using EQS, a program which employs a Full Information Maximum Likelihood (FIML) covariance structure model.[38] Our initial intent was to estimate the full theoretical model presented in Figure 2. This three-wave panel model anticipates lagged reciprocal relationships from parental attachment, commitment to school, and delinquent behavior at one wave to each of those same variables at the next wave. In addition, contemporaneous reciprocal relationships are anticipated among these variables. The model also includes stability effects for variables from one wave to the next. This aspect of the model allows one to predict changes in delinquent behavior, parental attachment, and commitment to school from other lagged and instantaneous variables. Furthermore, when both lagged and contemporaneous effects of exogenous variables are called for, the model allows one to predict *changes* in the endogenous variables from both level of and changes in exogenous variables. In estimating all of these coefficients, the effects of age, sex, and ethnicity are controlled.

Numerous heartbreaking attempts, employing various minor changes in specification, were made to estimate this model. After properly identifying the model, estimation proved unsuccessful if one includes both cross-lagged and instantaneous effects in the sys-

---

[37] To determine that the offenses reported are "actionable," respondents are asked to describe the most serious (or only) act committed in a category. Coders rate the act as being actionable or not. The interrater reliability for the three waves ranged from 90% to 95%. If the most serious delinquency described is not rated as delinquent, the item is coded as a zero.

[38] P. BENTLER, EQS: STRUCTURAL EQUATIONS PROGRAM MANUAL (1989).

tem of equations. This is true for both the second and third panels of the model. These findings, as well as those of previous research using this data set,[39] suggest that collinearity may be a serious problem when both lagged and instantaneous reciprocal effects are included in the same model. Because of this collinearity concern, a model that includes only lagged reciprocal effects is estimated in this study. This causal order (see Figure 3) is employed, because a model retaining *only* the instantaneous reciprocal effects implies that current levels of attachment and commitment can predict changes in delinquency over the prior six months. The same logical problem holds for the other endogenous variables. Thus, if only one class of relationships can be retained because of collinearity, the cross-lagged model is the only one consistent with proper temporal and causal ordering.

In addition to the lagged reciprocal relationships, the estimated model includes stability effects, error terms, appropriate correlations among the errors, and three unidirectional contemporaneous effects at each wave. We predict that delinquency has a contemporaneous effect on both attachment and commitment since, at each wave, delinquency measures behavior over the prior six months, and attachment and commitment are contemporaneous measures. In essence, these relationships are also lagged even though the measurement occurs at the same time.[40] The choice of including an effect from attachment to commitment is discussed below.

Results for this model are presented in Figure 4 and Tables 2 and 3. The traditional chi-square goodness of fit test for the model is insignificant ($X^2 = 11.48$; $p = 0.12$), indicating that the model is a very good representation of the data.[41] This is somewhat surprising, given the sensitivity of chi-square to large sample sizes like the one here.

A.   STABILITY EFFECTS

The stability effects in the model are generally larger between

---

[39] T. Thornberry, A. Lizotte, M. Krohn & M. Farnworth, The Role of Delinquent Peers in the Initiation of Delinquent Behavior (RYDS Working Paper No. 6) (presented at the annual meetings of the American Sociological Ass'n, Washington, D.C., Aug. 1990) (available through authors).

[40] For a discussion of this point, see Paternoster, *supra* note 12.

[41] Standardized effects are reported, and all effects are significant at the 0.05 level of a one-tailed test. With one exception, which is discussed below, results of the multiple LaGrange test (explained in Bentler & Dijkstra, *Efficient Estimation Via Linearization in Structural Models*, in VI MULTIVARIATE ANALYSIS (P. Krishnaiah ed. 1985)) suggest that we have not made unreasonable assumptions about excluding other relationships among these variables.

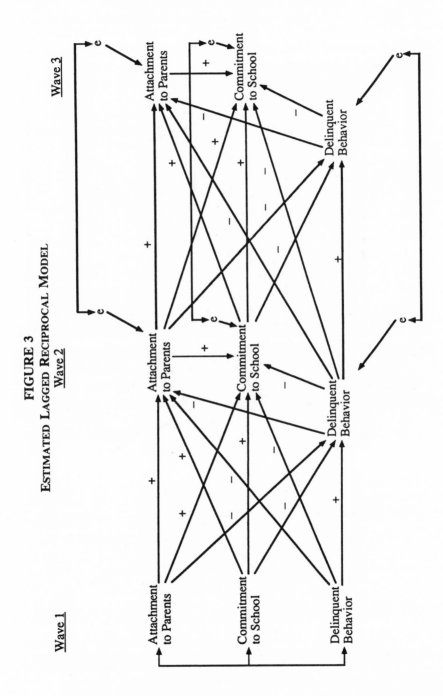

FIGURE 3
ESTIMATED LAGGED RECIPROCAL MODEL

FIGURE 4

EMPIRICALLY SUPPORTED LAGGED RECIPROCAL MODEL

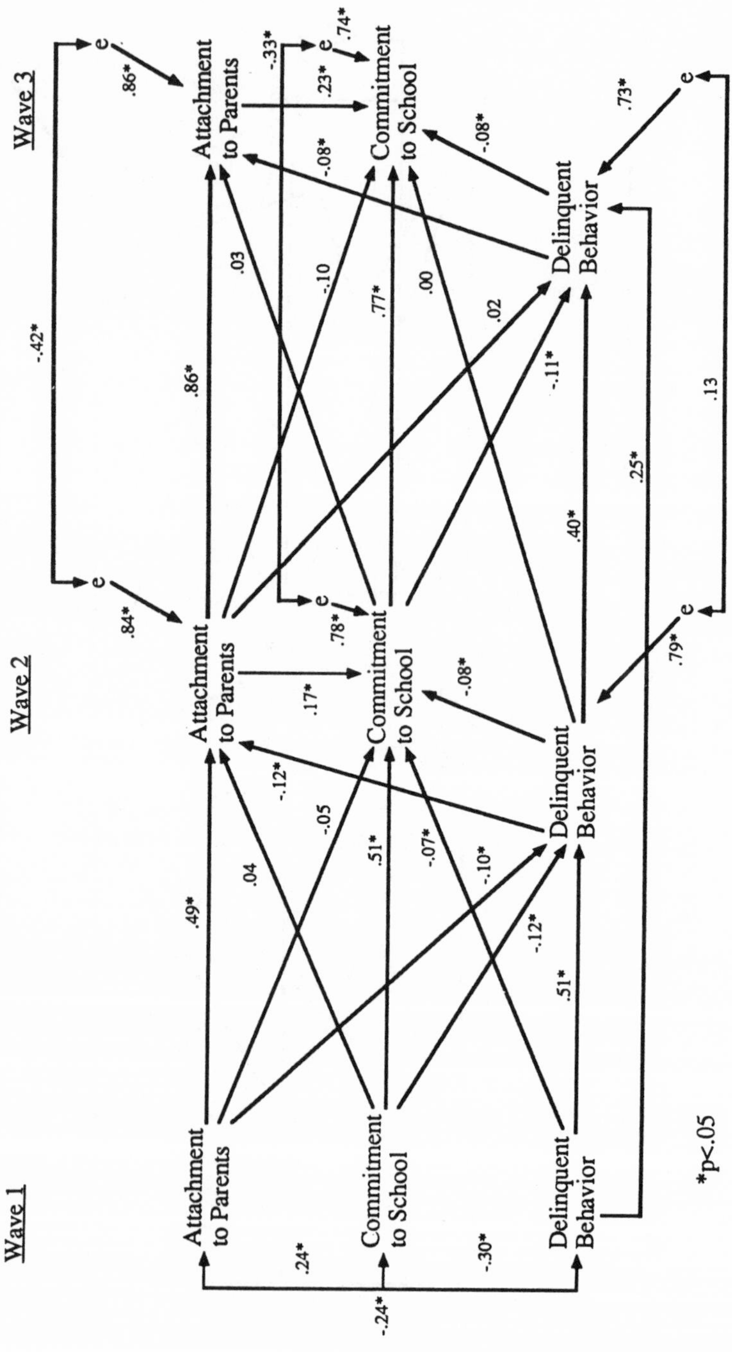

Waves 2 and 3 than they are between Waves 1 and 2. For example, for attachment to parents, the Wave 1 to 2 effect is 0.49 while the Wave 2 to 3 effect is 0.86; for commitment to school, the first stability effect is 0.51 and the second is 0.77. For delinquent behavior, the LaGrange test indicated the importance of adding the stability effect of delinquent behavior at Wave 1 to delinquent behavior at Wave 3. At Wave 3 both one-wave and two-wave lagged stability effects are significant, with the one-year lag being about half the size of the six-month lag. If one adds the two direct stability effects for Wave 3 together, the combined direct effect (0.65) is again somewhat larger than the stability effect from Wave 1 to Wave 2 (0.51).

Overall, one might think of the stability effects for these variables as a sort of momentum of past behaviors encouraging future behaviors. This implies that, for this age group, adolescents are moving toward a sort of equilibrium on these variables. As time passes, the probability increases that the level of a variable at one point will be positively related to the level of that same variable at a subsequent point.[42] These findings also suggest that one-year time intervals between interviews are too long, because they would tend to homogenize the more rapidly changing and divergent six-month effects and the yearly effect.

There are moderate negative correlations of the residuals for the attachment to parents and commitment to school equations between Waves 2 and 3. This implies that large errors in predicting commitment to school at Wave 2 are associated with small errors in prediction at Wave 3.[43] The negative correlation might be removed by including the Wave 1 to Wave 3 stability effect. When this effect was added for delinquent behavior (see above), the correlation between the error terms changed from negative and significant to positive and nonsignificant. In fact, the multiple LaGrange test[44] suggests adding the two-wave lagged stability effect to the Wave 3 equation predicting attachment to parents. When this effect is added to the model, the maximum likelihood function does not converge, making model estimation impossible. The LaGrange test did

---

[42] Of course, at later ages, teens decline and even desist from delinquency. Hence, at some point in the analysis involving later waves of data, it will become increasingly important to locate the factors associated with declining stability over time. These factors would separate the career delinquents from those who desist. At even later ages, stability would again increase because of more uniform desistance in the population.

[43] For a discussion of how omitted causal factors could account for these correlations, see Luskin, *Estimating and Interpreting Correlations Between Disturbances and Residual Path Coefficients in Nonrecursive (and Recursive) Causal Models*, 22 AM. J. POL. SCI. 444 (1978).

[44] Bentler & Dijkstra, *Efficient Estimation, supra* note 41.

not call for the inclusion of the Wave 1 to Wave 3 effect for commitment to school.

B.   CROSS-LAGGED EFFECTS

The theoretically expected lagged reciprocal relationship between the two bonding variables is not evident in this model. Attachment to parents has significant instantaneous effects on commitment to school, such that high attachment increases commitment. However, the anticipated reciprocal effects from commitment to attachment, either lagged or instantaneous,[45] are absent. Therefore, it would appear that these variables are involved in a unidirectional relationship with attachment to parents increasing commitment to school.

In addition, for both Waves 2 and 3, the lagged effect of attachment to parents on commitment to school is negative but insignificant if evaluated using a one-tailed test. One expects the level of attachment in Wave 1 to produce decreasing commitment to school in Wave 2, having also controlled for changes in attachment to parents in Wave 2. After having accounted for change, those with high initial levels of parental attachment will experience decreasing commitment, and those with very low levels of attachment will experience increasing commitment. One could think of this result as an example of regression toward the mean of attachment to parents over time.

For the substantive predictions concerning the cross-lagged effects involving delinquency, considerable correspondence exists between the hypothesized and estimated models. Attachment to parents and commitment to school in Wave 1 are significant and negative predictors of delinquent behavior at Wave 2. The standardized coefficients are -0.10 and -0.12, respectively. In other words, high levels of both attachment to parents and commitment to school in Wave 1 lead to decreases in delinquency from Wave 1 to Wave 2. In addition, however, there is a significant cross-lagged reciprocal effect from delinquent behavior at Wave 1 to commitment to school at Wave 2 (-0.07); high levels of initial delinquency are associated with reductions in commitment to school.[46] At Wave 2,

---

[45] The model including instantaneous effects from commitment to attachment is not shown in this article. The model is the same as that presented in Figure 4 with the addition of an instrumental variable—family involvement—that has a direct effect on attachment to parents at each of the waves.

[46] Lagged effects from delinquent behavior to attachment to parents are not shown in Figure 4. Initial estimates indicated that they are essentially zero, and they were eliminated from final estimations to improve the fit of the model.

there are also instantaneous negative effects of delinquent behavior on both attachment to parents (−0.12) and commitment to school (−0.08). High delinquency during the last six months produces decreases in attachment to parents and commitment to school.

In combination, these results suggest that low levels of attachment to parents and commitment to school at one time, lead to more delinquency in the next time interval; and high delinquency, in turn, further attenuates attachment to parents and commitment to school. The model shows that even in a relatively short interval, relationships between attachment and commitment on the one hand, and delinquency on the other, can propel one towards or away from delinquency.

Commitment to school and attachment to parents play central roles in the model. At Wave 2, delinquent behavior and attachment to parents both drive commitment to school. Furthermore, increases in attachment to parents cause increases in commitment to school.

The model also shows how these variables interact over time to propel individuals into or out of a delinquent career in the long run. The level of commitment to school at Wave 2, and the stability of delinquency from Waves 1 and 2, lead to increases in delinquency at Wave 3. This starts the cycle again, with higher delinquency at Wave 3 leading to lower attachment to parents. Again, at Wave 3, both delinquent behavior and attachment to parents determine commitment to school.

C. INDIRECT EFFECTS

To this point, analysis has focused on direct effects—the effect of one variable on another—without taking into consideration indirect pathways via intervening or mediating variables. Yet the structure of interactional theory suggests that substantial indirect effects among these variables should occur as well. Since the variables are all interrelated in a relatively dense causal web (see Figure 2), change in any single variable should not only have a direct impact on another variable, but should also have indirect effects as the consequences of that change ripple throughout the causal system. To examine this possibility, Table 2 presents the sum of all indirect effects from each predictor variable to each of the endogenous variables. One can calculate the specific pathways that contribute to these sums from the coefficients presented earlier in Figure 4.[47]

---

[47] In the parlance of path analysis, these are the causal indirect effects. They are calculated by simply multiplying adjacent indirect effects. They include neither non-

TABLE 2
INDIRECT EFFECTS FOR ENDOGENOUS VARIABLES†

Predictor Variables	Endogenous Variables					
	Attachment to Parents W2	Commitment to School W2	Delinquent Behavior W2	Attachment to Parents W3	Commitment to School W3	Delinquent Behavior W3
Attachment to Parents W1	.01	.09*	—	.44*	.08*	-.04
Commitment to School W1	.01	.02	—	.07*	.42*	-.10
Delinquent Behavior W1	-.06*	-.05*	—	-.09*	-.14*	.22*
Attachment to Parents W2	—	—	—	.01	.33*	-.02*
Commitment to School W2	—	—	—	.01*	.02*	—
Delinquent Behavior W2	—	-.02*	—	-.14*	-.12*	.01
Attachment to Parents W3	—	—	—	—	—	—
Commitment to School W3	—	—	—	—	—	—
Delinquent Behavior W3	—	—	—	—	-.02*	—

† Dashes indicate that no indirect paths were estimated.
* Significant at the level of .05 (one-tailed test)

The top panel of Table 2 displays the indirect effects of Wave 1 variables on Wave 2 and 3 endogenous variables. The most informative results concern the Wave 3 endogenous variables (the upper right panel of Table 2), since these variables have the greatest number of indirect paths leading to them.

The main diagonal of the upper right panel presents "indirect stability effects," or, more specifically, the indirect effects of a variable measured at Wave 1 on that same variable measured at Wave 3. These indirect effects are significant and quite high, but almost all of the effect is due to the multiplication of the first and second stability effects, as revealed by an examination of Figure 4.

The off-diagonal entries in that panel are more interesting theoretically since they represent indirect effects across variables. Attachment to parents at Wave 1 has an indirect effect on commitment to school at Wave 3 (0.08), and commitment at Wave 1 has an indirect effect on attachment at Wave 3 (0.07). Interestingly though, neither bonding variable has a significant indirect effect on delinquency. On the other hand, delinquent behavior at Wave 1 has significant effects on both of the Wave 3 bonding variables— attachment to parents (-0.09) and commitment to school (-0.14). Thus, delinquent conduct attenuates a person's bond to conventional society both directly and via a number of indirect pathways.

The one-wave indirect effects, seen in the upper left and the middle right panels of Table 2, are substantially smaller than the two-wave effects just discussed.[48] Nevertheless, the pattern of results is similar. Indirect effects of the bonding variables on delinquency and on each other tend to be smaller than the indirect effects of delinquency on the bonding variables.

In sum, results for both the direct and indirect effects estimated in this model are quite similar. While attachment to parents and commitment to school tend to reduce delinquent behavior, it appears that delinquent behavior has somewhat stronger and more consistent effects on reducing attachment to parents and commitment to school.

D.   BACKGROUND VARIABLES

Table 3 shows the effects of sex, age, and ethnicity on the endogenous variables in the model. The most notable findings are

---

causal indirect effects (traversing backwards on an arrow) nor spurious effects (effects traversing correlations among exogenous variables).

[48] There is one exception to this statement. The indirect effect of Wave 2 attachment on Wave 3 commitment is large (0.33), primarily because this effect includes two pathways that involve stability effects.

TABLE 3

EFFECTS OF BACKGROUND VARIABLES AND GOODNESS-OF-FIT STATISTICS FOR LAGGED RECIPROCAL MODEL

Variable Names	Wave 2			Wave 3		
	Attachment to Parents	Commitment to School	Delinquent Behavior	Attachment to Parents	Commitment to School	Delinquent Behavior
Sex (Male)	.03	.04	.02	-.01	-.04	.08*
Age	.02	-.10*	.05*	.05	-.03	.01
Ethnicity (Afro-American)	.04	.08*	.07*	.01	.06	.06
Ethnicity (Hispanic)	.01	-.03	-.01	.02	-.00	.02

* p<.05 (one-tailed test)

Note: Goodness-of-fit indices for the total model
　　　Chi-square: 11.48 with 7 degrees of freedom (p=.12)
　　　Bentler-Bonett Normed Fit Index: .997

that age decreases commitment to school at Wave 2; males are more likely to experience increases in delinquent behavior at Wave 3; and Afro-Americans report more increases in commitment to school and increases in delinquency than others. None of these effects are particularly strong, however, suggesting that this model applies reasonably well to each of these major demographic subgroups.

VI. DISCUSSION

The classical version of control theory, epitomized by Hirschi's presentation, has generated much research over the past two decades. Although some of that research has supported hypotheses derived from that perspective, other examinations have pointed to deficiencies in the theory. Integrated theories, which combine propositions from control theory and social learning theory, address one of these deficiencies—the failure to include the impact of differential associations in predicting delinquent behavior. Integrated control theories, however, share with classical control theories a static theoretical structure, failing to attend to developmental issues and not allowing for reciprocal causal influences.

In contrast to these models, interactional theory explicitly recognizes that causal influences vary at different developmental stages and that many causal relationships are reciprocal. To account for these issues, interactional theory is necessarily more complex and less parsimonious. The current analysis has addressed the question of whether such complexity is warranted by focusing on the part of the overall model that includes the interrelationships among attachment to parents, commitment to school, and delinquent behavior for early adolescence.

Results warrant such theoretical complexity. In terms of the hypotheses of reciprocal relationships offered by interactional theory in the present analysis, only the relationship concerning the two bonding variables is unsupported. While attachment to parents has an instantaneous effect on commitment to school, commitment to school does not exert a significant lagged or instantaneous effect on attachment to parents.

Commitment to school and delinquent behavior are involved in a mutually reinforcing causal relationship over time. Low commitment increases delinquency, and delinquency in turn reduces commitment to school. Reciprocal effects for these variables are quite stable over the three waves of this panel model.

The relationship between attachment to parents and delinquent behavior is somewhat more complex. From Wave 1 to 2 these variables are reciprocally related: low attachment leads to increases in delinquency and delinquency further attenuates the adolescent's attachment to parents. From Wave 2 to 3, however, the relationship between these variables appears to be unidirectional; delinquency has a negative impact on attachment, but attachment to parents does not have a significant effect on delinquency. The latter finding, while not anticipated by either classical or integrated control theory, is suggested by the model for middle adolescence presented in interactional theory.[49] That model posits that parental influences in accounting for delinquency diminish considerably over time as adolescents gain independence. Indeed, by middle adolescence, attachment to parents is viewed as an effect of delinquency rather than a cause of it. The findings reported here are quite consistent with this developmental perspective.

These reciprocal effects and the significant indirect effects observed here are also consistent with interactional theory's concept of behavioral trajectories. This concept suggests that for adolescents who are weakly bonded to society,

> the initially weak bonds lead to high delinquency involvement, the high delinquency involvement further weakens the conventional bonds, and in combination both of these effects make it extremely difficult to reestablish bonds to conventional society at later ages. As a result, all of the factors tend to reinforce one another over time to produce an extremely high probability of continued deviance.[50]

On the other hand, of course, there are adolescents who are highly attached to parents and committed to school, and they are unlikely to engage in delinquency. In turn, their generally conforming behavior patterns further cement their bond to conventional society. In this case, a behavioral trajectory is established that leads to increasing conformity.

While these results support interactional theory, it must be emphasized that they address only a part of the overall theoretical argument. Whether the reciprocal relationships found in this study remain once variables like association with deviant peers are entered into the model has yet to be determined. The estimation of such a model is the ultimate objective of the Rochester Youth Development Study, and the present findings offer encouragement to pursue that objective.

Perhaps more importantly than what the results suggest about interactional theory is what they suggest about research strategies in the study of delinquency causation. By collecting and analyzing

---

[49] Thornberry, *supra* note 1, at 877-79.
[50] *Id.* at 893.

panel data and allowing for reciprocal effects, this study calls into question the interpretation of results from studies that examine only unidirectional relationships. It has been argued that unidirectional hypotheses that ignore causal effects from delinquency to commitment and from delinquency to attachment are theoretically implausible. The results of this study join with the relatively few previous investigations of reciprocal relationships to suggest that such hypotheses are also empirically implausible. However, if researchers confine their investigations to cross-sectional studies or do not examine bidirectional hypotheses when they have access to panel data, they will continue to make important errors in interpretation. Although this study did not directly investigate the developmental aspects of interactional theory, some of its results also suggest that future studies should examine developmental changes more thoroughly as well.

## VII.	Policy Implications

The results of this study have a number of implications for programs designed to prevent and treat delinquency. The remainder of this article discusses some of these implications. Our intent is to identify issues that should be addressed by intervention programs; we do not attempt to recommend how one should design those programs or what specific modalities one should offer. The design of programs goes beyond the inferences that one can draw from these data and requires the special expertise of treatment agents. Nevertheless, the findings of this research have a number of implications for policy.

First, this study highlights, once again, the importance of bonding adolescents to conventional society as an important step in reducing delinquency. In doing so, however, programs should begin to treat delinquent behavior as an active rather than a passive element in the causal system. Because of its reciprocal relationships with the bonding variables, delinquent behavior contributes, in a very real sense, to its own causation. Once exhibited, delinquency causes a deterioration in attachment and commitment, which, in turn, leads to further increases in delinquency. Treatment agents need to be aware of this causal pattern and should design intervention strategies that reduce or mitigate the negative consequences of delinquency on family and school. If this is not done, then the adolescent's continuing delinquency may simply "undo" the success of intervention programs in improving attachment to family and commitment to school.

Second, the interlocking nature of the causal relationships suggests the need for comprehensive, holistic treatment strategies. Since delinquency appears to be embedded in a rather complex causal network, there is no single, direct pathway to delinquency. For this reason, programs need to address all of these causal influences as a coherent package. Precisely because of the reciprocal nature of delinquency causation, single focus interventions are less likely to be successful than programs that deal with multiple factors and their interrelationships simultaneously.

The emphasis on holistic programs that flows from an interactional perspective has both positive and negative features. On the negative side, it suggests that interventions need to be comprehensive and interdisciplinary and therefore are likely to be both expensive and difficult to manage. On the positive side, however, it suggests that successful intervention in any one part of the system will tend to ripple throughout the system, helping intervention efforts targeted at another factor. For example, family interventions that improve attachment to parents should also indirectly improve commitment to school, thereby making the efforts of teachers and counselors to improve academic performance in school a little easier.

Third, these findings suggest that family interventions should start relatively early in the life-course, since the causal impact of attachment to parents on delinquency appears to weaken as these subjects begin to enter middle adolescence. If this pattern continues, it would highlight the importance of intervening in other aspects of the adolescents' lives as they mature.

Fourth, results of this study suggest the importance of the educational arena as one of the other aspects of the adolescents' lives. Commitment to school and delinquent behavior have strong reciprocal effects on one another. Programs that attempt to break the cycle of alienation from school increasing delinquency, and delinquency increasing alienation from school, appear to be particularly important at these ages. At still later ages, other intervention targets are likely to become more salient. For example, by late adolescence, providing for a smooth transition from school to work is likely to be a central issue for reducing criminal involvement. The more general point is that intervention strategies need to be both holistic in scope and flexible enough to be developmentally appropriate.

Finally, results reported here suggest that if problems in the family or school, or initial delinquency itself, are left unattended, a behavioral trajectory is established that increases considerably the likelihood of a delinquent career. After some initial impetus is provided, the reciprocal nature of the causal system tends to be self-perpetuating, and delinquency becomes more and more likely. On the other hand, however, if early problems are successfully treated, then the same reciprocal quality of the system works to decrease the chances of delinquency and increase the chances of conformity. For example, successful family intervention should both reduce delinquency and increase commitment to school, which should begin a set of mutually reinforcing relationships that make delinquency less and less likely. The most important point from an interactional perspective is that all of the causes of delinquency need to be identified and dealt with in a coordinated fashion to take advantage of the reciprocal quality of the system, thereby establishing a behavioral trajectory that makes delinquency increasingly less likely.

APPENDIX A

FACTOR ANALYSIS AND RELIABILITY ANALYSIS FOR BONDING VARIABLES

Items	Wave 1		Wave 2		Wave 3	
	Factor Loading	Alpha	Factor Loading	Alpha	Factor Loading	Alpha
Attachment to Parents						
How often would you say that		.82		.87		.87
(1. Never 2. Seldom 3. Sometimes 4. Often)						
1. You get along well with your ____?	.662		.716		.698	
2. You feel that you can really trust your ____?	.644		.736		.700	
3. Your ____ does not understanding you?	.304		.406		.407	
4. Your ____ is too demanding?	.401		.408		.447	
5. You really enjoy your ____?	.782		.814		.795	
6. Your ____ interferes with your activities?	.358		.382		.382	
7. You think your ____ is terrific?	.772		.774		.769	
8. You feel very angry toward your ____?	.482		.517		.547	
9. You feel violent toward your ____?	.458		.531		.548	
10. You feel proud of your ____?	.667		.739		.722	
11. You have a lot of respect for your ____?	N.A.		.565		.566	
Commitment to School						
How much do you agree or disagree with these statements?		.76		.80		.83
(1. Strongly Disagree 2. Disagree 3. Agree 4. Strongly Agree)						
1. Since school began this year, you like school a lot.	.465		.478		.553	
2. School is boring to you.	.391		.533		.605	
3. You do poorly at school.	.487		.591		.613	
4. You don't really belong at school.	.491		.551		.560	
5. Homework is a waste of time.	.593		.641		.632	
6. You try hard at school.	.600		.587		.679	
7. You usually finish your homework.	.494		.567		.617	
8. Getting good grades is very important to you.	.600		.622		.626	
9. Sometimes you do extra work to improve your grades.	.428		.452		.450	
10. If you could choose on your own between studying to get a good grade on a test or going out with your friends, would you . . .:	.304		.357		.435	

(1. Definitely go out with friends 2. Probably go out with friends 3. Probably study 4. Definitely study)?

APPENDIX B
SELF-REPORTED DELINQUENCY ITEMS

Have you ever . . .

1. Run away from home?
2. Skipped classes without an excuse?
3. Lied about your age to get into some place or to buy something? (for example, lying about your age to get into a movie or to buy alcohol)
4. Hitchhiked a ride with a stranger?
5. Carried a hidden knife, gun, or other weapon?
6. Been loud or rowdy in a public place where somebody complained and you got in trouble?
7. Been drunk in a public place?
8. Damaged, destroyed or marked up somebody else's property on purpose?
9. Set fire on purpose or tried to set fire on purpose to a house, building, or car?
10. Avoided paying for things, like a movie, taking bus rides, using a computer, or anything else?
11. Gone into or broken into a building to steal or damage something?
12. Tried to steal or actually stolen money or things worth $5 or less?
13. Tried to steal or actually stolen money or things worth between $5 and $50?
14. How about between $50 and $100?
15. How about more than $100?
16. Snatched someone's purse or wallet or picked someone's pocket?
17. Tried to buy or sell things that were stolen?
18. Taken a car or motorcycle for a ride without the owner's permission?
19. Stolen or tried to steal a car or other motor vehicle?
20. Forged a check or used fake money to pay for something?
21. Used or tried to use a credit card, bank card, or automatic teller card without permission?
22. Tried to cheat someone by selling them something that was worthless or not what you said it was?
23. Used a weapon with the idea of seriously hurting or killing someone?
24. Hit someone with the idea of hurting them? (other than what you just told me about)
25. Been involved in gang fights?
26. Thrown objects such as rocks or bottles at people? (other than events you have already mentioned)
27. Used a weapon or force to make someone give you money or things?
28. Sold marijuana, reefer or pot?
29. Sold other drugs such as heroin, cocaine, crack, or LSD?

Acknowledgments

Agnew, Robert. "Foundation for a General Strain Theory of Crime and Delinquency." *Criminology* 30 (1992): 47–66. Reprinted with the permission of the American Society of Criminology.

Beirne, Piers. "Inventing Criminology: The 'Science of Man' in Cesare Beccaria's *Dei delitti e delle pene* (1764)." *Criminology* 29 (1991): 777–820. Reprinted with the permission of the American Society of Criminology.

Braithwaite, John. "Poverty, Power, White-Collar Crime and the Paradoxes of Criminological Theory." *Australian and New Zealand Journal of Criminology* 24 (1991): 40–58. Reprinted with the permission of Butterworths.

Burton, Velmer S., Jr., Francis T. Cullen, T. David Evans, and R. Gregory Dunaway. "Reconsidering Strain Theory: Operationalization, Rival Theories, and Adult Criminality." *Journal of Quantitative Criminology* 10 (1994): 213–39. Reprinted with the permission of Plenum Publishing Corp.

Cohen, Lawrence E. and Richard Machalek. "The Normalcy of Crime: From Durkheim to Evolutionary Ecology." *Rationality and Society* 6 (1994): 286–308. Reprinted with the permission of Sage Ltd.

Gibbons, Don C. "Talking About Crime: Observations on the Prospects for Causal Theory in Criminology." *Criminal Justice Research Bulletin* 7 (1992): 1–10. Reprinted with the permission of the Criminal Justice Center.

Gottfredson, Denise C., Richard J. McNeil III, and Gary D. Gottfredson. "Social Area Influences on Delinquency: A Multilevel Analysis." *Journal of Research in Crime and Delinquency* 28 (1991): 197–226. Reprinted with the permission of Sage Publications Inc.

Grasmick, Harold G., Charles R. Tittle, Robert J. Bursik Jr., and Bruce J. Arneklev. "Testing the Core Empirical Implications of Gottfredson and Hirschi's General Theory of Crime." *Journal of Research in Crime and Delinquency* 30 (1993): 5–29. Reprinted with the permission of Sage Publications Inc.

Hagan, John. "Destiny and Drift: Subcultural Preferences, Status Attainments, and the Risks and Rewards of Youth." *American Sociological Review* 56 (1991): 567–82. Reprinted with the permission of the American Sociological Association.

McCord, Joan. "The Cycle of Crime and Socialization Practices." *Journal of Criminal Law and Criminology* 82 (1991): 211–28. Reprinted with the special permission of the Northwestern University School of Law, *Journal of Criminal Law and Criminology*.

Messner, Steven F. and Reid M. Golden. "Racial Inequality and Racially Disaggregated Homicide Rates: An Assessment of Alternative Theoretical Explanations." *Criminology* 30 (1992): 421–45. Reprinted with the permission of the American Society of Criminology.

Milovanovic, Dragan. "Dueling Paradigms: Modernist versus Postmodernist Thought." *Humanity and Society* 19 (1995): 19–44. Reprinted with the permission of the Association for Humanist Sociology.

Nagin, Daniel S. and Raymond Paternoster. "Enduring Individual Differences and Rational Choice Theories of Crime." *Law and Society Review* 27 (1993): 467–96. Reprinted with the permission of the Law and Society Association.

Sampson, Robert J. and John H. Laub. "Urban Poverty and the Family Context of Delinquency: A New Look at Structure and Process in a Classic Study. *Child Development* 65 (1994): 523–40. Reprinted with the permission of the Society for Research in Child Development.

Simpson, Sally S. "Caste, Class, and Violent Crime: Explaining Difference in Female Offending." *Criminology* 29 (1991): 115–35. Reprinted with the permission of the American Society of Criminology.

Stafford, Mark C. and Mark Warr. "A Reconceptualization of General and Specific Deterrence." *Journal of Research in Crime and Delinquency* 30 (1993): 123–35. Reprinted with the permission of Sage Publications Inc.

Thornberry, Terence P., Alan J. Lizotte, Marvin D. Krohn, Margaret Farnworth, and Sung Joon Jang. "Testing Interactional Theory: An Examination of Reciprocal Causal Relationships Among Family, School, and Delinquency." *Journal of Criminal Law and Criminology* 82 (1991): 3–35. Reprinted with the special permission of the Northwestern University School of Law, *Journal of Criminal Law and Criminology*.